Praise for *Small Wars, Faraway Places*

"A well-researched and readable account of two tumultuous decades . . . Burleigh has synthesized a wide range of material to create a valuable introduction to the political and military events of the early Cold War." —*The New York Times Book Review*

"Michael Burleigh chronicles the end of the British, French, and Dutch empires in the wake of World War II and looks into what replaced them and why—a topic, he argues, that has special relevance because 'generals and military experts have ransacked this period for "how to do it" lessons for contemporary Iraq and Afghanistan.' . . . It is a rollicking journey in the company of such dynamic figures as British General Gerald Templer, who won the Malayan Emergency and popularized the phrase 'hearts and minds,' and French President Charles de Gaulle, who lost Algeria after a brutal counterinsurgency campaign that relied heavily upon torture."
—John A. Nagl, *The Wall Street Journal*

"An enjoyable, breezy read—perfect for a lazy afternoon at the beach—and it is full of nicely evocative descriptions. . . . Burleigh has a particularly good eye for the telling detail."
—Max Boot, *National Review*

"Burleigh writes with engaging wit."
—John M. Taylor, *The Washington Times*

"Burleigh nails his cast of politicians, generals, and revolutionaries to turn the page in a series of ruthlessly observed character sketches."
—Keith Lowe, author of *Savage Continent*

"The book contains a series of vivid, vigorous narratives, illuminated by telling snippets of information, compelling but rarely flattering portraits of the key characters, and some trenchant judgments. Burleigh has little interest in grand theories and does not dwell on the deep, impersonal social and economic forces at work or the big ideas that gripped collective imaginations. Instead he concentrates on the choices made by flawed and fallible men (and in this book they are almost all men) in the turbulent two decades from 1945 to 1965."

—Lawrence Freedman, *The Washington Post*

"[A] penetrating and often sardonic narrative of the struggles that formed the world as we know it. Blending engaging character sketches and telling vignettes with geopolitical analysis, [Burleigh] presents the two decades after 1945 from a vantage point that provides illuminating perspective. . . . Burleigh's wide-ranging account brings out the relationship between political challenge and response, along with the difficulties in understanding very different societies from the outside."

—William Anthony Hay, *The American Conservative*

"Slyly humorous and wonderfully detailed, Burleigh's vivid narrative does justice to the lesser-known struggles of a complex era."

—*Publishers Weekly* (starred review)

"Burleigh is an equal opportunity moralist, not an ideologue, and he stalks his prey with feline grace."

—Christopher Silvester, *Financial Times*

"The vault of knowledge that followers of current events have been seeking. . . . From the Mau-Mau Emergency in Kenya to the Korean War . . . to the French misadventure in Indochina and the clash between Arab nationalism and Zionism in the British Mandate in Palestine, Burleigh traces eighteen distinct story lines of terrorism, counter-terrorism, intrigue, nationalism, and Cold War rivalry. With these stories, the reader can find the tangled roots on nearly all of today's nasty hotspots; he or she can even foresee the sort of messes that modern-day conflicts are likely to create down the road. . . . That *Small Wars* eschews easy answers or one-size-fits-all theories about the conflicts that it documents is a tribute to its author."

—*The Christian Science Monitor*

"Vividly written and stimulating . . . the raw truth, conveyed in scintillating language by a master of historical irony and of the grimly entertaining. If history for grown-ups is what you're after, this is it."
—George Walden, *Sunday Telegraph* (London)

"The violent geopolitical shifts of the immediate postwar years constitute a dramatic saga, which Burleigh recounts with panache and wit. . . . Lucid and persuasive."　　　—*The Sunday Times* (London)

"Burleigh is the don of elegant, historical writing, and every vignette in this book is arresting. His ability to command his material is truly breathtaking. . . . Damnably good."
—John Lewis-Stempel, *Sunday Express* (London)

"Terrific . . . Burleigh writes with a keen eye for self-righteousness, hypocrisy and unintended consequences. He is quite brilliant at puncturing the vanities of history's great and good."
—Dominic Sandbrook, *Evening Standard*

"Harsh and vivid."　　　—Max Hastings, *Financial Times*

SMALL WARS, FARAWAY PLACES

Global Insurrection and the Making of the Modern World,

1945–1965

MICHAEL BURLEIGH

PENGUIN BOOKS

PENGUIN BOOKS
Published by the Penguin Group
Penguin Group (USA) LLC
375 Hudson Street
New York, New York 10014

USA | Canada | UK | Ireland | Australia | New Zealand | India | South Africa | China
penguin.com
A Penguin Random House Company

First published in Great Britain by Macmillan, an imprint of Pan Macmillan 2013
First published in the United States of America by Viking Penguin,
a member of Penguin Group (USA) LLC, 2013
Published in Penguin Books 2014

Map illustrations by Hugo Bicheno

THE LIBRARY OF CONGRESS HAS CATALOGED THE
HARDCOVER EDITION AS FOLLOWS:
Burleigh, Michael, 1955–
   Small wars, faraway places : global insurrection and the making of the modern world,
1945–1965 / Michael Burleigh.
      pages cm
   Includes bibliographical references and index.
   ISBN 978-0-670-02545-9 (hc.)
   ISBN 978-0-14-312595-2 (pbk.)
   1. Low-intensity conflicts (Military science)—History—20th century. 2. Military
history, Modern—20th century. 3. United States—Military policy—History—20th
century. 4. World politics—20th century 5. Imperialism. 6. Cold War. I. Title.
II. Title: Global insurrection and the making of the modern world, 1945–1965.
   D431.B87 2013
   909.82'5—dc23
   2013017207

Printed in the United States of America
10 9 8 7 6 5 4 3 2 1

Set in Sabon LT Std

For Vidia and Nadira Naipaul,
Nancy Sladek and Andrea Chiari-Gaggia

CONTENTS

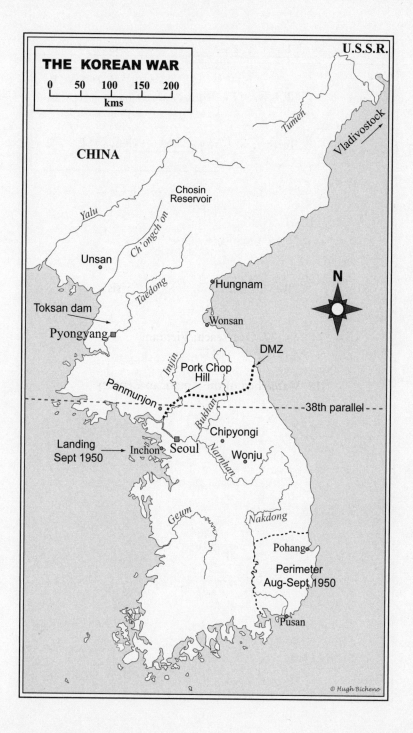

THE KOREAN WAR

0   50   100   150   200
kms

U.S.S.R.

CHINA

Tumen

Vladivostock

Yalu

Ch'ongch'on

Chosin
Reservoir

Unsan

Taedong

Hungnam

N

Toksan dam

Wonsan

Pyongyang

Imjin

DMZ

Pork Chop
Hill

Panmunjon

Bukhan

38th parallel

Chipyongi

Landing
Sept 1950

Inchon   Seoul

Namhan

Wonju

Geum

Nakdong

Pohang

Perimeter
Aug–Sept 1950

Pusan

© Hugh Bicheno

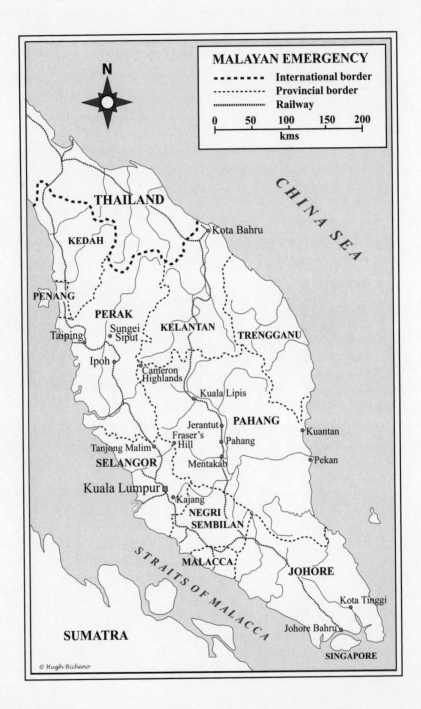

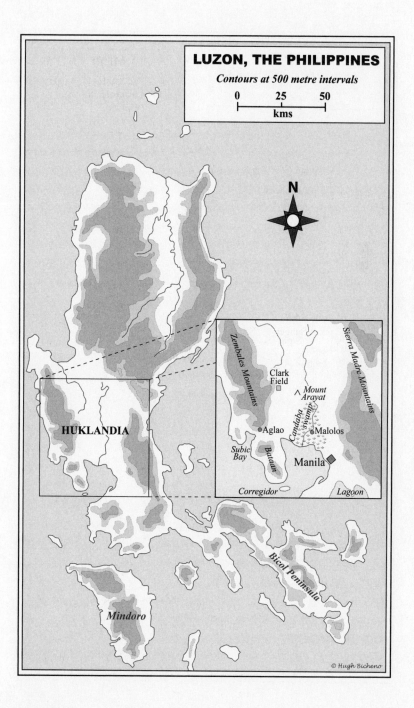

LUZON, THE PHILIPPINES

Contours at 500 metre intervals

0   25   50
kms

N

HUKLANDIA

Zembales Mountains

Clark Field

Mount Arayat

Sierra Madre Mountains

Aglao

Candaba Swamp

Malolos

Subic Bay

Bataan

Manila

Corregidor

Lagoon

Mindoro

Bicol Peninsula

© Hugh Bicheno

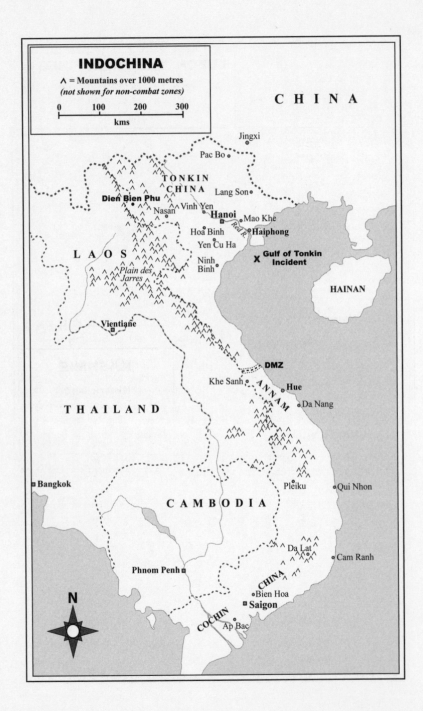

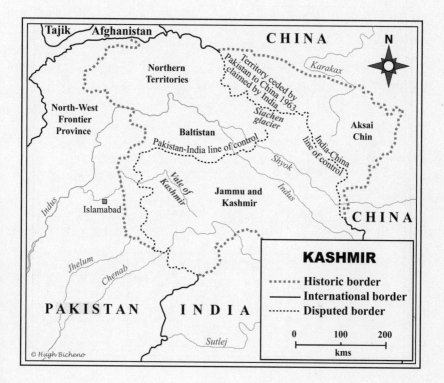

Tajik Afghanistan   CHINA   N

Northern
Territories
                          Territory ceded by
                          Pakistan to China 1963
                          claimed by India   Karakax

North-West
Frontier   Aksai
Province   Baltistan   Siachen   Chin
                Pakistan-India line of control   glacier
                                                      India-China
                          Vale of   Shyok   line of control
                          Kashmir
        Indus   Jammu and   Indus
Islamabad   Kashmir   CHINA

        Jhelum

                Chenab   ┌──────────────────────────┐
                                            │ **KASHMIR**   │
PAKISTAN   INDIA   │ ••••••• Historic border │
                                            │ ────── International border │
                        Sutlej   │ ------- Disputed border │
                                            │   │
© Hugh Bicheno   │ 0   100   200   │
                                            │ ├────────┼────────┤   │
                                            │   kms   │
                                            └──────────────────────────┘

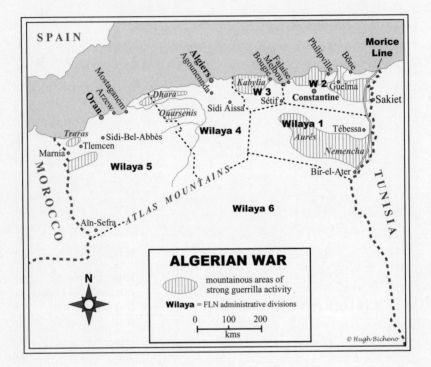

SPAIN

Morice
Line

Philippville · Bône

Algiers · Agoumennda

Falaise
Melbou
Bougie

W 2 · Guelma

Kabylia

W 3

Constantine · Sakiet

Mostaganem

Dhara

Sétif

Oran · Arzew

Ouarsenis

Sidi Aissa

Wilaya 1

Tébessa

Traras

Sidi-Bel-Abbès

Wilaya 4

Aurès

Marnia

Tlemcen

Nemencha

MOROCCO

Wilaya 5

Bir-el-Ater

TUNISIA

ATLAS MOUNTAINS

Wilaya 6

Aïn-Sefra

N

ALGERIAN WAR

mountainous areas of
strong guerrilla activity

Wilaya = FLN administrative divisions

0   100   200

kms

© Hugh Bicheno

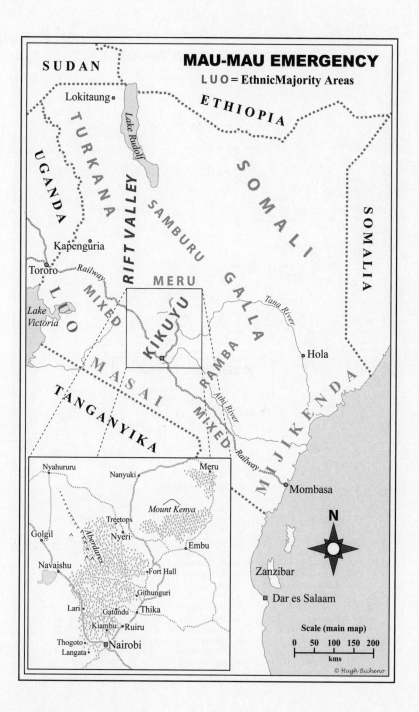

MAU-MAU EMERGENCY

LUO = EthnicMajority Areas

SUDAN

Lokitaung

ETHIOPIA

UGANDA

TURKANA

Lake Rudolf

RIFT VALLEY

SAMBURU

SOMALI

SOMALIA

Kapenguria

Tororo

Railway

MERU

MIXED

LUO

Lake Victoria

KIKUYU

GALLA

Tana River

Hola

MASAI

RAMBA

Athi River

TANGANYIKA

MIXED

Railway

MIJIKENDA

Mombasa

Nyahururu

Nanyuki

Meru

Mount Kenya

Golgil

Treetops

Aberdares

Nyeri

Embu

Navaishu

Fort Hall

N

Githunguri

Zanzibar

Lari

Gatundu

Thika

Kiambu

Ruiru

Dar es Salaam

Thogoto

Nairobi

Langata

Scale (main map)

0   50   100   150   200

kms

© Hugh Bicheno

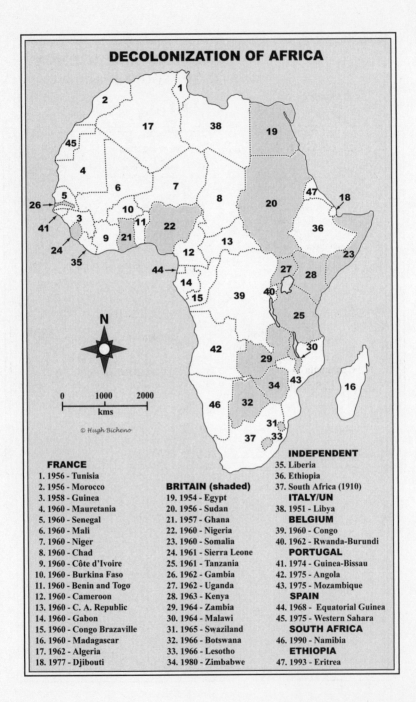

DECOLONIZATION OF AFRICA

© Hugh Bicheno

FRANCE
1. 1956 - Tunisia
2. 1956 - Morocco
3. 1958 - Guinea
4. 1960 - Mauretania
5. 1960 - Senegal
6. 1960 - Mali
7. 1960 - Niger
8. 1960 - Chad
9. 1960 - Côte d'Ivoire
10. 1960 - Burkina Faso
11. 1960 - Benin and Togo
12. 1960 - Cameroon
13. 1960 - C. A. Republic
14. 1960 - Gabon
15. 1960 - Congo Brazaville
16. 1960 - Madagascar
17. 1962 - Algeria
18. 1977 - Djibouti

BRITAIN (shaded)
19. 1954 - Egypt
20. 1956 - Sudan
21. 1957 - Ghana
22. 1960 - Nigeria
23. 1960 - Somalia
24. 1961 - Sierra Leone
25. 1961 - Tanzania
26. 1962 - Gambia
27. 1962 - Uganda
28. 1963 - Kenya
29. 1964 - Zambia
30. 1964 - Malawi
31. 1965 - Swaziland
32. 1966 - Botswana
33. 1966 - Lesotho
34. 1980 - Zimbabwe

INDEPENDENT
35. Liberia
36. Ethiopia
37. South Africa (1910)
ITALY/UN
38. 1951 - Libya
BELGIUM
39. 1960 - Congo
40. 1962 - Rwanda-Burundi
PORTUGAL
41. 1974 - Guinea-Bissau
42. 1975 - Angola
43. 1975 - Mozambique
SPAIN
44. 1968 - Equatorial Guinea
45. 1975 - Western Sahara
SOUTH AFRICA
46. 1990 - Namibia
ETHIOPIA
47. 1993 - Eritrea

MISSILE CRISIS 1962

US Bases
A Homestead
B Key West
C Guantánamo

Missile Sites
1 San Cristobal MRBM
2 Guanajay IRBM
3 Sagua la Grande MRBM
4 Remedios IRBM

Houston

New Orleans

Miami

A

B

Havana

1 2

3 4

Bay of Pigs

U-2 shot down

Santiago

C

Haiti

Dominican Republic

Puerto Rico

Jamaica

Mexico

British Honduras

Guatemala

Honduras

El Salvador

Nicaragua

CARIBBEAN SEA

Costa Rica

Panama

Colombia

Venezuela

Quarantine Interdiction Line

N

0   500   1000
kms

© Hugh Bicheno

INTRODUCTION

From the Halls of Montezuma to the
Green Zone of Baghdad

At the height of President George W. Bush's 2003 intervention in Iraq, bold spirits urged the United States to do as Rudyard Kipling once urged in 1899, following the lightning US conquest of the Spanish overseas empire:

> *Take up the White Man's burden –*
> *Send forth the best ye breed –*
> *Go bind your sons to exile*
> *To serve your captives' need . . .*

Yet in mid-1945, when the US assumed leadership of the free world, half a century after Kipling wrote and another before President Bush acted, history and tradition rendered such a choice a more equivocal affair for Americans than it is often made to seem. The pitifully needy condition of Europe after 1945, resembling the continent's million wandering orphans, sealed the fate of its distant colonies. In Asia these fell like ninepins to the marauding Japanese from early 1942 onwards. The example of Nazism more generally discredited the notion that race determined political destinies, as did Imperial Japan's occupation of Asia, with which this book begins.

It tells the story of the eclipse of those empires, of the birth of some of the nation states that replaced them, and of how the US (and the Soviet Union) reacted to these developments. These struggles for independence, in Africa, Asia and the Middle East, coincided with the intense super-power competition called the Cold War. The Americans had to suppress a long-standing disinclination to meddle in other countries – a view cari-catured as 'isolationism' – and an inherent dislike of colonial rule stem-ming from their own freedom fight against the British. That was notwithstanding an imperialist spasm of the Republic's own just before and after the dawn of the twentieth century, or intensified interference in Mexico and the Caribbean. Colonies shocked Americans, from the Presidents downwards, and despite racial segregation in the Southern states. After a wartime visit to Gambia, President Franklin D. Roosevelt wrote to his son Elliott: 'Dirt. Disease. Very high mortality rate. I asked. Life expectancy – you'd never guess what it is. Twenty-six years. These people are treated worse than livestock. Their cattle live longer!' In the case of French Indochina, Roosevelt agreed with Stalin that French rule there was 'rotten to the core'. As an article in *Life* magazine had it in October 1942: 'One thing we are sure we are *not* fighting for is to hold the British Empire together.'

However, by the late 1940s, when the Cold War had begun in ear-nest, the United States calculated that propping up colonial empires was cheaper than deploying US troops, while accepting the argument that European metropolises economically weakened by decolonization would become as susceptible to Communist subversion as their colonies. Because the Soviet Union was the sole Communist state, it was assumed that its directing hand was responsible for subversion everywhere: it had after all established the Communist International, or Comintern, for that purpose in 1919. In fact, despite being Lenin's former Commissar responsible for nationalities, Stalin was uninterested in the Third World. A red mist clouded the vision of America's governing class, even when Yugoslavia and then China took another route. State Department experts also sometimes failed to detect reds under every bed and Presi-dent Dwight Eisenhower warned of the dangers to democracy of a military–industrial complex. Of course, American inability to discrimi-nate between Communist regimes was as nothing compared with the incapacity of successive Communist regimes to learn from the disas-ters of those who went before them, so that Mao repeated many of the same 'errors' – meaning murderous experiments in collectivization – as Stalin, whose own radicality was eclipsed by Cambodia's Pol Pot.

Not all Americans were enamoured of their new world role. US Congressmen routinely opposed any spending on new embassy buildings the State Department thought commensurate with post-war US power, because they and their constituents resented 'striped pants' elitists bent on squandering their hard-earned cash on glass ziggurats in faraway places. Actually, foreign service officers often worked in dangerous places, where the air they breathed or the water they drank could kill them, not to speak of air travel, which was far more lethal than it is now. The resentments were reciprocal. US Secretary of State Dean Acheson, an East Coast elitist and Anglophile, once gave the game away by publicly remarking: 'If you truly had a democracy and did what people wanted, you'd go wrong every time.' That is more relevant than ever at a time when Western intervention in Afghanistan is massively unpopular in Europe and the US.

This US accommodation with late European empire was eased by the fact that the colonial powers had themselves adopted the rhetoric of happy families progressing towards self-rule (notably the British Commonwealth but also the French Union) even as they fought vicious rearguard actions against nationalists in their colonies. What commenced as a response to Britain's admission that it no longer had the means to support Greece and Turkey became the 1947 Truman Doctrine of potentially limitless global security undertakings. Republican Senator Robert Taft spoke up to oppose the conversion of the United States into 'a meddlesome Mattie, interfering in every trouble throughout the world'. This linked him to a venerable tradition in US foreign policy going back to John Quincy Adams's reluctance to support Greek nationalists in the early 1820s, no mean gesture in a land with a city called Philadelphia, and forward to the pre-9/11 foreign policy of George W. Bush, which defined itself in opposition to the fitful humanitarian interventions of William Jefferson Clinton. In the 1940s, the influential newspaper columnist Walter Lippmann was among the first to see that this newly achieved American 'globalism' also passed the initiative to the Soviets, who could defeat the US by 'disorganizing states that are already disorganized, by disuniting peoples that are torn with civil strife, and by inciting their discontent which is already very great'. The US would become embroiled in 'recruiting, subsidizing and supporting a heterogeneous army of satellites, clients, dependents and puppets', a highly prescient description of the decades covered in this book, 1945–65. Mindful not to alienate large numbers of West European Communists attached to their respective empires, the Soviets also reluctantly adjusted their theoretical doctrines so as to accommodate 'bourgeois' nationalists – for there were not many industrial proletarians in the Third World, before Khrushchev decided to compete with the US for influence in the developing world. By the end of the 1960s, Mao's China made a bid to lead all Third World revolutionary struggles. While relations with the Soviets cooled, Mao also grew impatient with India's pretensions to being an equal partner in the affairs of Asia. This led to war between the two most populous Asian nations over disputed territories in the Himalayas. Nations seeking to free themselves from colonialism were sucked into this vast superpower conflict, often with devastating local effects, despite attempts begun by Yugoslavia and taken over by India to non-align the new Asian and African states in a distinctive Third World camp at the April 1955 Bandung Conference. The two major empires were those of Britain and France, though there is some attention paid to the Netherlands East Indies too.

Books on empire seem to oblige the authors to give a verdict and/or statement or confession of views about the subject, although this is less contentious in the case of the Macedonian, Roman, Persian or Han empires of the ancient past where the 'civilizing' effects seem less controversial at such a great remove. Contemporary history is more sensitive, even though empires have been more normative than either democracies or nation states in the broad history of humankind. Just as many Americans disliked the US's global role, so not all Europeans were eager for empire, and nor did they all live in castles and chateaux either. There were and are many critics of imperialism. Emotional investment in empire was limited, except in Scotland, to the prefect class from the private schools, inspired by the Christian warriors depicted in the stained glass of their chapels. Its ethos was anti-democratic. As one proconsul wrote from northern Nigeria, 'the duty of colonial trusteeship lay . . . in protecting the virtues of northern [Nigerian] aristocratic life and its communal economy' from the 'barbarizing effects of European capitalism, democracy and individualism'. The British ruling classes enmeshed indigenous elites in all the fluff and flummery of chivalric orders and titles, for when all was said and done the British knew how to mount a damn good show. Though they may be suckers for 'our' royal weddings, most Americans can separate the fluff from statecraft. They are not Romans to British Greeks, a conceit with unfortunate contemporary undertones. This is not to deprecate or ignore such objective improvements as the eradication of tropical diseases or constructing telegraphs, railways and roads, not to speak of legal systems and (through schools) the Christian virtues, which nowadays are more pervasive in Africa than in the secular former imperial metropolises. Actual literacy rates often told another story. Long after it ceased to exist, empire also left a sense of mass national entitlement and elite Romantic ambition, which endures as Britain punching above its actual capacities and resources, or the assumption lower down the social scale that a defined pool of foreigners would always do the unpleasant jobs. While your author is not a crusader trying to right past injustices, he has a realistic view of empire and its unfortunate legacies to the former colonial powers, including the subconscious ways it affects so many international moralists, for that is part of punching above one's weight too, however much human rights advocates would not appreciate me saying so.

So, this book is about a crucial transitional era in which power tangibly passed from European capitals to the 'World Capital on the Potomac'. Beneath that secular process, dozens of new nations struggled into independent existence, many successfully, some disastrously. Since a book which discussed every struggle for independence would be impossibly long, I have selected those which most interest me, favouring depth of field rather than a wide-angled focus. As it is, I reluctantly decided to cut lengthy sections on Angola, Mozambique and South Africa, despite months spent researching them. In all cases the presence or absence of a charismatic leader such as Chiang Kai-shek, Chairman Mao, Ho Chi Minh, Fidel Castro, Patrice Lumumba or Jomo Kenyatta was determinative. Who remembers the Malayan Communist leader Chin Peng, one of the few among my cast of characters who, aged ninety at the time of writing, still lurks somewhere over the Thai border? Much blood was shed in what was not a sociological process, though it is worth recalling that in Africa – often regarded as uniquely savage – the initial wave of statehood cost less life than the number of Americans killed each year on the roads. That was certainly not true of Algeria or Indochina, where millions died, nor of Korea, where the death toll was similarly colossal as the superpowers fought a proxy war and the Americans came up against Mao's armies.

This period of small wars in faraway places is highly topical, not least in contemporary military circles, which study them obsessively. This book explores a number of those fought by the British and French, or the Japanese before them, questioning some of the received wisdom whereby bludgeoning incompetents were supplanted by quasi-heroic sophisticates practising 'population-centric' hearts-and-minds warfare. Generals and military experts have ransacked this period for 'how to do it' lessons for contemporary Iraq and Afghanistan, often by ignoring what tactics actually won atypical campaigns in favour of what best resembles what they want to do in the present.

I branch out into the parallel experiences of the US in the Philippines and Vietnam, where in the first case the Americans directed a highly successful counter-insurgency campaign, and in the second inherited and compounded the disaster left by the French. In reality, hearts-and-minds campaigns only worked once kinetic force – a euphemism for killing people – had achieved population and spatial control, as such contemporary adepts as General David Petraeus do not readily acknowledge in their apparent unawareness that the Japanese also pioneered this style of warfare long before the British in Malaya. The British triumphed in Malaya, which they were leaving anyway, against an enemy limited to part of an ethnic minority, just as in Kenya their Mau Mau opponents consisted of marginalized elements of the Kikuyu tribe. In Algeria and Indochina the French had the majority populations against them and lost against guerrillas who could weave in and out of neighbouring states. China and the Soviet Union also poured men and weapons into Indochina. Able to dissociate leftist Algerian nationalists from Communists, the Americans proved unable to do the same in the case of the Vietnamese and ended up fighting a disastrous war that became uniquely their own. Obviously the ability to discriminate between Communist states was hampered by their generic internal similarities, with secret policemen consigning broadly defined opponents to concentration camps, whether in Albania, Bulgaria, China or Vietnam.

Using counter-insurgency campaigns as paradigms for contemporary practice also involves ignoring their less savoury aspects. These were deliberately concealed by the destruction of incriminating written materials relating to brutality, murder and torture. Even the ashes of burned papers were pulverized by the British, while crates crammed with papers were dropped into deep sea, where there were no currents to wash them up again. The so-called legacy files handed on to the post-colonial successor governments were systematically weeded too. When a file flagged as a watch file (stamped W) was surreptitiously removed from an archive, a dummy twin was created to fill its place, with suitably anodyne content. This ever so deliberate work was to be done only by white colonial police officers. The archive policy was decreed by Prime Minister Harold Macmillan's Colonial Secretary Iain Macleod so that materials that 'might embarrass Her Majesty's governments' or 'members of the police, military forces, public servants or others e.g. police informers' or that might be 'used unethically by ministers in the successor government' would never see the light of day. The surviving files were secreted in a Foreign Office communications centre in Buckinghamshire until lawyers acting for Kenyan victims of British maltreatment forced their selective release into the public domain in 2011.

The period I have chosen to write about is one in which many contemporary developments can be discerned, like ships appearing on the horizon, from Cuba to China and Palestine to Pakistan, though I happen to believe that contemporaries also make their own destinies in a past that was no more determined than the present. For many contemporaries, some of the major transformations described here were inconceivable at the time, whether the coming to power of Mao's Communists in China or the swift demise of what seemed to be unassailable global empires. People probably once felt the same way about the impossibility of democracy or racial integration. Then there are the certainties which have been overturned in subsequent decades. How many Americans can

...can that Pakistan was among the US's most solidly reliable allies, whereas India was regarded as suspiciously pink? Who would have imagined, given the US's tragic invovements in Indochina, that nowadays it would be conducting joint naval exercises with Communist Vietnam designed to contain Chinese claims to a few submerged rocks in the northern Pacific as it asserts its own Monroe Doctrine?

Historians organize decades of history, impressing their own periodization on them – the Age of Discovery; the European Civil War 1890–1945; the Cold War 1947–1989 and so forth – as they have done since the Renaissance implicitly defined a Dark Age following classical antiquity. But the lives of contemporaries rarely fit such divisions neatly, especially since until recently youth was not mandatory for high political office. Throughout I have sought to convey the generational experiences of the men who were at the centres of these events, although it is worth noting how, for example, fear of repeating 1930s appeasement still haunts leaders far too young to have lived it, as it did Presidents Truman, Kennedy and Johnson. That is why I have included biographical sketches of the main players: to emphasize the myriad experiences they brought to the decisions they made during these two decades. What did future nationalist leaders from Africa or Asia think when as young men they gawped at the ornate buildings in huge European capitals, and from within whose elegant façades the destinies of their countrymen were arranged according to abstract or inaccurate anthropological principles, or in line with considerations of international balances of power that had little or nothing to do with them? Speaking of these future leaders, it requires an act of imaginative recovery to grasp the sheer vitality of Marxist-Leninism or the 'national socialisms', which in ensuing decades have in turn been swept aside by Communo-capitalism or political Islamism. I hope I give the worm's-eye view too, that is the perspective of the men and women amid whom cold and hot wars were waged as well as that of the intelligence officers who flit in and out of this story like shifting shadows. Many of the subjects dealt with here also have a remarkable pertinacity, for example Iranian belief in the almost occult role of the British in their national affairs, a form of paranoia they share with the Russians, as they uncover cameras placed by the Secret Intelligence Service (popularly known as MI6) in fake rocks in Moscow parks.

One can hear this paranoia in the words of the Iranian nationalist leader Mohammed Mossadeq, although he had every justification for feeling very afraid. The most tense borders in the world – in Korea or Kashmir – derive from this period, as do the unresolved problems of Israel and its neighbours, one of over twenty or more extant problems in the post-colonial Middle East.

The following narrative unashamedly swerves, turns in on itself and revisits key events in different contexts, in an attempt to weave them together in something approximating to their multi-layered complexity. It would be impossible for my readers to follow a simultaneous account of events in very different cultures thousands of miles apart from one another, as we would have to jump back and forth from Algeria to Kenya via Malaya and Indochina. Beneath whatever modish stances states struck were also what amounted to cultural demiurges, evident in, for example, India's far-from-smooth relations with China or the latter's with the Vietnamese, which have to be considered too. Although the military mind is often amnesiac, there were clear examples of one campaign influencing another, or of mindsets formed in one context, such as French Indochina, pre-programming a determination to win in another, in this case Algeria, even if this meant mutinous paratroopers descending on central Paris. The connections can be surprising, and the morality involved was usually obscure, most obviously in the Anglo–French–Israeli plot to overthrow Nasser or in the Kennedy brothers conniving with the Mafia to kill Fidel Castro, himself no slouch at assassinating his enemies. 'Good' decisions, such as Lyndon Johnson's not to use military force to stop China becoming a nuclear power, contributed to the 'bad' one of attempting to crush North Vietnam by conventional bombing to reassure Asia-Pacific allies made anxious by China's first nuclear-bomb test in October 1964. I have tried throughout to indicate these connections and ironies.

All maps fundamentally distort the reality they depict, including those using words rather than lines and shading. Thus, for effect, I have tilted on its head the map familiar to many Europeans and North Americans by beginning in East Asia with a series of cascading responses to the effect of the Japanese lunge south in 1941–2, followed by the impact of global war on the greater Middle East. This is primarily designed to encourage readers to think on a commensurate scale about places that may not come readily to mind. After the only occasion, in Korea, where US and Soviet forces fought one another in the air, we turn to what in reality were simultaneous counter-insurgency wars, mainly in South and East Asia, with the coup in Iran against Mossadeq in 1953 and the Suez Crisis in 1956 marking the midway point of the book, and the moment when US power was most nakedly revealed to its own allies. This was when thoughtful British people realized they were no longer a great power, although many of their fellows have still not grasped that reality in the twenty-first century.

The extremely costly struggles between colonizers and nationalist insurgents in Algeria and Kenya follow, until we revert to the global superpower contest, and the competition for influence in Africa and South Asia, culminating in the 1962 Cuban Missile Crisis, the most ominous crisis of the entire conflict. In a way all the small wars were surrogates for the avoidance of such a moment when people might have awakened to the northern hemisphere destroyed by huge arsenals of nuclear bombs. Throughout I have intermittently referred to the parallel growth of those deadly stockpiles, to remind readers what was ultimately at stake whenever American or Russian agents clashed in some remote country according to their own 'big boys' rules'. The book ends with the US acting as a colonial power amid the debris of its nation-building efforts in South Vietnam, the event which fixed the widespread perception of the US as another, infinitely more successful, imperial power that persists to this day. And so it may seem, with the Pentagon's thousand or more overseas military bases, ranging from the Green Zone in Baghdad to a drone hangar on the Seychelles, though even America's critics relentlessly continue to admire and consume its high and low material and intellectual cultures.

As Sir Vidia Naipaul has reminded me, historians of ancient Rome from Appian of Alexandria to Edward Gibbon were still striving to understand the long-term significance of major events that had taken place centuries earlier. That is a respectable justification for the endless rehashing of the history of the Second World War in Europe, and of more or less exiguous episodes within it. Here I want readers to focus on the two seminal decades of the Cold War, which for the older among them is the world they came from, or in my case the one in which I grew up. I wanted a depth of field that would be lost if the global story were dragged out through the 1970s and 1980s. This period really did result in the wider world as we have come to know it – obliged, as every sentient citizen is, to think much more globally than paradoxically was often the case in the first age of globalization.

Imperialism is a touchy subject, although I have tried to avoid a bland 'on the one hand, on the other' median tone. What follows is not a work of advocacy history, for I have little ideological and even less nostalgic investment in the events described, and your historian is not an ancillary to activist lawyers campaigning for empire's victims. But such questions as how to wage war on irregular opponents hidden among entire populations have a contemporary relevance, as do how societies claiming to represent civilization disguise torture with euphemisms. The book will not please those who wish for a reaffirmation of their simple dogmas, but then they seldom read anything outside their own approved canon. Fortunately, most readers do not fall into that narrow category, and people of many ages and national backgrounds will read this book. They include those living in societies still marked by empire's long recessional – such as my own – as well as those who have as yet to find ways of demythologizing the founding myths of their national liberation. The liberation-era pieties of Algeria's ruling FLN seem pretty hollow to many unemployed Algerians under twenty-five, particularly if they see the children of the governing elite driving around in Porsches. I hope the book has the same effect on the open-minded as the surprise of looking at a painting under X-ray to find a messy multi-layered affair of false starts and second thoughts beneath the smooth surface, in this case consisting of choices and decisions by people much as ourselves.

1. JAPAN OPENS PANDORA'S BOX

A War for the Future of the World

The end of the Second World War was like a starting pistol for what the uninvolved often dismiss as 'little' colonial wars. From December 1941 Japanese forces had swept all before them, defying the huge latent industrial capacities of their enemies. These were experienced warriors who had been at war in northern China since 1937. A series of powerful thrusts took the invaders into South-east Asia, the Netherlands East Indies and the Philippines, as well as across a vast oceanic Pacific theatre. Their intelligence officers prepared the ground well for a rampage that took imperial forces to the northern shores of Australia. Japanese fishermen mapped the coastlines, while barbers and brothel madams recorded their clients' careless gossip. Even the official photographer inside Singapore Naval Base was a covert Japanese intelligence officer.[1]

The Japanese advances caused panic among European colonists, among whom it was a case of *sauve qui peut*. Pet dogs and horses were put down, captive birds set free as their owners fled pell-mell from the Japanese. There were also personal betrayals. Leslie Froggatt in Singapore confessed:

I betrayed my Malay gardener. He cut my hedges, watered my flowers, cut and rolled my tennis lawn, and brushed up the leaves that blew down from the trees. I betrayed my round fat amah, who liked me, and amused me with her funny ways. I betrayed my Hokkien cook, who had a wife and four lovely children, whom he kept beautifully dressed at all times on the money he earned from me. I betrayed 'Old Faithful', our Nr. 2 Boy, who knew no word of English or Malay and padded round the house silently in bare feet . . . I betrayed the caddie who carried my bag, searched for my ball, and always backed my game with a sporting bet.[2]

When Japanese troops entered Singapore in early 1942, the clocks moved forward two hours to Tokyo time, and the year became 2602, in conformity with the Japanese calendar. Other changes deranged the cosmos of many Asians in more fundamental ways. Unless interned, the European masters and mistresses had to carry cash and stand in line in stores, rather than signing a chit or sending a 'boy' (the general term for servants, even when they were greyheads) to shop in their stead. For the first time in their lives, Asian subjects of European colonial rule witnessed the white man abase himself in the dirt, hands raised in the air, or sullenly sweeping the streets. If disobedient, these white men were slapped, or had their heads chopped off with a samurai sword, wielded by conquerors who regarded themselves as liberating lords of Asia.[3]

The Japanese were given to massed cries of 'Banzai!' when they paraded or assembled. Lopping prisoners' heads off was a competitive sport for their officers, whose brisk manners owed something to classical operas familiar to other Asians. European and Dominion soldiers (half of the defenders of Singapore were Indians, while many of the whites were Australians) seemed slovenly and wilted, even before their morale collapsed amid defeat and heat.[4]

The surrender of 85,000 British and Dominion troops to 36,000 Japanese under General Yamashita Tomoyuki at Singapore in February 1942 was a comprehensive humiliation. As the opera-singer wife of the British Admiral superintending the docks wrote in her diary while Japanese shells whizzed overhead: 'One can have so little confidence in the powers that be here. It's a tragedy.'[5] Gross negligence before the war had been crowned by dithering incompetence during the campaign. 'Never have so many been fucked about by so few / And neither the few nor the many / Have fuck all idea what to do,' observed a British wit.[6]

The war with Japan pitted Washington's vision of a democratic United Nations against Tokyo's paternalist Greater East Asian Co-

Prosperity Scheme. The Indian Communist and nationalist Manabendra Nath Roy accurately described the conflict – in which he supported the democracies – as 'a war for the future of the world'.[7] When the Japanese attacked Pearl Harbor in December 1941, the Christian Methodist Chinese Nationalist Generalissimo Chiang Kai-shek responded by playing 'Ave Maria' on his gramophone. He hoped, and the US hoped too, that a reunited and revivified China would emerge as the world's fourth major power, occupying the vacuum that would one day be left by the defeated Japanese. It was not to be under his leadership, and by the time the People's Republic of China finally replaced the rump Republic of China in Taiwan as a permanent member of the UN Security Council in 1971 the old 'progressive' concept of the great powers presiding over a world of self-determined and democratic peoples seemed like a distant hallucination.

Broader geostrategic calculations forced actions blatantly at variance with the rhetoric of the August 1941 Anglo-American Atlantic Charter, which affirmed 'the rights of all peoples to choose the form of government under which they shall live'. The Japanese responded by claiming that each people within its Greater East Asia Co-Prosperity Sphere would 'have its proper place and demonstrate its real character, thereby securing an order of coexistence and co-prosperity based on ethical principles with Japan serving as its nucleus'. The Japanese granted Burma qualified independence in 1943, offered it to the Philippines a year later and pursued a fairly successful hearts-and-minds campaign in Malaya, an approach they had essayed fighting Kim Il Sung in Manchuria in the 1930s.[8] They also had some success in recruiting captured Indian Army troops to a new Indian National Army under their puppet Chandra Subhas Bose. Bose overstated the size of the INA for propaganda purposes, but at one point British intelligence estimated that it contained about 35,000 trained troops.

Some Asians regarded the Japanese as liberators, on the principle that 'my enemy's enemy is my friend', or believed the Japanese embodied an Asian form of modernity. They did, but it was racially supremacist and bound up with mystical nationalism, rather in the way of Nazi Germany. The benign view had gathered momentum ever since the crushing defeat Japan inflicted on Russia in 1904–5, proof indeed of the Meiji modernization of the previously backward island empire. That was why so many Asian nationalists sought to instrumentalize the Japanese against colonialism. This may seem remarkable in the light of the atrocities committed by the Japanese against civilians and prisoners of war, but from the point of view of Asian nationalists these were not greatly different to the methods employed on occasions by the Western powers, both before and after the war.[9]

The Japanese distinguished between what they called 'the rule of branches and leaves', meaning the day-to-day emergencies of fighting insurgents, and 'the rule of the roots', a metaphor for the fundamental social and political issues which needed to be tackled. Japanese policy in China included *minshin haaku* – winning the people's hearts – which went beyond mere propaganda to include reducing feudal dues, providing farmers with tools and seeds and above all ensuring competent government, in a land where officials were chosen and promoted on the basis of their calligraphy. The more intelligent Japanese officials were well aware that effective administration was the 'secret weapon' of the British Empire, and sought to emulate it. They also built on the foundations laid by Europeans to encourage opium addiction as a means of corrupting and pacifying the general population.

For all their belief in ancient paternalistic values, the Japanese employed modern techniques of mobilizing populations they claimed had been metaphorically emasculated by Western colonialism. Japanese propaganda films showed each martial triumph, from the blazing hulks of Pearl Harbor to victorious troops entering Rangoon or Singapore. When Chiang found himself ruling most of China after the Japanese capitulation, he popularized the rule of the Chinese Nationalist Kuomintang (KMT) with the aid of printing presses the Japanese had established in major Chinese cities.[10]

To the regret of some Japanese commanders, who appreciated the importance of winning popular support in a counter-insurgency campaign, the predominance of a purely military ethos ensured that these civilian-run programmes were never terribly effective and the bayonet was more conspicuous than the hand of friendship. Starting in 1934 the Japanese sought to isolate the guerrillas from the local population by corralling peasants in collective hamlets or *shudan buraku*, after burning their villages. The loss, disruption and increased costs caused by such programmes won the Japanese few friends, to the detriment of their simultaneous programme of intelligence gathering and the deployment of local collaborators to track down and kill insurgents.[11]

Perhaps the principal reason why Bose, Aung San of Burma and Sukarno of the Dutch East Indies took a broad view of Japanese atrocities was that they were mainly perpetrated in China, or against overseas Chinese in other conquered lands, where they were universally resented. *Minshin haaku* stood little chance against the particular racist loathing felt by the Japanese for the Chinese, and by the end of the war they had killed fifteen million of a people they regarded as uncultured vermin. Ominously, General Yamashita Tomoyuki's men fought boredom on troopships steaming to Malaya by reading a booklet in which the 'extortionist' overseas Chinese were excluded from any notions of 'Asia for the Asians' or 'Asian brotherhood'. This was heady stuff amid the diesel fumes and stale air.[12]

... amid the oil
fumes and the
hot desert air.

China

The Japanese military's aggression in South-east Asia and the Pacific was an extension of their earlier invasion of China, itself torn apart by ongoing civil war. In 1937, when the Japanese resumed their attempts to conquer China from the northern Manchurian bastion they had seized in 1931–2, the KMT and Communists only briefly stopped fighting each other. Even as the Japanese occupied most of the coastal areas, the two rival Chinese camps fought the invaders as competitors rather than allies. Nor were all Chinese opposed to the Japanese invasion. Wang Jingwei, a left-wing Nationalist politician who had fallen out with KMT leader Chiang Kai-shek, set up a collaborationist regime in Nanjing based on what he deemed the true principles of Sun Yat-sen, the godfather of the Chinese Revolution that deposed the Manchu Qing dynasty in 1910. Sun had modernized the surface of Chinese life, with men cutting off their long pigtail queues and adopting collarless Sun Yat-sen suits, the prototype for the garb of Mao. He also met with the Comintern in 1923, which resulted in the United Front pact with the Communists.[13]

In the mid-1920s the future Communist leader Mao Zedong had been one of Wang's political clients, a relationship subsequently obscured.[14] Born in landlocked Hunan in 1893, Mao was given a name (Zedong) that meant 'shine on the East'. His peasant-cum-soldier father made enough money dealing in grain to subsidize Mao's peripatetic student idleness, which consisted less of formal study than of whiling away entire days in university libraries, much like Lenin in Zurich before 1917. Mao was a shabbily dressed, long-haired layabout with a big fleshy face, but he had already decided that peace and prosperity only suited little folk: 'People like me long for its destruction, because when the old universe is destroyed, a new universe will be formed. Isn't that better?'[15]

Mao was also a poet, composing more than competently, often about nature, in the Chinese classical style. Yet he believed that much of traditional Chinese culture should be destroyed, while Confucianism did not appeal to one who defined morality as whatever suited his interests. After a spell in Beijing he returned to Hunan, where he eked out a modest living as a teacher, with a sideline in journalism, having rejected the opportunity to study in France because he did not want to learn the language. In June 1920 the twenty-seven-year-old radical was asked to open a bookshop by one of the founders of the Chinese Communist Party. Soviet Comintern agents provided him with subsidies to become a full-time professional revolutionary, which meant sleeping most of the day and reading and plotting through the night. His total loyalty to the Soviets meant that he was given a key role in infiltrating the KMT. Encouraged by the Soviets to take an interest in peasant themes that he had hitherto ignored, Mao realized that only the peasantry had sufficient numbers for a revolution in a vast country where the industrial proletariat made up only 5 per cent of the population. The history of Chinese peasant uprisings – notably the genocidal Taiping Rebellion in the nineteenth century – led him to the view that the Party and People's Liberation Army needed to win over the peasantry, while the prospect of another bloodbath appealed to him.

The Nationalists were appalled by the systematic violence unleashed by the Communists, and in 1927 Chiang Kai-shek, the head of the military section at the Soviet-inspired Whampoa Academy, moved against them, with an arrest list that included Mao's name. The Communists reverted to the defence of 'Soviet areas' in which their appetites for bloodthirsty purges of real and imagined opponents were indulged to the hilt and with indescribable cruelty. In 1934 Mao embarked on the 6,000-mile Long March, a year-long extraction of 82,000 Communist fighters from encirclement and destruction in the south, with 8,000 resurfacing as survivors in the remote north. There the Communists could pose as liberators and reformers without fear of attack by either the KMT or the Japanese. Mao gradually emerged as *primus inter pares* of a statelet that harked back to Plato, with the Party cadres being the philosopher kings while the guardians were the Red Army commanders and soldiers, below whom were the drones whose labour supported them. Since the majority of those who flocked to the remote Yenan redoubt did so merely from a patriotic desire to fight the Japanese, 'rectification' campaigns based on confessions and indoctrination were used to re-engineer their personalities, submerging the individual self in the collective as embodied by Mao himself.[16]

The KMT could not mobilize sufficient military power to defeat the Communists as well as resisting Japanese invasion. As elsewhere in East Asia, wealthy figures in cities such as Shanghai rallied to the Japanese cause.[17] But so did many collaborators who were also covert Communist agents, with instructions to direct the Japanese against their Nationalist rivals. While Chiang's armies fought the Japanese, Mao's Communists avoided main-force encounters, even when urged to fight them by Stalin, who feared that the Soviet Union could be crushed between the Japanese and German onslaughts. Mao's caution and evasiveness rankled with the Soviet leader and the only 'battle' against the Japanese, at Pingxing-guan in September 1937, hardly features in the annals of warfare.[18]

Communist guerrillas did have an impact in Manchuria, historically a lawless place which contained the world's densest concentration of villages run by outlaws. But it was also the most industrialized region in China, which was why the Japanese had conquered it. The guerrillas who fought the Japanese in this wild, grey-brown place were ethnic Koreans, who also made up 90 per cent of the local 'Chinese' Communist Party. The ethnic Chinese Communists claimed to be fighting the Japanese as they husbanded their resources in their northern regional redoubt of Yenan for the anticipated showdown with Chiang.[19]

Mao's forces were sustained by subsidies from Stalin as well as by a revived opium industry, which they wisely kept secret from the 'Dixie Mission' sent to Yenan by the US Office of Strategic Services (OSS) in July 1944 out of frustration with KMT military incompetence and venality and in order to glean actionable intelligence on Japanese strength in northern China from POWs taken by the Communists.[20] While a large pool of 2,000 American advisers stationed in Chongqing by turns publicly lauded and privately denounced Chiang Kai-shek, some of the Yenan Americans became admirers of the iron discipline of the Communists.[21]

Korea

Japan's 'backyard' was Korea, which it had ruled since 1910. There, geography arguably played a greater role than politics in the long sequence of events that was to result in one of the most intractably divided nations of the world. The north of the peninsula was bleak and mountainous, and it was among the million or so Koreans who migrated to Manchuria in search of industrial jobs that the Korean Communist Party was born. Among them was Kim Il Sung, the future Great Leader of the People's Republic of North Korea and grandfather of Kim Eun, the third generation of Kims who assumed power in 2012. Born in a village near Pyongyang in 1912, Kim migrated with his family to Manchuria in 1919. From 1932 onwards, he led a small but lethal guerrilla force against the Japanese, striking at Japanese police bases across the Korean border. The Japanese murdered his first wife; his middle brother died at their hands; and an uncle spent thirteen years in Japanese prisons. Like Mao Zedong, Kim Il Sung was steeled by conflict and struggle, another way of saying that his capacity for human sympathy was severely diminished, though for a rare photograph he managed a wide smile as he bounced his unsmiling son and successor Kim Il Jong on his knee.[22] In October 1939 the Japanese launched a huge punitive operation against the North-east Anti-Japanese Army, of which Kim's group was a part, forcing the latter to flee into Soviet Siberia.[23]

In the more agrarian south, many members of the Korean elite, including businessmen, landowners and soldiers, collaborated with the

Japanese colonial regime, which in the late 1930s banned the Korean language entirely.[24] A different path was taken by Syngman Rhee, who had been an advocate of Korean independence since the late nineteenth century, while becoming a Christian in a Japanese prison. After release he travelled to the USA and he took a BA at George Washington University, an MA at Harvard and a PhD at Princeton, where he became a protégé of Woodrow Wilson. Although the 'Fourteen Points' expounded by President Wilson at Versailles after the First World War were not extended to the Far East, the principle of self-determination was the theme of a 1919 conference of Korean independence movements in Shanghai. Syngman Rhee was elected president of the provisional government of the Republic of Korea, a post he held until 1925, when he was impeached for behaving in a dictatorial manner. In a prefiguring of their attempt to foist the supposedly safe (because US-educated) Ahmed Chalabi on Iraq in 2003, Syngman Rhee was the obvious candidate when the Americans needed a sympathetic strongman to govern South Korea in the late 1940s.

As we shall see, the US preference for charismatic individuals (who spoke fluent English) over mass political movements was to colour policy far beyond Korea, and in the process betrayed a profound lack of faith that their grand declarations of principle were a useful guide to the exigencies of war and the post-war settlement in the Far East that mobilized immense numbers of ordinary people.

India

With considerable high-handedness the liberal imperialist Viceroy John Hope, Marquess of Linlithgow, announced in 1939 that India was at war. When he refused the majority Indian National Congress party any role in the central direction of the Indian war effort, its members resigned en masse from provincial governments, and British governors assumed direct rule. The interruption of what the British had hoped would be orderly (for which read as slow as possible) progress towards representative government made little difference while the war was far away, but the Japanese came close enough to induce widespread panic. In April

1942 they raided the Ceylonese capital of Colombo, killing 800 British sailors in two successive attacks on the naval base at Trincomalee. They struck next at southern Indian ports as well as coastal Madras, causing many British administrators to flee to the interior hills. Japanese agents were especially active in Calcutta, capital of Bengal, where Subhas Chandra Bose envisaged a nationalist army on the lines of the Irish Republican Army of the 1920s.

The fact that the US would undertake the main burden of reversing Japanese expansion in South Asia meant that Washington baulked at Prime Minister Winston Churchill's insistence that the affairs of India were none of their business. Large numbers of American servicemen were stationed in India, where, oblivious of their own racially segregated society, they criticized British racism.[25] However, both American meddling and Churchillian obduracy were irrelevant – India was well on its way to independence before the war, and its massive contribution to the war effort made the case for prompt post-war independence overwhelming. Two million sub-continentals, the largest volunteer army in history, served with the British armed forces, many of them in North Africa or Italy. London agreed to underwrite the costs of Indians serving abroad, the result being that Britain owed India £1,321 million by the end of the war, an often overlooked 40 per cent of its colossal £3,355 million post-war debt. Sixty-five per cent of the Indian Army troops were Punjabi Muslims from the north of the sub-continent, which in turn was to make a compelling case for a Muslim-dominated area in the north of a loose, secular Indian federation. Events moved so swiftly and violently that the result was an independent Pakistan.

Indian nationalist politicians had long ago discovered the advantages of alternating constitutional politics with passive-aggressive non-violent protest. They knew the British close up, and saw their weaknesses. Such a strategy had enabled them to occupy the moral high ground, with the British cast in the role of clumsy and violent oppressors.[26] Once war with Japan began, Hindu leader Mahatma Gandhi – who knew Linlithgow well and judged him to be weak and out of his depth – launched a renewed wave of resistance, demanding immediate independence and neutrality, encapsulated in the slogan that the British should 'Quit India'. It was a tactical error that split the Congress and damaged Gandhi's prestige, not only because it was foolish to expect the Japanese to respect Indian neutrality but also because it gave Linlithgow no choice but to invoke emergency powers. British rule became an occupation, deploying more troops – fifty battalions – to quell Indian unrest than were being used to fight the Japanese.[27]

Beginning on 9 August 1942 the British rounded up 60,000 Congress supporters, including the leaders. Jawaharlal Nehru, the radical lawyer and nationalist politician, was comfortably installed in the old Mughal fort at Ahmednagar, but Gandhi was locked up in the Aga Khan's insalubrious prison at Pune. While Nehru read, gardened and wrote, Gandhi embarked on one of his carefully calibrated fasts. The 'Quit India' campaign degenerated rapidly from non-violent strikes into mass riots and acts of sabotage. A hundred police stations were burned down, and there were attacks on 250 railway stations. Track was dismantled and telegraph wires cut. The British response was robust, with 900 people killed and 600 flogged by their own estimate. In and around Patna, the capital of Bihar, RAF fighters were used to strafe Congress supporters who under the cover of lying down on the tracks were tearing them up.

The disparity between how India's two major religious groups responded to metropolitan Britain's existential crisis enhanced the claims of Muhammad Ali Jinnah and his Muslim League to an independent Pakistan following the war, drowning out the voices of Muslim members of the Congress party who disputed Jinnah's claims to speak for all of India's Muslims. Of course the Western-educated lawyers who dominated Congress did not speak for all Hindus either. British emissaries and viceroys vainly endeavoured to retain an all-Indian framework as Hindus, Muslims and Sikhs slid towards an inter-communal bloodbath. In addition the 562 independent feudal princes, some ruling enormous territories such as Hyderabad, represented a further layer of complexity because Britain acknowledged their autocracies through the doctrine of paramountcy.

In the course of 1943 these political problems were joined by a humanitarian one, as some two million Bengalis starved to death when a combination of hoarding-induced inflation and bureaucratic bungling by mainly Indian civil servants resulted in famine. Six million tons of wheat, reserved for military use, bobbed on ships in the Indian Ocean, while other shipping capacity was reserved for the planned D-Day landings in Normandy.[28] Churchill insisted that Indians should 'feel the pinch in the same way as the Mother Country has done'. If humiliating military defeat stripped away the illusion of British power, and emergency laws revealed the mere force that underpinned it, the Bengal famine revealed the supposed efficiency of British administration to be a sham.[29]

India was, of course, the jewel not only in the crown of the British Empire but also by an order of magnitude (with nearly 400 million people) the most intrinsically powerful possession of any of the colonial powers. As such it was able to defend its own frontiers and so buy time for the British to make a swift exit in 1947, once they realized that more was to be gained from a free India within the Commonwealth than from trying to hang on in a situation where the balance of effective power had already tipped to the native population, whether in provincial politics or in the composition of the Indian Civil Service. Unfortunately, in the phrase employed by Field Marshal Lord Wavell, who replaced the hapless Linlithgow as viceroy in 1943, the momentum of past prestige prevented the imperial boat from slowing before it hit the rocks.

Other minds turned from the Raj to an independent future, although much of that future would retain the DNA of the Raj. The key problem, as Nehru acknowledged, was how to create a secular state in a religious country. The future Prime Minister was a Harrow- and Cambridge-educated leftist lawyer. He was well travelled, including Russia in his peregrinations, and well imprisoned, since he spent nine years of his adult life in the Raj's jails. How on earth, he asked, was he to deal with a society in which the questions whether cow dung should be left piled up in the streets or rabid sacred monkeys should not be shot were regarded as issues of fundamental import, and for which human life could be lost in instantly combusting riots.[30] Although many of his Congress party colleagues resented it, the British valued Nehru's dispassionate approach, sharing his concern that Partition would lead to the wholesale Balkanization of the sub-continent as micro-communities descended into religiously inspired anarchy and violence.

The British withdrew in 1947 amid scenes of horror in which a million people were slaughtered and another fifteen million physically displaced, with many women subjected to rape. One Sunday in September 1947 the last Viceroy, Lord Mountbatten, took Nehru in his Dakota to get a close look at the mass exodus of refugees fleeing communal violence. They swooped down to 200 feet above one such column, of Muslims heading north to Lahore. It took a quarter of an hour at 180mph to fly along the forty-five-mile length of the column.[31]

Unsurprisingly, the British retreat from India bulks large in many British accounts, but other Asian empires were more directly victims of Imperial Japan's rampage. European authority in the lesser Far Eastern colonies was irretrievably destroyed by the ease with which the Japanese had conquered them. However, as with the Nazis in Eastern Europe, Japanese assumptions of racial supremacy caused them to behave in most respects worse than the Europeans they had defeated.

The Philippines

The US conquest of the Philippines in 1898 had been followed by a decade-long counter-insurgency against Filipino nationalists. Having previously and piously denounced the use of 'reconcentration camps' by the Spanish in Cuba and the British in South Africa, the Americans adopted them in the Philippines, along with the routine employment of torture including the 'water cure' of drowning and reviving guerrilla suspects, a practice they had learned from the Apaches. US imperialists regarded the Philippines as the key to the door of China and an unsatisfactory post-conquest settlement resulted, with local Hispanic elites utterly dependent on US patronage using the rhetoric of nationalism. As always the Americans talked the talk about democracy, but deferred independence while ensuring that the tame and corrupt native elites remained in power. In the mid-1930s the Tydings–McDuffie Act promised the so-called Commonwealth of the Philippines independence, but with its external relations controlled by the US. The archipelago's defences were entrusted to the ambitious General Douglas MacArthur, son of a former US military governor, who was loaned to Manila to organize a Swiss-style citizens' army.[32]

In the event, by May 1942 the Japanese had overrun the Philippines, forcing the US to surrender its forces after dogged rearguard actions at

Bataan and Corregidor. MacArthur was evacuated, accompanied on his retreat to Australia by the Commonwealth's President Manuel Quezon. The Japanese stationed an enormous occupation force, some 625,800 soldiers, in the Philippines, which were rightly regarded as crucial to defence of the home islands and to the entire Japanese position in South-east Asia. Few members of the Hispanic elites who had collaborated with the Americans had qualms about switching their allegiance. The Japanese met them halfway, explaining, 'Like it or not you are Filipinos and belong to the Oriental race. No matter how hard you try, you cannot become white people.'[33] Tokyo offered its collaborators independence more rapidly than the defeated Americans had done. In July 1943 they were instructed to draft a constitution, the *quid pro quo* being that they declare war on the US, which after much foot dragging they did in September 1944.

Meanwhile, large numbers of brave Filipinos retreated to the hills to wage guerrilla war against the occupiers. The largest group was the Hukbong Bayan Laban sa Hapon (People's Anti-Japanese Army), known as Hukbalahap (Huks) for short. The Huks had their roots in several pre-war militant peasant groups that had coalesced to defend the traditional rights of peasant tenant farmers on the central plain of Luzon, in an area bounded by the Candaba Swamps, the lone peak of Mount Arayat, and the longer ranges of the Sierra Madre and Zimbales. Their desire was to 'get what was just if landlords were honourable and good men'; for, like most peasant movements in history, they were nostalgic for supposedly venerable customs and times when the *patron* wore a human face. The trend was otherwise: landlords took up to 50 per cent of each rice harvest, charging extortionate interest rates in return for emergency loans, and introduced machines to replace men. They also abused land registration to appropriate land with insecure titles, getting away with it because of their corrupt influence in the courts and the Constabulary. On haciendas they had their own strongarm squads to rough up troublesome peasants.[34]

The complex relationship between the Huks and the Philippines Communist Party will be discussed separately. Many of the Huks were in their twenties and had witnessed Japanese brutality at first hand when their relatives were raped, tortured or shot. One in ten of them were young women, although they usually acted as couriers, instructors and nurses rather than as guerrilla fighters. Their weapons were those they took from the Japanese, which they taught themselves to use. It was a desperately savage conflict, in which the Japanese relied on hooded informants to identify Huk sympathizers, while the Huks kidnapped, tried and shot local mayors and policemen who collaborated with the occupiers. The US also inserted its own force into this conflict, recruiting guerrillas whose task was to keep a watching brief on Japanese troop movements, but increasingly they also came into conflict with the Huks. All of this would be replayed after MacArthur's grandiose return and the liberation of the Philippines, when the pre-war elite was restored to power.[35]

Indochina

Indochina was a French colony, consisting of the petty kingdoms of Cambodia and Laos, as well as the southern colony of Cochin China, and the protectorates of Annam and Tonkin in the north. These last three comprised 'Vietnam' in the eyes of nationalists, a very long country about a thousand miles north to south, and wider in the north and south than in a middle, where it narrows to thirty miles. It is roughly the length of California but half the width, and much of it consists of mountainous jungle. Forty thousand French ruled twenty-three million indigenous peoples, the bureaucrats mostly ensconced in the administrative capital of Hanoi in the north, and the settlers concentrated in Saigon in the south, to be near their coffee, rubber and tea plantations. The overseas Chinese constituted the majority of the urban entrepreneurial class.[36]

In 1943 Franklin Roosevelt famously commented to Stalin that 'after a hundred years of French rule in Indochina, the inhabitants are worse off than they had been before'.[37] This was because the ramified interests of the Banque d'Indochine syphoned off the nation's wealth, so that Indochina was actually an economic and political liability. Roosevelt's preferred solution was to place such dysfunctional colonies under international trusteeships, to be supervised by the United States, the Soviet

Union, Britain and China, for in his view France did not merit a place in such exalted company. China's manifold incapacities were the first blow to this solution, while on the altar of inter-Allied solidarity he eventually bowed to Churchill, who supported the exiled Free French leader Charles de Gaulle from 1940 onwards as much to pre-empt US threats to Britain's own colonial interests as to restore France. As Churchill said, he had not become prime minister to preside over the liquidation of the British Empire. Roosevelt also reluctantly awoke to the probability that the colonial issue might compromise the larger security architecture he envisaged for the post-war world, chiefly by weakening the already debilitated imperial metropolises by stripping away their overseas resources.[38]

Wartime Indochina had special complexities, largely because the colonial power fractured into two inimical groupings: adherents of Marshal Pétain's Vichy regime and the Free French followers of Charles de Gaulle. From 1940 to 1944, Vichy French forces coexisted with 65,000 Japanese troops, a minor concession being that they were not obliged to salute each other. For the Japanese, Indochina was the pivotal hinge of the fan they used to spread across South-east Asia, as well as a means of preventing Allied supplies reaching Nationalist China overland. As the war turned against them, the Japanese feared a US invasion from the liberated Philippines, which might be co-ordinated with a local French uprising, after Vichy influence had been subverted by de Gaulle's Free French.

In March 1945 Japanese commander General Tsuchihashi Yuichi swept the colonial regime aside. He gave Admiral Jean Decoux two hours to ponder whether to subordinate French troops to the Japanese. When Decoux asked for more time, the Japanese took over all French bases and installations, crushing such French resistance as arose. Wherever French troops baulked at this coup, as they did at Lang Son in the far north, they were captured and beheaded, poignantly singing the 'Marseillaise'. Those French troops who escaped to a remote north-western airfield at Dien Bien Phu found that their requests for US arms fell on deaf ears. They eventually straggled into southern China, barefoot and hungry.

In Indochina the French had ruthlessly suppressed every manifestation of anti-colonial sentiment, from mutinous troops via rebellious peasants to striking schoolboys, but there was one implacable opponent who eluded them for three decades: Ho Chi Minh. This was the final iteration of multiple aliases Ho would use. Nguyen Tat Thanh (He Who Will Succeed) was born in about 1890 to a farmer's son who had joined the mandarin elite, achieving the equivalent of a doctorate. Whether because of pride or temperament, Ho's father refused to work directly for the puppet emperor who ruled supposedly autonomous Annam, working instead as a rural teacher and then as a magistrate. In 1910 in a drunken rage he caned the wrong person to death and was dismissed from office. He died poor in Saigon.

The future Ho was a bright boy who shed the long hair that marked him out as a country bumpkin at school. He realized early on that a mastery of Western culture – including its revolutionary tradition – was the way to defeat Western imperialism. By his late teens Thanh was involved in anti-French demonstrations, which resulted in expulsion from his French school. Already marked out by the colonial police, he eventually embarked for France, as 'Ba', an assistant cook and stoker on a small liner bound for Marseilles. A truly remarkable odyssey had begun.[39]

When Ho arrived in Marseilles in July 1911, he noted that 'the French in France are better and more polite than in Indochina'. In cafés waiters called him 'Monsieur'. He applied without success for a scholarship to attend the Colonial School. After he had opted for the merchant marine his movements were necessarily opaque; but, wherever he ventured ashore, he moved in political circles as Nguyen Ai Quoc (Nguyen the Patriot).

In July 1923 he slipped his French police shadows through the rear exit of a Parisian cinema and boarded a train to Hamburg and on to Russia by ship as the Chinese merchant 'Chen Vang'. In Moscow he enrolled in the University of the Toilers of the East, which was informally known as the Stalin School since it was under his Commissariat of Nationalities. By July 1923 Ho was deemed important enough to move into the Lux Hotel, albeit into a small room with a bed infested with bugs. In January 1924 his face and fingers were damaged after queuing for hours in deep winter to view Lenin's body. After impressing his

Comintern comrades at the Fifth Congress in 1924, speaking of the need to strike imperialism in the colonies from which it drew its resources, he persuaded his superiors to send him to Canton to organize exiled Vietnamese revolutionaries.[40]

Ho moved into the Canton villa of Mikhail Borodin, the leader of twenty Bolshevik agents attached to the United Front of the KMT and CCP (that is, the Chinese Communist Party). He became 'Ly Thuy' to confuse the French Sûreté officers operating from the French enclave. Officially a journalist, his covert Comintern activities involved recruiting members of an exiled Vietnamese Anarchist group called Tam Tam Xa (Society of Beating Hearts) who, shortly before his arrival, had attempted to assassinate Martial Merlin, the new Governor-General of Indochina, at a banquet, with a bomb that sent knives and forks into the bodies of five other guests. These radicals became the initial recruits of an Indochinese Nationalist Party attached to the CCP and the KMT, but also the covert kernel of a separate Vietnamese Communist group. In early 1925 Ho founded the Vietnamese Revolutionary Youth League, the feeder pool for a future Vietnamese Communist Party. The mandarin's son gave a distinctly Confucian ethical stamp to a movement that blended nationalism and Marxist-Leninism, at a time when the relationship between the two was unresolved by the Soviets.

His relatively stable life in Canton with wife and child ended when in 1927 Chiang Kai-shek's KMT broke with the Chinese Communists, many of whom were tracked down and shot. Ho fled to Hong Kong, where he was refused entry, then to Vladivostok and back to Europe. One night in Paris a friend met him on a bridge, looking down sadly into the Seine. 'I always thought I would become a scholar or a writer, but I've become a professional revolutionary,' he said. 'I travel through many countries, but I see nothing. I'm on strict orders, and my itinerary is carefully prescribed, and you cannot deviate from the route, can you?'[41]

He eventually took ship to Siam, home to 20,000 Vietnamese exiles. In 1929 the French colonial authorities sentenced him to death *in absentia*. When three rival Vietnamese Communist parties emerged, Ho was smuggled into Hong Kong in February 1930 to resolve their differences. This resulted in the formal foundation of the Dang Cong san Viet Nam, the Vietnamese Communist Party. Arrested and put on trial by the British, Ho eventually fled to the Soviet Union, where he remained until 1938.

Lengthy British custody meant that he laboured under suspicion of being a spy in the years when Stalin murdered 650,000 of his comrades, in purges which reached into the foreign denizens of the Lux Hotel, who got used to sleeping with one eye open. Ho survived because Stalin did not regard Indochina as a serious place, and by shrinking into near invisibility. In 1938 he was allowed to leave for China, where the CCP and KMT had re-formed their alliance to resist the Japanese. He used the name Hu Guang first in Yan'an, where the CCP were massed, and then in Guangxi, whence he repaired to establish closer links with his homeland.

By 1940 he was in Kunming, the capital of Yunnan, where he met two fellow sons of Vietnamese mandarins: Pham Van Dong and Vo Nguygen Giap. The former had spent years in the notorious 'tiger cages' of the French prison of Poulo Condore, the latter was a law graduate who had developed a fascination with military history, in particular guerrilla warfare. Giap's father and sister had died in, or just after release from, French jails by the time he reached ten years of age. His sister-in-law was executed by the French and in 1943 his young wife would perish in Hanoi's Central Prison – later known to captured Americans as the Hanoi Hilton. These experiences left him a cold, unforgiving man wholly dedicated to the cause of armed struggle, in which he was to reveal military genius.[42]

The fall of France in June 1940 triggered a new stage in a hitherto spasmodic revolution. By then Ho had thoroughly studied the strategy and tactics of the Chinese Communist Party and he had read Mao's works on guerrilla warfare. He decided that the first priority should be to build a political infrastructure throughout the country, while creating a small military force that, when the moment came, could launch insurrections which would trigger a general uprising. While Ho had close contacts with the Chinese Communists, and in particular with Zhou Enlai, he also needed to maintain good relations with the Kuomintang, who would be providing Ho's forces with a safe rear area in southern China. He cleverly negotiated his way through the complex eddies of Chinese politics, by stressing a simple anti-imperialist line, in which the

enemy was the Japanese and the French. Moving nearer to the border
with Tonkin, Ho helped form a united patriotic front or League for the
Independence of Vietnam, which in Vietnamese was the Viet Nam Doc
Lap Dong Minh – better known as Viet Minh. In 1941 he was the lead
instructor at a camp at Jingxi on the Vietnamese border at which Giap
provided the military training. The course ended with a kiss of the red
flag with its gold star, after which graduates were sent back to Vietnam,
gathering in a mountainous area called the Viet Bac. In early 1941 Ho
returned to Vietnam for the first time in thirty years, setting up an HQ
in a limestone cave near the remote village of Pac Bo. By this time he had
adopted the identity of a Chinese journalist and the name Ho Chi Minh
(He Who Enlightens).[43]

Although Ho was not Party general secretary, the French police had
eliminated most of his internal Vietnamese rivals and he enjoyed enormous prestige not just as the Comintern's senior man, but because of the
sacrifices his life had manifestly entailed. In Vietnamese terms he was
also quite old, and hence deserving of the affectionate name Uncle. The
final incarnation had occurred: Uncle Ho. Ever in character, he dodged
French checkpoints and patrols by pretending to be a shaman, dressed in
a black robe and equipped with magic texts, joss sticks and a live chicken
for sacrifice.

Japanese destruction of French rule forced crucial decisions on the
Viet Minh. It also provided the Americans with an opportunity to use
the Vietnamese to fight the Japanese. The US began dropping arms from
aircraft based in southern China, while the Viet Minh provided valuable
weather reports and helped locate shot-down US aircrew. In March
1945 the OSS sent 'Deer Team' into Vietnam to liaise with the 'old man'
who led the Viet Minh. One of these agents, Archimedes 'Al' Patti,
penned an account of their stay in a jungle encampment. The emaciated
Viet Minh leader, already tubercular, lay ill with dysentery and malaria,
but rallied enough to chain-smoke Patti's Chesterfields after the team
doctor had treated him.[44] The OSS agents taught guerrillas, commanded
by Giap – 'a wiry little man with large calculating eyes and a perpetually
angry look' – how to use modern weapons. The Americans spent many
agreeable hours with Ho Chi Minh, who at one point inquired in English:
'Your statesmen make eloquent speeches about helping those with

self-determination. We are self-determined. Why not help us? Am I different from Nehru, Quezon, even your George Washington? Was not Washington considered a revolutionary? I, too, want to set my people free.[45] Privately he thought that the Americans were all about business. As Ho heard news of the dropping of the atomic bombs and the Japanese surrender that August, he and Giap decided to launch their insurrection, their task aided by widespread peasant anger over a famine in the winter of 1944–5 that killed a million people, after the Japanese had refused to stop exporting rice to Japan from their state granaries.[46]

Then the Japanese managed to cause a political crisis. Following their disarming of the French in March 1945, they encouraged Emperor Bao Dai to declare Vietnamese independence, a step they urged neighbouring Cambodia's Prince Sihanouk to follow. Bao Dai's authority was entirely notional in northern Tonkin, where real, lethal power was increasingly exercised by the Viet Minh from their Viet Bac bases, from which they sortied to cut communications and terrorize government officials and policemen.

The Potsdam conference arranged in the summer of 1945 to reorder the world is often viewed through an exclusively European optic, as reflected in the fact that the Big Three were actually the Big Four, for Generalissimo Chiang Kai-shek was present along with Harry S. Truman (Roosevelt's successor), Stalin and Churchill. The conference was concerned with winning the ongoing war with Japan and unmaking its empire in South-east Asia. It was decreed that China and Britain should occupy Indochina above and below the 16th parallel, but Al Patti's OSS units returned to Vietnam, nominally to secure Allied POWs and civilian internees still in Japanese captivity. This gave them a ringside seat to observe how Ho created a *fait accompli* to pre-empt the restoration of colonial authority. He sent his men into Hanoi across the Doumer Bridge over the Red River to force the abdication of Bao Dai. The capital of Tonkin was bedecked with lanterns, flowers and red banners with the five golden stars, all under the eyes of 30,000 Japanese troops. On 2 September 1945 at a massed meeting on Place Puginier in front of the former Governor-General's Hanoi Palace, Ho proclaimed Vietnamese independence. There were some deliberate nods to his OSS friends in the wording of his speech:

'All men are created equal. They are endowed by their creator with certain unalienable rights; among these are life, liberty, and the pursuit of happiness.' This immortal statement appeared in the Declaration of Independence of the United States of America in 1776. In a broader sense, it means: All the peoples on earth are equal from birth, all the peoples have a right to live and to be happy and free. The Declaration of the Rights of Man and the Citizen, made at the time of the French Revolution, in 1791, also states: 'All men are born free and with equal rights, and must always remain free and have equal rights.'[47]

He asked the crowd, 'My fellow countrymen, have you understood?' 'Yes!' the crowd roared back. Standing alongside Patti, General Giap gave a clenched-fist salute when the band struck up the 'Star Spangled Banner'. The French were appalled by this. A more senior US team tried to pin down Ho's political views, but was fobbed off with evasive vagaries: 'I have difficulty remembering some parts of my long life. That is the problem of being an old revolutionary.' Meanwhile his regime in Hanoi made short work of any ideological opponents. In addition to a new state security apparatus, the Communists encouraged the creation of 'traitor elimination committees' and an 'Assault Assassination Committee' whose victims were liberal nationalists, Trotskyites and women who had married French men.[48]

As the new government established itself, 150,000 Chinese KMT Nationalist troops crossed into Vietnam under a drug-addict warlord Chiang was keen to divert from China. The Viet Minh tried to secure their good conduct by supplying him with opium, but the Chinese looted everything up to the roof tiles. Meanwhile, in the southern capital of Saigon, where the Viet Minh played a much weaker hand as part of a broader nationalist coalition, attempts to celebrate Independence Day led to violent clashes between French and Vietnamese residents. Watching the celebrations from high vantage points, the French ostentatiously refused to join in the applause when independence was proclaimed. French snipers started shooting, and in retaliation Europeans were assaulted and their business premises looted.

Four days later 600 men from the 20th Indian Division arrived in Saigon under General Douglas Gracey to disarm 50,000 surrendered

Japanese troops. He was not a political general and inflexibly followed his orders, with disastrous consequences. One of his first acts was to use his Gurkha guard to evict the Southern Provisional Executive Committee from the former Governor-General's Palace, after they had tried to welcome him. He next rearmed liberated French internees, who promptly attacked any 'native' they encountered. Angry Vietnamese retaliated, slaughtering 150 Europeans. With fresh French troops slow to arrive, Gracey relied on his Gurkhas and surrendered Japanese to expel the Viet Minh. He declared martial law to break a general strike and used liberated French Foreign Legionnaires to impose their simulacrum of civil order.

In a remarkable example of intra-Allied incivility Gracey ordered Lieutenant-Colonel Peter Dewey, the senior OSS officer in Saigon, to leave Indochina because of the OSS's 'blatantly subversive' involvement with the Viet Minh. Dewey was shot dead en route to the airport after Gracey forbade him to fly the Stars and Stripes on his Jeep and the Viet Minh mistook him for a Frenchman. The following day Gracey threatened Japanese General Numata with prosecution for war crimes if he did not order his men to help the British and French fight the Viet Minh; and so it was that the British coerced the soldiers who had humiliated them in 1942 to reimpose French rule over Vietnam, which the Japanese had overthrown seven months previously.[49]

By early October 1945 there were sufficient French forces in Cochin China for Gracey to relinquish authority south of the 16th parallel to the Free French war hero General Philippe Leclerc, who re-established French rule in Cambodia and Laos, before turning his attention to the northern Democratic Republic of Vietnam. By 20 January 1946 the British forces were gone. A French high commissioner designate, Jean Sainteny, was flown to Hanoi accompanied by Patti's OSS team. They noted that Hanoi was swathed in red banners and bedecked with other banners which, in English, read 'Independence or Death' and 'Vietnam for the Vietnamese'. Only a cordon of Japanese troops prevented the French from being lynched, but Patti and his team settled into a comfortable and unthreatened existence at the Hotel Metropole.

Sainteny was bitter about the role of the Americans: 'We seemed to the Americans incorrigibly obstinate in reviving a colonial past to which they were opposed, in the name of an infantile anti-colonialism which blinded them to almost everything.'[50] Nothing is so simple, for there were also OSS agents of French-American extraction, or passionately Francophile veterans of the Gaullist resistance. But the Americans were certainly more popular than anyone else. One night Ho invited a relatively junior OSS agent to dinner. Major Frank White noticed to his horror that he was seated next to Ho himself in a room awash with Chinese and French dignitaries. The Chinese quickly became drunk and the French were uncommunicative and as stiff as broomsticks. When White remarked on the resentment caused by the seating plan, Ho replied, 'Yes, I can see that – but who else could I talk to?'

Leclerc despatched motorized and waterborne columns, one commanded by Colonel Jacques Massu, whom we will encounter later, to surprise Viet Minh troops in the countryside, which was then ravaged by follow-up infantry sweeps. Otherwise he was careful to minimize civilian casualties in ways which prefigured British hearts-and-minds efforts in Malaya. As far as northern Annam and Tonkin were concerned, Leclerc prevailed on the Chinese to withdraw – they were needed by Chiang Kai-shek to fight the Communists – in return for a renunciation of French concessionary enclaves in China. Ironically, Chiang had earlier declined Roosevelt's offer to take over the whole of Vietnam.

Ho was careful to do nothing to upset the Franco-Chinese negotiations. As he explained to his sceptical Party comrades: 'Can't you understand what would happen if the Chinese stayed? You are forgetting our past history. Whenever the Chinese came, they stayed a thousand years. The French, on the other hand, can stay for only a short time. Eventually they will leave.' His summing up was less delicate: 'Better to sniff French shit for a while than to eat China's for the rest of our lives.'[51] To that end Giap led talks with Sainteny at the mountain resort of Dalat, although there was little trust on either side. The French agreed to a Democratic Republic of Vietnam, within the French Union, with the possible future inclusion of Cochin China subject to a referendum – although in reality the French had no intention of relinquishing control. Almost as soon as the Vietnamese thought they had a deal, the French tried to write their continued control of justice, economic planning and communications into it. Ho even agreed to allow the French to station

15,000 troops in the north for a five-year period. At a rally where Ho explained his strategy to activists, someone threw a grenade, forgetting to take the pin out.

While Leclerc was commander-in-chief Indochina, de Gaulle's new High Commissioner was Admiral Thierry d'Argenlieu, a militant right-wing Catholic and former Carmelite friar. A member of his staff said he 'had one of the greatest minds of the twelfth century'. He intended to restore French rule in Cochin China and, unlike Leclerc, refused to negotiate with Ho over the fate of the North. While Ho flew to Paris to finalize the settlement drafted with Leclerc, on 1 June 1946 d'Argenlieu returned from home leave and unilaterally proclaimed a new Autonomous Republic of Cochin China to scupper the talks in France. While he had the backing of businessmen and colonists, the Admiral had no authorization from Paris to do this. In November 1946, when Ho was still engaged in talks at Fontainebleau, the Admiral ordered the French cruiser *Suffren* to shell Haiphong, killing around 6,000 people, under the pretext of interdicting arms shipments.

In retaliation, Giap ordered the killing of about 350 village headmen who refused to co-operate with the Viet Minh, and the slaughter of the entire leadership of the nationalist movement who were members of the coalition government of the Democratic Republic. At Fontainebleau the talks collapsed and after Sainteny had stated that the French must triumph militarily, Ho replied: 'You will kill ten of my men while we kill one of yours, but you will be the ones to end up exhausted.' The larger irony involved in this story was that the Radical, Socialist and Christian Democrat French politicians who were at the forefront in advocating a federal Europe were the most intransigent supporters of an authoritarian and centralized colonial empire. Empire was essential to France's ongoing pretensions to be a global power after years of defeat and humiliation and dependence on the Anglo-Saxons for liberation.[52]

Emboldened by increasing numbers, in Hanoi the French troops acted in a cavalier fashion towards what was a democratically elected northern government. Giap readied the population for rebellion, with holes drilled in trees into which dynamite could be inserted to create instant roadblocks. After Ho returned in December, he reluctantly called for a war of resistance. Sainteny was an early casualty when a mine destroyed his armoured vehicle, and another forty French nationals were also killed. Although the French gained control of the capital, the night of 19–20 December 1946 was when the first Indochina war between the French and Viet Minh formally began.

The Communists fell back on their former liberated areas in Viet Bac near the Chinese border, around eighty miles from Hanoi, in a country where moving a couple of miles could take a month. *Ad hoc* arms factories churned out weapons to supplement old British or Japanese stocks, or those purchased from the Chinese, who also supplied modern radio communications equipment. Japanese instructors taught the Viet Minh how to use modern weaponry, and in some cases joined operations against the French. Giap rigorously applied the basic principles of modern insurgency warfare which he had acquired through a reading of Mao's works on guerrilla warfare. He added some tactical tips of his own:

> If the enemy advances, we retreat.
> If he halts, we harass.
> If he avoids battle, we attack.
> If he retreats, we follow.

He was a keen student of domestic French politics and knew that the here-today, gone-tomorrow caravanserai of squabbling Fourth Republic politicians would always go for a quick fix, that the French public had little appetite for the drip of death thousands of miles away, and that much of the equipment that arrived in Vietnam would be sabotaged by a fifth column of French Communist workers. In this war of wills, it would be a rash man who would put money on the French. Leclerc was among those who realized that there was no military solution. Shortly before his death in Africa in 1947 he wrote: 'France will no longer put down by force a grouping of 24 million inhabitants which is assuming unity and in which there exists a xenophobic and perhaps a national ideal . . . The main problem is political.'[53]

The French drifted into war against a masterly tactician leading a people whose warlike propensities had been evident – to their neighbours – since the Middle Ages.[54] But there were signs that the French would not be fighting alone. As Al Patti's OSS team was withdrawn from Indochina on 30 September 1945, he had already realized how far US policy was changing from Roosevelt's coolness towards colonial regimes. He felt that a new policy had evolved almost by stealth after Truman took over. By January 1946, this favoured the French, as evidenced when the State Department approved a British request to give the French 800 US military vehicles from their Lend-Lease pool. The 'Made in America' markings disappeared, in a minor concession to the disregarded anti-colonial line. This was the first step on a winding road, which would lead, over the protracted agony of France's involvements in Indochina, to the US taking on Giap and his steely troops themselves.[55]

Indonesia

Starting in late December 1941 and concluding in March 1942, successive attacks by the Japanese resulted in their conquest of the resource-rich archipelago of the Netherlands East Indies (modern Indonesia). In March 93,000 men of the Dutch colonial army surrendered, not bothering to consult their Australian and British allies, who joined many European and Australian civilians in brutal and degrading captivity. The Dutch had made no attempt to arm native Indonesians, typical of a colonial regime that had managed to educate 207 native children a year to high-school level from a total population of sixty-seven million.

The 300,000 Japanese troops based on these islands managed to make Dutch neglect seem benign. Native women were abducted to work in military brothels, while men were deployed as slave labour on railways, roads and the like. Of a quarter of a million Javanese abducted to work for the Japanese, only 70,000 came home alive. Drought, typhoons and Japanese rice requisitioning caused the death by starvation of two and a half million Javanese. Sumatra was administratively detached and merged into a Southern Region with Malaya, all ultimately governed by Tokyo from Singapore, renamed Syonan or 'Light of the South'. Suspected of aiding Chiang or Mao, the large ethnic Chinese community was treated with appalling brutality, with 40,000 of them murdered.

Richer Chinese saved their skins by paying a $50 million levy in 'atone-ment' for past support of Chiang Kai-shek. This was not the only respect in which domestic Chinese politics had contaminated the diaspora. In Malay forests, the Japanese corralled villagers in stockades to isolate them from Communist guerrillas who were supported by Force 136 sent by the British Special Operations Executive (SOE).[56]

By a unique accident, the Japanese occupation of the Dutch East Indies laid the foundations for an independent nation. Although the Jap-anese navy swept the Dutch and their British and American allies aside with ease, one Allied submarine managed to sink a transport carrying half the trained administrators sent by Tokyo to take over the govern-ment of the vast Indonesian archipelago – it is as wide as the United States, and Sumatra alone is the size of California. Among some Indone-sians the Japanese, and their erasure of Dutch-language street signs and place names, were welcomed, although their earliest actions included the dissolution of political parties and the prohibition of the red and white Indonesian nationalist flag. However, the mass internment of Dutch administrators and the deaths of their Japanese replacements meant that educated Indonesians filled thousands of middle- and upper-echelon administrative and technical jobs. These officials soon gained confidence and realized that they did not need Dutch – or Japanese – tutelage to run their country.[57]

The middle-aged civil engineer and nationalist activist Sukarno (Java-nese has no first names) was one of the first to beat a path to the Japa-nese high command; he left the meeting in a Buick loaned to him to facilitate his collaborative activities. Yet he was not quite the Quisling the Dutch claimed him to be to discredit him with the Americans. With one eye towards a post-imperial future, Sukarno calculated that it was better to collaborate with the Japanese, whose overstretched empire seemed potentially ephemeral, than to support what even in defeat he regarded as more durable European empires. Although he was as aware as many other nationalists of the nature of Japanese imperialism, unlike the others he had not been educated in metropolitan Holland and had no residual loyalty to the Dutch, who had repeatedly imprisoned and exiled him in the preceding years.

Everywhere they conquered, the Japanese authorities created submissive local claques to replace nascent political parties. They invariably involved the word 'New' in their titles. In China there was Wang Jin-wei's New Citizens' Movement; in the Philippines the Association for Service to the New Philippines. In Indonesia the Japanese crudely tried to co-opt both modernized and traditional Islam by requiring their adherents to bow towards Tokyo's Imperial Palace rather than Mecca. They also established a Triple A movement: Japan the Leader of Asia; Japan the Light of Asia; and Japan the Protector of Asia. The limited appeal of this movement afforded Sukarno his chance; he offered to associate Indonesian nationalism with the conqueror-liberators through a movement called Centre of the People's Power or Putera, the Indonesian word for Son of his Mother. 'Long Live Japan! Long Live Indonesia!' was its slogan.

As the tide of war turned, the Japanese conceded limited representative institutions, perhaps with a view to lumbering the Allies with the most awkward customers among the latter's former colonial subjects while reducing the number of problems they had to deal with themselves. In September 1943 Sukarno was appointed president of a Central Advisory Council, at whose sessions Indonesians could raise grievances as they simultaneously rubber-stamped Japanese demands for labour or rice levies. As similar bodies were elaborated down to local level, so an embryonic national administration emerged. Collaborating also licensed Sukarno to traverse Indonesia, which in itself enabled him to become a national figure. He may have been strident in his denunciations of the Americans and British, and extravagant in his praise of the Japanese, but he did so in an elliptical Indonesian tongue via a national network of 'singing trees' or village radios suspended from branches. It was easy in these speeches to bamboozle the largely monoglot Japanese, but they had also learned – too late – that a policy of ruthless exploitation was counter-productive. One senior Japanese commander wrote:

If we judge the trend of native sentiments correctly and, while advancing their education, promise in the near future to meet their desires, the extremely sensitive natives will be impressed and although there may be material shortages they will tolerate this and steadily strengthen their cooperation . . . On the other hand, if we regard the natives as ignorant people and err in the ways of winning their hearts, we shall receive an unexpected counterblow – as the saying goes, 'Even a small work has a large spirit' – and we must then be prepared to partake of the same bitter cup suffered by the former Dutch regime at the time of its collapse.[58]

In accordance with this new line, the Japanese formed quasi-military youth movements and an Indonesian volunteer army which would become the core of a future republican Indonesian army. In November 1943 Sukarno made his first foreign trip to Tokyo, where he was decorated by Emperor Hirohito and entertained by Prime Minister Tojo. In May 1944 he attended a conference in Singapore, where he publicly enunciated the five principles which would guide a future Indonesian state. These were belief in God, social justice, representative government, internationalism and unity of the archipelago from Sumatra to Papua New Guinea. In a complex society of sixty-seven million people, this was probably the maximum aspiration.[59]

Sukarno's strategy appeared to pay dividends as in September 1944 the Japanese promised independence to what they had hitherto called the Southern Regions, meaning all the territory they had conquered in South-east Asia. In March 1945 they established an Investigative Committee for the Preparation of Independence. That August they appointed Sukarno chairman, and Mohammed Hatta his deputy, with 24 August set to be the date when power would be formally transferred – a date rendered irrelevant by the abrupt end of the war following the dropping of atomic bombs on Hiroshima and Nagasaki.

After 8 August Sukarno took matters into his own hands and on the 17th in the courtyard of a house in Jakarta simply declared, 'We, the people of Indonesia, hereby declare Indonesia's independence.' This was followed by demonstrations, under the nervous eyes of Japanese troops, in the lengthy interval before the Allies arrived to take their surrender. As originally planned, that should have been the Americans, with the Dutch East Indies destined to become a part of MacArthur's vast Pacific command. He fully intended to restore Dutch rule, but while an invasion of Japan was still on the cards US Chief of Staff General George Marshall had decided that MacArthur should not dissipate forces he needed for

Operation Olympic, the invasion and occupation of Japan. Marshall's growing dislike of MacArthur gave him a further reason to cut him down to size.

Following agreement at Potsdam, the British had already subsumed the Dutch East Indies into Mountbatten's hopelessly overstretched South East Asia Command (SEAC), an enterprise known to American cynics as 'Save England's Asian Colonies'. This sleight of hand resulted in some confused loyalties in Indonesia two months later, when Australian and Indian Army troops landed, the delay caused by the US reluctance to provide ships. Red and white flags flew openly and 'Merdeka!' (Freedom!) was daubed on walls; but there were also such pro-US slogans as: 'We are fighting for government for the people, by the people, of the people.' A British officer sourly noted to an American observer: 'Your damned American revolution is still giving us trouble.' After Indonesian nationalist gangs tried to kill anyone with a white face, a larger force of Seaforth Highlanders was despatched under General Sir Philip Christison. With demobilization beckoning, none of these British or Indian soldiers wished to tarry in Indonesia and, since his Muslim Indian troops would be highly unlikely to coerce Muslim Indonesians, Christison wisely announced that 'British and Indian troops will not become involved in internal politics,' leaving the maintenance of civil order in the hands of the Japanese. His aim was to fulfil only the limited role of freeing 100,000 Europeans from atrocious conditions of confinement, but circumstances dictated otherwise.

The new Labour government in London endorsed Mountbatten's proposal that the Dutch negotiate with the Indonesian nationalists. Unwilling though they were, the Dutch had little choice, since their homeland was devastated and the country had no armed forces to speak of. Negotiations were complicated by the fact that the government in The Hague was provisional, and unwilling to wave farewell to a colony that was at least as important to the Netherlands economy as India was to Britain. Overseas colonies also bolstered Dutch pretensions to being a significant player in newly liberated Europe. Not unreasonably, Sukarno pleaded with the British: 'Indonesians will never understand why it is, for instance, wrong for the Germans to rule Holland if it is right for the Dutch to rule Indonesia. In either case the right to rule rests on pure force and not on the sanction of the populations.' Mohammed Hatta put it more bluntly: 'the Dutch [are] about as popular as the pox'.[60]

The British tried to stand aside from the murderous tensions between Indonesian nationalists and incoming Dutch officials, who behaved as though they would simply take up where they had left off three years earlier. However, in Surabaya in eastern Java a British force was surrounded and shot up by a much larger number of Indonesian militiamen after they tried to extract civilian internees. A British general based in Batavia made the mistake of leafleting these militias from the air, telling them to disarm. When the British commander on the spot, Brigadier Aubertin Mallaby, tried to negotiate an exit for his forces, he was killed. The 5th Indian Division, supported by aircraft and tanks, went in to avenge the Mallaby's death and killed around 9,000 Indonesian fighters.

Since the Dutch lacked the forces to reoccupy Indonesia, the fate of their colony devolved on the Americans and the British. US policy initially reflected the anti-colonial sentiments of the late President Roosevelt, but his idea of international trusteeships for former European colonies was quietly abandoned, partly because the Joint Chiefs of Staff in Washington did not want this logic extended to the new overseas bases the US had acquired, and also because US corporations had a keen interest in Indonesia's oil, rubber and tin.

But Indonesia was affected by a more fundamental clash over policy between different departments of the US foreign service, which was to bedevil the making of policy towards other parts of the world in the post-war years. The State Department was bitterly divided between Europeanists, who wanted to support Britain, France and the Netherlands, and Asianists, who thought that the (outrageously circumscribed) independence the United States granted to the Philippines on 4 July 1946 should be paradigmatic for all former European colonies. A compromise formula that sought to reconcile the 'natural aspirations' of indigenous peoples and the 'legitimate rights and interests' of the colonizers revealed some of the tensions in US policy-making. The advent of Harry Truman with his less cynical and more broadbrush view of the world enabled the Europeanists to quietly bury Roosevelt's more ambivalent policy, which, in truth, would have unravelled anyway under the weight of its own contradictions.

The main British concern was that the spirit of independence evident in Indonesia should not spread to Malaya, but at the same time the British wished to withdraw their forces as rapidly as possible. The solution was to rely on 65,000 Japanese troops to maintain order, as they were legally obliged to do under the terms of the surrender agreement. They were good soldiers, as a British officer noted when he used them to rescue European hostages taken in Bandung. 'I watched the Japs closely as they went in. Couldn't fault 'em – absolutely first class!' When Mountbatten visited in April 1946, the guard of honour consisted of a thousand Japanese with their officers presenting arms with Samurai swords.[61]

The threat of peremptory British withdrawal forced the Dutch into negotiations, not with Sukarno, who was unacceptable to them, but with Premier Sutan Sjahrir, who met with them at Linggadjati under the chairmanship of Lord Killearn. The agreement, concluded in November 1946 but not ratified until six months later, accepted the existence of an independent Indonesian Republic as part of a Netherlands Union headed by the Dutch Crown, with joint control of defence and foreign affairs. Pausing only long enough to slip 55,000 Dutch troops into Java, the British withdrew.[62]

The Dutch hoped to establish a series of puppet states organized as an Indonesian federation under Dutch control. This resulted in fighting between the Dutch troops, who took major cities on Java and Sumatra as well as the Outer Islands including Bali, and the army of the Indonesian Republic and *ad hoc* militias. The Dutch launched two major 'police' campaigns in July 1947 and December 1948, the first called Operation Product, the second Operation Crow, after an intervening armistice known as the Renville Agreement broke down. These operations were extremely brutal. On 9 December 1947 Dutch forces massacred all 431 men in the village of Rawagede after they refused to betray the whereabouts of a leading independence fighter – tragically, they did not know who he was. After the Indonesian nationalists also breached the Renville Agreement, in December 1948 the Dutch launched a surprise attack on the nationalist capital of Jogjakarta, their actions aided by their having broken the enemy's military codes. They took the city and captured Hatta and Sukarno, who were about to depart for a meeting with Nehru in India, and exiled them to Bangka island.

The Dutch had failed to spot the significance of an earlier event. Between September and November 1948, Soviet-backed Indonesian Communists had launched the Madiun revolt in Central Java, which the Indonesian army had suppressed with considerable violence. This brought the Americans into play. A senior agent of the CIA (which had succeeded the OSS in 1947 as America's main external intelligence agency) arrived in Jogjakarta, one of his tasks being to select members of the Police Mobile Brigade, who were flown to US bases for advanced training. The US was not going to allow a minor power like the Netherlands to mess up the incipient United Nations and used the threat of ending the Netherlands' participation in the European reconstruction assistance plan known as Marshall Aid to to induce the Dutch to comply with UN ceasefire demands. Under the terms of the final settlement which gave the Indonesian Republic its independence, the Dutch clung on to Netherlands New Guinea, while Indonesia was obliged to take over £4 billion of Dutch East Indies debt, half of which was the cost of the campaign Holland had waged to frustrate Indonesian independence.[63]

2. HARRY TRUMAN'S WORLD

Much to be Modest About

Other than a general commitment to a liberal economic order, and to his fundamental Four Freedoms, before his death in April 1945 Roosevelt was vague about how the world might be ordered for the peace, for this was one of those seminal moments, like 1815 or 1919. He was credulous towards Stalin, regarded Churchill as an out-of-date imperialist, detested de Gaulle and reposed great faith in China. FDR thought in terms of something like the nineteenth-century Congress of Europe from the era of Metternich and Castlereagh. When updated this meant that four policemen, the US, Britain, the Soviet Union and Nationalist China, would police the world. The disguising mechanism for this quadrumvirate was the United Nations, where they would dominate the Security Council, and a General Assembly front-loaded with their allies in the pre-decolonized era.[1]

How the US dealt with the world was inevitably subordinated to more immediate problems. The Americans had experienced nothing of the domestic civilian death and destruction experienced by Asian and European belligerents and so failed to grasp how deeply the war had disordered the world. While the rest of the world was laid waste, US GNP rose from $886 million in 1939 to $135 billion in 1945. Nonetheless, on Victory in Japan Day there were over twelve million personnel in the US armed forces, including seven million overseas. The first task was to get them home as their families adopted the slogan 'No boats, no votes'. Repatriated at the rate of 15,000 per day, GIs teemed into an economy undergoing painful civilian reconversion. For example, Boeing laid off 21,200 of the 29,000 men in two aircraft plants on one day, while 6,000 naval ships were mothballed at the stroke of a pen. Within a single week, $15 billion worth of arms contracts were cancelled.[2]

Among workers and their representatives there was fear that wartime economic expansion was only a hiatus before the return to Depression-era conditions. As prices and rents were freed, rationing was phased out and forty-eight-hour weeks with overtime ceased, union leaders contrasted their members' newly modest incomes with the colossal profits corporations had made in wartime. A rash of ugly strikes swept the US, involving automobile and steel workers, coal miners and meat packers. Regardless of whether they were homebound veterans or civilians who had followed wartime work to remote locations, everyone wanted a place of their own, but there was a chronic shortage of new housing. This was only partly solved by loans to GIs or the application of Fordist assembly-line methods to basic suburban housing. The reality was many families doubling up, with people also camped out in cars, barns, cellars and streetcars.

Although Americans had forced savings in bonds and cash amounting to $140 billion in 1945 as a result of the wartime dearth of consumer goods, there was still remarkably little to spend their money on. For this was a lean America, where a weekly hot bath was a luxury, almost impossible for us to imagine from the vantage point of the twenty-first century. It was not concerned with whether the Russians wanted a small piece of Turkey, or which permutation of crooks and villains came to power in Athens. It did not want US armed forces permanently stationed 3,000 miles away to defend former enemy lands against a former ally. At the same time most Americans passionately believed in the universal value of the United Nations. In a poll held in late 1947, as many as 82 per cent believed that it was 'very important that the UN succeed', while 56 per cent wanted it converted into 'a world government with power to control the armed forces of all nations, including the United States'.[3]

The burden of reconciling the hopes of many Americans for a better life with the responsibilities of global power fell to Harry Truman. He was a seemingly mundane Mid-Westerner, the son of a failed Missouri farmer who had gone on to fail himself as a haberdasher. Too poor to go to college, and hence the last non-graduate US president, Truman distinguished himself as an artillery officer in the First World War. He was five feet eight, with grey-blue eyes and steely hair. His personal integrity, based on a strong Baptist faith, somehow managed to coexist with being part of the deeply corrupt regime of the Democrat Tom Pendergast in St Louis. Chosen to put an honest face on the Pendergast machine in Congress, Truman was elected to the Senate in 1934, aged fifty.

His experiences of the havoc debt played on families such as his own gave him a horror of government overspending and waste. The profligacy of the armed forces and defence contractors with taxpayers' money was a particular bugbear. Washington DC was not Truman's kind of town, certainly not the smart salons of Georgetown. He was quick to resent the East Coast 'pinko pansies', 'striped pants' patrician snobs and impertinent journalists who darkened his path.[4]

Nothing about Harry would have mattered much in broader historical terms, until on the evening of 12 April 1945 he was summoned to the White House. A grieving Eleanor Roosevelt said: 'Harry, the President is dead.' 'Is there anything I can do for you?' he asked, to break the silence. Mrs Roosevelt replied, 'Is there anything we can do for you? For you are the one in trouble now.'[5] The intimacy of this scene contrasted with the fact that FDR had met Truman only three times before he drafted him to replace the left-liberal Henry Wallace, and then three times more, perfunctorily, after Truman had become vice president. Now, aged sixty, Truman was president. While conscious that there were a dozen people who could do the job better, he told friends and colleagues that Providence had destined him for the role.

Truman quickly dumped Secretary of State Edward Stettinius, 'a fine man, good looking, amiable, cooperative, but never an idea old or new'. His replacement was a dud for different reasons. Relations with James Byrnes, a South Carolina politician who thought he should have been FDR's running mate and successor, were soon strained by Byrnes's lengthy absences at overseas conferences and by disagreement over how to react to Soviet provocations as the wartime Grand Alliance came apart like an accelerating row of burst threads. Byrnes conducted diplomacy with one eye on his domestic political ambitions, seeking agreements as much for their headline value without adequately informing either Truman or Congressional leaders, his vanity making it easy for Stalin and his Foreign Minister, Molotov, to manipulate him. In January 1947 Truman recalled Marshall from China to replace him.[6]

The new President rapidly realized that the Soviets were bent on taking 'here a little, there a little, they are chiselling from us'. Not long after becoming president he lectured Molotov on Soviet bad faith. In Truman's recollection, Molotov said, 'I have never been talked to like that in my life.' 'Carry out your agreements and you won't get talked to like that,' Truman snapped back.[7] By January 1946 Truman had decided: 'Unless Russia is faced with an iron fist and strong language another war is in the making. Only one language do they understand: "How many divisions have you?"' He would endeavour to get along with the Soviets, and work with them within the new UN Security Council, but he was never going to appease them, the common nightmare of his generation.[8]

An inquiry from the US Treasury as to why the Soviets had rejected the International Monetary Fund and other global organizations established at Bretton Woods and Dumbarton Oaks elicited a significant response from the US embassy in Moscow, becalmed during its celebrations of George Washington's birthday.

The diplomat and Soviet expert George Kennan dictated a powerful 'Long Telegram' (at 5,000 words the longest such document in US diplomatic history) in which he argued that Marxism had combined with the deep-seated neuroses of the old Russia. The Soviets would seek to dominate such neighbours as Iran and Turkey, while spreading subversion through so-called liberation movements in the undeveloped world, and via labour unions and youth organizations in the West itself. Read without the author's later discovery of nuance, the telegram seemed to call for the US to wield a big stick: 'Soviet power is impervious to the logic of reason, and it is highly sensitive to the logic of force.' Through the actions of this 'expanding totalitarian state' the world was dividing into hostile armed camps. Kennan's Long Telegram was one of the most influential diplomatic ruminations of modern times. It used history and ideology to explain the nature of the Soviet menace, while creating a potential job for the author by calling for a level of peacetime strategic planning, resembling the girding of the sinews more customary to states at war. 'My reputation was made. My voice now carried.'

Born in 1904, Kennan had an unremarkable early life, and – judging by a diary of his dreams – one that was not as prim and proper as it seemed on the daytime surface. He was a Presbyterian from Milwaukee who had studied history at Princeton University, before entering the US Foreign Service. A distant relative, also called George Kennan, who had written about exiles in nineteenth-century Siberia, sparked his initial interest in Russia. His diplomatic stints in Russia (whose language he thoroughly mastered) lay either side of the Second World War, during which he was interned for a while in Hitler's Berlin before being repatriated. His illustrious mentors in Moscow's Spaso House US embassy included such ambassadors as William Bullitt and Averell Harriman, the latter one of the few men Kennan was in awe of; his diplomat contemporaries included Charles 'Chip' Bohlen and Loy Henderson, subsequently ambassadors and senior officials, whom we shall be seeing more of.

Seconded to the National War College, Kennan began to generalize the psychology of chess: 'Our task is to plan and execute our strategic dispositions in such a way as to compel Sov. Govt. either to accept combat under unfavourable conditions (which it will never do) or withdraw.' Since the Soviet Union was an empire, by now ruling a majority of non-Russian speakers, Kennan thought that the judicious application of counterforce would not only contain Soviet expansionism but possibly trigger the collapse of the Soviet system. His main caveat was that the US should act 'only in cases where the prospective results bear a satisfactory relationship to the expenditure of American resources and effort'.[9] At the prompting of Navy Secretary Forrestal, Marshall and his deputy Dean Acheson selected Kennan to run the State Department's Policy Planning Staff, which fed seventy major strategy papers, totalling 900 pages, into the newly created National Security Council (NSC), a body Britain would emulate in 2010. Kennan was also part of the CIA's Office of Special Projects, set up by Marshall and the Agency's director, Admiral Roscoe Hillenkoetter, to mount covert operations.

Kennan found it hard to adjust from being the lone supreme expert to being part of complex bureaucratic teams staffed by equally ambitious men, serving politicians who had to exaggerate and simplify his ideas, whether to secure Congressional funding or obtain popular approval.

There was also a tension between the policy-maker and the historian, for the grand strategy of containment (as it came to be called) jibed with John Quincy Adams's 1821 warning that the young Republic should not go seeking monsters to destroy, a view that still resonated 130 years later. To the alleged disquiet of its intellectual architect, the chess game degenerated into a crude affair of nuclear-armed bombers at all points of the compass, and messy peripheral wars in countries Kennan cared not one jot about. Propping up Third World clients and puppets might also incite the very revolutionary turmoil containment was supposed to prevent. Put out to grass, Kennan spent the rest of his long life (he died in 2005 aged 101), defending policy subtleties that no one else had noticed at the time.

In fact his more cultural-philosophical approach to grand strategy seemed to inhibit practical decision-making and it was White House adviser Clark Clifford who set about turning Kennan's rather abstract thoughts into concrete policy. In a Top Secret Study dated 24 September 1946, Clifford argued that a robust global US security mission encompassing 'all democratic countries which are in any way menaced by the USSR' would eventually trigger the systemic collapse of the Soviet Union, which needed constantly to expand to disguise how a small ruling clique had latched themselves on to the basically decent Russian people. Identifying the potential weakness of the Soviet system was among the highly prescient insights of an article Kennan published anonymously as 'X' in July 1947 in the influential journal *Foreign Affairs*: 'If . . . anything were ever to occur to disrupt the unity and efficacy of the Party as a political instrument, Soviet Russia might be changed overnight from one of the strongest to one of the weakest and most pitiable of national societies.'[10]

One further intervention helped shape the emerging consensus on Soviet intentions. Truman relayed an invitation to Churchill to speak in Fulton, Missouri, in March 1946. They took a caravanserai of journalists and photographers on a thousand-mile train journey, during which the two men whiled away the time boozing and playing poker. In his speech Churchill revisited an earlier metaphor, coined by Goebbels, to speak of an 'iron curtain' behind which historic European peoples were subject to repressive Soviet control. The domestic US response to Churchill's call for a union of the English-speaking peoples was largely negative, with protesters in New York shouting, 'Winnie, Winnie, go

away, U-N-O is here to stay.' The conservative *Wall Street Journal*
declared: 'The United States wants no alliance, or anything that resembles an alliance, with any other nation.' Stalin mischievously accused
Churchill of Nazi-style racism in his harping on about the unity of the
Anglo-Saxons, and purported to regard the speech as a 'call to war'. In
a letter to his mother, Truman explained that he was not yet ready to
endorse the belligerent Briton's advanced opinions in public. He wrote to
Stalin offering to bring him by ship to Missouri to deliver his own riposte
to Churchill's speech, which Truman falsely claimed not to have read in
advance. Indeed the supposition must be that he and Churchill discussed
it thoroughly during the long train journey and he applauded enthusiastically as it was delivered.[11]

At the same time news reported from within the Red Empire was not
encouraging. US journalists who penetrated Soviet-occupied Manchuria
found factories being dismantled and removed by the trainload. If they
managed to interview a local, the person was invariably shot shortly
afterwards. Sniper fire kept most reporters embedded in their hotel
rooms. Some American liberals began to change their minds under the
influence of one of their own – John Fischer, who reported from Russia
for a variety of magazines. The columnist Brooks Atkinson of the *New
York Times* put the grim anecdotes into a wider policy framework:

> Friendship in the sense of intimate association and political compro-
> mise is not wanted, is not possible, and is not involved . . . The Rus-
> sian people are admirable . . . but between us and the Russian people
> stands the Soviet government. Despite its sanctimonious use of the
> word 'democracy' it is a totalitarian government . . . There are no free-
> doms within the Soviet Union . . . The government is a machine for
> generating power within the Soviet Union and as far outside as the
> power can be made to extend; and all attempts to deal with it in terms
> of friendship are doomed to failure.[12]

This was very much the view emerging among top US policy-makers,
leading to the dumping of Henry Wallace, the former vice president who
had been brought back in as secretary of commerce, after he became an
apologist for Russia and a proponent of its moral equivalence with the

US. Under Truman out went Roosevelt's casual hunches about other world leaders and in came cold-blooded assessments of long-term threats and how to respond to them.[13] The incoming Secretary of State Marshall was dry, laconic, solid and reliable, unfazed by talented subordinates. He had a keen sense of history and thought that no one who had not read about the Peloponnesian Wars should conduct foreign policy. He knew how to delegate policy formation to Under Secretary Dean Acheson, who in turn knew the difference between an endless seminar and how to steer tight groups of experts in the required direction, giving them time and space to air their opinions. Although Acheson was a supple intellect, there was nothing subtle about such *obiter dicta* as 'the United States was the locomotive at the head of mankind and the rest of the world was the caboose [guard's van]'.[14]

Who were the men who devised and determined US policy during what the journalist Walter Lippmann had already dubbed the 'Cold War' in the title of a 1947 compilation of his articles? He probably borrowed the term from the French, who had used *la guerre blanche* or *la guerre froid* in the 1930s.[15] Much of the top talent hailed from elite East Coast prep schools and Harvard or Yale, who served lengthy spells as Wall Street investment bankers and corporate lawyers, with a few exceptional academics drawn directly from the Ivy League schools. Some were extremely wealthy, like Averell Harriman, whose sad demeanour belied a fortune of $100 million, and whose, manners as those who crossed him discovered, were those of a crocodile. All of them believed in the obligation of public service, although few were averse to making money too. They may have been gentlemen players – with a strong sense of duty and loyalty when the McCarthyite mob hounded their patrician friends – rather than trained foreign policy professionals, but after the First World War they had ranged far and wide to invest their clients' money, sometimes doubling up as intelligence gatherers. In an intermission between recurrent bouts of American puritanism, policy was thrashed out, passionately, over highballs and whiskey sours in smart houses in Georgetown. Culturally, these men felt most at home among Europeans, although only Acheson affected British tailoring and a Guards officer's moustache. Harriman advised him to lose it: 'you owe it to Truman', he remarked.[16]

This was sage advice, as this elite group could easily appear alien to many of their fellow countrymen, especially after their resentments had been mobilized by the likes of newly elected Californian Congressman Richard Nixon, or the new Senator for Wisconsin, Joseph McCarthy.[17] Every time the State Department's Office of Foreign Buildings sought funds from Congress for a new embassy building – needed to house the increased number of aid programmes, CIA agents and military advisers that accompanied containment – some awkward Congressman would pipe up about constituents' hard-earned money being frittered on 'increased booze allowances for cookie pushers'.[18] If the foreign policy elite had one collective flaw it was a snobbish disdain towards the 'rest' in a world of great powers. According to the future Secretary of State Dean Rusk, Acheson 'did not give a damn about the little red-yellow-black people in various parts of the world'.[19] Yet this was also government on a human scale. Every day Acheson walked the mile and a half to work alongside his friend Judge Felix Frankfurter, with not a car or body-guard in sight. As the son of an Episcopalian minister and the daughter of a whiskey distiller, he claimed to have known both good and evil from an early age, though in his official role he maintained that the two could exist side by side and he was sceptical of moral absolutes.[20]

Truman's foreign policy was complicated by the November 1946 Congressional elections in which the Republicans won 246 to 188 seats in the House, and 51 to 45 in the Senate. Even many Democrats, such as the new Massachusetts Congressman John Kennedy, found it opportune to employ militantly anti-Soviet rhetoric. There was also the problem of Communist sympathizers, when not outright Soviet agents, occupying key government posts. In late March 1947 Truman issued an executive order setting in motion loyalty investigations of employees of the executive branch of government.[21] Although Truman was not entirely convinced by the Communist 'bugaboo', the investigation sparked rancorous hostility between populist Congressmen and a State Department that held them in contempt. Acheson habitually referred to McCarthy as a 'primitive', but the Senator found popular resonance when he portrayed the State Department as a nest of red subversives who had deliberately 'lost' China.[22] The climate of suspicion crept steadily, like a sinister fog, from the State Department to the CIA and the armed forces, with even the patriotism of Marshall impugned by the demagogues.

Immediately after the war Truman sought to amortize a wartime debt of $250 billion. One obvious target was the defence budget, which he cut from $90 billion to $10.3 billion, and hoped to cut further. In 1947 the armed forces shrank to 1.5 million men, the majority occupation troops living pampered existences in Germany and Japan. Mainly because he disliked its Republican chief, General William 'Wild Bill' Donovan, in September 1945 Truman abruptly wound up the wartime OSS. These cuts in defence expenditure were hard to reconcile with the worsening state of US–Soviet relations and the unpreparedness of the US armed forces was to be shockingly revealed in the opening months of the Korean War. But the turning point came when Britain's formal admission of impending bankruptcy forced the US to put a much larger footprint on the wider world.

On 21 February 1947 the British embassy in Washington told Acheson that it wished to deliver an important note. Acheson called the contents 'shockers': the British government was abandoning commitments to support Greece and Turkey because it could no longer bear the financial strain. In a moment that Acheson over-dramatically compared with creation in Genesis, he urged economic and military assistance for Greece and Turkey. Intensive discussions ensued: were the British bluffing? Were they expecting the Americans to refuse aid to Greece and Turkey, to make it easier for Britain to accommodate rather than confront the Soviet Union? The removal of the British Empire as a global shock absorber might bring a third world war much closer. Should the US regard Greece and Turkey as separate issues, or did it need to treat the threat of Communism at a more global conceptual level? Then there was Greece itself. What level of involvement in Greece was appropriate when the 'extreme Right' was 'not averse to playing on the fears of the Greek public to brand all opposition as Communistic and foreign inspired, with the hope of justifying strong measures to stamp out Left factions and to render impotent any real Center republicanism'? The 'extreme Left' was equally adroit at playing this game by ramping up the threat of Fascism to destroy all manner of opponents of Stalinism.[23]

With a Republican Congress demanding 20 per cent tax cuts, pumping money towards the Aegean was going to be a tough sell, particularly since the threat to Turkey was unproven and it was Yugoslavia rather than the Soviet Union that was supporting the Reds in Greece. Although an eloquent public speaker, Secretary of State Marshall flunked it at the first informal gathering of select Congressional leaders, making what was not yet called containment sound as anodyne as another aid programme, until Acheson took the rhetorical reins. The present was comparable to the struggle of Athens and Sparta, Rome and Carthage. Simple fractions helped too, as Acheson spoke of the prospect of two-thirds of the world's population and three-quarters of its land area turning a bloody red, an initial outing for the 'domino theory' of states falling sequentially to the red menace.

Senator Arthur Vandenberg, chair of the Foreign Relations Committee, urged Truman to make his pitch to a joint session of Congress. Although the text of the speech was batted back and forth with appropriate amendments, it is important to stress that it was the President himself who insisted, 'I want no hedge in this speech. This is America's answer to the surge of Communist tyranny.' The minor sleights of hand in the address when delivered on 12 March 1947 included the rash promise that money sent to Greece would not be embezzled, and that the US was not simply pulling British chestnuts out of the fire. There was a lot of tear-jerking detail about Greece's immense suffering during the war, and particularly its legions of tubercular children. Truman was less forthcoming about Turkey, which had been neutral, but it was going to get its share of the $400 million too. This was apparently not much to ask. Fiscal conservatives were reminded that it was a tenth of 1 per cent of the $341,000,000,000 the US had spent winning the war. The President then turned to the 'broad implications' of his proposal. The United Nations could not function properly if its individual elements were subject to internal or external coercion. Truman spelled out the stark choices:

At the present moment in world history nearly every nation must choose between alternative ways of life. The choice is too often not a free one. One way of life is based on the will of the majority, and is distinguished by free institutions, representative government, free elections, guarantees of individual liberty, freedom of speech and religion, and freedom from political oppression. The second way of life is based on the will of the minority forcibly imposed on the majority. It relies on terror and oppression, a controlled press and radio, fixed elections, and the suppression of personal freedoms. I believe that it must be the policy of the United States to support free peoples who are resisting attempted subjugation by armed minorities or by outside pressures.[24]

The authors of the Truman Doctrine were careful to disavow anything as militant as an ideological crusade, and nor were they interested in Churchill's idea of a further grand summit to negotiate a deal with a bombless Stalin. It was not a matter of rolling back Communism from places like Hungary or Poland, but of ensuring that Communism did not spread. In 1940 Roosevelt had warned that the US should never become 'a lone island in a world dominated by the philosophy of force'. The US needed to restore Germany and Japan to the free community of nations. This was to ensure that no potential aggressors would ever be able to use their enormous industrial resources and technical flair against the United States itself.[25] The US should build up its armed might, and assume responsibility for restoring the economic health of the free world.

Truman was fortunate that the Congressional Republican leadership included the internationalist Vandenberg. Despite objections to the potentially open-ended nature of these commitments, in April the aid packages were approved by Congress. Congress allocated $400 million to Greece alone, with Loy Henderson despatched to Athens to bang heads together. A rapidly deteriorating economy worsened the security situation. As a result much of future US support went towards military assistance programmes, namely a 450-strong military advisory group under General James Van Fleet, which helped the Greek government crush Communist guerrillas in what on both sides was a prototypical dirty war. An added bonus of such resolution was that when Stalin got cold feet about indirectly aiding the Greek Communists, his efforts to rein in the Yugoslav comrades further soured his relations with their leader Marshal Tito.[26]

Truly great powers do national security strategy rather than simply react in ill-thought-out spasms. The Truman Doctrine required a review of national security structures and under the July 1947 National Security Act the US revamped its defence and intelligence apparatus. The wartime Joint Chiefs of Staff became a standing entity, while instead of secretaries for war and the navy, the armed services, which included a freestanding air force, were represented by a new cabinet-level defense secretary. This important post was dogged by bad luck. James Forrestal drove himself mad through overwork and in 1949 threw himself from a sixteenth-floor window in Bethesda Naval Hospital. His successor, Louis Johnson, who in 1948 amassed the campaign funds that enabled Truman to win a surprise second term, saw himself as his heir apparent and tried to ratchet down defence spending – airily announcing that he wished to abolish the navy and the Marine Corps – while talking tough on Communism. When he justified the cuts in defence spending by boasting that the US 'could lick Russia with one hand behind its back', the first Chairman of the Joint Chiefs of Staff, General Omar Bradley, remarked that Truman 'had unwittingly replaced one mental case with another'.[27]

Long-term grand strategy was the domain of the new NSC, with the State Department more confined to diplomatic relations. Ironically, afraid that the NSC might cramp his style, Truman attended only twelve of the forty-seven Council sessions between 1947 and 1950. Not the least of Truman's attributes was a rare willingness to admit error, and while he had abolished the wartime OSS, sacking 'Wild Bill' Donovan with an insultingly brief note, two years later he availed himself of Donovan's own recommendations and of a large number of former OSS officers when he established the new and well-funded Central Intelligence Agency. Kennan's Office of Special Projects linked the CIA to the State Department.[28]

The sharpest end of national security had been established in 1946. Air Defense Command consisted of radar stations and interceptor aircraft to protect the continental US. Fighter aircraft and fighter-bombers made up the Tactical Air Command. The jewel in the crown was Strategic Air Command (SAC), whose B-29s could drop the Bomb on industrial targets in the Soviet Union. The US atomic stockpile was modest, with nine bombs in 1946, thirteen in 1947 and fifty by the end of 1948.[29] But in 1947 the Atomic Energy Commission was authorized to build 200 further devices. By the end of 1947 SAC had 319 B-29s, one in ten of which had been modified to carry nuclear weapons, each weighing about 10,000 pounds. These thirty-odd planes packed the punch of 70,000 conventionally armed aircraft. The introduction of air-to-air refuelling tankers in 1948 gave their missions longer range and made them less suicidal.

The biggest change was the appointment of General Curtis LeMay as bomber commander-in-chief. He was responsible for the Emergency War Plan called 'Offtackle', under which 104 Soviet cities would be hit by 292 atomic bombs, with a further 72 bombs for targets identified by parallel reconnaissance flights. The B-29s and newer B-36s would fly from Britain and Morocco as well as the US, arriving in small groups, in which only one plane would carry the most deadly ordnance. While much of what SAC did was necessarily secret, it had no difficulty recruiting 300,000 people to watch for Soviet aircraft seeking to fly under the US's rudimentary radar shield, while the Nevada test site spawned a whole subculture of 'atomic cocktails' (four ounces combined of grapefruit and pineapple juice, half an ounce of Galliano and one of Plymouth Gin) or picnic baskets for families who wanted to gawp at mushroom clouds expanding in the clear skies of the desert.[30]

Cocktail hour turned to deep dread when in early September 1949 US reconnaissance planes registered unusually high levels of radiation of a thousand counts per minute where normal background radiation counts were around fifty. Stalin had acquired and tested an atomic bomb, called RDS 1 or 'First Lightning' at a site named Semipalatinsk-21 in Kazakhstan. The Soviet spy chief Lavrentii Beria was on hand to watch the blast from the twenty-kiloton device. Afterwards he recommended such medals as Hero of Soviet Labour or the Order of Lenin for the scientists involved: the recipients did not know that the specific decoration they received was determined by their ranking on a list of those to be shot or imprisoned had they failed.[31] Americans dubbed the weapon 'Joe 1'. Fear of Communist subversion was thenceforth overshadowed by the prospect of mushroom clouds rising from US cities, even though the Soviets had no means of delivering such a weapon on a US target. After several months of secret debate, Truman decided in late January 1950 to authorize a hydrogen device whose explosive power dwarfed that of the bombs he had dropped on Hiroshima and Nagasaki.[32]

The restoration of Europe's economic fortunes was integral to its conversion into an effective bastion against the Soviets. US attempts to interest the Soviets themselves in post-war European reconstruction proved pointless. In March 1947, Under Secretary Acheson set in motion planning to rebuild Europe's shattered economies, in a more comprehensive and permanent way than was suggested by the word 'relief'. Reconstruction would benefit the US economically and strategically, while inoculating European societies against the conditions in which Communism thrived. The process was made more urgent by the failure of the Moscow conference to agree the future of Germany and Austria, for the industrial Rhine basin was the lynchpin of any efforts to revive the continent's economy.

The joint stakes which several US states had in the Tennessee Valley Authority became a template for how many US policy-makers saw the future of Europe, which was as a single entity, preferably with the British inside it.[33] The eponymous Marshall Plan reflected the Secretary of State's own concern that in Europe 'the patient is sinking while the doctors deliberate', as he put in it an April 1947 radio address.[34] Acheson trailed the gist of it to an audience of farmers in the unlikely setting of the Delta State Teachers College in Mississippi, before it was reprised by Marshall in the grander setting of a Harvard commencement ceremony. Drafted by the former Ambassador to Moscow 'Chip' Bohlen, Marshall's speech to Harvard alumni was focused on the need to combat 'hunger, desperation and chaos', rather than Communism – though that lurked in the background as the beneficiary of such abstract evils.

There was no formal exclusion of the Soviets and their satellites; indeed the ideal was to secure their collaboration in return for loans. However, Soviet participation was out of the question since it would mean revealing the economic reality of Soviet weakness through data Stalin would never share.[35] Stalin also realized that such a plan would undermine the Soviets' lock on their satellites, if they were enticed into the orbit of the powerful sun that was the US economy.

Between 1945 and 1953 total global US aid was $44 billion, of which $12.3 billion was pumped into European economies after 1948. This permitted European governments an extended range of policy choices while lubricating recovery that was often already under way. All wished to introduce welfare states, but there were wide divergences in how US aid was used in each national case, with the French and Germans making most intelligent use of these funds.[36] If the strictly economic impact of the Marshall Plan is contentious, it undoubtedly contributed to the consolidation of the West as an Atlantic political entity. No similar effect was achieved in Asia, where equally vast sums were invested, but not under a similar unifying plan. Reflecting what was a truly remarkable enterprise, the phrase Marshall Aid recurs again and again when a major crisis calls for boldness of vision. Marshall Aid gave Bruno at BMW and Giuseppe at FIAT something to believe in. In former Axis countries, where nationalism was under a cloud, productivity became a consensus-building vocation, a miraculous *Wunder* as the Germans called it. The rapid revival of West Germany in turn accelerated French efforts to contain it, which took the form of intra-European institutions from which the British excluded themselves.

The Soviets responded to the Marshall Plan in September 1947 with the formation of Cominform, and the use of sinister methods to cement their hold on Hungary and Czechoslovakia in 1947–8.[37] The takeover in Czechoslovakia, where Foreign Minister Jan Masaryk 'fell' from a high window, accelerated the creation of the North Atlantic Treaty Organization, one of the great achievements of the British Foreign Secretary Ernest Bevin, who therewith dodged a solely European defensive alliance. NATO bolted the US into Europe's defence, in a sort of 'empire by invitation', and in 1955 locked in West Germany too, frustrating Soviet gambits for a neutral unified Germany. It was sold to Congress as a new kind of alliance, allegedly directed against 'armed aggression' in general, rather than any specific enemy. It was a precedent-setting novelty in US foreign policy, a cardinal tenet of which had always been to avoid 'foreign entanglements'.[38] Together these confident policies hugely benefited centrist Christian Democrat, Liberal (meaning free-market) and Social Democrat politicians, marginalizing Stalin's West European Communist puppets.

The burgeoning commitments demanded by globalized containment encountered plenty of critics in the US itself. On the left there were many who deplored the amorality of propping up, or installing, regimes with dubious records of repression. This is familiar enough, but criticisms from the right are less so. Conservative anti-interventionists and realists criticized the indiscriminate nature of what was being undertaken, much of which they found hard to relate to American national security. What business of America's was it who ruled in Greece, Iran or Laos? Were revolutionaries nationalists or Marxist-Leninists? To what extent did more venerable national pathologies – for example Vietnamese hostility towards China – cancel out any ideological sympathies? It is almost impossible to imagine what the world would have been like had 'isolationist' Senator Robert Taft become Republican president, for he was implacably opposed to both the Marshall Plan and NATO.

US aid had ramifications far from Western Europe, for it indirectly freed up resources used to cling on to overseas colonies. In the Dutch case, Marshall Aid was used to blackmail America's fifth-ranked strategic partner into relinquishing control of a former colony. In what was a travesty of the reality of moderate Indonesian nationalism, the Dutch played to US enthusiasms by highlighting the 'Communist' character of the independence movement. That gambit failed when in September 1948 the Indonesian Republic swiftly crushed an Indonesian Communist rising in the town of Madiun. Since Indonesia instantly became 'the only government in Far East to have met and crushed an all-out Communist offensive', the CIA immediately sent an agent to Jogjakarta to assist in such operations.[39]

Thus when in December 1948 the Dutch resumed their military offensive, capturing Jogjakarta and arresting Sukarno, Hatta and half the Republic's cabinet, the US was outraged. American Congressmen, of all political stripes, were especially angry over how Marshall Plan dollars were indirectly financing Dutch military activities in Indonesia on behalf of 'a senile and ineffectual imperialism'. Moreover, the CIA coolly warned that 'The Dutch "police action" provides ample material for a prolonged Communist propaganda campaign and the greater part of this material will seem irrefutable when presented in the context of Asiatic nationalism versus Western imperialism.'[40] Ten Republican Senators introduced a resolution amending Marshall Aid funding and calling the Dutch action 'a crushing sneak attack like Japan's on Pearl Harbor, like Nazi Germany's on Holland itself'. The resolution's author, Owen Brewster of Maine, pointedly inquired: 'Do we intend to support nineteenth-century

Dutch–British–French imperialism in Asia which will create a climate for the growth of communism? Or do we intend to support the moderate republican nationalists throughout Asia?'[41]

While the US threatened to suspend Marshall Plan funding to the Netherlands, Dutch forces on the ground were running into stiff guerrilla resistance, and support among the anti-Republican federal states they had created began to fray. In the end, as Acheson put it, 'money talked' and the threat to end all Marshall Aid to the Netherlands forced the Dutch to resume negotiations with the Indonesians. With considerable US pressure to resolve the many issues over which talks stalled, the Dutch eventually conceded Indonesian independence, which took place at a formal handover ceremony in Jakarta on 27 December 1949. Here was a precedent not pursued elsewhere.

'Losing' China

If the huge red expanse of the Soviet Union seemed disconcerting on maps, how much more so once China, with its population of some 600 millions, had turned red too. A struggle which had been waged for decades was coming to its grim conclusion, its outcome partly due to the different temperaments of Chiang Kai-shek and Mao Zedong. 'Old Mr Chiang was not like old Mr Mao. Perhaps this was why Chiang was beaten by Mao.'[42] Their reversals of fortune were as swift and striking as this apparently simple peasant diagnosis, for Mao possessed another order of ruthlessness. He was known to like Aesop's Fables, one of which, 'Evil for Good', concerns a peasant boy who, on finding a snake frozen rigid by cold, decides to nurse the serpent. When the snake revived from the boy's warmth, it bit him and he died. Mao would quote the dying boy's lament: 'I've got what I deserve for taking pity on an evil creature.' Mao was pitiless.[43]

In mid-1945 Chiang controlled less than 15 per cent of China's territory. Following the surrender of Japan, and after the US had flown his troops into liberated northern territory, Chiang controlled 80 per cent of the whole. Or so it seemed, for control is relative and the corrupt, inept and reactionary KMT government alienated the population wherever it was imposed.[44] The position of Mao's Communists in a few north-eastern pockets above the Great Wall seemed so weak that most Western newspapers had written them off. Stalin was not overly impressed either. Yet four years later Mao's peasant army rolled into the historic capital in US trucks, brandishing American weapons – rather than their standard Soviet issue – to further demoralize what was left of Chiang's forces, for which the arms had been destined.

Mao had not been in Beijing for thirty years, the last time as a poorly paid junior librarian. It was the only big city he knew. This was one reason he revived it as China's capital; another was that there he was closer to the Soviets than in the former capital Nanjing. On 1October 1949 Mao appeared on top of Beijing's Tiananmen Gate, where, despite suffering from low-level malaria and bronchitis, he inaugurated the People's Republic of China. Chiang withdrew to Shanghai and then to Taiwan, where his incomers were as unpopular among the natives as they had been on the mainland. Nine months before, the heads of the US intelligence agencies had met in Washington DC to discuss what was happening in China. The Chief of Naval Intelligence Admiral Inglis said: 'One thing that puzzles us is the superiority and the strategic direction of the Chinese Communists and their ability to support themselves logistically and in communications. It just doesn't seem Chinese.' General Irwin, Director of US Army General Staff Intelligence, mused: 'I don't think it is.'[45]

Stalin's ideal solution for China was that it would function as a weak buffer zone, protecting his empire's eastern flanks against any resurgence of Japan. To that end he backed both Chiang, from whom he extracted territorial concessions in return for recognizing his legitimacy as ruler of China, and Mao, whom the Soviet dictator regarded as a naive peasant or a potential troublemaker in the mould of Yugoslavia's Tito, architect of a revolution that owed little to Soviet support. Stalin's appreciation could not have been more wrong. US policy towards China blew up in the Truman administration's face. While the powerful, and largely Republican, China lobby regarded Chiang as a Christian hero resisting Mao's godless hordes, the administration became increasingly frustrated with the huge sums they disbursed down what Truman called Nationalist 'rat holes'. But the money had to be paid to ensure Republican assent in Congress to the aid more usefully pouring into Europe. Informed observers had warned for years that Chiang Kai-shek was a loser, though that message had not been allowed to become widespread in the US. 'Why, if he is a generalissimo,' asked Texas Senator Tom Connally of the Foreign Relations Committee in a possibly unconscious solecism, 'does he not generalize?'[46]

While the Nationalists endeavoured to fight a war at the further reaches of their supply chain, Mao imposed his iron grip on rural Manchuria, using class war and terror to meld peasant society and the People's Liberation Army (PLA) into one lethal whole. Chiang's military efforts were hampered by commanders who acted as warlords with headquarters riddled with Communist spies. They included the personal secretary to General Hu Zongnan, who in March 1947 managed to take the Communist capital of Yan'an, and both an adviser to and the daughter of Fu Zuoyi, the KMT commander in Beijing.[47] Armed with this intelligence, Mao's commanders were able to ambush and destroy every KMT force sent against them. Mao compared this approach with prising open an attacker's fist to chop the fingers off one at a time.

In April 1947, the French counter-insurgency expert David Galula was briefly captured by Communist troops in a town in Shanxi Province. As a guest of honour, Galula was allowed to explore his hosts' camp, where it was explained to him that Nationalist prisoners were treated leniently to promote their demoralization. If they chose, prisoners were simply incorporated into the PLA; officers who defected to the PLA were accorded the same rank they had reached in the KMT armed forces. If they decided to return to the Nationalist fold, the Communists calculated that no one would trust them.[48] Mao's Soviet-advised forces successfully made the transition from guerrilla operations to sophisticated main-force manoeuvres of the kind the Red Army had practised to such effect in Eastern and Central Europe. Although Mao took much of the credit for a series of stunning battles – culminating in the decisive Huaihai campaign of November 1948–January 1949 – he relied on such capable commanders as Lin Biao and Liu Bocheng. On they swept, driving the Nationalists towards the southern coast, or across the borders into Burma and Vietnam.

Although his forces were like rude and insecure interlopers in the fertile south, Mao was obsessed with China's future place in the world. In August 1946, on the first anniversary of the atomic bombing of Hiroshima and Nagasaki, the exiled American radical feminist journalist Ann Louise Strong had interviewed Mao. The subject of the Bomb arose, as well it might on such an ominous date. Mao brushed such a weapon aside: 'The atom bomb is a paper tiger that the US reactionaries use to scare people. It looks terrible, but in fact it isn't. Of course, the atom bomb is a weapon of mass slaughter, but the outcome of a war is decided by the people, not by one or two new types of weapon.'[49] He claimed that nuclear bombs would make no appreciable impact on the vast turbulent zone between the USA and the USSR, a concept he illustrated by positioning several small wine glasses between two teacups. To conquer the Soviet Union, the US would have to subjugate the huge number of smaller powers within this intermediate zone, or what would be called the Third World. While Mao was prepared to concede primacy to Stalin's Soviet Union, he was also indicating that China and the intermediate zone as a whole were as much players as pieces on the chessboard, assets as much as burdens. While the US State Department devoted a thousand-paged China White Paper in August 1949 in defence of policies that were under ferocious domestic Republican attack, Mao and Stalin looked forward rather than back.

A Chinese mission led by Liu Shaoqi went to Moscow in the summer of 1949. Stalin met them six times, which was more direct contact than he allowed Mao when he arrived in December of that year, partly to celebrate the Great Master's birthday on the 21st.[50] Their first encounter was frosty. Stalin abruptly changed the subject when Mao asked for an apology for Russia's fitful and duplicitous support for the Chinese Revolution. Stalin was also bewildered by the elliptical way in which Mao (through his translator) expressed his need for aid. Nonetheless the result was the Sino–Soviet Treaty of Friendship, Alliance and Mutual Assistance of 14 February 1950, from which China received a relatively modest $300 million credit and increased military aid. The Soviets got the Chinese to exclude all non-Soviet foreigners from Manchuria and Xinxiang, while retaining humiliating naval and railway concessions made to tsarist Russia. A secret appendix excluded from the ambit of Chinese law Soviet advisers who committed crimes.

While the Soviets promised to come to China's aid in the event of Japanese or 'other' aggression, Stalin conceded China a subaltern role in fomenting revolution in South-east Asia. He advised extreme caution in the case of Vietnam, lest Mao's intervention on behalf of Ho embroil him in a war with either the French or the US. Nonetheless Mao had a Chinese Military Advisory Group and PLA troops operating in North Vietnam from the autumn, by which time newly built roads connected the two countries. There was a major conflict of interest here, although Mao and Stalin suppressed it in favour of the international revolution. Mao regarded Vietnam as the most likely launching pad for any imperialist attempt to wrest southern China from his control; Stalin was more worried about how overt support for Ho might impact on his relations with France, the lynchpin of his attempts to stymie German rearmament through membership of NATO. In the event, the first major contest of the Cold War would come in Korea, as a civil war took on international ramifications.

The Korean Civil War

Korea, roughly the size of the Japanese island of Honshu, was once an independent kingdom but one successively subjected to Chinese and Japanese rule. It had rarely prospered except by emulating the hermit crab, but a keen desire for independence remained among its twenty-seven million people. Korea had been divided at the 38th parallel on 9 August 1945, notionally so that Japanese troops would surrender to Chiang Kai-shek in the north and to the Americans in the south. The bleaker more industrialized north had ten million people, the more agrarian south seventeen million. The line was entirely arbitrary, the work of a late night in Washington DC by Colonel Dean Rusk, whose source material was a copy of National Geographic; he was unaware that imperial Russia and Japan had chosen that line of division forty years previously. There was no obvious physical feature on which to base a border and Rusk and his colleague Colonel Charles Bonesteel were determined to keep Seoul in the southern zone. These arrangements were upset when Soviet, rather than Nationalist Chinese, forces arrived in the north a month before the first Americans were shipped in from Japan and the Philippines. Soviet troops systematically plundered the country, raping the Japanese women and robbing fifty million yen from the main bank. They also dismantled and removed such assets as the Hungnam petrochemical plant and the Sup'ung hydroelectric plant on the Yalu River.

In September 1945 a Russian ship, the *Pugachev*, docked in Wonsan. Aboard was Kim Il Sung, who in 1940 had slipped into Siberia to evade the Japanese. In the interim Kim had become a captain in the Red Army's 88th Special Reconnaissance Brigade within the Twenty-fifth Army. He deftly formed his own North Korean Communist Party in June 1946 with Soviet support, murdering any older or more charismatic rivals. Nearly 60 per cent of the 4,500 members were intellectuals, entrepreneurs and 'others' rather than workers. At the same time Kim, a fluent Mandarin speaker, built up his credit with Mao by allowing Lin Biao's PLA troops to flee into Korea when they were hard pressed in Manchuria in late 1946 by Chiang's troops. While Mao's fortunes in China hung in the balance, Soviet influence in Korea was undisputed, the most powerful Russian being General Terentii Shtykov, Stalin's *de facto* viceroy.[51] Many Korean Communist-nationalists were nonplussed when, in a lacklustre debut at a mass rally, Kim was flanked by three Red Army generals who listened gravely to his lengthy paean to Stalin. Kim implemented a programme of land reform and nationalization of industry. Around a million northerners fled south after experiencing the beginnings of Communist rule.[52]

The lands south of the parallel had been occupied by troops from a US corps stationed on Okinawa. Their commander was General John Reed Hodge, who answered to General Douglas MacArthur, America's supremo in the Pacific theatre. MacArthur had little interest in this part of his imperium, and visited it only once in the five years before the outbreak of the Korean War in June 1950. Initially the Americans found the orderly Japanese occupiers more congenial than Korea's fractious politicians. The US relied on former collaborating elites – including soldiers and policemen – and Korea's own Flying Dutchman, Syngman Rhee, as governing institutions took shape. Although Syngman Rhee was regarded with suspicion by the US State Department, the tough old septuagenarian, known as the Walnut because of his leathery skin, had the immense advantage of being one of the few Koreans the Americans knew. Rhee understood 'his' Americans too. His devout Methodism, anti-Communism and authoritarianism fitted the job description of the sort of charismatic leader the US hoped would do their bidding in Asia. Members of the conservative Korean Democratic Party dominated the eleven-man advisory council established to aid the US Military Governor, while the rival Korean People's Republic grouping and the labour unions were suppressed as Communist fronts, which they were not.

In December 1945, the Russians agreed to an American proposal that Korea should be entrusted to a Four Power International Trusteeship lasting five years. This would ease the transition to an independent and unified Korean state. In reality, both the Americans and the Soviets encouraged the consolidation of their own client governments, as they had been doing in Germany. A provisional legislature and interim government emerged in Seoul, dominated by conservatives who had collaborated with the Japanese. The Chief of Staff of the new South Korean Army was a former colonel in the Japanese army and his successor was also a former soldier in the Kwantung Army in Manchuria. While the Russians proposed that they and the US simply pull out of Korea, leaving local rivals to battle it out, the US persuaded the United Nations to support nationwide elections under UN supervision as a preliminary to US–Soviet withdrawal.

After North Korea had refused to accept these arrangements, the majority of members of a UN General Assembly Interim Committee on Korea allowed elections to proceed only in the South.[53] Although Rhee's 'police goons' used considerable brutality to rig the outcome of elections, which the opposition boycotted, the UN accepted a result that brought Rhee to power in a coalition of conservative parties. After the establishment of the Republic of Korea (ROK) in July 1948, Syngman Rhee became its first president. Although he made a stab at eliminating former collaborators, under the December 1948 National Security Law some 58,000 leftist South Koreans were jailed amid endemic political violence, while the press was brought under stringent controls. In June 1949 one of Rhee's most prominent critics was assassinated.[54]

The regime emerging in the South was far from universally popular, and not all the opposition came from so-called Communists, a term

Americans were bandying around with decreasing discrimination. The political consolidation of the ROK ran into a regional insurgency that owed little to the guerrillas the North Koreans infiltrated into north-eastern Kangwon Province. Throughout South Korea People's Committees had spontaneously come into existence amid the collapse of Japanese rule. Some of these were dominated by adherents of the left, notably in south-westerly Cholla and Kyongsang, and on the island of Cheju. In November 1946 US troops joined the police in repressing a peasant rebellion in Cholla. Known as the Autumn Harvest Rebellion, it was sparked in part by a dry monsoon season and a poor rice crop.[55]

On the island of Cheju socialism and separatism combined to fight against attempts by Syngman Rhee's supporters to sideline the People's Committees that had run the island's affairs with minimal interference by the Americans since late 1945. The regime in Seoul introduced a rightist militia, called the North-west Youth Corps, to aid and abet the police in suppressing leftists with murderous violence. The rebels formed an insurgent force called the People's Democratic Army. The US Army provided advisers to the police and militias, who then used Japanese counter-insurgency tactics to rid the island of rebels. This involved destroying interior villages and removing their inhabitants to the coast, where they could be closely controlled. The guerrillas were then attacked when the winter snows impeded their mobility and made them more visible. Anywhere between 30,000 and 60,000 islanders were killed in this pacification campaign, with a further 40,000 fleeing overseas to Japan.

Many members of the North-west Youth Corps were incorporated into the police, while a senior policeman from Seoul became one of the island's deputies to the National Assembly. The rebellion on Cheju spread to ROK troops who refused to embark at a port called Yosu to fight the insurgents and then linked up with guerrillas. Korean officers who had fought for the Japanese in Manchuria used Japanese counter-insurgency methods to suppress them, with the Americans providing intelligence, aerial reconnaissance and C-47 transporters to move Korean troops into the war zones. It has been estimated that 100,000 Koreans died in these counter-insurgency operations, which ended a year before the Korean War broke out.

With the rebellions crushed, and a South Korean state in being, the

US withdrew Hodge and the two remaining US divisions, confident that the 60,000-strong ROK armed forces could cope with any future challenges. All that remained of the US presence was a 500-man Korean Military Advisory Group. North of the parallel, Kim had proclaimed a Democratic Republic of North Korea in September 1948, rather as the establishment of the German Democratic Republic postdated the creation of the Federal Republic. Although the Soviets withdrew their forces in late 1948, their 120,000-strong Twenty-fifth Army handed its weapons to the newly formed Korean People's Army as well as the arms the Soviets had earlier confiscated from two entire Japanese armies.

From May 1949 onwards, cross-border clashes between North and South intensified, involving ever greater numbers of troops. Although the US had denied the South Koreans heavy artillery, tanks and aircraft, this did not stop South Korea's leaders from engaging in bellicose rhetoric. In October 1949 Syngman Rhee told a senior US journalist, 'I am sure we could take Pyongyang . . . in three days.' The same month the South Korean Defence Minister told the press that his troops were 'ready to drive into North Korea. If we had our own way, we would have started already . . . We are strong enough to march up and take Pyongyang within a few days.'[56] What some historians call a civil war to unify Korea, after forty years of Japanese occupation, was about to become the most dangerous crisis of the post-war years.[57]

3. ARAB NATIONALISM, JEWISH HOMELAND

It's about Oil

With the defeat of Germany and Japan, some perspicacious American observers reckoned that the Soviets would focus their attention on the Middle East, where the British position seemed enfeebled. In addition to promoting Communist activity in Greece, the Soviets sought concessions from Iran and Turkey, using increasingly strongarm methods to achieve them. But were the Americans justified in seeing this as a pathological pattern, or was Stalin acting much more opportunistically as each new chance arose? Was he acting within the historic tradition of tsarist Russian policy, or was a more ideological ambition involved? Moreover, British imperial power throughout the region was being contested by nationalist movements that had almost nothing to do with Communism, towards which cultural Islam often proved a major obstacle.

The collapse of European authority in the Middle East after the Second World War was much less precipitate than what happened to the colonial powers in Asia. Although the British had a long-standing presence in Egypt and close relations with the Trucial Emirates of the Persian Gulf, their involvement in the area had only deepened in the final year of the First World War, when British Imperial forces drove the Germans' Ottoman allies from their historic Arab dominions. Hegemony over this enormous area came to be seen as crucial to the survival of the

British Empire, not only to ensure communications between Britain and India but also because of the strategic importance of oil deposits in Mesopotamia and Persia. Mesopotamia was the ancient Greek toponym for 'land of the two rivers', the cradle of ancient civilization between the Tigris and Euphrates where modern Iraq now sits; Persia was the vast ancient empire ultimately beneath modern Iran.[1]

After the First World War the British and French became the administrators of hugely increased imperial territories in the Middle East, usually as mandates from the League of Nations for a specified time. The trick was to turn them into the equivalent of perpetual tenancies through puppet rulers. Amir Abdullah's Hashemite kingdom of Transjordan became the most dependable after the British had expelled his independent advisers in 1924. But it was Iraq that was supposed to exemplify the 'civilized tutelage' the British elites envisioned for these mandates, although in reality it was a defence in depth of the Anglo–Persian Oil Company, whose majority shareholder was the British government. In 1918 Anglo–Persian increased its controlling share of the Turkish Petroleum Company (renamed the Iraqi Petroleum Company) to 75 per cent after expropriating the 25 per cent formerly held by Deutsche Bank. Hashemite Amir Faisal, first proclaimed king of Syria, was transferred to the Iraqi throne in 1921 after a referendum from which the British subtracted rival contenders, shipping one of them to Ceylon. That Faisal was a Sunni and that the majority of Iraqis were Shiite simply perpetuated the divide-and-rule strategy employed by the Ottomans. At his pre-dawn coronation ceremony, the band played the British anthem, 'God Save the King'.

The Anglo–Iraqi Treaty of 1922 cemented British influence over a nominally independent Iraq for twenty years, during which resistance was ruthlessly suppressed. Iraqi crude was not even refined locally and was of little benefit to the local population, 90 per cent of whom were still illiterate in 1950. When the British mandate expired in 1932, a new treaty pared down the British presence to a military minimum, retaining two air bases at Habbaniyah and Shaiba and the right of their armed forces to transit the country. Two years later Iraq became the first Arab state to be admitted to the League of Nations. Its independence remained a sham in the eyes of Iraqi nationalists, and it was also a hotbed of ethnic and sectarian animosities between Kurds and Arabs, Sunnis and Shias, and political tensions between the army, the elites and left-wing reformers.

Resentments grew towards a monarch who was nothing more than a British client, and the resentful seized their moment when fate resulted in that shaky moment for all monarchies, a period of regency and minority rule. After Faisal had died in Switzerland in 1933, his son Ghazi, a Harrow-educated playboy with a love of fast cars, took over until he drove one at high speed into a lamppost in April 1939. The throne passed to three-year-old Faisal II under the regency of Ghazi's twenty-six-year-old cousin Abdullah, with a pro-British prime minister called Nuri as-Said. Once the Second World War had broken out, opponents of the regime were naturally drawn towards Fascist Italy and Nazi Germany. In April 1941 the pro-Axis Rashid Ali al-Gayani deposed Abdullah and Nuri and appointed the Mufti of Jerusalem to his new cabinet, prompting the British to intervene in strength in what Iraqis call the 'Thirty Days War'. Baghdad's Jewish community fell victim to a terrible pogrom in the period before the British established control. As the chief inciter of these riots, the Mufti had blamed an alleged Zionist fifth column for the fall of the Rashid Ali regime. Unlike Iraqi Christians, the Jews had indeed been indiscreet in their warm welcome for the British. Rashid Ali and the Mufti fled, the latter to the Japanese embassy in Tehran, which proved an uncertain sanctuary.

Meanwhile Faisal II was sent to Harrow to become more thoroughly anglicized than his Bedouin father. Commercial sharp practice ensured that the Iraqi Petroleum Company kept the lion's share of Iraq's oil profits, with very little of the remainder invested in anything that might have benefited ordinary Iraqis rather than their profligate rulers. The arrangement continued until 1958, when King Faisal, his Crown Prince and Nuri As-Said were brutally murdered in a popular uprising and Iraq embarked on its future as a republic.

Oil also figured very prominently in British calculations regarding Iran – or Persia, as foreigners insisted on calling it. In October 1941 what had been an almost frantically neutral government issued a resigned armistice plea: 'We have done whatever possible to prevent this nefarious war from breaking out on our land. But against all international rules and moral principles, our two neighbours invaded our country. There can be no other reason for this dastardly act but their wish to destroy our system and our progress, which we have achieved with so much labour and human struggle.'[3] The victim was not Poland, but Iran. The aggressors were Great Britain and the Soviet Union, whose forces occupied the country to secure Allied Lend-Lease supplies going to the Red Army defending the Caucasus, as well as to protect the oil refinery at Abadan, on which the Royal Navy depended.

The deep background to this unhappy story reached back to the turn of the twentieth century, when Persia had been a *de facto* colony of Great Britain in the south and of tsarist Russia in the north, leaving the ruling Qajar dynasty in precarious power in the centre. Russians staffed the Persian army's elite Cossack forces, while the British had their own South Persian Rifles, whose main task was to protect the burgeoning interests of the Anglo–Persian Oil Company. This rapacious organization (renamed the Anglo–Iranian Oil Company in 1932, before eventually becoming British Petroleum) paid derisory royalties to the Iranian government from its colossal revenues.

Every trick in the accountants' book was used to swindle the Iranians. This was easy as two British government officials sat on AIOC's board and there were no Iranian representatives. Taxes to the British Exchequer were deducted before profits were distributed to Iran, which meant that in 1949 the Iranian government received £1 million in tax revenue while Whitehall received £28 million. The British Admiralty paid twenty US cents per barrel of oil when the market price was $1.50 and similar discounts were made to American oil concerns to help liquidate Britain's massive post-war debt to the USA.

European operatives enjoyed a plush lifestyle while local workers were paid 50 cents a day and lived in shacks made from beaten oil drums amid the giant refinery complex on the island of Abadan and in what were called 'The Fields', where the oil was extracted. Under the 1933 agreement the AIOC was obliged to improve the infrastructure with roads, hospitals and schools, but none of this was done. Abadan was an immense complex of metal pipes, valves and tanks, all burning to the touch and shimmering like a mirage in the heat. Asphalt roads had the consistency of marshmallow, and grocers served customers while standing in a barrel of water. Two thousand British administrators and technicians worked there, although it could have functioned with fifty.[4]

In the early 1920s the British had backed an officer in the Cossack guard in his quest to discipline and modernize the country along the lines of Atatürk's Turkey. A little English general stood on tiptoe to whisper in the giant Reza's ear, 'Colonel, you are a man of great possibilities.' This was the tall, pockmarked, illiterate soldier who in 1921 deposed the Qajar monarch. Five years later the Iranian parliament, or Majlis, offered Reza Shah Pahlavi – as he styled himself – the Peacock Throne; he crowned himself and preferred to sleep on the floor. Reza Shah wanted to eradicate what he regarded as the backward effects of Arab conquest on Iran. He only ever ventured west as far as Turkey, for he feared the humiliating shock of visiting developed Western Europe.[5]

After having some of the old order poisoned or strangled, Reza Shah dragged urban Iran into the new century. In 1935 he banned the name 'Persia' in favour of the more ancient Iran. In 1936 he outlawed the Islamic chador and introduced peaked caps to make it hard for pious Muslims to bump their foreheads on their prayer rugs. He tore down much of medieval Tehran, often before the residents could evacuate their possessions, replacing it with expansive boulevards and swanky public buildings. People were prohibited from photographing symbolically backward camels. He insisted on providing the country with a modern infrastructure, notably the Trans-Iranian Railway, completed in 1938, even though most freight was carried on trucks. Nomads were forced to settle and the tribes were cowed. Mullahs without demonstrable theological training were banned from preaching and the raggedy mullah became a common sight.[6]

Washington was asked to send a team of experts to sort out the country's bankrupt and corrupted finances. Reza Shah created a civil service as well as a national army, while instituting secular courts. He could be brutal if he needed to be. When clerics gathered in the Khorasan mosque to protest against the ban on veils, his troops stormed it and killed a hundred of those inside. When bakers hoarded wheat, causing a famine, he had one of them thrown in his own oven. Dissenting liberals were bricked up in a tower.[7]

One of those who opposed the Shah's modernizing military despotism

ammed Mossadeq, a scion of Iran's ramified ruling Qajar
dy... Having studied public administration in Iran's mandarin manner in order to work as a tax collector, the aristocratic Mossadeq went
to Paris in his mid-twenties to acquire modern Western culture. His second long stint in Europe was in Switzerland, where he completed a doctoral thesis, in Latin, on testaments in Islamic law, the first Iranian to
achieve such a higher degree. On his return home he was elected to parliament. There he bravely opposed Reza Shah's 1925 coup and the latter's increasingly tyrannical behaviour. Mossadeq was a committed
parliamentarian – not quite the same beast as a democrat – who hated
foreign interference in Iranian affairs. He spent virtually the entire 1930s
living in rural isolation, the alternative to being murdered by the Shah.[8]

For if Reza Shah's initial model was Atatürk, by the 1930s he had
become entranced by Europe's Fascists. In his quest to find a source of
investment capital and expertise independent of the British and Russians,
Reza Shah opened Iran to the Germans, who flooded into the country in
some numbers. The British and Soviets combined to insist that Reza Shah
expel them so as to protect supply routes to the desperate Soviets, and,
although he complied, they occupied his country anyway and he went
into exile. The Allies put his twenty-one-year-old son Mohammed Reza
Shah on the throne, in events witnessed by the young Ayatollah Ruhollah
Khomenei. Mohammed was a soft pastiche of Daddy.

A British consular official, Sir Claremont Skrine, was based throughout the war in Meshed, a city within the increasingly closed Soviet north
of Iran. His main task was to expedite transhipments of war materials
going to the Soviet Union. In his peripheral vision Skrine also noted
another power in the land, the third party to a tripartite treaty which
guaranteed Iran's sovereignty and territorial integrity, with a supplemental promise to evacuate the country six months after the cessation of
global hostilities. Thirty thousand US troops radically increased the carrying capacity of the Trans-Iranian Railway bearing Lend-Lease materials northwards. The fiscal expert Arthur Millspaugh returned to run
Iran's public finances. Colonel H. Norman Schwarzkopf, the founder of
the New Jersey State Police, was imported to reorganize the Iranian
paramilitary Gendarmerie. He was to return in 1953 as part of a joint
CIA–SIS operation to overthrow Mossadeq and reinstate the Shah.

Although his relations with the Soviets began amicably enough, Skrine noticed that, following a few changes of key personnel, the atmosphere deteriorated. In 1941 the Soviets helped camouflage the Iranian Communists as a more populist Tudeh or 'Masses' Party, to attract a wider range of those who sought reform and an end to foreign rule. Although it numbered only a few thousand core members, it had hundreds of thousands of sympathizers, particularly in the unions. The Soviets also backed separatist movements among the Azerbaijanis under Mir Bagirov and Kurds under Jafar Pishevari, even though this threat to Iran's integrity was anathema to the Tudeh Party.

The British responded by supporting such conservative forces as the Shia clergy and the monarchy, while encouraging an anti-Communist Party called National Will. In the event, power in the Majlis passed to liberal nationalists such as Ahmed Qavam and Mossadeq. Stalin gradually dropped the Tudeh party in favour of using the northern Azeri and Kurdish nationalists to lever oil concessions out of the Iranian government. Of course the northern nationalists were expendable pawns too, as Molotov admitted when he said that Pishevari 'could die or become ill' should he prove awkward.[9] The Iranian government sought to interest a wider range of Western oil companies in Iran, partly to counter the hegemony of the British. This annoyed the Soviets, who in October 1944 demanded a northern oil concession of their own. The Soviet Ambassador, Sergei Kavtaradze, tried to bully the Iranians by encouraging the Tudeh Party to demonstrate outside the parliament building, calling for the Prime Minister's resignation, and then deployed Red Army troops to protect the demonstrators from the Iranian government. No wonder the US was worried about how the Soviets conducted themselves towards a 'friendly' power.[10]

While Mossadeq took to railing in parliament against both the British and Russians, the new Prime Minister Qazam encouraged deeper US involvement in Iran's oil industry, while simultaneously double-crossing the Soviets over their northern concession. Qazam promised Stalin oil concessions and took three Tudeh Party members into his government. Stalin duly dropped the northern separatists and withdrew his forces in May 1946. He explained to his despondent separatist clients that their analysis of events was faulty, and that at this stage of the infant Iranian revolution it was necessary to support a progressive bourgeois like Qazam to isolate the Iranian Anglophiles.

It was Stalin's analysis of the situation that proved flawed. The Shah's forces crushed the Azeri and Kurdish separatists with extreme violence, the three Communists were ejected from the Tehran government and the oil-concessions treaty was never ratified by the Majlis, where opposition to Qazam was led by Mossadeq. Resembling a cartoon vulture, Mossadeq was much given to fainting, weeping and long bouts of hysterical laughter, which played well among emotional Shias but which lent themselves to self-serving foreign insinuations about his sanity. He was emerging as the one figure who had suffered twenty years of exile and house arrest for his loyal opposition to the old Shah, and who could unite all shades of nationalist opinion, including the Shia clergy. The door closed on Stalin was one which opened for the US, reluctantly drawn into ever closer support for the young Shah of Iran, whose pretensions to restoring the empire of Darius the Great otherwise struck the Americans as absurd.[11]

Stalin's parallel demands on Turkey, for military bases on the Straits and the return of Kars and Ardahan to the Armenian Soviet Republic, and his alleged backing for Communists in Greece led many US policy-makers to see ominous patterns in his behaviour.[12] One who did so was Loy Henderson, who in the spring of 1946 became head of the State Department's Near Eastern and African Affairs division, having served in Moscow in the 1930s. In a major policy paper, written two months before Kennan's Long Telegram, Henderson argued that with Germany and Japan out of the way, the Soviets would turn their attentions to an enfeebled British position in the greater Middle East. He played a major role in following Soviet troop movements in northern Iran – the Vice Consul in Tabriz spent many nights counting tanks by moonlight – and in persuading Secretary of State Byrnes to let the Russians know that the US were fully aware of what they were doing.[13]

In fact Stalin pursued a policy that might be called an immoderate *sauter pour mieux reculer* to make a more moderate gain, always testing his ideological enemies' resolve. Thus Soviet demands for a military presence on the Dardanelles in August 1946 led the Americans to elaborate war plans (codename Pincher) for the region. There was talk of the knock-on effects, not just in Greece, but in the Middle East, India and even China, the prototype of the domino theory that came to dominate US policy-making. A US carrier group, led by the USS *Franklin D. Roosevelt*, was moved into the eastern Mediterranean, while by October plans had been worked out for air strikes on Soviet oil installations, and for nuclear war. Fully informed of US plans by his many agents in the US government, Stalin backed down and made more emollient noises to Ankara.[14]

Egyptian Resurgence

If the Soviet threat drew the US into the affairs of Iran and Turkey, to the west and south its British ally was the main problem. Egypt had never formally been a British colony, unusual in that since the time of the ancient pharaohs foreigners, from the Hellenic Ptolemys to the Ottoman Turks, had always ruled Egypt. But because the French-designed and Egyptian-built Suez Canal was the jugular vein for the wider British Empire, the British used financial power and military might to install themselves on and around this major artery. Interwar monarchical Egypt was a paradise of liberality compared with anywhere in the Middle East. There were regular elections to a bicameral legislature, which dated back to 1866, full adult male suffrage and a free press. Only the last was true of contemporary Britain. Alexandria and Cairo were lively cosmopolitan cities. Of course, one should not idealize modern Egypt for in the late 1940s as little as 5 per cent of Egypt's population controlled 65 per cent of the country's commercial and industrial assets, while 3 per cent owned 80 per cent of its land.[15]

As the first entrant into the field, the liberal nationalist Al-Wafd (Delegation) Party dominated the politics of the period. Its main concerns were to wring further constitutional concessions from King Fuad, and from 1936 his child heir Faruq, and to limit British dominance of what, since 1922 when the British relinquished financial controls, was a nominally independent country. Although the 1936 Treaty of Preferential Alliance, negotiated by Anthony Eden, conceded that 'Egypt was an independent and sovereign state' – it joined the League of Nations a year

later – two major points of tension were unresolved. First, Britain refused
to acknowledge exclusive Egyptian suzerainty over the much vaster
Sudan, which since 1899 had been ruled as a condominium; and second,
the British retained an enormous military presence in the Suez Canal
Zone as well as in Cairo and Alexandria. Suez was the juncture where
the British Empire could be split in half. The Suez complex included
some ten airfields and forty other major encampments capable of sustaining half a million troops or more in the event of war, in which the
Canal was a vital strategic route for the defence of India. Ironically, one
minor detail in the 1936 Anglo–Egyptian Treaty was that the Military
Academy was opened to all of Egypt's social classes. Among the beneficiaries was Gamal Abdul Nasser.

Nasser was one of eleven children, who moved frequently in the tow
of their postmaster father until he settled in the capital. Despite the inevitably cramped conditions in a four-room Cairo apartment, Nasser managed to supplement the rote learning common at the time with extensive
if somewhat indiscriminate reading about Julius Caesar, Nelson and
Gandhi, even tackling the novels of Dickens and Hugo. Schoolboys and
students were sufficiently uncommon in a society where peasants earned
£15 a year for them to assume vanguardist functions. While still young,
Nasser was smashed in the face with a truncheon during a demonstration. By late adolescence he had to face the fact that his family were too
poor for him to study law. Instead he joined the army, which had something of the Kemalist cum Prusso-Japanese air of being a school for the
nation. Various desultory provincial postings ensued, including three
years in the Sudan, but already he had become firm friends with a group
of like-minded nationalist officers, including Anwar Sadat, who chafed
at the continuance of British informal rule behind the puppets on the
Egyptian throne.

Sadat was tantalized by the discipline and mobilizing powers of totalitarian dictatorships, but above all this group looked at neighbouring
Palestine and saw a majority Arab population held down in order for the
British to import European Zionist refugees, bent on creating a settler
society resembling what the French had established in Algeria. Among
these Egyptian officers the Palestinian Arab revolt of the late 1930s elicited the same passionate response as the Spanish civil war among

European and US intellectuals. On the outbreak of war in Europe, Sadat was most assiduous in seeking an Axis victory, establishing contacts with Italian and German agents, as well as with the Muslim Brotherhood leader, Hassan al-Banna, with a view to overthrowing Faruq's regime along the lines of Rashid Ali al-Gayani's coup in Iraq. The British had little difficulty keeping tabs on German agents so incompetent that they established their base next to a houseboat inhabited by the city's best belly dancers. Sadat was duly rounded up and imprisoned.[16]

The British engineered the dismissal of Prime Minister Aly Mahir in June 1940 and of the Egyptian Chief of Staff in August. In early 1942, they persuaded the Egyptian government to break off relations with Vichy France, although they did not consult young Faruq about this development. The entire government collapsed when Faruq demanded that his Foreign Minister resign. The British Ambassador, Sir Miles Lampson, was a bullying giant at six feet five and seventeen stone, who had the unfortunate habit of referring to Faruq as 'the boy'. Lampson insisted that Faruq form a new pro-British government and sent him an ultimatum warning that 'unless I hear by 6pm that Mustafa Nahas Pasha has been asked to form a cabinet, his Majesty King Farouk must expect consequences'. When Faruq ventured rhetorical defiance while otherwise complying with this demand, Lampson had tanks surround Abdin Palace. Lampson stormed in, accompanied by two South African officer cadets brandishing guns, and told the King he should appoint Nahas or abdicate immediately. He had a letter of abdication already prepared for the browbeaten King lest he baulk at dismissing his own Prime Minister.[17]

This incident, which has hardly registered in British consciousness, was of the utmost importance in the evolution of Egyptian nationalism. It discredited both Faruq and those who benefited from the brutal intervention. To Nasser and his friends it was an appalling affront to their sense of national dignity and honour. Of course it also discredited the British, although other factors had contributed more to that process. Throughout the war all colonial peoples observed white men killing other white men in vast numbers, while the influx of thousands of lower-class soldiers undermined the carefully cultivated image of the white men as a superior race. This was particularly the case in Egypt.[18] A capital where the Circassian-Egyptian elite had interacted happily with their British equivalents was suddenly invaded by a horde of British and Dominion troops, the Australians in particular distinguished by their drunken boorishness. Amid the bars and brothels of the Fish Market, there was much knocking off of red tarboosh hats and raucous chants of 'Faruq the Dirty Old Crook'. Although the King was still in his twenties, the refrain was otherwise accurate about his lifelong pursuit of teenage girls.

By the end of the war Nasser was a captain in his late twenties, happily married to a woman with a considerable private income of £800 a year. He and Sadat quietly organized cells of so-called Free Officers within the army of the late 1940s, a clandestine group numbering in the low hundreds with a larger group of civilian sympathizers. Meanwhile, successive Egyptian governments sought to renegotiate the 1936 Treaty with Britain, seeking to force it to relinquish control of the Sudan and to withdraw its troops from the Suez Canal Zone. The British were able to resist these efforts, but were not strong enough to reassert their control over Egypt as a whole.

In 1948 Egypt was one of seven Arab nations to send troops to Palestine, ostensibly to crush the new nation of Israel in support of the Palestinian Arabs, but in reality to prevent King Abdullah's Jordan absorbing the areas the UN had ceded to the Arabs under the partition arrangements. Nasser was one of the officers involved in a shambolic campaign where he had to buy food for his men, who were equipped with Spanish grenades that blew up in their hands. He suffered a superficial wound and, although his troops may have acquitted themselves with honour, the political and military deficiencies of the Arabs were laid bare. Returning to his duties as a Staff College instructor, Nasser blamed the West's royal Arab puppets for military humiliation at the hands of the Israelis, who at that time enjoyed the support of both the USA and the Soviet Union. Defeat also brought the Free Officers an important recruit in the form of the influential General Mohammed Naguib. In 1951 Faruq's government unilaterally abrogated both the 1936 Anglo–Egyptian Treaty and the 1899 convention on the Sudan but then, unwisely, authorized a guerrilla campaign against British forces in the Canal Zone, which was run by the Free Officers. Heavy-handed British reprisals triggered mass protests in Cairo and Alexandria that Naguib and the Free Officers exploited to topple the monarchy.

Asking for Trouble in Algeria

In Arabic the Maghreb signifies the western tip of an Arab world whose heart is in the Gulf. France had two protectorates in the Maghreb – Morocco and Tunisia – while the three departments of Algeria were legally and constitutionally as much a part of metropolitan France as Normandy. Algeria was France's oldest and most integrated colonial possession. Hard, sun-baked *colons* faced hard, dour native Muslims, for, as the nationalist leader Ahmed Ben Bella himself acknowledged, the peoples of Algeria are not known for their winning charm.[19]

Algeria was a classic settler colony, with some 800,000 Europeans – many of them Corsicans, Italians, Maltese and Spanish rather than *français de souche* (of the stump), as native French are known. Collectively these settlers were known as *pieds noirs*, after the shiny black shoes they wore amid the bare feet and sandals. The European settlers were French citizens – the indigenous Muslim population were unenfranchised subjects, to whom the repressive 1881 Native Code applied. One of Algeria's nationalist leaders acknowledged that there was no Algerian nation: 'such a fatherland does not exist. I questioned the living and the dead. I searched through the cemeteries: nobody could speak to me of it. You cannot build on air.'[20]

The introduction of private property law based on written contract gave Europeans key advantages over an indigenous population based on oral lore and tribal ownership. Muslim prohibitions on usury also gave Europeans an advantage in buying land on credit. By 1936, a century after the initial French conquest, European *colons* owned 40 per cent of the land once owned by Arabs and Berbers, the indigenous people who predated the Arab conquests.[21] Agricultural mechanization diminished the importance of physical labour.[22] The Muslims migrated into shanty-towns or the pullulating courts of the cities' various kasbahs, the Arab word for tight warrens of streets, steps and alleyways. As long as they were docile, these migrants would not be regarded as a threat by the Europeans who lived in the tonier quarters of towns.

The French divided Algeria into three departments – Oran, Algiers and Constantine – whose *colon* voters sent deputies and senators to the national legislature in Paris. The franchise was extended only to a very select group of Muslims who were deemed capable of being educated up towards full citizenship, as suggested by the paternalist Darwinian term *évolués* for such men. Since only 10,000 of three and a half million Muslims attended primary schools in 1890, evolution was a glacial process. Sharia law, governing marriage, the family and inheritance, was a convenient obstacle to granting Muslims full civic rights, a role played by polygamy in black Africa.

Although many nationalist leaders were secular French-speakers married to French women – and spoke Arabic haltingly – they regarded Islam (in its typically Algerian animist Sufi form) as a non-negotiable part of their cultural identity. Fanatical Islam was something they associated with medieval Almoravid conquerors. Football was as important as religion in forging a sense of national identity. In the 1920s Muslim Algerians formed separate football teams such as the Mouloudia Club in Algiers, whose red and green strip celebrated Mahloud, the festival of the Prophet's birthday. Nervous of allowing Muslims to occupy any public space unsupervised, the authorities insisted that each Muslim team must include three *colon* players, regardless of their lack of skill.

There were three outstanding figures in the first wave of Algerian nationalists. Their precise ideological identities should be taken with a pinch of salt since in their part of the world these were often fluid. They were the Islamist cleric Sheikh Abd al-Hamid ben Badis, a student politician called Ferhat Abbas, who stemmed from the Francophone Muslim bourgeoisie, and finally the First World War veteran and factory worker Messali Hadj, who spent long periods in French prisons in between nondescript jobs in Paris's Red Belt. The guru of the Egyptian Muslim Brotherhood, Hassan Al-Banna, influenced ben Badis, whose Association of the Algerian Ulema rejected French influences and sought to align Algeria within the wider Muslim *umma*, the global community of believers. Ferhat Abbas was a chemistry graduate married into an Alsatian settler family. He reluctantly moved from advocacy of citizenship through total integration to demanding an Algerian state based on parity of rights 'within the fold of the French community' and based on the principles of 1789. Messali Hadj was a shoemaker's son who married the daughter of a French anarchist miner. He became the leading light of the Etoile Nord-Africaine (North African Star), an organization which flourished chiefly among the half-million Algerian workers living in metropolitan France. Politically, he moved from adherence to the French Communist Party to something more nationalist and Islamic, but the link with Communism would always play against him.[23]

The Second World War crystallized Algerian nationalist demands, not for integration but for complete independence. The army had always been an exit route from the grim economic conditions Muslim Algerians experienced, although a few managed to become soccer stars in France. The future nationalist leader Ahmed Ben Bella joined the army in 1936, while playing midfield too for Olympique de Marseilles.[24] Ben Bella was a natural soldier, who loved the army mainly because he experienced no discrimination in it. He won the Croix de Guerre and the Médaille Militaire fighting as a warrant officer at such epic battles as Monte Cassino. His elder brother had died of wounds sustained during the First World War. Other soldiers included such former non-commissioned officers as Omar Ouamrane and Belkacem Krim. 'I never had a chance to know adolescence,' said Krim. 'My brother returned from Europe with medals and frost-bitten feet. There, everyone was equal. Why not here?' It was a very good question, which could just as easily have been asked by any non-white soldier returning to a racially stratified colony, or by Afro-American GIs who returned to the segregated South, where they could not even enter a bar.[25]

After 1940 the monolithic face of French authority was compromised, with Vichy being especially popular among the *colons*. Then a much more powerful 'Anglo-Saxon' actor arrived on the North African stage in the wake of Operation Torch, the Allied invasion in late 1942. Abbas was politely received by Roosevelt's personal envoy Robert Murphy – mainly, it should be said, to solicit Muslim support for the war. In 1943 most of the Algerian nationalist factions combined into an Association des Amis du Manifeste et de la Liberté (Friends of the Manifesto and of Liberty), which became the first mass political movement in Algerian history.

In March 1944 de Gaulle in principle opened all government posts to Muslims and Frenchmen alike, and included 65,000 deserving Muslims on the French electoral roll. All Muslim males over twenty-one were declared eligible to vote for local assemblies, which had to include 40 per cent Muslims in their membership. This was too little, too late in an atmosphere rendered febrile by the end of a war that had pushed so many Muslims to the wall. By mid-1945 parts of Algeria seethed with discontent, with nationalists organizing boycotts of collaborating businesses and the intimidation of Muslims who drank alcohol or worked for the French. The eastern department of Constantine, next to Tunisia, became a flashpoint, with some of its nondescript towns harbouring concentrations of nationalists. One of these was Sétif, where Ferhat Abbas had worked as a pharmacist. On 8 May a noisy Muslim procession, led by the Muslim Boy Scouts, wound its way through Sétif to celebrate Victory in Europe Day and calling for the release of Messali Hadj from house arrest. Hadj was instead transferred to detention in the desert before being flown to Brazzaville in the French Congo – where, ironically enough, de Gaulle had made a declaration during the war embracing broad colonial reform, albeit without independence, to placate the Americans.

In Sétif twenty gendarmes faced around 8,000 demonstrators, boldly intervening to confiscate the green and white banners emblazoned with calls for a 'free and independent Algeria'. In the increasingly ill-tempered encounters between demonstrators and policemen, shots were fired, which led to wholesale Muslim attacks on any passing Europeans. A priest had his heart ripped out and hung round his neck, while the hands of the Secretary of the Communist Party were chopped off. Word passed quickly to the surrounding countryside that 'jihad' had been declared, to cries of 'Holy War in the name of Allah!' Although control was restored by nightfall in Sétif itself, out in the countryside armed groups of Muslims bushwhacked isolated settlers, killing 103 of them with clubs, guns and knives. There were instances of women being raped.

One hundred and ten miles east of Sétif lay the small town of Guelma, with around 4,500 Italian, Maltese and Jewish European inhabitants amid 16,500 Muslims. The Association of the Friends of the Manifesto was well represented among them. Again there was an initially peaceful VE Day demonstration which turned ugly, after the local police commissioner, André Achiary, fired warning shots in the air, shortly followed by his men opening fire on the foremost demonstrators. After imposing a curfew, Achiary restored a semblance of order in the town, before launching a series of arrests of nationalist leaders, some of whom were summarily killed by the police and their *colon* vigilante helpers, who in an echo of Vichy's paramilitary police dubbed themselves the *milice*. By the time the bloodshed stopped, around 1,500 Muslims were dead.[26]

The French government's response was swift and hard. On arriving in Algiers to congratulate the French Governor-General on victory in Europe, the liberal Ferhat Abbas was arrested despite having denounced the uprising in Sétif. French troops, including Foreign Legionnaires and Senegalese, neither trained in counter-insurgency warfare, saturated Muslim villages, aggressively 'raking them over' to identify Muslim militants. Remote villages were attacked with US-supplied Douglas dive-bombers, armed with anti-personnel bombs supplied by the RAF. A cruiser shelled a coastal road used by Muslim militants. Muslims suspected of political activism were arrested and shot, their bodies disposed of in kilns, wells and ravines.[27]

Quite how many Muslims were killed remains contentious. After gaining independence the Algerian nationalist government claimed that 50,000 or 80,000 people had been killed (the number rose over time), but a more realistic estimate seems to be between 6,000 and 8,000. What is not in doubt is that the French authorities were determined to overawe the Muslims. After a hotelier and his daughter had been killed by Muslims in Falaise, the army commander in Constantine ordered 15,000 Muslims to assemble on a beach at Melbou, marshalled behind their headmen or *caids*. French navy ships manoeuvred offshore; aircraft swooped past at alarmingly low levels; artillery salvoes boomed. A mufti praised the steps taken by the French and invoked Allah before leading a collective prayer. The terrified crowd were given slices of 'peace cakes', which they received with applause and ululations.[28]

By way of concession to Muslim opinion, and in the teeth of settler opposition, the French National Assembly agreed to a revised electoral statute for Algeria. A new Algerian Assembly would have 120 seats, half chosen by a European electoral college of 460,000 French citizens plus 58,000 assimilated Muslims, and the other half elected by 1,400,000 unassimilated Muslims. Even these slanted arrangements had to be comprehensively rigged on polling day in April 1948, to secure European dominance. Right-wing parties won fifty-four of the sixty European seats, but only nineteen of the sixty Muslim seats went to socialists and nationalists. Forty-one went to government stooges, known as *béni-oui-ouis* (Uncle Toms) to the locals.[29] All of this was the handiwork of a 'Third Force', socialist-dominated French government, whose Governor-General in Algiers, Marcel Naegelen, was an Alsatian anti-Communist leftist fanatically opposed to 'separatism'. Thus the range of non-violent options open to Algerian nationalists was diminished while the incentives for armed resistance increased.

Not So Holy Land

A year before the Second World War erupted, the newly appointed British Colonial Secretary, Malcolm MacDonald, calculated that, although he was responsible for fifty colonies around the world, the Palestine Mandate alone occupied half of his time. Churchill would describe the war between Arab and Jew in Palestine as the 'war of mice', for it continued – as it still does more than sixty years later – even as the world's bull elephants clashed. In essence, the conflict between the mice was about the semantic ambiguity of the phrase 'national home' as promised to the Jews in the 1917 Balfour Declaration, avoiding the commitment embodied by the word 'state'.

There has never been an historic Palestine, except as a Roman province, though there certainly were two ancient Jewish kingdoms long before that. Palestine had no separate identity during the centuries of Ottoman rule either, in the latter part of which, from the 1880s onwards, the 25,000 Orthodox Jews who lived in Jerusalem were augmented by two major waves of East European immigrants who farmed on the plains. The Balfour Declaration had served two circumstantial purposes. One was to defuse Bolshevism, whose internationalism was widely attributed to the influence of the perennially homeless Jews. The other was as a wartime expedient to win the support of US Jews, much as the Russians were promised Constantinople, and probably no more sincerely meant.

Following a three-year Arab revolt, which the British crushed ruth-lessly, in 1939 MacDonald published a White Paper that drastically restricted Jewish immigration to Palestine, limiting it to some 75,000 persons over five years, even though he recognized that it was largely the employment opportunities created by these industrious immigrants that had led to an increase in the local Arab population. In Zionist eyes the White Paper was a cold-blooded betrayal of a desperate people, for it coincided with the intensified persecution of European Jews in Nazi Germany and in Poland. The rest of the world (with the notable excep-tion of dictator Leonidas Trujillo's Dominican Republic) had responded by agreeing at the 1938 Evian Conference that there was no more room in their respective inns. The British issued the White Paper to ensure that the wider Arab world, from which Britain derived 60 per cent of its oil, did not switch to the Axis side during the imminent war. As MacDonald explained, 'We could not let emotion rule our policy. We must accept the facts of the extremely dangerous prospect with absolute, unsentimental and, some people would say, even cynical realism. The Jews would be on our side in any case in the struggle against Hitler. Would the indepen-dent Arab nations adopt the same attitude?'[30]

While this local example of appeasement did not lead to a recrudes-cence of the Anglo-Arab alliance of the First World War, it did mean that no major trouble jeopardized trans-Jordanian oil pipelines or threat-ened British bases in Egypt, even when the British heavy-handedly deposed the Egyptian Prime Minister. Nor, given the Nazis' pathologi-cal hatred of the Jews, did the British have cause to worry where the latter's sympathies might lie. The Zionist-Fascists led by Vladimir Jabot-insky were a tiny if noisy minority, although one of Jabotinsky's most devoted disciples was Menachem Begin, later leader of the Irgun terror-ist organization. The majority Zionist response to a war that was exis-tential for the Jewish people was encapsulated by David Ben Gurion's formula that 'we shall fight with Great Britain in this war as if there were no White Paper, and we shall fight the White Paper as if there was no war'.

When the Zionists offered to raise a Jewish army to fight the Axis, the British prevaricated, eventually conceding a joint Arab and Jewish bat-talion attached to the East Kent Buffs in which the Jewish contingent fought and the Arabs deserted. Ten thousand or so Palestinian Jews (and 7,000 Palestinian Arabs) served as individuals in the British armed forces. In late 1944 the British at last sanctioned a Jewish Brigade, which fought with distinction. British equivocation, however justifiable in terms of keeping the Arabs on side, was to give the Zionists a potent propaganda weapon to use against them once the mass murder of European Jews was revealed to an uncomprehending world. As evidence built up of Nazi murder of Europe's Jews, so Zionist insistence on a secure Jewish state of Israel intensified. If all else failed, the world's Jews could repair there. This meant that the Jews were never going to accept the preferred British fix of Arab and Jewish enclaves with a bi-national Palestine.

A murky human traffic had developed between Palestinian Jewish agents and the Nazi paramilitary SS to expatriate Jews down the Danube to Romanian ports and hence out of Europe. These ships were vermin-infested freighters, rusting cattle boats and leaking tankers, into which men, women and children were crammed. When these overloaded hulks appeared off Palestine the British ordered them to turn back, and in one instance opened fire, killing two refugees. Thus began a war of boat propaganda, a tactic Israel's Turkish and NGO enemies have since turned against it. In November 1940 the British transferred 1,700 refugees from two ships which had arrived at Haifa on to a larger vessel called *La Patria*, which was destined for Mauritius. Early one morning the ship's alarm was sounded and the refugees leaped into the sea. Shortly afterwards *La Patria* blew up and sank. Two hundred and forty refugees drowned or died in the explosion, along with a dozen policemen. The Jewish Agency, founded in 1929 to promote settlement of Palestine, promptly claimed that the refugees had opted to kill themselves rather than go to the hell of Mauritius – in fact one of the most agreeable islands in the world. The true cause of the tragedy was a bungled attempt by the Irgun to cripple the ship's propulsion. Further incidents included a ship denied entry to Turkish harbours that sank with the loss of 231 lives during a storm, and the *Struma*, a well-publicized floating hell moored off Istanbul, which sank after another mysterious explosion. Although the fanatical Begin regarded the British as Nazis with better manners, the Irgun respected the call of the mainstream Jewish Agency and its militia army the Haganah to refrain from attacking the British.

But the Zionist movement itself was also highly fissiparous, and included extremists as well as moderates. No such restraint inhibited the Lehi, known as the Stern Gang from its charismatic leader Avraham Stern, revered as 'Yair' (the Illuminator) by his followers. Stern was killed 'trying to escape' from British custody in 1942, but the gang continued to carry out terrorist attacks during the war, murdering at least fifteen men and attacking police stations, official buildings and oil pipelines.[31]

Initially, British life in the Mandate had differed little from that of colonists elsewhere, reflecting the way most of the British administrators and soldiers thought about a situation whose complexities generally eluded them – for Palestine was not a colony. There were official receptions at Government House, flower shows and tea parties. The more active could hunt jackals with the Ramle Vale Hunt, or tee off on the Sodom and Gomorrah Golf Course, about which there was much ribald wit. But this was not India or the Sudan; it was more a dead end than a chance to shine as part of an elite, among people too 'clever' to be patronized, and one with no real strategic significance until the British had to consider alternatives to a restive Egypt. In a word, Palestine was a boring backwater posting, except perhaps to those of a religious bent.

Zionist terrorism began in retaliation for Arab atrocities during the 1936–9 Arab Revolt, providing perplexing evidence for the British of peoples' inability to 'get along', as if they were neighbours quarrelling over a suburban hedge or party wall.[32] The military response was in line with a simple-minded speech Brigadier Bernard Montgomery had delivered in Haifa in 1937: 'I do not care whether you are Jews or Gentiles. I care nothing for your political opinions. I am a soldier. My duty is to maintain law and order. I intend to do so.'[33] The countenance of the Mandate changed, with official buildings heavily sandbagged behind barriers of barbed wire, and police stations turned into imposing forts constructed from reinforced concrete. In November 1944 the Stern Gang excelled themselves when two of their operatives murdered Resident Minister of State Lord Moyne, Churchill's friend and his wife Clementine's exotic travel companion, in Cairo. The reaction among the British governing class was so negative that the Jewish Agency, Haganah and Irgun declared a 'hunting season' against Sternist sympathizers. The two young assassins were quickly caught, tried and hanged.

Although the British in Palestine could rejoice at victory in the war, that mood proved evanescent in the troubled Mandate, where concrete police forts were dubbed 'Bevingrads' after Ernest Bevin, the new Labour Foreign Secretary. As the British pulled back their forces in Egypt to the Canal Zone, so Palestine assumed greater importance should they have to beat a strategic retreat from there, with the port of Haifa substituting for the naval facilities at Alexandria. That was why the British concentrated so many troops, at an annual cost of £40 million, in a place where two irreconcilable national identities had long clashed. The 100,000-strong force stationed in Palestine became the object of a campaign in which Jewish children were encouraged to spit on its members while crying 'English bastards' or 'Gestapo'. British airborne troops, in their maroon berets, were dubbed 'red poppies with black hearts' when they marched past sullen Jewish onlookers. The emotional atmosphere was further ratcheted up over the well-publicized plight of Jewish Displaced Persons languishing in former Nazi camps.

As British statesmen were only too aware, Palestine threatened to poison their relations with the US, largely because of the electoral clout of a Jewish lobby that had been bitterly divided before and during the war, but which was now speaking with the enormous moral authority derived from the Holocaust. Disinclined, like his illustrious predecessor, to open America's doors to them, in August 1945 President Truman requested the admission of 100,000 refugees to Palestine to assuage agitation among Jewish Democrat supporters in New York. Many ordinary Americans, especially the more fundamentalist Christians, supported the Zionists but were ambivalent about America's own Jews and hated their strong presence in the New York financial district. Truman's demand thwarted British efforts to decouple the problems of refugees and Palestine, while Washington's standard combination of opportunism and self-righteousness was bitterly resented in London.

US policy in the Middle East was almost as subject as the British to competing pressures. In an echo of the Balfour Declaration, Roosevelt had both endorsed the idea of a Jewish state and solemnly promised Saudi Arabia's King Abd Al-Aziz Ibn Saud that he would not aid the Jews or do anything detrimental to Arab interests. Perspicacious diplomats also noted that there was no point in bolstering the imaginary arch represented by the Northern Tier of Greece, Iran and Turkey if 'we are going to kick out the pillars' to the south on which the arch rested. While Arabs had a few advocates like Loy Henderson within the US State *Buche* Department, they could not match the Zionist organizers, who knew how to mobilize public emotion and had many sympathizers extending to the very top of the administration.

Truman himself put the main problem succinctly: 'I do not have hundreds of thousands of Arabs among my constituents.' Specifically, only once since 1876 had a candidate won the presidency without winning the forty-seven electoral votes of New York, and – though he did in fact lose New York in 1948 – Truman was not going to take that risk. He may have been occasionally exasperated by Zionist lobbyists, but they had the ear of some in his inner circle nonetheless, notably his right-hand man and campaign manager Clark Clifford, who was also to be a highly influential member of the administrations of Presidents Kennedy and Johnson.

Many of Truman's advisers were dismissively racist towards the Arabs, while other influential figures were simply naive about the complexity of such conflicts. Loy Henderson, who had been a consul in the Irish Free State as well as chief of mission to Baghdad, was aghast when Eleanor Roosevelt optimistically opined in 1947: 'Come, come . . . a few years ago Ireland was considered to be a problem that could not be solved. Then the Irish Republic was established and the problem vanished. I'm confident that when a Jewish state is set up, the Arabs will see the light; they will quiet down; and Palestine will no longer be a problem.'[34] Not for the last time, Ireland's idiosyncratic history was wrongly taken to be exemplary. Rather than encouraging Americans to overcome their own aversion to Jewish immigration, US policy-makers expected the Arabs to do so.[35]

While some of the British governing class were as reflexively anti-Semitic as their US peers, others simply refused to accept that the remnants of the Jewish people had no further destiny in Europe.[36] They could not grasp that they were asking the Jews to assimilate into a charnel house. The pro-Zionist Labour politician Richard Crossman accurately described the irresponsible aspects of US moral grandstanding: 'By shouting for a Jewish state, Americans satisfy many motives. They are attacking the Empire and British imperialism, they are espousing a moral cause, the fulfilment for which they will take no responsibility, and, most important of all, they are diverting attention from the fact that their own immigration laws are one of the causes of the problem.'[37]

If Americans felt common cause with rebellious colonial frontiersmen, the British were unused to colonized peoples who were modern, democratic, self-assertive and prone to moralizing about general European guilt for what was not yet called the Holocaust. British anti-Semitism and anti-Zionism (which should not be casually conflated) received powerful impulse from what was too crudely described then, and now, as 'Jewish terrorism', a term akin to calling the IRA 'Catholic terrorists'.

While the Haganah focused on destroying British coastal radar installations, bridges and railway lines, Irgun and the Stern Gang stepped up their terrorist campaigns. In April 1946 they gunned down seven British soldiers in a car park and stole their weapons. In June Operation Agatha saw the large-scale deployment of British troops to detain leading Zionists, including many ostensibly moderate Jewish Agency figures, and to unearth arms dumps. The primary object of this operation was to prove connections between the Jewish Agency and the Haganah underground, and in that respect it was successful, despite seemingly hysterical women on rural kibbutzim who tore off their sleeves to reveal German concentration-camp tattoos to distract the searchers from weapons dumps.

Irgun documents seized in such raids found their way to British Criminal Investigation Department offices situated, alongside other Mandate bureaucracies, on various floors of Jerusalem's King David Hotel.[38] Even by British standards it was an act of astonishing casualness to have conflated business and pleasure in one major complex, for the King David Hotel was both an administrative centre and a functioning luxury hotel. On 22 July 1946 fourteen or fifteen Zionist terrorists, dressed as Arabs, drew up in a truck and unloaded milk churns packed with explosives into the basement nightclub called the Régence. These exploded at 12.36 p.m., when the hotel was at its most crowded, and demolished most of its southern wing, killing ninety-one people including British soldiers and Arab and Jewish administrators. A few days after the attack the British launched Operation Shark to round up further Zionist extremists, 800 of whom were detained in Rafah camp. Onerous controls were placed on the general Jewish population through random searches, curfews and roadblocks.[39]

The terrorists responded by extending their campaign to British interests in Europe (the British embassy in Rome was bombed in October 1946), as well as to the imperial metropolis itself. In March 1947 the Stern Gang bombed the British Colonial Club off Trafalgar Square, injuring black servicemen and African students. In June the gang despatched the first ever letter bombs, with Churchill, Bevin, Clement Attlee and Eden among the addressees. The Security Service, MI5, kept Zionist sympathizers under close surveillance and successfully frustrated terrorist attacks.[40] Unsurprisingly, the British authorities in Palestine responded to Zionist attacks with strongarm methods that many of their policemen had learned fighting Irish republicans in the 1920s, the model of choice too for many Zionist terrorists in the 1940s. The ranks of the undercover police also included such war heroes as SAS Major Roy Farran, whose robust approach to counter-terrorism (which has been normative in Israel itself for the last half-century) was denounced by those indulgent of the malignancy of Zionist terrorism. By the end of 1946 the terrorists had murdered 373 people, the majority civilians.[41]

High-level British policy was conflicted between those who believed in the primacy of a political solution and military men who regarded any negotiated settlement as appeasement. The chief advocate of a hard line was the star general, Field Marshal Montgomery, who easily overruled the more political approach of Colonial Secretary Arthur Creech Jones, who had been jailed for pacifism in the First World War. British troops were forbidden to visit such public places as cafés and cinemas, while non-essential family members were repatriated. The British retreated behind more fortifications, in the process 'transforming the Mandate into a prison, and locking themselves in as well'.[42] They also relied upon collective reprisals for terrorist atrocities, something modern Israel practises too. As one British officer noted: 'when the security forces have to deal with a thoroughly non-cooperative, unscrupulous, dishonest and utterly immoral civilian population such as the Jewish Community in Palestine, who systematically and continually hide and refuse to give up to justice the perpetrators of murderous outrages, reprisals are the only effective weapon to employ, saving time, money and unnecessary bloodshed'.[43]

Events in Britain and India compelled a decision in the winter of 1946–7. While the bankrupt British froze in their own homes, in India communal violence forced them to put a date on withdrawal. In the House of Commons on 25 February 1947 Richard Crossman fatuously maintained that a bit of creative conflict might bring resolution, just as a strike might settle a domestic labour dispute after failed negotiation and arbitration.[44] Such facile analogies made it easy enough to let Palestine go, a decision arrived at that month when the cabinet acknowledged that there was no obvious political solution. It also declared martial law, although that proved no more help than the abortive quest for a political solution.

Meanwhile the Zionists continued to utilize what has been called 'boat propaganda', which MI6 sought to frustrate with Operation Embarrass, in which they damaged or sank five refugee ships in Italian harbours.[45] They did not manage to get at the *Exodus 1947*, which after being repulsed from Palestine was in turn refused entry to Marseilles, ending up in Hamburg, where British troops and German policemen manhandled the refugees ashore. The captain subsequently recalled that Zionist intelligence agents 'gave us orders that this ship was to be used as a big demonstration with banners to show how poor and weak and helpless we were, and how cruel the British were'.[46]

The *Exodus* story was played up in an inflammatory way in the US by the Zionist screenwriter Ben Hecht. Any emotional capital the *Exodus* saga accrued in Britain was immediately dissipated when the Irgun hanged two British sergeants and booby-trapped their bodies in response to the execution of three convicted terrorist killers in Acre jail – and Hecht gloated about it. The outrage caused British troops in Palestine to riot and contributed to anti-Semitic incidents in Britain itself.[47]

These incidents took place under the noses of the delegates to the UN Special Committee on Palestine, who arrived in Palestine in mid-June 1947. Three of its members personally witnessed British mismanagement of the *Exodus* saga in Haifa harbour. UNSCOP eventually recommended partition, by eight votes to three, although under these arrangements the Arab and Jewish areas were to be entwined like two fighting snakes. The British rejected the proposal on the grounds that the US refused to underwrite it with aid or troops. Unable to impose a solution on either Arabs or Jews, in late 1947 the British informed the UN of their intention to withdraw unilaterally, fixing the date at 14 May 1948. The precedent of India lay to hand, except that there they had patched up a settlement of a sort. Although the British claimed to represent law and order, this was notional in a country given over to a civil war between Jews and Arabs. To British surprise, both the US and the Soviet Union backed partition, tacitly uniting under the banner of anti-imperialism.[48]

The Soviet attitude was interesting. Stalin always sought to disrupt and divide what was coalescing as a single Western opponent. In this respect Palestine seemed ideally designed to cause trouble between the US and Britain. There was much for the Soviets to like in the incipient Zionist state. Young Zionists like Amos Perlmutter had eagerly charted the onward march of the Red Army into Germany with maps and pins on their bedroom walls, and Stalin was certainly aware of how rife pro-German sympathies had been in the Arab world, as well as among Muslims in the wartime Soviet Union. Trade unionism had a much stronger purchase among Palestine's Jews than it did in any surrounding Arab country. Interwar Palestine had the largest Communist Party in the Middle East, dominated by its Jewish members. Unlike Egypt, where most land was in feudal ownership, the Zionist kibbutzim bore a generic resemblance to Soviet collective farms. Stalin could imagine that, should the Arabs emulate these modern features of Zionism, they might then enter into a more revolutionary phase of their own development. No wonder the Soviet Union was the first country to recognize Israel.[49]

The Zionists had achieved international recognition for a Jewish state, rather than a 'national home', within Palestine, even though with 600,000 Jews to 1.2 million Arabs the Jews were only a large minority in a country where most of the land was owned by absentee urban Arab landlords. There were some obvious weaknesses on the Arab side. They lacked the military experience and European training of Haganah, nor did they have the sophisticated war-surplus German weapons that Haganah was sourcing from Czechoslovakia. Illiterate Arab villagers had a much less visceral sense of nationhood than educated European immigrants who had survived attempts to exterminate them all.[50] The internal Palestinian Arab leadership was bitterly divided between rival clans, while the notorious Mufti Hajj Amin was hated by other Arab leaders and damned as a Nazi collaborator in the wider world.

The only Arab ruler to support partition, King Abdullah of Jordan, did so with a view to absorbing a small Arab Palestine into Transjordan itself. His wider regional ambitions frightened the Syrians, whom he wished to subsume into a greater Hashemite kingdom, the Egyptians, who thought they were leaders of the Arab world, and finally the Saud dynasty, who were the Hashemites' main regional rivals. But since Arab emotions had been whipped up by the prospect of a Jewish state in their midst, Arab rulers had to be seen to act, for their own febrile street mobs might easily be turned on them. In view of their rivalries, it suited Arabs rulers to send a free-floating Arab Liberation Army into battle with the Jews, whom the Arabs regarded as an alien European excrescence in their part of the world. They could not understand why the Europeans or Americans could not find the Jews a homeland elsewhere.

The Jews responded with a similar argument vis-à-vis the leaderless Palestinian Arabs, who began fleeing the fight they had spasmodically begun. Why couldn't they be relocated to the huge desert spaces of the Arab kingdoms? A Palestinian Arab and Jewish war began, fought under weary British eyes and with mounting ferocity on both sides. Believing that they were going to be massacred by the Jews, up to 300,000 Arabs fled their homes, convinced that they would return with neighbouring Arab armies to exact their own vengeance. One day after the British had sailed away, five Arab armies attacked the newly declared state of Israel and comprehensively lost. Israel would survive further wars as the sole modern democratic state in a Middle East dominated by dictators and autocratic monarchs. But it would carry forward both a wider sense of Jewish victimhood and militarism in its DNA. That so many military men have also figured in its political class testifies to what it means to live in a neighbourhood of fanatics and maniacs.

4. SOME MORE VICTORIOUS THAN OTHERS

The View from the Potomac

The US emerged from the Second World War with its industrial power mightily boosted, as well as being sole possessor of the most destructive weapons invented by humankind. The Pacific had become an American lake. US warships alone had routed the Imperial Japanese Navy and US Marines had stormed Pacific islands in the teeth of suicidal resistance. The US also had the world's only significant long-range bomber in the B-29 Superfortress with its 3,250-mile combat range, given a nearly global reach by the acquisition of new oceanic bases, and the US attitude to colonies subtly shifted as it prepared to hang on to those bases for strategic reasons.

US policy towards China was always overshadowed by events in Europe, where the Soviet threat grew more menacing by the day. Nazi occupation and the bloodiest fighting of the war had ravaged the Soviet Union's heartlands, but it too was manifestly a bigger player than the battle-scarred imperial giant represented at Potsdam, not by the exhausted Churchill, but by the new Labour Prime Minister Clement Attlee. Unlike the British, the Soviets defined themselves in opposition to US interests, time and again showing a pattern of aggressive behaviour that the US felt obliged to counter. These points of friction condensed into global ideological conflict between free and totalitarian camps in which issues of national sovereignty took second or third place to how individual countries aligned themselves. The passions aroused by the broader struggle were to distort perceptions of lesser conflicts whose origins were more local.

While Americans, Russians and Britons celebrated peace, and others the liberation of their countries from Nazism, the wider world in 1945 was hardly a peaceful place. But from 1945 onwards the destinies of many of the world's peoples depended no longer on the colonial powers but on Washington and Moscow, united only in common hostility towards colonial empires. The Soviet heirs to imperial Russia's overland dominions forcibly imposed a Red Empire over Eastern Europe and sought to make mischief in Asia, and the US response was to intervene in much less benign ways in the affairs of Asia, not least to bolster European allies against threats which they convinced themselves were Communist, a perception eagerly encouraged by these self-interested colonial powers.

Long before any American dreamed up the domino theory, the French had the 'ten-pin theory', which was much the same. Thus General Jean de Lattre de Tassigny told an American colleague: 'Tonkin is the key to Southeast Asia, if Southeast Asia is lost, India will burn like a match, and there will be no barrier to the advance of Communism before Suez and Africa. If the Muslim world were thus engulfed, the Muslims in North Africa would soon fall into line and Europe itself would be outflanked.'[1] Sub-Saharan Africa had yet to become part of this global struggle. Amid the conflict and chaos of 1945 one key trend emerged: the rise of the Soviet Union and its willingness to kick at the rickety doors of declining British and French global influence. There was no way back to the merely dollar diplomacy of the 1930s, however much many Americans might have wished it. Events in China gave powerful impetus to the belief that the onward march of global Communism had to be stopped, though only after attempts to rescue Chiang Kai-shek had failed.

The Americans restrained Chiang from definitively strangling Mao's Communists in their Yan'an fastness, and then suggested he incorporate them into a coalition government. Quite possibly Chiang could not have achieved a military solution, but the constraints put on his freedom of action by the Americans ruled it out altogether. One would not think it from British historiography, but China, untainted by either Communism or imperialism, was Roosevelt's favourite ally in the Second World War.

'The people of China', he said in 1943, 'have been, in thought and in objective, closer to us Americans than almost any other peoples in the world – the same great ideals. China in the last – less than half a century has become one of the great democracies of the world.' The will to see a world full of potential Americans, struggling to cast off the shackles of imperialism, tribalism and other unAmerican cultural accretions, has deep roots. Many influential Americans looked at China and saw evolving a more populous version of their own country.[2]

Real China, as distinct from this fantasy, fascinated and frustrated Americans in equal measure. It was vast, with desert, mountains and then coastal plains crisscrossed by irrigation canals. The currency fluctuated with bewildering rapidity, while palms had to be greased for every encounter with officialdom. Gangsters, such as Shanghai's Green Gang, had fluid relations with government agencies including the KMT secret police, which reminded Americans of the Gestapo. Although the US sought a unified, democratic China, its chosen instrument for achieving this goal, Chiang's Nationalists, denied elementary Western freedoms even as they experimented with constitutions and assemblies.

An alarming percentage of US aid went to the territorial warlords who dominated the Nationalist military. The US sought a moral basis for supporting the Nationalists, but grew frustrated when it could not find one in a regime whose corruption was epic. Misreading Mao's Communists as honest agrarian socialists, Washington thought they could be persuaded to become a loyal opposition within a democratic framework. To that end financial pressure was brought to bear on the Nationalists, who after a twenty-year struggle knew their Communist opponents far better than the Americans did. As Chiang once remarked: 'The Japanese are a disease of the skin; the Communists are a disease of the heart.'[3]

US policy was not well served by its Ambassador to China from late 1944 onwards, a former Republican secretary of war called Patrick Hurley, a drunken idiot given to Choctaw war cries. Oblivious of China's delicate protocols, he referred to Chiang as 'Mr Shek' and Mao Zedong as 'Moose Dung' in the course of shuttle trips designed to bring the two together to convert China into a springboard for the final showdown with the Japanese. Mao's cronies called Hurley 'the Clown'; his US diplomatic colleagues dubbed him 'the Albatross'.[4]

Although in 1943 the Western powers had given Chiang's nationalist credentials a boost by renouncing most of the (Japanese-occupied) urban territorial concessions wrung from the Qing empire, foreign dabbling in China continued. The Soviets (who had the largest enclave of all) encouraged Muslim Uighur separatists in Xinjiang, who in 1944 established an East Turkestan Republic. The British sought to maintain a buffer between China and India by promoting Tibetan autonomy, personified by the boy Dalai Lama, but neither they nor the Americans were prepared to subsidize it with loans in return for yak tails.[5]

On 8 August 1945, in accordance with the Yalta agreement to create zones of influence, a million Soviet troops made a devastating attack on Manchuria in an operation codenamed August Storm, seizing Port Arthur and usurping the railway rights that Churchill and Roosevelt had agreed to. Some 600,000 Japanese civilians and POWs were deported to the Siberian gulags, where it was said a corpse lay under every sleeper of the railways they built. The Soviets dismantled and removed around $2 billion worth of plant, while subjecting local women to attentions as infamous as those they had imposed on the women of Germany. OSS teams were sent to Soviet-occupied China to investigate the fate of US POWs. One agent had studied Russian in the US and had long harboured a theoretical admiration for all things Soviet after joining a US–Soviet friendship society. In Manchuria he advanced on the first Red Army troops he spied, optimistically bellowing 'Tovarischi!' (Comrades!). The Russians swung their sub-machine guns towards him, while their leader bore down on him: 'Give me your watch,' he said.[6]

Stalin played a typically Machiavellian hand. His aim was a weak China in which he could meddle at will, so, while using a ten-month phased withdrawal to allow Mao's troops to establish themselves in Manchuria, he simultaneously extracted a treaty from Chiang reaffirming economic concessions to the Soviets, a treaty which acknowledged Chiang as sole ruler of China. This was an extraordinary slap in the face to Mao, perhaps a *quid pro quo* for Mao's refusal to aid the Soviets against the Japanese in their hour of greatest need in 1941. The seeds of the later Sino–Soviet split were sown in this period, resentments which festered in already dark hearts.

Following Japan's abrupt surrender, Chiang used stranded Japanese

soldiers to assert his authority throughout coastal China, while despatching his own best troops to seize urban centres in Manchuria ahead
of the Communists. This race saw the first fighting of a civil war which
would cost a further three million Chinese lives. Although it claimed to
be neutral, the US helped Chiang redeploy his forces in one of the greatest airlifts of all time, in which half a million Chinese troops were flown
north in US transport planes.[7] The Soviets turned over to Mao's forces
prodigious quantities of Japanese weapons, as well as Japanese instructors to help establish a Red Chinese air force. Two hundred thousand
North Korean troops were loaned to Mao, who could also avail himself
of northern Korea for strategic depth, as Chiang's armies pressed him in
Manchuria. It created a sense of obligation on Mao's part towards Kim
Il Sung, who was otherwise a servile Soviet client.

Since neither Mao nor Chiang wanted the sole responsibility of plunging China into a civil war hard on the heels of fourteen years of genocidal conflict with Japan, they made a stab at negotiations. Mao
undertook the first flight of his life – he deemed it 'very efficient' – to the
Nationalist headquarters at Chongqing, although he took along the US
Ambassador as a precaution against assassination. Despite superficial
cordiality, these talks achieved nothing, since Mao refused the absorp-
tion of his forces into a national army. Nor would he cede control of key
provincial administrations in the north, where his cadres were winning
peasant support through agrarian reforms and the murder of anyone
who opposed them.

The situation became far too complex for Ambassador Hurley, who
flew home and resigned in a blaze of self-publicity, convinced that China
had been betrayed by Communist sympathizers in the State Department
or by those liaising in Yan'an with Mao. This stance sat oddly with his
own recent flirtations with Moose Dung, but played well with domestic
right-wingers at a time when the Chinese Communists had just murdered an American Baptist missionary and OSS officer called John Birch
after he unwisely tried to test the resolve of some juvenile cadres at a
roadblock (they shot him).[8]

China and Chiang, as if the two were synonymous, were highly
emotive subjects in the US. China had long been a major field for American Protestant and Catholic missionaries, who roused the American

public to outpourings of charity for good works among little girls with bandaged feet. Among the Christian Sinophiles was Henry Luce, the publisher of *Time* and *Life* magazines and the son of missionaries, who believed passionately that China's destiny was both Christian and capitalist, an Asian version of the US. Such sentiments were politically useful both to isolationists (for whom China's great virtue as a client was that it was so geographically remote) and to 'China-Firsters' (who believed America's destinies lay in the Pacific rather than the Atlantic). A neologism – Asialationists – combined these positions, which expressed the paradox that, although these people emoted about a vision of China that had little contact with reality, few were prepared to make the major commitment that would have been required to bring it about. It would be the bane of US foreign policy thenceforth that Chiang's Nationalists operated the most successful lobby group in modern US domestic history, and that the Republicans alighted on China's plight as a powerful unifying issue to attack a Democrat government whose fiscal conservatism otherwise made it a slippery target for inveterate tax cutters.

Even under Roosevelt, US policy towards China was focused on winning the war against Japan. But behind that simple goal there were different perceptions of what was happening in China. Foreign Service officers in Chongqing and Yan'an had a higher opinion of the honesty and efficiency of the Communists than of the Nationalists. The pro-Soviet Vice President Henry Wallace convinced himself that Mao's adherents were, as Stalin put it, 'margarine Communists' rather than real butter. The State Department's Division of Chinese Affairs (part of the Office of Far Eastern Affairs) were under no illusions about the Communists, but rather hoped that a liberal, pro-Western third force might emerge to supplant both them and the Nationalists, an illusion special unto itself. Then there was the US military mission to Chongqing, under 'Vinegar Joe' Stilwell, whose vocal contempt for Chiang (and Roosevelt, and the British, and so on) made it necessary to replace him with the more diplomatic Albert Wedemeyer, whose primary role was to get the Chinese to draw off as many Japanese as possible while the US converged on the home islands. It is easy to see how policy towards China was always incipiently a blame game in the making.[9]

Truman harboured no sentimental delusions about China. He knew that US support for Chiang (around $2.5 billion before 1949) was like gambling on a three-legged horse. It would take an authentic American hero to broker a deal between the Nationalists and Communists, whereby the latter would take their place in a democratic China, and he trusted military men far more than diplomats. In December 1945, Truman telephoned General George Marshall, around six days into a well-earned retirement from directing the US war effort, at his home in Leesburg, Virginia. 'General, I want you to go to China for me,' said the President. 'Yes, Mr President,' replied Marshall before he hung up, lest Mrs Marshall overhear his acceptance of a new appointment.[10] The architect of US victory embarked on a mission which was one of the few failures in his career. He was revisiting his own past. He had been posted to Tianjin for three years in the 1920s as commander of an infantry regiment. On 20 December 1945 he was back in China and remained there until January 1947.

The poker-faced General was determined to deal honestly with a country whose elites had turned graft and corruption into a higher art form. His bargaining chips were the threat to cut off relief supplies and to withdraw the 100,000 Marines in China. While the ideal was to unify the Communists and Nationalists into a democratic China, Marshall's bottom line was that the Communists were not going to emerge as sole rulers. To improve the Nationalists' mixed popular image in the US, Marshall attached a journalist, John Robinson Beal, to advise Chongqing on public relations. Since Beal's knowledge of China derived from reading a chapter in an American academic book, he had the grace to recognize that Chiang might have known more about the pitfalls of attempting to deal with the Communists than he or Marshall. Beal's account of Marshall's thirteen months in China includes a statement of basic US objectives:

> We undertook to promote unity in China in the interest of world stability, which was in our own interest. At the same time we believed the solution to both corruption and political intrigue was to seek establishment of a unified China, in which the army would be divorced from politics, and devote itself to defending the country; a China in which KMT and Communists alike would compete democratically within a

reorganised governmental structure, exchanging power as often as they won such support. Given the climate of the times in the Western world, given the fostered belief that the Chinese Communists were really honest agrarians and not the undemocratic Russian type, this was not unsound as a concept on which to base the mediation effort.[11]

Marshall was adamant that the US would commit no forces to fight in China, for he could see no clear exit route and the country was too vast. He also urged Chiang to spend less on the military, and not to chase after the Communists at the very end of his supply chain. Frustrated by Chiang's cavalier response to his considered advice, he used the threat to withdraw US aid to force Chiang into repeated ceasefires with the Communists, which merely enabled them to cement their hold on territories roughly the size of Germany. However honourable Marshall's intentions, these ceasefires were a lifeline to Mao as both sides embarked on the final round of a struggle which would determine the destiny of China.

Wearied by his futile mission, when General Eisenhower, his successor as army chief of staff, sounded him out about becoming Truman's secretary of state, Marshall replied: 'Great goodness, Eisenhower. I'd take any job in the world to get out of this one.'[12] After being appointed on 8 January 1947, Marshall had to weigh up much conflicting advice on China, which did not help matters. The new NSC afforded service chiefs considerable influence over foreign policy.[13] This tipped the balance in favour of those in the military and State Department who felt that the fate of China was unimportant relative to that of Europe. The newly founded CIA also warned that it would cost the US $2 billion to intervene in the Chinese civil war, while noting that aid to a Communist China would be a drain on the Soviets' already depleted resources, leaving them with fewer options to intervene elsewhere while perhaps stoking Chinese resentments. At no point did the administration seriously analyse what a Communist China might mean beyond construing it as just part of a monolithic bloc. It was as if imaginations ceased whenever the term Communism was used, to the neglect of how far China's long imperial history might impact on its international stances, not to speak of how its many proud nationalists might baulk at Soviet tutelage, the latest example of interference by foreign devils. Confessing that 'I have tortured my brain and I can't now see the answer,' Marshall opted for aid but nothing more. He told a session of the House Foreign Affairs Committee in February 1948 that underwriting the Nationalists 'would involve obligations and responsibilities which I am convinced the American people would never knowingly accept'. He added that 'the magnitude of the task and the probable costs thereof would clearly be out of all proportion to the results to be obtained'. Chiang got an economic and military aid package of $400 million, but without the benefit of deeper US involvement or supervision of how it would be spent. The important thing, Marshall said, 'was to do this without getting sucked in'. According to a Gallup poll in late 1948 this decision was fully in line with US public opinion, despite the clamorous efforts of the China lobby.[14] But not getting involved militarily in China was not the same as 'losing' China, as if it were a high card in America's hand rather than an old and great civilization in its own right. That loss would come as a very powerful shock and finally confirm the belief that the US was facing a global Communist conspiracy.

The View from Red Square

On 24 June 1945 Generalissimo Stalin watched his legions tramp across Red Square, clattering captured Nazi standards on to a vast red, black and white pyre of Gothic lettering, eagles and swastikas. This was how the collective racialized fantasy of German industrialists, professors, soldiers and workers met its nemesis, their country a ruined wasteland a mere seventy years after its unification under Bismarck. Even reunited, German power has never recovered; it may be an economic giant in Europe, but it is a pygmy in world affairs, of less moment nowadays than India or Brazil. Attempts to congratulate Stalin on Hitler's demise were rebuffed and the closest he came to praising his own people was an oblique reference to the toiling 'little cogs'.[15] The following month, attired in splendid white uniform, he travelled by special train to the Potsdam Conference with Churchill and the new US President Harry Truman. He arrived late, intentionally.[16]

Honouring his promise at Yalta to the dying President Roosevelt,

Stalin had set the Red Army in motion to launch a massive attack on Manchuria as soon as the Germans surrendered. In the event the Japanese capitulated sooner than expected following the annihilation of Hiroshima and Nagasaki on 6 and 9 August, but Truman could not be sure the bombs would work when, on 24 July, he told Stalin that the US had tested a weapon of 'unusual destructive power'. Truman recalled that Stalin did not seem surprised. 'That's fine,' he replied. 'I hope you make good use of it against the Japanese.'[17] His nonchalance was due to Soviet intelligence penetration of the Manhattan Project.[18]

Had the welfare of his people mattered to Stalin, the Soviet Union should have devoted its entire energy to domestic reconstruction. When Eisenhower flew low to Moscow, he surveyed a wasteland, but not the twenty million dead. However, Stalin correctly perceived that foreign policy was the key to the survival of the Soviet regime. Not only had he extended the boundaries of the Russian Empire far beyond the limits reached by his tsarist predecessors, but he was also deeply committed to Marxist-Leninist universalism. Traditional Russian security concerns and imperial objectives readily fused with the Bolshevik mission to bring the Communist version of modernity and revolutionary social justice to the peoples of the world. From the beginning relations between the Bolshevik regime and the West were characterized by justified paranoia. How could the Soviets trust powers that had intervened to smother the Bolshevik Revolution at birth? The diplomacy of the 1920s and the mass murders of the 1930s perpetuated this mistrust, culminating in the August 1939 Molotov–Ribbentrop Pact, which allowed Stalin to grab the Baltic States and half of Poland.[19]

Stalin was no less brutally realistic once the Germans had swarmed across his new borders. The global revolutionary aspects of Soviet foreign policy had been abandoned and the international revolutionary Comintern organization liquidated long before it was formally dissolved in May 1943. Despite the sentimentality displayed at both public and private occasions whenever 'Uncle Joe' and his brave legions were mentioned, in reality Soviet relations with foreigners of all kinds remained poisonous and the Russian intelligence services redoubled their efforts to penetrate Western governments. As the war ended Stalin believed that the victorious Western powers might fall out, as inherently unstable cap-italist powers were bound to do, leaving him in a good place, with mil-lions of his troops on the ground, to leverage the Soviet Union's position through diplomacy, guile and force.[20]

In 1943 the British Post-Hostilities Planning Committee, chaired by Labour leader Attlee, was already discussing the Soviet threat, and by August 1944 the American OSS had three dozen experts assessing 'Soviet intentions and capabilities', co-opting the Italian military intelli-gence service (SIM) to spy on Russian officials even as the war in Italy ground on.[21] Along with the rest of Europe, Britain's exhaustion would result in the subordination of its security to that of the United States, which would emerge as the defender of the democratic and capitalist free world. But before this had hardened into established fact, domestic iso-lationist reservations in the US about assuming such responsibilities, and hopes that the United Nations would resolve all international problems, created a window of opportunity for Stalin to realize ambitions that had thwarted the tsars. Like a burglar he tried every door, hoping to find one unlocked: in Greece, Iran, Turkey and even western Libya, where he sought a toehold in the British-dominated Mediterranean as his rightful share of the Italian war in which he had not participated. His hopes for a piece of Japan as the reward for smashing the Japanese armies in Man-churia were limited by Truman's Far Eastern proconsul MacArthur to recovering the southern half of Sakhalin Island, lost in the war of 1905. MacArthur also infuriated Stalin by treating General Kuzma Derevy-anko – the head of the Soviet mission in Tokyo – 'like a mere piece of furniture'.[22]

Stalin enjoyed the public aura of a god but, like Churchill, his health had suffered from the colossal strain of directing an existential war. He reminded one senior US diplomat of a battle-scarred tiger. Aged sixty-five in 1945, Stalin had seen off Roosevelt, and in July Churchill was replaced by the seemingly meeker Attlee. 'Mr Attlee does not look to me like a man who is hungry for power' was Stalin's comment when Churchill left Potsdam to hear the shock result of the elections, which Stalin would have preferred Churchill to win.[23] Any pretence at formal government in Moscow collapsed into a weird regimen involving cinema shows, followed by late-night bacchanalia at his Kuntsevo dacha. The inner cronies of the Politburo were obliged to attend these glum festivities.[24]

A hundred million people fell under Stalin's sway after 1945, with a further eighteen millions directly incorporated into his inner Red Empire. Using the tried and trusted method of coalitions or 'fronts' to satisfy the democratic proprieties of the West, Stalin installed his thoroughly winnowed Marxist-Leninist clients in Eastern Europe, who then systematically culled their democratic allies of convenience. The myths of the Great Patriotic War added indirect lustre to Communism in Western Europe too. In the Far East Stalin was the *de facto* arbiter in the Chinese civil war, sticking with Chiang Kai-shek because he was unconvinced that Mao could dominate much more than a region. He drew a few key lessons from history, using external tensions with the West to tighten his domestic grip. In 1945 many Russians similarly hoped that their wartime sacrifices were going to be rewarded; the novelist Boris Pasternak felt sure that 'so many sacrifices cannot result in nothing'.

Such hopes were dashed. Stalin tightened control, starting with all those he imagined had been contaminated by even the briefest brush with the freedom and prosperity of the West. Nearly three million repatriated Red Army troops were interrogated by the secret police, and half of them were consigned to the gulags. Any signs of cultural liberalization were crushed in the process known as the *Zhdanovshchina*, named after Stalin's henchman Andrei Zhdanov; the poet Anna Akhmatova was sent to mop floors while the composers Prokofiev and Shostakovich were told to write music proletarians could whistle as they worked harder than ever.[25]

It is not hard to see that there were many internal reasons for the Soviets to welcome the Cold War. Anti-Western paranoia helped to perpetuate the extremities of wartime mobilization, needed to rebuild the Soviet economy without relaxing the grip of the Communist Party. Stalin also took the opportunity to realize a traditional tsarist quest for spheres of influence in a post-war situation where it was no longer checked by other European imperial powers. Behind it all lurked a profound ideological suspicion of the West, and the belief that war was inevitable because of the ultimate, systemic irreconcilability of capitalism and Communism. On that Stalin was clear even as the war was ending: 'We shall recover in fifteen or twenty years, and then we'll have another go at it.'[26]

Domestic recovery was sacrificed to military imperatives. The war-time defence budget had been halved by 1948 and the Red Army shrunk by three-quarters, but following the creation of the North Atlantic Treaty Organization (NATO) Soviet defence had vaulted back to pre-1948 levels by 1953. In between those dates, however, Mao had surprised Washington and Moscow alike by winning the Chinese civil war with ease. The Sino–Soviet Treaty of February 1950 gave Stalin a priceless ally and the realistic prospect of an entirely Communist Asia, while freeing up the resources the CIA had hoped would be tied down in the Chinese civil war, to the detriment of the balance of forces in Europe.[27]

US leaders had the perennial problem of determining whether Stalin's belligerent rhetoric was largely for domestic consumption or a credible external threat. When he spoke in especially challenging tones in early February 1946, vowing to triple expenditure on armaments, the liberal Supreme Court Justice William Douglas saw it as a 'Declaration of World War III'.[28] That Russia was increasingly acting unilaterally, making major geopolitical changes to the map of Europe and beyond without consulting its former allies, should not have been in doubt – yet the American hands-across-the-caviar set were always willing to deny reality in favour of sentimentality about the Soviets. There was also the no less perennial distortion of equating manifestations of alien cultures to those with which US leaders were familiar. Thus Truman insisted that Stalin's belligerent speech was akin to the more demagogic tones any democratic politician adopted before an election.[29]

Like his august predecessor, or for that matter Chamberlain with Hitler, and Churchill with Stalin, Truman was susceptible to the tempting illusion of the personal breakthrough. Stalin could be candid, charming and emollient, as well as shockingly brutal, as many foreigners discovered. Having invested so much in propagandizing a benign Uncle Joe, even US presidents yearned to discover such a being, despite all the evidence to the contrary. 'If we could only get Stalin to unburden himself to someone on our side he could trust, I thought we could get somewhere,' explained Truman hopefully. At Potsdam the President marginally preferred Stalin's laconic grunts to the flattery with which

Churchill smothered him, for, as Truman astutely remarked, it hurts when soap gets in one's eye.[30]

The Glorious Loser

By the end of the war the world's largest imperial power was bankrupt, owing £1,321 million to India and even £400 million to Egypt. Britain anticipated a gradual cessation of US aid, but the atomic bombs dropped on Japan abruptly terminated hopes of a decent interval in which to reconvert the British economy to peacetime production. Lend-Lease to Britain was halted even as it was extended to Nationalist China. Britain experienced other strains. The cost of maintaining 18.6 per cent of the country's manpower in the armed forces was prohibitive, not to speak of the men it subtracted from post-war reconstruction and Labour's quest for a New Jerusalem of cradle-to-grave welfare socialism. Many of these troops and airmen were demoralized and restive because of the slow speed of demobilization and repatriation. Nor could the military resources of India, which had underpinned the empire in the East, be depended on. In early 1946 there was a major mutiny in the Royal Indian Navy after a British commander insisted on calling his ratings 'black buggers' or 'coolie bastards'. Trouble spread to the Indian Air Force and police too.

What a moment it might have been, with Germany and Italy reduced to ruins. France, its liberation entirely attributable to what the French call the Anglo-American *disembarcation*, was grudgingly readmitted to the top table only at Churchill's insistence. But at the end of the war Britain was both triumphant and prostrate. In 1945 the British (and their white Dominions and colonies) celebrated victory in a war whose high point had been its own dogged survival until the crushing might of its two major allies was brought to bear on Nazi Germany. Although only one in ten of the troops who fought the final battle for Germany were British, at Potsdam Churchill acted as if there were no fundamentally changed international realities. Field Marshal Alan Brooke, the British Chief of the Imperial General Staff, recorded Churchill's response to Truman's news about successful tests of the US atom bomb:

we now had something in our hands which would redress the balance
with the Russians! The secret of this explosive, and the power to use
it, would completely alter the diplomatic equilibrium which was adrift
since the defeat of Germany! Now we had a new value which redressed
our position (pushing his chin out and scowling), now we could say if
you insist on doing this or that, well we can just blot out Moscow,
then Stalingrad, then Kiev, then Kuibyshev, Kharkov, Stalingrad [sic],
Sebastopol etc etc. And now where are the Russians!!!'[31]

A few days later, in one of the most dramatic elections of modern times,
Labour won the general election in a landslide, winning 393 seats to the
Tories 213, which translated into a 146-seat majority in the House of
Commons. Churchill was not the man to carry through the fundamental
reforms so many British people yearned for, and which were envisaged in
the 1943 Beveridge Report that he had commissioned. He did global
strategy rather than free dentures. By contrast with Churchill, voters saw
Clement Attlee as a reassuring schoolmaster. British servicemen voted for
him in droves, identifying the Tories with the armed forces hierarchy.[32]

At Potsdam Stalin and Truman found themselves sitting across from
the laconic 'Little Clem' flanked by his tough Foreign Secretary Ernest
Bevin, who Stalin instantly realized was not one of life's 'gentlemen'.
Truman simply thought Bevin boorish. Even so, in many respects there
was less fundamental change than there seemed. Most Labour politicians subscribed to the same delusions of great power that animated the
Conservatives, with the added interest their industrial-worker constituents had in defence jobs. Labour's many Scots were always suckers for
tough talk about national security. Worse, they sought to combine the
enormous costs of global strategic overstretch with the creation of a
domestic New Jerusalem, paid for by huge US loans that might instead
have been used – as they were intended – to give the creaky economic
legacy of the first industrial revolution a thorough overhaul. The Germans eventually spent more on welfare, but only after their economic
miracle had taken off in the late 1950s.[33]

The decline of a nation is seldom abrupt, and always far more nuanced
than professional Cassandras imagine, usually in the cause of stiffening
the sinews and girding the loins in the present. In 1945 the British ruled

over 457 million people, with vast tracts of every schoolboy's atlas still coloured imperial red, as they had been from the 1880s onwards. Britain had enormous military and naval bases in such locations as Mombasa and Simonstown, Suez and Singapore. It had a very substantial army, and a large navy and air force, the continuance of conscription being one considerable cost of pretensions to being a global power.[34] Already in September 1944 the Treasury economist John Maynard Keynes had warned: 'We cannot police half the world at our own expense when we have already gone into pawn to the other half.'[35] But it was wholehearted British investment in Truman's Cold War, rather than the needs of imperial defence, that saw defence spending rise from an interwar norm of 3 per cent to 7.7 per cent in the late 1940s, and to 12 per cent by the time of the Korean War. This meant that Britain was massively over-spending each year, burning through the $3.75 billion US loan to support dubious global commitments as well as the new welfare state, which increased domestic spending by a comparatively modest 50 per cent.[36] The vast sprawl of commitments maintained around the world lacked strategic logic, for with India independent in 1947 what was the point of the 'vital' linking presence in the Middle East? It was all about global 'influence', 'prestige' and 'status' rather than about how to defend Britain itself and its immediate north-west European neighbourhood.[37]

The pock-marked and smog-blackened architectural pomp of the metropolis was the stage set for this world of dreams and romantic delusions. The broad avenue of Whitehall was abutted by a Colonial Office, a Dominions Office (renamed the Commonwealth Relations Office in 1947) and a separate bureaucracy for India, not to speak of the Foreign Office in its pseudo-Italianate palace. These were conveniently situated for the gentlemen's clubs of Pall Mall, where the Establishment did things with a quiet word over indifferent school food. The business of government was carried out by an allegedly Rolls-Royce civil service, consisting of men who had been to the same public schools and Oxford or Cambridge, with a few numerate interlopers from the London School of Economics. Britain was not unique in being governed by a cosy club – witness the salience of *énarques* from the Ecole National d'Administration in France – but at least the French were trained in Cartesian logic and did not celebrate the amateurism of classicists. Elsewhere there was still evidence of burgeoning productive capacity in the post-war years. Britain produced such successful brands as Massey Ferguson tractors and Land Rovers, which one could find from Africa to Australia. Viewed from the Dominions, London was also a major cultural mecca.[38]

Complacent ignorance was just as well represented among Labour's gritty trade unionists as among the Tories, particularly if they represented constituents with defence-sector jobs at stake. The working class, which Labour nominally represented, was the most resistant to change, with its trade unions defending the most corrupt and retrograde practices. Thirteen of Attlee's twenty-strong Cabinet had no experience of industry whatsoever, with the trade unionists, who specialized in frustrating change, balanced by members of the left-liberal progressive Establishment, whose backgrounds were in academia and journalism. The preferred *modus operandi* was the committee, vividly described by the British scholar Correlli Barnett as a 'claustrophobic hell of boredom imagined by [the author of the sentiment "hell is other people"] Jean-Paul Sartre', as well as the ability to hone a well-written essay – as if that could alter deep cultural and structural realities.[39]

Although Britain imagined it was a great power, the role was impossible to sustain. The wartime Sterling Area was one liability misconstrued as a national asset, as an international currency to rival the US dollar. Huge quantities of 'unrequited exports' flowed to India or the Middle East, in return for British debts incurred fighting the Germans and Japanese. Britain also assumed occupation responsibility for the least agricultural part of Germany, into which millions of refugees from the East poured. That involved spending a further £80 million a year and providing this zone with 70 per cent of its food. One consequence was that in July 1946 bread rationing was introduced for the first time to Britain itself, as wheat was exported to its defeated foe. Soon it was anticipated that potatoes and other essential foodstuffs would be rationed too. Then there was the cost of maintaining armed forces four times the size, and at between two and three times the cost, of those extant in 1939, despite the intervening loss of 25 per cent of the nation's wealth.[40] The breaking point came in early 1947 when the country froze up in one of the bleakest winters on record. Here is *The Times* on 20 February 1947:

> From many parts of the country there were reports of renewed snow-falls threatening roads cleared after days and nights of work by thousands of troops and German prisoners of war, of Lincolnshire villages still isolated by snowdrifts, and of other villages in West Stirlingshire whose water supply is endangered by frost blocking the feeder streams in the Campsie hills. Ice floes in the North Sea are proving a menace to British trawlers and other shipping. As they drift westward they are carrying away buoys marking wrecks and shipping channels between mined areas. One huge floe was reported to be about 40 miles east of Great Yarmouth and gradually drawing nearer. A radio warning to shipping has been broadcast from the Humber. Shortly before noon yesterday the sun penetrated the clouds over London [for the first time in seventeen days] but an official at Kew Observatory said it was not strong enough to record on their instruments.[41]

Electric power ebbed and flowed, gas pressure for ovens and fires fell to scarcely perceptible levels and the railways juddered to a halt under deep snowdrifts driven by Siberian winds.[42] The spring thaw in 1948 brought catastrophic flooding. In that year, rationing reached its nadir. The weekly food allowance for an adult was thirteen ounces of meat, one and a half of cheese, six ounces of butter, one of cooking fat, eight of sugar, two pints of milk and an egg. Pallid, putty-faced people patiently and resentfully waited in line for hours for these basic foodstuffs.[43]

The sixteen-year-old J. G. Ballard debouched into this grim and grey environment, after being interned by the Japanese for two years in Shanghai: 'The whole nation seemed to be deeply depressed. Audiences sat in their damp raincoats in smoke-filled cinemas as they watched newsreels that showed the immense pomp of the royal family, the aggressively cheerful crowds at a new holiday camp, and the triumph of some new air-speed or land-speed record, as if Britain still led the world in technology. It is hard to imagine how conditions could have been worse if we had lost the war.'[44]

There was little investment in modernizing the railways, the road network, bridges and tunnels, the docks, telecommunications or, in fact, any industries of future importance, such as machine tools and plastics, even though British scientists had made many important wartime breakthroughs. All resources were devoted to avoiding deflation and maintaining full employment, which reduced the welfare bill at the cost of suffocating the price signals that guide a healthy economy and the productive reallocation of labour.

In the industries kept on politically driven life support, amateur managers faced militant trade unionists who opposed all innovation. When new labour-saving machines were grudgingly accepted, the surplus labour was retained to do nothing, notably in the thieves' kitchens located in the nation's docks. Then there were the illusions of 'punching above our weight', of sustaining a global role beyond having to choose between being with the US or being in Europe.

The Foreign Office regarded having a belligerent son of toil in their midst with some trepidation, until Bevin became their trade union spokesman. Early on, Assistant Under Secretary Gladwyn Jebb (Eton and Magdalen College, Oxford) found himself summoned to Bevin's office where, after a contrived silence, the new Secretary of State said in his West Country burr: 'Must be kinda queer for a chap like you to see a chap like me sitting in a chair like this?' George III gazed down benignly as Jebb shrugged off this jibe, forcing Bevin to continue: 'Ain't never 'appened before in 'istory.' Jebb smilingly reminded Bevin of Henry VIII's Chancellor Cardinal Thomas Wolsey, a butcher's son, 'and incidentally he was not unlike you physically'. From then on Bevin determined to like the British upper classes, finding common ground in detestation of the 'self-righteous and narrow-minded' middle. He and they probably had in mind people who ran businesses that made and sold things.[45]

Bevin was a burly fellow and plug-ugly with it. He had about three years of schooling before starting life delivering water on a little truck. He had risen to command the Transport and General Workers, Britain's largest trade union, equivalent to the US Teamsters, in which capacity he travelled widely. While he had no objections to the Bolshevik Revolution, he did mind the Communists trying to take over 'his' TGWU. He had first been elected to parliament aged sixty, allowing him to be, from

1940 onwards, Churchill's Minister of Labour. By 1943 he was already a very sick man, with his doctor 'finding not a sound organ in his body, apart from his feet'. He had angina, cardiac trouble, arteriosclerosis, an enlarged liver and kidney damage. He was obese and smoked and drank to excess, sleeping poorly and taking no exercise.

After 1945 Bevin maintained the bipartisan spirit of the wartime coalition, regularly consulting his Conservative predecessor and opposition shadow Anthony Eden – the joke of the moment was: 'Hasn't Anthony grown fat?' Many of Bevin's troubles stemmed not from the Conservatives but from the Labour left, and especially the Hampstead intellectual contingent of caviar leftists. Bevin stood for a more pragmatic approach based on a keen awareness that international alliances were the only way of compensating for Britain's diminished role in the world, a role which emphatically included a reformed empire. Bevin was a patriot who believed in the hard-headed pursuit of national interest – albeit construed in misguided terms of world power – rather than socialist internationalism. He had no time for those who saw no moral difference between the USA and the USSR, let alone those whose self-delusion about the 'Workers' Paradise' made them Soviet stooges. He disliked the Germans, telling General Brian Robertson, 'I tries 'ard, Brian, but I 'ates them.' This was a widespread view, in a party nominally affiliated with the Social Democrats, but which preferred to divide rather than unite Germany. A united Europe was a Pandora's Box concealing what Bevin called 'Trojan 'orses'.[46]

The Labour Party also had long-standing ties with socialist Zionists, both in the diaspora and in the Palestinian Yishuv. In 1944 the Party's National Executive Committee had called for unrestricted Jewish immigration, and the subsidized transfer of the Palestinian Arabs elsewhere, but in office the Party did no such thing. Whether Bevin's hatred of Germans extended to Jews is controversial. Since Bevin had never obtrusively commented on Jews in his sixty-five years, it seems unlikely that he somehow revealed this animadversion once ensconced in King Charles Street, where, admittedly, there was much class sentimentality about Arab sheikhs and fondness for Arab boys. Palestine grated on account of the time and effort it required, and because the creative ambiguity embodied in the Balfour Declaration disintegrated on Bevin's watch.

Unsurprisingly, Bevin objected to being called an anti-Semite or a Nazi by Zionists whose terrorist arm attempted to murder him. He also resented the way Jewish voters in New York seemed to be holding Truman's Democrats to ransom. Bevin was in no doubt that a stable Middle East was doubly important to Britain in terms of imperial defence and strategic oil supplies.[47]

Then there were the parts of the world that really mattered to British self-esteem and sense of family kinship, for after the war hundreds of thousands of British people flooded into the white Dominions. Relations with Australia or New Zealand were smoothed by the fact that until 1949 they also had Labour governments and, along with Canada, majority populations who strongly identified themselves as British, by allegiance to the King, culture, ethnic origins and common institutions. The trouble was that the Dominions did not want to fall in line behind some general British foreign policy and were as far away as the planet could devise. Canada rejected centralization of defence and foreign policy, and never joined the Sterling Area, while the (many hyphenated Irish) Australians were defining their sense of nationhood in anti-British terms. Both concluded defence treaties with the US before the war was over. Dealing with Nehru's independent India was like trying to grasp fog. Even though the rise of Afrikaner nationalism had ousted the Anglophile President Smuts, only South Africa remained a dependable ally.[48]

There was also Labour 'racism'. Whatever their fraternal ties with Black African nationalist leaders, the private views of leading Labour Party members were like any Tory dilating about the fecklessness of 'Mr Woggy'. Herbert Morrison, who in March 1951 would succeed Bevin as foreign secretary after he was stricken with cancer, insisted that granting self-government to black Africans was akin to giving a ten-year-old 'a latch-key, bank account and a shot-gun'. The Chancellor of the Exchequer, Hugh Dalton, wrote in his diary that he declined the office of colonial secretary because 'I had a horrid vision of pullulating, poverty-stricken, diseased nigger communities, for whom one can do nothing in the short run, and now, the more one tries to help them, are querulous and ungrateful; [and] . . . of white settlers, as reactionary and troublesome in their own way as niggers.'[49]

The First World War pacifist Arthur Creech Jones, a leading light of the Fabian Society Colonial Research Bureau, became colonial secretary in 1946 and focused the Labour Party's own humanitarian and missionary zeal on the eradication of 'tropical East Ends' (the East End of London being synonymous with slums).[50] He and his advisers were responsible for the oxymoronic ethical colonialism, based on economic improvement and political advancement, more recently and grandiosely called nation-building. From 1948 onwards, £100 million was pumped into Africa, Asia and the Caribbean through a Colonial Development Corporation. This resulted in such lamentable failures as producing eggs in the Gambia, or clearing huge tracts of Tanganyika to produce groundnut oil as a substitute for scarce fats. £38 million were expended clearing the wrong trees (some sacred) with machines that constantly broke down.

An Overseas Food Corporation had more success in bulk-purchasing staples such as cocoa, cotton and tobacco, either to earn precious dollars or to satisfy domestic British consumers. In truth, the only colony to be of any value in terms of earning US dollars was Malaya, but this was slighted in the cause of promoting Africa as a fall-back for a lost India. Bevin dreamed that 'If we only pushed and developed Africa, we could have the United States dependent on us, and eating out of our hand, in four or five years . . . The US is very barren of essential minerals, and in Africa we have them all.' The eminent historian Ronald Hyam coined the term 'cosmoplastic' to describe this degree of magical thinking.[51]

Initially, Labour imagined no major difficulty in funding its vast domestic welfare project at the same time as defending and maintaining a sprawling overseas empire, both of which, together with the cost of supporting its temporary German colony, soaked up resources even as conditions at home became ever bleaker. In the minds of Britain's elites, even when shorn of India the empire was what kept Britain Great. To become 'little' Sweden was the *cauchemar* that many of us can only dream of nowadays. For the essence of Bevin's foreign policy was to prevent Britain becoming either the forty-ninth state of the Union or the Soviet Union's seventeenth republic, coupled with resentment towards the US for demanding its pound of flesh for wartime aid. The US desire to see Britain integrated into a restored Western Europe, particularly in the field of defence, was resisted by cunningly submerging the traditional concerns of imperial defence within the new parameters of the Cold

War. Yet this was to ignore the fact that, Malaya apart, with India gone the empire was nothing more than a colossal burden.

The first breaking point came in 1947 when, having pumped £132 million into supporting the Greek government over the preceding two years, Britain told the US that it could no longer bear the cost.[52] As we have seen, the same economic imperative led Britain to liquidate its presence in Palestine with unseemly haste. Yet in the same crisis year the British decided to retain military conscription and, without public fanfare, to develop their own atomic bomb. They may have been facing financial ruin, but the Labour government was going to maintain Britain as an independent great power. At the same time, through the creation of NATO, Bevin succeeded in locking the US into the immediate defence of Western Europe against the Soviets, denying itself the luxury of letting the Western European nations ruin themselves once more before joining the war. The payback came a few years later in Korea, when the British felt compelled to respond to US calls for military solidarity in an area of no geopolitical concern to Britain whatever.

Bevin took Britain further down the road of a 'special relationship' at the expense of what might have been an Anglo–French-dominated Europe, which developed instead around a Franco–German axis, in which a powerfully revived Germany allowed the French to play the dominant political partner. His belief that Britain might enjoy a special status as a bridge between Europe and the US failed on both sides of the divide, with the rest of Europe regarding Britain as a US Trojan horse – as a continental Bevin might have put it – even though the Americans had no interest in any such subterfuge.

One way in which the British liked to highlight the virtues of their empire was to denigrate those of everyone else as cruel and despotic. In reality they burned or buried their own files on atrocities committed in the colonies in the bowels of the Foreign Office, much as the Italian Ministry of Defence did with documentation regarding colonial Ethiopia and Libya.[53] Leaving aside whatever responsibility adheres to Britain for the bloody partitions in India and Palestine, its activities elsewhere contributed to the restoration of regimes it purported to deplore. As we have seen, General Gracey played a significant role in the restoration of French rule in Indochina, though when he withdrew his forces in January

1946 he declined the decorations a grateful French nation offered to pin on him.

Nearly sixty Labour MPs were sufficiently exercised by British support for the French in Indochina and the Dutch in Indonesia to sign a letter denouncing it. More worryingly for Bevin, Asian nationalists in Burma, Ceylon, India and Malaya refused to allow ports and airfields to be used to supply the French with either troops or munitions. Some of them even attempted to enlist with the Viet Minh. Gracey had withdrawn partly because of Nehru's objection to his use of Indian troops to restore the French in Saigon and elsewhere, and for the same reason the British restricted French transport flights through New Delhi to one per week.

While Bevin maintained the public fiction that France was merely restoring order to build conditions 'in which her liberal programme can find its realisation', in secret Attlee's government shipped weapons to France for reshipment in French vessels to Indochina, such that a British official boasted that 'sten guns in Tonkin are as common as umbrellas in Piccadilly'. They did this partly to bolster France's position in post-war Europe, but mainly because of a version of domino theory more usually applied to the Americans. If the French overseas empire went down, the thinking went, it was likely to be contagious. The alternative and equally erroneous view, expressed by such as Malcolm MacDonald in Malaya, was that the Viet Minh were nationalists who had only turned to the Communists for want of an alternative, a misreading of the likes of Ho Chi Minh, whose entire biography told a different story.

The dominant strategic view was expressed as early as February 1944 by the Foreign Office mandarin Alexander Cadogan, who wrote: 'Any such attempt to abrogate French rule in Indochina cannot fail to react on the position of other nations holding possessions in the Far East, e.g., the Dutch and ourselves.'[54] Some years later another British official warned that 'the frontiers of Malaya are on the Mekong' because, like the Japanese, the Communists might use Vietnam as a launch pad for the conquest of the rest of South-east Asia. Since the British were aware of their own economic limitations, they insisted that the US remain a member of Mountbatten's SEAC command, despite US attempts to withdraw in late 1945, and thereafter did their best to drag a reluctant US

into Indochina. That reluctance stemmed from the US perception that
the line must be held at Japan, Formosa, the Philippines and Indonesia.
In due course the British got their wish as the US formally recognized
Bao Dai's puppet government – something the British blithely forgot but
the Americans coldly remembered when Britain later refused to participate in what became America's long war in South-east Asia.

Loser Twice Over

Considering its abject collapse in 1940, France made an impressive
post-war recovery, whether in terms of regaining great-power status, a
goal on which most Frenchmen could agree, or fitting its economy for
rapid growth through judicious planning, modernization and nationalization of the major banks and key industries. Part of that recovery
involved the restoration of an overseas empire, for 'La France n'est rien
sans ses colonies.'

Wartime and post-war relations between France and the US were
extremely fraught. Backed by Churchill in the teeth of Roosevelt's
intense hostility, the relatively obscure Charles de Gaulle had made himself the only plausible representative of France in Allied councils. Devoid
of Gallic charm, de Gaulle used hauteur and stunning ingratitude to
play a weak military hand exceptionally well, gaining a French-occupied
zone in Germany and a permanent seat on the UN Security Council, not
to speak of large tranches of US economic aid and covert CIA funding
for what would be his personal political party. His government swiftly
neutered the grassroots activism of the wartime resistance which gave
birth to a leftist mythology about the Liberation in 1944 as a revolutionary moment betrayed.[55]

Post-war France was torn by labour unrest and economic problems.
Coal production in 1946 was a third of what it had been in 1938, itself
not an outstanding year for the industry. Nineteen-forty-seven was a
nadir in terms of food supplies, when in June the government cut the
bread ration from eight and a half ounces to five per day. A very powerful Communist Party, which enjoyed the support of a quarter of the
adult population, including the intellectual herd, repeatedly plunged the

nation into industrial strife, at the loss of two million working days in 1947, with some violent strikes repressed with gunfire.[56]

If the Communists were one destabilizing force on the left wing of the French political spectrum, the Gaullists performed an analogous role on the right, with the major caveat that they did not take their marching orders from an alien power. Indeed most of them despised the gum-chewing and informal Americans. Like Churchill, de Gaulle lost political power soon after the war, when he dramatically resigned as prime minister of the tripartite provisional government in January 1946, flouncing out after the Socialists insisted on defence cuts. Behind that issue was a more fundamental disagreement about the relative powers of a democratic assembly dominated by political parties, each 'cooking its little soup, on its little fire in its little corner', as he contemptuously described it. De Gaulle's authoritarian vision was of a strong presidential executive soaring above a bicameral legislature. 'A military man can never adapt himself completely to the business of politics,' said the diplomat Jacques Dumaine.[57]

After he retreated to Colombey-les Deux-Eglises in Lorraine, there ensued twenty-one governments in the years 1946–55, one managing to last fifteen months, while another only existed for hours. These were usually coalitions, involving the Socialists, Radicals and Progressive Catholics as the nuclear elements.[58] Both the Communists, dismissed from government in May 1947, and the movement de Gaulle himself founded in April 1947 (the Rassemblement du Peuple Français, or RPF) played a spoiling role by seeking to overturn the Fourth Republic's constitution. The Stalinist Communists banked on their (inflated) wartime resistance record – the party of the 70,000 dead – while de Gaulle's appeal was that 'he is not like the others'.[59]

France still retained an overseas empire second only in scale to that of Britain. Indochina alone was much larger than metropolitan France, though we are accustomed to think of it as small because of the war with the mighty US. In January 1944, de Gaulle had convened a conference at Brazzaville in the French Congo, where promises of administrative reform were coupled with refusal even to contemplate independence. As the provisional Colonial Minister René Pleven said: '[France] refuses all idea of autonomy, all possibility of an evolution outside the French bloc of empire; the eventual, even distant establishment of self-government is rejected.'[60] Parallel with the British substitution of Commonwealth for empire, the French dropped the term empire in favour of the federalist concept of the French Union. This included the pre- and post-Revolution colonies, not least Algeria, but excluded the protectorates of Morocco and Tunisia. The French President was president of the Union, and French politicians were generously represented on both the Supreme Council and in the Assembly of that entity. As school textbooks explained: 'European France is a medium-sized power, with overseas France she is a great power, the French Union.'[61] Although France would fight two terrible colonial wars in Algeria and Indochina, it is worth noting that it also managed the decolonization of French West Africa and French Equatorial Africa with as much skill as the British did in West Africa, although bluntly linking continued close association with future aid.

As we have seen, in Indochina the French piggybacked to precarious power on British Indian Army troops and their rearmed Japanese prisoners. The withdrawal of Chinese forces by the hard-pressed Chiang Kai-shek enabled General Leclerc to get a grip on the north by using a nuanced form of counter-insurgency warfare whose objects were the hearts and minds of the population. De Gaulle's resignation inclined Ho Chi Minh to believe that a political settlement might be possible and he concluded a ceasefire in March 1946. Leclerc acknowledged at the time that 'since we do not have the means to break Vietnamese nationalism by force, France should try by every possible means to align her interests with those of Vietnam'.

Unfortunately Leclerc's realistic appreciation of French possibilities was trumped by the fanatical High Commissioner d'Argenlieu, who compared Leclerc's dealings with Ho and his Defence Minister Giap with Chamberlain's and Daladier's meeting with Hitler at Munich in 1938, an analogy which ensured Leclerc's abrupt recall to France. It is hard to say whether there was ever a possibility that an independent (Communist) Vietnam might remain within the French Union, but if there was the opportunity was lost, and in purely military terms Leclerc's successors, Generals Jean-Etienne Valluy, Roger Blaizot and Marcel Carpentier, were not of his calibre.

Ironically the tripartite French government that replaced de Gaulle pursued a more implacable line, despite the Minister for Overseas Territories being the Socialist Marius Moutet, who might have been expected to view Ho more favourably. The French Communists were also initially opposed to Vietnamese independence, fearful of losing the patriotic vote and dreaming of a Communist Vietnam within a Communist French Union. In early 1947, on orders from Moscow, the Communists left the French government over defence appropriations, weakening the remaining Socialist component vis-à-vis their Progressive Catholic (Mouvement Républicain Populaire, or MRP) coalition partners. In opposition the Communists became vociferous opponents of the 'dirty war'. The ruling coalition tilted to the centre right as strikes and riots disrupted France throughout late 1947. In November the MRP's former War Minister, Paul Coste-Floret, replaced Moutet as colonial minister. History virtually locked him into a losing position since he claimed that withdrawal from Indochina would be tantamount to another 1940. While French troops vainly battled the Viet Minh in terrain ideally suited to guerrilla warfare, Coste-Floret sought to build Bao Dai into a national figure. An agreement was eventually reached in 1949, which left Bao Dai as the nominal ruler of an 'independent' Vietnam within the French Union, although France retained control of the country's defence and foreign affairs.

At home the Indochina war became progressively more unpopular. In the summer of 1947, 37 per cent of French people favoured continuing the conflict, with a similar percentage wanting negotiations with the Viet Minh. Two years later those favouring the war had fallen to 19 per cent, with nearly 50 per cent advocating complete withdrawal. As the domestic will to win collapsed, so did the morale of the troops in the field. This was despite the fact that they were overwhelmingly regular soldiers, including paratroopers, Foreign Legionnaires and North African and Senegalese *tirailleurs*, for only volunteers were sent to Indochina. Their numbers rose from the 60,000 commanded by Leclerc in 1946, to 100,000 under Valluy, and then 150,000 when Carpentier was in charge, still too few to do the many things the French attempted.

Events in China in 1949 also had an adverse impact on the French position. Defeated KMT troops who fled over the southern border usually sold their weapons to the Viet Minh, while once Mao had taken charge southern China became a useful bolt-hole for Viet Minh guerrillas operating in northern Tonkin. In July 1950, the Chinese sent military advisers and opened training camps south of their border, by which time the Viet Minh had 20,000 regulars of their own, organized in divisions and battalions. Whatever villages the French army appeared to control by day were usually forfeited during the night, as Viet Minh cadres slipped in to reimpose their iron brand of discipline. The French gradually lost their nerve in isolated bases that were subject to constant nocturnal attack, consoling themselves with drugs, whores and copious amounts of beer and wine while in the front line, and more of the same along with frenzied gambling when on local leave.

By contrast the Viet Minh subsisted on rice, with rat meat considered a delicacy, and their free time was occupied with political indoctrination sessions. Ruthless internal discipline was accompanied by the torture and assassination of real, potential or putative collaborators. Systematic brutality occurred in a context where every civilian, regardless of age or sex, was potentially an enemy fighter. The conduct of this 'dirty war' in which only French brutalities were publicized by the French press further undermined domestic support among liberal-minded people. Left-wing celebrities from Picasso to Jean-Paul Sartre did their best to subvert the war effort.[62]

Algerian nationalists closely followed the course of the war in Indochina. In the wake of Sétif, French reforms were modestly cosmetic. An Algerian assembly was established to deal with local questions. Dominated by *colon* members of the right-wing Union Algérienne, the Assembly exercised a veto over any reforms initiated by Paris, which required a two-thirds local majority to be passed. Such arrangements meant that the more liberal assimilationist Muslim alternative represented by Ferhat Abbas lost ground to the more extreme nationalism of the Front de Libération Nationale (FLN). By the late 1940s the FLN had taken their struggle underground, with their own regionally based structures to collect funds and to administer (rough) justice, and the beginnings of an army called the Organisation Spéciale (OS). In the Kabyle region this consisted of 500 men under a formidable commander called Belkacem Krim.

Other members of the OS would go on to lead the FLN, whether based in Cairo after fleeing French captivity like the decorated war veterans Ahmed Ben Bella, Mohammed Khider and Hocine Ait Ahmed, or like Mostafa Ben Boulaid, Larbi Ben M'hidi, Rabah Bitat, Mourad Didouche and Krim himself within Algeria. These were physically tough and implacable men, with an average age of thirty-two at the time.[63] Algeria was on the brink of a protracted war, whose outbreak required events in Indochina to take a further turn, with the French bowing out and the US coming in.

That would require a significant dilution of the hostility towards European colonialism that lay at the heart of the founding myth of the United States. The rapidly growing perception that colonies were essential to the ability of weakened European states to resist Soviet expansionism – an argument also applied to the future immunity to Communism of a democratic Japan – meant that criticism of imperialism would become little more than a muted grumble under Truman, before reviving with a vengeance in the era of Eisenhower and John Foster Dulles.

5. 'POLICE ACTION': KOREA

The Master's Last Throw

The US and the Soviets only once fought directly and openly during the Cold War, save for a few aerial clashes on the inner German border, when Soviet MiG-15 jets clashed with US F-86 Sabres over North Korea and the Manchurian borderlands. But the Korean War could have led to a far greater clash between the superpowers, for the US might have used atom bombs to take the war to China, activating China's mutual defence alliance with the Soviet Union.

The fuse for the Korean War was lit between 4 March and 7 April 1949, when the North Korean dictator Kim Il Sung visited Moscow, cap in hand, after the failure of North Korea's first two-year economic plan. The North had only half the population of South Korea, and was losing people in droves.[1] During these talks, after Stalin had casually inquired, 'How's it going, Comrade Kim?', the Korean replied that 'the southern-ers are making trouble all the time. They are violating the border; there are continuous small clashes.' Of course he was doing the same; both sides had mounted cross-border incursions, using up to 1,500 troops at a time. Stalin was outraged on Kim's behalf: 'What are you talking about? Are you short of arms? We shall give them to you. You must strike the southerners in the teeth. Strike them, strike them.'[2]

But while Stalin encouraged the thirty-seven-year-old Kim to strike hard, the US warned the aged Syngman Rhee that it would not come to his aid unless the North attacked in strength. Stalin provided Kim's forces with heavy weapons and fighter aircraft; the US denied such arms to Rhee, whose forces had only a week's supply of ammunition. The disparity in armaments was an opportunity not to be missed. In the first half of 1950 Kim persistently lobbied Stalin to green-light a North Korean onslaught. He claimed that his well-equipped army of 100,000, called the In Min Gun, would destroy Rhee's 60,000-strong Republic of Korea (ROK) force. In a boast to a French Stalinist journalist after his invasion was under way, Kim claimed to have predicted that he would celebrate the liberation of Korea in Seoul by the end of August 1950.

The North Korean leader knew how to play on Stalin's sensitivities as paramount leader of the world Communist movement. In January 1950 Kim entertained Terentii Shtykov, the Soviet Ambassador, to a well-lubricated lunch during which he casually remarked that 'Mao Zedong is his friend and will always help Korea,' words which were relayed back to Stalin.[3] The victory of the Chinese Communists in December 1949, and Mao's oft-repeated desire to foment revolution throughout East Asia, suggested to Stalin that he might be able to sanction Kim's war plans while shifting the burden of dealing with any negative consequences on to Mao. However, it seemed most unlikely that the US would intervene in Korea, a view indirectly confirmed on 12 January 1950, when Secretary of State Dean Acheson, in unscripted and unwise remarks to the Press Club, publicly excluded Korea and Taiwan from the US defence perimeter in Asia.

That was also the considered view of the US Chiefs of Staff, Eisenhower, Nimitz and Spaatz, who in 1949 got their way in withdrawing the majority of US troops from South Korea. The newly established CIA predicted that a North Korean invasion was unthinkable. Lastly General Douglas MacArthur, Supreme Commander of Allied forces in the Pacific and *de facto* Shogun of Japan, was uninterested in Korea, which he regarded as a satrapy of the hated State Department. The feeling was mutual, as Acheson was outraged when MacArthur halved the number of occupation troops in Japan without even consulting the State Department.[4]

Although it seemed that the US cared little for South Korea's fate, the earlier loss of China to the Communists and the Soviet testing of an atom bomb in August 1949 prompted a thoroughgoing restatement of US policy in a document known as NSC 68. Written in early 1950 by a

committee chaired by the former banker Paul Nitze, this sought to cali-
brate foreign and defence policy at a time when the administration was
trying to reconcile increased Soviet threats with defence expenditure
cuts, to be achieved by what many regarded as an over-reliance on
nuclear weapons. NSC 68 was a powerful attempt, largely on Acheson's
part, to concentrate minds on the huge disparity (approximately thirty
Soviet to seven US divisions) in conventional forces.

As George Kennan might have argued, had he been invited to this
party, this was to conflate capabilities with intentions, for the policy
document was strong on alarmist statistics of Soviet military power but
weak on what Stalin intended. The strength of the Soviet air force was
extrapolated from the floor space of aircraft hangars and factories;
ominous numbers of divisions were counted without regard to their
actual operational strength, leading to an overestimate of overall Soviet
troop numbers by around two million. The fact that the Soviets had torn
up the railway lines linking Germany to Russia went unmentioned, as
did their lack of a transcontinental strategic bomber force, the biggest
gap in their arsenal. The policy document recommended that the US
must not only have the capacity to deter a Soviet nuclear attack but also
the wherewithal to fight non-nuclear wars in a flexible manner.[5]

Cost-cutting Defense Secretary Louis Johnson fought NSC 68 tooth
and nail, but he was weakened in the face of the State Department by a
Congressional investigation prompted by leaks from the navy, which
was bearing the brunt of Johnson's cuts. When the policy document
reached Truman's desk that April it stayed there until the Korean War
broke out. Truman and Johnson sought to cap defence spending at
around $13 billion by depending heavily on the nuclear deterrent, but
adoption of NSC 68 would increase expenditure by anything from $30
billion to $50 billion. Although the Korean War itself only cost an addi-
tional $3–5 billion, it ensured the adoption of NSC 68 and an overall
rise in defence expenditure to $48.2 billion in 1951. This translated not
only into hundreds more nuclear weapons, but also into an army of
1,353,000 men, 397 major warships and an air force with ninety-five
wings. If Stalin wanted a war anywhere on earth he would get it, and the
US intended to win.[6]

NSC 68 eschewed the nuances of a doctoral thesis (this a jibe at

Kennan) in favour of bludgeoning the official 'mass mind' with basic data and a Manichaean vision of a free world menaced by religoid fanatics. There should be heavy investment in covert, economic, psychological and political warfare, all designed to counter Communist advances and to subvert satellite countries and the Soviet Union itself.[7] Since the US was engaged in 'completely irreconcilable moral conflict' with the Soviets, 'total diplomacy' would be required to mobilize America's domestic resources and those of the entire free world too. As one of the key drafters of NSC 68 remarked, 'if we can sell every useless article known to man in large quantities, we should be able to sell our very fine story in larger quantities'.[8]

Korea and NSC 68 were very bitter pills for Truman to swallow. It was a war he could not shy away from for reasons of face and prestige, but one in which he could not use America's unilateral military advantage in nuclear weapons without risking escalation into a new world war. There was also a strong element of 'for want of a nail' in the voting down by Congress in January 1950 of $11 million in defence assistance for Seoul. Although a compromise package was subsequently approved, Moscow, Beijing and Pyongyang took it as a green light for a military solution to the Korean problem.[9]

War in Korea had many positive aspects for Stalin, provided it remained limited. A unified Communist Korea would extend the depth of this buffer on the Soviet Union's south-eastern Asiatic flank and it might be a useful springboard for an assault on Japan in the global war he thought inevitable. The US would be bound to shift forces away from Europe towards the Far East, which would weaken the newly established NATO, the Western response to the crises Stalin had engineered over Berlin and in Prague in 1948. If the US intervened in Korea, Mao's dependence on Stalin would increase, diminishing the likelihood of his becoming an Asian Tito. A war between China and the US would exact a terrible price in blood and treasure on the US, which the 'soft' Americans would be unwilling to pay. As for the North Koreans, Stalin said they would 'lose nothing, except for their men', a view he later extended to the Chinese.[10] At meetings with Mao, Stalin recommended that Mao put the 14,000 remaining Korean troops in the PLA's 156th Division at Kim's disposal. Mao had already allowed the 164th and 166th Divisions to return to North Korea, making a total of 30,000 to 40,000 battle-hardened veterans of China's civil war ready for action in Korea. There really was no downside from the Kremlin's point of view.

During a secret visit to Moscow between 30 March and 25 April 1950, Kim brought along the leader of the South Korean Communists, Pak Hon-yong, who declared that there were 200,000 disaffected South Korean leftists waiting to spring into action, a gross overestimate that omitted to mention that thousands of them were in prison. Comrade Pak, who was to be shot three years later, hoped that when Seoul was liberated the balance of power within the united Korean Communist Party would tilt towards the southerners and away from Kim's Soviet Korean group.[11] During the visit he assured Stalin that there would not be time for any US intervention because his blitzkrieg would be over in two to three weeks. Stalin bluntly told him that he was more exercised by events in Europe, and insisted that Kim turn for more concrete assistance to Mao with his 'good understanding of Oriental matters'. His parting shot to Kim was 'If you should get kicked in the teeth, I shall not lift a finger. You have to ask Mao for all the help.'

On 13 May 1950 Kim flew to Beijing for three more days of secret talks. When he told Mao that Stalin had approved his invasion of the South, Mao cabled Stalin to confirm this story. While he did not discount potentially adverse consequences, Mao regarded war in Korea as a useful way of consolidating the Communist regime in China – through anti-American nationalism – and as a means of subverting the world order in the Asia-Pacific region.[12] He was also simultaneously reassured, and offended, when Kim insisted that his troops did not require any Chinese military assistance, including the deployment of troops along the Chinese–Korean border. This ran contrary to Stalin's last words to him, and caused the Soviet dictator to take a bigger stake in the venture. There was a significant spike in the quantity of arms arriving on Soviet ships in North Korea's main port, and three Soviet generals with extensive combat experience arrived in Pyongyang, where they scrutinized and rejected the North Korean invasion plan. They imposed an alternative 'counter-offensive' based on the useful fiction that their ally was responding to South Korean aggression.

The North Korean invasion began at 4 a.m. on Sunday 25 June 1950,

a timing seared on the minds of Soviet planners by Hitler nine years earlier. A hundred and fifty Soviet T-34 tanks enabled the In Min Gun to
penetrate sixty miles in a couple of days, in a thrust which brought them
to Seoul. North Korean secret police made short work of any 'rightists'
who fell into their hands. Syngman Rhee's ROK troops had already
taken 30,000 imprisoned leftists out of the city to shoot them in ditches,
the fate of many more suspects who had been compulsorily enrolled in
an organization called the Bodo League. News of the invasion reached
MacArthur's headquarters before dawn on Sunday morning. Because of
huge time differences, Washington did not learn of the attack until 3
p.m. on what was still Saturday 25 June. Truman was in his hometown
of Independence, Missouri, Acheson was gardening at his Maryland
farm, and Defense Secretary Johnson and Chairman of the Joint Chiefs
Omar Bradley were exhausted after a long flight home from Asia.

The news reached the State Department's Far Eastern Desk at 8 p.m.
and was relayed to Dean Rusk, who was dining with the journalist
Joseph Alsop, and then to Dean Acheson, who telephoned Truman. In
response to Acheson's initial grim tidings, Truman made his position
clear: 'Dean, we've got to stop the sons of bitches, no matter what.'
Simultaneously John Hickerson, who dealt with UN business, telephoned Secretary-General Trygve Lie at his home on Long Island. 'My
God Jack, this is war against the United Nations' was Lie's response. In
the early hours of Sunday morning, Lie summoned the members of the
Security Council for a meeting to be held that afternoon. Meanwhile
Truman flew back from Independence on the eponymous presidential
aircraft and had the radio operator summon all the relevant principals
for a meeting to be held at Blair House, his residence while the White
House was undergoing much-needed refurbishment. Arriving back in
Washington by early evening, during the drive to Blair House he
exploded: 'By God, I am going to let them have it.' After a dinner the
fourteen men discussed how to respond, with 'an intense moral outrage'
pervading the room.[13]

The USAF began planning to wipe out Soviet air bases in the Far
East. The Seventh Fleet was sent north from the Philippines to patrol the
straits between mainland China and Taiwan. All Americans were to be
evacuated from Korea, while the ammunition previously denied to Rhee

was to be rushed there from Japan. Over the following days Truman authorized US air and naval operations up to the 38th parallel to slow the momentum of the North Korean advance. The big imponderable was who stood behind Kim Il Sung, for, as one US official remarked, 'Can you imagine Donald Duck going on a rampage without Walt Disney knowing about it?' Truman accurately calculated that 'the Russians are going to let the Chinese do the fighting for them', although at this stage the Chinese were nowhere in sight.

With the Soviets absent from the UN Security Council, which they were boycotting because Chiang's regime still represented China, on 27 June the UN sanctioned an international armed response to North Korean aggression. Some thirteen nations would eventually join the US-led coalition. That decision coincided with the day the North Koreans overran Seoul, bringing terror in their wake, and sending ROK forces into headlong retreat. In a move which would strain his relations with MacArthur, Truman first accepted and then declined Chiang's offer of 33,000 KMT troops, on reflection deciding to keep the fates of Korea and Taiwan separate.

On Friday 30 June Truman committed two divisions of US ground troops from MacArthur's command in Japan to what he described as a 'police action' in Korea. MacArthur had sought five divisions, including some from the West, but the Joint Chiefs were anxious lest the Soviets make a counter-move in Germany. The terminology helped avoid a wider war, for a formal declaration of war would have activated Chinese treaties with North Korea and the defence elements of the 1950 Sino–Soviet Pact.[14] In Congress, the loudest cheers were for Representative Charles Eaton when he said: 'We've got a rattlesnake by the tail and the sooner we pound its damn head in the better.' Most Congressmen accepted the administration's citation of eighty-seven precedents for presidents who despatched troops without prior Congressional authorization. In fact the alleged precedents were all limited efforts to extract US citizens from foreign war zones; in retrospect Truman's action was an ominous step on the road to the imperial presidency.[15]

MacArthur's new title was commander-in-chief, Far East. US forces were thereby entrusted to an egomaniacal seventy-year-old, who suffered more than most from the general's generic disease of being surrounded by yes-men. He also resembled the actress who complained that the movie screens had grown too small for her talents. A colleague always referred to him as 'Sarah' in letters to his wife, alluding to the actress Sarah Bernhardt. The General had alabaster skin dotted with age spots and a craggy profile. His hair was thinning and its colour derived from a bottle. He was routinely kitted out in sunglasses, a battered peaked cap, pilot's blouson and pleated slacks, with a corncob pipe jutting from his mouth, a contrived common touch designed to contrast with his exalted five-star rank.

MacArthur ruled Japan at a time when Hirohito had wisely abdicated the role to become a low-key constitutional monarch. The General commuted between a huge colonial-style embassy residence and the Dai Ichi insurance building opposite the Imperial Palace. He was a master of public relations, from dealing with the Emperor Hirohito to a humble carpenter who bowed back out of a lift the General entered. Suitably manipulated by MacArthur's propagandists, the carpenter became a local celebrity. The General had long affected an oracular, third-person mode of speech, in which 'History' did this or that, and 'MacArthur paid a visit'. His vast headquarters staff were dedicated believers in the cult, clones with his rigidity of opinion but without his flashes of genius.

MacArthur had grown contemptuous of his political masters, and became both anti-Semitic and a little loopy. Roosevelt had been 'Rosenfeld', but Truman was 'that Jew in the White House'. When an aide was confused by this remark, MacArthur said, 'You can tell by his name. Look at his face.'[16] Yet fate made him uniquely indispensable to the administration, despite the ties he had with Truman's domestic political opponents. Ironically one of them, the future Secretary of State John Foster Dulles, was in Tokyo when the invasion started and privately recommended to Truman that he find another commander since the elderly warrior's mind wandered. It did not wander far from his principal preoccupation with himself. MacArthur thought himself superior to any other general, dismissing his (four-star) titular boss Omar Bradley as 'a farmer', and was convinced that he was an expert on 'the oriental mind'. In fact the oriental minds he was acquainted with were those of upper-class Filipinos and his wartime comrade Chiang Kai-shek. The

Japanese were the policemen who bowed and saluted along his daily progress, or the people who beamed at him from the newsreels he watched at night as a substitute for visiting real places.[17]

The Tokyo high command was a case of too many chiefs and not enough Native Americans. The General's intimates were called the Bataan Gang, that is the officers who had played supporting roles in the redemptive myth MacArthur had constructed about the Philippines. They had bitterly resented the prominence given to the war in Europe and hence anyone connected to Marshall or Eisenhower. It was therefore a blow to them when Marshall became Truman's defense secretary a month into the Korean War, while Bradley became the fifth and last US five-star general in September.

MacArthur's initial strategy was to trade space for time, but little time was bought because the two US divisions shipped from Japan as the Eighth Army under General Walton 'Johnnie' Walker performed lamentably. They were unused to marching on foot and had little or no battlefield situational awareness. The North Koreans ambushed their lumbering motorized columns as they crawled through the zig-zagging hills that made up the spine of Korea, or exhausted them by always attacking their positions at night. It did not help that many GIs could not fathom why they were there at all. 'I'll fight for my country, but I'll be damned if I see why I'm fighting to save this hell hole,' remarked a Corporal Stephen Zeg of Chicago.[18] The occupation troops had gone to seed in a fantasy world of cheap servants and cheaper whores, where their main preoccupation was making a fast buck on the enormous black market in American consumer goods. One of the most effective US commanders, Colonel John 'Iron Mike' Michaelis, described his troops as follows:

> When they started out, they couldn't shoot. They didn't know their weapons. They had not had enough training in old fashioned musketry. They'd spent a lot of time listening to lectures on the differences between communism and Americanism and not enough time crawling on their bellies on manoeuvres with live ammunition singing over them. They'd been nursed and coddled, told to drive safely, to buy War Bonds, to give to the Red Cross, to avoid VD, to write home to

mother – when someone ought to have been telling them how to clean
a machine gun when it jams.[19]

The blame was shared between Truman's cuts to the military budget,
which had led to a sharp reduction in combat training, and MacArthur's
own lack of diligence. The result, by August, was that the North Koreans, although suffering 40 per cent casualties according to Chinese estimates, had the retreating US and ROK forces contained within a large
rectangular perimeter around the southern port of Pusan. That was
where MacArthur made his stand, pumping in huge additional resources
while his air force pounded the enemy. The 90,000 besieged soon outnumbered the besieging force by 20,000.

North Korean hubris gave MacArthur his chance to execute one of
the most brilliant moves of his career. He would strike by sea at the
North Koreans' extended supply chain, trapping them in a pincer movement when Walker's heavily reinforced army moved north. After initially ruling out an amphibious landing, codenamed Bluehearts, because
of the poor quality of his army troops, MacArthur grasped an offer
from General Lemuel Shepherd of the US Marines to deploy a
combat-ready force that was threatened by Truman's budgetary cuts.
The revamped plan, Operation Chromite, was for a landing at the port
of Inchon. If successful the landing would give him a forward air base at
Kimpo and a mere twenty miles to cover in order to seize the logistical
bottleneck of Seoul. Inchon, however, was very far from being an ideal
place for an amphibious landing. It had the second greatest tidal rise and
fall in the world, only high enough for one day per month to permit
landing craft to avoid getting stranded on viscous mud thousands of
yards offshore. The troops would have to land straight on to piers and
concrete seawalls and the harbour might also be mined. At a crucial
meeting MacArthur won over sceptical naval commanders by asking:
'Are you content to let our troops stay in that bloody perimeter like beef
cattle in a slaughterhouse? Who will take the responsibility for such a
tragedy? Certainly, I will not.'[20]

On Wednesday 13 September, 261 ships began disembarking a massive invasion force that rapidly secured Inchon. MacArthur marred this
act of brilliance by appointing his chief Tokyo crony, General Edward

'Ned' Almond, as the titular head of an operation conceived and led by Shepherd, on the thin grounds that Almond was to have command of the army's post-invasion X Corps. Meanwhile Walton Walker's Eighth Army command broke out of Pusan and smashed the besieging force. The In Min Gun was shattered, and although 50,000 soldiers eventually managed to flee across the 38th parallel, they did so without their equipment. MacArthur flew into liberated Seoul on his personal Constellation, the *Bataan*, to preside at the reinstallation of Syngman Rhee. Both men were overcome with emotion, weeping tears of joy. The ceremony took place in the badly damaged National Assembly building, with shards of glass falling down as MacArthur led the Lord's Prayer. His entourage nervously donned their steel helmets, but he carried on with head bared.

With his forces halted at the 38th parallel, MacArthur waited on instructions. The UN Security Council resolution had called for the 'complete independence and unity of Korea' and Acheson dismissed the parallel as 'a surveyor's line'. Truman resolved that MacArthur should 'conduct the necessary military operations either to force the North Koreans behind the 38th Parallel *or to destroy their forces*'. MacArthur could cross the parallel to occupy North Korea, provided there was no indication of Chinese or Russian intervention. When MacArthur, correctly, sought clarification, Marshall cabled: 'We want you to feel unhampered tactically and strategically to proceed north of the 38th Parallel,' although he was supposed to use only South Korean forces for such operations. Simply put, MacArthur was in no way responsible for the decision to extend the war.

He was, however, responsible for not equipping his troops for the Korean winter, when temperatures commonly fell to 20 or 30 degrees below zero, or for the mountainous terrain they would encounter further north, where the country expands into a vast and inhospitable landscape. Although MacArthur was scrupulous in leading with ROK troops, the US Eighth Army and X Corps were not far behind. They were closing on an area thick with hydroelectric plants, which provided power not just to Korea but also to China and the Soviet Union. On 9 October two US aircraft, badly off course, attacked a Soviet air base near Vladivostok, sixty miles inside the Soviet Union.

It was at this moment that Truman flew to confer with MacArthur on Wake Island. With the Congressional elections on his mind, the President wanted to be seen to be associated with a successful commander, but he was also ensuring that MacArthur took his full share of responsibility for the next step.[21] The two men barely talked about possible Chinese intervention. When the subject was raised, MacArthur dismissed as minimal the numbers of PLA who could have crossed the Yalu River already, and spoke confidently about the capacity of the air force to wipe them out. Truman made a public show of parting amicably from the General, but was privately furious that MacArthur did not salute him either when he met or when they parted.

In late October MacArthur's troops took the northern capital of Pyongyang. In an act of extraordinary hubris the General diverted incoming reinforcements to Hawaii and Japan while persisting in his drive towards the border with China on the Yalu River. He promised reporters that 'the war very definitely is coming to an end shortly'. Again, it must be emphasized that Truman fully endorsed his plan to drive the North Koreans beyond the Yalu.[22] There was also an ominous coda. Legally speaking, the South Koreans were not entitled to administer the North, which was supposed to be a task devolved upon the US by the United Nations. In reality, thousands of South Korean policemen arrived in Pyongyang, where they embarked on a murderous witch-hunt for Communist functionaries and Party members – the latter some 14 per cent of the population. Sometimes individual US units participated in the resulting atrocities.[23]

Phantoms with No Shadows: Enter the Dragon

By August 1950, a total of 260,000 People's Liberation Army troops had moved to the North Korean border. The Chinese leadership had lost all faith in Kim Il Sung's military competence when he over-extended his supply lines to Pusan, but Stalin goaded Mao, insisting that unless he intervened North Korea was about to be erased as a Communist state. Having once refused offers of men from China, Kim now sent ever more desperate messages for China to intervene. When Pyongyang fell to US and ROK troops, China's supreme leader – safe inside one of his many nuclear shelters – decided to go to war. The Party began mass mobilization behind the slogan 'The Great Movement to Resist America and Assist Korea'.[24]

The Chinese leadership had discussed how to act throughout the first week of October 1950. They knew that it would not be like fighting the KMT in the civil war, where secret deals were more important than combat. Apart from Mao, party leaders worried that war with the US would jeopardize the consolidation of their victory in China itself. Their most distinguished soldier, Lin Biao, raised concerns that the US might intervene in Manchuria, or along the southern coast from Taiwan. He also told them that the firepower of a US division was ten or twenty times greater than that of an equivalent PLA formation, and warned that the Chinese would have little defence against enemy naval and air forces.[25] Lin prudently used the excuse of imminent medical treatment in the Soviet Union to decline the command of China's intervention forces.

Mao turned instead to the highly experienced fifty-two-year-old Peng Duhai. He was from a very poor peasant family and had been forced by circumstances to work as a child labourer in a coal mine before becoming a soldier in Chiang's army. He joined the Communist Party in 1928 and rose to be one of Mao's top commanders. It proved unnecessary to win him round to the plan, as he was passionately convinced that the Americans had to be defeated in Korea to defend the revolution in China.

To a degree the choice of field commander was irrelevant, as Mao himself directed the war in great detail. Like Hitler in his bunker, he pored over maps of Korea through the nights that followed; unlike Hitler, he smoked incessantly and drank so much tea that his teeth seemed to turn green. Mao's paramountcy, born of his reputation as a strategic sage, was at stake. He was determined to show Stalin what the new China could do, with the blood price conveniently paid by KMT troops recently assimilated into the PLA. Stalin himself made his own calculations about eroding American strength with the aid of what Russians called *limonski*, or yellow-skinned cannon fodder. For these were not allies in the Roosevelt–Churchill mould. Only Stalin's enormous prestige kept Mao's resentments just beneath boiling point. On 8 October Mao informed a relieved Kim Il Sung of his decision, and Peng was sent to lead an army he had never commanded before, in a theatre about which he knew very little.[26]

After being put on a state of alert in mid-August, the North-east Border Defence Army was renamed the Zhiyuanjun (Chinese People's Volunteers, or PVA), a cosmetic change to permit the Chinese leadership to claim that the intervention was the expression of spontaneous mass support rather than state policy. The Chinese leaders believed that US soldiers were rubbish and that mass and stealth could overcome superior US technology, but Zhou Enlai and Lin Biao were despatched to the Crimea on 10 October to firm up Stalin's earlier offer of support. Accustomed as he was to knowing American intentions in advance through his network of spies, Stalin had been rudely surprised by the US readiness to fight for Korea and baldly reneged on his promise to provide air cover to a Chinese invasion force. After a tense, ten-hour meeting, he agreed only to provide air cover north of the Yalu River.

Stalin's treachery imposed a delay on the intervention, planned for 15 October. Faced with well-reasoned dissent from his subordinate commanders about the frozen ground conditions as well as the lack of air cover, Peng himself threatened to resign and was recalled to Beijing for a face-to-face interview with the Chairman. Mao's will prevailed and on the night of 19 October 1950 some 300,000 Chinese Volunteers began crossing the Yalu into North Korea in an operation so skilfully carried out that it has been described as 'a phantom which cast no shadow'.[27]

The shadow might have been identified if the Americans had been looking for it, but they were totally caught up in the euphoria of what had become a military procession through North Korea. At this stage there were only eight unoccupied towns left in North Korea, and resistance was so slight that B-29s switched from dropping bombs to dropping leaflets, while a loudspeaker-equipped Dakota known as 'The Voice' flew over the remaining enemy territory, booming out calls to surrender. Charles Willoughby, MacArthur's egregious chief of intelligence, even denied the presence of the large contingent of 'Chinese Koreans' that Mao had deployed months earlier. When CIA operatives attached to the Seventh Fleet reported secret radio messages from former KMT soldiers who had been merged into the PLA, Willoughby threatened to expel the CIA from MacArthur's command.

US troops operating around Unsan captured prisoners who were taller than the North Koreans, and wore distinctive, heavily quilted uniforms. One of them admitted he was PLA and not a volunteer. When this information was relayed to General Walker he said, 'Well, he may be Chinese, but remember they have a lot of Mexicans in Los Angeles but you don't call LA a Mexican city.' Further reports arrived of enemy dead equipped with American weapons and neatly packed gear, and carrying no personal identity papers or letters. US reconnaissance planes also began to notice massed footprints that suddenly seemed to vanish in the snow – in fact these were large numbers of Chinese lying still in their white camouflage suits – and dense rows of trees where none had stood before, and which on closer inspection seemed to move.[28]

The self-styled expert on the 'oriental mind' failed to read it. MacArthur ignored all the contrary evidence and ordered X Corps and Eighth Army north to the Yalu. Later he would claim it was a reconnaissance in force, designed to pre-empt a Chinese attack, but that was a lie. On 1 November US and ROK forces in the Unsan area were surprised by ferocious attacks by Chinese troops, who then melted away. Again, MacArthur wilfully misunderstood its significance. The preliminary attack was a warning from the Chinese of what they could do, and that UN forces had advanced too far. In essence they were redrawing the border well south of the Yalu River. Ignoring the warning, ROK troops pressed on to the river and ceremonially urinated in it.

Starting on 25 November, the forces which MacArthur sent north in his 'Home by Christmas' offensive were attacked along a 300-mile front by 300,000 PVA, who compensated for their lack of radios by using bugles, cymbals, drums, whistles and even flutes for battlefield communications. They also attacked by night to neutralize the impact of US air supremacy and avoided roads, marching instead along Korea's hilly central spine. They had a mere 300 trucks to move supplies (always at night because of US bombing) and were otherwise totally reliant on mules and human bearers to move ammunition, food and equipment south, and their wounded north. Yet an army whose doctrine relied on the co-operative attitude of surrounding peasants found itself as disliked by the North Koreans as the Americans were. The feeling was mutual, as the Chinese really did not like the North Koreans. The country was bleak, the women unappealing and the national dish of fermented and highly spiced cabbage produced epic flatulence.

The troops themselves could move fast because they carried very little kit, and whereas a US division required 610 tons of supplies a day, the equivalent figure for the PVA was 50.[29] PVA soldiers carried an odd assortment of mainly American and Japanese weapons, and lacked heavy artillery. Their reversible brown and white cotton-filled jackets were impossible to dry when they became wet because they dared not light fires. When the temperature really plummeted, they smothered their faces with pork fat and stuffed straw in their rubber-soled canvas sneakers. The only sleeping bags they possessed were captured from the enemy. Two-thirds of Chinese casualties were caused by frostbite, and it was certain death to fall into exhausted sleep without huddling together for warmth. They could eat only cold food, usually *shaoping*, unleavened bread made from a mixture of sorghum, millet, lima beans and flour which they carried with them. Chinese soldiers rarely received leave, except on extreme compassionate grounds, and their recreational activities were minimal. Medical provision for the wounded was primitive, only amputees were repatriated and the Chinese dead were rarely buried.

In addition to dealing with primitive communications and tenuous logistics, Peng was constantly harassed by Mao and Kim. What was he to make of such exhortations as 'Win a quick war if you can; if you can't, win a slow one'?[30] He did his best to make it quick. After destroying an ROK corps on the Ch'ongch'on River, he smashed the US 2nd Infantry Division on the right flank of the UN advance. US Eighth Army's headlong retreat was covered by the suicidally brave stand of the Turkish Brigade. At Chosin Reservoir the US 7th Infantry Division Regimental Combat Team and the US 1st Marine Division were nearly encircled and suffered some 15,000 casualties before they escaped thanks to concentrated bombardment by the USAF and the massed guns of US X Corps.

By mid-December the PVA had driven US Eighth Army from north-west Korea across the 38th parallel. In the north-east US X Corps inflicted devastating losses on the PVA 9th Army Group and established a hedgehog position around the port of Hungnam, but had to be withdrawn to bolster Eighth Army. The evacuation involved over 100,000 soldiers, almost as many civilians, 17,500 vehicles and 350,000 tons of supplies. Before departing they levelled Hungnam city, rendering the port unusable for the duration. On 16 December Truman declared a national emergency.

Although victorious all along the line, Peng's army had taken terrible punishment from US firepower. The Chinese leadership had the option of accepting an Indian-brokered ceasefire, but chose to order Peng to push south beyond the 38th parallel. Peng was compelled to press further south, even though he was acutely aware of his army's logistical vulnerabilities and stiffening resistance as the 'compressed spring' effect made itself felt.[31] On the last day of 1950 he launched a further offensive and took Seoul on 4 January 1951, but the cost was heavy.

Just before Christmas 1950 General Walker was killed in a freak jeep accident. MacArthur had already decided to replace him with General Matthew Ridgway, a flinty, taciturn paratrooper who in June 1944 had jumped with his men in Normandy, and who had been director of athletics at West Point when MacArthur was superintendent. Rather than spoil the Christmas arrangements of his staff officers Ridgway flew to Tokyo alone on Christmas Eve. MacArthur told him: 'The Eighth Army is yours, Matt. Do what you think best.'[32]

The wider context in which Ridgway had to find his feet had become febrile. During a press conference on 30 November, Truman had declared that the use of all weapons at his disposal, including atomic bombs, was under 'active consideration' and that the field commander would be 'in charge of the use of all these weapons'. He should have been more careful in his choice of words, or at least aware that they would be welcomed all too eagerly by a frantic MacArthur, who was desperate to redeem his error in advancing to the Yalu. His PR men played up the arrival of the 'hordes' they had hitherto dismissed as 'mere laundrymen'. At one briefing a cynical correspondent asked, 'Will you tell us how many Chinese battalions go to a horde, or vice versa?'[33]

On Christmas Eve 1950 MacArthur submitted a targeting list that required twenty-six nuclear weapons, sixteen of which were to be used against Chinese industrial and military targets.[34] The prospect of nuclear escalation brought a large British contingent to Washington, led by Attlee and Bevin. They insisted that they should have a say in the use of nuclear weapons, while underlining that they regarded a widening of the war as disastrous, not least for their outpost of Hong Kong. They were also angling for a US subsidy towards their £3,800 million rearmament programme, but that is another story.

In fact, US policy-makers realized that select nuclear strikes would probably not impact much on China's overall ability to wage war in Korea, while courting the real risk of the Soviets coming to the aid of their ally, in Europe rather than Asia. Unilateral use of atomic weapons would also turn the UN against the US, while alienating European (and Japanese) allies. This led US policy-makers to favour a local draw, but none of his titular superiors had the courage to inform MacArthur of this major change of policy, a moral lapse that slightly mitigated his future conduct.[35]

On arrival in Korea, Ridgway spent time acquainting himself with his troops and with battlefields he surveyed from a small plane. He quickly decided that he could expect little of the ROK army; but his own men were cold and demoralized, mainly because they did not know what they were fighting for. They regarded Truman's euphemism of a 'police action' as a bad joke – this was a very real war. Ridgway took care of their creature comforts and addressed a rousing message to them on 21 January 1951:

> The real issues are whether the power of Western civilization, as God has permitted it to flower in our own beloved lands, shall defy and defeat Communism; whether the rule of men who shoot their prisoners, enslave their citizens and deride the dignity of man, shall displace the rule of those to whom the individual and his individual rights are sacred; whether we are to survive with God's hand to guide and lead us, or to perish in the dead existence of a Godless world.[36]

Ridgway's mantra was 'Find them! Fix them! Fight them! Finish them!' Behind the tough talk, however, he knew that his task was to strip the PVA of its sustaining belief in overwhelming invincibility, pitting US military technology against Chinese numbers. In essence, he was less concerned with battlefield victory than with increasing the rate of attrition that had already slowed the Chinese offensive until Beijing accepted the reality of a stalemate.

Mao used the Korean War to whip up nationalist hysteria in China to consolidate Communist rule. Few regimes in history – other than the one in North Korea – have so completely mobilized hysterical levels of enthusiasm or hatred, as well as enthusiastic hate too. Pride in China would lead to pride in Mao's regime, a tactic the Communist Party has exploited ever since. The paradox of a 'social imperialist' war wrapped in the slogans of anti-imperialism is not often remarked by left-wing commentators, who invariably accuse regimes that do not pretend to be socialist of waging war for domestic political reasons.[37] Mao was also the ultimate back-seat driver, constantly interfering in tactical decisions. An army trained for guerrilla warfare, and in which institutionalized command structures took second place to charismatic personalities, was not best suited to the needs of war against a well-equipped modern army. PVA troops could sustain a ferocious pace in battle for about three days, but after that failures of supply and support would lead to collapse. Lower-level officers and NCOs were forbidden to use their own initiative and lacked the authority to call in such support as was available – unlike their opponents, who could call in almost unlimited artillery and, when weather permitted, terrifying air attacks.[38]

While Ridgway worked out how to achieve a draw, the seventy-one-year-old MacArthur was determined to close out his career with an unambiguous victory. On 30 December 1950 he lobbied the Republicans in Washington to be allowed to blockade the Chinese mainland, even though most PVA supplies came overland. He wanted to bomb China's strategic defence industries, even though the results of such bombing during the Second World War had been questionable. He wanted Chinese Nationalist troops to be sent to Korea as reinforcements and to launch diversionary attacks on the Chinese mainland from Taiwan, apparently unaware that Chiang Kai-shek's forces lacked amphibious capacity. He was also not slow to ventilate his belief that the war in Korea was being fought half-heartedly, dismissing Ridgway's approach as 'an accordion war' in which the combatants seesawed back and forth. Truman set his staff to investigate the analogous precedent of General

George McClellan, whom Abraham Lincoln had sacked during the American civil war for blaming his military failure on the political direction of the war. Their findings confirmed what the amateur historian Truman believed already. The trouble was that in the popular mind MacArthur was more like the victorious Ulysses Grant than the hapless McClellan. But in the end it was intolerable that a serving officer should be openly conspiring with the political opponents of the administration. MacArthur's wild talk of extending the war to China threatened the international backing the US enjoyed in Korea and invited Soviet retaliation in Europe, but the sacking point was his flagrant attempt to usurp the power of his constitutional Commander-in-Chief. Truman summarily dismissed MacArthur in April 1951, a decision so unpopular that supporters of the President were ordered out of taxis by irate drivers and married couples ended up in jail after brawling over it.

Three months before this melodrama unfolded, Ridgway had to deal with the renewed Chinese onslaught that took Seoul but then ran into well-prepared UN defensive positions at the intersection of the main east–west and north–south rail and road routes that quartered Korea. PVA losses in the battles of Chipyongni and Wonju were catastrophic, and to add to his troubles Peng now had to guard against being cut off by a second Inchon landing.[39] Seoul was untenable and the war settled down to a struggle along what Ridgway called the 'Main Line of Resistance' around the 38th parallel. Ferocious battles still occurred, the doomed stand of the 1st Battalion of the British Gloucestershire Regiment on the Imjin River taking place at the end of April. Peng returned to Beijing, where he took his life in his hands by interrupting Mao's sleep to argue the folly of further massed offensives. Mao was already halfway persuaded that the political gains from the PVA intervention were sufficient and agreed to a new strategy of 'fighting while negotiating', with the exhausted Chinese troops permitted to create strong defensive positions as arrangements were made for them to be rotated back to China. Once Stalin had endorsed it, Kim was compelled to accept it.[40]

The Korean War had served many useful purposes for the Soviet dictator, who fought it to the last Chinese. It confirmed his low view of US fighting prowess and the sentimental weakness of US public opinion, as he revealed in comments to Zhou Enlai in autumn 1952:

Americans are not capable of waging a large-scale war at all, especially after the Korean War. All of their strength lies in air power and the atom bomb. Britain won't fight for America. America cannot defeat little Korea. One must be firm when dealing with America. The Chinese comrades must know that if America does not lose this war, then China will never recapture Taiwan. Americans are merchants. Every American soldier is a speculator, occupied with buying and selling. Germans conquered France in 20 days. It's been already two years, and the USA has still not subdued little Korea. What kind of strength is that? America's primary weapons are stockings, cigarettes and other merchandise. They want to subjugate the world, yet they cannot subdue little Korea. No, Americans don't know how to fight. After the Korean War, in particular, they have lost the capability to wage a large-scale war. They are pinning their hopes on the atom bomb and air power. But one cannot win a war with that. One needs infantry, and they don't have much infantry; the infantry they do have is weak. They are fighting with little Korea, and already people are weeping in the USA. What will happen if they start a large-scale war? Then perhaps, everyone will weep.[41]

The war consolidated Chinese dependence on the Soviets, while digging a huge trench between China and the US, where residual sympathies for China had been supplanted by images of menacing 'Mongol' hordes. Stalin took a keen interest in the fighting, especially the air war, where he was testing his own resources and acquiring US technology when it fell out of the sky. The Soviets had around seventy search parties roving around the battlefields, hoping to get their hands on downed F-86 fighter jets, as well as G-suits and radar bomb sights. With the flow of technology from British sympathizers interrupted, these salvage operations played a role in the development of equivalent Soviet weaponry second only to espionage.

Stalin authorized the armistice talks that began in July 1951 at Kaesong, where the subjects of whose chair was higher or faced north or south (in China victors always face south) occupied many a week, before the talks were relocated to a permanent site at Panmunjon. Meanwhile the opposing sides constructed formidable lines of underground defences across the 150-mile width of the peninsula, with the US-led coalition digging in deep in opposed positions. Both sides continued to pressure each other with offensive action, with the infamous battles for Pork Chop Hill taking place in the spring and summer of 1953, ending three weeks before the armistice was signed. Fighting while negotiating had simply added to the enormous human cost of what had long since become a futile struggle for geographical features of no strategic value whatever.[42]

On the UN side, Curtis LeMay's Strategic Air Command was turned loose to prove that air power could win a war, the untested conceit of the British and American air force commanders during the Second World War, and his default solution too to Russian missiles being based in Cuba a decade later. Whereas the USAAF had dropped some half a million tons of bombs throughout the entire Pacific theatre during the Second World War, 635,000 tons were unloaded on North Korea, with a further 32,557 tons of napalm.[43] The cities of North Korea were reduced to ruins and dams such as those at Toksan breached, washing away roads and railways, without significantly diminishing the fighting power of the armies along the 38th parallel. The B-29s suffered rising losses once the enemy deployed the new MiG-15, some of them flown by Soviet pilots over the Yalu River in dogfights with US F-86 Sabres escorting the bombers. Ominously, Operation Hudson Harbor saw lone B-29s flying dry runs for using nuclear weapons, a bluff called by Chinese expertise in dispersion, which meant that there were never any troop concentrations large enough to merit the use of such weapons.[44]

On the other side, Mao may have abandoned the hope of winning the war but he still poured troops and supplies into Korea, so that the PVA had 1.35 million men there by early 1953, with 120,000 tons of ammunition and a quarter of a million tons of grain. It was more than sufficient to launch another offensive, but, if one was contemplated, Stalin's sudden death in early 1953 forestalled it. The war had done nothing to prevent Mao asserting his grip on the wider Chinese empire at a time when he was allegedly still under Stalin's thumb. In 1950–1 Chinese forces invaded Tibet, all the while proclaiming respect for Tibetan autonomy, and Han Chinese, mainly demobbed ex-KMT troops, were sent to colonize strategically vital Xinjiang, the Muslim Uighur-dominated region which bordered on four of the Soviet republics as well as Mongolia, Afghanistan, Pakistan and India, and also contained large reserves of oil and natural gas.[45]

In the United States, from enjoying overwhelming initial public support the Korean War had become deeply unpopular, a fate shared by the Democrats, who had been continuously in power since 1933. By early 1951 as many as 66 per cent of Americans wanted 'to pull our troops out of Korea as fast as possible', while 49 per cent regarded the war as a mistake. Truman's personal popularity plummeted to a miserable 26 per cent and MacArthur did his best to send it further downwards. He returned to a hero's welcome in the US and, after his bathetic address to Congress about old soldiers never dying, Truman sneered at 'damn fool Congressmen crying like a bunch of women'. In fact the ensuing Congressional inquiry pricked MacArthur's bubble by exposing his professional errors and his outrageous attempt to dictate global strategy in the service of the single theatre for which he was responsible.[46]

The ceasefire talks dragged on because of the vexed issue of prisoner repatriation. While all but a handful of UN converts to Marxist-Leninism wished to flee the Chinese people's paradise as soon as possible, most of the 116,000 POWs held by the Americans did not wish to return to Communist China or North Korea. Even when the US, in a morally abject exercise of realpolitik, offered to return at least 70,000–80,000 of them against their will, the Chinese sensed a loss of face and sought to deny the Americans the moral high ground by fabricating claims that the US was using biological weapons, supported by the testimony of a handful of coerced POW pilots. Truman found this war without end intensely frustrating, using his diary to give vent to apocalyptic fantasies of blockading China's coast, destroying its industrial cities and taking on the Soviets in an all-out war.

Eisenhower, the Republican presidential nominee universally known as 'Ike', rode the wave of domestic weariness with this faraway war. His prestige quite as strong as MacArthur's, Ike seemed both more moderate and entirely at home in civilian garb, and promised to fly to Korea to end the conflict. At the same time he won over the rabid anti-Communist right by choosing Richard Nixon as his running mate and associating himself with McCarthyism: 'find the pinks: we will find the Communists; we will find the disloyal', he declared on the stump in Montana.

After winning the 1952 election but before taking office, he kept his promise and went to Korea, where he flew over the lines and observed an exchange of artillery fire. Desultory struggles over burned-out hills, he decided, would not bring victory in the wider struggle with Communism.[47] On his return he indulged MacArthur with an audience, but rejected his loose talk about nuclear warfare. After their meeting MacArthur growled that Eisenhower 'never did have the guts, and never will'.

In fact Ike wanted a summit with Stalin designed to agree the neutralization of democratic Germany, Austria, Japan and Korea, failing which the US would launch an all-out nuclear assault against North Korea and China. More immediately, the Chinese were discreetly informed that, if they did not enter talks, then Eisenhower would wage war with every weapon at his disposal, as he had done to devastating effect against Hitler's Germany.[48] The new President also increased the tension by withdrawing the US Seventh Fleet from the Taiwan Straits, seeming to clear the way for a Nationalist invasion of the mainland. Mao judged the threats to be credible.

When UN Commander Mark Clark, who replaced Ridgway in May 1952, offered an exchange of sick and wounded POWs, the Chinese responded in kind. The wider POW repatriation problem was resolved by putting the prisoners in UN custody, which defused the issue. Serious negotiations resumed at Panmunjom, although the Chinese launched some late offensives to maximize their negotiating position. A fly in the ointment was Syngman Rhee's devil-may-care desire to go on fighting to liberate the North. When in June 1953 he unilaterally turned loose some POWs whose fate was still under discussion, Eisenhower's cabinet discussed removing him through a military coup or an assassin's bullet. Even though a ceasefire had been declared, and signature of an armistice was imminent, the Chinese launched another limited offensive to punish Rhee.

The armistice was signed at Panmunjom on 27 July 1953, although internal Korean crises continue to flare up to this day, bringing the real threat of global nuclear war in their wake.[49] The war had cost China 152,000 dead and 230,000 wounded. The US lost 33,629 dead and a further 105,000 wounded; their UN allies 1,263 dead and 4,817 wounded. Korean casualties were far greater, since both North and South carried out vicious purges when they occupied each other's territory. South Korea lost 415,000 killed and 429,000 wounded, plus another half-million civilian dead. North Korea suffered over half a million military fatalities, with anywhere between one and two million civilians killed. The 38th parallel, and particularly Panmunjom itself, remains one of the most febrile flashpoints in the world, where the miserable hermit kingdom of Kim Il Sung's grandson Kim Jong Eun still trains guns and atomic missiles on a democratic and thriving South Korea.[50]

The war in Korea also underlined the strategic importance of South-east Asia, to the extent that the US felt obliged to support the European powers in their colonial wars. Economic interests played a role, but they were not those of the US itself, which was an exporter of rice and could access all the region's raw materials elsewhere. Rather it was a strategic decision related to the economic health of Britain, France and Japan, for which the US judged South-east Asia to be vital. This was also why the British were prepared to fight a long counter-insurgency war in Malaya so that its independence would be on their terms.[51]

6. 'EMERGENCY': MALAYA

Yesterday's Heroes, Tomorrow's Enemies

Malaya was the only place where in their empire's twenty-year post-war collapse the British fought an insurgency based specifically on Maoist doctrines of revolutionary warfare, as distinct from nationalists seeking their country's independence. Having lost Malaya under humiliating circumstances, the British stole back late in 1945 under the shadow of the atom bombs, directed by Mountbatten's South East Asia Command based in Ceylon. The Americans wanted the European colonial powers to follow their lead in promising the Philippines independence, and in Malaya the British would do enough to satisfy the Americans by highlighting their desire for an integrated multiracial outcome. Once Washington appreciated that the loss of their colonial assets would undermine the ability of the colonial powers to withstand Communism in Europe, British policy adjusted to the new anti-Communist imperative.[1]

The insurgency was born in May 1948 when fifty men converged on an isolated jungle encampment in Malaya's Pahang state, one of nine sultanates of the newly minted Federation of Malaya. Elaborate security measures, including concentric rings of sentries and relays of escorts, ensured that the leadership of the Malayan Communist Party would be undisturbed. Fearing that the Party was about to be declared illegal by the British High Commissioner, Sir Edward Gent, these men had to decide what future strategy to pursue.

The key decision-maker in the party of equals was a twenty-four-year-old Malay Chinese called Chin Peng (pronounced 'Pong', a source of wry amusement to the British). He was the son of the owner of a cycle-repair shop who, as a schoolboy, helped raise aid for mainland Chinese resistance to Japanese occupation. In 1940 he shifted his political allegiances from the KMT to the Communists. Chin Peng followed many other Communists into Force 136, a stay-behind operation directed by British SOE agents.

Eventually numbering around 5,000 guerrilla fighters, they called themselves the Malayan People's Anti-Japanese Army (MPAJA) to disguise the British connection. Most fighters were ethnic Chinese, part of the Chinese diaspora which the Japanese had targeted with genocidal savagery. They were under twenty-five, former rubber tappers, mining coolies, woodcutters, shop assistants and domestic servants. In so far as there was any effective resistance to the Japanese in Malaya, it came from these brave men and women.[2]

Communal violence began the moment Japan surrendered, when these mainly ethnic Chinese guerrillas emerged from the jungle to wreak vengeance on predominantly Malay 'collaborators', which in turn triggered an ethnic Malay pogrom against the Chinese.[3] By December 1945 the British had formally disarmed the Communist guerrillas. There was a parade in Kuala Lumpur at which each fighter received a campaign medal, M$350 (about £45) and a copy of General Sir Frank Messervy's speech praising their gallantry. Fifteen Communist leaders were also honoured, to the accompanying strains of a band of the Royal Marines, at an even grander parade in Singapore presided over by Mountbatten. Chin Peng was judged sufficiently meritorious to be appointed to the Order of the British Empire (subsequently rescinded). An ex-MPAJA Comrades' Association kept the flame of resistance alive, and enabled the Communists to tap the former fighters' modest military pensions.[4]

The Emergency, a choice of name we shall explore below, erupted in one of the most beautiful lands on earth, and probably the greenest, its humidity relieved only by monsoons in which the wind-driven rain can be almost horizontal. The size of England without Wales, the country is surrounded by sea except for a 170-mile land border with Thailand. Four-fifths of Malaya is covered by equatorial forest, in the depths of which dwelled *orang asli* aboriginal tribes. European settlers and Chinese immigrants were responsible for Malaya's two main wealth generators. Britons imported Brazilian rubber plants that flourished in Malaya's climate once the jungle had been cleared, and the Chinese began open-cast mining of tin, leaving muddy smudges on the landscape. By the twentieth century there were around 3,000 rubber plantations, the smaller run by single traders and the larger managed on behalf of such tyre manufacturers as Dunlop or Goodyear. There were also 750 tin mines, operated by Chinese as well as by Europeans and a large number of Americans.[5]

At the time of the Emergency Malaya's population was 5,300,000, the narrow majority (46 per cent) being Muslim Malays, plus 600,000 Tamil labourers recruited from southern India. However, 38 per cent of the population were ethnic Chinese, immigrants since the fifteenth century. The Chinese were clannish and culturally insular, but also in reaction to Muslim clannishness over dietary matters and marriage with infidels. The British had governed the Malay Chinese through a separate Chinese protectorate, which it was said 'was not so much to protect the Chinese as to protect the country against them'.

After the war, the British sought a progressive goal by regressive means, largely with an eye on changing American attitudes. They abrogated the sovereignty of the five independent sultans (four others were already in a mini-federation) and attempted to integrate the Chinese into a multiracial Malay Union. This was unpopular. The British next alighted on a federation as a more acceptable alternative, partially restoring the powers of the sultans over religious matters, which in a Muslim society meant over much of the law. Throughout Malaya, the British were like a class apart – interaction with the locals, apart from elite or rich 'honorary Europeans', being confined to much beloved servants or, on isolated estates, Asian concubines. British society was highly stratified itself, with a major fault-line running between 'officials' of the Malayan Civil Service and the 'unofficial' men of business and trade, with a sort of apartheid even as to who could occupy which end of the various club bars, and an acronym-heavy code based on civil service rank, company name or job title. As elsewhere in the empire, the unwritten rule was to get native elites to play the game of ritual and status, luring them in with medals and titles.[6]

The insurgents received a psychological boost from the victory of

Communism in China, whose regime was recognized by London in January 1950. The Viet Minh concurrently inflicted severe defeats on the French in Indochina. The advent of a Communist regime in China meant that it was no longer possible for the British to deport suspected Communists there, while it also encouraged Chinese millionaires (who in Malaya were more numerous than British) to hedge their bets, in case their extended families were subjected to intimidation. The British received support from Australia and New Zealand, while the US Consul in Kuala Lumpur and the CIA's Singapore station kept a watchful eye on events.

The outbreak of the Korean War helped the British in two ways. Firstly, it brought increased demand for Malayan rubber and tin, which meant that counter-insurgency efforts were virtually self-financing. In 1949 the Malayan colonial government had received $28.1 million in duty on rubber and $31.1 million on tin. A year later, the rubber duties were $89.3 million, and those on tin $50.9 million, and by 1951 the figures were $214.1 million and $76.2 million.[7] The cost of fighting the insurgency rose from $82 million in 1948 to $296 million in 1953, virtually all of it defrayed from tax receipts on these two commodities. Secondly, what the Americans might otherwise have regarded as a sordid little colonial war designed to benefit British commercial interests could be depicted as part of a wider crusade against Communism, mirrored by eager British participation in the UN coalition fighting Communism in Korea.[8]

The Malay Chinese were hardworking and entrepreneurial, including the 600,000 so-called squatters among their number. That was largely why the Malays resented their community, whose businessmen *towkays* dominated Kuala Lumpur and other towns. Yet the Chinese community was very complex and fractured, not least into supporters of the Communists and the Kuomintang and by membership of rival societies, while there were those who still yearned for China and others who saw their future in Malaya.[9] The Chinese squatters had fled the murderous racial violence of the Japanese to eke out a living cultivating small plots of land etched from densely forested hillsides with no formal legal title. Officials claimed they were damaging valuable stocks of timber, while planters resented the relative independence such plots gave to people they wanted as a low-paid workforce on rubber plantations. Both labour and planters organized for confrontation, with Communist-infiltrated labour unions calling for strikes and the Incorporated Society of Planters demanding dismissals, evictions, floggings and the like. In 1947, some 700,000 working days were lost in 300 major strikes, which sent ripples far beyond the peninsula. In 1948 the US imported 371,000 tons of rubber and 155,000 tons of tin, worth some $170 million at a time when the sterling area owed $1,800 million. The bonanza gave the labour unions greatly increased leverage and there was a superabundance of combustible materials before the Malayan Communist Party decided to strike a match, without any known direction or interference from Moscow.[10]

Chin Peng had become Communist secretary-general in 1947 after the Party's much respected leader, an Annamite migrant called Lai Teck, had fallen under a cloud of suspicion. Lai Teck's dogged advocacy of moderation began to be read by his comrades in the sinister retrospective light of how he had survived arrest by the Japanese unscathed in 1941, or why he alone had not attended a September 1942 conference of Party members that was wiped out in a Japanese ambush. Sensing that the noose was tightening, Lai Teck fled to Singapore, taking with him the bulk of Party funds. It transpired that he had been a British agent, inherited by Singapore Special Branch after his cover had been blown while spying for the French in Indochina. His former comrades subsequently assassinated him in Bangkok. Apart from Peng, other Force 136 veterans included Ah 'Shorty' Kuk and Lau Yew, an experienced jungle fighter who had led the Malay contingent to London's VJ parade. The only Muslim Malay veteran of Force 136 was Che Dat bin Abdullah, always known as Abdullah CD, who would command Communist operations in Pehang, Malaya's largest state. The British owed most of these men wartime pensions.

At their jungle meeting they decided to rename their organization the Malayan People's Anti-British Army and to divide it into a small strike force of full-time paid guerrillas, operating from hidden bases and organized as eight regiments, together with a larger pool of active supporters who would provide funding, food and intelligence gathering. The guerrilla regiments varied in strength from 300 to 800 fighters, of whom around 10 per cent were women. A bizarre component consisted of a hundred Japanese soldiers, unreconciled to the outcome of the Second

World War. The Communists wore rudimentary uniforms, with three stars on their caps called *tiga bintang* to symbolize the major ethnic groups in Malaya. In practice 90 per cent of Communists were ethnic Chinese.

The civilian supporters' network was called the Min Yuen or Masses Movement, and included people well placed to gather intelligence such as clerks and waiters working in offices or clubs used by the habitually indiscreet British. The Communist Central Executive controlled the entire structure through a network of political commissars and political cells. Chin Peng agreed an overall strategy which would begin with attacks on British managers and 'collaborating' local overseers on isolated mines and plantations, as well as against government and police outposts in small towns and villages. The idea was to reveal the nullity of government power by exposing its inability to offer protection. It would also force the British to vacate the countryside in favour of the larger towns. Under Phase Two, in rural areas liberated from the British, the Min Yuen would be co-opted into the guerrilla force and prepared for Phase Three, an all-out assault on communications links and the major towns to force the British out of Malaya completely.

Until subsequent events in southern Iraq disabused them of the conceit, the British liked to congratulate themselves on their expertise in a softly-softly, hearts-and-minds approach to counter-insurgency warfare, and were inclined to sneer at the more robust 'cowboy' approach of the Americans.[11] Although part of the deeper class illusion of the British as Greeks to American Romans, this attitude was born of the success of the Malayan counter-insurgency and persisted into the early 2000s. The lessons of Malaya have been incorporated into current US and British counter-insurgency warfare doctrine, by among others generals David Petraeus and Rupert Smith, but this may only involve selectively raiding the past to justify the prescriptions of the present. Modern armies are obsessed with the military learning cycle, of learning from past 'best practice' and mistakes. The problem is which part of the past provides the lessons, something to be explored below.[12] Much hard fighting and coerced population transfers had to have occurred before hearts-and-minds warfare could ever be implemented. Moreover, there is a large silence over who the British may have learned from themselves, for the

Boer War was a very long time ago, even in the late 1940s. Fortified villages, the key element of British counter-insurgency tactics, had been pioneered by the Japanese occupiers, something the British never acknowledged – except, that is, for a district officer called Howe. 'The Japs put barbed wire around Titi and Pertang, garrisoned these towns with troops and made all Chinese of the locality live within the defended areas,' he observed. 'Could we not try the same idea?'[13]

On 14 June 1948 the head of the Malayan Security Service (MSS) reported to London: 'There is no immediate threat to internal security in Malaya although the position is constantly changing and is potentially dangerous.'[14] Seldom has an official assessment been proved wrong so swiftly. The tin-mining town of Sungei Siput in the state of Perak lay to the west of Malaya's central mountains. Twenty miles east of Sungei Siput was an isolated rubber plantation called the Elphil Estate, run by a British manager called Arthur Walker. For Walker, 16 June 1948 was a special day since he and his wife, who had been in Malaya for twenty years, were going on leave to England. Mrs Walker had already left for Sungei Siput to do some last-minute shopping, while Walker was busy with paperwork in the estate office. At around 8.30 a.m. three Chinese men rode up on bicycles, walked into the office saying 'Tabek, Tuan!' or 'Greetings, Sir!', shot Walker dead and then left the office, ignoring a large sum of money in the open safe. A terrified Indian clerk looked at one of the men who stared back and then contemptuously spat on the ground before cycling away. Ten miles east, twelve armed Chinese burst into the offices of Sungei Siput estate and tied up two British managers, one a twenty-one-year-old trainee called Christian. Both men were murdered, the first of ninety-nine planters killed in the Emergency.[15] One of the Chinese reassured a Malay clerk, 'Don't be afraid. We're only out for the Europeans and the running dogs,' a Maoist term covering collaborators of all kinds.[16] Ambushes on roads and railways rounded out what was to be the *modus operandi* of the 'bandits', the term the British initially alighted upon to delegitimize their opponents.

These events gave thirty-two-year-old Chinese Affairs Officer Robert Thompson a welcome escape from daily routine in Ipoh. Thompson set off for the Elphil Estate where Walker had been murdered, arriving just as a company of Gurkhas drove in. He then went on to the Sungei Siput

Estate, where he ate Christian's food, but could not bring himself to sleep in the murdered man's bed. While he drove home, more atrocities were occurring. At the Voules Estate in Johore, Communist terrorists (CTs) identified the Chinese headman, Ah Fung, demanding that he furnish them with fifty cents a week from every tapper on the estate. When Ah Fung refused he was tied to a tree and in full view of his wife and daughter had both his arms hacked off. A note reading 'Death to the Running Dogs' was pinned to his chest. Atrocities were not entirely one-sided. In December 1948 Scots Guards massacred at least twenty-four Chinese prisoners at Batang Kali, all allegedly shot while trying to escape in a miracle of marksmanship.[17]

Many of the planters blamed the outbreak on High Commissioner Sir Edward Gent, a liberal Whitehall mandarin who had not concealed his disdain for them. He had certainly been remiss in not believing their warnings, and the over-optimistic MSS assessment undoubtedly reflected his wishful thinking. The planters were so nervous that in Perak they began a sweepstake based on when, where and against whom the CTs would strike next within a given forty-eight-hour window.[18] Faced with an editorial in the influential *Straits Times* that told him 'Govern or Get Out', Gent declared a 'State of Emergency', the choice of words dictated by planters whose London-based insurers would not pay out in the case of civil wars, but who would cover losses due to civil disorders and riots. The insurance companies had withdrawn cover in Palestine from 1945 to 1948 and by 1949 were threatening to do the same in Malaya. The British were also loath to introduce martial law and relied instead on the March 1939 Emergency Powers (Colonial Defence) Order-in-Council, which granted governors extensive arbitrary powers to preserve public safety and order.

Police leave was cancelled and guns were handed out to the planters. The European population of around 12,000 soon bristled with weapons, which they had to deposit on entering the bar of the 'Spotted Dog', the nickname for the Selangor Club.[19] On paper it seemed an uneven contest between about 8,000 Communist guerrillas and over 10,000 full-time police, ultimately backed by 11,000 regular troops including Gurkhas, Seaforth Highlanders and the King's Own Yorkshire Light Infantry. In reality, more than half these were support troops, and there

were only about 4,000 combat effectives available for fighting in the
jungle. The main burden of the conflict was carried by the police force,
which swelled to around 70,000 men, the vast majority of them Malay
special constables.

The British were a fractious bunch, plagued by animosities old and
new. The planters believed that Gent's shortcomings were an expression
of policy emanating from the despised 'Socialist regime' in London. In
fact the Labour government's Commissioner-General for South-east
Asia, Malcolm MacDonald, urged London to recall Gent, who died on
4 July when the plane bearing him home suffered a mid-air collision as it
landed at Northolt airport outside London.[20] It took three months for
his successor to arrive. This was Sir Henry Gurney, an experienced colonial official who had served in Africa and Palestine, his practical understanding of terrorism there perhaps outweighing his ignorance of
Malaya. Not the least of his problems was that the security forces were
bitterly divided between officers who had fled the Japanese occupation
and those who had stayed and had been interned under terrible circumstances. There were tensions between the Police Commissioner, the
Criminal Investigation Department (CID) and the tiny Special Branch,
which functioned as an intelligence-gathering agency. London-based
MI5 also had a local presence.

Although the Communists launched raids on isolated police stations,
their preferred targets were the planters who ran rubber estates, which
ranged from vast 14,000-acre enterprises, owned by London-based
firms, down to more humble affairs consisting of a thousand acres
owned by absentee Chinese. American mining operators were left alone,
not least because they were formidably well armed. The rubber planters
and their families lived in bungalows at the heart of their estates, places
sometimes so isolated that three-week-old copies of the London *Times*
were prized. They were a tough lot, many of them having survived
internment by the Japanese before reverting to their lonely lives where
the nearest neighbour was five or ten miles away. Whether they deserved
the contempt visited on them in the stories of Somerset Maugham is
debatable, but bridge, golf and whisky sodas (*stengahs*) played a major
part in their lives, as did the *amahs*, boys, *syces* and *tukan ayers* who
catered to their families' needs.[21] Their women, 'mems', who went by

nicknames like Billy or Tommy, were often as adept with a Bren gun or grenades as their husbands. Planters learned to vary their routine as they ventured out to inspect the native men and women harvesting white sap oozing from spiral cuts in the trees, or when and where they sat down to lunch, lest a grenade fly through the window. Their sleep was periodically interrupted by bursts of gunfire from the pitch-black jungle beyond their homes.

As a former RAF officer attached to Orde Wingate's Chindits, Robert Thompson was fertile in schemes to protect the planters. Bachelors were under special stress, so Thompson organized 'sleep with planters parties', whereby three or four male companions would drive out to the estates at dusk to provide additional firepower through the night.[22] Major-General Charles Boucher, GOC Malaya, asked Thompson to organize an irregular 'Ferret Force', in which he and two others led company-strength patrols into the jungle to fight the CTs on their own turf. Dyak tribesmen from Borneo and Ibans from Sarawak were brought in to assist as trackers, with the black tattoos on the thumbs of the older Dyaks indicating success as head-hunters. The Ferret Force had some limited successes against the enemy, certainly more than the easily evaded large-scale military sweeps organized by the army.

Luck played its part in the early death of Lau Yew, Chin Peng's right-hand man. Former navy stoker Police Superintendent Bill 'Two-Gun' Stafford, so called because he carried a revolver under each armpit, learned from his barber-informant in Kuala Lumpur that the Communists were to hold a meeting in a village south of the capital. Stafford and a team of Chinese detectives lay in wait, but were spotted by three men who exited a hut firing wildly. Two of them were shot dead and the third mortally wounded. After identifying the body of Lau Yew, Stafford and his men handcuffed five women, including Lau Yew's wife. Attacked in turn by a large number of insurgents, Stafford earned his Chinese nickname 'Iron Broom' by charging the attackers shouting 'Here come the Gurkhas!' The Communists fled rather than confront the deadly little Nepalese, who were not in fact present. Stafford was also responsible for a huge haul of Communist weapons, acting on a tip-off from an informer eager for the reward posted for every gun or bullet. The two men met in the back row of a dingy cinema showing a

Tarzan movie. The next night Stafford and four men went to a lonely spot near the village of Karang, where after strenuous digging they unearthed a cache which included dozens of machine guns, 237 rifles and 10,000 rounds of ammunition. The informer was due M$100,000 for this haul, but eventually settled for M$60,000. Stafford stoutly refused an offer of a share in the proceeds.

Gurney and Briggs

Army sweeps through the jungle commonly failed to find the enemy, and when they did the CTs normally evaded attempts to surround them. Some of the most withering criticism of the role of the British army came from Brigadier 'Mad Mike' Calvert of the newly re-formed SAS, which the Labour government had disbanded in October 1945. After a five-month inspection of Malaya in 1950 he wrote that the army was 'making a lot of noise, but achieving very little'. His efforts to inject small British and Rhodesian SAS units into the conflict collapsed when he suffered a major nervous breakdown in June 1951 and was sent home. Using the RAF to bomb suspect villages simply increased local support for the Communists. In any case, since the RAF was prohibited from bombing rubber plantations because of compensation claims, the guerrillas found them to be a useful hiding place. Thompson, who had been seconded to co-ordinate intelligence gathering in Kuala Lumpur, argued that 'the very size of an army foments political instability because political power inevitably rests with control of the army'.

The arrival of Gurney led to the adoption of a counter-insurgency strategy in which the military were subordinated to police work and politics. When Gurney and Boucher lobbied Whitehall for their respective strategies to defeat the insurgency, Gurney's approach won – although Boucher continued to act as though he were in overall command until recalled by Chief of the Imperial General Staff Field Marshal 'Bill' Slim. Apart from relying on Thompson, Gurney made further key personnel changes which were important to the outcome of the Emergency long before Gerald Templer arrived on the scene as dynamic wonder-worker.[23] The ineffectual Police Commissioner, Harold Langworthy, was replaced by Colonel Nicol Gray, former head of the Palestine Police. Among the established practices Gray encountered on arrival in Malaya was a police communications system which shut down every night after 6.30 p.m. until the next morning, and which closed from lunchtime on Saturday until Monday morning.

Gray was a tall Scot who had been chief instructor at a Royal Marines training base before leading commando operations after D-Day.[24] He recruited hundreds of his former subordinates, in particular sergeants accustomed to using boots and rifle butts on Arabs and Jews. The journalist Harry Miller was an eyewitness to 'a British sergeant encouraging a heavy-booted policeman to treat a suspect like a football. The young Chinese was kicked all round the room until a threat to report this treatment to headquarters brought the game to a stop.'[25] Promoted to the rank of lieutenant, these 'Palestinians' were resented by the already rancorous British police in Malaya, but they played an important role in training over 40,000 special constables for static guard duties on isolated plantations. Gray was not popular among his subordinates, not least because he ordered them to take greater risks, including driving out on lonely roads in unarmoured trucks, daring the Communists to ambush them. On its first trial run this resulted in the loss of sixteen police dead and nine wounded. Others were sent out on patrol in what his critics called 'jungle-bashing', which brought him into conflict with Boucher until the General was recalled.

The second key appointment was Lieutenant-General Sir Harold Briggs, at the age of fifty-five already a couple of years into retirement after a distinguished wartime career in the Indian Army that had culminated in his appointment as commander-in-chief Burma. Briggs was persuaded to come to Malaya for eighteen months as director of operations. The aim of his appointment was that he should co-ordinate army and police counter-insurgency operations, although Briggs had no executive control over either service. His Directive Number 1 established a Federal War Council, replicated at state, settlement and district levels. These co-ordinated all branches of government, police and military activity.[26] Some twenty months into the insurgency the government also established a Malaya Committee in London. Briggs – together with Thompson, who was transferred to his staff – had the job of converting Gurney's views on how to win this war into a plan of operations, which they delivered in June 1950. Its full title was 'Federation Plan for the Elimination of the Communist Organisation and Armed Forces in Malaya'. Based on what the British had earlier essayed in Burma in the 1930s, the gist was to concentrate and control the rural Chinese to force their armed comrades to seek supplies in British killing grounds. The army were divided into small units assigned to local areas, with a larger strike force to take on main Communist units.

Chinese who had recently immigrated and who were suspected of Communist sympathies could be despatched to China under Regulation 17C of November 1948. Around 12,000 of them were deported. 17D permitted the collective removal and detention of all inhabitants of a proscribed area, while 17E and F licensed compulsory eviction and forced resettlement of entire villages, which were then burned down. A series of Emergency Regulations issued in July 1950 greatly extended the powers of the police, who became the main instrument for applying pressure on the Communist insurgency. The death penalty was imposed on anyone convicted of terrorism or aiding and abetting it, suspects could be detained without trial for up to two years and searches required no warrants. The Malayan Security Service had proved a broken reed, its end accelerated after it was reported to the visiting head of MI5, Sir Percy Sillitoe, who had started his career as a Glasgow policeman, that the head of the MSS had referred to him as 'a Glasgow corner boy'. After the MSS had been abolished, the onus of combating the insurgency devolved on Special Branch, which in 1952 was separated from the CID. Old-fashioned Special Branch officers with their intuitive 'nose' for villainy are the real but unsung heroes of every war the British have fought with insurgents and terrorists, not least in Northern Ireland and in the present against Islamists.

One of their prime tasks was to identify the enemy's order of battle and the relationships between the Communist Party, the Malayan People's Anti-British Army and the civilian Min Yuen support network. Getting an overall picture was very difficult since the Communists relied upon self-contained cells. All of this data was combined with known kills and plotted with the aid of coloured pins on large maps to make sense of a bewildering kaleidoscope of events. One major source was intercepted messages written in minute Chinese characters on rolled rice paper, carried either by couriers or left in jungle dead drops, interpreted and collated in the Special Branch headquarters situated on the outskirts of Kuala Lumpur. Another key location was a complex of buildings known as the Holding Centre (or White House), where captured or surrendered terrorists were taken for interrogation in rooms equipped with listening devices and two-way mirrors. Since few British Special Branch officers spoke China's Mandarin lingua franca and even fewer the Cantonese or Hokkien dialects, the questions were posed by Chinese policemen, or terrorists who had already been turned. There was less brutality and more emphasis on psychologically overwhelming a detainee with information about his or her own life. A system of financial rewards was designed to induce people to betray the whereabouts of CTs, with up to M$250,000 (£29,000) offered for Chin Peng himself, the reward halved if the terrorist was brought in dead. CT informers were paid only half the rewards in a carefully calibrated system of inducements designed to avoid seeming to rewarding the enemy. A nationwide identity-card scheme was introduced, based on a model pioneered by the Japanese, involving photographs and thumbprints, so effective that the CTs assassinated eleven Chinese commercial photographers.[27]

The guerrillas depended on ordinary villagers to provide them with food and intelligence, which was either freely given or extorted by acts of exemplary brutality such as hacking off a child's arms. The Chinese squatters were the most vulnerable to this extortion, although the Chinese business community also sullenly paid the equivalent of protection money. The principal aim of the Briggs Plan was to protect the population in a fashion which isolated the insurgents, forcing them into deep jungle camps where they would compel the aboriginals to grow food. Briggs moved 600,000 Chinese squatters into a network of resettlement areas on agricultural land provided by the Malay sultans. The army established headquarters in towns and villages in areas plagued by guerrillas, with smaller outposts on the fringes of the jungle. The resettlement areas were heavily fortified, with rings of barbed wire and searchlights, but also with electricity and fresh water from standpipes. A single entrance facilitated close monitoring of the population's movements. Each family would receive an 800-square-yard plot within the perimeter on which to build a house, together with a two-acre field cleared from the jungle beyond. Cash payments and food would tide them over the five or six months before their own crops could be harvested. Every village was supposed to have a police post, health clinic and school, all supervised by 'European' camp officers, many of them young idealists drawn from Australia and New Zealand.

British soldiers had the delicate task of transferring complete village populations from their existing homes to these new locations. The entire operation was carried out swiftly, and by mid-1951 a total of 423,000 Chinese had been placed in 410 resettlements. Although there were a few model settlements, exploited for propaganda purposes, many of them were wretched and squalid. A Chinese doctor married to a Special Branch policeman wrote, 'The dirt road was a red gash across the jungle. There at the fetid edge of a mangrove swamp, the barbed wire manned by a police post, was the "new village", spreading itself into the swamp. Four hundred beings, including children, foot-deep in brackish mud . . . there was no clean water anywhere.'[28] Life within these villages was so monotonous that at least one captured female terrorist said that 'I saw my life stretching out interminably, a drab and dreary existence, until I became too old to work and had to depend on others to look after me. I hated the thought of it.'[29] While the British remained in overall charge, new village councils were elected with the power to levy modest local taxes. A conspicuously mishandled part of this programme involved the parallel resettlement of many of the aboriginal mountain peoples who had acted as guides and trackers for the MPAJA during the war. Moving them to the plains and denying them their customary forest diet proved disastrous, and 8,000 of them succumbed to disease or lost the will to live. When the MPC retreated to deep jungle, they found the residual aboriginals more than willing to act as scouts.[30]

Resettlement was part of a wider effort to thwart Mao's dictum that the guerrilla fish should swim in the popular sea, forcing them to come looking for supplies in areas where the security forces had an advantage. A restricted-goods policy ensured that there had to be precise records of each purchase and sale of rice, or such goods as the paper and printing materials the CTs needed for their own propaganda. Other measures included hampering the circulation of uncooked or tinned foods by dispensing only punctured tins and rice that had already been boiled. In the case of those new villages which functioned as dormitories for plantation workforces, tappers had to return for communal meals rather than taking ingredients for lunch out amid the rubber trees. This 'food-denial operation' forced the guerrillas to cultivate their own food crops, which were vulnerable to herbicides sprayed by the RAF, until the Communists learned how to deceive through irregular planting patterns. Police and troops became adept at spotting how food was smuggled, dismantling bicycles that might have rice concealed in the frame or handlebars, and searching those whose bulky clothing might conceal bags of food.

The British also sought to divide the Communists by exploiting internal ideological and strategic fissures and by encouraging defectors. When Malacca political commissar Shao Liu criticized the leadership for embarking on revolutionary violence without having secured the support of Malaya's three major races, he was called to account for 'deviationism' and put under surveillance. When he continued to criticize the leadership, Chin Peng ordered his execution along with his wife and three closest supporters. Lam Swee, a trade unionist who had joined the insurgents as a political commissar in the state of Johore, was angered by the disparity between the rigours and risks facing fighters in jungle encampments and the high life enjoyed by members of the Communist Politburo, who had three square meals a day and kept mistresses at their base near Mentakab. After a gruelling six-week trek to what was supposed to be a new base, Lam Swee and forty men were refused food and money by the local political commissar, who Lam Swee knew possessed M$2,000 in cash. After the Politburo learned of a meeting between Lam Swee and his platoon leaders at which the Central Committee was heavily criticized, one platoon commander was shot and Lam Swee was stripped of his rank and weapons and arrested. Fearing that he was about to be shot, he fled and surrendered himself at a police station. His capture was a major triumph for the British.

Such individual stories of dissent, hypocrisy and betrayal were grist to the men running British psychological warfare operations, who got Lam Swee to write a tract called *My Accusation*, copies of which were air-dropped into the jungle. One key player was C. C. Too, a thirty-year-old Malayan Chinese. He grasped that, since the object was to encourage CT defection, depicting them as hateful adversaries was counter-productive. Instead he exploited the personal animosities within CT ranks, in particular those arising from sexual frustration. During the Emergency the British dropped 500 million leaflets into the jungle, all written in the languages of the insurgents, or using comic-style graphics for the illiterate. About 10,000 were showered down on each square on a map. Some of them contained images of insurgents who had been killed by the British, posing the question whether anyone wished to share this grisly fate. But others had photographs of the mistresses of the Communist leadership, which was especially effective since the soldiers in the camps were supposed to abjure sexual relations with female comrades on pain of death. Lam Swee ghosted a letter, allegedly for an illiterate surrendered terrorist, which read: 'Comrades, I surrendered after my commanding officer had stolen my girl friend. The officer was not only well fed but he had girl friends whenever he wanted. Have you any girl friend? The upper ranks can make love in their huts, but if you want to find a lady friend then you have to wait until there is one left over from the upper ranks.'[31] The issue demoralized many CTs, with married comrades surrendering to be reunited with their wives and children, or young men fleeing to experience a normal sex life. Most of the printed propaganda material involved photos of surrendered terrorists in rude health, or copies of personal letters in which a former comrade, parent or spouse urged surrender. Some leaflets mentioned a named individual fighter, blinded in battle, with a commissar poised behind him ready to finish off the unfortunate with a knife. One leaflet, depicting a happy baby, was targeted at a pregnant Communist fighter, Lim Yook Lee, with the wording 'How safe and comfortable is this baby in a government maternity hospital.'[32] Starting in late 1949, there were also safe-conduct passes for defectors, signed by the High Commissioner, which carefully avoided the word 'surrender' in favour of the more anodyne 'coming out' to diminish the loss of face involved.

Terrorists who surrendered found themselves housed alongside captured Min Yuen operatives in the Academy of Peace and Tranquillity at Taiping racecourse. This was run by George Rotheray, a Malay Civil Service official. The Hok Uens or 'students' could learn a trade, play sports or cultivate allotments. The prototypes for this experiment were

Wilton Park, where captured German officers had been comfortably interned amid concealed microphones to capture their every word, and Macronissos in Greece where captured Communists were prepared for service in the Greek army. The guiding philosophy was that the devil made work for idle hands, a principle evident in contemporary efforts at rehabilitating Islamist extremists in Indonesia and Saudi Arabia. The apparent freedom enjoyed by the inmates was designed to prevent the dominance that hard-core activists exert inside regular detention facilities and prisons. The Taiping Academy resembled a modern open jail, with minimal security arrangements and opportunities for the inmates to learn a useful trade and to work outside under daily licence at such trades as hairdresser or mechanic. Inside there were such recreational facilities as a cinema (American Westerns were popular), a radio which could be tuned to Beijing and opportunities to play badminton and basketball.[33]

These measures were combined with military operations that sought to drive the Communist leadership over the border with Thailand. Although in the long run these combined policies would succeed, in 1951 the outlook for the British looked bleak. By then 3,000 men, women and children had been killed, the death toll including a planter's wife and their two-year-old child. The CTs also killed Sir Henry Gurney, ironically after he had tendered his resignation from frustration at the pace of the counter-insurgency. One weekend in October, Gurney and his wife Florence set off towards the hill resort of Fraser's Hill in a three-vehicle convoy, but did so in the official Rolls-Royce flying the Union Jack. As they slowly negotiated a climbing S-bend, they were ambushed by thirty-eight guerrillas lying in wait for a troop convoy. The lead jeep and the Rolls were hit by small-arms fire and Gurney decided to get out of his car to draw fire away from his wife. He was mortally wounded almost immediately. The Rolls was hit by thirty-five bullets, but Lady Gurney and Sir Henry's secretary survived by crouching down on the floor.

Gurney had made a significant contribution to the future success of counter-insurgency operations, not just with the new villages, but with a Malayan Chinese Association, which co-opted wealthy businessmen to the government side, and a Provident Fund for employees of all races. He had also forced the Communists to divert fighters into helping grow food deep in the jungle, while their combatant forces carried out a more selective range of attacks. All of this was evident from the October 1951 Resolutions in which the Communists acknowledged the effects of British activity. Insurgent attacks declined from 506 a month in 1951 to 295 in July 1952 and 198 in September.[34] Gurney's chief failure was not to put Briggs in overall command of military and police operations, something Briggs recommended to the new Prime Minister Winston Churchill before he himself retired to Britain with broken health.

The Tiger Years

The idea of fusing civil and military functions appealed to both Churchill and his new Colonial Secretary, Oliver Lyttelton, who on a flying visit to Malaya rapidly decided to dispense with the police chief, Nicol Gray, and William Jenkin, the head of Special Branch, who by this stage were no longer on speaking terms and had indicated a wish to retire. In London, Churchill and Lyttelton tried to find a general who would combine civil and military power as the next high commissioner. They consulted Field Marshal Montgomery, who sent Lyttelton a terse note:

> Dear Lyttelton,
> Malaya
> We must have a plan.
> Secondly we must have a man.
> When we have a plan and a man, we shall succeed; not otherwise.
> Yours sincerely
> Montgomery (F.M.)

Lyttelton commented, 'I may, perhaps without undue conceit, say that this had occurred to me.'[35]

They tried Brian Robertson in Suez, who declined a further overseas post so late in his career, and then Field Marshal Slim, who said he was too old, before alighting on fifty-four-year-old General Sir Gerald Templer. Templer was of Northern Irish ancestry, with a background in staff work and intelligence. His back had been broken in Italy by debris from a truck that left the road to avoid a collision with his jeep and ran over a mine. He was an energetic martinet, with a habit of poking interlocutors in the chest or stomach with his cane. His colourful language was translated with care by his Chinese interpreters. Thus 'You bastards' became 'His Excellency informs you that he knows that none of your fathers and mothers were married when you were born.' He came to be known as the 'Tiger of Malaya', a title previously enjoyed by Japan's General Yamashita, who had inflicted the greatest ever defeat on the British when he conquered Malaya and Singapore in 1942.

Summoned by Churchill to a summit in Canada, Templer eventually gained audience with the Prime Minister and the Defence Secretary Field Marshal Alexander at one in the morning. Churchill had been drinking and was in a lachrymose mood. Putting his hand on the General's knee, he promised: 'You must have power – absolute power – civil power and military power. I will see that you get it. And when you've got it, grasp it – grasp it firmly. And then never use it. Be cunning – very cunning. That's what you've got to be!' After that Churchill retired, making reference to Montgomery's terse note by saying, 'Well, Alex, there we are. We've found a man.'[36]

Indeed. Templer was given political authority as high commissioner and effective control of the police and all services of the armed forces as director of operations. No British soldier since Oliver Cromwell had enjoyed such extensive powers. He had spent virtually his whole military career in intelligence, reaching the rank of director of military intelligence, but his more recent experience had been in nation-building as the head of the military government in the British Zone in Germany. During this time he had acquired notoriety for sacking the Oberbürgermeister of Cologne, Konrad Adenauer, for being too old for the job, thereby launching Adenauer's meteoric career to become chancellor of Germany. That aside, Templer was a wise, intelligent and humane administrator.

His strategy was to build a unified Malaya, following Whitehall's line of promising its peoples independence once the insurgency had been defeated. It may have been he who decided to abandon calling the enemy 'bandits' in favour of 'Communist terrorists'. This served to locate the war in Malaya in a broader Cold War context. Talk of Communists would have greater purchase on American audiences, who could not otherwise comprehend why so much state power was being directed at mere 'bandits'.[37] Although Templer was unaware of it, his appointment coincided with a change in strategy by his opponents. In October 1951 the Communist Central Committee 'resolved' that indiscriminate terror was counter-productive, and that violence should be confined to such symbolic targets as British officials and the security forces.[38]

Ensconced in the mock-Tudor King's House in Kuala Lumpur, Templer refined the legacy of Harold Briggs, rather than doing anything startlingly new. He brought charisma and a brisk clip to his new job. Emulating Churchill's notorious 'Action this Day' memos, he sent out 'Red Minutes', to which he expected answers and solutions by the end of the day. From the start Templer realized that the Emergency was not going to be resolved by military means alone. 'The shooting side of the business is only 25% of the trouble and the other 75% lies in getting the people of this country behind us,' he wrote in 1952.[39] Captured terrorists were better than dead terrorists since they had valuable information.

There was a clean sweep at the top: Major-General Hugh Stockwell, with vast experience in Burma and Palestine, came in as GOC Malaya; a senior Metropolitan Police officer, Sir Arthur Young, was brought in to civilianize the police; and Jack Morton was made director of intelligence, with Guy Madoc as head of a separate Special Branch. C. C. Too was retained and backed fully. Hugh Carlton Greene, a wartime propagandist and future director-general of the BBC, was appointed to run information warfare from the same complex which housed Special Branch, convenient for getting his hands on turned CTs.[40] The US Consul-General was an *ex officio* member of the British Defence Co-ordination Committee, and received regular briefings from Special Branch. Templer told him that 'If I have anyone who can't work with the Americans I'll fire him.' Visiting US Aid Survey Missions also satisfied British requests for such things as radios, outboard motors, shotguns, armour plate, barbed wire and Chinese interpreters.[41]

Templer believed in the value of seeing conditions on the ground. To that end, during the twenty-eight months he spent in Malaya he undertook 122 tours of the country, covering 30,000 miles by air and 21,000 by road. Each tour involved multiple stops, with the General firing sharp questions at officials and listening to the locals, whether villagers or planters. He made it clear from the outset that he was capable of acting ruthlessly. Almost as he arrived a dozen people, engineers and policemen, were killed in an ambush at Tanjong Malim, including Assistant District Officer Michael Codner, renowned as one of the men who had successfully fled German captivity in the Wooden Horse escape. Templer descended on the town, where he harangued the inhabitants for cowardice in allowing the Communists to operate in their vicinity. 'This is going to stop,' he declared. 'It does not amuse me to punish innocent people, but many of you are not innocent. You have information which you are too cowardly to give.'[42] He then stripped Tanjong Malim of its status as an administrative capital, which hit the townspeople in their wallets, and halved the rice ration. He also imposed a twenty-two-hour curfew policed by 3,500 guards covering a double barbed-wire fence, with fifteen watchtowers and powerful perimeter lighting. The villagers were also required to complete confidential forms giving information on Communist suspects and sympathizers. The first batch was transported in sealed boxes to King's House, where Templer read them himself, passing the highlights to Special Branch. The forms were then destroyed to preserve anonymity.

    He and his staff endeavoured to reduce the ethnic tensions which underlay the Emergency. One problem was that the police were predominantly ethnic Malay, partly because Chinese families thought the rank of humble constable was beneath them. As the Chinese proverb goes, good men do not become soldiers, any more than good iron is used to make nails. Chinese businessmen were encouraged to subsidize police recruits. An essentially paramilitary police force was renamed a 'service', and its badge redesigned to include two clasped hands. The resettlement areas were renamed new villages, with all the connotations of a fresh start, and their amenities were constantly improved. Voluntary associations were encouraged to flourish, with Templer taking a particular interest in the Boy Scouts. His redoubtable wife Peggie threw herself into voluntary work and learned enough rudimentary Malay to broadcast in it. She also played a part in popularizing Women's Institutes to help form an indigenous multi-ethnic middle class, with its own direct experience of democratic organization.[43] Together with the Girl Guides and Red Cross, the WI was important in making younger women aware of wider social obligations than their mothers had accepted. Lady Templer also threw open King's House to everyone from select groups of Malay villagers to aboriginal headmen, who delighted in eating bars of chocolate with the paper and foil wrapping still on.

Templer set the tone at King's House in eradicating instances of petty racist snobbery, becoming the first High Commissioner to shake hands with his own domestic servants, with whom he also danced the conga on special occasions. In a speech to Kuala Lumpur's Rotarians, he made it clear that he had little time for the lotus life of many European colonists. 'You can see today how the Communists work. They seldom go to the races. They seldom go to dinner parties or cocktail parties. And they don't play golf.' One St George's Day, even the Sultan of Selangor found himself barred from celebrations at the Lake Club, of which he was the landlord rather than a member. Templer summoned the Club's committee and read the riot act, pointing out that the British army in Malaya was a multiracial force including Africans from Nyasaland, Gurkhas, Indians and Fijians, not to speak of Australians, New Zealanders and white Rhodesian SAS men, and threatened to close down the Club. In a major address to the Chamber of Commerce, Templer stressed the responsibilities of European colonizers:

> The British community as citizens of a leading democratic country have a special responsibility for leadership and example . . . Europeans must learn to see themselves not just as transients without roots in Malaya but as part of a tradition of partnership between Britain and Malaya which has endured in the past and will endure in the future. They must take an active part in the life of the local Malayan community. They must crusade against racial barriers or discrimination wherever they may be found. They must set an example in employer–employee relationships and business ethics. They must be prepared to devote some time to voluntary activities.[44]

Templer secured an invitation to the 1953 coronation of Queen Elizabeth II for the (Indian) General Secretary of the Plantation Workers Union and did not hesitate to bypass obstructive plantation managers by writing directly to their masters in the City of London if he felt that conditions and wages on their plantations were inadequate. Templer also had to guard against seeming to favour the Malay Chinese over the ethnic Malay majority, who reminded him of the superficially passive but secretly angry Arabs he had seen during his year in Palestine in the mid-1930s. Some Malays even sought relocation in dedicated resettlement in new villages to escape the squalor of their existing kampongs. One measure was to use government subsidies to alleviate the rapid drop in rubber prices following the Korean War boom. The army was in the vanguard of integrating the races, since in addition to an exclusively Malay regiment Templer established a multiracial Federation Regiment, with a surrogate Sandhurst in the shape of the Federation Military College.

Templer did not neglect the role of armed force in driving the Communists to the negotiating table. Its role should not be downplayed in the interests of highlighting softer forms of counter-terrorism based on protecting the population, just because this has become modish in contemporary Iraq or Afghanistan. The cardinal principle was that guerrillas were best placed to combat guerrillas, especially if the security services had use of Surrendered Enemy Personnel to guide them to the lairs of their former comrades. A specialist jungle warfare school was established in a former lunatic asylum at Kota Tinggi in 1953, where the new lunacy, as taught by a veteran of Force 136, included getting used to such delicacies as fried iguana and python soup. An Anti-Terrorist Operational Manual, colloquially called ATOM, fitted into every squaddie's sweat-soaked jungle greens.

Troops were expected to combine the qualities of a cat burglar, gangster and poacher. They learned to whisper when speaking – for sound carries in the jungle – and how to use the noise of heavy rainfall to get into position for ambushes. Companies of soldiers competed with one another to have the best score-card of kills, with a hundred dead referred to as a 'century', as in cricket. In an environment where visibility was a matter of yards and everyone ended up looking ragged after lengthy patrolling, the danger of friendly-fire incidents was constantly stressed. Ambushes remained an ever-present risk on the country's roads, but armoured trains secured the railways. There were amusing incidents. A

Green Howards company commander saw three heads ducking down 200 yards ahead alongside the road his convoy was travelling. He ordered his men to dismount and launched a flanking attack on what turned out to be monkeys sheltering in a hollow.[45]

Aircraft and Sikorski helicopters were used to resupply long-range patrols inserted into remote regions, and to boost army morale by rapidly evacuating casualties. A ten-minute helicopter flight covered the same distance as ten hours of walking through the jungle. Elite special forces, known as the Malayan Scouts but derived from the SAS, were dropped by parachute, or abseiled from helicopters to ambush CT squads. Six men would drop down in as many seconds. The use of former head-hunters from Sarawak led to a minor scandal when in 1952 the Communist *Daily Worker* published a photo of a Royal Marine commando proudly brandishing the severed heads of two terrorists, although they had been collected for identification purposes as a necessary alternative to hauling the bodies back to base through dense jungle.

In a departure from the Briggs strategy of systematically working south to north, Templer and General Stockwell decided to use mobile patrols to combat CTs everywhere, while larger formations held areas that from September 1953 onwards were designated 'white' after being cleared of terrorists through intelligence-driven operations. In the 'white' areas, copied from the Japanese 'Model Peace Zones' of wartime Malaya, curfews and other restrictions were lifted. They spread like ink blots and within them normal life was restored, so that children could play in village streets rather than being cooped up indoors, and young couples could go for meaningful walks.

By the end of 1953 around 7,000 MCP fighters had been killed or captured or had surrendered, although since their recruitment ran at an estimated 1,600 a year their numbers remained fairly stable at around 5,500. But they were decreasingly active. Incidents involving exchanges of gunfire declined from around 6,000 in 1950 to a thousand four years later. The last five years of the Emergency saw patrols chasing ever smaller groups of terrorists.[46] Anticipating the Americans' use of Agent Orange and the like in Vietnam, the British also used the chemical defoliant sodium trichloroacetate, manufactured by ICI, to clear roadside vegetation from which ambushes were mounted, and to spray clearings where the CTs grew their own food. The government claimed that these chemicals were non-toxic weedkillers or hormone plant agents.[47]

The British also made use of Voice aircraft, codenamed Loudmouth, as employed by the US in Korea. The Americans supplied Dakota aircraft, which contained a diesel generator that powered four large loudspeakers attached to the undercarriage. Since the tree canopy inhibited anti-aircraft fire, these planes could cruise at low altitudes along square boxes of airspace, booming out pre-recorded messages to the guerrillas below. Some recordings had the authoritative tones of the voice of God. After three days spent mastering the Mandarin pronunciation, Templer's voice announced from the sky: 'This is General Templer speaking. To all members of the Malayan Communist Party. You need not be afraid and you can surrender. This is my personal pledge to you. You will not be ill treated.' Others were messages from already turned terrorists, which were disconcertingly addressed to individuals. By 1955 all surrendered guerrillas claimed to have heard such messages.[48] Chinese-language leaflets read, 'Don't feed the Communist mad dogs: they will bite you,' illustrated with a Chinese farmer dropping a rice bowl as a fierce dog wearing a cap and Communist stars bit his behind. Flyers aimed at Communist fighters included some that showed the corpse of a Tamil called Ramesamy with the caption 'He was shot dead like an unwanted dog.' Broadcasts dwelled on former insurgents enjoying their New Year roast-duck meal after leaving the jungle.[49]

Chinese officers in Madoc's Special Branch won the intelligence war. They had the necessary cultural sensitivity and language skills. Locating enemy bases was one priority, sometimes achieved by planting homing devices in radios which were then sold on to dealers known to sell goods to people involved in the Min Yuen. Breaking into the Communist courier network was also important. Women were often preferred as couriers since the mainly male police force would be inhibited from giving them a thorough body search in societies where personal modesty is valued. A woman carrying a baby, often on loan from another Min Yuen member, was even better.

The women courier network became the special target of a young Chinese detective, Irene Lee. She was a woman of deadly purpose; the Communists had killed her detective husband. Special Branch got its initial break after three weeks spent idling amid the racks and shelves of Robinson's department store in Singapore watching Ah Soo, wife of the leader of Singapore's Communist protection squad. Ah Soo eventually met with another woman carrying an identical plastic shopping bag which the two surreptitiously exchanged. Irene Lee followed Ah Soo out of the store, poking a Beretta in her back to force her into an unmarked car which was cruising alongside the pavement. Back at Special Branch HQ a tin of Johnson's Baby Powder was found to contain a message concealed in its false bottom. Ah Soo was induced to reveal her next contact by threats that she would be photographed between two smiling policemen and that 50,000 printed copies would be dropped in the jungle.

At Yong Peng, where the second courier lived, Irene Lee persuaded her that she was a terrorist herself, inviting her out to celebrate a recent kill. The courier was abducted in a taxi and found herself in a room in Special Branch HQ, occupied by strange equipment, mirrors and two women in white coats. Terrified that she was going to be tortured, the courier readily confessed after they merely gave her a manicure and a perm. This confession took Irene Lee to a rubber plantation near Ipoh, whose workforce she joined as a humble tapper. For several weeks she observed a fellow worker called Chen Lee, known to be a member of the Min Yuen. She confronted him after luring him to a darkened taxi parked at a lonely spot, showing him the rice he had smuggled inside a bicycle pump and medicines he had buried on the edge of the jungle. She also said she had evidence that he had passed three cartridges to terrorists, at which point he broke, knowing that possession of guns or ammunition carried a mandatory death sentence.

Chen Lee's information brought Irene Lee near the end of the chain: a book store on Batu Road in Kuala Lumpur. Somehow Special Branch had to get inside, although the only entrance was via the front from a busy street and Min Yuen agents kept permanent watch on the shop. Special Branch set up an import-export company based on a pineapple estate and cannery in Johore. They acquired a large truck, which each week plied between Johore and Penang, stopping every Sunday in Kuala Lumpur before taking its load onward to Penang's docks. One Sunday morning the truck had a puncture outside the bookshop and the driver persuaded the Min Yuen agents to unload the cases of tinned pineapple to make it easier to jack the vehicle up. The driver, himself a Special Branch detective, sent off for bottles of Tiger beer, for it was hot work. The cases were piled up in front of the bookshop and in one of them Irene Lee waited to exit through a trap door. She picked the shop's lock, photographed the store's contents and was back inside the case before it was loaded back on to the vehicle. She had found two vital clues: the head courier was in Ipoh and it was a young woman.

In July 1952 Irene Lee and six other Special Branch officers sat in the FMS Bar in Ipoh, waiting for a team of local Special Branch officers who would conduct the arrest. Their goal was to crack open the cell structure the Communists relied on to commit terrorist attacks. Their target was Lee Meng, a twenty-four-year-old former teacher, the Communists' top courier who had previously organized multiple grenade attacks in the Ipoh area. These included attacks on the offices of a KMT newspaper, another which killed five civilians watching a Chinese circus, and another on a cinema audience. She had also attempted to kill leading members of the Malayan Chinese Association, including its president, Ten Cheng Lock. After Irene Lee had entered her apartment, Lee Meng (who used a false identity) claimed to be employed in a tin mine, and stuck to her well-rehearsed story for over two hours. The pace of questioning picked up, and ceased to be friendly, after Lee Meng faltered over details about her earlier life in Singapore. She could not recall the name of the store opposite her home, or of a coffee shop near the street where she claimed to have lived. A thorough search of her room revealed Communist documents in a false drawer inside an old Chinese desk. Lee Meng was arrested under her real name and sent to Taiping prison.

To conceal how she had been detected, Lee Meng was charged with possession of a hand grenade, an offence committed not in 1952 but some time between 1948 and 1951, for there was a photograph showing her holding one. Nine former terrorists testified that she was a guerrilla leader, responsible for grenade attacks. She was quickly dubbed 'The Grenade Girl' in the press. To prevent the intimidation of jurors, under the Emergency justice system two lay assessors sat with a British judge. The two non-European lay assessors found her not guilty, but the judge simply ordered a retrial, with a European acting as one of the assessors.

Lee Meng was found guilty and sentenced to hang. The case attracted worldwide publicity and her appeal eventually went before the Privy Council in London. The Hungarian government intervened, offering to release a British businessman convicted of spying in return for Lee Meng's life, and public pressure, in both Britain and Malaya, persuaded a reluctant Whitehall to authorize the swap, although it was technically the Sultan of Perak who reprieved her. She subsequently spent eleven years in jail before being deported to Communist China.[50]

The interception of messages translated into invaluable intelligence for the security forces. They were often written in lemon juice or soluble aspirin, which revealed the text with the application of heat. The messages used crude codes, so that 'the weather over here has been horrible for the past two months' referred to ongoing harassment by the security forces. After discovering messages concealed in a toothpaste tube and an evil-smelling durian fruit, Special Branch discovered the identity of a Min Yuen member in touch with Liew Kon Kim, the notorious 'Bearded Terror of Kajang'. Troops from the Suffolk Regiment surrounded a forest hut where Kim, his mistress and four comrades were snoozing after a hearty lunch. The Bearded Terror and his mistress were killed.

Other terrorists succumbed to the considerable bounty on offer for leading Communist cadres. The rewards offered for the top echelon of terrorist leaders led to the death of twenty-nine-year-old Shorty Kuk after he made the mistake of bragging to his comrades about the $200,000 reward posted on his head. A few days later, the driver of an express train was forced to stop by two men and a woman beside the track, who appeared to be waving a severed head. This turned out to belong to Shorty Tuk, terminally abbreviated. The trio, who were surrendering, also brought along two rucksacks filled with Communist documents, including Chin Peng's policy statements and military plans, and letters detailing tensions between the guerrillas and Min Yuen. Evidence of demoralization was confirmed when in the spring of 1953 Chin Peng decided to withdraw across the Thai border with eighty companions. This was dismal news after five years of fighting. Many of the remaining guerrilla groups were suffering from low morale, caused by an inadequate diet, jungle sores and bouts of malaria and dysentery. This was especially true of Communist Party intellectuals, whose previous existence had not prepared them for the leeches and massed insects of the jungle.

In 1954 three terrorists used aboriginal intermediaries to indicate that Osman China, the Party's chief propagandist, was ready to surrender with his group. With something like relief, Osman gave himself up to David Storrier, the Special Branch officer who went into the jungle to meet him. After the two men had established trust, Osman China offered to bring in his comrade Hor Leung, simply by writing to him. Hor Leung soon surrendered. The two top terrorists then agreed to bring in more of their comrades. After a fortnight eighteen men had surrendered and both men received large cash rewards.

Aboriginal intermediaries were rewarded too, stocking up on such goods as refrigerators and radios, without realizing that they needed electricity to power them. After 1957 the insurgency lost its anti-colonial aura with the establishment of an independent Malayan government under Tunku (Prince) Abdul Rahman, and by the late 1950s CT activity was confined to Kedah and Perak near the Thai border. One of the final major operations concerned a Communist leader called Siu Mah, who had led the group that killed Sir Henry Gurney. He and his group had been holed up in caves in limestone cliffs, severely short of food. Two of Siu Mah's three bodyguards sent to contact the Min Yuen for supplies instead surrendered to Special Branch, under a plan already hatched with a third bodyguard who remained with Siu Mah. A Chinese Special Branch officer, posing as a member of the Min Yuen, accompanied the two turncoats back to the caves. As they arrived they rang a bicycle bell twice, the signal for the remaining bodyguard to assassinate Siu Mah.

Life in the jungle involved contracting horizons, so that the main preoccupations were food and somewhere warm to sleep. The wider world was represented, if at all, by crackling voices on a radio. Early CT camps were large, with the days and nights packed with an orderly round of activity. Iron discipline prevailed, and commanders awarded merits and demerits for bravery or dozing off while mounting an ambush. As the larger formations gave way to small bands, the rigid discipline seemed gratingly petty-minded. Worse, the delusion of being a cog in a huge machine (present whenever messages came from the South Johore Regional Committee or the Press and Propaganda Unit) gave way to the reality of being like animals on the run, pursued not just by the British, but by Dyak head-hunters, fierce black tribesmen from Nyasaland with arrow-shaped initiation scars on their faces, and beefy Fijians, incredibly fleet of foot and prone to singing as they killed people.[51]

When Templer returned to Britain in 1954, he commented on a *Time* magazine report that 'the jungle had been stabilized' by saying, 'I'll shoot the bastard who says that.' His powers were divided between a civilian high commissioner, Donald MacGillivray – Templer's former deputy – and General Sir Geoffrey Bourne, who was firmly subordinated to the civilian leadership. Fears that Malaya had become a police state, as voiced in the House of Commons and by a pair of visiting academics from Oxford and Cambridge, proved groundless, though the two dons persisted in their accusations long after all the evidence had proved them false. In reality it was being turned into a democracy, as promises of independence drew nearer to being realized. The first task was to encourage elite Malays to co-operate with elite Chinese, which eventually gave birth to a multi-ethnic Alliance Party, led by the easy-going Tunku Abdul Rahman. From September 1953 onwards, members of the Alliance were encouraged to join the Executive Council to Malayanize responsibility for the conduct of the Emergency and to ready them for self-government. Chinese were also encouraged to join the Malay-dominated civil service, thereby discouraging their belief that they were a money-making class apart. In addition to co-opting elites, the British worked on the minds and hearts of Chinese farmers who felt ambivalent towards the Communist insurgents.

Although the British had declared that Malaya would achieve independence in twenty years, the timetable was repeatedly stretched. This was partly because the ethnic Malays wished to get into power quickly before the Chinese were fully mobilized politically. Elections to a federal legislature were held in 1955, with the Alliance scooping fifty-one of the Federal Council's fifty-two seats. Tunku Abdul Rahman became chief minister. That year the Tunku also had secret talks with Cheng Peng in the English School at Baling in an unsuccessful attempt to find a peace settlement. Peng's pride would not permit him to recognize that the Tunku represented a genuine national movement that was achieving independence. Partly as a result, when Malaya reached independence a multi-ethnic identity had not been forged and the Emergency still had three years to run until its formal end in July 1960.

When Britain and the Malaysian governments negotiated a new Malayan Federation between 1958 and 1962, some nationalists in both oil-rich Brunei and Sarawak preferred to take their bearings from Indonesia and the Philippines, which disputed the proposed extent of the Federation. The Royal Marines, Gurkhas and Green Jackets crushed the rebels in Brunei, which became an independent statelet of extraordinary wealth, while Sarawak eventually joined the Malaysian Federation. British policemen continued in a purely advisory capacity as the Malaysians themselves defeated the remaining Communist insurgents. In 1961 Chin Peng embarked on a life in exile in a special compound in Beijing, though he was eventually relocated to the southern Thai borderlands where he was still residing in 2012. He and the MCP only finally threw in the towel in 1989. In due course the 12,000 white planters and managers disappeared beneath successive waves of Malayanization.[52]

Malaya was not the first (Palestine) nor the last (Aden) counter-insurgency campaign waged by the British, but it was the most outstandingly successful. In January 1957 an official in Cyprus suggested to his superiors in the Colonial Office that it might be useful to compare and contrast counter-insurgency campaigns. The Security and Intelligence Adviser concurred in terms that echo drearily through the years and are as true today as they were then:

> I think that in the past we have failed to make proper use of previous experience. When the emergency was declared in Kenya, that Government set about its problems of detention, propaganda, rehabilitation, etc., as if they were new and strange phenomenons [sic]. Cyprus in turn did much the same thing. I do not think that this was the fault of either Government. It was merely that the experience gained in Malaya was nowhere summarised in a form available for reference. Cyprus, in turn, suffered from a lack of any systematic collation of experience gained in Kenya.

A couple of years later, a policeman who had served in Malaysia touched on a deeper problem: 'This secrecy and a traditional British distrust of general principles has caused much unnecessary trouble in the past. Lessons painfully learned in one campaign are forgotten, so that they must be learned again, or rigidly enforced in a different situation, where they no longer apply.'[53] The lesson, for our time, is that one should be careful to learn the lesson from the right phase of any earlier campaign, rather than imagining that what you prefer to do in the present worked like magic in the past. Was the Malayan Emergency really won through 'hearts and minds' and the herculean efforts of a charismatic general? Or did victory result from prior establishment of population and spatial dominance through military force, with hearts-and-minds warfare as a parenthesis before the democratic co-option of Chinese elites? Few of the basic conditions in Malaya were evident in Vietnam, whether under the French or later the US and its local ally, so its vaunted lessons were not really applicable. Not much of that 'military learning experience' seems replicable either in contemporary Afghanistan.[54] But before we get to Indochina, we need to visit a counter-insurgency war, in the Philippines, which with a few deft strokes the US undoubtedly won.

7. BY HUK OR BY CROOK:
THE PHILIPPINES

Peasant Rebels

When the Philippine Socialists and Communists merged in 1938, the Vice Chairman of the combined Party made one thing clear:

> We have no intention of importing the Russian brand of Communism into this situation. Russian conditions are utterly different . . . In fact, I feel free to severely criticise the Soviets. Indeed, we would welcome . . . twentieth century capitalism in the Philippines. If our workers could approximate the living conditions, status, and rights that . . . American workers have obtained under modern capitalism, we would be satisfied.[1]

That message was comprehensively forgotten when in 1950 a US Air Force colonel called Edward Lansdale landed in Manila to defeat what by then had become part of the global Communist threat to the Philippines. In fact he was about to become, on the basis of his work in the Philippines, America's leading expert on counter-insurgency warfare. His story is so extraordinary and paradigmatic that he is almost a signature theme for much of this book. But why was he in the Philippines at all?

Following the Japanese occupation of the Philippines in early 1942, Filipino ruling elites faced the unenviable choice of flight, resistance or collaboration. Most chose collaboration, while a tiny handful of resisters, 300 at most, fled outwards from the plain that dominates Central

Luzon to the Candaba Swamp, Mount Arayat or the Sierra Madre and Zimbales mountain ranges. They formed a guerrilla movement called the Hukbong Bayan Laban sa Hapon, or People's Anti-Japanese Army. In the original Tagalog, the predominant language in a country with over a hundred local tongues, this was shortened (as we have seen) to Hukbalahap or Huks, pronounced 'hooks'.

The Huks had their roots in several pre-war grassroots organizations, formed to defend the traditional rights of peasant tenant farmers on the central plains of Luzon. They wanted 'to get what was just if landlords were honourable and good men'. Like peasant movements throughout all periods of history almost everywhere, they were nostalgic for good old days when the bosses wore a familiar human face, or at least did not threaten to replace their labours with machines.[2] Their demands were modest: landlords should not take 50 per cent of the rice harvest or charge extortionate interest for loans of rice or cash needed to tide their tenants over the bad times. Landlords were also using land registration to snatch land from peasants who often had insecure or non-existent titles. They got away with this because of their intimately corrupt involvements with the regime in Manila, which meant that they could use the courts and the brutal Philippines Constabulary to suppress any peasant protests.

Many of the Huks were in their twenties and had witnessed Japanese brutality at first hand when their relatives were raped, tortured or shot. One in ten of them were women, although they normally acted as couriers, instructors and nurses rather than guerrilla fighters. Using weapons whose numbers increased with each hit on a Japanese post or patrol, and which they taught themselves to use, the Huks contested Japanese control of the countryside. It was a desperately cruel conflict. The Japanese used hooded informers to identify Huk sympathizers among the peasants; the Huks kidnapped, tried and shot local officials and policemen who collaborated with the occupiers.[3]

There was considerable overlap between the Huks and the Philippines Communist Party, but the Huks were primarily motivated by a 'Red Christ' vision of social justice and a visceral hatred of the occupiers, whereas the Communist leaders were aloof theoreticians who despised their own lower ranks as much as any *haciendero* viewing his peasants. Marxism was far too sophisticated a creed for poorly educated peasant fighters, many of them devout Christians and pro-American.[4] A putatively socialist Jesus meant more to them than Lenin or Stalin, let alone Mao Zedong.

In late summer of 1943, senior Filipino politicians were summoned to Tokyo to be congratulated on their draft constitution for an independent Philippines republic, a document commissioned by the Japanese commanders in Manila. This striking concession reflected mounting Japanese awareness of the extent to which US material and military might had tipped the strategic balance against them. They would trump US promises of independence for the Philippines, but there was one catch: Japanese Premier Hideki Tojo required the new republic to declare war on the US. After much agonizing, the politicians decided that the future wrath of the Americans was preferable to the immediate vengeance of the Japanese. While the elites grovelled, 10,000 Huks fought a hot war against the Japanese occupiers, observed rather than joined by a rival guerrilla force sponsored by the Americans, known as US Armed Forces Far East (USAFFE). While its watching brief was perfectly comprehensible, since it gathered valuable intelligence for MacArthur's forces, such fighting as it did do tended to be with the rival Huks, who refused to submit to US command.

Although powerful voices wanted to bypass the Philippines en route to Japan, MacArthur felt a debt of honour to a people he had been forced to abandon. Ignoring Japanese snipers and flanked by his media team, MacArthur waded through the surf in October 1944 as 160,000 US troops landed at Leyte. The Japanese under Tomoyuki Yamashita suffered colossal casualties in protracted battles to repel the invaders, as did the Filipinos, with 100,000 civilians slaughtered in the battle for Manila. The city was ruined, with 60 per cent of the housing destroyed by bombing, shelling and fire. According to Dwight Eisenhower, only Warsaw suffered more damage in the war. In the countryside, villages were burned, rice fields were maliciously flooded or sown with mines and unexploded ordnance, while the carcasses of carabao buffalo rotted.[5]

The existence of a government that had collaborated with the Japanese posed delicate problems for the US. Since the number of educated Filipinos capable of governing the country was modest, MacArthur decided that even collaborators were indispensable to post-war reconstruction and identified one of them, the Nationalist Party's Manuel Roxas, as a future president of the independent state the US had promised. Under this former army brigadier, Filipino judicial proceedings against collaborators were a desultory affair, with only 156 convictions in 5,000 cases before a general amnesty was issued three years after the war. This was pathetic, even by the general low standards of the times.

In contrast to such indulgence, the Americans endeavoured to disarm and demobilize the Huks, falsely portrayed as extreme Communists by the rival guerrillas of the USAFFE, who it should be recalled had not strained themselves to fight the Japanese. Hoping to obtain government pensions for veterans, the Huks naively provided the authorities with the names of their fighters. The lists led to arrests, or allowed landlords to blacklist or evict those listed. At Malolos in Bucalan, a USAFFE colonel named Adonias Maclang had 109 Huk fighters shot into a mass grave, in the presence of US Counter Intelligence Corps officers. The Americans rewarded Maclang by making him mayor of Malolos.[6]

While the Huks were disarmed or murdered, the USAFFE guerrillas were converted into a paramilitary Military Police, their wages paid from the budget of the Philippines Constabulary and given 5,000 machine guns by the Americans. They became a strongarm force, whose main role was to reimpose the authority of the large landowners on the peasants whose campaign for social justice resumed where it had been interrupted by war. The main demand was a 60:40 split in the rice harvest in the peasants' favour; a subsidiary demand was that they should not have to pay back rent covering three years of occupation to landlords who had fled to Manila the moment the Japanese appeared. Legal chicanery was employed to stop restive peasants from holding public meetings, which, when they happened, were broken up by Military Police in armoured cars armed with machine guns. An uprising might, just, have been averted had the political system functioned as a ventilator for pressures which many peasants likened to rice boiling over in a pan; but it was not to be.

The de facto Japanese Shogun Douglas MacArthur intoned that 'America buried imperialism here today' when the Philippine Republic was proclaimed on 4 July 1946, but this regime was scarcely an advertisement for self-determination in the Asia-Pacific region. Manuel Roxas and his Liberal Party won the April 1946 national elections and quickly ratified the Bell Trade Act, which prohibited the manufacture or sale of any products that might compete with US goods and required the Philippines constitution to grant US citizens and corporations untrammelled access to Philippine markets and natural resources. It also pegged the Filipino peso to the US dollar. How this could be construed as anything other than colonialism stripped of administrative costs is a mystery. The new Supreme Court rushed ratification of this treaty to avoid scrutiny, while false charges of fraud were employed to disqualify six elected Congressmen from the Democratic Alliance. This was a new party whose candidates included the charismatic Huk military commander Luis Taruc. Permanent US air and naval basing rights further compromised the country's sovereignty, with Roxas granting the US vast facilities at Clark Field and Subic Bay.[7]

Needless to say, the Huks reverted to armed struggle, once all efforts to disband them had failed. Much of Central Luzon, which had voted heavily against Roxas, rapidly resembled an occupied country. Military Police in armoured cars dominated the main roads, while squads of them imposed their control on the *barrios* (shanty towns) strung along the side lanes while going on marauding 'Huk Hunts'. This persuaded many former Huk supporters to go underground, with weapons they had retained or purchased from US servicemen. Younger people outraged by Roxas's farce of democracy joined them, together with those who sought vengeance for police abuses. The leaders of the Democratic Alliance, the Huks and the Communist Party jointly offered to broker a truce between the Military Police and the growing number of peasants who were resorting to armed self-defence. Their initiative failed after one of them, Juan Feleo, disappeared in August 1946 while under Military Police escort; his decapitated body was later found floating in the Pampanga River. Months of police strongarm tactics in the *barrios*, involving innocent people tortured or kidnapped and killed, led the much abused peasants to a revival of the wartime resistance movement, initially an essentially defensive campaign against their police oppressors.

The Roxas government responded with an iron fist, using artillery and dive bombers against *barrios* suspected of sheltering Huks. It deployed a police death squad named 'Nenita' under a commander called Napoleon Valeriano. The Nenitas had skull-and-crossbone insignia on their sleeves and on their banners, and lived down to their reputation as the 'Skull Squadron' by decapitating their prisoners. Detained Huk sympathizers were tortured with electric shocks and by a revival of the 'water cure' employed by the US Army when it suppressed the Filipino rebellion at the turn of the century. Suspects had water poured down their throats and their swollen stomachs were then jumped on by booted Nenitas. Many were then 'shot while trying to escape'. None of this found its way into reports by the chief of the US military intelligence branch in the Philippines, which treated the Huks as part of a Communist conspiracy. In March 1946 he reported:

> [The leaders of the Huks] have made their boast that once their membership reached 500,000 their revolution will start. Meanwhile, in the provinces of Pampagna, Nueva Ecija, Tarlac, Bulacan, and Pangasinan, they are establishing or have established a reign of terror. So ironclad is their grip and so feared is their power that the peasants dare not oppose them in many localities. On liberation, their members were about 50,000; sources now report some 150,000 tribute-paying members . . . [The Huks] are now organised into trigger men, castor oil boys, and just big strong . . . ruffians to keep the more meek in line.[8]

In fact, the Communist Party – whose members were to be found among unionized workers in Manila rather than in the countryside – said that 'it does not believe in the use of force and violence or in conspiracy as its methods to achieve its programme', which it sought to realize through constitutional means and the labour movement. The upper-class intellectuals and trade unionists who dominated the Party took a cooler view of things than simple peasants who were on the receiving end of government repression, and they did not alter this line until May 1948.

The Man with a Mouth Organ

Manuel Roxas died of a heart attack on 15 April 1948, while delivering a speech at Clark Air Force Base. Many Filipinos derived employment from the Americans, but 2,000 tenant farmers had been evicted to make way for the expansion of the base. It was so vast that Huk guerrillas commonly crossed the runways unhindered. Roxas's successor was another Liberal, Elpidio Quirino, who 'won' the shamelessly fraudulent elections of 1949. Wits remarked that even the birds and trees had voted. Like Roxas, his principal activity was embezzling US aid, but Quirino also made a show of seeking to negotiate with the Huks. The talks collapsed when Luis Taruc learned of a police conspiracy to murder him and Quirino reverted to naked repression.

US policy towards the Philippines was overshadowed by the loss of China to Communism, which concentrated minds and injected a sense of urgency lest the vast archipelago go the same way. However, the greatly increased funds made available once Congress accepted the policy of containment were not disbursed as indiscriminately to the Philippine government as they were in Europe, and as they had been to Chiang Kai-shek's KMT. In the Philippines the US learned how to make aid grants dedicated to particular projects and contingent on the recipients delivering specific reforms.[9]

In Septembr 1950 Edward Lansdale arrived in the Philippines. He was born in 1908, the son of an automobile industry executive. After dropping out from UCLA, he drifted into the advertising industry in San Francisco, acquiring such clients as the Wells Fargo bank and Levi Strauss, manufacturer of the eponymous jeans. He had an ear for the catchy phrase and an eye for the striking image. In December 1941 Lansdale sought to reactivate the college student reservist commission he had won at UCLA, but was deemed unfit for active service. His high-level connections won him a billet at the Washington DC headquarters of the OSS.

He was put to work devising training courses. One exercise involved seeing how far a recruit would go in trying to knife a stranger, identified as a German agent, on the Manhattan subway. He also compiled detailed reports on foreign countries, based on the observations of travellers and academics. His involvement with the Philippines began when he interviewed an ichthyologist with extensive knowledge of the types of poisonous fish invading US troops might encounter around the archipelago. Long before Lansdale was posted to Manila, he insisted that his brother, who had served there, teach him local songs that he could then play on his ever-handy harmonica. While it is not entirely clear where Lansdale served in the last years of the war, he spent ten months in the Philippines from late 1945 to the summer of 1946, dealing with the complex aftermath of the Pacific conflict and reporting on the Huks.[10]

Lansdale persuaded his wife, with whom he was reunited while on leave, to bring their two sons to Manila, a city still in wartime ruins. Helen Lansdale detested life there and the two became estranged, with Lansdale striking up a close friendship with Pat Kelly, a vivacious Filipino journalist with whom he toured the remoter parts of the country. The quietly spoken Landsdale was also cultivating other relationships, whether with the oligarchs in the Malacañang Palace, or with raiding parties of Huk guerrillas across whose trails he loitered to strike up conversations in return for cigarettes. Even though at this stage the Americans were still invested with the aura of liberators, these acts of fraternization required strong nerves as well as an easy smile. Frustrated with army bureaucracy, Lansdale had himself transferred into the newly established US Air Force while retaining his job as an army press officer.

On returning to the States, the Lansdales separated. Bored in a teaching job on a base in Denver, he was rescued by being reassigned to the Office of Policy Coordination (OPC) in Washington, a covert organization created in 1948 at the urging of George Kennan to carry out psychological and paramilitary operations (a.k.a. dirty tricks). At first nominally independent, it was merged with the CIA in 1952. The OPC's director was Frank Wisner, a New York lawyer who had served with the OSS in Romania. The new group flourished as the Cold War intensified, growing from 302 personnel to nearly 3,000 in 1952, and its budget from $4.7 million in 1949 to $82 million in 1952, running covert operations in over fifty countries.[11]

After an initial period working on the Soviet desk, he persuaded his superiors that the Agency's Far East division needed his services more. After all, he knew about poisonous fish. Soon he was running seminars in Washington for Filipino army officers who had completed training courses elsewhere in the US, his object being to improve the capabilities of an army whose indiscriminate violence was swelling the ranks of the

Huk guerrillas. He eventually fastened on a visiting Filipino congress-man who had fought the Japanese in the USAFFE, finishing the war as a captain. This was Ramon Magsaysay, a former bus company mechanic and a big man, full of nervous energy. He had grown up in a hut made of bamboo and cogon grass, spending his youth milking water buffaloes and working his family's modest plot. The two men quickly realized that each could be very useful to the other, their common objective being the defeat of the Huk insurgency. Lansdale's superiors organized a lunch to take a closer look at Magsaysay, before the decision was taken to send a delegation to President Quirino to tell him to appoint Magsaysay as his secretary of defence instead of his own candidate, a notorious wartime collaborator called Teofilo Sison. Quirino also appointed Lansdale as his adviser on intelligence.[12]

Lansdale and his sidekick Lieutenant Charles 'Bo' Bohannan landed in Manila and took up residence in a two-storey bungalow on the city's outskirts in an area reserved for Americans, ringed with barbed wire and guarded by Filipino troops. Lansdale was treated with extraordinary deference by everyone from the US Ambassador and the general commanding the US Military Advisory Group (MAG) to President Quirino, who once interrupted a cabinet meeting rather than keep Lansdale waiting.

By this time 50,000 Filipino government troops and policemen were fighting around 15,000 Huk guerrillas, who operated amid a further million sympathizers. The centre of Huk activity was the mountainous areas of Central Luzon, known as Huklandia. There the Huks had their forest camps, linked to each other and the population of the village in the plains by a sophisticated courier system akin to the system developed by the CTs in Malaya, which made much use of girls. Lectures and communal songs were used to drill into recruits the 'Fundamental Spirit' guiding the movement and there was intensive training in weaponry and tactics. Women were not limited to support activities but were also recruited as combatants. Some of them married older male comrades in ceremonies where the newlyweds passed under an arch of guns, but did not for that reason cease to be fighters. In a very conservative Catholic country, people were fascinated by tales of Huk 'Amazons', some of whom insisted on putting on makeup before going into battle. It did the

Huk cause no harm that some of their female commanders, such as Remedios Gomez (a.k.a. the Joan of Arc of the Philippines) and Celia Mariano were strikingly beautiful.[13]

The main recruiting agent for the guerrillas was the brutality, corruption and ineptitude of a police force that daily heightened popular perception of gross social injustice. In the countryside it operated like a criminal gang, stealing at will, and in the cities even the traffic police regarded their job as a licence to extort bribes. In 1948 the US military commander in the Philippines reported to Chief of Staff Omar Bradley on a level of theft from his command that put even wartime Naples in the shade. Gasoline was stolen wholesale, trucks hijacked and goods thrown from moving trains to gangs of thieves. The leading black marketeers included the sons of the Mayor of Manila, the Chief of Police and the Secretary of Labour. When American investigators probed into a case of stolen army jeeps, the lead agent's young daughter was shot dead by policemen under the orders of the Mayor of San Luis, who also killed a US officer outside a supply depot.[14]

Lansdale and Magsaysay made improving the reputation of the security forces their first priority, with Magsaysay setting an example by being seen to live on his $500 a month ministerial salary, plus a smaller amount as chairman of Philippines Airlines. Magsaysay immediately took on the army's hopelessly corrupt system of promotion, rewarding combat merit over seniority and connections. In 1951 the Americans suspended all aid until Quirino dismissed the armed forces Chief of Staff, General Mariano Castañeda, and the Chief of Constabulary, General Alberto Ramos. Brutalization of the civilian population was diminished by setting up a system whereby peasants could send telegrams to Magsaysay himself at a very cheap rate, their complaints followed up with inflexible rigour. He also increased soldiers' pay so that they would no longer be obliged to steal in order to eat.[15]

The relationship between Lansdale and Magsaysay deepened when, fearing Huk assassins, Magsaysay sent his wife and three children away and moved into Lansdale's bungalow inside the 'country club', as Filipinos called the American quarter. The two men slept in separate single beds in the same room. The breakfast table became Magsaysay's surrogate office, so that all defence department business was conducted in this bungalow. Lansdale held parallel informal meetings with Filipino soldiers, with the deliberate intention of having these casual conversations overheard by the Defence Secretary. Some thought that the ferociously ambitious Magsaysay was merely Lansdale's creature – they called Lansdale 'Frank' and Bo Bohannan 'Stein' – and it was true that one of the Colonel's talents was to make his own ideas seem like someone else's, and another the capacity to seem invisible in any room where he was the dominant influence.[16]

Their relationship was so close that Lansdale claimed the two men were brothers, with Lansdale playing his harmonica to lull 'Monching' to a sleep often troubled by phantoms. Magsaysay sometimes woke, grabbed his rifle and stuffed his pockets with cartridges after nightmares about a Huk raid in November 1950 on his home town of Barrio Aglao, in which the Huks had killed twenty-two people, many hacked to pieces with bolo knives, in retaliation for the government's capture of virtually the entire Communist leadership in Manila. The relationship between the Filipino and the American was not always congenial and on one occasion, when they were travelling on a US internal flight, Lansdale knocked Magsaysay out for presuming to use a speech written by a Filipino aide instead of the one prepared by Lansdale.

Lansdale also believed in getting about to see conditions for himself, rather than relying on second- or third-hand reports or on experts who had never been to a Filipino *barrio*. He persuaded Magsaysay to undertake similar trips, sometimes even hitching lifts, with Lansdale in uniform and Magsaysay dressed like an American tourist. Magsaysay took note of everything from the tell-tale cardboard used by soldiers to resole worn-out boots to officers showing signs of debauchery, and cashiered those responsible. All units were also issued with cameras to photograph captured or killed Huks, which would be circulated to boost army morale.[17]

The dynamic duo's ultimate objective was to capitalize on Magsaysay's success in the counter-insurgency war to propel him to the Filipino presidency. Building Magsaysay into a heroic figure came naturally to Lansdale from his background in advertising, and a reformist Magsaysay presidency, which emphasized justice, would secure long-term US strategic and commercial interests. That it represented gross interference in the internal affairs of an independent country was undeniable, but Lansdale argued that the coming to power of a representative of the ambitious new middle classes was better for the average Filipino than the survival of a corrupt oligarchy in hock to powerful landowners. Was it a crime to order a polling station burned when the ballot papers it contained were all fakes? Or to organize counter-gangs against the electoral thuggery of President Quirino's brother Tony? Was it not fair enough to disseminate forged leaflets in which the Huk leadership enjoined sympathizers to boycott a presidential election? And so on. Lansdale was the consummate practitioner of the philosophy that the end justified the means.[18]

Night of the Vampires

As a veteran guerrilla himself, Magsaysay instructed his commanders to forget all they had been taught: 'Gentlemen, I know you all have graduated from military establishments here and in the United States. Now I am telling you to forget everything you were taught at Fort Leavenworth, Fort Benning, and the Academy [at West Point]. The Huks are fighting an unorthodox war. We are going to combat them in unorthodox ways. Whatever it was that hurt me as a guerrilla is what we are going to do now to the Huks.' They rather than the Philippine Communist Party were evidently the enemy. The Constabulary were brought under army control and large-scale operations were replaced by the constant pressure of smaller units.[19]

Lansdale made his own unorthodox contributions. One of his earliest suggestions was to introduce doctored ammunition and faulty hand grenades into the military supply system, knowing that soldiers sold such materials to the Huks. Lansdale claimed that this stopped once Huks were blown up with their own grenades or had rifles explode in their face.[20] It is a truism of revolutionary warfare that guerrillas command the night, while counter-insurgency troops dominate the day. The night was when the guerrillas ventured into populated areas, extorted levies of money or food, conducted kangaroo courts or proselytized their creed. Lansdale brought all the black arts of psychological warfare to bear on both the guerrillas and their civilian sympathizers. His favourite Filipino instruments were the 7th Battalion Combat Teams commanded by Colonel Napoleon Valeriano, once the leader of the notorious Skull Squadron. One of the teams, known as Force X, disguised themselves as Huk guerrillas carrying men supposedly wounded in a staged battle with police to get close to real Huk groups. Over a few weeks they killed over a hundred Huks, and induced two Huk units to shoot each other to pieces, each thinking the other was Force X. Lansdale also fitted Piper aircraft with Second World War-surplus naval loudhailers to broadcast messages to the Huks and their village sympathizers. As already noted, the content of these broadcasts could be unnervingly specific:

> You hiding down there. We see you. Yes, I mean you in Squadron 17. I mean you Commander Sol. I mean you, Juan Santos. And you Bulacan Boy. And you, Pepe and Ramon and Emiliano. Borro and Dario, Carmelo and Baby. We know all about you. We are coming to kill you. Stay there. And now I must go while our troops are coming to attack you. To our secret friend in your ranks I say thank you! Run and hide so you won't be killed. Sorry I can't call you by name but you know who I mean. Thank you and goodbye.[21]

This not only caused Squadron 17 to relocate in panic but also triggered a witch-hunt for the fictional 'friends' within their ranks who had revealed such information. Lansdale had the further bright idea of making the 'eye of god' an icon, based on the all-seeing Masonic eye on the US dollar bill. Once he had produced a suitably menacing version, Philippine army troops were instructed to sneak into villages at night and paint the all-seeing eye on walls. Villagers would awake to find it glaring at them, the shock multiplied by a profound peasant belief in evil spirits so widespread that even Huk guerrillas wore amulets to ward them off.

Building on the success of the 'eye of god' campaign, Lansdale exploited the notoriety of an old soothsayer called Ilocos Norte, who had accurately predicted the death of President Roxas. Taking the old man's name in vain, Lansdale had it rumoured that Norte had said that men with evil in their hearts would perish in the fangs of a local vampire called an *asuang*. One night soldiers seized the last man of a Huk column

village from a jungle trail, throttled him and made two pune-
neck before hanging him by his heels to drain off his blood.
In the morning the Huks came across the blanched body sprawled across
their trail and fled the area. Lansdale also did his best to curb indiscriminate killing. On one occasion he accompanied a unit which captured, killed and decapitated a Huk guerrilla. Seizing the head, Lansdale
began to ask it questions, to which, obviously enough, there were no
answers. He grew angrier and started slapping the head, until the Filipinos piped up: 'Colonel, Colonel, it is dead. It cannot talk to you.' Lansdale rounded on them: 'No, you stupid son of a bitch! Of course it can't!
But it could have, if you hadn't been so fucking stupid as to sever the
head from the body!' He threw the head to the ground.[22]

Feeding primitive fears and causing the Huks to doubt themselves
was only part of Lansdale's strategy. The other part was to encourage
Huk defectors and to win over the peasant population. Cash rewards
were used to encourage informants, while Huks were encouraged to give
up after Magsaysay promised a general amnesty for past crimes. Lansdale and Magsaysay were acutely aware that the peasants had turned to
violence because of a lack of land and justice. Justice was easier to provide: Magsaysay deputed military lawyers serving in the judge advocate's
department of the army to represent peasants *pro bono* in provincial
courts, which tipped the balance in a system previously weighted against
them. The Chinese business community, deeply grateful to Lansdale for
curtailing police extortion, was prevailed on to advance peasant farmers
affordable loans, further curtailing the power of the big landowners.
The land issue itself was addressed by a variant of the ancient Roman
system of military colonies, which became the template for an Economic
Development Corporation established in late 1950. Army units were
posted to remote areas of southerly Mindanao and encouraged to
develop agricultural plots which became their property once the conscripts had completed their term of service. Some of the plots were
reserved for captured or surrendered Huks and their sympathizers, who
found themselves farming alongside men of unimpeachable loyalty to
the government.

Many Huk prisoners did not want to become farmers, and vocational
training in such trades as carpentry or mechanics was laid on within

their detention camps. Attention was drawn to the fact that one of the trainees had tried to assassinate Magsaysay, symbolic of forgiveness of past sins to the truly repentant from the highest level.[23] Lansdale also attacked the high moral ground claimed by the Huks by publicizing the fate of babies abandoned when the Huks had to make a rapid retreat from a threatened camp. The plight of these 'Huklings' did much to discredit the Huk 'Amazons', whose neglect and abandonment of their young was underlined by photographs showing the children being tended by army nurses or by soldiers armed with milk bottles, and gazed on lovingly by Magsaysay's fetching daughter Teresita.[24]

Lansdale's larger aim of getting Magsaysay elected president required resolving one of the Huks' key recruiting grievances. In 1949 the Huks had used the slogan 'Your ballot isn't counted. Join us and use a gun to get a new government. It's the only way.' In fact one of Magsaysay's political associates had been tortured and murdered during that notorious election, and a picture of him cradling the mangled body was used when he subsequently bid for the presidency. As a preparatory step Lansdale determined to prevent fraud and intimidation in the elections of December 1951 – while still ensuring a favourable outcome – when a third of the seats in the Senate and many local elected posts were in play.[25] Summoning US experts to help him prevent electoral fraud Lansdale created a new National Movement for Free Elections to teach voters how to leave clear thumbprints on their polling card to avoid the ballots being disqualified, and to take pictures of government thugs loitering around polling stations. The lay organization Catholic Action deployed the discreet power of the Roman Catholic Church, while the no less influential Iglesia ni Kristo did the same among evangelical Protestants.

At a time when President Quirino was out of the country on one of many trips to the US for medical treatment, Lansdale persuaded Magsaysay to substitute his soldiers for the police supposedly guarding the polling stations. A million more people voted in 1951 than in 1949 and the results were gratifying. The presence of the soldiers undoubtedly strengthened the vote for those candidates favoured by Magsaysay, without the traditional coercion. Even the 'Huk' leaflets that Lansdale and his team had printed inside Clark Air Force Base in fact reflected a genuine call by the Communists to boycott the elections. Thoroughly manipulated by the Americans though it was, the election almost certainly reflected genuine public opinion.

However accomplished at engineering elections, Lansdale could have done nothing without the political astuteness of Magsaysay, who decided to run in 1952 as the Nacionalista candidate, even though until then he had been a Liberal. This swung some members of the traditional elites behind him and Lansdale kept a copy of a secret agreement by which the Nacionalista barons would be allowed to nominate most of the cabinet in US Ambassador Raymond Spruance's safe. Meanwhile he set about raising Magsaysay's profile in the US, planting a puff piece in the *New York Times* and persuading the magazines *Newsweek*, *Fortune* and *Time* to run cover stories of the tough guy with a heart of gold running for the Filipino presidency. The local news media were even easier to nobble, as Americans owned three of Manila's main newspapers and the Voice of America controlled twelve of the country's forty-one radio stations. Major US corporations active in the Philippines such as Coca-Cola were also encouraged to make campaign contributions, much of it in untraceable cash.

The distinctive hucksterish flavour of the 1952 election was provided by Lansdale, employing standard US electoral techniques. A 'Magsaysay is my guy' button soon adorned many chests, and Lansdale composed a 'Magsaysay Mambo' as well as the hugely popular 'Magsaysay March':

> We want the bell of liberty
> Ringing for us once more;
> We want the people's will to be
> Free as it was before!
>
> We want our native land to lie
> Peaceful and clean again;
> We want our nation guided by
> God-fearing honest men!
>
> Men who'll serve without the nerve
> To cheat eternally;
> Who'll do the job and never rob
> The public treasury!

Only the man of destiny
Our need will satisfy;
This is the cry for you and me;
We want Magsaysay![26]

Although the candidate was being sold as an antidote to endemic corruption, Lansdale had at his disposal a secret CIA fund of $500,000 as well as movie cameras, projectors and sound trucks provided by the Agency. He also employed a full range of dirty tricks to counter the dirty tricks of Quirino's supporters, including incapacitating their speakers with drugs before they were due to make major speeches.[27] His hyperactivity was not without risk, and on several occasions he narrowly avoided being beaten up or killed by gangsters sent by Tony, the President's brother and chief enforcer. Quirino himself tried to get Ambassador Spruance recalled and Lansdale sacked, openly referring to him as the 'mastermind' of 'an American Army party organized to foist a "man on horseback" on the Filipinos'.

The dangers (and the accusation) were sufficiently well founded to cause Spruance – clearly an ambassador with clout – to reassign Lansdale to the lowly post of assistant to the underemployed historian attached to Clark Air Force Base, whence he continued to direct his covert activities until six weeks before the election. He took a working vacation in Indochina, which was to be his next major assignment, before returning to Manila to watch Magsaysay win the election with nearly three million votes to Quirino's 1,313,991. Seventy per cent of the votes in Huklandia went to Magsaysay. The Indian Ambassador wittily suggested that 'a certain American' should change his name to 'Colonel Landslide'. Just in case Quirino decided not to go quietly, the USS *Wasp* battle group appeared off the coast of the Philippines.

The Huk rebellion petered out by 1955, with the capture, surrender and imprisonment of many Huk leaders. A mistake often made in reviewing counter-insurgency campaigns is to focus on what the winning side did right, without giving due weight to what the losers did to undermine their own cause. The Huk rising against the Japanese had been a visceral response to occupation by an alien and brutal enemy. ➤ Things were not so clear cut in a civil war that divided a society with densely meshed kinship structures, in which a policeman might be a rebel's cousin. When, in April 1949, a Huk unit ambushed and killed Aurora Quezón, the widow of the exiled wartime President, and her daughter as well as several government officials, it was a seriously damaging blunder.

But the insurgency dealt itself a death blow in late 1950, after Magsaysay had rounded up virtually the entire leadership of the Communist Party in Manila, including its leader Jose Lava. It is worth noting that this coup depended on intelligence gathering put in place by Quirino, for one should not exaggerate Magsaysay's contribution. Lava's brother Jesus took over as general secretary and promptly fell out with Luis Taruc, the Huk head of military operations, over revolutionary strategy. Divorced from the political leadership and sensing that the Huks were forfeiting the support of the *barrios* through increasingly onerous exactions, Taruc tried to initiate peace negotiations through the young journalist and future charismatic political leader Benigno Aquino. Under sentence of death for deviationism, Taruc eventually surrendered to the government. He would spend twelve years imprisoned until he was pardoned in 1968 by Ferdinand Marcos, his published memoirs in the interim inspiring Nelson Mandela, leader of the armed wing of South Africa's African National Congress (ANC).[28] Taruc's testimony on internal Huk discipline was revealing:

A young nurse named Lita asked permission to go home, to rest and recuperate and to get a new supply of clothes. She was suspected of planning to surrender and was 'liquidated' on the orders of the leaders ... A Huk women's organizer who was known as a nagger was liquidated by a fellow Huk, allegedly for suggesting that her husband surrender. But it seems that he had grown tired of her nagging and was then living with another woman. Her brother, a Huk commander, turned against the movement when he learned of the murder ... A minor error of an eighteen-year-old girl who was the number two of a cadre caused her death. She had committed her 'crime' when she had fallen into the hands of government troops and was interrogated [and] she revealed the address where she slept when she visited a nearby barrio. The storeowner was not killed and there were no official repercussions of any sort. But still, she was shot without a trial ... Executed with her was a platoon commander of the GHQ security force named Etti. He had fallen ill one day and left his post, after appointing his assistant to take over. He was court-martialled, charged with dereliction of duty, and executed by a firing squad ... Half a dozen young boys were executed for similar offences.[29]

Since the Philippines are an oceanic archipelago there were no foreign sanctuaries where exhausted fighters could recuperate. Even within the Philippines the Huks were never very successful in extending their operations to islands south of Luzon, especially after one expeditionary team raped a local woman. Although there were unconfirmed reports of Chinese agents, in reality there was no external Communist involvement, except for occasional supportive articles in Soviet magazines. The US and Philippines had much history in common, and Filipino admiration for US institutions extended well into the ranks of the Huks. There was a unity of purpose in how the US dealt with the Philippines, which contrasted with the bitter domestic divisions over China. The US also directed huge sums of money into the Philippines, including from 1951–6 some $383 million in economic assistance, and a further $117 million in military aid. This was on top of around $700 million in reconstruction funds in 1946–50, although much of that was embezzled before the US learned how to target aid more discriminately. The US armed the Philippine army with modern weapons and deployed its own air power in their support.

Helped by American advisers, Magsaysay's reformed Filipino army also killed more Huks with less indiscriminate violence meted out to civilians, innocent or culpable. Between 1950 and 1955, the army claimed to have killed 6,000 Huks, with a further 2,000 wounded, 4,700 captured and 9,500 who voluntarily surrendered.[30] Relentless pursuit by the Filipino military isolated the Huks from their sources of supply in the *barrios*, and left them grubbing for food in the mountains or swamps. William Pomeroy, a former US soldier and war correspondent who joined the Huks, reported that he and his wife Celia Mariano were starving for months on end. Many Huks with less iron will than the Pomeroys were worn out by such an existence, in which betrayal and violent death were never far away. The fact that the Huks lacked a rear area in a neighbouring country critically impacted on their ability to withdraw to recover strength.

But above all the rise of Magsaysay confused many of the Huks' peasant supporters, as he seemed to promise (and practised) the simple virtues which had led them to support the guerrillas. He spoke to their concerns in ways that the elite Marxist intellectuals of the Communist Party who had latched on to the pre-existing peasant movement did not. Like Lansdale's all-seeing eye, Magsaysay's presence was felt everywhere, working to stimulate the dormant conscience of even a humble postmaster contemplating stealing a few stamps.

Sadly, once he was in power Magsaysay found himself shackled by the deal with the old landowning elite brokered by Lansdale. It was not he and the Americans who had tricked them, but they and the Americans who had tricked him. He could not keep the promises made to get him elected and the betrayal pained him until his death, when his presidential aeroplane crashed into Mount Manunggal on Cebu in March 1957. The Americans were not about to tolerate structural reforms in the country that was the keystone of their policy of containment in Asia, least of all at a time when they were being drawn into the strategic black hole created by French defeat in Indochina.

8. PARACHUTE THE ESCARGOT: INDOCHINA

France's Vietnam War

In the late 1940s the Viet Minh made the arduous transition from a hit-and-run guerrilla force into a regular army capable of sophisticated conventional operations. They ultimately outgunned, and outfought, their French opponents, culminating in May 1954 with victory at Dien Bien Phu, which broke France's will to remain in Indochina. The Viet Minh had much help. From 1950 onwards the Chinese afforded the Viet Minh crucial advantages, not counterbalanced by mounting US financial assistance for France's flagging war effort. Ho Chi Minh joined the Sino–Soviet alliance talks in Moscow, where Stalin deftly palmed responsibility for the Asian revolution on to the willing Chinese. Mao was more indulgent towards Ho than was Stalin, who harboured suspicions about Ho's ideological reliability after his wartime flirtations with the OSS. In January 1950, Communist China formally recognized Ho's northern Democratic Republic of Vietnam, followed shortly by the Soviet Union and the Communist bloc. Mao agreed to supply the Viet Minh with armaments, opening Chinese military training facilities to Vietnamese volunteers and conscripts.

In August 1950 some seventy-nine PLA commanders, including Chen Geng of the Twentieth Army, were sent to Vietnam, where they played a vital role in shaping the strategy and individual battle plans of their less experienced Vietnamese comrades.[1] By October 1951 the Chinese had built a direct rail link across the border, over which flowed the first shipment of 4,000 tons of munitions, including howitzers, anti-aircraft batteries and ten million rounds of rifle ammunition. By 1954 they would be delivering the same tonnage of armaments *every month*. What the Chinese or Soviets could not supply was bought on the open market, using the $1 million which accrued to the Viet Minh annually from the sale of opium produced by Meong tribesmen.[2]

Nonetheless the war was fought by Vietnamese rather than Chinese. As eventually constituted, Giap's forces had a pyramidal structure. The base consisted of a vast part-time peasant militia, called the Dan Cong, which acted as Giap's local eyes and ears, as well as being a part-time pioneer corps available for up to fourteen days' service away from their home hamlets. Then there were full-time guerrilla forces which operated within a circumscribed region. Those who distinguished themselves then joined Giap's regular force, which consisted of divisions of around 10,000 men, organized into regiments, battalions and companies. Each division had its own staff officers and specialist sections, including battalions of artillery as well as intelligence units. Careful staff work meant that these regular forces could be on the move for months, with the part-time pioneers putting in place the food and munitions they needed to survive. Chinese influence resulted in the omnipresence of political commissars, with every third soldier acting as their eyes and ears among the ranks, and interminable self-criticism sessions so rigorous that suicide often resulted.

Facing them were 160,000 French Expeditionary Corps troops, only 42 per cent born in France itself. They were mostly regulars, for young national-service conscripts had to volunteer to serve in Indochina, which a decreasing number of them did as metropolitan Radicals, Socialists and Communists turned against this remote 'dirty war'. Communist trade unionists sabotaged supplies destined for Indochina, while high-placed sympathizers within the civil service informed the Viet Minh regarding key shifts in government policy. The war eventually became so unpopular that, when French people donated blood, the health service had to specify that it was *not* destined for the army in Indochina.

The main French forces derived from the (North) African Army, that is Algerian and Moroccan Berbers and Arabs, colonial regiments (sub-Saharan African and Indochinese), and the multinational but

French-officered Foreign Legion. The Legion and the parachute regiments, which included Moroccans and Vietnamese, were the hard-core warriors. The Legionnaires were bludgeoners and brawlers, as slow and sure as their strange formal march, while the wiry little Paras – who had to jump out of narrow aircraft doors carrying a huge weight of equipment – specialized in going fast and hard into any fight.

Apart from aggressive mobile formations of Legionnaires and paratroopers, the French external intelligence service, the Service de Documentation Extérieure et de Contre-espionnage (SDECE), experimented with deep-penetration units modelled on Orde Wingate's Second World War Chindits. There was a special forces training base at Ty-Wan where anonymous Americans, Britons and Nationalist Chinese contributed to the instruction. French NCOs led groups of Cambodians, Meong or T'ai tribesmen (who were known as Black or White T'ai after the colour of their women's shirts), in sowing murder and mayhem behind Viet Minh lines. At Coc-Leu in late 1953 one unit was joined by French paratroopers, and together they killed 150 Viet Minh.[3] The Meong attached only one condition to their contribution to the French war effort: that the French should replace the Viet Minh in marketing their opium crop. Although the French had banned opium in 1945, the SDECE arranged for secret flights which took the opium from Laos to Saigon, where General Binh Xuyen processed it inside his stronghold of Cholon and returned part of the profits to the Meong.

Under US pressure there was a growing effort to Vietnamize the war, called *jaunissement* – yellowing – through the creation of a Vietnamese National Army. Recruitment was a slow process and the VNA numbered no more than 38,000 by the end of 1951, although it grew rapidly thereafter. The war was waged mainly in the north, but there were constant grenade attacks on those Saigon bars and cafés that failed to pay protection money to the Communists. After 10 p.m. the suburbs were hit by desultory mortar fire from the countryside, with return tracer fire arcing through the darkness. In many places, which the French or Bao Dai's troops seemed to control by day, the Viet Minh took over as darkness suddenly fell and all traffic halted on the roads until sunrise.[4]

French strategy in Tonkin was to control the major roads and the populous rice paddies of the Red River Delta, while interdicting Viet

Minh supply routes from China. The frontier forts on the Chinese border north of where Laos indents into Vietnam were a tempting target for the Viet Minh. Low cloud, fog and dense jungle foliage neutralized French air power, while the jungle terrain made relief laborious. In October 1950, twenty-three regular Viet Minh battalions, equipped with American artillery from KMT stocks left on the mainland, smashed the French defence lines along the Chinese border, shrinking the French position in northern Vietnam to a perimeter around the Red River Delta. The Viet Minh now held a continuous band of territory from the Chinese border to within 100 miles of Saigon. The overwhelming victory led Giap to believe that with one bold push in 1951 he could take overrun the Delta, including Hanoi and Haiphong, where French staff officers were evacuating their families and burning documents.

The First Indochina War coincided with the 'police action' in Korea. In one amusing incident a French colonel called Wainwright – his English grandfather had been captured by Napoleon and remained in France – had the strange experience of trying to call in an air strike as his mobile group came under heavy attack. Due to peculiar atmospheric conditions his radio operator could hear nothing but an American sergeant dully enumerating equipment required at a supply depot in Korea. Eventually, an American colonel attached as an adviser to Wainwright's force shouted, 'Get the hell off this radio channel! There's a war going on here.'[5]

The Chinese intervention in Korea was the reason why an American adviser was serving with the imperialist French forces. Truman, Marshall and Acheson lumped the Chinese Communists, North Koreans, Huks and Viet Minh into one Soviet-inspired global conspiracy, ignoring the possibility of exploiting divisions between the Soviets and the Chinese, and between them and the insurgent forces. As we saw with the Huks, their relationship with the Communists was not exactly straightforward. The US gave France $133 million, with conditions attached to how the French might improve their performance in Indochina.[6] A key recommendation was coldly spelled out by a State Department official: 'Much of the stigma of colonialism can be removed if, where necessary, yellow men will be killed by yellow men rather than by white men alone.'[7]

What they were looking for, and never found, was a Vietnamese

Magsaysay or Sukarno. They wanted France's puppet ruler Bao Dai to be given enough latitude to function as a rallying point for all non-Communist Vietnamese nationalists. But Bao Dai was a hopeless choice, his support derived from southern landowners and the Cao Dai religious sect with its Disneyland cathedral and armed militia. He was also a sybaritic playboy, preferring his yacht or French Riviera villa to his Norodom Palace, which was inhabited instead by French generals. It is most unlikely that he would have exercised meaningful power even if it were not circumscribed by a book-length document that listed the areas of policy that France reserved to itself.

Giap's 1951 offensive coincided with the appointment of the sixty-two-year-old General Jean de Lattre de Tassigny, who from December 1950 combined the roles of high commissioner and theatre commander-in-chief in ways that anticipated the British proconsul Gerald Templer. He was a Vendéan Catholic who had fought in the First World War and in the North African Rif, and had escaped from Vichy captivity using a saw smuggled to him by his wife; he went on to join the Free French in the liberation of France from the Nazis, with the future US Ambassador Henry Cabot Lodge as his US liaison officer. During his stellar career de Lattre had been wounded eight times, receiving forty-six decorations, on the first occasion for killing two Prussian lancers with his sabre. On arrival in Hanoi, accompanied by his redoubtable wife, he promised to win the war inside fifteen months. 'From now on you will be commanded,' he told his men, who nicknamed him either 'King Jean' or 'DDT' after the highly effective pesticide. On arrival he scrapped his predecessor's plans to evacuate the north, obliging all French women and children to remain in Hanoi too. Whiners were awarded 'the order of the steamship' – a ticket home. His twenty-three-year-old-son Bernard was serving as an army lieutenant in Indochina and was to be killed at Ninh-Binh within the year, one of the twenty-one sons of senior French commanders killed in this savage war.[8]

Fighting in Indochina had its ebb and flow, determined by the monsoons which oppressed different parts of a country shaped like an elongated letter S. From January 1951 Giap focused his main attack on the town of Vinh Yen, thirty-two miles from Hanoi. De Lattre rushed in reinforcements from Cochin China and sent every available aircraft to support them, many of them British or German surplus from the Second World War. The aircrews hurled high-explosive bombs and canisters of napalm out of the doors and loading bays. A Viet Minh officer described the effects on the ground:

I order my men to take cover from the bombs and machine gun bul-lets. But the planes dived on us without firing their guns. However, all of a sudden, hell opens in front of my eyes. Hell comes in the form of large, egg-shaped containers, dropping from the first plane, followed by other eggs from the second and third plane. Immense sheets of flames, extending to over a hundred metres, it seems, strike terror in the ranks of my soldiers. This is napalm, the fire which falls from the skies. Another plane swoops down behind us and again drops a napalm bomb. The bomb falls closely behind us and I feel its fiery breath touching my whole body. The men are now fleeing and I cannot hold them back. There is no way of holding out under the torrent of fire which flows in all directions and burns everything on its passage. On all sides flame surrounds us now ... I stop at the platoon com-mander ... His eyes are wide with terror. 'What is this? The atomic bomb?' 'No, it is napalm.'[9]

From January to June Giap launched repeated attacks, led by suicide teams to flatten barbed wire and to detonate explosive satchels against French bunkers, but each was repulsed at very great human cost on both sides.[10] One attacker, whose badly wounded arm was trapped in barbed wire, ordered a colleague to hack off the limb before crawling with his explosive satchel charge to blow up a bunker. When the battle ended, the Viet Minh had been defeated with at least 5,000 casualties. The Chinese correctly anticipated that de Lattre would strike next at Hoa Binh, which straddled the main Viet Minh supply routes between North and South Vietnam, and Giap reinforced it. French attempts to take the town were all repulsed.[11]

After Vinh Yen and further victories at Mao Khe and Yen Cu Ha, the craggy-faced 'French MacArthur' was given the full American media blitz, culminating in his visit to the US in September 1951. In Washing-ton, doubts about French colonialism were smoothed with talk of a

Soviet-inspired 'red colonialism', as much of a menace in Indochina as in Korea or Malaya. De Lattre spoke darkly of the red legions occupying North Africa to lunge at southern Europe in a variant of the increasingly influential domino theory.[12]

Assured of US support, the General built a chain of fortresses called the De Lattre Line to defend the Red River Delta. The Line consisted of two concentric rings, but the whole project exuded the same nervous hubris as the interwar Maginot Line along the French border. A subordinate once questioned the cost and the manpower needed to garrison these positions. De Lattre replied, 'Fuck the cost. As for the men, we'll put the real *cons* [politely: useless fellows] down there.'[13] The outposts were supported by long-range artillery, and mobile units, with light tanks and armoured cars, acted as a fire brigade. One such group consisted of the French battalion which had fought with distinction in Korea; it would prove useful in calling in a debt of honour from the US as it stepped up funding for the war in Indochina.

In 1952 de Lattre died at home of cancer, eight months after his adored only son was killed under his command. His successor, General Raoul 'Chinese' Salan, was probably the senior French officer with the most experience of fighting in South-east Asia and instituted a policy of building 'hedgehogs', strongly defended bases, each with an airstrip and ringed by smaller perimeter forts, from which the French could launch powerful raids into Viet Minh territory. On the other side of the hill Giap followed Chinese advice to stretch and thin French resources by maintaining pressure in Cochin China while opening a new front along the border between Vietnam and Laos. Between October and December 1952 the Viet Minh drove the French out of north-western Vietnam, and one of the many governments that came and went during the Fourth Republic replaced Salan in January 1953 with General Henri Navarre, an intelligence specialist with far less combat experience than his predecessors.

The ending of the Korean War the following summer meant that both the Chinese and the US focused on the war in Indochina, ramping up support for their proxies. It is impossible to determine whether Giap or his Chinese advisers were mainly responsible for the Viet Minh's successes on the battlefield. Certainly there were frictions between the two, since the Vietnamese had long memories of Chinese dominance of their country. The Chinese generals also had to refer all their major recommendations back to the Central Committee, where Mao took a keen interest in this campaign.

Giap is frequently lauded as a military superman, but his principal strength was that his men were able to tolerate casualties akin to the trench warfare of the First World War.[14] The Viet Minh had many merits from a strictly military viewpoint, but their greatest advantage lay in the part-time pioneers who made it possible for the regular army to fight. Each division relied on 50,000 porters. The gruelling nature of their work can be gauged from Giap's calculations that a porter could carry fifty-five pounds of rice fifteen miles by day, or twelve miles in darkness, and half that amount over mountains, but only forty pounds of other stores because a rice sack conveniently moulded itself into the human body, whereas artillery shells or other hardware did not. Since the roads were too vulnerable to air attack, the Viet Minh pioneers laboriously cut their own alternative routes through the jungle, preserving the overhead canopy and surfacing them with whatever lay to hand.

The Viet Minh also stoically endured conditions unthinkable to Western soldiers. The food consisted of cold rice, sometimes enlivened with pungent fish sauce, carried in a rolled towel around the waist. Their medical facilities were rudimentary, with men expected to 'sweat out' bouts of endemic malaria, and quinine tablets, when they were available, were divided into therapeutically valueless ten parts. No time was wasted on badly wounded men and once, when a captured Algerian found his path obstructed by a dying Viet Minh, his guard ordered him to tread on him.

Life among the Viet Minh was extremely regulated, akin to membership of a religious order in which everyone was 'Brother' except Giap himself. Cards, alcohol, sex and smoking were forbidden; instead there were communal singing and endless political indoctrination sessions. In a country where pre-colonial universal literacy (necessary for any civil service post) had sunk to 20 per cent under the French, the Viet Minh taught that illiteracy was unpatriotic. One needed to read to understand their propaganda.[15] To neutralize French aerial surveillance each Viet Minh soldier carried a wire-mesh dish, regularly adorned with the varying foliage of the different areas of vegetation he traversed. Viet Minh militias were also adept at making even more lethal an environment which already had everything from tigers and panthers to poisonous snakes, ants, rats and scorpions. Concealed pits contained sharpened bamboo poles, smeared with excrement to make wounds fester, while every step through waist-deep water could mean a spiked caltrop piercing the sole of a soft boot and at least two men to take the wounded third away.

The Viet Minh were supremely adept at tunnelling, in both defence and offence. Tranquil village ponds would sometimes have the equivalent of a modern washbasin's siphon, concealed by undergrowth, beyond whose S-bend lurked tunnels and storerooms with concealed ventilation shafts. The sound of the Viet Minh digging proved almost as ominous as their massed cries of 'Forward!' Chinese engineers with experience of Korea taught the Viet Minh how to inch assault trenches almost up to French hill-top fortifications, using coal miners to tunnel under them and insert huge quantities of explosives. Unfortunately the Viet Minh also accepted Chinese advice on 'human wave' attacks to overwhelm defenders, which proved as needlessly expensive in Vietnam as they did in Korea. In part this was a self-perpetuating aberration, as experienced officers died early and their replacements relied heavily on written orders.

Giap was perfectly prepared to write off any unit that got into trouble, refusing to react to French raids and offensives in order to maintain the initiative. While the Viet Minh did not torture prisoners in the manner of the wartime Japanese, and even made some effort to win them over, captured French troops often starved to death on the basic Viet Minh diet. Cruelty was used with cold deliberation. US foreign service officer Howard Simpson encountered an embittered French planter who was waging a private vendetta against the Viet Minh operating in his area. He had the bodies of Viet Minh couriers laid out neatly in a storeroom designated 'Cold Meat'. His savagery was born of an attack on his plantation when he was absent, in which the Viet Minh slaughtered his Cambodian guards and humiliated his Vietnamese mother-in-law in front of the workforce. When he returned, the planter saw her, as he thought, buried up to the neck in a mound of earth. By the light of his headlights he rushed to excavate her, only to have her head roll away.[16]

Amoebic dysentery, malaria, jungle sores and leeches were plagues common to both sides, but undermined the morale of the French Expeditionary soldiers more. Paddy fields were a particular horror. To avoid the punji stakes and other booby-traps lurking under the putty-coloured water, French troops trudged along the embankments, which were often mined with devices improvised from dud French shells and bombs, and which exposed them to sniper fire. Steady attrition, especially from mines, led to retaliation against nearby villages, whose miserable inhabitants had to hope the French would not kill them for not giving them information, for the Viet Minh certainly would if they did.

The French soldiers much preferred life in Saigon, the fabled 'pearl of the Orient', to the colder and greyer northern capital of Hanoi. The epicentres of life in the southern capital were along the Rue Catinat, notably the terrace bar of the Continental Hotel. Nets to prevent grenades being lobbed in protected all such premises. This was where French officers in their camouflage fatigues had their last drink before going out on missions, their movements and the takeoffs of aircraft from Tan Son Nhut air base being carefully recorded by Viet Minh agents. Another favourite watering hole and superb restaurant was the Arc-en-Ciel in the Chinese quarter of Cholon, whose nightclub boasted such visiting stars as Charles Trenet and Josephine Baker. Howard Simpson was deeply offended by a notoriously sybaritic army that insisted on life's pleasures even out in the field, and wrote the following contemptuous doggerel:

> *Camembert for the Colonel's table,*
> *Wine in abundance when we're able.*
> *Indochina may be lost,*
> *Our Colonel eats well despite the cost . . .*
> *. . . Parachute the escargot!*
> *Follow them with old Bordeaux.*
> *And on our graves near Dien Bien Phu*
> *Inscribe these words, these very few,*
> *'They died for France, but more . . .*
> *Their Colonel ate well throughout the war.'*[17]

Although there were itinerant military brothels, staffed by brave and colourfully dressed women from the Algerian Ouled Nail tribe that honoured the activity as a way of earning matrimonial dowries, many French troops acquired a permanent *congai* or common law wife, a popular practice too among their Vietnamese comrades, who simply moved their real wives into *camps de mariés*. The vulnerability this created was manifest, and a third of the French posts that fell were betrayed from within by Viet Minh Trojan whores.[18]

In what was to become a drearily familiar tactic, the mechanization of the French forces became another Achilles heel. In wooded or hilly terrain, truck convoys were regularly stopped by destroying the lead vehicle, usually a Sherman tank, with bazookas and then assaulting the soft-skinned vehicles from either side of the road. The French never acquired the armoured bulldozers that could have cleared the roads of obstacles in an ambush. The constant attrition on the roads led them to depend more and more on aerial resupply, materials which, when dropped by parachute, were as likely as not to fall into Viet Minh hands. While French air force and naval pilots did their best, there were more planes than pilots, and never enough bombers to make aerial bombardment effective. From 1953 the CIA's Civil Air Transport front company – the forerunner of the more famous Air America – loaned transport planes and US aircrews with colourful names like James 'Earthquake' McGoon. There was also an acute shortage of helicopters – never more than ten until April 1954 – with which to make morale-boosting casualty evacuations.

Enter the Americans

Although the Pentagon had major reservations about how the French were conducting the war, adoption of the domino theory led them, grudgingly, to provide ever greater assistance, theoretically under cost-effective scrutiny by the burgeoning Military Assistance and Advisory Group (MAAG) headed by Generals Thomas Trapnell and his successor John 'Iron Mike' O'Daniel. No strings were attached to a tranche of $150 million in 1952 when it dawned on the Americans that the French might 'leave us holding the baby'. In addition the prospect that France might reduce its contribution to the defence of Western Europe acted to blackmail the US into underwriting French operations in Indochina. US funding climbed from 40 to 75 per cent of France's war costs by October 1952. The Americans became more visible, cruising the streets in their black sedans, while poolside parties in the grounds of US-rented villas became the places where power lay. The French responded with their usual proud ingratitude, treating 'les Amerloques' (crazy Americans) with cool indifference or ill-concealed hatred born as much of resentment about the US role in liberating France in 1944 as of the conceit that their experience as colonialists gave them unique insight into how to win the war in Indochina.[19]

The Eisenhower administration inherited involvement in Indochina from its predecessor and, like any new broom, sought to inject vitality into what it chose to depict as the Truman gang's failing investment. There was much manly talk about refusing to pick up the tab which had enabled the French to 'sit in their Beau Geste forts on champagne cases', and that it was time 'to put the squeeze on the French to get them off their fannies'. This translated into calls for an expansion of the Vietnamese National Army and for a new commander who would go on to the offensive.

General Navarre tried to conceal his lack of practical experience with Gallic hauteur. At his welcoming reception in the Continental an American official gave him a book by the Chindit commander 'Mad Mike' Calvert, which Navarre disdainfully passed to an aide. American assessments were surprisingly optimistic about the new arrival, although one report said: 'There is an eighteenth-century fragrance to him ... One almost expects ruffles and a powdered wig.' He was personally wealthy and, in addition to his storied name, Navarre's chic blonde wife was descended from Marshal Murat. 'Logically victory is certain,' Navare told his staff with staggering hubris, 'but victory is a woman. She does not give herself except to those who know how to take her. One cannot win without attacking.'[20] He decided to fight during the May-to-October monsoon season, to force the Viet Minh into a pitched battle some time in 1954, weakening their hand in the negotiations for which secret preliminary talks were already taking place. The US provided another $400 million for the Navarre Plan, which met with early successes, including wiping out an entire Viet Minh division sent to infiltrate the Red River Delta.

Dissatisfied with these reactive fire-fighting operations, Navarre determined to build on Salan's initiative to create more heavily manned artillery fortresses with airstrips as the rocks against which the Viet Minh waves would break, or, should they concentrate their forces against one of them, as the anvils on which the hammer of a relief force under the Red River area commander General Cogny would smash them. At the same time he also planned Operation Atlante, in which mainly Vietnamese forces with a French spearhead would deliver a long coastal strip in Annam from the 30,000 Viet Minh who controlled it. Navarre believed he could overcome the strategic incoherence of pursuing divergent objectives with air power. Overstretching French resources while seeking a 'decisive' battle that would hinge on the effectiveness of air supply was madness, but nobody appears to have whispered the word 'Stalingrad' in his ear.

The Viet Minh threat to northern Laos and its lucrative opium traffic determined where Navarre would seek his decisive battle: at Dien Bien Phu, a collection of hamlets of 10,000 to 15,000 inhabitants strung along a remote valley with a small airstrip in the north-west corner of Vietnam, five miles from the Laotian border and about 185 miles from the Red River Delta. The project was originally Salan's, who had planned to squeeze the Viet Minh between Dien Bien Phu and another bastion at Nasan, which had withstood an all-out assault in December 1952. Yet in August 1953 Navarre evacuated Nasan on the grounds that it was too costly to resupply even though, unlike Dien Bien Phu, it was not commanded by surrounding hills.[21]

Bizarrely, it was Dien Bien Phu's vulnerability that appealed to Navarre. When his subordinate commanders expressed strong reservations about the site, Navarre replied that it was supposed to tempt the Viet Minh to attack, making it the poisoned bait in what he hoped would be a huge trap. The first step was to clear the valley of the under-strength Viet Minh division that had moved into it a year earlier, accomplished with ease because the French had broken the Viet Minh operational cipher, which enabled them to plot the whereabouts of enemy forces. Incredibly, this intelligence coup was leaked to the press and, when Giap directed five new divisions towards Dien Bien Phu, he used a new cipher.[22]

Navarre initially thought in terms of using Dien Ben Phu as a safe haven from which to launch powerful thrusts against the Viet Minh, while also signifying a strong presence to encourage bolder action by T'ai guerrillas. Such forays ceased in mid-February 1954 after one massacre too many. The remnants of the T'ai had to walk more than forty miles to Dien Bien Phu, where they proved completely unsuited to the static warfare they were co-opted into. Rather than think again, Navarre decided to use the fortified valley as an Asian Verdun, against whose defences the Viet Minh would be cut to pieces. The human cost of this would make the Viet Minh political leadership more amenable in the peace talks which were about to commence in Geneva in April 1954.

On the other side, Giap did not realize that the Chinese had already decided to endorse a Soviet-inspired 'peace offensive' to resolve both Korea and Indochina. As they had done in Korea before the armistice talks, the Chinese wanted one major offensive to maximize their ally's position at the talks and did not really expect the outright victory that Giap was to achieve at Dien Bien Phu.[23]

'Annihilate Them Bit by Bit'

Airborne insertions played a greater part in the First Indochina War than they have done in any conflict since. The day before his paratroopers dropped into the Dien Bien Phu valley on 21 November 1953, Navarre learned that the French government had refused his request for the reinforcements he needed for this and related operations, even as Operation Atlante also got under way on the coast of Annam. Navarre and Cogny went ahead with the Dien Bien Phu plan (Operation Castor) anyway, the first of many decisions that made sense only if Navarre felt confident that he could pin any defeat on the despised politicians.[24] The Paras quickly took control of the valley, which is about eleven miles long and three miles wide around the winding Nam Youm River. Over the coming days Navarre dropped more paratroops, and then flew in a division-sized force numbering over 10,000 men; further reinforcements during the battle brought the Dien Bien Phu garrison to around 15,000.

The first task of troops that preferred dash to digging was to build an enormous central camp on the west bank of the river, repair the larger of the two heavily sabotaged airstrips and cover it with welded metal plates, and transform a series of outlying hills into redoubts that would be covered by the artillery concentrated in the central camp. On average the hills were 130 feet high, and each had to be cleared of trees and brush to create clear fields of fire for the bunkers. Dismantled tanks were reassembled after being flown in by transport aircraft, along with anti-aircraft guns to be used against the expected massed infantry assaults. The fortress had a water-purification plant, ample fuel and large ammunition dumps. Much of the work was done by a couple of thousand former Viet Minh, who had opted for hard labour rather than life in a prison camp.

Legend has it that the resulting forts were named after the many mistresses of Colonel Christian Marie Ferdinand de la Croix des Castries, the fifty-one-year-old former cavalry officer and Moroccan Spahi commander who would command the defence of Dien Bien Phu. Anne-Marie, Béatrice, Claudine, Dominique, Eliane, Gabrielle, Huguette (containing the main airstrip) and Isabelle (with another) were duly cleared and fortified. Each had numbered internal strongpoints – Eliane 1, 2, 3 and so on. It must have looked an impressive sight to the streams of visiting dignitaries who were flown in, but it soon became a muddy hell when the monsoon rains began and water streamed down from the surrounding heights, where Giap's troops were to enjoy a comparatively dry existence.

It took time for Giap to divine the significance of what Navarre was doing at Dien Ben Phu. When he did, he was inclined to accept the challenge of the major pitched battle the French had been seeking since the time of de Lattre. In early December the Communist Party leadership and their Chinese and Russian advisers agreed with his plan to mount only harassing raids while spending months preparing the battlefield. Artillery was to play a major part in the battle and Mao reassured Giap that there would be no limit on the supply of shells from China. When he was ready, the Chinese Central Military Commission recommended that he should not make an all-out general assault, but instead progressively isolate individual enemy positions 'to annihilate them bit by bit'.[25]

The preparatory phase took about three months. Giap had to move

25,000 men and their equipment 300 miles from the hills of the Viet Bac and the southern Delta, with his supply lines stretching some 500 miles from the Chinese border. Over 100,000 porters took the perilous and precipitous jungle routes, lugging dismantled artillery pieces up and down steep slopes with the aid of ropes, and built concealed roads with streams bridged by logs hidden below the water's surface for 600 Russian trucks to move vast quantities of food and ammunition. Extreme precautions were taken against aerial surveillance. At the first sound of aircraft engines, spotters in the tree tops used triangles and whistles to halt the convoys in camouflaged way stations. Even if they had seen them, French pilots had too little fuel to loiter for any meaningful time over an area so far from their land and sea bases. This was soon to be the least of their problems, as Giap also positioned anti-aircraft batteries to cover the limited number of air approaches to the valley. Aircraft that successfully ran the gauntlet would then be shelled on the airstrip. The Chinese also emphasized the importance of guarding against airborne forces being dropped to attack the besiegers from outside the perimeter.

During the preparatory period Giap must have felt like a cat pondering a bowl full of oblivious goldfish. Undisturbed by French patrols, the Viet Minh were even able to use the darkness to excavate deep gun emplacements on the forward slopes of the hills around Dien Bien Phu to give the guns direct lines of fire, as Giap's gunners lacked the training to fire effectively from reverse slopes. One by one the guns were set up and aimed over open sights, and then the gunners waited inside their dugouts like the cannon crews of Napoleonic-era warships. Giap himself moved into a cave 300 feet deep. Every feature of the fortress was carefully logged, sometimes by Viet Minh commandos who crept around inside the main camp at night, with particular attention paid to command bunkers bristling with radio antennae.

After dark on 13 March 1954 Giap opened his attack with a colossal artillery barrage, including fire from 155mm cannon that the French had thought it impossible for the enemy to bring to the party and which outranged their own battery of 155mm howitzers. Viet Minh sappers had dug assault trenches right up to the wire, and then used waves of troops to overwhelm the outermost redoubts, Béatrice from the Legion that night and Gabrielle the following day, despite the French firing around 30,000 shells in support of them. During the night of 14–15 March Lieutenant-Colonel Charles Piroth, the one-armed French artillery commander who had been confident his guns could keep the Viet Minh at bay, killed himself by holding a grenade to his chest.

Anne-Marie was held by T'ai troops who had been showered with leaflets telling them they could leave without hindrance. In the morning of the 17th most of them did and the remainder retreated to the main camp. The loss of the northern redoubts closed two avenues of approach to the airstrip and not long afterwards Isabelle, too far south of the main defensive perimeter, was cut off. It became extremely perilous to land or even to fly low enough to make accurate parachute drops. Navarre and Cogny had never envisaged such an outcome and lacked sufficient parachutes, a matter rectified when the Americans flew in 60,000 chutes from the Philippines. But as the anti-aircraft fire forced supply planes to fly higher, their cargoes were as likely to land in the hands of the Viet Minh as inside the fortress perimeters. After a while the valley floor was strewn with thousands of piles of white silk and shattered crates. The Americans had a device that delayed the opening of parachutes to ensure greater accuracy, but the French never acquired it.[26]

There was a two-week lull while Giap called in 25,000 reserves and replenished his depleted supplies of ammunition. While sporadic skirmishes and artillery exchanges never ceased during this lull, the Viet Minh concentrated on surrounding the remaining redoubts with a spider web of assault trenches. On 24 March Castries' chief of staff was flown out of Dien Bien Phu after suffering a nervous breakdown and Castries himself effectively surrendered command to the tough commander of the Airborne Group, Lieutenant-Colonel Pierre Langlais. Lower down the ranks others were cracking up in different ways, and by the end up to 3,000 internal deserters hid in the reed-covered banks of the Nam Youm River, scurrying forth at night like rats to filch food from the littered battlefield. On 28 March the last aircraft to land at Dien Bien Phu, a Dakota taking out wounded, was destroyed on the runway.

On 30 March Giap launched attacks on the Dominiques and Elianes, and bitter fighting continued throughout April. The Viet Minh suffered appalling casualties, not least when the defenders of overrun positions called in artillery strikes on their own positions, sheltering in their bunkers while the enemy in the open outside were shredded by air bursts and by fire from the French anti-aircraft guns. The few tanks also proved to have a combat weight of gold. Time and again the hard core of the defence, the French, Foreign Legion and Vietnamese Paras, cobbled together shattered units to beat off attacks and to retake lost positions, fighting beyond exhaustion with the aid of Benzedrine-like stimulants. And all the while incredibly brave soldiers without parachute training volunteered to jump into the shrinking perimeter, which was too small for the defenders to be able to collect more than a fraction of the supplies dropped to them, at terrible cost to the French and American transport aircraft pilots. On 29 April the defenders went on half-rations.

It is no great mystery that the Viet Minh prevailed: including auxiliaries, the Viet Minh outnumbered the French by six or seven to one. The only hopes were that a relief force might punch its way north from Laos, or else that a massive US intervention might be launched. Equivocal French evidence of increased Chinese military involvement led the US to consider sending in B-29 Superfortresses from the Philippines, picking up jet fighter escorts from carriers in the Gulf of Tonkin for their final run. In the event they did carry out covert bombing raids. There was also loose talk – notably from Vice President Richard Nixon – of using tactical nuclear bombs, but even if the weather conditions had not been so unfavourable, mass bombing from high level was unrealistic in a battle where the Viet Minh were 'holding the enemy by the belt-buckle', a tactic they were to refine in battle with US airmobile units in the 1960s.

Eisenhower's view of Dien Bien Phu was unsentimental: 'Who could be so dumb as to put a garrison down in a valley and then challenge the other guy, who has artillery on the surrounding hills, to come out and fight?' When the CIA Director Allen Dulles tried to discuss the matter further Eisenhower waved him away, saying, 'Do you think I have to be bothered with that god-forsaken place?'[27] When his Chiefs of Staff brought up the nuclear option the President angrily rounded on them: 'You boys must be crazy. We can't use those awful things against Asians for the second time in ten years. My God!'

Many Americans were vocal in opposing any involvement in Indochina. Army Chief of Staff Matthew Ridgway was a paid-up member of the 'Never Again Club' and strongly resisted embroiling US ground forces in another Asian war so soon after Korea. Vice Admiral Lawton Collins made a lapidary remark about limited US military intervention: 'one cannot go over Niagara in a barrel only slightly' – a view shared by the Senate Minority Leader, Lyndon Baines Johnson, who pounded a desk to make his opposition forcefully. When a senator worried that defeat at Dien Bien Phu would represent a Western loss of face, another senator rejoined: 'I'm not worried about losing my face – I'm worried about losing my ass.'[28]

There were, anyway, insuperable obstacles in the way of US intervention, even before the CIA noted shortly after the lost battle that Dien Bien Phu had involved only 4 per cent of overall French forces, and that it need not result in a complete collapse of their position in Indochina. There had to be Congressional approval (no chance), joint commitment by allies (British premier Winston Churchill declined to send troops) and a firm French commitment to Vietnamese independence (which would not be given). That left the French to dig their way out of their own mess. Operation Condor, the hastily cobbled-together relief force from Laos, never really got under way, crippled by the logistical problems of crossing the rough terrain dominated by the Viet Minh between the Laotian plain and Dien Bien Phu. The truth was that the French in Laos were barely able to hold their own.[29]

When Giap's troops launched their final offensive on May Day 1954, their gunners had won the artillery battle and their sappers had covered what was left of the French position with a dense network of assault trenches, while at Eliane 2 former coal miners dug a tunnel to put tons of TNT under French defenders who could hear them excavate their doom. Inside the main camp, facilities for dealing with the mounting number of wounded were overwhelmed, and the survivors would never forget the heroism of the little Ouled Nail prostitutes, now nurses, who comforted the dying. To the end, extraordinary heroism was commonplace on both sides, most poignantly among the colonial paratroopers who insisted on being dropped by night to join their comrades battling to the last.

Before nightfall on 7 May the fighting gradually stopped, with men who had fought more or less continuously for fifty-six days succumbing to exhaustion. Wary Viet Minh soldiers checked each remaining bunker to make sure the scarecrows inside no longer wished to fight on. Nine thousand men surrendered, of whom half would die over the following four months, including virtually every Vietnamese soldier the Communists captured.

The Agency Invents a Country

The day after the fall of Dien Bien Phu, formal peace talks opened in Geneva with delegations from the Democratic Republic of Vietnam, France, Britain, the Soviet Union, China and the US, as well as representatives of Bao Dai and the Laotian and Cambodian monarchies. Though the Viet Minh appeared to hold all the cards after Dien Bien Phu, they had not reckoned on the overriding concern of the Soviets and Chinese to keep the US from filling the vacuum left by the departing French. Zhou Enlai and Molotov closely co-ordinated their negotiating strategy and imposed it on Pham Van Dong, the chief Viet Minh negotiator.

Pham wanted independence for the whole of Indochina and elections which the Viet Minh believed they would win. Molotov and Zhou Enlai favoured the division of Vietnam between the Democratic Republic and Bao Dai's southern government, and rejected Pham's wish to include the Laotian Pathet Lao and Cambodian Khmer Rouge in the talks, calculating that neutralist monarchies would be enough to keep the Americans from intervening.

They were almost right. President Eisenhower's Secretary of State John Foster Dulles, brother of Allen Dulles, believed that, with the French out of the way, the US could economically bolster Cambodia, Laos and South Vietnam as bulwarks against the further spread of Communism in Asia, without getting involved too deeply and incurring the taint of colonialism. Together with Burma, Indonesia, Thailand and Malaya, Indochina was also vital for Japanese economic recovery, functioning collectively as substitutes for the vast lost market in China.

American-sponsored reforms would ensure that Vietnamese nationalists would rally to South Vietnam, its prosperity discrediting the 'false' nationalism peddled by Ho Chi Minh. This was a momentous shift in US policy in Indochina since it meant commitment to the survival of the southern regime.[30]

With the future of Cambodia and Laos artfully subtracted from the discussion, efforts focused on finding an acceptable dividing line across Vietnam. The negotiators eventually agreed on a provisional division of the country at the 17th parallel, and national elections in 1956 to decide a government for the whole country. Free migration across the parallel was to be permitted for 300 days after the Geneva Accords were signed on 21 July 1954. As many as 800,000 people moved from north to south, the majority of them Roman Catholics, while 50,000–90,000 Viet Minh sympathizers went north.

On 9 October the Viet Minh took over from the French in Hanoi under the loose supervision of Canadian, Indian and Polish monitors. Amid wild cheering and with red and gold flags sprouting from every window and balcony, Giap's troops marched into the city on sandals made from rubber tyres. Most of them peasants, they marvelled at multi-storey buildings for the first time. Ho Chi Minh modestly took up residence in the gardener's cottage in the grounds of the former Governor-General's Palace. Meanwhile, away from the international monitors, the Viet Minh security service rounded up long lists of people identified as collaborators, who were never heard from again.[31]

Peace of a sort was patched up in Geneva in 1954. The US took part as a grudging 'interested nation' and Dulles refused to shake hands with Zhou Enlai. While it suited the big powers to stop the fighting, the US declined to ratify what amounted to recognition of North Vietnam as a separate state. In September it called into being the South East Asian Treaty Organization (SEATO), which included the United States, Britain, France, Australia, New Zealand, the Philippines, Thailand and Pakistan. Burma, India and Indonesia refused to join and thereby significantly weakened the alliance. In an act that breached the terms of the Geneva Accords, which prohibited either Vietnamese state from contracting external alliances, SEATO's mandate extended to Indochina.[32]

French politics was in such disarray following the loss of Indochina that the French Assembly voted against the creation of a supranational European Defence Community that France itself had proposed as an alternative to admitting a rearmed Germany to NATO, thereby bringing about precisely the outcome that Paris had sought to avoid.

Meanwhile in Saigon, Bao Dai reluctantly appointed Ngo Dinh Diem, a nationalist from a Hué Mandarin family, as prime minister. Ho had once offered Diem a post in a popular-front cabinet, which Diem had rejected because the Viet Minh had assassinated his elder brother and nephew. Bao Dai's reluctance was understandable: Diem was a Cold War warrior and a militant Roman Catholic in a predominantly pacifist and Buddhist country. He owed his elevation to the fact that during a lengthy sojourn in the US he had been adopted by former Ambassador Joseph Kennedy and Cardinal Francis Spellman, spending three years living in the Maryknoll seminary at Ossining in New York State. With an eye to helping fellow Democrats counter Republican jibes about being 'soft on Communism', Senators John F. Kennedy and Mike Mansfield became leading lights of an association that backed Diem called American Friends of Vietnam, and Kennedy declared that Vietnam was 'the cornerstone of the Free World in Southeast Asia, the keystone to the arch, the finger in the dyke'.[33]

The Saigon Diem returned to was an Asian version of Roaring Twenties Chicago, with the police in the pockets of gangsters who openly ran casinos, opium dens and brothels. Prime Minister Diem set out to become the boss of bosses, favouring fellow northerners and making nepotism the basis of his rule. He depended on his megalomaniac librarian brother Nhu for advice, and his sister-in-law Madame Nhu for imperious glamour with her long red nails and tight *ao dais*. She may have banned both abortion and dancing, but her husband was an opium addict, heavily involved in the drug trade. Other relatives were given the ambassadorships to London, the UN and Washington. Thuc, the eldest surviving brother, became archbishop of Hué, outdoing his corrupt siblings with his own brand of genial clerical extortion.

The Eisenhower administration was divided about whether to back Diem, since he seemed to have such limited support amid the treacherous political shoals of what as yet lacked any identity as a distinctive country. 'We are prepared to accept the seemingly ridiculous prospect that this yogi-like mystic could assume the charge he is apparently about to undertake only because the standard set by his predecessors is so low,' wrote one US official. Initially, Eisenhower's emissary to Saigon, General 'Lightning Joe' Collins, thought Diem would not survive. He changed his own and Eisenhower's mind when Diem struck hard at the sects, while the rebellious generals melted away. The Cao Dai and Hoa Hao sects, and the shadowy Binh Xuyen gangsters, all had powerful paramilitary elements of the kind accurately depicted in Graham Greene's 1955 novel *The Quiet American*. In this shadowy world, loyalties turned like quicksilver.

With the odds on Diem's survival improved to 50 per cent, the US would back him, with an annual subsidy of $250 million, which from 1955 to 1961 translated into 58 per cent of South Vietnam's entire government revenue. In these years France's influence diminished as US exports to Vietnam overtook French, and 20,000 bureaucrats returned to France. Although most educated Vietnamese spoke fluent French, the prudent started to learn English, which an ever greater number of US cultural agencies ensured was taught.[34] The US embassy in Saigon became the largest such mission in the world. The Military Assistance and Advice Group (MAAG) quietly circumvented a cap on its personnel of 700 to grow to a total of 1,500, coexisting, for the time being, with General Paul Ely's French troops, still responsible for maintaining order until France pulled out. They jointly trained the Vietnamese National Army, although in tactics which might have been relevant to Korea – where many of the Americans had fought – but which were ill suited to what these troops would have to face in their own country.[35] Through a quiet process of osmosis, the US military displaced French training efforts, externally evident from the adoption of US-style insignia and the replacement of berets with steel helmets. The growing US influence was also apparent in street names changed from Rue Catinat to Tu Do (Freedom Street) and in stores called Chicago rather than Catinat.[36]

British advice, based on the experience in Malaya, was also beside the point, since the Viet Minh had a far larger basis of popular support than the CTs had enjoyed. Attempts to make the South Vietnamese wage a hearts-and-minds campaign among their own population were not a success. To have authority meant a right to beat people and steal. Instead of going about 'with a guitar under the left arm, a sub-machine gun under the right', as hearts and minds was poeticized, brutality and torture were the norm.[37]

Diem was adamantly opposed to democratic elections, rightly fearing that Ho Chi Minh would win. A CIA assessment concurred, claiming that Ho would receive 80 per cent support in a free election. Diem initiated a 'Denounce the Communists' campaign, in which thousands of southern Viet Minh sympathizers, or anyone who opposed him, disappeared into concentration camps. Newspapers which criticized him were closed. His brother Nhu supplied a political creed to bolster Diem's reactionary desire to be a latter-day emperor, as evidenced by the little shrines which flourished around his photographed image. By October 1955, Diem was sufficiently sure of himself to hold an illegal referendum in the south, in which people could choose between him and Bao Dai. He was chosen, becoming president for five years under the October 1956 constitution. Diem's political clients packed the new 123-seat National Assembly. Eighteen of its members were told to act as an opposition, while always voting with the government. They included Nhu, who won a seat as an Independent in an assembly he never graced with his presence.

That April, the last French troops withdrew from South Vietnam. The First Indochina War had cost the multiracial French forces 90,000 dead or missing in action. On the other side, the Viet Minh had lost maybe 200,000. Almost without a pause for breath, French veterans of this war found themselves transferred to Algeria, where their FLN opponents included Algerian Army of Africa soldiers who had been captured, and retrained in guerrilla warfare, by the Viet Minh.

New Dog, Same Tricks: Lansdale in Vietnam

In June 1954 a new assistant air attaché reported for duty at the US embassy in Saigon. The Air Attaché hated this confident fellow on sight, and so did the local CIA station chief, a querulous drunk who was soon replaced. For the new man was Colonel Edward Lansdale, who had automatic contact with CIA Director Allen Dulles and with his brother John Foster, the Secretary of State.

Lansdale took up residence in a spacious house with a swimming pool, trailed everywhere he went by a Filipino bodyguard called Proculo Mojica, who wore sunglasses all the time and visibly carried a large gun inside his jacket. Lansdale selected twenty men to join his new Saigon Military Mission, which operated in uneasy parallel to the Saigon CIA station. Their new premises soon overflowed with boxes of arms, ammunition and grenades. Some of these men were quiet scholarly types, proficient linguists with a background as wartime paratroopers; others were of a more buccaneering disposition, including Major Lucien Conein (pronounced Con*een*). Conein was known as 'Two Fingers Lou' or 'Black Luigi', nicknames derived from different episodes in his vivid career. A former wartime OSS agent, he claimed to have lost two fingers while serving in the French Foreign Legion, although in fact they were cut off when he was repairing the fan belt of a car in which he had been having sex with his best friend's wife. But he *was* an honorary member of the Corsican Brotherhood, a criminal organization that made the Sicilian Mafia seem tame. Bo Bohannan also came along, because Lansdale's essential task in Saigon was to repeat with Diem his success with Ramon Magsaysay. From then on a portrait of Magsaysay stared at Diem from his office wall, and from an autographed photo on his desk. But Magsaysay was a charismatic, dynamic leader admired by most Filipinos; Diem was an aloof religious zealot presiding over a regime riddled with corruption.

Still, Lansdale could but try. On the first day he simply walked into Diem's palace and volunteered his memo 'Notes on How to Be a Prime Minister of Vietnam'. Initially his help involved telling Diem the meaning of such arcane terms as 'chain of command' or 'floating a loan'. The men grew close, although Lansdale declined Diem's offer to move into the palace. Diem was encouraged to get out and about, if necessary allowing mud to splash on his white sharkskin suits. Peasants in need found themselves recipients of presidential largesse organized by Lansdale. Although Diem was an austere bachelor who had opted for celibacy, to counter rumours that he might be homosexual Lansdale had him shyly but publicly call on a woman who was supposed to be his one and only 'girlfriend', although the timid Diem never even knocked on her door.

The hand of the CIA was at work in the population transfers, or Operation Passage to Freedom. The US Navy and the CIA's Civil Air Transport, helped with the moving, while a Filipino charity provided doctors and nurses as part of a public health exercise for refugees, funded by the CIA front Operation Brotherhood. Mysterious rumours were circulated in the Communist North. One was that 'the Blessed Virgin Mary is going south'; another that two divisions of Chinese troops had arrived in the North bent on rape and pillage, ramming chopsticks in people's ears as a torture. When challenged about this last one, a smile invariably spread across Lansdale's face. Eminent astrologers were co-opted into producing cheap almanacs, which predicted disasters set to befall Viet Minh leaders even as an era of prosperity blossomed in the South. Forged Viet Minh leaflets did the rounds. One told southern Viet Minh supporters to take warm clothing north, since they were about to work as volunteers on Chinese railways, and denied that it would be necessary to confine northbound passengers in ships' holds because of likely enemy air or submarine attack. The effect of this denial on those contemplating taking passage in rusty Soviet freighters can readily be imagined.

Meanwhile, in Hanoi, Conein recruited men who were removed to a training base on Saipan where they learned the blacker forms of warfare before being infiltrated back to North Vietnam. Lansdale smuggled some eight and a half tons of weapons into the North, where Conein's favoured ruse was to smuggle coffins laden with grenades, rifles and explosives via fake funerals. Although the inserted teams of guerrillas had a comprehensive list of targets for sabotage, in the event they merely disabled Hanoi's bus service with acids added to the engine oil, and the railways by mingling explosives disguised as bricks of coal into the stocks piled at Hanoi's railway yards.

Lansdale drew heavily on his Filipino contacts, after Magsaysay had sanctioned the Freedom Company, which was designed to share lessons from the war against the Huks. Since Diem rightly feared assassination, Napoleon Valeriano – who had headed the most notorious Skulls commando force fighting the Huks – was flown to Saigon to train presidential security guards. Lansdale personally dealt with negotiations with the leadership of the sects, each of which had its own armed militia, with a view to integrating the latter into the National Army. The simplest approach was to bribe the leaders from the fund of $10 million which Lansdale had at his disposal, invariably disguised as back-pay owed to their soldiers to save face.

Diem successfully thinned out those who contested his regime's power. A gun battle that destroyed an entire suburb of Saigon saw off the gangsters of the Binh Xuyen, whose vice lord Le Bay Vien fled to Paris. The Cao Dai pope left for Cambodia; the Hoa Hao leader known as 'Ba-Cut' (he had severed a finger when vowing to fight the French) was publicly guillotined.[38] The prospect of a putsch against Diem by his own army's Chief of Staff General Nguyen Van Hinh, who enjoyed support from the US embassy, was neutralized by flying key officers for a week of debauchery in Manila, and allowing the General to transfer into the departing French army. In this manner any threats to Diem from the armed sects or the army were neutralized. This increased his attractions to the Americans.

At the same time, Lansdale was active with the Franco–US Training Relations Instruction Mission (TRIM), designed to modernize the Vietnamese National Army along the lines he had essayed in the Philippines. In addition to encouraging the army to undertake civil affairs programmes to improve their standing among the people, Lansdale flew select cadres to Clark Air Force Base in the Philippines to learn the rudiments of counter-insurgency warfare. Lansdale knew that the primary threat would come from Viet Minh guerrillas implanted in the South – whom Diem in a contraction of the Vietnamese for 'Communist Traitors to Vietnam' christened Viet Cong, a name which stuck. Their likely camps and operational areas were mapped and army communications improved, while Lansdale started recruiting Vietnamese rangers to patrol the jungle. He employed Communist Chinese military manuals to teach hearts-and-minds methods to sceptical South Vietnamese soldiers who preferred using rifle butts and boots on uncooperative farmers. Plays were organized involving a cast of Good and Bad Soldiers, Villagers, Guerrillas and a chicken, designed to illustrate the political ill-effects of soldiers' stealing food from peasants.[39]

Lansdale was also responsible for persuading Diem not simply to declare himself president, but to hold the referendum with the choice between himself and Bao Dai. Brother Nhu was invited not to stuff the ballot boxes with fake votes. In a largely illiterate country, Lansdale had the bright idea of making Diem's ballot papers red – a colour signifying good fortune, while Bao Dai got green, a colour signifying a cuckold. In the event, Diem received 98 per cent of the vote, his 5.7 million eclipsing Bao Dai's 63,000. In Saigon, Diem received a third more votes than the total number of registered electors. Lansdale deprecated such incompetence.

With his brother elected president, Nhu established a pro-Diem caucus – the Can Lao or Revolutionary Personalist Labour Party – which was compulsory for all public servants. It was a cross between a political party, a religious order and the Gestapo, since those who refused to join were often tortured or murdered. Nhu drew on his French Catholic background for the Party's creed of 'personalism', which would emphasize the dignity and value of the individual person as against Communist idolization of the masses. It was essentially the ideology of Vichy, with similar formations to integrate youth, women and so forth. Whenever the Nhus sought to explain it – and they could easily talk for eight hours without pause – their eager American auditors could not fathom their reactionary social views since these were so successfully obscured by theological mumbo-jumbo.

The reality behind the fog was that Nhu had ten separate secret intelligence agencies, in an opaque structure that prevented him from knowing anything at all since each had an investment in thwarting the other and inventing intelligence.[40] Lansdale was incensed about the Can Lao, knowing that it would result in all opposition to Diem going underground. He flew to Washington to persuade the Dulles brothers that he was right and the US embassy, which approved of the Can Lao, wrong: 'I cannot truly sympathize with Americans who help promote a Fascistic state and then get angry when it doesn't act like a democracy.' Ordered to return to Saigon, Lansdale found that Diem had cooled towards him, chiefly because the touchy President felt a loss of face whenever the bold Filipino Magsaysay was held up as an exemplar.[41]

Not only did Diem terrorize his opponents, but by excluding Buddhist leaders and professional people from its ranks the Can Lao virtually drove them into opposition. Worse, from 1956 onwards Diem did away with Vietnam's venerable tradition of elected village leaders and replaced them with his own appointees, while doing very little to purge the central civil service of time servers inherited from the French. There was no prospect of land reform, given Diem's close ties to the old landowning class. Instead Diem experimented with corralling villagers into *agrovilles*, failing to give them enough money to purchase any land, coercing them to undertake communal forced labour. Worst of all, this bastard imitation of the successful British tactics in Malaya breached the intense attachment the Vietnamese peasants felt for the graves of their ancestors. In 1959 Diem reintroduced the guillotine, which was used by mobile tribunals to rid the South of suspected Communists as well as criminals. Instead of softening their treatment of the peasantry, as Lansdale had recommended before he left Vietnam, Diem's troops were known to deal with truculent farmers by cutting off their heads and playing football with them.[42]

In North Vietnam Chinese advisers were helping the more militant Communists to carry out what was euphemistically called land reform. Peasants were encouraged to denounce their 'feudal' exploiters, who were humiliated or shot after kangaroo court hearings. By late 1956, several thousand people had been executed as 'class enemies', with estimated dead ranging from 3,000 to 15,000, depending on whether one counts victims of agrarian reform or people killed for other political deviations. When these policies touched former members of the Viet Minh army, or Catholics in Ho Chi Minh's home province, there was a popular backlash, which in the latter case required the intervention of an entire army division.

There was also the problem of how to respond to the southern comrades who were reeling under the repressive measures taken by Diem and his security forces. Moscow's enthusiasm for peaceful coexistence and the North's desire to devote its energies to post-war reconstruction initially meant that restraint was urged on the southern Communists. The Soviets even sought admission of both Vietnamese states to the UN, a gambit which appalled Hanoi. The favoured slogan was 'Build the North, look to the South', although it should be stressed that there were plenty of militants (including Giap) who wanted to unify the country through renewed war. After the southern Party leader Le Duan became acting general secretary, this line was gradually modified over a period of years and in December 1956 the Central Committee in Hanoi sanctioned a limited campaign of terrorism against southern government officials. The new tactic simultaneously retaliated for Diem's repressions while subverting any consolidation of a permanent southern state.

The limited campaign by southern Communists was transformed into something larger during the Fifteenth Plenum of the Central Committee in January 1959. The number of assassinations in the South rose from 700 a year in 1958 to 2,500 two years later, and to 4,000 in 1961. Teams of southerners who had moved north in 1954 and had received extensive military training near Hanoi were infiltrated back into South Vietnam, where they assumed command of a major campaign of revolutionary violence. Others remained in Laos, converting rudimentary jungle tracks into the major supply route later known as the Ho Chi Minh Trail; the politically schooled devoted their energies to the newly formed National Liberation Front, so called to broaden the opposition's base beyond Communists. The Viet Cong easily incited major peasant uprisings, especially in the Mekong Delta, where Diem had reimposed landowners who had fled when the French regime collapsed, while appointing his clients and cronies as provincial and village officials.

The Eisenhower administration successfully propped up Diem for six years, in line with the strong-man strategy pursued elsewhere. To his immense credit, Ike refused to commit US troops to South Vietnam. But efforts to link US aid to nation-building reforms were a complete failure, and the hatred once felt for the French transferred readily to the Americans, who were disparaged as big clumsy people. The differences with the Philippines experience were fundamental. The Vietnamese were treated not as manly partners but as feckless dependants, and no effort was made to find a Vietnamese Magsaysay, if such a being existed in this altered context. The result was that Diem became indispensable, in the apt words of an American official 'a puppet who pulled his own strings – and ours as well'. Diem's solution to Communist violence was to militarize a provincial bureaucracy already crawling with his own Catholic cronies and protégés. Their violence alienated many southern peasants, driving them into the arms of the Viet Cong, whose violence was tightly focused. It was they, not the Diem regime, which won the hearts and minds of the rural population through a genuine understanding of their concerns and by simple but effective measures.

The Diem regime spouted pretentious French metaphysics (shorn of the tradition of administrative efficiency) while practising corruption, torture and arbitrary murder.[43] And it was into this rat-hole that the Eisenhower administration poured more than $1 billion in aid between 1955 and 1961, as much as 78 per cent of it military. Superficially, Saigon took on the countenance of a modern city – it reminded the economist John Kenneth Galbraith of Toulouse – with the added charm of exceptionally pretty girls in pyjamas riding around on bicycles. Much of the non-military US aid was frittered away on consumer goods, rather than invested in ways that might have improved the lot of Vietnam's peasantry, who were 90 per cent of the population.

From 1956 onwards the American MAAG took over from the French the task of training the South Vietnamese Army. Its supremo, Lieutenant-General Samuel 'Hanging Sam' Williams, was a conventionally minded soldier who had served in Korea. This meant that such reforms as MAAG oversaw involved preparing the South Vietnamese Army for a conventional conflict, in which the threat would be a North Vietnamese invasion. Even this aim was subverted by Diem's interference. Loyalty trumped competence when it came to promotions, and dispositions were made that suited Diem's political instincts. As for the local Civil Guard, disagreements broke out among the American advisers as to whether this should be a village home guard or a mobile strike force. Diem simply starved it of resources and used it as a dumping ground for officers he disliked. As the Communist insurgency gained terrifying momentum, the Americans were also divided between those civilian officials, led by Ambassador Elbridge Dubrow, who wanted Diem to reform to widen his popular support, and MAAG, which looked for a purely military solution. Ironically, an increased US presence did not translate into control over America's client, for Diem knew how to play on US divisions, and had his own ideas on where Vietnam should stand in the wider world. He wanted to demonstrate that he was not another Chiang Kai-shek or Syngman Rhee. By 1958 forty countries had formally recognized South Vietnam, and it participated in some twenty UN-affiliated organizations. Diem hoped that his non-Communist and non-colonial country would become a leading light of the non-aligned world. Even as the Americans were pouring millions into modernizing his country, Diem's preferred model was to be an Asian de Gaulle. There was plenty of scope for disillusionment on both sides.[44]

After Lansdale had left Vietnam, he dealt deftly with how the shadowy role of men like himself was being presented to a wider public. He was not the real-life prototype for Graham Greene's 1955 *Quiet American*, since Greene had finished the first draft of his novel before the two men briefly met amid a large French crowd. A more likely candidate would be the younger Howard Simpson, with whom Greene once shared a plane and jeep ride followed by a boozy lunch. Nonetheless, in the small world of Westerners in Saigon, Greene's book was read as a novel in which actual persons and events are disguised as fictional characters. Lansdale certainly took the character of Greene's American anti-hero Alden Pyle very personally even if, at forty-six on arrival in Saigon, he was hardly naive young Pyle idealistically blundering around in a Saigon he barely understood. Pyle vies for the love of a Vietnamese girl called Phuong with an opium-addicted, worldly-wise British correspondent called Thomas Fowler, tempted to escape his loveless marriage with an English Roman Catholic wife. Fowler realizes that Pyle is deeply involved in Cao Dai terrorism, and indirectly has him assassinated by the Viet Minh. The book snobbishly insinuates that Pyle is merely a vulgar interloper from a Coca-Cola and chewing-gum culture in a dying colonial world that was not all bad, for Greene had much fellow feeling for the supposedly sophisticated French.

Although he could do little about the book, Lansdale strongly influenced the 1958 Hollywood movie based on it, since the producer Joseph Mankiewicz made him a technical adviser and submitted the draft script for his comments. Partly by casting the much decorated American war hero Audie Murphy in the role of Pyle, and Michael Redgrave playing Fowler like a maiden aunt in drag, Mankiewicz reversed the Greene's own sympathies for the two protagonists. The most memorable parts of the drama are the forceful monologues of Audie Murphy's Pyle defending the US mission in Vietnam, while Redgrave blanches with queenly horror. Lansdale also ensured that the film-makers received the full co-operation of the CIA's Saigon station, which may explain why the movie includes vividly authentic footage of the city's raucous street life, although the actress who played Phuong was an orientalized American starlet. The proceeds of the film's premiere were donated to American Friends of Vietnam. Greene was furious about this travesty of his political analysis, which probably did not scratch the surface of what Lansdale and his kind really did.[45]

9. SOMETIMES SPECIAL RELATIONSHIP

'In God We Trust' and 'More Bang for the Buck'

Dwight 'Ike' Eisenhower was the last US President to be born in rural nineteenth-century America. The son of a failed farmer and store keeper of the Mennonite River Brethren, Eisenhower – thanks to the patronage of Army Chief of Staff George Marshall – vaulted over hundreds of more senior officers to become one of the greatest military commanders of the twentieth century.[1] Stalin made one of the most astute comments about Ike, when he told Averell Harriman: 'General Eisenhower is a very great man, not only because of his military accomplishments, but because of his human, friendly, kind and frank nature. He is not a *grubi* [meaning coarse or brusque] like most military.'[2]

But he was still a poor boy made good and, as he approached retirement age, concern about how to ensure a comfortable living loomed larger in his mind than whether to throw his hat into the political ring. The matter of comfortable living was resolved by a coterie of rich Republican businessmen he befriended while playing golf at Augusta, Georgia. He made more cash with his wartime memoirs. A spell as president of New York's Columbia University was a waste of his energy. Between 1951 and 1952, while he served as commander of NATO forces in Europe, Ike played the reluctant bride to Republican suitors, while quietly having experts flown over to brief him about mortgages, farm subsidies, public housing and the economy.[3] He was so careful to hide his political views that in November 1951 Truman offered to back his candidacy as a Democrat – even as his rich Republican friends were organizing a Citizens for Ike movement. These friends also paid the salaries of the personal staff he retained after leaving the army, including the Democrat-supporting journalist Emmet John Hughes, seconded to his campaign teams in 1952 and 1956 and author of one of the sharpest insider memoirs of that era, *The Ordeal of Power* (1963).

Ike knew that, as in love, so in politics 'the seeker is never so popular as the sought. People want what they can't get.' Robert Taft, a scion of the great Ohio political dynasty whom we encountered earlier in this book as the chief Republican isolationist, was the last serious anti-interventionist presidential candidate in US history, at least until George W. Bush, who started out with such views. He feared that the expanded overseas commitments represented by Truman's doctrine of containment would put the US in the same boat as nineteenth-century Britain, perpetually squandering resources in fire-fighting insurgencies in places of little or no value to the metropolis, while federal government would grow like Jack's beanstalk. Although highly intelligent and popular in the Mid-West, Taft did not appeal to the Republicans' more international-minded East Coast elite, or to younger Americans who had experienced the wider world while in uniform.

In January 1952 Ike allowed his name to be entered for the New Hampshire primary. Despite remaining in Paris, where he spent the election night playing bridge, he comfortably beat Robert Taft. On 12 April he resigned his NATO command to fight for the Republican nomination. After a notoriously ill-tempered battle he won the nomination, putting the Californian Senator Richard Nixon on his ticket to appease the McCarthyite right and to increase his appeal in California. He had to get used to indignities for which his military career had not prepared him, including insinuations that he was a Jew (the name, you see). Arriving in Kansas City, the vast Governor Dan Thornton, wearing a ten-gallon hat, slapped him on the back with a 'Howya, pardner!' Eisenhower temporarily froze and glared at the Governor, before extending his hand to say, 'Howya, Dan.'[4]

Ike's Democrat opponent was a similarly shy bride. Adlai Stevenson was the Governor of Illinois who, with a firm sense of dynastic entitlement, had achieved this august position on his initial foray into politics. He was in no hurry to run for the presidency, prompting Truman to exclaim: 'Adlai, if a knucklehead like me can be President and not do too badly, think what a really educated guy could do in the job.'[5] Stevenson had difficulty in pacing his speeches, and his forced smile flashed on and off in the wrong places. He found politics vulgar.

Stevenson's greatest weakness was that his heart was not in the contest. He had contemplated Eisenhower's gambit of paying a 'let's end the war' visit to Korea before he did, but rejected it as too populist.[6] He even conceded that the Democrats had been in power too long and that Ike was a decent fellow. As George Ball remarked, the Democrats had exhausted the ranks of poor people to sentimentalize in an abstract way, while running into the quagmire of Korea.

Eisenhower ran his campaign like a military operation, compiling orders with bullet points detailing the sequence of actions to be taken. Aged sixty-two, he also had the stamina for travelling over 50,000 miles and speaking in 232 towns and cities. In addition to his prestige as the supreme commander of the wartime campaign in Europe, Ike was blessed with a winning smile that made him an ad man's dream. He was skilfully packaged for television, a medium his opponent held in snobbish disdain. Ad execs advising his team had no time for the exalted political rhetoric that came naturally to Stevenson and focused on the 'fifteen-second spot' that would be remembered when all the other words were forgotten. Heavily scripted Q&A sessions translated when broadcast as short spots into a housewife asking: 'You know what things cost today. High prices are driving me crazy.' To which the General would reply: 'Yes, my Mamie [his wife] gets after me about the high cost of living. It's another reason why I say it's time for a change. Time to get back to an honest dollar and an honest dollar's work.' After a long day spent recording these spots, Ike grumbled, 'To think that an old soldier should come to this.'[7]

Popular desire for change was so great that Ike would probably have won handsomely anyway, but what clinched it was his dramatic last-minute promise to go to Korea immediately after he was elected, thus making it clear that ending the war would be his first priority once he entered the White House. He won 33.9 million votes to Stevenson's 27.3 million, and 442 to 89 votes in the Electoral College. Republicans also won majorities in both Houses of Congress.

US presidents have around ten weeks to assemble their governing team. Ike was adamant in avoiding cronyism, preferring big business-men who would take a financial hit through government service as opposed to 'business failures, college professors [crossed out and replaced by 'political hacks'] and New Deal lawyers'. His appointments included 'Engine Charlie' Wilson, the President of General Motors, as secretary of defense, George Humphrey, the President of the Mark Hanna Com-pany, to the Treasury, while the Boston banker Robert Cutler became national security advisor. The cabinet consisted of 'eight millionaires and a plumber' – a token and useless trade unionist. Engine Charlie in particular was 'a classic type of corporation executive: basically apoliti-cal and certainly unphilosophic, aggressive in action and direct in speech – the undoubting and uncomplicated pragmatist who inhabits a world of sleek, shining certitude'. He combined an ability to be coldly callous towards the ordinary worker with credulousness about doing a 'package deal' with the Soviets over Korea. After one too many Wilsonian mono-logues, a fellow cabinet member scribbled: 'From now on, I'm buying nothing but [Chrysler] Plymouths.'[8]

The millionaire lawyer John Foster Dulles was appointed secretary of state. He was a difficult man to like: big face, big ears, big glasses and a mouth like a shark. There was something relentless about him, as sym-bolized by the 559,688 miles of diplomatic travel he clocked up while in office. A shy man, Dulles appeared to lack social graces. Arguably the most knowledgeable Secretary of State in recent US history and certainly the most hard working, he would spend between twelve and fifteen hours preparing a thirty-minute speech, using the process to think through each problem. His favourite word was 'moral', which State Department officials tried regularly but unsuccessfully to remove from his draft speeches.[9]

Dulles's maternal grandfather General John Watson Foster had been secretary of state in 1892–3 and his 'Uncle Bert', Robert Lansing, served Woodrow Wilson in the same capacity in 1915–20. No less significantly, a paternal grandparent had been a Christian missionary and Dulles's father a Presbyterian minister of the liberal persuasion. At Princeton his teachers included Wilson, then the university President, and during a graduate year at the Sorbonne he was taught by the Nobel Prize-winning philosopher Henri Bergson, from whom he acquired a sophisticated understanding of the role of time in diplomacy. Dulles passed out top of his law-school class at George Washington University, joining the prestigious Wall Street law firm Sullivan & Cromwell, who were aggressive seekers of business opportunities for their clients – lobbyists rather than trial lawyers. Uncle Bert used him as an international negotiator. His younger brother Allen also joined Sullivan & Cromwell, but with a lengthy intermission as a diplomat and in the wartime OSS.

While John Foster was a Republican isolationist, close to the Nazi apologist Charles Lindbergh, brother Allen was firmly in the internationalist camp of the same party. Both brothers regularly attended the influential Council of Foreign Relations, where rich men and their tame intellectuals discussed the world over port and cigars. John Foster talked and wrote extensively about foreign affairs, where his main interest became the role of religious faith in securing peace through international institutions. After 1941, for the first and only time in their lives, Allen eclipsed his brother, running one of the OSS's most effective agent networks from Switzerland. Beneath the Santa Claus manner – he laughed 'ho, ho' without any humour – this was a tough, complex and cunning man.[10]

Neither brother was in good odour with the new Truman administration, which quickly closed down the OSS. Even so, John Foster occasionally served Truman, without securing a senior permanent post. This was no reflection on his competence, rather on his profound disagreement with the foreign policy of Truman and Acheson. In particular he judged the doctrine of containment as advocated by Kennan and other realists to be 'non-moral'. Freezing the status quo, he said, left hundreds of millions of wretched people languishing under Communist totalitarian domination.[11]

Ike met Dulles for the first time in April 1952, and immediately earmarked him for the State Department, although he did require him to tone down his comments on what he would like to do with the containment policy.[12] Both men were conservative Cold War internationalists, and Ike said of him, 'there's only one man I know who has seen more of the world and talked with more people and knows more than he does – and that's me'.[13]

Ever more outrageous claims by Senator McCarthy were failing to maintain the red scare, and with Ike and Dulles in power and the compromised Democrats out, much of the heat went out of the domestic foreign policy debate. Although the competition is fierce, John Foster Dulles may be the American statesman most tendentiously vilified and misrepresented by leftists on both sides of the Atlantic. The reason is not hard to identify: he had strong Christian views and uncompromisingly condemned Communism as evil. A bit like Marxists, Dulles believed 'there is a moral law which, no less than physical law, undergirds our world'. This was not exclusive to Christianity but common to many religions, as he had found when dealing with people of other faiths. Nonetheless, he believed that with its God-given form of government, the US had a unique mission to extend the values it incarnated to the rest of the world. A spiritually robust America would operate as a moral force, breathing life into such international organizations as the United Nations, through overseas aid and by the promotion of individual freedom and human rights.

Dulles had strong ethical objections to the survival of Woodrow Wilson's progressive spin on 'racial segregation', if only because it undermined the US case in the struggle with Soviet anti-imperialists.[14] He discussed the difficult ethical choices he had to make with his high-level contacts in the American Churches, to which he also appealed to mobilize popular support for the administration's foreign policy. He recruited the evangelist Billy Graham, a confidant and supporter of the President, as a roving US ambassador, notably to darkest Britain. Dulles's relations with Church leaders were not without frictions, particularly over the issue of nuclear weapons, with the religious supporting disarmament and Dulles insisting on the necessity of maintaining a massive nuclear deterrent. The *Time-Life* journalist and presidential speechwriter Emmet Hughes judged that Dulles's greatest failing as a statesman was that he thought and spoke like a lawyer, engaged in prosecuting the Soviet Union in a long-drawn-out case in the court of history. He was absolutely invested in his case, 'quickly excited by small gains, suddenly shaken by minor reverses, and ever prone to contemplating the drastic remedy of the massive retort'.[15]

Although Dulles was the more cerebral of the two, Ike had the edge in a key respect, for as a former general he was calmer in the face of major setbacks, never allowing the detail to obscure the big picture. Religious faith was important in cementing their relationship. A day before his inauguration, Eisenhower was baptized into the National Presbyterian Church by a pastor, Edward Elson, who had served as a military chaplain in occupied Germany. Ike personally insisted on prefacing his inauguration speech with a prayer of his own devising. He opened his first cabinet session with a prayer, and the practice was institutionalized at the urging of his Mormon Secretary for Agriculture. The President also held regular National Prayer Breakfasts, where religious leaders mingled with the powerful, as well as, from 1954 onwards, a National Day of Prayer. 'In God We Trust' became the national motto and henceforth appeared on US banknotes. The Pledge of Allegiance was emended to include the phrase 'one nation under God'.

The symbolic elaboration of an older civic religion was important to a nation whose global enemy marched under the banner of materialistic atheism. America of the 1950s may have been 'about' McDonald hamburgers, Holiday Inns, Levittown suburbs, Lucille Ball, Elvis, Marlon, Marilyn and James Dean, but it also witnessed an astonishing religious revival. 'I believe fanatically in the American form of democracy, a system . . . that ascribes to the individual a dignity accruing to him because of his creation in the image of the supreme being,' wrote Ike to a friend in 1947. The US may have been a deeply consumerist society itself, but Ike deprecated the Soviets' obsession with technology, secure in the knowledge that the US was, and would remain, far ahead without having to make the sacrifices that the Soviet leadership imposed on their people. When the Soviets scored a major propaganda coup on launching the first space satellite in October 1957, which did little more than emit beeps to radio hams, Ike responded by helping raise $20 million to build a new National Presbyterian Church in Washington, while continuing to invest quietly in Intercontinental Ballistic Missiles (ICBM) and in the long-term development of a spy satellite system to replace the interim U-2 spy plane.[16]

Realizing that spirituality was another potential weapon in the Cold War, Ike did not rely on such establishment bodies as the National

Council of Churches, but co-opted evangelicals, Catholics, Jews and Muslims, while carefully excluding the more intemperate Protestant fundamentalists. In reality, relations with US Jews were cool, because Ike suspected them of divided loyalties over Israel, and Dulles resented incessant Zionist lobbying ultimately orchestrated by the Israeli government. This was the first and last US administration to refuse tax exemptions to the American Israel Public Affairs Committee (AIPAC), which affected its funding prospects. The crux of the problem was that the US needed amicable relations with Arab states to contain the Soviets, and hence could not over-identify with Israel, which for its part needed harmonious relations with the Soviets to expedite the exit of Russian and Polish Jews.[17] Instead, aided by Pastor Elson, the chairman of American Friends of the Middle East, Ike went out of his way to be respectful towards Islam, sensing its utility in repelling Communism, and opening the US's first national mosque.[18]

Ike's conundrum was how 'not [to] destroy what we are attempting to defend' – how to reconcile fiscal probity with international responsibilities.[19] The administration's first challenge was to reduce a defence budget that had nearly quadrupled under Truman, without impairing the nation's future security. Truman's parting gift in the field of national security, the day before he left office, was to approve a continental air defence system and a massive civil defence programme, all requiring a further $20 billion on top of defence expenditure of $53 billion in 1953, or 61 per cent of all government spending and 12 per cent of GNP.[20] Ike believed that such an order of expenditure must harm America's economy and so undermine the nation's security, while the resulting 'garrison state' would subvert its own citizens' cherished freedoms. The Bomb was seen as a means of squaring this circle.

Ike's 'New Look' policy relied on devastating nuclear retaliation as a cheaper option to interminable peripheral wars that could not be won, a strategy summed up by the jokey phrase 'more bang for the buck'. Dulles believed in the certainty/uncertainty principle by which an opponent had to be convinced that aggression would trigger a response, but the opponent would not know what that would be. Eisenhower deplored nuclear weapons, but he never dispelled the belief that he would not hesitate to use them, and all in one massive blow.

Nuclear weapons and the means to deliver them were rapidly evolving. By 1954 the USA and the USSR had respectively 2,063 and 150 nuclear bombs of various potencies, for their yield could be 'dialled' up or down. Obviously this information was highly classified and was not shared by the two major nuclear powers. The US significantly changed the game when on 1 November 1952 it tested its first thermonuclear device on the islet of Elugelab in the South Pacific. The 10.4 megaton weapon exploded with the force of 700 Hiroshimas and the flash of light was seen 400 miles away from a fireball three miles wide. Eighty million tons of coral, sand and water became a giant vapour cloud. Elugelab ceased to exist. Nuclear tactics evolved too. Operation Quick Strike in October 1953 showed it was possible for the new B-52 Stratofortresses to take off from the continental US, refuel in mid-air, hit their Soviet targets, refuel again and land in Britain or Morocco. To shorten the lengthy time it took to deploy the bombs, Eisenhower authorized the final assembly of the devices in flight.[21] The Soviets' counter to the B-52, the Myasishchev-4 (NATO codename Bison), lacked the range and the mid-air refuelling capability to reach the US. The Soviets also had no aircraft carriers, and no ships or submarines capable of launching nuclear missiles. But even their medium-range Tupolev Tu-16 (Badger) could hit London or Paris. Nuclear testing took a frightening turn when the thermonuclear device codenamed Bravo was detonated at Eniwetok Atoll in 1954. It had been thought the component Lithium-7 would remain inert, but it did not and an explosion predicted to be in the eight- to ten-megaton range yielded a runaway fifteen. The fireball was four miles wide, while three condensation rings formed around the debris cloud which ascended at a thousand feet per second. A radioactive cloud extended a thousand miles away.[22] The scientific search for a strategic edge also took bizarre forms. Looking for an alternative to nuclear warfare, in August 1953 Ike created the Presidential Advisory Committee on Weather Control to follow up on experiments in the late 1940s that had shown it was possible to induce snow by releasing dry ice from a plane flying inside clouds. Mercifully, weather-warfare projects were allowed to lapse.[23]

Eisenhower inherited a vastly expanded range of global commit- ments. The State Department had mushroomed from 5,000 employees

to 20,000, with US embassies becoming a conspicuous and often jar-
ringly modernistic presence in foreign capitals. The embassy in Seoul
alone had 2,000 staff.[24] There were three and a half million men and
women in the US armed forces, of whom a third were deployed in 800
overseas bases in fulfilment of treaty obligations to defend forty-two
countries. Thanks to the end of active hostilities in Korea, Ike was able
to cut their numbers to 2.8 million, and to reduce the defence budget by
nearly $5 billion in 1954–5, and he brought it below $50 billion during
the rest of his presidency. Only the air force saw an increase, its budget
rising by $1 billion in line with the new emphasis on nuclear deter-
rence.[25] Strategic Air Command alone represented $8.5 billion of fixed
capital investment, twice that of the giant Standard Oil of Ohio.

The National Security Council assumed a new importance, with
Eisenhower chairing 339 sessions.[26] His past experiences made him a
superb manager. His view was that 'a platoon leader doesn't get his platoon to go that way by getting up and saying "I am smarter, I am bigger,
I am stronger, I am the leader". He gets his men to go with him because
they want to do it for him, because they believe in him.'[27] The new permanent special assistant for national security affairs, Robert Cutler,
co-ordinated relations between the White House and the NSC, while for
the first time the US Treasury Secretary was made a member of the NSC
to underline the links between the economy and national security strategy. Eisenhower also increased the power of the Chairman of the Joint
Chiefs of Staff in an attempt to bring wasteful inter-service rivalry under
control. Service chiefs were told to cut costs. As a general, Ike knew
every trick the Pentagon used to increase its budget and how much fat
could be cut from the bone. Cutler set up a subordinate Planning Board
and a separate Operations Coordinating Board for implementation, to
accustom board members to work within their areas of expertise on the
nation's long-term security.[28] The NSC itself became the scene of sophisticated group discussions, with Ike and John Foster Dulles not always in
agreement about future strategy. Dulles was sceptical of the value of the
'shattered old people' who ran Europe, and insisted that the US should
make strenuous efforts to liberate Eastern Europe. With the authority of
a former NATO commander, Ike believed in the capability and will
of the Europeans to defend themselves, while seeing the Cold War

more as a battle for hearts and minds than for territorial control. The final word, as expressed in NSC 162/2, was the result of profound and far-reaching discussion, influenced by circumstances in the world beyond Washington.[29]

Ike believed in the maxim 'Planning is everything; plans are nothing.' Ideas were subject to creative competition. Project Solarium, named after the White House sunroom where Mamie's canary chirped, but in fact conducted at the National War College under cover of redesigning the curriculum, was an attempt to game-play and to cost alternative national security strategies. Ike was looking for a strategy which toned down the harsh pre-election rhetoric of John Foster Dulles, while reverting to the more considered approach of his wartime boss George Marshall. The exercise involved three seven-man teams that spent five weeks perfecting their play. Team A was led by George Kennan, the others by a general and an admiral. Team B's position was straightforward and involved drawing a line in the sand and telling Moscow to go no further. Team C argued for the more aggressive liberation of areas under Communist domination. Kennan's team turned in a 150-page report, which advocated watchful but unaggressive containment to bring about peaceful liberation when Communism collapsed from its own inner contradictions, thus avoiding the transformation of the US itself into an armed camp. At the plenary NSC meeting where Team A's work was adopted, Kennan had the satisfaction of observing Dulles being saddled with his policy even though the Secretary of State had 'disembarrassed' himself of Kennan's person.[30]

Parallel with these discussions, the new men on the Joint Chiefs of Staff – notably Admiral Radford and General Ridgway – were asked for a new set of military strategies, which would also shape NSC policy. To Dulles's alarm, they took him at his word, advocating a huge build-up of nuclear capacity, and the withdrawal of forces from defending all points of the compass, a combination which would also save money. He worried that such a defence posture would frighten Europeans into neutralism because of the unlikelihood that the US would risk total annihilation on behalf of Belgium. Consequently, after lengthy sessions with the President, Dulles emerged as a leading advocate of collective security, as well as of instant nuclear retaliation, with room left open for subversion of the Red Empire or its clients, provided this stopped short of provoking all-out war. That was where his brother Allen came in.

Greater attention was paid (in National Security document NSC 162/2 of October 1953) to psychological warfare, covert operations and subversion, all of which were relatively cheap. Eisenhower was also keen on such catchy propaganda campaigns as Atoms for Peace, which stressed the civil uses of nuclear energy, and Open Skies, an abortive attempt to introduce mutual and voluntary aerial monitoring of US and Soviet nuclear and missile sites. Both were intended to maintain an American grip on the moral high ground of international opinion.[31] No less importantly the giant US Information Agency aggressively sponsored the teaching of English in the Third World, arguably the best way of interesting people in the Western way of life. The radio station Voice of America's most popular programme behind the Iron Curtain was Willis Conover's *Music USA – Jazz Hour*, so much so that an entire generation of young people in Communist countries tried to speak English with the host's tobacco-enriched accent.[32]

Darker practices were the domain of the CIA and the newly founded National Security Agency responsible for communications intelligence. Truman had botched the establishment of the CIA by appointing orthodox military types to run it. Admiral Roscoe Hillenkoetter and General Walter Bedell Smith lacked the creative flair of many of their subordinates, including such legends as David Bruce, Kermit Roosevelt, Cord Meyer, William Bundy, Richard Bissell and William Colby. Far from being a collection of right-wing ideological fanatics, they were often registered Democrats who shared the outlook and sophisticated tastes of the East Coast liberal elite, and consequently incurred particularly malignant attention from Senator McCarthy. They admired Jackson Pollock, whose exhibitions the CIA covertly sponsored to advertise Western freedoms against Soviet socialist realism.[33]

At the time of the riots in Bogotá during the 9th Pan-American Conference in 1948 which had menaced Secretary Marshall in person, Defense Secretary Forrestal commissioned a wide-ranging review of the CIA. The report was cleverly drafted by Allen Dulles to create a job description that fitted him perfectly. Although he made many sensible suggestions, NSC 10/2 of 18 June 1948 fatefully linked covert intelligence collection with the very different activity of covert operations – active intervention in the domestic affairs of foreign countries often involving contracted paramilitaries. The report gave birth to the blandly named Office of Policy Coordination to carry out such operations under the leadership of former OSS agent Frank Wisner. After the election of Eisenhower, the sixty-year-old Allen Dulles became the first civilian director of the Agency, his satisfaction at achieving a lifetime's ambition marred by a messy marriage to Clover and the death of his son in Korea. Poolside weekend parties at their sister's home in suburban McLean, where Allen and Foster dressed in Hawaiian shirts and baggy shorts, the one all bonhomie, the other like the grim reaper, was one unlikely venue where US policy was made.

Britain: The Long Goodbye

Eisenhower's presidency coincided with a changing of the guard in Great Britain. In the general election of February 1950, the overall Labour majority was cut from 146 to 8. The result revitalized the seventy-five-year-old Churchill, who mercilessly harassed government spokesmen in Parliament for the next twenty months, finally forcing another general election in October 1951. Churchill captured people's smouldering resentment of Labour's regimentation of every aspect of daily life. 'We are for the ladder,' he said. 'Let us all do our best to climb. They are for the queue. Let each wait in his place until his turn comes.' The election saw him return to power with a majority of seventeen, although Labour still won a plurality of the popular vote (48.8 per cent against the joint Conservative and National Liberal 48 per cent). Had there been any major policy differences between the two main parties, the result would have indicated a dangerously polarized society. Instead it simply meant a needed change in personnel to administer the post-war settlement, as the attrition of office had consumed the limited pool of talent in the Labour Party.[34]

The big political question was how long Churchill would remain in 10 Downing Street.[35] All the many insider diarists of the period agreed that his character flaws became more pronounced with age: rambling monologues at the cabinet or dinner tables, and an obsessive interest in playing bezique rather than reading important state papers. Lachrymose bouts became simply embarrassing when detached from the high emotions generated by wartime. 'He starts confused and wrong on almost every issue, hardly listens to argument and constantly reverts to wartime and post-war analogies,' wrote Eden's private secretary Evelyn Shuckburgh. He seemed 'old, weary and inconsequent'.[36] In June 1953, Churchill collapsed after suffering a major stroke while entertaining Italian premier Alcide De Gasperi in Downing Street. It was a moment to retire with dignity, but Churchill recovered and soldiered on, perpetually discovering fresh excuses to delay retirement. It was the final, desperate act of a wholly self-centred life, for he repeatedly said that he would die quickly once he left office, which was his reason to go on living.[37]

He remained in office because none of the other Conservative leaders had the necessary killer instinct. His prissy young Chancellor of the Exchequer, Rab Butler, was coping with young children after his wife's premature death. The dynamic Housing Minister, Harold Macmillan, was in his private life a knowing cuckold to Churchill's bisexual crony Bob Boothby; he also suffered chronic pain from a First World War wound and had his gall bladder removed in 1953. That same year, two botched operations for the same condition nearly carried off Eden, who had to go to the US to have the damage repaired. Chronic bad health, as well as the loss of his son in Burma late in the war and a painful divorce in 1950, exacerbated Eden's volatile nature, although marriage to Churchill's niece Clarissa in 1952 had a stabilizing effect. From April to October 1953 Churchill acted as his own foreign secretary, implicitly putting another question mark over the capacities and stamina of his would-be successor, whose stock fell the longer Churchill remained in harness.[38] There was much truth in Macmillan's bitchy 1975 comment: 'The trouble with Anthony Eden was that he was trained to win the Derby in 1938; unfortunately he was not let out of the starting stalls until 1955.'[39]

Although on a good day Churchill fussed over Eden like a son, on a bad day he could be vicious. Lavishing praise on the bearing and elegance of Acheson, who did indeed resemble a parody of a British Guards officer, Churchill turned to Eden and said, 'Dean looks like you're supposed to do.' In Eden's case it was difficult to decide whether he was a strong man with weak tendencies, as his ambiguous record on appeasement in the 1930s suggested, or a weak man neurotically pretending to be strong, which was Churchill's private opinion of him.

Churchill was more willing to subordinate Britain to the new realities of US power and was sentimental about the land of his mother in a way that Eden emphatically was not. Like most of his generation Eden deeply resented the Americans' late entry into the two world wars and the huge profit they had made from them, as well as their primary responsibility for the Great Depression and their brutal cut-off of financial aid and nuclear collaboration in 1946. The feeling was mutual. Acheson was contemptuous of Eden's habit of calling males 'my dear', and on one occasion his diplomatic mask slipped right off. In November 1952, accompanied by an aide, Acheson wandered from a cocktail party into Eden's hotel room in New York, requiring 'a real martini, meaning mainly gin' despite already being four sheets to the wind. The British delegation had been trying to get the Americans to accept an Indian scheme to resolve the prisoner-repatriation issue in Korea, and Acheson let go with a rapid fire of contemptuous assessments of Commonwealth leaders and even of his uncomfortable British hosts.[40]

Churchill's wartime role meant that he was indulged in Washington, where his anti-Communism and flights of grandiose generalities about a commonality of culture and purpose were warmly received. Crossing the Atlantic aboard the *Queen Mary* to bid farewell to Truman and to salute President-elect Eisenhower, Churchill spoke of the need for an Anglo-American common front, 'from Korea to Kikuyu and from Kikuyu to Calais'.[41] Unfortunately he sought a continuing leading role in world affairs that neither he nor his country had the strength to justify, as evidenced in an obsessive quest for one last 'Big Three' summit conference with the Americans and the Soviets. His cabinet were privately appalled, as they could foresee his alcohol-fuelled grandiosity leading him to enter into unsustainable commitments and to make damaging concessions. Dulles did not believe in summits with the Soviets.

Churchill had worked closely with Eisenhower during the war and shared the general British view that he was 'a genial and dynamic mediocrity'.[42] Ike's account of his first encounter with Churchill as president in January 1953 reveals that the self-styled 'dumb bunny' had a more accurate understanding:

> Mr Churchill is as charming and interesting as ever, but he is quite definitely showing the effects of the passing years. He has fixed in his mind a certain international relationship he is trying to establish . . . This is that Britain and the British Commonwealth are not to be treated just as other nations would be treated by the United States in our complicated foreign problems. On the contrary, he most earnestly hopes and intends that those countries shall enjoy a relationship which he thinks will recognize the special place of partnership they occupied with us during World War II . . . Winston is trying to relive the days of World War II. In those days he had the enjoyable feeling that he and our President were sitting on some rather Olympian platform with respect to the rest of the world, and directing world affairs from that point of vantage. Even if this picture were an accurate one of those days, it would have no application to the present. But it was only partially true, even then, as many of us who, in various corners of the world, had to work out the solutions for nasty local problems, are well aware. In the present international complexities, any hope of establishing such a relationship is completely fatuous . . . the two strongest western powers must not appear before the world as a combination of forces to compel adherence to the status quo.[43]

In Bermuda in late 1953, the British noticed that the President no longer smiled much and chewed the arms of his glasses during meetings. But they also noted how Churchill cut a sad figure beside the ramrod posture of the President when they took formal salutes. During one session, riled by Churchill's claims that Russia had changed and needed to be wooed, Ike retorted: 'So long as you mean what I think you mean, I agree – that it is the same old woman of the streets, even if she has on a new hat.' Ignoring the pained expressions on British faces, when Eden asked when the next session might be Ike snapped: 'I don't know. Mine is with a whisky and soda.'[44] The British were also chilled by Ike's apparent nonchalance about nuclear weapons, and his casual comments about the cost-effectiveness of using them against Chinese military bases as a means of bringing the Korean War to a swift close.

Given Britain's abrupt decline, relations between any foreign secretary and the US secretary of state were bound to be delicate. Eden passionately believed that the British Commonwealth should play an autonomous role in world affairs, which entitled the British to be treated as equal partners by the Americans. Washington's traditional anti-colonialism and its attempts to direct British policy in the Middle East towards accommodation with Arab nationalism were constant irritants. Eden was also indifferent to Europe and resented US pressure for Britain to participate in tentative schemes for enhanced European economic and defence co-operation. What with one thing and another, Eden had a growing chip on his shoulder about US power, though his class tended only to see chips on those of others.[45]

In the first year of the new administration relations with Dulles were a considerable improvement, despite Eden's attempt in May 1952 to dissuade Ike from appointing him. Dulles may have been deliberate and ponderous in manner, but he was also an experienced and highly professional operator.[46] Churchill detested on sight the Secretary's 'great slab of a face', ever after lisping his name as 'Dullith' or punning 'Dull, duller, Dulles'. On learning that a brother, Allen, was the new head of CIA, Churchill commented: 'They tell me that there is another Dullith. Is that possible?'[47]

The first indication that all was not smooth sailing between Dulles and Eden was evident when the former claimed to have been 'double-crossed' and 'lied to', as Eden subverted Dulles's attempts to establish SEATO *before* the convening of the Geneva peace conference on Indochina.[48] The mood at Geneva in 1954 was not good: 'A.E. is fed up with Dulles, refuses to make concessions to his feelings, and almost resents seeing him . . . A.E. is now hoping Dulles will go away as soon as possible . . . there is no doubt that Dulles and A.E. have got thoroughly on each other's nerves, and are both behaving like prima donnas. Dulles is said to be irritated by the "imprecision" of A.E.'s mind . . . A.E had a terrible dinner with Dulles last night.'[49]

With reference to his failed attempt to include India, which the US deeply distrusted, in SEATO, Eden commented that 'Americans may think the time is past when they need consider the feelings or difficulties of their allies . . . We, at least, have constantly to bear in mind all our Commonwealth partners, even if the United States does not like them.'[50] At the Geneva conference, which he regarded as a personal triumph, Eden shared with Molotov the worrying thought that Britain and the USSR were respectively the inside right and inside left, with the 'wilder' Americans and Chinese on the outside extremes. The more Eden tried to act independently of the US, with a view to distinguishing himself from Churchill, the more the Americans would resent his interference in their global schemes.[51]

Churchill's last government was mainly devoted to digesting the massive overload of change it had inherited, with little effort made to identify, still less address, the major structural flaws on which the edifice of the New Jerusalem rested. Historians have found little to say about this administration, which testifies to its generally emollient management of the nation's affairs. One can be too censorious about Churchill's lack of interest in tackling domestic issues, because he was surely correct to focus on the danger of nuclear war, which clouded his optimistic vision of 'broad sunlit uplands' in the future far more than the Nazi menace ever had. Britain's inferiority and vulnerability were manifest. A month after Britain had tested its first, Nagasaki-sized atomic bomb in October 1952, the US exploded the first hydrogen bomb. After Ike had partially restored the wartime nuclear weapons co-operation the US had broken off in 1946, Churchill authorized work on a British hydrogen bomb, keeping most of his cabinet in the dark about it. It was partly a British version of 'more bang for the buck', partly a way of securing Britain's continued place at the top table.

During the early 1950s elections Churchill had been stung by Labour's revival of its 1930s taunt that he was a 'warmonger'. He was acutely aware that the Soviets, who in November 1955 tested their first hydrogen bomb, might not be able to hit the US but could certainly drop them on Britain; and that ten H-bombs targeted on Britain would bring its civilization to an end.[52] To some degree this deep concern lay behind Churchill's vain obsession with a Big Three summit, which he pursued despite the indifference of Ike and Dulles and the alarmed lack of support of his own ministers.[53]

When Churchill's ministers, prompted by Macmillan, finally summoned up the collective courage to urge the old man to go, Eden went to Buckingham Palace on 6 April 1955.[54] With strikes afflicting the docks, transport and newspapers, he decided to seek a fresh mandate from the electorate and in May won a majority of sixty seats. Macmillan was rewarded with the office of chancellor of the exchequer, with Butler demoted to leader of the House, while the Welsh lawyer Selwyn Lloyd became foreign secretary, a tricky remit since Eden regarded the field as uniquely his own.[55]

If one subtracts the concluding disaster of Suez, the most striking feature of the Eden government was its inconsequentiality beneath the facile Etonian glamour. Eden had no grasp or interest in economics – which lay at the heart of Britain's problems – and, having been foreign secretary for so long, he found it difficult to adjust to a job in which Jack is obliged to be master of all trades. Even in his area of greatest expertise, he haughtily abstained from participation in the institutions of the European Common Market. The monuments to his domestic policy were meagre – a dozen technical schools founded half a century after the Germans had instituted theirs – and overall one must conclude that he was more of man of the past than the high-Victorian throwback he replaced.[56]

'Luck be a Lady'

One notable upward blip in the generally downward trend of Anglo-American relations was the two countries' collaboration in the 1953 overthrow of Prime Minister Mohammed Mossadeq of Iran. Mossadeq had become the *de facto* leader of a National Front in which secular nationalists such as himself combined with the supporters of Ayatollah Abolqassem Kashani, speaking for the Shia clergy. Following the assassination of Prime Minister Haj Ali Razmara in March 1951, the Majlis (parliament) imposed Mossadeq on the reluctant Shah and voted to nationalize the oil industry in the same parliamentary session.[57]

As we have seen, the Anglo-Iranian Oil Company (AIOC) had it coming. It had behaved in a manner outrageous even by the generally low standards of the oil industry, paying the Iranian government a pittance for its vastly profitable monopoly and treating Iranian employees like helots. It bribed parliamentary deputies to get its own way, and all promises of better pay or improvements to local amenities were broken. The company's scabrous Glaswegian chairman, William Fraser, refused to negotiate a more equitable settlement, confident that the AIOC could always rig Iranian politics to suit its interests.[58] In this he was encouraged by Labour's Foreign Secretary Herbert Morrison, of whom it is difficult to decide whether his diplomatic or his genetic legacy – in the form of his grandson Peter Mandelson, New Labour's fixer-in-chief at the turn of the twenty-first century – has done more to depress Britain's international standing.

A month before Mossadeq became prime minister a new US ambassador had arrived in Tehran. This was our old friend the Anglophile Loy Henderson, who had won a reputation as the man who had cleaned up after the British in Iraq, Greece and Turkey, Palestine and India, his most recent posting. Iran was the final mess the British got him into. The State Department was aware that Morrison's intransigent stance served only to increase the popularity of the volatile Mossadeq, and at this stage the US administration was reluctant to accept British attempts to depict Mossadeq as a fanatic or madman. Objectively, the melodramatic Iranian was an aristocratic secular-minded man who wanted neither political soldiers nor clerics in power. His problem was that he excelled in the negatives; he offered no positive vision to replace what he hated.[59]

Confident that the Iranian Majlis could be rigged into compliance, the AIOC had offered the Iranians a Supplemental Agreement, allegedly improving on the original terms forged with Reza Shah in 1933 and, like them, set to run until 1993. Popular outrage prevented the parliamentarians from simply accepting this, and Fraser refused to improve his offer. With nationalization in the air the Majlis formed a committee chaired by Mossadeq to study the Agreement, while the British pressured the Shah to sack his Prime Minister and replace him with General Haj-Ali Razmara, a former head of the army. On 3 March 1951 Razmara addressed the Majlis with an appeal not to vote for nationalization in view of Iran's treaty obligations and lack of capacity to run its own oil industry. Four days later he was assassinated at prayer in a mosque by a member of the militant Muslim group Fadayan-e Islam.

Iranian outrage had been stoked when the US oil corporation Aramco signed a 50:50 profit-sharing deal with its Saudi Arabian partners, in line with arrangements already in place in Venezuela since the late 1940s. Indeed, in November 1950 four Venezuelan diplomats arrived in Iran, proposing something very like the Organization of Petroleum Exporting Countries (OPEC), the international oil cartel which only came into existence a decade later.[60] Although the AIOC unwillingly offered Iran the same deal, it did so too late to halt the momentum towards outright nationalization. The inept combination of Fraser and Morrison could think of no better response than to reduce oil workers' pay and to station five Royal Navy vessels in the waters off Abadan. Instead of caving in, the Majlis rejected the Shah's (and AIOC's) nominee Prime Minister and elected Mossadeq, who nationalized AIOC's assets in May 1951. Morrison's attempts to garner US support collided with the State Department's assessment that 'Mossadeq's National Front Party is the closest thing to a moderate and stable political element in the national parliament.'

After Fraser had ordered all British managers and technicians to leave, in a preview of the attack on the US embassy in Tehran in 1979 raids on the AIOC's offices and the homes of senior personnel found proof that the AIOC had run its own intelligence service in Iran, whose personnel were in regular social contact with SIS officers in the vast British embassy, which occupied fifteen acres of central Tehran. At the home of the head of the AIOC's Tehran office enough papers were left unincinerated for Mossadeq to show the world how the company's tentacles had reached into every corner of the Iranian government, bribing some and forcing others from office. There was even documentary proof that the company had paid overtly nationalist newspapers to print the canard that National Front leaders were AIOC stooges.[61]

Mossadeq refused to pay compensation to the AIOC, instead demanding £50 million in unpaid taxes. He also refused to accept the mediation of the International Court of Justice in The Hague, on the grounds that AIOC was a private company, leading the apoplectic Morrison to entertain the idea of military intervention to depose him. Apprised of this, Acheson observed that Morrison knew nothing of foreign affairs. Both Britain and Iran looked to the US for support, and Truman's judicious response was to send to Tehran the most venerable emissary available, tycoon and diplomat Averell Harriman. Despite his close wartime dealings with London, Harriman had no hesitation in identifying as the root of the problem the AIOC's mismanagement and a total failure by Whitehall to comprehend Iran. This was despite being greeted by a huge demonstration shouting 'Death to Harriman,' which was violently suppressed with some loss of life.

Accompanied by oil-industry experts and with the future CIA Director Vernon Walters acting as his interpreter, Harriman sought to defuse the situation by concentrating on the technical difficulties thrown up by precipitate nationalization: how would the Iranians make up for their lack of expertise, where were their oil tankers? But Mossadeq, who when he met Harriman's wife kissed her hand as far as her elbow, was – to put it kindly – elliptical in his approach to negotiations. When Harriman spoke of oil prices, Mossadeq mused that 'it all started with that Greek Alexander' who had burned ancient Persian Persepolis 2,000 years before. Nor was Harriman prepared for the depth of Mossadeq's resentment towards the British. 'You do not know how crafty they are,' he raged. 'You do not know how evil they are. You do not know how they sully everything they touch.'[62]

Indeed. Before departing, AIOC personnel attempted to sabotage vital equipment at Abadan, while both the company and the British government discouraged foreigners from taking jobs with the new Iranian Oil Company. Legal threats were used against countries which sought to import Iranian oil. Meanwhile Robin Zaehner, a brilliant linguist who had run Britain's counter-intelligence and counter-sabotage operations in the north of Iran during and after the Second World War, was recalled to Tehran by SIS from his post as lecturer in Persian at Oxford. He was unsuccessful in organizing a plot to overthrow Mossadeq and return the oilfields to the AIOC, after which he returned to Oxford, where he was elected Spalding professor of Eastern religions and ethics in 1952.

Failing to sway Mossadeq, Harriman turned to the Shah, who was terrified of the mob, and then to Ayatollah Kashani, the leading clerical member of the National Front. When Kashani pointedly brought up the subject of an American oil man who had been murdered in Iran before the First World War, Harriman calmly replied: 'Eminence, you must understand that I have been in many dangerous situations in my life and I do not frighten easily.' 'Well, there was no harm in trying,' shrugged the cleric. Before leaving, Harriman indicated to the Shah that Mossadeq might be the obstacle that would have to be removed before a settlement could be patched up with the British. Under the Truman administration, this was but a thought left in the air.

By the summer of 1951 Morrison had persuaded Prime Minister Attlee to impose sanctions on Iran and to permit planning for military operations, codenamed Buccaneer and Plan Y, that were unrealistic at a time when Britain was committed to the Korean conflict and when 'Mossadeqism' in Egypt made it imprudent to use troops normally stationed there. British military thinking had still not adjusted to loss of the Indian Army, which had previously maintained British power in the Middle East. British hopes that the US would support intervention were unequivocally dashed by Acheson and Truman, as well as by much of the US press. The *Wall Street Journal* deprecated 'nineteenth century methods' and the *Philadelphia Inquirer* warned of a third world war. Attempts to talk up the minimal prospect of a Communist Tudeh Party takeover in Iran did not at this time resonate in the US and Attlee cancelled the military preparations. He later lamented that Morrison was the worst appointment he had ever made.

Mossadeq rubbed it in during a visit to the US, where he trounced Britain's Ambassador Gladwyn Jebb at the United Nations. The Labour government had gone in for wholesale nationalization itself without damaging world peace, he said, adding slyly that Iran had no gunboats patrolling the Thames. This went down very well with the delegates of the many countries that had past experience of British high-handedness.[63] Mossadeq also knew which buttons to push to win over the Americans, posing beside the Liberty Bell in Philadelphia to remind them that they, too, had once rebelled to win independence from Britain. When he met Truman and Acheson in October 1951 he kissed the Secretary of State but was stopped by the President's cold glare. 'Mr President, I am speaking for a very poor country, a country all desert – just sand, a few camels, a few sheep . . .' he ventured. 'Yes, and with your oil, just like Texas,' Truman interrupted.

To British ears, the thud of the other shoe dropping was plainly audible when the US government tried to broker a deal by creating a neutral company to extract and market Iran's oil, which was seen as an advance guard for the US oil interests the AIOC had long battled against. Unsurprisingly the US gambit was rejected by the new Churchill government in Britain; but it was also rejected by Mossadeq, perhaps too exalted by being named *Time* magazine's Man of the Year to recognize a lifeline when it was thrown to him.[64] Acheson had belittled the British argument that Mossadeq would necessarily turn to the Tudeh Party for support, and in the process help to push Britain towards bankruptcy; the Eisenhower administration was to take another view.[65]

During 1952 Mossadeq's domestic position weakened. He tried unsuccessfully to wrest control of the armed forces from the Shah, but desisted when he heard sabres rattling. Suspecting, not without reason, that British agents were fixing elections to the Majlis in the more rural provinces, he suspended them. In addition to his always erratic behaviour, his conduct became increasingly arbitrary and he resorted more often to raving radio appeals directly to the people. The economic situation deteriorated sharply, with the small but influential middle class badly squeezed, but it did not affect the 80 per cent of the population who were subsistence farmers.

Real trouble loomed after the Royal Navy had intercepted a tanker attempting to ship oil to Italy. The seizure, legitimized by a court in the British colony of Aden, meant that no more oil would be exported from Iran. Japan strongly protested against the British action, thereby winning a friend for life in Tehran, a relationship that endures to this day. Mossadeq tendered his resignation, to be replaced by his elderly cousin Ahmad Qavam, an SIS asset. His appointment did not last a week since it united Mossadeq's supporters, the Muslim clergy and the Communists against him. Uncertain of the loyalties of the army in the face of protesting crowds, the Shah recalled Mossadeq, which came as a shock to the CIA and SIS station chiefs who were on trout-fishing vacation together.

Mossadeq's reinstatement coincided with victory for Iran in its dispute with Britain at the International Court in The Hague, to whose judgments he had reluctantly submitted, but he was not content with that and compounded his earlier misstep of rejecting the US compromise solution by trying to blackmail Ambassador Henderson with the threat of turning to the Soviets for economic aid. Henderson patiently sat through bedside meetings with the hypochondriac Mossadeq, but began to wonder whether he was entirely sane.[66] Previously distant contact between the Americans and Mossadeq's opponents at court and in the army began to get closer.[67]

Before Iran broke off diplomatic relations with Britain in October 1952, the SIS station had developed what would become the essentials of any future anti-Mossadeq plot. Since street protesters sustained Mossadeq against both the British and the timid Shah, there would have to be a countervailing force. There also needed to be a plausible alternative ruler to Mossadeq, but not from the old elite, who were tainted by their association with the British. Their candidate was General Fazlullah Zahedi, the Nazi-sympathizing commander of Iranian forces in Isfahan who had been kidnapped in 1942 by the Member of Parliament and irregular warrior Fitzroy Maclean and had spent the rest of the war interned in Palestine. The General was perfectly ready to let bygones be bygones in return for a slice of the action when he reinstated the AIOC.

Whatever might have come of the second British conspiracy became moot when the embassy had to close and the SIS station lost its ability to keep in close contact with its many agents. Once again in a preview – in reverse – of the events of 1979–81, it had to pass its assets to a CIA station made markedly more co-operative by the imminent Republican victory in the November 1952 election. Planning for the coup now went forward on a joint basis, with the CIA's Donald Wilber and SIS's Norman Darbyshire laying the groundwork in Cyprus during May 1953.

When CIA station chief Roger Gioran showed insufficient enthusiasm for gambling his nexus of agents in a coup against Mossadeq, Allen Dulles appointed Kermit Roosevelt, a senior officer in the CIA's Middle Eastern division and a grandson of President Teddy Roosevelt, to go to Iran and co-ordinate what was now named Operation Ajax; the British bluntly codenamed it Operation Boot. Kermit Roosevelt, a graduate of the elite Groton private school and Harvard, was polished, courteous, tall and lean, and had the intelligence officer's blessing of a forgettable face. Throughout the events that followed he endlessly played on the gramophone and hummed 'Luck be a Lady', a song from the hit musical *Guys and Dolls*. She needed to be.

In early June, Kermit Roosevelt flew to Beirut to review the plan, and then to London, where he took part in discussions at SIS headquarters. Meanwhile Monty Woodhouse of SIS was in Washington representing Winston Churchill, who had given the green light to the operation while acting as his own foreign secretary in the absence of the ailing Eden. Woodhouse dispelled his CIA friends' reservations by agreeing that Fraser and his AIOC co-directors were 'stupid, boring, pigheaded and tiresome', while emphasizing the threat of a Soviet-backed Tudeh coup in Iran. He had been a stellar Oxford classicist whose academic career had been truncated by the war, in which he saw distinguished service with SOE.[68] Gradually the number of people in Washington, London, Nicosia and Tehran with intimate knowledge of the coup grew to nearly ninety.[69] The key players were SIS's George Young, CIA London station chief Ray Clines, Darbyshire in Nicosia and Roosevelt's team in Tehran. Others included the American political warfare expert Miles Copeland.[70]

The key assets SIS brought to the table were the rich and influential Rashidian brothers, 'head agents' who were given £10,000 a month to recruit influential figures as well as the leaders of urban gangs, notably Shaban 'The Brainless' Jafari, for any move against Mossadeq. More money had been spread around restive tribal leaders in southern Iran, who would also play their part in preliminary destabilization, while certain Majlis deputies had received cash hidden inside boxes of biscuits. SIS also had a list of seventeen prospective prime ministers as alternatives to General Zahedi, who was on the run after Mossadeq had ordered his arrest.[71]

Once the Americans came on board the money available increased exponentially. The decision to go ahead was made on 25 June at a State Department meeting chaired by John Foster Dulles. After Roosevelt had outlined what the CIA had in mind, Dulles took a vote. The Dulles brothers and Bedell Smith, now Under Secretary of State, were the most enthusiastic, while Ambassador Henderson remarked, 'Mr Secretary, I don't like this kind of business at all . . . [but] we have no choice.'[72] Ike signed off on the operation following a dubiously spontaneous breakdown of public order in Tehran, when a mob led by Shaban the Brainless broke into Mossadeq's Tehran home. The Dulles brothers won over the President by stressing that the only beneficiaries of urban anarchy would be the Soviets, who might then take over the entire Middle East. The first domino had to be propped up.

Preparations proceeded apace. The CIA Art Group set about producing anti-Mossadeq cartoons which would find their way into Iran's major newspapers, along with 'grey' propaganda. One editor was paid $45,000. Rumours were spread that Mossadeq was a Jew.[73] The money passed through the Rashidians became a torrent, with $150,000 for suborning an anti-Mossadeq mob alone. To play up the Communist threat the Rashidians organized the abduction and murder of the Tehran Chief of Police and further 'black' attacks were made on clerics. General Zahedi was given $135,000 to win friends among his fellow officers and $11,000 a week was directed to bribing members of the Majlis, with Asadollah Rashidian personally handling sensitive payments to the more senior figures. When the day came the rent-a-mob would bring Tehran to a standstill, prompting bribed members of the Majlis to vote out Mossadeq. If he resisted, the army would step in.

In mid-July 1953 Mossadeq engineered the resignation of his supporters in parliament to force an election that was to be a referendum to dissolve the Majlis entirely. By this act he usurped the constitutional role of the Shah, while dispersing his own supporters back to their constituencies.[74] That month one James Lockridge crossed Syria and Iraq by car, faintly amused when a dopey Iranian border guard copying his passport details wrote down 'Scar on Right Forehead' as his surname. This was Kermit Roosevelt, coming to orchestrate the crescendo that was to end in the overthrow of Mossadeq. The weakest link in the chain was the Shah, in defence of whom all the 'spontaneous' newspaper campaigns and demonstrations were notionally to take place. He was, not to put too fine a point on it, a coward. Such backbone as he had was provided by his twin sister, Princess Ashraf, whose own resolve had been strengthened when Darbyshire came to her Paris hotel bearing a mink coat and a large packet of cash 'which made her eyes light up'.

Another key player was General H. Norman Schwarzkopf, who had organized the Iranian Gendarmerie in the 1940s and who now arrived back in Tehran accompanying several million dollars in the diplomatic bag. It was Schwarzkopf who brokered the first meeting between the Shah and Kermit Roosevelt – for which Roosevelt entered the royal palace concealed under the back seat of a car. At last the Shah agreed to sign two *firmans* (decrees) dismissing Mossadeq and appointing Zahedi, but only after he was assured he could leave the country before the coup took place. He flew via Baghdad to Rome, leaving in such haste that Queen Soraya left her Skye terrier behind. By coincidence the Iranian royals took up residence in the Excelsior Hotel, where Allen Dulles was on vacation.[75]

Roosevelt moved into the basement of Henderson's US embassy in the second week of August, when the operation went into high gear with bombing attacks on clerics falsely blamed on the Tudeh Party.[76] On 15 August Roosevelt's chosen instrument, Colonel Nematollah Nasiri, an ultra-royalist in the imperial guard and the future head of Savak, the Shah's secret police, led a detachment of troops to Mossadeq's home. To his surprise he found his path blocked by loyalist troops under General Taqi Riahi, who arrested him. The plot had been betrayed. As his coup unravelled, Roosevelt ignored orders from CIA headquarters to get out fast and braved the streets of Tehran, where the security police were rounding up suspected conspirators, to attend a meeting with General Zahedi to learn whether he was prepared to try again. He was.

While the Shah and Queen Soraya waited in Rome, Roosevelt had the *firmans* dismissing Mossadeq and appointing Zahedi copied and distributed throughout Tehran and sent to army officers in the provinces. Newspapers headlined that Mossadeq had tried to depose the Shah, only to be thwarted by army loyalists. Roosevelt despatched the US Military Attaché to Isfahan and garrisons in the capital with additional money to motivate the officers and their troops. He also gave two leaders of Tehran mobs the simple choice between $100,000 in cash to organize anarchy and being shot. Ayatollah Kashani received a further sweetener of $10,000.

The following day pretend pro-Mossadeq mobs began rampaging through the streets, toppling a statue of Reza Shah and leaving only his bronze boots on the plinth. Genuine nationalists and Communists were drawn out to join the protests and Mossadeq ordered the police not to interfere. This was not what the plotters wanted and Ambassador Henderson called in person to protest against the threats and vandalism to which US nationals had been subjected by hostile mobs. Mossadeq duly ordered the police to suppress the riots and mobilized the Tehran army garrison, unaware that this was the crucial next step in Operation Ajax.

On 19 August a huge counter-demonstration flooded central Tehran untroubled by the confused police. The crowds were led by hundreds of athletes and strongmen, somersaulting and flexing their biceps, and all crying 'Long Live the Shah!' Even the city's more exotic prostitutes took part. The army moved in with tanks that fired on government buildings and the few pro-government newspaper offices went up in flames. By late afternoon tanks and troops had surrounded Mossadeq's strongly guarded home, and while a two-hour gun battle raged he made his escape over a series of adjacent garden walls. About 150 people died in the battle, some of them members of the rent-a-mob with Roosevelt's largesse still in their pockets.

As Roosevelt lunched with Henderson and his wife, a Radio Tehran announcer reported that 'the Mossadeq government has fallen'. Roosevelt did not recognize the voice of the agent he had recruited for this broadcast, but the eager interloper did the trick nonetheless. It was the signal for the army to rise up in Isfahan, Meshed and Tabriz, whose radio stations reported back when they were in control.[77] At the US embassy Henderson, Roosevelt and Ardeshir Zahedi, the son of the new Prime Minister whom the CIA had recruited as a direct link to the British asset, toasted each other with champagne. Roosevelt later attended the prolonged celebration at the Officers Club where General Zahedi held court. The Americans were to ensure that he knew where his loyalties now lay by giving him $5 million for starting-up expenses with a further $1 million for himself.

The following evening Mossadeq surrendered and after a short interval the Shah and his consort flew home from Rome, stopping off at the venerable Shiite tomb of Ali in Iraq for pious photographs. Prime Minister Zahedi fell to his knees on the tarmac to kiss the imperial hand. Loy Henderson and Shaban the Brainless were among those who came to welcome him back. For the first time Roosevelt was driven openly to meet the Shah, with the message that 'the outcome is full repayment' and that Iran owed the US nothing, although he did accept a gold cigarette case as a personal gift. As he left the palace he passed General Nasiri, as he had become, and caught a few hours' sleep before flying out the next morning. He was awarded the National Intelligence Medal, though he would decline the offer to repeat his Iranian escapades when the CIA decided on a repeat coup in Guatemala. Henderson was recalled to Washington as a deputy under secretary of state to supervise a purge of New Dealers.

Mossadeq was tried and sentenced to three years in solitary confinement, to be followed by house arrest for life at Ahmadabad. Henderson made sure he was not killed, but around sixty army officers who remained loyal to him were executed. The National Front and the Tudeh Party were proscribed. An international consortium called the National Iranian Oil Company took over the industry, with BP (the rebrand of the AIOC) and a group of five American majors both owning 40 per cent and the rest split between Royal Dutch Shell and others. Oil revenues were divided 50:50 with the Iranian government, in line with the earlier Aramco deal with Riyadh. These arrangements were brokered by Sullivan & Cromwell, Foster Dulles's old firm. After he left the CIA, Kermit Roosevelt worked as a political consultant to one of the US oil majors involved in the new Iranian consortium.

In the 1960s the Shah was to spend much of this revenue on British tanks and American aircraft, for his rule rested on the armed forces and on Savak, the secret police trained by CIA operatives who had taken part in Operation Ajax.[78] The Americans believed that the Shah's authoritarian modernization would marginalize the reactionary Muslim clergy, as Iran progressed into a Western society. It did, and they struck back. While it would be absurd to blame the 1979 Iranian Revolution on the CIA, they did enable the Shia clerics to posture as Iranian patriots, notably Ayatollah Khomeini, who had remained aloof during the struggle between Mossadeq and the Shah. The always perceptive Loy Henderson summed it up in an early report from Tehran: 'Religious fanaticism can be used to combat communism, but it cannot be employed as a constructive force for the country's progress.'[79]

Before returning to Washington Roosevelt paid a courtesy call on Winston Churchill. He was shepherded into Churchill's bedroom, where he was recovering from a stroke. Roosevelt noted that he 'seemed in bad shape physically. He had great difficulty in hearing; occasional difficulty in articulating; and apparent difficulty in seeing to his left.' As usual in his contacts with Americans the old man laid it on with a trowel. He praised Roosevelt for pulling off 'the finest operation since the war' and said he would have liked to have served under the young American. The weight of history was immense: as first lord of the Admiralty in 1911–15, Churchill had ordered the Royal Navy to switch from coal to oil, and to secure supplies had ensured that the British government bought a controlling stake in the old Anglo-Persian company. In Iranian eyes the US was forever linked with British duplicity and skulduggery; but Britain would still be regarded as the ultimate malign force in Iranian affairs, long after it had lost the ability to fulfil such a role.

10. HUNGARY AND SUEZ

The Kremlin: Old Guard, New Look

As New Year dawned in 1953 Stalin was in such a good mood that he grabbed his daughter Svetlana by the hair to take her on to the dance floor to shuffle some steps. By 5 March he was dead. The succession was settled quickly. The ruling group consisted of Yegor Malenkov, Lavrentii Beria, Viacheslav Molotov, Kliment Voroshilov – and Nikita Khrushchev, fifth in seniority. None of the others rated the autodidact Khrushchev, who could read but could write only his name, and whom they regarded as a conscientious slogger.

Nikita Sergeyevich was born in 1894, into a peasant family too poor to afford either shoes or more than a couple of years of schooling. As a teenager he cleaned the insides of industrial boilers in one of Russia's hellish mining towns before becoming a skilled metal worker. He was a good organizer, something that saw him rise rapidly in the Communist Party, which he joined in late 1918. He did well in successive industrial managerial roles and eventually caught Stalin's eye when he drove forward construction of Moscow's extraordinary Metro project. Khrushchev was a willing participant in the purges of the 1930s, when even close friends were culled, and while still in his forties he was made first secretary in the Ukraine, where he was as active as the Boss in signing arrest and death-sentence warrants. Power brought material comforts. In addition to an outsized villa overlooking Kiev, the Khrushchevs had a huge apartment, with staff, a few blocks from the Kremlin.

During the Great Patriotic War Khrushchev served as political commissar-in-chief, and was promoted to lieutenant-general. He lost his fighter pilot son Lyonia, who sought death in battle to atone for a drunken incident when he accidentally killed a comrade as he tried to shoot a bottle off his head. After the reconquest of Kiev Khrushchev resumed his earlier role of viceroy in the Ukraine, ruthlessly crushing nationalists who had sought to piggyback on the German occupation, and who would still be fighting into the early 1960s. Ukraine was a vast charnel house of pulverized towns and charred villages, with millions of decomposing bodies hastily buried or not interred at all. It remains astonishing that the Western media were to highlight Khrushchev's roly-poly appearance and ragged-toothed smile without reference to his record.[1]

At five foot one and 200 pounds Khrushchev was no threat to Stalin, who was touchy about his height, and by acting like an enthusiastic teddy-bear he won the role of court jester, enduring the Boss's jape of tapping his pipe on his subordinate's bald pate to show that it was hollow. The teddy-bear showed his teeth after Stalin's death, when Khrushchev was the prime mover in the conspiracy to get rid of Beria, the psychopathic Mingrelian secret police chief, who was arrested, tried and after a few months shot. In September 1953 Premier Malenkov and the others rewarded him with the post of first secretary of the Communist Party, apparently hoping that this would keep him busy and leave the running of the state to them.

In fact real power rested with the Presidium, which operated in the name of the Party Central Committee, and not with the Premier and the Council of Ministers. Khrushchev used his extensive powers of Party patronage to outmanoeuvre Malenkov, who in a novel departure was not executed when he was forced to resign in 1955.[2] Next, Khrushchev went after the long-time Foreign Minister Molotov, who continued to conduct a Stalinist foreign policy. Khrushchev wanted a competitive but less confrontational relationship with the capitalist world so as to avoid a nuclear war, and a more tolerant relationship with whatever 'progressive' forces stirred in the Third World.[3] Molotov also failed to achieve a united and neutral Germany and was held to have given too much away in a May 1955 state treaty with Austria. Unlike Stalin, Khrushchev was a keen traveller. He led a delegation to China and took the lead in repairing relations with Yugoslavia, both wounded by Molotov's high-handedness. He would meet Eisenhower at Camp David in 1959 and Kennedy in Vienna in 1961.[4]

Khrushchev blamed Molotov for creating a world of enemies, a theme he took up during the 20th Congress of the Soviet Communist Party when it convened from 14 February 1956. But the real meat came in an unscheduled secret session, in which Khrushchev devoted four hours to Stalin's 'mania for greatness', summed up in the dictator's remark 'I'll wag my little finger – and there will be no more Tito.' Fortified by brandy, Khrushchev committed such heresies as accusing Stalin of cowardice and incompetence in 1941–2. Since most of those present had been complicit in Stalin's crimes, not least the speaker himself, the speech was greeted with an excruciating silence punctuated by an audibly anxious hum, even though he neglected to mention the terror famine in the Ukraine or the ordinary people scythed down in the purges.[5]

Khrushchev ordered the release of some of the 2.5 million people confined in the gulags, together with an investigation into the crimes Stalin had perpetrated against members of the Party, without, it should be noted, questioning its continuing legitimacy. By June, he had ousted Molotov, and other such prominent Stalinist cronies as Lazar Kaganovich, bringing in ambitious younger men like Leonid Brezhnev and Ivan Serov, his KGB (Committee for State Security) chief in Ukraine, to replace them. The relatively young Dmitri Shepilov, a former editor of *Pravda*, was given a major foreign policy role. Smartly turned out, he came as a pleasant surprise to Westerners used to dealing with grim old bruisers in baggy suits.[6]

Shepilov's ministry shared a twenty-three-storey building on Smolensk Square with the Ministry of Foreign Trade. Imposing on the outside, this Stalinist edifice had dull dun-coloured corridors, with high-ceilinged offices containing too many people crammed together. A separate elevator took Foreign Ministry staff higher than the first six floors, where the 'tradesmen' operated. Another transported a select few to the top, where it was all hushed carpets and wooden panelling. That was where the ministers and senior bosses lurked. Several checkpoints monitored all internal movements.[7] There were also the 'near neighbours' at the KGB headquarters in the Lubyanka and the 'far neighbours' of the military intelligence GRU, both heavily represented in any Soviet mission like their counterparts in the CIA or SIS.

During the purges 90 per cent of the old Commissariat of Foreign Affairs had been shot or sent to concentration camps. Their instant replacements were poorly educated and utterly orthodox. Shepilov was an economist. By ordering all Foreign Ministry staff to retake courses in political economy, he weeded out many of the more concrete-headed Stalinists. New recruits came from the Moscow State Institute of International Relations, or MGIMO in Russian, housed in a sooty building near Krymsky Bridge. This prestigious school recruited heavily from the golden youth: that is the children of higher Party and state officials. There were no Jews and only a token woman – Molotov's daughter. Dialectical materialism dominated the curriculum, although the elite cadres were also despatched each autumn to a *kolkhoz* to harvest potatoes.

The Soviet foreign service had its own pecking order, which resembled that of the US. The top assignments were Germany, nuclear disarmament, the US and Europe. The lowliest were the 'provincials' who dealt with Africa and Asia, a destiny consisting of 'unpleasant climates, low salaries, and lack of consumer goods' and few opportunities for promotion.[8] All employees were subject to constant Communist Party scrutiny of their behaviour, from boozing and philandering to smuggling foreign goods. The KGB vetted those seeking an overseas posting, an opportunity open only to the really reliable, who would come back. Pay was poor. Those serving at the UN – and many did because of the opportunities for espionage in the US – were paid in dollars by the Secretariat, from which all but the official's lower salary in roubles was deducted by a penny-pinching Moscow. Half of Soviet UN staff were KGB or GRU agents, identifiable by their better suits and shoes.

The Soviet Union was going out into the wider world, initially concentrating on newly independent India, Indonesia and Egypt. In 1953 Moscow signed a trade deal with Cairo, providing kerosene in return for Egyptian cotton.[9] But this was a question not just of improving trade, but of finding a forum where the Soviets could compete with the Americans without triggering a nuclear war. That was why they became so active in the Third World, where the US's colonialist allies were facing ever more active national liberation movements.[10]

The reverberations from Khrushchev's speech were greatly magnified when Israeli intelligence provided Allen Dulles with a copy of the text and the CIA made sure it became widely disseminated within the Soviet bloc. After workers had rioted in Poznan in June 1956, the Polish Party resolved to recall Władysław Gomułka, who had been purged and jailed in 1948 for 'Titoist deviationism' after opposing the collectivization of agriculture. When they also sought to depose Marshal Konstantin Rokossovsky, the Russified Pole whom Stalin had made Poland's defence minister, Khrushchev flew to Warsaw with a high-powered delegation including twelve bemedalled generals. The two sides met at Warsaw airport, where Russian fists were waved under Polish noses while Red Army armoured units were motoring towards the frontier. The tanks were halted, and then set in motion again before being halted for a final time.[11] They did so because Gomułka pulled off the remarkable feat of persuading the sceptical Russians that his proposed reforms would not undermine either Communism or the unity of the Communist bloc, and that he had no intention of making his country vulnerable to West German 'Fascist revanchists'.

In Hungary the challenge to Soviet power was much more overt. From 1953 to 1955 the Marxist intellectual Imre Nagy had promoted a 'New Course', declaring that Marxism must evolve or fail. Under Soviet pressure he was deprived of his Party functions and then sacked as chairman of the Council of Ministers on 18 April 1955. Gomułka's success in Poland led Hungarians to hope that they could bring Nagy back, but pro-Nagy demonstrators tore down a giant statue of Stalin, planting Hungarian flags in the empty boots on the plinth. The CIA, with only one officer in Budapest, was taken totally unawares by these developments, but its Radio Free Europe broadcast arguably irresponsible encouraging noises that may have led Hungarian patriots to overplay their hand.[12]

Anastas Mikoyan and Mikhail Suslov, who arrived in Budapest to monitor developments in conjunction with the Soviet Ambassador Yuri Andropov, initially consented to the appointment of Nagy as prime minister and János Kádár as first secretary of the Communist Party. This occurred even as Soviet tanks and troops entered Budapest to restore order and were met with fierce resistance from mainly young Hungarians, who erected barricades and attacked the tanks with petrol bombs. Hundreds of Hungarian patriots and Soviet soldiers died, and members of the hated secret police (AVH) were hunted down and lynched until Khrushchev ordered the troops to pull out of Budapest and the Presidium issued a declaration including an apology for 'egregious mistakes and violations of the principle of equality in relations with socialist countries'.

Nagy was no Gomułka. With an intellectual's inability to see the wood for the trees, he asked Mikoyan and Suslov to reinforce the Soviet troops but also mooted the idea of Hungary becoming a constitutionally neutral state, like Austria.[13] With tragic timing he announced his intention to take Hungary out of the Warsaw Pact on the same day (1 November) that the Presidium published the declaration that might have laid the basis for a phased decompression, not only for Hungary but for all the Soviet satellites. The role of China remains unclear – Mao had advised moderation in Poland, but at first urged strong repression in Hungary. Then he changed his mind, perhaps influenced by the Presidium's call for greater mutual respect among fraternal socialist nations. Either way, it is noticeable that, whereas once the Soviets had been the ultimate arbiter of Communist orthodoxy, the arrival of several Marxist-Leninist states raised the possibility that they would have minds of their own, shaped by their distinctive national experiences and the personalities of their leaders. This was despite the obvious commonalities in how these states were ruled, with a single party, secret police and concentration-camp apparatus that made a nonsense of the rule of law. Yugoslavia's Marshal Josip Broz Tito was the first to stray from the true path in the late 1940s, not just because he failed to mention Stalin's name in his speeches, but because his machinations in the wider Balkan neighbourhood queered Stalin's larger geostrategic concerns with the US and its allies. While Yugoslav estrangement was manageable, this would not be true when China broke ranks too.

The respect Mao had felt for Stalin did not transfer to his Soviet successors, and was further diminished by Khrushchev's denunciations of 'the Master'. There were non-ideological tensions also arising from an adverse balance of trade and the Soviet refusal to share nuclear weapons with China. Adding insult to injury, Khrushchev's decision to create a fleet of nuclear ballistic missile submarines would require Chinese co-operation if they were to operate at will in the Pacific since the Soviet port of Vladivostok iced up in winter and could easily be blockaded.[14] Khrushchev rather too easily assumed that Mao would grant him the use of Chinese ports, and permit the Soviets to base on Chinese territory a coastal radio system to communicate with the submarines. Mao saw this as an affront to Chinese sovereignty and resented being treated as a backward, 'inferior . . . dumb, careless' nation by his Soviet patrons.[15] It was not yet a Sino–Soviet split, but the mood of the relationship portended that way.

In Europe, unrest in Romania and among students at Moscow State University led Khrushchev to act as the Soviet military was urging him to do. In an operation aptly codenamed Whirlwind the Red Army rolled back into Budapest and crushed the Hungarian Revolution, killing 20,000 people at a loss to themselves of 1,500 troops. A further 20,000 Hungarians were arrested and imprisoned (Nagy was secretly tried and hanged) and 200,000 Hungarians went into exile, an exodus of talent from which the free world benefited enormously. The diplomatic fall-out after Hungary reverted to being a grim Stalinist state was diluted by the simultaneous attack on Egypt by the British, French and Israelis, who Khrushchev believed were acting with US approval. Despite the Soviet Union's vast investment in espionage, he could not have been more badly informed.

Munich on the Nile?

Before the Suez Crisis in 1956 the British were confident that they were still one of the great powers in the world. Afterwards the more realistic of them grasped that this was no longer so. At the eye of the ensuing storm was Anthony Eden, whose mental and physical ruination symbolized the burdens that Britain could no longer bear. The crisis involved oil, complex legal issues about ownership, and the wider strategic architecture of the Middle East.

The Suez Canal was operated by an Anglo–French company whose commercial concession would expire in 1968. Around 122 million tons of cargo passed along the Canal each year, 40 per cent of it oil, which included two-thirds of Western Europe's oil supplies; in contrast, only 5 per cent of US oil imports went through Suez. In the early 1950s the Egyptian government received just $3 million of the company's annual profits of $100 million, a source of burning resentment to the Egyptian ruling elite.[16]

Britain controlled an area the size of Wales on either side of the Canal, in which it stationed 80,000 troops, a legacy of its armed intervention against the Egyptian military uprising of Ahmad Urabi in the 1880s.[17] Potentially, this force could be used to determine who ruled in Cairo, though by the early 1950s it was just another brick in the global containment of the Soviets. The 1936 treaty governing this last arrangement was renegotiated in 1953–4, with the British agreeing in October 1954 to withdraw their troops within twenty months. By that time it had been decided by defence experts that the Soviets could be contained elsewhere. So when the British and their allies returned in force by air and sea in November 1956, they did so for no strategically valid reason.[18]

The ejection of the British from the Canal Zone became an obsession for Egyptian nationalists, particularly among army officers who saw themselves as Urabi's twentieth-century heirs. From late 1951 there were fitful attacks on British forces, and there was organized unrest among the 60,000-strong Egyptian workforce. What would be the last Wafdist government turned a blind eye to these disturbances, which often involved armed auxiliaries attached to the police.[19] A more robust British response became inevitable when the Conservatives were returned to power in October 1951. The party harboured a vociferous Suez Group with whose strident views Churchill was in sympathy even though their leader, Captain Charles Waterhouse, had been a diehard appeaser in the 1930s. At this stage, Foreign Secretary Eden was not of their persuasion. Late one well-watered December night, Churchill rose from his chair to advance with mock menace on Eden: 'Tell them [the Egyptians] that if we have any more of their cheek we will set the Jews on them and drive them into the gutter, from which they should never have emerged.'[20]

Yet Churchill's views varied, depending on whether he was thinking atavistically or strategically. In the first case, he passionately believed that 'scuttling' from Egypt and Sudan would be followed by the sudden collapse of colonies in Africa, the British version of the domino theory. But when he thought strategically, as in remarks to three American journalists in January 1952, the Canal was not so vital: 'Now that we no longer hold India, the Canal means very little to us. Australia? We could go round the Cape. We are holding the Canal not for ourselves but for civilisation. I feel inclined to threaten the Americans that we will leave the Canal if they don't come in.'[21]

In January 1952 British troops with tanks stormed the police post at Ismailia, killing forty-six of the occupants and wounding a further seventy-two. The post had been harbouring nationalist fighters who took pot shots at the British. In response policemen, students and the Cairo mob turned on the symbols of British power and Egyptian collaboration. Shepheard's Hotel and the Turf Club witnessed scenes of wild violence, while the offices of such firms as BOAC, Barclay's Bank and travel agent Thomas Cook were ransacked. Muslim Brotherhood supporters destroyed the city's ten largest cinemas, for there were multiple agendas at play, including those of the tiny Egyptian Communist Party. A total of twenty people were killed, including eleven British subjects, one of whom was hacked to death after he broke his back leaping from a burning building. As the British Ambassador pondered whether to summon British troops from the Zone to restore order in Cairo, neither King Faruq nor the army leadership made any effort to bring 'Black Saturday' to a halt. Churchill railed against 'degraded savages', but in Washington Acheson sneered at Britain's 'splutter of musketry' at Ismailia.[22]

Faruq's parliamentary monarchy limped on, until the King attempted to purge the self-styled Free Officers who had defeated his placemen in the executive committee of the Army Officers Club in Heliopolis. This seemingly obscure social issue was really about control of the armed forces and it triggered a coup long in the making. Colonel Gamal Nasser played a key part, motoring from base to base in his little black Austin to secure each individual unit's support. He was also in regular contact with the CIA's political action officers Kermit Roosevelt and Miles Copeland, who had fastened on him after failing to find a Muslim Billy Graham among Cairo's mystic Sufi whirling dervishes to replace a king they privately referred to as 'FF' or 'Fat Fucker'. The officers overthrew FF and installed the fifty-four-year-old General Mohammed Naguib in his stead, the front man of this bloodless revolution. Faruq was exiled to a life of limitless debauchery and international celebrity, finally choking to death in a Rome restaurant.[23]

Churchill acknowledged the justice in the stated aim of the revolution, which was to close the yawning chasm between the Egyptian elite and a peasant population that struggled to survive on $50 a year, with an average life expectancy of thirty-six. He welcomed the advent of 'Neg-wib', scribbling on a memo 'Down with the Pashas and Up the Fellaheen!' In fact, real power lay with a thirteen-strong junta that met in Faruq's boat house at night, which was dominated by Deputy Prime Minister and Interior Minister Nasser. Nasser received CIA political coaching from learning to smile more frequently to designing a more effective security, immigration and customs service. The CIA discovered that in Egypt it was sometimes more 'socially efficient' to redirect 500 employees to copying the Koran than to make them redundant, thereby alienating their numerous dependants and kinfolk. Copeland had soup and sandwiches two or three times a week with Nasser, either in the Interior Ministry or at the Revolutionary Command Council HQ in Zamalek.[24]

In August 1952 the new regime suppressed a textile-factory strike by executing the leaders. In January 1953 they banned all political parties except their own Liberation Rally mass movement. A year later they proscribed the Muslim Brotherhood on the grounds that it was a political party in disguise. The relationship between Naguib and Nasser was fraught, with Nasser playing Lenin to this 'Kerensky in a fez' until he forced his rival into retirement in late March 1954. Since Naguib was an ethnic Sudanese, Nasser became the first native Egyptian to rule Egypt since the time of the ancient pharaohs.[25] In October a member of the Muslim Brotherhood tried to assassinate him as he addressed a huge crowd in Alexandria. Eight shots miraculously missed their target. Nasser put Brotherhood leaders on trial and executed them, going on to eliminate sharia courts too. The CIA brought in a New York policeman to improve his security, and even concocted anti-American propaganda for him, to boost his image of incorruptible independence.[26]

As we have seen, the British had agreed to withdraw their forces from the Canal Zone, accomplishing this by June 1956. A committed devotee of international institutions since the 1920s, Eden forswore 'the methods of the last century' and knew that a compromise was necessary with Egyptian nationalism.[27] Churchill's views oscillated between resistance and compromise, often depending on whether he viewed the Egyptians through the prism of the past, the dimension he increasingly lived in. During the negotiations he dilated on appeasement, saying that 'he never knew before that Munich was situated on the Nile'.[28] Yet reality also impressed itself on him. Britain could not afford the luxury of maintaining 80,000 troops at Suez at an annual cost of £56 million. Respected military advisers advised him that such concentrated bases were a compact target for atomic bombs, and that the garrisons should be dispersed to Cyprus, Gaza, Jordan, Kenya and Libya.

Churchill hoped the Americans would help him square the circle. Presuming on his wartime relationship with Eisenhower, he tried to inveigle the US into stationing a few troops on the Canal as part of a regional defence organization, to permit continued Egyptian subordination under a new guise. His letters to Eisenhower, Dulles and Under Secretary Bedell 'Beetle' Smith conjured up a host of useful demons: the Cairo mob, the 'dictator' Naguib, the interloping Russian 'bear', the strain of anti-Americanism in the British Labour Party, German Nazis in Egyptian employ (unknown to him, mainly there courtesy of the CIA) and even '50,000 British graves' in the western desert. This emotive and incoherent guff made little impact on Ike, for like Dulles he was determined not to find himself on the losing side of the argument between 'old' imperialism and 'new' post-colonial nationalism, least of all in a region whose oil was vital and where America's only firm friend was Saudi Arabia. The Americans also simply did not understand the importance of the Canal to the British government and to French shareholders, for whom it was like a family heirloom.[29] The Americans wanted as many Arab states as possible gathered in a regional alliance to repulse the Soviets, not a scrappy colonial conflict which would divide those states from the West, not least because of the wild card of Israel, which feared such an Arab alliance being armed by the US.[30]

In the event, with Eden ill and Churchill felled by a stroke, the negotiations were concluded by Lord 'Bobbety' Salisbury, who took over the Foreign Office between late July and early October 1954. He was the author of the phrase 'too clever by half' to describe the many people who were not as stupid as he, but he had some help from the CIA station in Cairo, which helped to distinguish between what was posturing and what substance in the Egyptian negotiating stance. The final terms agreed that British forces were to evacuate the Suez bases, although 4,000 technicians would keep the bases in readiness should the troops have to return to defend Egypt and other states of the region from Soviet attack. The new treaty was to run for seven years, until 1961.

The Suez Crisis is a notorious instance of misfires from bad historical analogies. Fresh from the horror of a world war most believed could have been prevented by confronting Hitler when he bluffed his way into the Rhineland in 1936, men with little or no knowledge of modern Egyptian history accommodated every assertive move by Nasser to a misleading Hitlerian template. This was a bipartisan affair since the Labour leader Hugh Gaitskell was as keen on comparisons between Nasser and Hitler as any Tory.[31] Nasser's writings outlining his vision of Egypt's role in the world were read by the light of *Mein Kampf*, yet in reality his view that Egypt was simultaneously a Middle Eastern, African and Muslim power was entirely comparable to the belief widespread among the British that their islands' destiny was linked to the Commonwealth, Europe and the US.[32] One who knew him well was the British Ambassador to Cairo, Humphrey Trevelyan, who memorably described him as a charming man of modest tastes, who never lost his temper or raised his voice, but who was also an inveterate conspirator whose suspicions of others were not dependent on the existence of plots.[33]

Different visions of how the strategic architecture of the Middle East should be organized contributed to the general air of tension. Nasser's desire to lead the Arab world – evidenced day and night by Radio Cairo broadcasts – received a major setback with the signing in February 1955 of the Baghdad Pact, linking Britain to Iraq, Iran, Turkey and Pakistan. Only Iraq was an Arab power, one moreover with the most pro-British rulers: Harrow-educated King Faisal and his Prime Minister Nuri as-Said. It seemed as if Britain was cunningly shifting power in the Middle East northwards – to the Northern Tier in fact – and away from a country which saw itself as being the most important in the Afro-Arab world, with a civilization older than that of the Greeks and Romans. Nasser used every means, fair and foul, to ensure that other Arab countries, and especially Jordan and Syria, did not follow the treacherous Iraqis into this alliance.

It was against this background that Eden, who was touring the Middle East and Asia in his final month as foreign secretary, met Nasser in the British Embassy in Cairo. Eden was dressed to kill; Nasser wore a military tunic. As they were being photographed, Nasser awkwardly clutched Eden's hand. Having read oriental languages at Oxford, Eden spoke to Nasser in Arabic, inquiring whether this was the first time he had been in the embassy. It was, Nasser replied, his first chance to see where Egypt was governed from. 'Not governed, advised perhaps,' replied the silky Foreign Secretary. Over dinner, when Eden tried to explain the benefits of his new northern alliance, Nasser shrewdly replied that it was a flimsy construction involving unpopular rulers, no substitute for defence deeply anchored in the national sentiment of a country's people. Nasser came away from the meeting with the feeling that Eden was behaving 'like a prince among beggars'.[34]

Although Nasser was careful not to get drawn into a hot war with his Israeli neighbours, the opposite consideration was uppermost for such Cairo-based Palestinian exiles as the student activist Yasser Arafat, an engineering student busily converting himself into Mr Palestine.[35] In response to Palestinian raids, launched mainly from Jordan but also from Egyptian-occupied Gaza, the Israeli leader David Ben-Gurion and his Chief of Staff, Moshe Dayan, unleashed the bull-like young airborne commander, Ariel 'Arik' Sharon, against both Jordan and Gaza. With his characteristic finesse Sharon botched an attack on Egyptian headquarters in Gaza, killing thirty-six Egyptians at a loss of nine of his own men. Nasser was incensed, but Egypt only had six functioning aircraft and enough artillery shells for a one-hour bombardment. Instead, the Egyptian army combed Gaza's jails for recruits to Palestinian *fedayeen* groups to wage a limited-liability proxy war against Israel.

Nasser hoped to buy weapons from the US, and in principle agreed a deal involving $20 million of arms and a further $40 million in economic aid. But Washington stalled, belatedly realizing that the weapons would be used against the Israelis, or even the British. Nasser made no bones about it in talks with John Foster Dulles in early 1953, when Britain and the US were still trying to interest him in an anti-Soviet Middle East Defence Pact: 'How can I go to my people and tell them I am disregarding a killer with a pistol sixty miles from me at the Suez Canal to worry about somebody who is holding a knife a thousand miles away?'[36]

Although Nasser hated the Egyptian Communist Party and its analogue in the Sudan, which was lobbying for independence, when the deal with the US did not prosper he turned to the Soviets, who saw a chance to neutralize the Baghdad Pact at a stroke and gave Nasser a deal based on barter and a cheap loan. The arms were to come through Prague, the back channel they had used to sell arms to the Israelis. This was astute, and gave Kermit Roosevelt and Miles Copeland just enough wriggle room when they flew to Cairo in September 1955 to minimize the fall-out from the Egyptian–Soviet deal. They persuaded Nasser to emphasize that the arms deal was with 'the Czechs', from whom the Israelis had themselves purchased arms, and also drafted a speech including the words 'reduce the tensions between the Arabs and Israel', although they could not get him to speak the word 'peace'. Nasser and the CIA men watched with amusement as the lights came on in the British embassy and Sir Humphrey Trevelyan's car drove across a Nile bridge for a meeting with Nasser, who told him the lies the CIA men had recommended. They joked about how Sir Humphrey would have reacted had they popped out from behind the arras to inquire, 'Excuse me, Gamal, but we're out of soda. Where do you keep the soda?'[37]

The US might be able to live with an Egypt armed by the Soviets, but the arrival of medium-range Ilyushin bombers in Cairo created an existential threat to Israel, which began to shop around to upgrade its own military capability. The Americans did not want to get into an arms race by proxy, and the only regional war the British thought they might get involved in was in defence of Jordan against Israeli retaliation for the guerrilla raids launched from Jordanian territory. The French stepped into the breach, cheerfully selling the Israelis Mirage jets and their new AMX-13 light tank. In a parallel development the two countries developed the 'Super Sherman', with a French gun turret married to the better-armoured hull of the old American M4 Sherman, the standard tank of the Israeli Defence Forces (IDF) in the 1950s. The Israelis began planning ambitious strikes against Gaza and south through Sinai to Sharm al-Sheikh, where the Egyptians could throttle access through the Red Sea to the developing Israeli port of Eilat.[38]

Once the Soviet arms deal was in place, London urged Washington to trump the Soviet gambit by offering, with Britain as a junior partner, to arrange the vast loans needed to finance the High Aswan Dam, a project dear to the hearts of Egypt's military rulers. The dam would indeed generate hydroelectricity while irrigating around three million more acres of the Nile Valley; but the longer-term environmental impact of interrupting the annual flooding of the Nile has included the death of once-abundant fisheries off the delta and disastrous soil salination. An outline deal emerged in which the initial funding would come from the US aid budget – which required the approval of Congress – to be followed by the main funding from the World Bank. Established at Bretton Woods in 1944, after the Marshall Plan had focused attention on Europe, this specialized in loans to the developing world. Neither side was happy with the arrangement, Nasser because of the historical echoes of foreigners gaining a degree of control over the Egyptian economy, while in the US Southern Congressmen were hostile to it because it would help out a rival cotton-growing nation, as were Cold War hardliners because Nasser had recognized the People's Republic of China.

Despite the CIA's best efforts, Dulles was never enthusiastic about Nasser or the Aswan project, and even imagined an alternative scenario in which it might cripple the Soviets in perpetuity should they be rash enough to get involved. How would they explain giving over $1 billion to Egypt when people in the satellite countries were cold and hungry? In July 1956 he withdrew the offer of loans and the World Bank pulled out of the scheme. Since Nasser had no desire to become dependent on the Soviets, the only alternative appeared to be to nationalize the Suez Canal and use its revenues to service the required loans. That possibility had certainly been at the back of Anthony Eden's mind when he lobbied for Washington to fund Aswan, but even so Nasser's quick reaction to the collapse of the US deal came as a surprise.

On 26 July 1956, addressing 250,000 people in Alexandria and a wider radio audience throughout the Arab world, Nasser used a confidential mode and colloquial Arabic to rehearse the sins of the British since the time of Cromer's semi-viceregal regime in the 1870s, conflating them with the recent actions of the US and the World Bank. 'I started to look at Mr [Eugene] Black [President of the World Bank], who was sitting on a chair,' he said, 'and I saw him in my imagination as Ferdinand de Lesseps [constructor of the Suez Canal].' In the rest of his rambling speech, Nasser contrived to mention de Lesseps fourteen times, for the name was a codeword for the seizure of the Canal. The news reached London while Eden was hosting the Iraqi King and his Prime Minister, Nuri es-Said. The latter's advice to Eden was 'Hit Nasser, hit him now, and hit him hard.' Descending the stairs of 10 Downing Street, Nuri glanced at a portrait of Benjamin Disraeli. 'That's the old Jew who got you into all this trouble,' he remarked, with reference to Disraeli's 1875 purchase of a controlling interest in the Canal.[39]

Eden's view of Nasser went from patronizing to pathological after he had convinced himself that Nasser was behind the March 1956 Jordanian sacking of Lieutenant-General Sir John Glubb (a.k.a. Glubb Pasha), who had trained and led Jordan's Arab Legion since 1939. In fact Glubb was well past his sell-by date and had long ago gone native, and Nasser had nothing to do with it. But the Egyptian leader gave that impression to the Foreign Office Minister Selwyn Lloyd, who was dining with him the night of Glubb's dismissal. Lloyd was infuriated by Nasser's smirk and by an evening of being treated much as Eden had treated Nasser during their meeting a year earlier. Eden's mind was clouded by the morphine and benzedrine he took to cope with chronic ill health and weariness and he told a junior Foreign Office official, on an open phone line, 'I want him [Nasser] murdered.' SIS turned to the CIA for advice and Dulles instructed his brother Allen to seem to play along, while in Cairo Copeland casually discussed it with the would-be victim:

Copeland: How about poison? . . . Suppose I just wait until you turn your head and slip a pill into your coffee?

Nasser: Well, there's Hassan standing right there. If I didn't see you Hassan would.

Copeland: But maybe we could bribe a servant to poison the coffee before bringing it in?

Nasser: Your New York policeman seems to have thought of that. The coffee would only kill the taster. And when the taster fell over dead, wouldn't that alert us to your plot?[40]

Eden's belligerent response to Nasser's actions reflected a deeper anxiety about loss of face and the country's international standing, as well as guilt about 1930s appeasement. Eden drew a totally false analogy between Nasser's *coup de main* and Hitler's occupation of the Rhineland in 1936, although Nasser was perfectly entitled to nationalize the Canal with due compensation, and the Egyptian takeover was not in breach of the Constantinople Convention governing the free use of the waterway. In addition the supposedly indispensable expertise of the Canal Company's foreign employees was revealed to be bogus when Egyptian pilots handled a record number of 254 vessels in one week without incident, and insurance premiums for passage of the Canal did not rise.

In a pattern grimly familiar from the resort to pseudo-legalism by more recent British governments, Lord Chancellor Kilmuir, the senior lawyer in the Eden administration, endorsed its aggressive policy with learned paragraphs, declaring Egypt to be in breach of international law in the teeth of contrary advice from the Attorney-General Reginald Manningham-Buller. Foreign Office lawyers also demurred, but they could be safely ignored, as they were programmed to find legal justification for an institutional predisposition to submissiveness.[41] The result was a disjunction between the Foreign Office's meek attempts to resolve the issue through diplomacy and the very real threat of force. It is instructive to compare the British government's futile attempts to gain international approval and the elusive moral high ground with the forthright belligerence of the French, where both left and right were one big Suez Group, further infuriated by Egypt's role in arming rebels in Algeria.[42]

On 27 July 1956, the British cabinet invited the Chiefs of Staff to prepare war plans, while a crisis group was formed known as the Egypt

Committee. This grouping deserves the epithet 'war cabinet' only if one believes that the British were hell bent on war from the start. It was much more anaemic than such a name suggests, and besides, with a combined membership of over fifty, it was too unwieldy for an effective conspiracy. The caution of Britain's service chiefs obliged Eden to explore diplomatic ways of discrediting Nasser to trigger his downfall. There was also the problem of gaining US support and 'moral cover', both of which the French regarded with disdain.

On 2 September 1956, Eisenhower wrote to Eden explaining: 'I must tell you frankly that American opinion flatly rejects the thought of using force, particularly when it does not seem that every possible peaceful means of protecting our vital interests has been exhausted without result.' The smooth operation of the Canal was one thing, Nasser's pan-Arab pretensions another. US policy was to avoid war by spinning out technical negotiations about the nationalization of the Canal. Based on their comprehensive bugging of the US embassy in Moscow, the Soviets were able to assure Nasser that the US would not take a confrontational stance over Suez.[43]

Dulles was sufficiently concerned by the bellicose tone of British ministers, notably that of the Chancellor of the Exchequer Harold Macmillan, to fly to London. A lawyer of considerable standing himself, he brushed aside Lord Kilmuir's disingenuous arguments to concentrate on the likely reverberations of armed Anglo–French intervention across the Arab world. Thanks to the likes of Copeland and Roosevelt, who reported to his brother Allen, Dulles knew that there was no plausible successor to Nasser, whose popularity increased with every tweak of the Lion's tail. He won Eden's support for a conference of all the major maritime users of the Canal, which would enable it to be passed from the Suez Canal Company to international control, with an equitable proportion of the revenues paid to Egypt. It appears Eden wrongly concluded that Dulles had consented to use of force as a last resort, whereas Dulles merely regarded it as an ulterior threat within the framework of tough negotiations. With a presidential election due in November, there was no way he was going to countenance old-school gunboat diplomacy. Dulles may have said Nasser should 'disgorge' his spoils, but he also stressed that Britain 'should make a genuine and sincere effort to settle the problem and avoid the use of force'.[44]

Even as the first of two conferences convened in London from 16 to 23 August, military planning for Operation Musketeer continued. There was, unsurprisingly, disagreement between the French and British staff officers over the extent and focus of the operation. Meanwhile the Australian Prime Minister Robert Menzies went to Cairo on behalf of the London conference to find out whether Nasser would consent to the establishment of an international users' association. Nasser's reaction to the 'Australian mule' was unequivocally negative. With the 'last resort' looking more likely, the Anglo–French military planners revised Musketeer to a limited attack on Port Said. The aim was to concentrate the issue on the Canal, hoping it would deflate Nasser's image as the champion of Arab nationalism without being seen to be seeking his overthrow. It was an idiotic premise, made worse by the French insistence that weather considerations made it necessary to mount the operation in October.

Dulles tried again with a second London conference in September, called the Suez Canal Users' Association, although Eden was already resigned to referring the issue to the United Nations Security Council. He had put himself in the worst of all positions. If he went for a negotiated settlement, his own fire-eating backbenchers would brand him an appeaser; if he used force against Nasser, the less belligerent Tory ministers and backbenchers would resign, and combine with Labour to defeat him. Meanwhile, on 20 September, Macmillan went to the US on a ten-day trip. His sole concern should have been to ensure that the US would not crack the financial whip, but instead he made the rounds of wartime colleagues in positions of power and gave Eden the entirely false impression that Eisenhower would tacitly back an Anglo–French operation against Egypt.

This was extremely dishonest. It flew in the face of repeated warnings, including a press conference on 2 October, when Dulles publicly distanced the US from anything reeking of colonialism, an antipathy which Roger Makins, the British Ambassador to Washington, reported rose to the surface within him like lava in a volcano. While perhaps we can acquit Macmillan of consciously pushing Eden into a hopeless situation in order to replace him as prime minister, we know enough about subconscious motivation to cast a very cold eye on his visit to Washington and the advice he gave the man he hoped to replace if it all went wrong.[45]

In truth Eden needed replacing. He was seriously ill, with recurrent bouts of fever which pushed his temperature to 106, and his attempts to keep the US abreast of every twisting development meant that he was on the telephone throughout the night rather than sleeping. When hope loomed on the horizon, in the form of a Six-Point Agreement devised by foreign ministers Selwyn Lloyd and Mahmoud Fawzi at the UN, Eisenhower, perhaps inadvertently, wrecked it in a speech that made it clear he did not support Britain's tough negotiating stance, while also refusing to oblige Eden with a public statement about sharing nuclear-missile technology. Any such statement at this stage was certain to be interpreted by Arab minds as indicating that the US did indeed support the British in their confrontation with Nasser.

The Lloyd–Fawzi formula was doomed to fail anyway, since the French opposed it and Eden could not stomach most of the Canal's revenues going to Egypt, thereby rewarding Nasser's aggression. With the French government colluding with the 'Anglo-Gaullist' Suez Group of Tories, who blamed him for frittering the Canal Zone away in 1954, Eden opted for a path which would end his career ignominiously and permanently alter Britain's standing in the world. For at the root of the crisis was a weak man compelled to act strong by those who had not fully grasped that Britain's post-war position was fundamentally altered. What had been obvious to outside observers now pricked the bubble of delusion of men who still thought they ruled the world.[46]

Revealed Realities

On 14 October Eden met with Albert Gazier, the acting French Foreign Minister, and General Maurice Challe, Chief of the French General Staff. Challe outlined a bold plan: Israel would strike into Sinai, with a feint towards the Suez Canal, the latter operation solely designed to win

Anglo–French approval for its attack by giving London and Paris a pretext to issue an ultimatum demanding that an Anglo–French force insert itself into the Canal Zone to restore 'peace'. Having sought a peaceful outcome for three months, Eden's sensitivity to the fact that he was not his august predecessor led him to succumb to pressure to use force. This came from the French, the Suez Group and much of the Tory press. A particularly questionable role was played by Sir Ivone Kirkpatrick, Permanent Under Secretary at the Foreign Office, whose hawkish views on Nasser were influenced by postings to Rome and Berlin in the 1930s. He went against the consensus view of his department and ensured that warnings from missions all over the world went unaired in cabinet.[47]

The cautiously deliberative processes of British cabinet government were abandoned. Eden and Selwyn Lloyd flew to Paris for more detailed discussions about the Franco–Israeli conspiracy to incite an Israeli attack on Egypt. These decisions were imparted to a narrow group of half a dozen key ministers and civil servants in Whitehall, who alone had access to all the facts and who then smoothed their passage through the full cabinet by being less than forthcoming about what was afoot. At a cabinet meeting on 18 October the Anglo–French–Israeli plot encountered no resistance, although the Leader of the House of Commons Rab Butler, who had the informal role of deputy prime minister, recommended pursuing the same course through an open alliance with Israel, while the Defence Secretary Viscount Monckton tried to dodge responsibility by requesting a lateral move to paymaster-general. Eden and his associates might, just, have got away with misleading their cabinet colleagues if they could have limited their role in the Israeli provocation.[48]

But on 21 October a message arrived from Paris; the Israelis would not make their move against Suez without more explicit British involvement. Both they and the French suspected *perfide Albion* would leave them hanging out to dry and demanded that the RAF should make the first move from its bases in Cyprus to take out the Egyptian Ilyushins. Selwyn Lloyd was despatched for a secret meeting with the Israelis and French, the two peoples he most mistrusted, at a villa in Sèvres. Joking that he should have worn a false moustache, Lloyd did not conceal his distaste from Israeli Prime Minister David Ben-Gurion as they haggled over the timing of pre-emptive air strikes, which Ben-Gurion insisted must take place first. Lloyd's instructions were to maintain the fiction that Anglo–French intervention was not the result of a conspiracy, but Ben-Gurion insisted he sign a protocol outlining the secret plan agreed at Sèvres. Lloyd did so provisionally, with the reservation of referring the matter back to his superiors in London. When he did so, he misled them.

In a letter to the French Socialist Prime Minister Guy Mollet, Eden committed himself 'in the situation therein envisaged [in the protocol] to take the action decided'. Eden was not a party to a further secret agreement between the Israelis and French that put French warplanes on Israeli airfields, and he sent an emissary to retrieve the French and Israeli copies of the protocol signed by Lloyd, who was rebuffed by Foreign Minister Christian Pineau and Ben-Gurion with well-deserved contempt.[49] The Israelis were to attack on 29 October, wrongly believing that the prospect of alienating the Jewish vote on 6 November would prevent Eisenhower condemning them. In fact the Jewish vote was so overwhelmingly Democrat that the Republicans discounted it.

At a meeting on 25 October, Eden's cabinet acquiesced in arrangements about whose precise nature they were misinformed. Only some ministers were aware that the British could be charged with collusion, and that intervention lacked UN sanction or US support.[50] Meanwhile the CIA had responded to being shut out by its closest partners by looking for major withdrawals of Israeli funds from Wall Street banks, noting a massive surge in encrypted radio traffic between Paris and Tel Aviv without being able to decipher the contents, and increased the number of U-2 flights over the Mediterranean and the Gulf, a programme begun in September, to gain advance notice of air and naval movements.[51]

The Israelis invaded Sinai on schedule, dropping paratroops on 29 October in the distant vicinity of Suez, with which a larger force was supposed to link up after crossing the Negev desert. Even when told that collusion was suspected, Nasser could not believe that Britain and France could stoop so low, or that Israel would hook up with the old colonial powers, one of which it had forced out of Palestine. Ike was furious, saying 'nothing justifies double-crossing us', and instantly understood why the British Ambassador had returned home on 11 October, with his successor not due to arrive by ship until 8 November. While Ike suspected the worst of the French, he found it hard to credit that the British should have muddied the water when the Hungarian crisis was reaching its defining point. Eden pressed ahead regardless, and issued the agreed twelve-hour ultimatum to Egypt and Israel, but the subterfuge was exposed when Britain and France found themselves compelled to veto a US-sponsored motion at the UN Security Council calling for an immediate ceasefire. The Soviets were delighted to support the motion and were loud in their denunciation of colonialism, even as they prepared to suppress Hungarian aspirations to self-determination.

The Israelis encountered tough Egyptian resistance in Sinai, opposition which included Egyptian bombing raids. On the evening of 31 October the RAF attacked five different airfields around Cairo, hitting Cairo's civilian International Airport by mistake and narrowly aborting a mission that would have hit the 1,300 Americans being evacuated from the city. 'Bombs, by God,' Ike exclaimed. 'What does Anthony think he's doing?'[52] With Dulles in hospital for colon-cancer treatment, the President took sole charge and was especially shocked when a U-2 flight provided before and after images of the damage at Cairo airport, which coincided with the bad news coming in from Hungary. Ike ordered sanctions against Israel and told the British to expect no favours when they ran short of oil and the dollars needed to pay for it. The US Sixth Fleet also made a nuisance of itself as the slow British naval armada made its way across the Mediterranean from Malta, bearing the amphibious landing force that was supposed to reinforce Anglo–French airborne troops dropped at Port Said on the morning of 5 November.

Amid violent confrontations in the street of London between opponents and supporters of the intervention, the cabinet worms turned at a meeting on 4 November. Butler and Salisbury took the lead in opposing further escalation and the duplicitous Macmillan, when he learned of Ike's blunt warning, exclaimed: 'Oil sanctions! That finishes it.' Five or six ministers favoured deferring the airborne assault, but Eden overrode them.

Meanwhile Ike had to deal with Soviet threats to send troops to the Middle East and to launch 'rockets' against London and Paris. Having been misled by the opinion of the defectors Guy Burgess and Donald Maclean, and the visiting Labour MP and KGB agent Tom Driberg, that Eden would not have the nerve to attack Egypt, Khrushchev was provoked into a dangerous bluff. Ike called it with a message to Premier Nikolai Bulganin that he would support his allies if they were attacked. The London CIA station chief, Chester Cooper, reassured a fearful Joint Intelligence Committee that the Soviets had no missiles capable of hitting London.[53]

Even as British amphibious forces landed in Egypt on 6 November, there was a US-driven run on sterling and the US blocked British efforts to draw on deposits held by the International Monetary Fund. That morning Ike spoke to Eden on the telephone. Whatever was said, within the hour Eden ordered a ceasefire. Later he informed the French, in conclave with the Germans at a Paris summit: 'I don't think we can go on. The pressure on sterling is becoming unbearable. The English can take a lot of things, but I do not think they would be willing to accept the failure of sterling which would have considerable consequences for the Commonwealth . . . I cannot hold out any longer.'[54]

The Suez Crisis was a remarkable advertisement for the impact of economic sanctions, although Macmillan played a part by deliberately painting the financial position a great deal blacker than it was. On 13 November he claimed in cabinet that gold and currency reserves had fallen by £100 million, whereas the real figure was £31.7 million.[55] Petrol rationing was introduced in Britain and France after Nasser had sunk fifty ships to block the Canal. Finally Ike, although publicly describing it as a 'family spat', made his private and personal displeasure with Eden clear, by first inviting him and then disinviting him to celebrate his re-election to the presidency. The large British diplomatic and security community in Washington also found itself excluded from official events.

Troops were withdrawn even as others landed, prompting the overall British commander (Sir Hugh Stockwell, whom last we saw in Malaya) to comment: 'We've achieved the impossible. We're going both ways at once.' To complete the disaster, the 'wogs' rounded up the entire British intelligence network in Egypt, which SIS was shocked to learn had been thoroughly penetrated for years but left intact as a means of feeding London disinformation. Over the ensuing month a UN force was transported by the US Navy to replace the British and French. Nasser vetoed Canadian participation on the grounds that Canada shared the Queen and had a British-styled army, while insisting that the non-European elements be increased.[56]

Eden and his wife left for Jamaica on 21 November for a period of medically decreed rest at Goldeneye, the home of Ian Fleming, author of the James Bond thrillers. Even Ann Fleming knew this was a political error, commenting: 'Torquay and a sun-ray lamp would have been more peaceful and patriotic.' There was no telephone at Goldeneye, and Eden had effectively abdicated. The Americans concentrated on the succession. Macmillan had two advantages over his younger rival Rab Butler. He knew many of the key US players from the war, and he had a camouflaged deviousness that the equivocating Butler clearly lacked. On the 20 November Ike had the following conversation with Winthrop Aldrich, the genial Republican businessman who was his Ambassador to London:

Eisenhower: You are dealing with at least one person – maybe two or three – on a very personal basis. Is it possible for you to get together, without embarrassment, the two you mentioned in one of your messages?

Aldrich: Yes, one of them I've been playing bridge with. Perhaps I can stop him.

Eisenhower: I'd rather you talk to both together. You know who I mean? One has the same name as my predecessor at Columbia University Presidency [Rab Butler]; the other was with me in the war [Macmillan].

Aldrich: I know the one with you in the war. Oh yes, now I've got it.

Eisenhower: Could you get them informally and say of course we are interested and sympathetic, and as soon as things happen that we anticipate, we can furnish 'a lot of fig leaves'.

Aldrich: I can certainly say that.

Eisenhower: Will that be enough to get the boys moving?

Aldrich: I think it will be.

Eisenhower: Herb [Under Secretary of State Herbert Hoover] will send you a cable later tonight. You see, we don't want to be in a position of interfering between these two. But we want to have you personally tell them. They are both good friends.

Aldrich: Yes, very much so. Have you seen all my messages? Regarding my conversations with them all?

Eisenhower: Yes – with at least two.

Aldrich: That is wonderful. I will do this tomorrow.

Eisenhower: Yes, first thing in the morning.

Aldrich: I shall certainly do it. And then I will communicate with you at once. I can do it without the slightest embarrassment.

Eisenhower: Communicate through regular channels, through Herb.[57]

On 22 November Macmillan turned in a bravura performance at the influential Tory 1922 Committee; unable to rise to this occasion, Butler faded from contention. Eden returned to London on 14 December, his deep suntan only accentuating the sick man within. His cabinet colleagues coldly informed him that he had until Easter to improve his health. On 20 December he sank further into ignominy by assuring the House of Commons that 'there [had been] no plans to attack Egypt', and that 'there was no foreknowledge that Israel would attack Egypt'. On 9 January 1957 Eden resigned and did nothing of note save breed prize Hereford cattle and take exotic holidays for the remaining twenty years of his life.

The British, inevitably, take a solipsistic view of the Suez Crisis, viewing it in terms of end of empire. The wider ramifications of Eden's decisions in 1956 were much more serious than that. The first reform Communist government to declare formally that it was leaving the Warsaw Pact would have been crushed anyway, but Suez so reduced the cost the Soviets paid for the violence they inflicted on Hungary, for the Americans had to deal with this totally unwanted distraction in Egypt. British and French influence in the Arab world was destroyed and, save for Jordan and some minor autocratic Gulf states, trust has never recovered; nor has it been between France and Britain, not that there was much in the first place. France threw its influence behind Israel, equipping it in 1957 with its Dimona nuclear reactor, which it would use to produce an arsenal of atomic bombs it pretends it might not possess. In Arab eyes Israel would be indelibly identified with Western imperialism – a latter-day crusader state – and Nasser's mere survival was construed as a victory, which became a wider impediment to political realism in the Middle East.[58]

11. WITH US OR AGAINST US: THE SUB-CONTINENT

Out of Sight, Out of Mind

After independence, despite containing a fifth of the world's population – India was a nation of 361 million people, and there were seventy million more in Pakistan – the sub-continent was of limited importance to the US, which was mainly preoccupied with Western Europe, Japan, the Middle East and South-east Asia, in that order. Stalin regarded India and Pakistan as reactionary stooges of their former colonial power and his only interest in the area seems to have been to monitor the ideological purity of the Indian Communist Party aided by the British Communist Party, which assumed a role of tutelage as though the Raj lived on.[1] The US and USSR alike mistrusted the neutralism professed by the Indian leaders.[2]

The British had expected greater American commitment after Franklin Roosevelt's wartime preaching, but their attempts to get the US involved fell on stony ground. In particular the Americans slighted an opportunity to play a constructive role in resolving the Kashmir dispute, which had India and Pakistan at each other's throats from the start, and which poisons relations between them to this day. Kashmir was a princely state, its ruler Hindu but the majority of his subjects Muslim. Perhaps more to the point, the family of Jawaharlal Nehru, India's first Prime Minister, were Kashmiri Hindu Brahmins. At partition the Prince opted to join India, a decision Pakistan sought to overturn by sending armed tribesmen into Kashmir to rouse the inhabitants to rebellion.

New Delhi sent troops to secure the province and Britain, disqualified by its own history, vainly tried to get the US to act as mediator.[3]

In July 1948 Loy Henderson came to take up his last post prior to the Tehran appointment reviewed in Chapter Nine. He had been eased out of the Near Eastern and African Affairs department at State because of his refusal to subordinate US policy in the Middle East to the vocal Zionist lobby. On the way to New Delhi he stopped off in London. During a relaxed dinner with Foreign Secretary Bevin and senior Foreign Office officials, Bevin said of India: 'There is a country where we must keep together, although you must let us be in the shop window.' Aware that being seen to collaborate with the former imperial power would be the kiss of death in Indian eyes, Bevin joked that 'If it is ever convenient for you to have a public row with [Sir Archibald] Archie Nye [Britain's High Commissioner to India] then I'll be happy to play that game with you.' An early sign that Henderson's new adventure would be difficult came when he called on Krishna Menon, the Indian High Commissioner to the Court of St James's, who rose from his desk but did not offer to shake hands. He informed Henderson that he was 'the first US ambassador to darken his door', a theme he kept repeating, and would revert to when they met again six months later.[4]

Initially there were good grounds for a US tilt towards India. The new nation's democratic and legal institutions were truly impressive, whatever complaints many had about a 'licence-payer raj' run by pedantically inefficient jobsworths. Almost all shades of political opinion were encompassed by the ruling Congress party, which in some respects resembled the catch-all Liberals of nineteenth-century Italy, as an organization through which an educated elite managed the largely illiterate mass. For, although its record was allegedly superior to those of other colonial powers, Britain's legacy to India was a literacy rate of only 14 per cent (1 per cent higher in Pakistan).[5]

There was nothing akin to the Congress party in Pakistan and unlike India, which broadly made do with the governing structure it had inherited from the Raj, the tribalist political factions in Pakistan could not even agree how the country should be governed. It took almost a decade to devise a constitution, perhaps because they sought the advice of American political science theorists from the Dearborn Foundation, whose well-meaning suggestions prioritized the optimum over the workable. Although Pakistan was technically a democracy, elections were rare and political legitimacy elusive. Its corrupt civilian politicians were despised by an efficient army, whose rituals and uniforms would not have seemed alien in Surrey or Wiltshire. The fundamental problem was that Pakistan came into existence as an Islamic state and the vast majority of the people were conservative and religious – yet the Western-educated feudal elite was secular, as it remains today.

A glance at a map showed the fundamental problem of a state with 1,100 miles of India bulging between West and East Pakistan. It was as if Massachusetts and Texas formed a single state, with all the intervening states being hostile. The Pakistani capital was situated in Karachi because Lahore was too close to the giant neighbour. In the 1960s it would be relocated to Islamabad, cooler than Karachi but regrettably more susceptible to military coups organized from the army HQ at nearby Rawalpindi, a chronic problem India's politicians were spared. However, the same glance at the map revealed the geopolitical importance of the new state, for as early as 1948–9 both the CIA and the US Joint Chiefs of Staff highlighted Pakistan's proximity to the Soviet Union and China.[6]

India had little resonance in the American imagination, whatever fitful curiosity there was about Gandhi in illustrated magazines. Although 350,000 US engineering and logistics troops had been stationed in wartime India, including Kennedy's future Secretary of State Dean Rusk, many more GIs had fought and died in Europe and on the islands of the Pacific. In so far as Americans had a view of India, beyond a handful tantalized by its 'spirituality', this derived from Rudyard Kipling or Katherine Mayo's 1927 bestseller *Mother India*, which popularized British views of the sub-continent for a US audience. While pushing for the early independence of the sub-continent, US policy-makers overlooked the likelihood of partition. They hoped the Muslim League would stop short of an independent Pakistan, but did nothing significant to discourage it.

The Americans underestimated the physical and cultural shock they would encounter in the sub-continent. During the Raj, the long sea voyage had given the British a gradual induction into the heat and the pervasive smell, with the shift to the exotic starting at Suez. Air travel meant travellers were hit in the face as they disembarked. Visiting US dignitaries blanched as they progressed through fetid slums from the airport to their sweltering quarters. The crush of people overwhelmed them, as did the ordure in the streets and the stray cows. Everywhere dusty heaps of rags stretched out begging bowls. Naked, wild-looking holy men went about with painted faces, and sepulchral Hindu temples, teeming with lascivious sculpted idols, were another shock to anyone disposed to moral outrage. The *New York Times* correspondent Cyrus Sulzberger wrote of a major place of worship in Old Delhi as being 'hideously ugly'.[7] Visiting academics spoke of 'the dysentery circuit'. When John and Robert Kennedy visited in 1951 they both succumbed to 'Delhi belly', hiding curried chicken under lettuce leaves to avoid the perils of eating it.

The cultural gulf yawned even wider for the few Indians who visited the US, with the requirement of demonstrating an income of $12 per diem in order to obtain a visa proving a challenge even for junior diplomats. Although the Indian caste system, with light-skinned Brahmins and dark-skinned Untouchables, was self-evidently racist, Indian visitors purported to be outraged by white American attitudes to African-Americans. Meat-eaters also smelled bad to vegetarian Hindu visitors, despite the obsessive American concern with hygiene, while they loftily judged that cities filled with cars betokened an anomic absence of human solidarity that was no more evident in Brahmins outraged whenever an Untouchable Dalit crossed their cast shadow.[8]

At least at elite levels, Indians and Americans shared a common language, and words like 'goons', 'thugs', 'Boston Brahmins' and 'Hollywood moguls' reflected some cultural cross-fertilization. Yet there was little mutual interest. There was no oil at stake and the US did not have domestic Hindu or Muslim lobbies. The deep emotional bonds that existed with Chiang Kai-shek's China were entirely lacking, even though India had also attracted large numbers of American missionaries, including John Welsh Dulles, author of *Life in India* and the Presbyterian missionary grandfather of Foster Dulles. There was a feeling that despite Mountbatten's culpable mismanagement of partition and his responsibility for the trouble in Kashmir, the British could be left to take care of Western interests. Under Truman the US adopted a stance of neutrality between India and Pakistan, imposing an arms embargo and – after heavy British lobbying – urging Nehru to submit the Kashmir dispute to international arbitration.[9]

Relations with India were personalized to an unfortunate degree, chiefly because Prime Minister Nehru thought that his cosmopolitan background uniquely equipped him to act as minister for external affairs. As such he did not deign to consult the cabinet on foreign policy or world affairs, about which (from memory) he had written a remarkable epistolary history while in British captivity in the early 1930s called *Glimpses of World History*. Here one might learn that the empire of Genghiz Khan was more significant than that of Julius Caesar. Nehru's colleagues were content to leave world affairs to him since they were much more interested in domestic portfolios, which brought real powers of patronage and self-enrichment. Snobbish attitudes and poses Nehru had acquired from the British also combined with Gandhian moralism to conceal a conventional ambition for India to be recognized as a great power. Every conversation with him felt like a lecture, in which his Fabian socialist self-righteousness grated on American nerves. He fashioned an ideology of non-alignment, based, he claimed, on recognizing what was worth while in the rival Cold War social systems. It was a poor choice to adopt the standard Western leftist's pose of moral equivalence between the two systems when, in the absence of any alternative, India would be reliant on US aid to embark on a London School of Economics-inspired bureaucratic socialist economic model that proved no less stultifying in India than in Britain and, indeed, anywhere else it was adopted.

Nehru's India would also be in the vanguard of denouncing imperialism and racism, and worked to give Southern Asia a coherent voice in the vacuum left by departing European empires. Still containing more Muslims than lived in Pakistan, India would also seek to dispel any negative impression resulting from its undemocratic land grab in Kashmir by being uncritically supportive of Muslim interests in the Middle East. Yet, during the first interview between Nehru and Ambassador Henderson, when Henderson touched on the need to resolve the conflict in Kashmir if there was to be any prospect of US aid, Nehru rejected American 'moral dictation', adding that there could be no compromise between a secular India and an Islamic Pakistani 'theocracy' engaged in a 'crusade' – an unfortunate but highly revealing choice of word that not only Westerners have used.

Before Nehru embarked on his first visit to the US in the autumn of 1949, Henderson advised Washington that the Indian leader was a 'vain, sensitive, emotional and complicated person'. For an agnostic he talked a lot about spirituality. Many of his less attractive characteristics stemmed from an America-hating English nanny and his education at Harrow, where 'he consorted with and cultivated a group of rather supercilious upper middle class young men who fancied themselves rather precious . . . He acquired some of their manners and ways of thinking.' Unlike them, being just a drunk or deeply stupid did not mitigate Nehru's snobbery, for he was neither. Prolonged exposure to the fashionably 'progressive' Mountbattens, including an intimate – although perhaps non-sexual – relationship with the promiscuous Edwina, had coloured his view of Americans as 'a vulgar, pushy, lot, lacking in fine feeling' with a culture 'dominated by the dollar'. Although the Americans were anxious to make the visit a success, they contrived to send a plane known as *The Sacred Cow* to convey Nehru from London to Washington. This did not augur well.

Every encounter with senior US policy-makers, from Assistant Secretary of State George McGhee to Secretary of State Dean Acheson, left a sour taste in the Indians' mouths. The CIA reported that the view of Nehru's inner circle was that Americans were 'elementary and material', while from Truman downwards the Indian Prime Minister felt he had encountered only 'mediocrities'. At a dinner with bankers intent on giving India a loan, the fastidious Nehru was so appalled by the 'vulgarity' of being told that 'twenty billion dollars were around the table' that he refused to pick it up. Exhausted by the pace of his whirlwind tour, he failed to press the fact that India urgently needed a million tons of wheat.[10]

Enter the Dragon, Again

More than bad personal chemistry explains why the US would ultimately favour Pakistan. The early Cold War was a time of 'with us or against us' on both sides. India's desire to be master of its own destinies was reflected in its response to the 1949 ascendancy of Mao's Communists in China. The US withheld recognition of Mao's regime and sought to generalize this line among all democratic powers. India made it clear that it intended to break ranks, arguing that the nationalistic Chinese Communists would not indefinitely accept Soviet tutelage. Although proved right in the longer term, in the short term Nehru was to be painfully reminded that Chinese nationalism was a greater threat to India than Communism would ever be. But for the moment India needed peace with China so as to build the new nation, while China did not need a problem on its western flank when it had trouble in the east with the Americans over Korea and Taiwan.

Nehru's rosy view of Mao's regime was influenced by his Ambassador to Beijing, a product of Christ Church, Oxford, called Kavalam Panikkar, whose daughter was married to Govindan Nair, the leader of the Communist Party of India, and who totally misrepresented the Red Chinese regime. Consequently Nehru took the amiable and urbane Premier Zhou Enlai to be representative of the rest of the Chinese leadership, which was neither. In fact Zhou's private response to Nehru, taking him under his wing, was 'I have never met a more arrogant man than Nehru.' India was as surprised as anyone by the North Korean invasion of the South, but after voting to condemn North Korean aggression, the Indian UN delegation did not support military action to defeat it and then tried to act, unbidden, as mediator, which succeeded only in annoying the Americans. India further irked the US by voting against UN condemnation of the Chinese intervention, on the grounds that the US had ignored Indian warnings. Nehru's attempt to deal himself a hand in Korea had consequences. The Truman administration had sent a proposal to Congress requesting $190 million in food aid for India once it was clear it was facing catastrophic famine. But Nehru's public anti-Americanism caused the proposal to limp through Congress, where it was transformed into a loan.[11]

In the 1950s Nehru favoured the slogan 'Hindee Chinee bhai-bhai' (India–China brotherhood) to characterize what he hoped would be joint condominium over Asia. This survived China's sudden occupation of Tibet in 1950, a land that Indians were emotionally and mythically attached to, and which had gained a degree of independence in 1911. The Chinese did not even mind India hosting the exiled Dalai Lama after 1959, but they objected to the welcoming circus of 300 reporters this entailed, for they expected India to curb the Dalai Lama's political activities. But now Chinese troops were on India's northern borders, where vast expanses of nothingness on the roof of the world were provisionally mapped with dotted lines drawn by the departed British. While the Chinese surreptitiously built a long road to link Xinjiang with western Tibet, elsewhere Indian troops asserted claims India had inherited from the British. Although the Congress party dominated the Lok Sabha (India's parliament), sundry defectors and renegades from Congress provided a vociferous opposition, including thirty-one Communists. Many Indians were appalled by harsh Chinese behaviour in Tibet – throwing rotten eggs and tomatoes at posters of Mao – and accused Nehru of appeasement, for this concept really travelled well. Even the Deputy Prime Minister Vallabhbhai Patel castigated Nehru for his naivety towards Mao's 'agrarian reformers', pointing out that Communism merely cloaked a series of historical, national and racial claims that could be fairly described as imperialist. Nehru got a taste of that when he met Mao in 1954 and found himself 'ushered into a presence, as someone coming from a tributary or vassal state of the Chinese empire'. He tried the empty platitudes of 'Panch Sheel' or Peaceful Coexistence based on Respect, and even mysticism, about the 'striving of the Indian spirit towards these Himalayas'. To this the Chinese drily responded that 'myths and legends could not be cited as a basis for the [territorial] alignment claimed by India'. They had seized one huge area around Aksai Chin by stealth, and by 1959 they were looking for an even bigger area below the disputed McMahon Line, which from 1914 onwards established the border between Imperial India and Tibet, and duly became the disputed frontier which separated India from China.[12] Nehru complacently thought of the Himalayas as a natural Maginot Line, and cut the defence budget accordingly.

Meanwhile, deepening relations between Washington and Pakistan also infuriated India. Initially, Pakistan did not seem to amount to much, with only 17.5 per cent of the financial assets of the Raj. Its Ministry of Foreign Affairs had six officials, three of whom were British hold-overs, none of whom even possessed a typewriter. A month after independence, 40 per cent of Pakistan's central government staff was stranded in New Delhi because savage communal violence had interrupted rail travel. They had to be flown to the new capital on chartered flights.[13]

Americans knew even less about Pakistan than about India. One US ex. millionaire thought that the visiting Pakistani Prime Minister and his entourage were Palestinians. Another, perplexed by the blank space separating West and East Pakistan on his menu card, thought it might be in Africa. In more populous East Pakistan, Bengalis and others resented western Punjabi domination of the new state. Everything about the new nation seemed provisional and not destined to last. Although the Punjab in West Pakistan had once been the granary of the Raj, India's control of the Indus headwaters meant that it could, and did, divert water away from Pakistan's irrigation canals, making Pakistan dependent on US food aid.

Apart from the wound in Kashmir, Pakistan had problems with the hatchet-faced gang who ruled Afghanistan, a people whom non-Pushtun Pakistanis regarded as murdering savages. But India and Russia were covertly encouraging Afghan irredentism through demands for an independent 'Pushtunistan' to encompass Pakistan's North West Frontier, so as to accommodate the wild Pashtun tribesmen (known to the British as Pathans) who straddled that border. That is still the goal of today's Afghan and Pakistani Taliban, in so far as they will not manage to take over both of these states.

When the first US Ambassador to Karachi died of cancer within four months of arrival, it took two years to replace him; Pakistan mattered that little. Truman also deflected Pakistani appeals for economic and military aid; when Karachi requested $2 billion, it received $10 million. Although the Prime Minister Liaquat Ali Khan paid a highly successful visit to the US in 1950, it may or may not have been an accident that nearly 500 tons of weapons and ammunition destined for Pakistan blew up in New Jersey. Liaquat Ali was assassinated soon after arriving home in circumstances that have never been explained, as the assassin was instantly killed.

Official US attitudes began to change when Pakistan joined Muslim Turkey in wholeheartedly supporting US action in Korea, although

Pakistan sent no troops because of anxieties about India and Kashmir. Since Pakistan spent 70 per cent of its government revenue on defence, it was not keen to take on further military commitments. By contrast India seemed flaky, pink and unreliable. The warmth with which US officials and visiting journalists began to report on Pakistan is striking. Starting with Mohammed Ali Jinnah, the Shia leader of the Muslim League, Pakistani leaders emphasized the radical incompatibility of Communism and Islam. Jinnah's successors were jolly fellows, not given to the icy moralizing of their southern neighbour. George McGhee's dealings with Liaquat Ali were 'like a breath of fresh air' after the 'wishy-washy' Nehru, whose conversation reminded many Americans of a dense fog. The Pakistani army commander General Ayub Khan, the Sandhurst-trained son of a former Indian Army NCO, was a particular favourite. He was a no-nonsense type who liked expensive horses and fine shot-guns. The horse Sardar, which he had presented to Jackie Kennedy, would follow the gun carriage carrying her husband's coffin after his assassination. Unlike Nehru, who would not remain in a room where alcohol was served, the moustachioed Pakistani military crowd were convivial topers.[14]

US enthusiasm for Pakistan owed much to American adoption of the British view of the northern 'warrior races'. It was no accident that Loy Henderson regarded Nehru as 'essentially a feminine personality'.[15] McGhee's view was that, unlike the polytheistic Hindus, whose many gods and complex caste system gave them a highly conditional grasp of truth, the Pakistanis were fine fighting men whose Islamic faith impressed on them a keen sense of good and evil.[16]

The big tilt towards Pakistan began in the early Eisenhower era. How the two nations had responded to Korea was reflected in how aid was dispensed. Whereas a Republican Congress immediately halved the aid being granted to India, Ike easily persuaded it to give food aid to Paki-stan. The former generals Eisenhower and Ayub Khan would also get along famously, not least because Ayub had deep respect for the former Supreme Commander in Europe. Dulles and Nehru also had a history, starting with Nehru's refusal of Indian endorsement of Dulles's peace settlement with Japan on the grounds that only fellow Asians should be involved. By contrast, Dulles was mightily impressed by the good show

Ayub Khan put on when he visited Karachi after a grim sojourn in New Delhi. Months later Dulles enthused the Senate Foreign Relations Committee with his vivid tales of 'the lancers . . . fellows that had to be 6 feet 2 inches to be qualified and they sat there on these great big horses'. Such men 'are going to fight any Communist invasion with their bare fists if they have to'.

To reduce US defence liabilities the Eisenhower administration strengthened reliable clients to create regional defence alliances against the Soviet Union. This had major consequences for Pakistan. Dulles became captive to British 'Great Game' thinking about how Afghanistan and Pakistan might be marshalled to thwart the Russian drive south to the warm waters of the Arabian Sea. Following a shift discernible under Truman, Pakistan was increasingly construed as a Middle Eastern rather than South Asian power, at a time when the Soviet threat to the Middle East – source of 70 per cent of Western Europe's oil – loomed large. Of course, the governments of Egypt, Iran and Turkey were unhappy about Pakistani ambitions in their region. Pakistan's strategic reorientation would depend on whether outsiders could resolve the issue of Kashmir, thereby freeing up Pakistan's army for operations in the west. In fact, Kashmir would prove irresolvable.[17]

Pakistani governments played US geostrategic needs for all they were worth, eventually persuading the US, under a May 1954 defence assistance treaty, to equip five and a half divisions, plus six air squadrons and twelve naval vessels. What the Pentagon reluctantly envisaged as a one-off spend of around $30 million became a semi-permanent subvention that quickly rose to $500 million in the first three years. Rarely can so much money have been expended with so little reflection. Hardly anyone in the US administration questioned whether Pakistan would ever be in a position to deploy troops to check Soviet advances into Iran and the Gulf, where they were rightly viewed as cat's-paws of the Americans. Nor did many ask whether the growth of the Pakistani armed forces, which consumed 70 per cent of Pakistani government revenue, might result in the neglect of urgent economic and social reforms, therby further alienating the people from the feudal elites who ruled.[18]

Possibly all the US gained from its embrace of Pakistan were air bases near the Soviet Union, notably Budaber near Peshawar, from which the

U-2s operated and which housed a vast National Security Agency eaves-dropping operation. Pakistan eagerly joined a web of US-sponsored alli-ances that obliged it to do very little. It entered into a bilateral defence agreement with Turkey and it joined the South East Asian Treaty Orga-nization (SEATO), an odd alliance since the only South-east Asian mem-ber, if one discounts the Philippines, was Thailand. And what suited the Pakistani feudal elite appalled the average Pakistani, who resented his nation (for *her* views did not count) becoming a US client.

The influential columnist Walter Lippmann got to the heart of Foster Dulles's view of Pakistan in a famous encounter shortly after Pakistan joined SEATO:

'Foster . . . what do you think you're going to accomplish with that thing [SEATO]? You've got mostly Europeans, plus Pakistan, which is nowhere near Southeast Asia.'

'Look, Walter . . . I've got to get some real fighting men into the south of Asia. The only Asians who can really fight are the Pakistanis. That's why we need them in the alliance. We could never get along without the Gurkas.'

'But Foster . . . the Gurkas aren't Pakistanis, they're Indians [they are actually from Nepal].'

'Well . . . they may not be Pakistanis, but they're Moslems.'

'No, I'm afraid they're not Moslems, either, they're Hindus.'

Dulles shrugged that off as well and 'proceeded to lecture Lippmann for half an hour on how SEATO would plug the dike against communism in Asia'.[19]

Following the collapse of the British Middle Eastern Defence Organi-zation (MEDO) project, Pakistan joined its US-sponsored successor, the Baghdad Pact, which eventually metamorphosed into the Central Treaty Organization (CENTO). This was based on the idea of a Northern Tier, designed to deter the Russians from going on the rampage in the oil-producing states of the Gulf.[20] The involvement of Iraq automatically meant Egypt dropped out, which enabled the Soviets simply to leapfrog the imaginary rampart by arming Nasser directly. Towards the end of his first term Ike privately conceded that arming Pakistan had been a 'terrible error' from a purely military point of view, without regard to the way in which it had encouraged a bloated Pakistani military to usurp civilian politics.

An increasingly authoritarian President Iskander Mirza (another Sandhurst graduate) eventually proclaimed martial law in October 1958, only to be overthrown himself by the US darling General Ayub Khan. Thus was demonstrated Sandhurst's power to inculcate British 'values' in the hearts and minds of its foreign graduates. Rather archly Khan explained that he was merely copying the US Electoral College when he concocted a base democracy of 80,000 village councillors, 95.6 per cent of whom duly agreed that he should remain president in what he claimed was an election.

Then there was India. Although India had a four-to-one superiority in manpower, the arrival of Patton tanks and F-86 jet fighters in Pakistan to some degree offset it. The US could never grasp that such a large country as India lived in mortal dread of the military in Pakistan. Nehru retaliated by banning US freight planes from using Indian air-space to resupply the French in Indochina. He even made difficulties about allowing US commercial planes to cross Indian airspace, and ordered the closure of several US Information Agency centres for being nests of propagandists, as though that were not their declared function.

Quickening relations with Pakistan had consequences for US relations with India. The Soviets promised India economic assistance and cheap loans to supplant the meagre US effort and in 1954 they offered to construct a vast steel mill at Bhilai. In June 1955 the Soviets played expertly to Nehru's vanity with a resoundingly stage-managed welcome when he visited the Soviet Union. In November and December Premier Nikolai Bulganin and General Secretary Khrushchev made a return visit to India. In Calcutta, two million people turned out to greet them. No Pakistani leader would visit Moscow until 1965.

Ike was fully aware that support for Pakistan was alienating India, and resolved to use economic aid to woo it away from the generous Soviets. The problem was that Nehru's hostile comments about the US meant it was much harder to get these packages through Congress. When the President requested $70 million for 1956, Congress reduced it by $20 million in retaliation for Nehru 'playing both ends against the middle', as the New Hampshire Republican Congressman Styles Bridges put it. Undeterred, and following a visit from Nehru in which Ike cleverly indulged the visitor's fondness for abstract speculation, he decided to underwrite India's Soviet-sounding second five-year economic plan. This in turn worried Pakistan, which believed it would free India to acquire modern weapons and to erode the qualitative edge Pakistan enjoyed, which indeed it did. In fact, once Dulles was dead, Eisenhower assiduously courted India, which he visited in December 1959, partly because he realized that India was falling out with China, and that Soviet *neutrality* over their disputes was in turn alienating the Chinese from Moscow. No wonder Eisenhower quadrupled India's aid allocation.[21]

One of Nehru's achievements was not to get locked into Cold War logic, by consolidating India's relations with a much wider array of partners. A subtle formula was found to enable this great republic to belong to a Commonwealth whose head was the British monarch. That platitudinous forum suited Nehru's style very well, especially as the growing British Gandhi cult made London suitably obsequious to the Mahatma's heir. Nehru's disdain for the ideological simplicities of the Cold War led him to participate enthusiastically in the Bandung Conference held in Indonesia in April 1955. Twenty-nine nations attended, including India and Pakistan, as well as Nasser for Egypt, both Vietnams and Communist China. Zhou Enlai reached Bandung only thanks to missing his official plane, which blew up after leaving Hong Kong, killing the rest of his delegation. He quickly and keenly resented being treated as the younger brother of the older Asian power. Nehru took a close interest in the conference arrangements, since he did not trust the Indonesian hosts to do so.[22]

The aim at Bandung was to represent the one and a half billion people of the newly independent nations, who would become a powerful moral force between the Cold War superpowers. There was much discussion of racism on the part of people who had experienced it and who, in returning to the theme ever after, were like an enthusiastic football team playing the game after the referee had blown his whistle and the opposing side had departed. The subject of caste was not on the agenda. Non-interference in the sovereign affairs of others was another important theme, especially among those still subject to the interference of former colonial powers.

Though Nehru was correct about the mentally constraining effects of 'bloc thought', in which one was either Communist or anti-Communist, he was wrong to believe that the Cold War must result in a global nuclear catastrophe, and that consequently Soviet ambitions must be accommodated at all costs. While the participants rapidly condemned (Western) colonialism, Ceylon, Pakistan, Turkey and Iran ensured that Communist imperialism was also denounced. The Ceylonese Prime Minister, Sir John Kotelawala, was vociferous in denouncing Communist imperialism in Eastern Europe and Central Asia, a stance not unconnected with Soviet vetoing of Ceylonese membership of the United Nations.[23] Within a decade, the irenic simplicities of Bandung received a cold douche of reality.

In 1959 Nehru adopted a forward strategy, establishing more Indian military posts to define what he claimed was the border with China. Convinced of India's moral unassailability, he failed to notice that Gandhian non-violence had left his armed forces in a parlous condition, with defence budgets slashed to pay for India's crash industrialization. The armed forces had also stupidly declined British and US offers of military manuals, based on experiences in Korea, of Chinese infantry battle tactics. The Chief of the General Staff was a brave man, but he had no battle experience. Nehru was ill advised by his feeble intelligence services that the Chinese would not try to fight at such high altitudes and on such intractable terrain as the Himalayan foothills. On 20 October 1962 the Chinese invaded to occupy the whole of the disputed 40,000 square miles east and west of Nepal, crushing the poorly prepared Indian army. Much to Nehru's surprise, while the West supported India, Russia got off the fence and supported China – how else could it react in view of the Cuban Missile Crisis – and the non-aligned world remained non-aligned, notably Nkrumah of Ghana, in whom Nehru had invested much time and hope. A desperate Nehru asked the US for enormous military resupplies, which began arriving by jet freighters from Germany within a week. By November, when the Chinese launched a massive thrust that made their opening moves look like a jabbing feint, Nehru asked the US for fifteen squadrons of bombers and fighters to repulse the invaders before they arrived in New Delhi.[24]

The following year Pakistan officially ceded to China the disputed

Kashmiri border area adjacent to its own territory, which had been agreed some time before but held in abeyance because the area was also claimed by India. The good relations between Pakistan and China that persist to this day were born of this largely forgotten conflict between India and China. Contrary to General Ayub Khan's hopes, however, China did not support Pakistan in the Second Kashmiri War in 1965.

The effect on Nehru and the India he had led since independence was profound. His pose as the apostle of non-violence had been exposed as cant when he sent the Indian army into the Portuguese enclave of Goa in 1961. Domestically his democratic credentials had taken a battering when in July 1959 he arbitrarily dismissed the world's first democratically elected Communist government in the Indian state of Kerala. Now the Chinese had exposed India's weakness and rudely rejected his airy assumption of leadership of the developing world. He was never the same man again and for the remaining months of his life (he died in May 1964) his spirit was broken by his loss of domestic and international prestige. He did not seem to notice the large rat that regularly sped across his office carpet to a big hole in the wall.[25] India's defence budget doubled and US and British air forces were invited to conduct air defence manoeuvres from Indian air bases. Despite all the heady talk at Bandung, there was massive resentment against 'these amoral neutralists who have refused to give India the unreserved sympathy and support she had asked for'. The ghost of John Foster Dulles might have smiled.[26]

12. LOSING BY WINNING: ALGERIA

Birth of a Nation: Algeria's Fight for Independence

The eight-year war in Algeria began as one between French government forces and indigenous Arab and Berber nationalists. It encompassed a civil war waged by the supposedly socialist Front de Libération Nationale (FLN), which practised widespread 'compliance terrorism' to enforce popular support, against the rival Mouvement National Algérien led by the veteran nationalist leader Messali Hadj, which probably enjoyed covert French support. In 1957 alone, some 4,000 Algerian Muslim immigrants were killed in feuding between these two groups in mainland French cities. The conflict ended with French right-wing Organisation de l'Armée Secrète terrorists declaring war on the French authorities and bombing and shooting their opponents in Algeria and in metropolitan France. The OAS alone killed as many people as died in the entire thirty-year Troubles in Northern Ireland between 1968 and 1998. It was the worst of the dirty wars waged by European colonial powers, eclipsing even Britain's brutal campaign in Kenya.[1]

The Second World War had raised the national consciousness of many of the Algerians who fought for France, while the collapse of France in 1940 had lowered its prestige in the eyes of Arabs, who were treated like dirt by French settlers. Chronic food shortages added to the tensions. The first covert armed Algerian nationalist movement was established in 1947 as the Organisation Spéciale, but this had been crushed by 1951. Its ranks included Ben Bella, who after the war had declined a regular army commission to become a local government

councillor in Marnia, where his family had a farm. In 1947 he was subject to obscure chicanery about ownership of his farm, which like all
Arab land lacked title deeds. He fled after shooting one of his would-be
dispossessors. In 1949 he planned a robbery on the Oran Post Office to
garner funds for the underground 'army' which was not even a band.
Careful police work led to his arrest and imprisonment. In 1953 Ben
Bella broke out of jail with the aid of a file hidden in a baguette, fleeing
to Cairo, where he had to communicate with his fellow Arab nationalists in French since his own Arabic was poor.[2]

World events were encouraging. At Dien Bien Phu in 1954 the French
army suffered epic defeat. Perplexed Viet Minh interrogators asked captured Algerian Muslims why they were not fighting their own war of
national liberation. It was a good question.[3] Ben Bella was closely
involved in establishing the FLN on 10 October 1954, with an armed
wing called the Armée de Libération Nationale, or ALN. The FLN had
a collective leadership of nine, who divided the country into six *wilayas*
or administrative cum military districts. It had external representatives
in Cairo, for the rebels realized that international diplomacy would be
crucial to victory. Within Algeria its underground apparatus administered rough justice and extorted money, while nullifying local expressions of French power.

Beyond such exogenous triggers as Dien Bien Phu, it is not hard to see
why an armed revolt should have occurred in the mid-1950s. A visiting
French commission acknowledged that 90 per cent of Algeria's wealth
was in the hands of a minority of the European 10 per cent of its ten million people, the large landowners who produced cereals, cork and wine.
One-third of the nine million Muslims were either under-employed or
chronically unemployed. Low wages were the lot of those in work.
Eighty per cent of Muslim children did not attend schools, a trend accelerated after guerrillas took to burning them down. Eighty-five per cent
of Muslims were illiterate in a society whose masters harped on about
Western civilization. Whereas the European birth rate in Algeria corre-
sponded to European norms, the Muslim figure was ten times higher.
While the European population enjoyed a standard of living roughly
equivalent to those of Greece, Portugal or Spain, life for the majority
Muslim population resembled that of the poorest people in Egypt or

India. Western military buffs may be tantalized by tales of the Paras, but the reality for the majority of Algerians was grinding rural poverty and far from casual racism.[4]

The nationalist insurrection began on All Saints' Day 1954, with seventy co-ordinated attacks on army bases and police stations in the Aurès region. A French teacher and his wife, together with a *caid* (one of the village headmen cum judges through whom the French ruled), were dragged off a bus and murdered. Radio Cairo broadcast the FLN's essential aims: 'restoration of the Algerian state, sovereign, democratic, and social, within the framework of the principles of Islam' and 'preservation of all fundamental freedoms, without distinction of race or religion'. The guerrillas' initial military outing may have been unimpressive, but it had a defined strategy, which it would pursue with unerring purpose.[5]

The first phase of the war, from November 1954 to late 1955, was a struggle for survival by a small guerrilla force lacking modern arms except for those sold or abandoned during the Second World War. Most FLN violence was directed at other Muslims as it went about creating a counter-state. Although the FLN was a predominantly secular movement, it also espoused a grim Islamic puritanism. Political toughs cut the throats of any Muslims who served the colonial power, drank alcohol or smoked, the method deliberately chosen to resemble the *halal* slaughtering of sheep.

The French Premier Pierre Mendès-France, fresh from liquidating the French Empire in Indochina, declared that Algeria was different. 'The Algerian departments are part of the French Republic,' he said. 'Between them and metropolitan France there can be no conceivable secession.' The Socialist Minister of the Interior, François Mitterrand, flatly stated that 'the only possible negotiation is war'. French troops began to mount 'raking' operations (*ratissages*) through the hills from which the guerrillas conducted their raids. The mountain scrub known as *bled* was not like the jungle that served the Viet Minh so well, and initial French successes included the capture or killing of three of the historic nine FLN leaders. They were, however, replaced by even more implacable younger men, and the *ratissages*, carried out with brutal insensitivity, replenished the pool of potential nationalist recruits. They also caused Muslims in the Algerian Assembly to walk out, among them the moderate liberal Ferhat Abbas who flew to Cairo in April 1956 to join the FLN.

The view from Paris was that the restoration of law and order was the necessary prelude to political reform. How they did it was nobody else's business as this was an internal French affair. The 1.2 million Algerian Europeans calculated that reform could be indefinitely deferred if they made their disapproval sufficiently vocal, for with parliamentary coalitions so tenuous the colonial tail was adroit at wagging the metropolitan dog. The *pieds noirs* were alert to any sign that they were going to be sold down the river, as they believed France had done to settlers in the neighbouring protectorates of Morocco and Tunisia, granted full independence in 1956. Both countries functioned as external bases for the FLN and gave passports to its couriers and diplomats. Safe havens were the *sine qua non* for any insurgency, providing in this case distribution points for the initially small flow of arms from Nasser's Egypt, followed in due course by far larger shipments and training missions from Yugoslavia and the Soviet bloc.[6]

The *pieds noirs* were intensely suspicious of Jacques Soustelle, a respected ethnologist and close collaborator of General de Gaulle, when he was appointed governor-general of Algeria. Yet Soustelle believed that Algeria was as French as Brittany or Provence and urged the French Assembly to pass a series of emergency decrees which brought courts martial and extensive controls on the media. The British war movie *The Bridge on the River Kwai* was banned for two years – for depicting Europeans being humiliated by Asian Japanese – while *Ill Met by Moonlight* was permanently prohibited for showing Greek partisans abducting a German general.[7]

The *pieds noirs* were hard to like. The rich had the wherewithal to relocate to metropolitan France, but the bulk of the settlers, some of whom had originally fled Prussian-occupied Alsace after 1870, were determined not to flee again. There were also those with nowhere to run, such as the polyglot *petit blancs* of Algiers' working-class Bab el-Oued (River's Gate), a rough waterfront district known as the proletarian Riviera. There the *colons* were as likely to be Corsican, Italian, Maltese or Spanish as ethnically French. Before the war many of them voted Communist, which eased their later transition to temperamentally similar Fascism. They lived close by their Muslim neighbours, mixing penny capitalism with petty crime. By the early 1950s such people had discovered a new saviour in the movement created by Pierre Poujade, the voice of militant anti-state and anti-Semitic artisans and shopkeepers in the depressed southern departments of metropolitan France. Poujade's pretty wife was from Algiers, which gave *poujadism* its entrée into France's oldest colony.

Although many *petits blancs* were reflexively anti-Semitic, they had an unbounded admiration for Israel for demonstrating how to bash uppity Arabs around, a syndrome repeated among the Afrikaners of South Africa.[8] There were also complex allegiances on the Muslim side, leaving aside those who served in colonial regiments of the army. Many Muslim *caids* did well out of the colonial regime, which was not true of the many poor and unemployed Muslims, especially those crammed into Algiers' historic kasbah, where 80,000 people lived densely crammed into about forty acres. There was also the issue of vicious FLN sectarianism, which forced those who knew they were excluded into the arms of the French.[9]

One major problem in Algeria was of France's own making. There were thousands of bureaucrats in Algiers and Oran, but hardly an official in sight out in the rural areas. Soustelle soon discovered that his own bureaucracy was permeated by *colon* collaborators, so that the switchboard operators always found technical reasons not to put through his calls to Paris. To correct these problems, some of Soustelle's advisers, such as his fellow ethnologist Germaine Tillon, a Resistance heroine who had survived Ravensbrück concentration camp, encouraged him in a reforming direction. New *sections administratives specialisées* stationed Arabic-speaking teams of technical experts in remote villages, where they advised on farming methods and built roads, clinics and schools. These were implicitly intended to substitute for political reform. However, the teams had to live inside forts (*bordjs*) for safety and the guerrillas destroyed infrastructural improvements wherever they could, killing any Muslims who participated in the projects.

The work of the technical modernizers was also undermined by the army. As field maps recorded the inky spread of FLN terrorist incidents, so the army command resorted to indiscriminate air power, including the use of napalm, and collective reprisals against entire villages. A spiral of reflex violence ensued, for when French troops encountered atrocities, or just sullen hostility, they often responded by shooting anyone they suspected of FLN involvement or sympathies. Like Coalition forces in Iraq and Afghanistan half a century later, the French army also found itself vulnerable to lone actors among the ranks of its own indigenous troops, who might suddenly shoot their French comrades.

Guerrilla strategy was to provoke the French into brutal retaliation to polarize the sympathies of a Muslim population whose loyalties were undecided, and to this end, in August 1955, nationalist fighters in the Constantine area carried out horrific atrocities on Europeans of all ages and sexes, notably at a pyrites mining settlement at El-Halia near Philippeville. There, thirty-seven Europeans were murdered with knives and bill-hooks, including ten children under fifteen. Elite French paratroops who rushed to the scene rounded up anyone they thought responsible and machine-gunned them. Enthusiastic *pied noir* vigilantes simultaneously ran amok lynching any Arabs they encountered. The official death toll was of 1,200 Muslims slaughtered, although the FLN claimed ten times that number.

Soustelle acknowledged that the struggle had become a *guerre à l'outrance*, 'for there had been well and truly dug an abyss through which flowed a river of blood'. After visiting the wounded in hospital, he became an implacable opponent of the FLN. A change of government in Paris meant that in early 1956 Soustelle was recalled before his reforms had had much discernible effect. He would return as a committed supporter of the *pieds noirs*. By that date, the French security forces had lost 550 dead, as against guerrilla losses of 3,000. The civilian death toll was 1,035 Europeans and 6,352 Muslims, for the brunt of guerrilla violence was still directed at fellow Muslims who were deemed collaborators with the colonial power.[10]

As more battle-hardened leaders moved to the top of the FLN, it acquired greater discipline and even more ferocious purpose, although internal organization remained chaotic. By the summer of 1956 it had a rudimentary newssheet, *El Moudjahid*, and an external broadcasting service, the *Voix de l'Algérie*. It tried to impose its own parallel administration, marginalizing the village *caids* through whom the French habitually worked. At a twenty-day summit held in a cabin in Kabylia's Soumman Valley, the FLN leadership established a military chain of command, reaching from small sections via companies of over a hundred men, with the highest rank that of colonel. Overall coordination of the *wilayas* reposed in a Committee of Nine, while in emulation of the wartime French resistance political control was vested in a thirty-four-man Conseil National de la Révolution Algérienne. The leadership's view was that 'one corpse in a jacket is always worth more than twenty in uniform', which meant a preference for well-publicized killing of European civilians in the cities, attracting the attention of the global media in ways that clashes in mountain villages could not.

In February 1956 the pacifist Socialist Prime Minister Guy Mollet arrived in Algiers to anoint Soustelle's successor, the seventy-nine-year-old General Georges Catroux, who had held the same post in 1943. General Jacques Massu's 10th Colonial Parachute Division, distinctive in a spotted camouflage kit known as *tenue léopard*, augmented Mollet's security detail. The *pieds noirs* decided that Catroux was a liberal and, in a first spectacular demonstration that the European settlers had a mind and will of their own, they declared a general strike, while 20,000 veterans – led by the limbless, the blind and the much decorated – marched in silence to 'welcome' Mollet when he laid a wreath at the main war memorial in Algiers, a statue of Joan of Arc. On arrival he was pelted with cabbages, eggs and tomatoes, and screams of 'Mollet au poteau!' (the post to which those to be executed by firing squad are tied). They pursued him into the Governor's official residence while the police did nothing.

Poujadist storekeepers and right-wing Gaullist elements dominated settler opinion. The leading figures were the restaurateur Jo Ortiz, the Corsican lawyer Jean-Baptiste Biaggi and a student leader called Pierre Lagaillard, who dressed like a paratrooper. They were almost as hostile to the Fourth Republic as towards the FLN, for many of them had been sympathetic to the pre-war right-wing Action Français and had been supporters of Marshal Pétain. Mightily impressed by the fact that the sort of people who would have voted for him in France nearly lynched him in Algiers, Mollet caved in to settler opinion in a speech which endorsed all their demands and rescinded Catroux's appointment before the General had even reached Algiers. The message to the more hot-headed settlers was clear: 'We are going to organize violence by the Europeans and prove that that, too, is profitable.'

In place of Catroux, Mollet appointed his fifty-seven-year-old Minister of Economic Affairs, Robert Lacoste, a man with the bluff manner of Ernest Bevin. François Mitterrand, now Justice Minister, invested Lacoste with sweeping dictatorial powers which gave the army the right to arrest, detain and interrogate suspects. Troop numbers in Algeria were boosted from 100,000 in 1955 to 200,000 in 1956 and 500,000 by 1957. This involved lengthening the period of military service, and making use of conscripts and reservists, a decision fraught with potential problems for the French state as well as its armed forces. Not long after Lacoste's appointment a platoon of reservists was ambushed at Palestro, with the loss of all but one of twenty-one men. Massu's Paras were despatched to track down the perpetrators, while Lacoste ordered police and troops into the Algiers kasbah. He also went ahead with the guillotining of Abdelkader Ferradj, a farm worker convicted of arson because his bicycle was found near where a farm had burned down, and of Ahmed Zabane, a senior FLN officer who had tried to shoot himself in the head when trapped, succeeding only in blowing out his left eye.[11]

The FLN commander in Algiers, a former baker called Saadi Yacef, responded by despatching teams of gunmen to shoot Europeans, leaving notes reading 'Zabane and Ferradj, you are avenged' pinned to their victims' chests. These included four guards from the Barberousse prison, where nationalist detainees were routinely tormented.

Lacoste sought to combine toughness on terror with enlightened reforms. Half of civil service posts were opened to Muslims, and attempts were made to grant Muslims land owned by the state. Highly secret talks were opened with the exiled FLN leader Mohamed Khider as a preliminary to talks with Ahmed Ben Bella. French intelligence derailed the talks when in October 1956 Khider, Ben Bella and Ait Ahmed were skyjacked while en route from Rabat to Tunis, with the French pilot landing at Algiers instead. Although Mollet and Lacoste were appalled, it was politically impossible to release the kidnapped leaders. The opportunity to exploit division between the colonels who ran ALN operations in Algeria and their external political representation was forfeit, since the imprisoned Ben Bella felt tricked and threw his considerable prestige behind the internal military leaders.

Worse was to follow. Massu's Paras had been sent on the Anglo–French Suez escapade, mainly because the French had convinced themselves that Nasser was arming the FLN, whereas in reality his assistance was as modest in practice as it was extravagant in rhetoric. Not only did the failed Suez expedition lead Nasser to hand over to the FLN huge stocks of Lee Enfield rifles abandoned by the British, but the Suez debacle added a further grudge among professional soldiers against their government, to accompany the wound of Dien Bien Phu. This was a French version of the 'stab in the back' legend that undermined Weimar Gemany in the 1920s and 1930s. Moreover, with frequent changes of government in Paris and long querulous intervals in between, the disgruntled military became the principal actors in Algeria, performing their own redemptive drama.[12]

Recapturing the Night

The French Commander-in-Chief in Algeria was General Raoul Salan, a fifty-eight-year-old five-star general and the most decorated soldier in the French army, whom we last saw in Indochina. He was of medium height, with a straight back and the profile of a Roman proconsul. Known as *Le Chinois*, his skin had a jaundiced hue, which some attributed to opium smoked during nearly two decades in Asia, and he was also noted for an inscrutable, supposedly oriental serenity.

His immediate subordinate was the fifty-year-old General Massu, a tall, extremely fit man who went around with a pair of wolfhounds. His wife Suzanne called her husband 'Cro Magnon Man'. His motto was 'When you are not fighting, you're training.' While Massu used his 6,000-strong 10th Parachute Division to crush the FLN in Algiers, his wife went about doing good deeds among the Muslims, adopting two Arab orphans as part of the Massu family. She was also responsible for a decree issued by her husband that the troops should no longer use the familiar *tu* when speaking to Arabs.

Most of the fighting in Algeria took place out in the *bled*, the scrub- and rock-strewn mountains of Aurès and Kabylia. The French army brought a variety of experiences to the conflict, with tactics determined as much by institutional tradition and individual psychology as by pain- fully acquired tactical doctrine on a case-by-case basis. Not for nothing has a recent study of counter-insurgency warfare or COIN compared it to attempting to eat soup with a knife.[13]

The French counter-insurgency warfare expert, David Galula, last encountered with the People's Liberation Army in China, and then as an observer in Malaya and the Philippines, was stationed in Algeria from 1956 onwards as a battalion commander in the predominantly Berber Kabylia region. French strategy for dealing with FLN hit-and-run tactics in open country included attempting to interdict the flow of weapons and men across the open border with Tunisia, while a grid system was imposed on Algeria itself. Some field commanders, including Galula, sought to exploit in-depth knowledge of local society to win the hearts and minds of uncommitted Muslims. The army had to work with the grain of village society, notably the councils of elders which were promi- nent in Kabylia, through whom French orders and Muslim grievances were mediated. Anyone using cigarettes or alcohol were another poten- tial ally, given that the FLN cut the throats of those found using either.

Galula identified former members of the French armed forces as pos- sible counters to the covert FLN apparatus, and contrived tests of wills, including making individual householders responsible for anti-FLN posters, which the guerrillas would deface or tear down. A compulsory census enabled the French to pin down the population by name and resi- dence, making it easier to identify suspicious strangers. More and more information on each inhabitant of a village was added to index cards by way of what anthropologists call 'thick description'. This enabled Gal- ula to identify the FLN's peripatetic tax collectors and extortionists. Building on his own experience of detention by the PLA in China, Gal- ula believed in trying to turn captured insurgents, although he was not above locking them inside a dark bread oven to focus their minds. Physi- cal improvements to the villagers' miserable lives were also important, notably rudimentary health clinics or schools which educated girls up to the age of thirteen, when they customarily married.[14]

As in many counter-insurgency wars, this quasi-anthropological approach (which has no greater success rate than any other) had to be undertaken in an overall institutional culture which rewarded naked aggression with decorations and promotions, and in which the warrior ethos was paramount. In the Constantine area, the Indochina veteran General André Beaufre divided his territory into densely occupied *zones de pacification*, where the population was subject to indoctrination allied with improvements to their quality of life, and *zones d'interdites*, from which the population was cleared to make it a free-fire zone, which was to be repeated on a larger-scale version by the air force General Maurice Challe a few years later.

For most of the twentieth century, following the discrediting of militarism by the *fin de siècle* Dreyfus Affair, in which a Jewish officer had falsely been convicted of treason, the army was known as 'the Great Mute', because of its ostentatious eschewal of grubby politics. The war in Algeria brought nearer to home praetorian features already evident from the war in Indochina. The elite French troops were warriors pure and simple. The most feared formations deployed in Algeria were the red-bereted colonial parachute regiments and the green-bereted Foreign Legion, with recent service in Indochina.

One of the most outstanding commanders was Colonel Marcel Bigeard, the son of a railway worker from Toul who had left school aged fourteen. After a good war, by the early 1950s he was commander of a colonial parachute battalion, which in 1954 was dropped into Dien Bien Phu. He led the defence of the hills Eliane 1 and 2, and survived six months of captivity by the Viet Minh. On arrival in Algeria he weeded out misfits and then took his troops on a two-month training expedition into the *bled*, from which they returned super-fit and wearing long-peaked sun caps, which led to the appellation 'lizards'. Bigeard was a tall man with a big nose, a shaven head and extremely powerful hands. In July 1956 he was shot in the chest while on operations near the city of Bône. No sooner had he recovered than in September he was shot in the back while jogging by the city's harbour. Bleeding from wounds near the liver and in his right arm, he tried to stop a car. The *colon* driver sped off, saying 'You'll stain my seat.'[15]

By early 1957 the atmosphere in the Algerian capital was febrile. In mid-January, settler extremists attempted to kill Salan by firing a bazooka into his office. His chief aide was killed and Salan's ten-year-old daughter Dominique was hit by flying glass as she did her homework in the flat above. The reason for the attack was that the settlers had convinced themselves that Salan had been sent to Algeria to organize withdrawal.

Algiers had become a very violent place. In response to Yacef's terror campaign, settler counter-terrorist squads blew up an FLN bomb factory in the Rue de Thèbes, killing seventy innocent people living in adjacent houses. Left in sole charge when other FLN leaders fled, the twenty-nine-year-old Yacef decided to retaliate in kind. He moved frequently, his office being an imitation-leather briefcase, filled with fake IDs, FLN documents and 500,000 francs. His base was in the kasbah, a maze of houses built around courtyards that stretched back from dark and narrow alleyways, with wearying flights of steps and sudden corners. Many of the alleyways led to dead ends, where intruders could be trapped and killed. The windows in the courtyards had grilles designed so that women could see out without being seen themselves. The Algiers police called it 'the aquarium'.

Among Yacef's 1,400 fighters were a number of attractive young Muslim women who could pass as Europeans, sometimes using peroxide to lighten their hair. On 30 September 1956, two pairs of these young women bluffed and flirted their way past incurious Zouave sentries guarding the exits from the kasbah, to deposit duffel bags containing bombs in a milk bar opposite Salan's headquarters and at a café popular among European students. The bombs killed three people and injured fifty. A third bomb failed to detonate in the Air France terminal.

Yacef's chief hit man was a former pimp called Ali Ammar, alias Ali la Pointe, who had discovered he was a political victim while in jail. He had the Legion motto *Marche ou crève* tattooed on his chest and *Tais toi* (shut up) on his left hand. In December, Ali la Pointe shot dead Mayor Amédée Froger, the most senior and most militant elected official in Algeria. Shortly before Froger's funeral cortège reached the cemetery an FLN bomb exploded among the tombs, which led to a furious *colon* mob spreading out to lynch Arabs. Governor-General Lacoste summoned Salan, who turned the response over to Massu's 10th Parachute

Division and his right-hand man Colonel Yves Godard, who had close working connections with the French intelligence services and no qualms about using torture to extract information. The first battle of Algiers was on.[16]

Godard divided Algiers into quadrilaterals, and then used numbers painted on houses to order the chaos of the kasbah. He appointed individual 'block' leaders, with a duty to report on the inhabitants, and took hooded informants on surprise visits to identify FLN activists. Armed with police files on nationalist suspects, and intelligence on their precise whereabouts, Bigeard's 3rd Paras combed this human rabbit warren, dragging out their targets. The nationalists responded with a general strike, which Massu broke by using trucks and chains to drag away the steel shutters used to close stores and kiosks and by intimidating transport and office employees into returning to work. In other words, the French were starting to make war on the entire population. Yacef launched a further wave of female bombers, who brought carnage to more cafés and restaurants, killing five and wounding sixty. Bombs left among the packed stands at a racecourse killed ten spectators and injured forty-five. Patient police work enabled Bigeard to locate the guerrillas' main bomb factory, where his Paras found eighty-seven fully operational bombs and a rich haul of bomb-making paraphernalia. Meanwhile, Godard's torturers were compiling detailed 'organigrammes' of the FLN's organizational structure within the kasbah, with each fact written on to a large chart.

Although Catholic Church leaders, including Archbishop 'Mohammed' Duval of Algiers, opposed torture, the 10th Division chaplain Father Delarue justified it, on the grounds that it prevented 'the massacre of innocents'. The methods went beyond what the French call the *passage à tabac*, or a disorientating roughing up, by way of preliminaries. What Bigeard dubbed 'muscular interrogation' involved the wet and dry 'submarines', suffocation by water or plastic bag (which were to gain renewed notoriety when employed by the Argentine military in the 1970s), and the 'talking machines', hand-cranked telephone generators attached to sensitive parts of the body. Female suspects were raped, sometimes with inanimate objects. Torture took on its own humdrum routines, with the torturers breaking to eat or smoke. Loud music was used to drown the screaming, except in situations where screams were useful to terrorize those awaiting interrogation.

Other stratagems included writing the names of FLN members who had not been captured on the doors of empty cells, to deceive those arrested into revealing details about them. When victims died under torture, they were either buried in remote spots or dropped out at sea by helicopter. This was also the fate of many live prisoners, who were dubbed 'crevettes Bigeard' (shrimps à la Bigeard) by barrack-room wits. Major Paul Aussaresses ran a combined torture and murder operation in the Villa des Tourelles, where other victims of army torture were taken for elimination. Most of them were driven to a variety of locations, where they were supposedly shot in combat or while trying to escape. In the case of FLN leader Larbi Ben M'Hidi, who had organized the 1957 general strike, Aussaresses personally hanged him and then claimed it was suicide in a prison cell. Aussaresses reported his nocturnal activities to Massu, who grunted acknowledgement.[17]

Even though a handful of French officials such as Paul Teitgen, the senior civil servant responsible for police, resigned in protest because he had been tortured (in Dachau) during the war, in many situations victims make excellent victimizers, their psychology twisted by their own appalling experiences. Some of the torturers had also been tortured by the Germans, or had acquired a taste for it in the wartime resistance, when they tortured and executed captured Nazis or members of the collaborating Milice. Nor were the FLN wilting violets when it came to torturing those suspected of collaboration with the French. It was a nightmare spiral into moral nihilism on the part of a country whose civilizing mission obviously included the 1789 Revolution's Declaration of the Rights of Man and the Citizen. In practice, when in 1955 Mitterrand authorized an investigation into allegations of ill-treatment of prisoners, the report avoided the term 'torture' in favour of 'procedures', which medical experts in turn helpfully sub-divided into the harmless and the 'abusive'. This issue has haunted many other subsequent governments fighting irregular opponents who did not enjoy the protection of the Geneva Conventions, which France had ratified in 1951.[18]

In recognizing the right of colonial peoples to national independence, in December 1960, the UN General Assembly was mute regarding coercion, torture and violence by national liberation movements. For there were no international constraints on guerrillas, who, being mobile, did not take many prisoners. In Algiers Yacef intensified terrorist violence. In June 1957 a powerful bomb placed under the stage at the seaside casino killed nine, including band leader Lucky Starway, and injured eighty-five, many of them girls with their feet or legs blown off. Rescuers were sickened to find scattered shoes still containing dainty feet. Sinister men in dark glasses directed mobs of outraged *pieds noirs* in their retaliatory rampages through Arab districts, as the army and police looked on.

Information from detainees and informants eventually led Godard to Yacef's lair, in two adjacent houses. After threatening to blow up the houses, Godard secured Yacef's surrender. Although never tortured, Yacef volunteered the whereabouts of his most loyal lieutenant. Ali la Pointe and a twelve-year-old admirer refused to surrender and died along with seventeen innocent neighbours when plastic explosives placed by the Paras detonated a large cache of FLN explosives in their hide-out. With this the battle of Algiers was considered won by the Paras, who relaxed into the admiring arms of their sun-kissed sweethearts. The FLN called it their Dien Bien Phu.

During the battle the ALN mounted diversionary attacks in the countryside and at Agounennda the strategy backfired when Bigeard's regiment killed ninety-six guerrillas for the loss of only eight Paras. A key priority became to staunch the flow of arms and men from ALN bases in Morocco and Tunisia, which was achieved with electrified fences. Infiltration from the Tunisian border was halted by the Morice Line, backed by the Challe Line, which stretched 220 miles from Bône to Bir el-Ater, with the most vulnerable section fortified to a depth of twelve miles, including floodlights, mines and two wire fences capable of delivering a 5,000-volt shock, backed by 40,000 conscript troops. The Pedron Line divided the country, running for ninety miles from Sidi Aissa. In 1958, of 1,200 guerrilla fighters who tried to cross from Tunisia into Algeria, only two made it. Three million villagers were compulsorily moved into 1,840 *auto-défense* villages by 1960, in an attempt to drain the sea in which the guerrillas swam. Some 8,000 nationalist suspects were held in ten internment camps, which attracted international criticism despite being deemed humane by the International Red Cross.[19]

Meanwhile as factional fighting between external and internal leaders or within the *wilayas* divided the nationalist camp, the French institutionalized the more advanced thinking about counter-insurgency warfare. French conscript officers attended twelve-day courses at the Centre d'Instruction de Pacification et de Contre-Guérilla established at Arzew near Oran in March 1956. Notable practitioners, including David Galula and Roger Trinquier who had led commandos behind Viet Minh lines, were discussed in military journals or in books on theory and practice. Efforts were made to explain the purpose of the war to incoming conscripts, who were far less enthusiastic than the regulars. The means included a weekly magazine called *Le Bled*. The aim was for the conscripts to internalize the hearts-and-minds approach of the more intelligent French counter-insurgency experts, an approach undermined by emphasis placed by the regulars on body counts. The half-million men stationed in Algeria in 1957 were divided among three corps situated in Algiers, Constantine and Oran, with the elite troops acting as a mobile reserve. In addition to 40,000 Algerian, Moroccan and Tunisian *tirailleurs* and Spahis, there were 60,000 Algerian Muslim irregular *harkis*, who included disillusioned former insurgents.[20]

From the government's point of view, the most worrying development was within the elite units. They saw themselves as a cut above the inexperienced and under-motivated conscripts who arrived from metropolitan France like lambs to the slaughter. Disdainful of the settler elite, the colonial and Legion troops sympathized with the rough-and-ready working-class *colons*, especially as many of their sons volunteered to do their military service in the elite units. In 1958 these men fell into the gulf dividing them from a metropolitan French society identified with slimy politicians and traitorous intellectuals when their contempt led them to mutiny.

Winning the Wider War

Although the FLN had lost the urban battle, being excluded from Algiers for the next three years, the epic and vicious nature of the fighting had attracted the world's notice, while the moral costs of torture were starting to be paid in metropolitan France and in France's standing in the wider world after the Paras turned their attention on French FLN sympathizers. As usual the liberal press ignored nationalist barbarity.

The FLN were aided and abetted by human rights lawyers who waged what is nowadays called 'lawfare' to distinguish those for whom self-promotion is more important than their individual client. One such was Jacques Vergès, the son of a French doctor and diplomat and a Vietnamese woman, who grew up on the island of Réunion. A Communist sympathizer, Vergès was so hopeless at defending FLN suspects that he became known as 'Maître Guillotine'. But he was a master at attracting publicity by waging 'a strategy of disruption' in courtrooms. He eventually married one of his clients, the FLN bomber Djamila Bouhired, and would go on to defend the Lyons Gestapo killer Klaus Barbie, the international terrorist Ilich Ramírez Sánchez (a.k.a. Carlos the Jackal), Saddam Hussein's Foreign Minister Tariq Aziz and the former Khmer Rouge head of state Khieu Samphan.[21]

Regardless of the motives of persons like Vergès, French conduct of the war undermined claims that it was being fought on behalf of Western liberal values, even though the FLN actively rejected those values. In 1955 the FLN had been recognized as the authentic voice of Algeria by the non-aligned states meeting at Bandung in Indonesia. Despite French efforts to treat the war in Algeria as a purely domestic affair, the nationalists' adroit and cosmopolitan diplomats won over American opinion, especially after left-wing French intellectuals made it both fashionable and respectable to criticize France, notably on university campuses. It was the FLN and not the French who tantalized American big business with the prospect of Saharan oil.

The nuanced and informed voice of the novelist Albert Camus, who defended the humanity of the settler population, became a cry in the wilderness, the ambiguities too subtle for most of the liberal media. For the Algerian *colons* became the targets of the universal left's Manichaean demonology that divides peoples according to its own definition of history. The *colons* were on the wrong side of 'progress', a category subsequently extended to Ulster Unionists, Afrikaners and Israelis. In reality, as Camus knew, and anybody capable of independent thought knows, they are just one of two peoples competing for the same piece of territory, which in most cases had never been a nation at all before they arrived.

The Eisenhower administration had several concerns about Algeria. Foster Dulles's chief consideration was that support for France in Algeria would undermine US efforts to exploit its own anti-colonial past in boosting anti-Communism sentiment in Asia and sub-Saharan Africa. The constant subtraction of French forces from Europe weakened NATO, which in turn appointed fewer French officers to senior positions, thereby alienating the army and the French public from an alliance in which France counted for less and less. Nor did Dulles believe French claims that the nationalists were part of the global Communist threat he otherwise fervently believed in. Ike, drawing on his wartime experience in the region, wanted to cultivate moderate Arab leaders like Sultan (later King) Mohammed V of Morocco and Habib Bourguiba of Tunisia. He also rightly suspected the anti-American potential of French Socialist plans for a Eurafrica bloc running from France via Algeria to Francophone sub-Saharan Africa.[22]

The nationalists had absorbed individual members of the Algerian Communist Party without being contaminated by its doctrines. While its leaders took any aid they could get from Moscow, they had no illusions that the Soviets had their eye on the main chance represented by detaching France from NATO, and they regarded Tito's Yugoslavia as a better external partner.[23] It was odd that while France claimed to be fighting for Western civilization, it refused to hear the views of any Western power on its presence in Algeria, let alone those of Morocco and Tunisia which tried to broker peace. Dulles realized that French policy was liable to create conditions in which Communism might gain a wider purchase throughout North Africa, undermining a solid block of anti-Soviet Arab states. Moreover, France's unconditional support for Israel was complicating America's more subtle policies in the Middle East; ironically this was a claim Europeans would use against the US itself fifty or sixty years later.

US confidence in the French was not improved by the chronic instability of the Fourth Republic, nor by veiled threats that, if the US failed to support it to the hilt, France might opt for neutralism between the US and Soviets. That pipedream was encouraged by Moscow, with Molotov telling the French that Algeria was a purely internal problem about which the Soviets refrained from expressing a view.[24] Threats of future neutralism led to US impatience with France's residual pretensions to being a great power. The skyjacking of Ben Bella destroyed US efforts to build an anti-Communist alliance in North Africa, involving Morocco, Tunisia and, revealingly, an independent Algeria. The October 1956 Suez Crisis came as a shock to a French public that was much more united behind the invasion than the British public was because of Cairo's support for the Algerian insurgents. Next came the body blow of the FLN being allowed to open an office in Washington DC as well as at the UN in New York. The French were not wrong in imagining that US policy-makers were sceptical about France, as indeed they had been since FDR did his best to exclude France from any significant post-war role. Anti-Americanism swept France, with US tourists refused fuel at petrol stations and taxi drivers declining their fares.

On 1 July 1957 the young Senator John F. Kennedy gave a widely publicized speech in which he called for peace and independence for Algeria, urging Ike to abandon his limp support for France. The administration refused to follow French urgings to frustrate the ensuing Senate resolution, for Kennedy had merely said what Dulles wanted to do. A week later the French responded in similar fashion when the government of Félix Gaillard refused to obstruct a National Assembly resolution calling for France to recognize Mao's China. At the same time, it is worth emphasizing, the US continued to supply the French with weapons – including helicopters – and loans to help it during one of many balance of payments crises.

An incident on the Algerian–Tunisian border on 8 February 1958 was the next turning point in the deterioration of Franco–US relations. Since the autumn of 1957 the Tunisians had abandoned a frontier strip twenty-five miles long to the ALN, which opened a training base at the village of Sakiet Sidi Youssef, a short distance from the Algerian border. Two and a half thousand nationalist fighters were soon camped there in a disused mine near the village. This raised the perennial problem of whether the host state was colluding with the enemy or was too weak and ineffectual to control him. On 11 January 1958 a group of 300 Algerian fighters ambushed a French patrol, killing fourteen, wounding two and taking four captives. On 8 February the French air force, using US-supplied B-26 bombers assigned for NATO use, flattened Sakiet. Among the hundred people killed were many guerrillas, but the casualties included women and children, and two International Red Cross trucks were destroyed as well.

With the Tunisians besieging the French troops permitted to remain in the country after independence, the US offered to mediate. The Francophobe Robert Murphy represented the US, along with Harold Beeley of the British Foreign Office. It became apparent that Murphy was hoping to lever the FLN into the picture, expanding these talks into peace negotiations between the FLN and French. When in April 1958 the French government presented a much modified version of the US proposal to the National Assembly, it was defeated and forced to resign. The last but one of twenty-one governments since 1947 was formed on 16 May 1958. The last came just over two weeks later, when de Gaulle returned to power to wind up the hapless Fourth Republic.

The *colons* were caught in a crossfire. An increasingly fashionable Third World voice was the Martinique psychiatrist and writer Frantz Fanon, who served the FLN in a field hospital. On the basis of observing his own psychiatric patients, Fanon claimed that colonialism was responsible for crippling mental disorders, which could be purged only by the victims unleashing savage violence. In 1957 France's greatest public intellectual, the Sorbonne sociologist and *Figaro* columnist Raymond Aron, openly questioned the value of overseas colonies, other than as a source of false pride, when the sums they were costing could have been better invested in modernizing France. He saw that Algerian nationalism was a passion, which was not susceptible to reasonable compromise. Besides, if France continued to cling on in Algeria, while making political concessions to the Muslims, the exponential rate of Muslim population growth would ultimately impact on politics within France itself. Two years later Aron was despatched to Washington to argue, to little effect, that the US should more fully commit to the French war effort, to avoid Fascist praetorians using Algeria to take over France itself.[25]

Resurrection?

The last governments of the Fourth Republic seemed to the American observer Cyrus Sulzberger to be practising gymnastics rather than ruling. Events in Algeria swept them away. An anti-government conspiracy was coalescing which truly menaced the regime. It consisted of disgruntled professional soldiers, soured by Indochina and Suez, Gaullist (and Pétainist) war veterans, supporters of Poujade and those whose persuasion was even further to the Fascist and anti-Semitic right. A young law student union activist turned Foreign Legionnaire called Jean-Marie Le Pen was an early Poujadist deputy, and a vocal supporter of *Algérie française*. This opposition to the Fourth Republic had links with some of de Gaulle's most prominent political 'barons', men like Michel Debré, Jacques Chaban-Delmas and Jacques Soustelle, the former Governor-General, who found himself watched by up to ten secret policemen at a time to prevent his return to Algeria.

The object of their devotions was not in top shape: de Gaulle's eyesight was dimming, he broke an arm in a fall, and he had fleshed out; but he was still an outstanding political poker player. He had little time for political soldiers since, apart from his own, he did not rate the intelligence or political acumen of generals. His views on Algeria depended on whether or not his policies succeeded or failed, and relied on deft use of innuendo which political innocents might mistake for firm pledges.[26] In reality, De Gaulle used the *colons* and their military supporters in a temporary coincidence of interests which brought him back to power. They only gradually realized that they had been tricked.

After coming to power de Gaulle told the *colons*, from the balcony of the Governor-General's residence in Algiers on 4 June 1958, 'I have understood you.' This could be, and was, interpreted to mean 'I agree with you.' At Mostaganem a few days later he grudgingly uttered, for the first and last time, the potent slogan 'Vive l'Algérie française.' In private, while he acknowledged the venerability of Moroccan or Tunisian statehood, his view was that Algeria had never been more than 'a heap of dust' (*poussière*). His initial policies suggest that he wanted to retain Algeria for France.[27] But as time passed he became coldly realistic, realizing that it was a financial drain on France in an age when nuclear bombs rather than colourfully uniformed colonial soldiers were the true index of national power. Algeria rendered its last service to French military *gloire* on 13 February 1960, when France successfully tested its first nuclear bomb in the Sahara. Atmospheric tests continued there until independence, and underground tests until 1966.

For France to regain what de Gaulle believed with religious fervour was its historic mission in the world, outmoded burdens like Algeria had to be shed, particularly as integration meant swamping metropolitan France with Arab immigrants. For the essence of Gaullism was to restore France to the first rank of nations and to deliver it from 'subordination' to an Anglo-Saxon-dominated NATO. In June 1960 he said: 'It is altogether natural to feel nostalgia for what empire was, just as one may yearn for the soft light of oil lamps, the splendour of the sailing ship navy, the charm of the horse and buggy era. But what of it? No policy is valid apart from the realities.'[28] The ease with which he made the transition is partly to be explained by his origins and outlook. He had never served in North or sub-Saharan Africa, or Indochina, though he had been in Lebanon and Syria during the 1930s and had close wartime knowledge of French possessions in West and Equatorial sub-Saharan Africa. He was a man of Lorraine, and German was the only foreign language he spoke.[29] He certainly did not speak the sing-song language of Algeria's meridional *colon* demagogues and ended up hating them. 'They are not French,' he said. 'They do not think like us.'[30] Nor did he relish the prospect of his beloved home town of Colombey-les-Deux-Eglises becoming Colombey-les-Deux-Moschées.[31]

What he thought did not matter much until he was in power, put there by soldiers who did not like or trust him. On 9 May 1958 the FLN announced that it had executed three French prisoners of war it had held for eighteen months. Angry settlers called for a massive demonstration to coincide with the formal inauguration of Pierre Pflimlin's ephemeral new government in Paris. On the same day, the four senior army commanders in Algeria, who included Salan and the Admiral commanding the navy, gave Governor-General Robert Lacoste a text to transmit to the Chief of Staff Paul Ely, warning that 'the French Army would, to a man, consider the surrender of this part of the national heritage to be an outrage'. On the 13 May a vast crowd of *colons* made its way to the administrative centre of Algiers, sacking the American Culture Center en route. Cars streamed into the city, honking their horns to mimic the cry of AL-GÉR-IE FRAN-ÇAIS. They used a truck to force the iron gates of the seat of government, bursting into its offices and throwing the contents of filing cabinets out the windows. Armed paratroopers did nothing to stop them. The unpopular Salan and the highly popular

Massu appeared and announced a committee of public safety. This eventually included seventy-four members, including three token Muslims to represent nine million of their co-religionists. Salan cabled Paris, 'The responsible military authorities consider it an imperative necessity to appeal to a national arbiter with a view to constituting a government of public safety . . . A call for calm by this senior authority is alone capable of re-establishing the situation.' Remarkably, 30,000 Muslims joined the demonstrations in an open display of unity that belies the FLN's narrative of these events.

De Gaulle took advantage of what was almost but not quite a military coup, while never aligning himself explicitly with the mutinous soldiers or the frantic *colons*.[32] Two vocal camps were marshalling their forces, one in Algiers and the other on the streets of Paris, where a brief revival of the 'they shall not pass' spirit among the left restored some of the government's missing courage. Instead of capitulating Pflimlin won a vote of confidence in the National Assembly, which left the rebels in Algiers facing the prospect of charges of seditious mutiny, although Pflimlin confused things by conferring full local powers on Salan.

As for de Gaulle, on a visit to Paris he was asked about events in Algeria. 'What events?' he coolly replied. Although Salan did not care for de Gaulle, on 15 May he was encouraged to add 'Et vive de Gaulle' to the patriotic litany he declaimed from an Algiers balcony. This resulted in an expression of willingness to assume power from Colombey-les-Deux-Eglises. De Gaulle benefited from Pflimlin's reluctance to risk full-blown civil war, which seemed real enough. There were well-founded rumours of paratroopers being flown from Algiers to metropolitan France, where they would join with other mutinous formations in Toulouse who were similarly bent on overthrowing the government. Crafted by Massu, the operation was initially codenamed Grenade until a phrase in a speech by de Gaulle on 19 May afforded Operation Resurrection.

While the government filled Parisian boulevards with trucks loaded with black-clad riot policemen, and opened internment camps for right-wingers in Languedoc, de Gaulle grandly announced: 'I am the man who belongs to no one and belongs to everyone.' He posed as a Gallic Cincinnatus, reluctantly dragged from his rustic idyll to save

France. Affirming that at sixty-seven he was too old to play the dictator, he signalled his readiness to take power if it were formally ceded to him by a government whose writ was atrophying by the day. His pitch allayed US fears that he would lead a coup, although Washington took the precaution of explicitly warning the military leaders in Algeria that it would support Morocco and Tunisia against any attack, even one purporting to be in pursuit of FLN guerrillas.

Possibly there was such a plan, but instead the revolt spread to garrisons in Corsica, bringing the threat very much closer to France. The government's nerve cracked and Pflimlin tendered his conditional resignation. Neither the Assembly nor a sizeable public demonstration by defenders of the Republic indicated that de Gaulle was on the home run. Indeed, when a deputation of senior Assembly figures met him they rejected his demands for a simple transfer of authority, prompting him to return to Lorraine with a Parthian shot: 'If parliament agrees with you I will have no alternative but to leave you to have things out with the parachutists and go back into retirement, with grief as my companion.'[33] President René Coty was not prepared to run the risk and announced his readiness to call on de Gaulle to save France from civil war. De Gaulle had been quietly cultivating Socialist deputies such as the former Prime Minister Guy Mollet, and on 1 June 1958 a majority of 320 to 224 deputies in the Assembly confirmed his appointment as prime minister. De Gaulle's supporters had no less quietly established the goodwill of the Eisenhower administration, even as the CIA station in Algiers was reporting rebel troop movements to the Pflimlin government. On 3 June the Assembly voted the new government the authority to draft a new constitution, and another law granted it the power to rule by decree for up to six months, except on matters related to the basic rights of citizens. The new, presidential constitution was overwhelmingly approved in a referendum on 28 September and the Fifth Republic came into being on 4 October.

Throughout, de Gaulle said a minimum about Algeria. During his 4 June trip to Algiers, the first of five, he contrived (as we have seen) to leave the *colons*, the Muslims and the army with the pacifying impression that he 'understood' them. He confirmed Salan as delegate-general and commander-in-chief in Algeria, then 'promoted' him to inspector-general before forcing him into early retirement. Salan was replaced by the air force General Maurice Challe, and Massu was appointed prefect of Algiers.

Challe embarked on the most ruthless attempt yet to extirpate the FLN. Instead of merely responding to each FLN incident, he focused his forces on a sector at a time, pinning down ALN units and using air power and mobile reserves to pulverize them. He recruited large numbers of indigenous *harkis* to lend local expertise to the fight. Their logic was irrefutable. As one *harki* explained:

> You get up one morning and you discover that your neighbour has had his throat cut during the night. You, you know him, your neighbour, for a long time. You do not understand why he has been killed. You understand only that you must not ask questions. So, in the beginning, you say to reassure yourself: 'It is astonishing but the moudjahidin know undoubtedly what they are doing. The men killed were perhaps playing a double game.' And then after a while, with all these deaths, the old people, the youngsters of fifteen or sixteen years of age, you say to yourself there is something not right here, that tomorrow it could be your turn, like that, for nothing.[34]

The ALN body count rose dramatically, although that was an unreliable index of progress. At the same time huge areas were denuded of their inhabitants, corralled in strategic settlements to enable the army to kill at will anyone remaining. The carrot took the form of the simultaneous Constantine Plan, in which billions of francs of investment would build industry and infrastructure. The idea was to create 400,000 new jobs in four years, including a giant oil refinery and steel mill. Homes for a million people were to be built. The entire scheme was to be run by a committee of European and Muslim experts, but it depended on private sector French investment, which was not forthcoming. There was therefore an imbalance between extremely costly military operations – some of which involved up to 25,000 troops operating in the field – and a failed hearts-and-minds campaign.

The *New York Times* correspondent Cyrus Sulzberger visited Algeria in March 1959, affording vivid snapshots of ordinary people in each camp or none. He met an elderly *colon*, whose farmhouse amid 200 acres resembled an armed camp. Up on a hill, the farmer gestured: 'See there: burned. Over there, burned and the vineyards cut. And there, burned; the owner *égorgé* (his throat cut). In that field my neighbour was *égorgé* while he was working, just two years ago. Last week an officer was shot on this slope. That farm was burned one Sunday while the *patron* played at bowls. There is my nephew's farm, burned. And we have been here since 1858.'

Sulzberger asked him why he stayed: 'Some call us oppressors, feudal lords, exploiters . . . this is false. My Moslems like me, but they are archaic and need a tribal leader, me. They are like tractors or like donkeys. You must mount them to make them work. Otherwise they do nothing. They don't plant trees; they cut them; they let their goats devour saplings and move on . . . We are the pioneers who understand and made this country. Our bones are in its cemeteries.'[35]

The American journalist next visited the *gourbi* or peasant hut of a Muslim family. The man's chief worry was having enough food. He was plagued by ALN *mujahedeen* who threatened to cut throats if they did not receive free provisions. If he obliged, they would be plagued in turn by the *harkis*, the irregulars employed by the French, but this would virtually guarantee that the *mujahedeen* would one night cut their throats. 'Nobody leaves us alone,' said the farmer. Finally Sulzberger spent a night with some tough-looking boys from a guerrilla unit. They were capable of marching forty miles a night, for they had to lie up to avoid spotter planes by day. Every man had a personal reason to fight the French, from having taken part in a strike to seeing a French patrol kill his entire family. A sergeant explained: 'We have paid a great price for our liberty. But we thirst for human dignity and freedom. Nothing, absolutely nothing, can defeat us.' Both the French army and the FLN were agreed on one point: too much blood had been sacrificed to throw in the towel.[36]

Though by mid-1959 the ALN appeared to be a shadow of its former self after the pummelling it had taken from Challe, this was misleading since the FLN had become a major diplomatic presence on the world stage. Moreover, de Gaulle's abandonment of closer integration of Algeria as future policy created the impression that he was preparing to give

Algeria independence. In a national radio address delivered on 16 September 1959, de Gaulle unequivocally offered Algerians self-determination, he hoped in future association with France. This was followed by a mass amnesty for nationalist prisoners and the commutation of all death sentences.[37]

This tipped the more extreme *colons* over the edge, with elements in the armed forces eager to follow them. When in January 1960 General Massu made some disloyal comments to a German journalist, de Gaulle had him transferred to France. Organized *colon* groups responded by attempting to bring Algiers to a halt. Ominously, elements of the Colonial Parachute Division colluded in this so-called Barricades Week by opposing the riot police sent to break it. For a week a *colon* mob occupied the heart of government in the capital.[38] While de Gaulle said nothing in public to indicate his ultimate choices, if he had to choose between Algeria plunging France into civil war and splitting the army, or letting Algeria go, he would choose the last. By spring 1960 a military putsch had found its leaders: active General André Zeller and air force General Edmond Jouhaud – and Salan. After retiring to Algeria, a series of provocative public statements led to Salan's expulsion and exile in Franco's Spain, home to many unrepentant Nazis and Fascists. Although the Franco regime was usually careful to maintain good relations with France because of the threat posed by a large number of Spanish Republican and Basque exiles on the other side of the Pyrenees, it was Franco's brother-in-law Ramón Serrano Suñer who smuggled Salan out of his hotel and back to Algiers.

The crucial recruit to the putsch was Challe, who had been unjustly forced into early retirement for being too popular with the troops. He became the rallying figurehead for the mutinous colonels and captains who spearheaded the putsch. Like the rest, he had little understanding of politics or even of normal civilian life. Such intelligence, in both senses of the word, possessed by the plotters was supplied by ex-Para Yves Godard, Director-General of the Sûreté in Algeria, who had been Massu's indispensable chief of staff during the battle of Algiers. When, in April 1960, de Gaulle presented a cost-benefit case for abandoning Algeria, the plotters deplored his 'shopkeeper's approach'. But by now their political aims went far beyond Algeria. They wanted to halt France's slide into decadence, its reduction to medium-power status, and what they regarded as the spread of the red menace across the southern shore of the Mediterranean.[39]

De Gaulle played a complex game, fitfully insisting that he would not negotiate with the nationalists, whose leadership was torn between politicals led by Ferhat Abbas and military hardliners under Houari Boumédiène, with whom the imprisoned Ben Bella would eventually side. On 14 June 1960 de Gaulle spoke on television: 'in the name of France, to the leaders of the insurrection. I declare to them that we await them here to find with them an honourable end to the fighting that drags on.' Although the French army had scored many notable successes against the ALN, de Gaulle knew that the FLN was fully supported by Moscow and Beijing and that Boumédiène was committed to a long war of attrition, using cross-border artillery and mortar attacks to keep large numbers of French troops pinned down on the Tunisian frontier, while the ALN in the Algerian interior avoided combat. In the major cities, there were just enough terrorist attacks to keep the *colons* and any would-be Muslim collaborators in a state of insecurity.

In December 1960 de Gaulle toured Algeria, encountering extreme hostility from the *colons*, and a warm welcome from many Muslims. Israeli intelligence tipped off de Gaulle's security service regarding one of the four active plots to kill him that week. Angry *pieds noirs* fought pitched battles with the police in Algiers and Oran. Much to their surprise, on Sunday 11 December a mass of green banners and ululating Arab women indicated the recrudescence of the FLN in the Algiers kasbah. The demonstration turned violent, with randomly selected Europeans having their throats slit, while an Arab mob wrecked the Great Synagogue.

The long-awaited coup was launched on 10 April 1961 when German Foreign Legionnaires arrested the army Commander-in-Chief and a minister of public works, who were visiting from Paris. It proved to be almost laughably misconceived. Challe so despised the radicalized *colons* that he excluded them from participation, alienating Jouhaud, who was of *colon* stock. Godard had failed to square many commanders outside Algiers, imagining that they would follow the plotters' lead, but in the end only 25,000 of more than 400,000 French troops in Algeria supported the putschists.

De Gaulle was no Pflimlin. Tanks were stationed around the Assembly and government ministries, and trucks on airport runways, but while some of his supporters succumbed to panic at the prospect of paratroops descending on Paris, de Gaulle simply remarked: 'Yes, Fidel Castro would be here, but not Challe.' He went on television to deliver one of the great speeches of his life, imploring French men and women to aid him in this hour of emergency when he became France.[40] Thumping the desk for emphasis, he poured scorn on the gaggle of retired generals who in their 'frenzy' had embarked on this Latin-style *pronunciamiento*, like a lot of uniformed clowns. The main impact of the speech, however, was on conscript soldiers who heard it on transistor radios in Algeria; these youths had long resented the swagger of the Paras and Legionnaires, who regarded themselves as real soldiers and the rest as milksops. Realizing that the putsch had failed, Challe surrendered, while Jouhaud, Salan and Zeller fled. The green berets of the 1st Colonial Parachutists blew up their ammunition stores, departing to the strains of Edith Piaf's 'Je ne regrette rien'. Challe, and Zeller, who surrendered after a week on the run, received fifteen-year jail sentences and loss of rank and pensions. Salan, Jouhaud and Godard were sentenced to death *in absentia*. Hundreds of more junior officers were purged from the military list. 1st Colonial Parachutists were disbanded and ceased to exist.

Lost Soldiers

Shortly before the coup, de Gaulle had used his banker friend Georges Pompidou to offer the FLN a unilateral ceasefire together with talks about Algerian independence. These began at Evian on Lake Geneva in March 1961 but failed in the face of the uncompromising Belkacem Krim. Almost inexplicably, Camille Blanc, the young Mayor of Evian, was assassinated as these talks started. He was one of the earliest victims of the OAS, a terrorist organization that incorporated military deserters who fled after the failed putsch with existing *colon* counter-terrorist groups. Its earliest declarations of intent were apocalyptic and Spenglerian:

Frenchmen of every background,
The final hour of France in Algeria is the last hour of France in the world, the last hour of France in the West.
Today everything is ready to be lost or saved. Everything depends on our willpower. Everything depends on the National Army.
We know that the ultimate battle approaches. We know that, to win this fight, there must be total unity and absolute discipline. Moreover, all the underground national movements and their resistance organizations have unanimously resolved to unite their forces and their efforts in a single fighting force.[41]

Total unity and absolute discipline hardly characterized an organization riven with internecine conflicts. Ironically, the OAS modelled itself on the FLN, although another model was the Zionist Haganah and Irgun.[42] Jouhaud and Salan were notionally in command, with Godard responsible for strategy, but in reality the killers ran the show – men like Delta Commando leader Roger Degueldre, a veteran of Dien Bien Phu. People the OAS deemed collaborators were very publicly stabbed or killed in drive-by shootings. *Plastiques* (bombs made of plastic explosives) rocked Algiers, Bône and Oran, as well as Paris.[43] The *colon* political leadership used such techniques as pirate radio broadcasts or interrupting television services with their own news bulletins, and a series of 'weeks' involving banging pots and pans, flying streamers or paralysing traffic to mobilize the settler population.[44]

Algiers became a ghost town after dark, with rival gangs of murderers roving the streets. The age of gunmen dropped as wired-up teenagers stalked their victims. On a single day, 3 January 1962, the OAS killed 127 Muslims and left hundreds more wounded. These killings became so normal that pedestrians simply stepped round the corpses lying in the streets. The violence spread to Paris, where, on a single night in January 1962, there were eighteen explosions. On 7 February that year a young law student tried to assassinate the writer and Gaullist Culture Minister André Malraux, but instead his *plastique* blinded and disfigured

Delphine Renard, a four-year-old girl, in the apartment below. More were killed when a demonstration denouncing the attacks turned into a police riot. The incessant terrorist atrocities brought the French and the FLN back to the negotiating table, this time in the Chalet du Yéti, a glorified garage for snowploughs high up in the Jura, before reverting to Evian. De Gaulle was now determined to wash his hands of the Algerian problem, even if that meant forgoing Saharan oil and gas, whose reserves (and the costs of accessing them) were a matter of guesswork at the time. While these talks inched towards their denouement, the number of killings in Algeria rose to thirty or forty a day. By this time both the civilian government and the military command were in fortified redoubts outside the city. Having failed to rouse public support, General Salan formally declared war on the French state.

The Evian talks reached an agreement in mid-March 1962, the most salient feature of which was that after a three-year transitional period the *colons* would have to choose to become Algerians or resident foreign nationals. The nationalists had achieved its key objective of denying the *colons* dual nationality in an independent Algerian state. In fact their view was that the *colons* had to choose the suitcase or the coffin. The OAS reacted by firing four mortar bombs into a Muslim crowd celebrating in an Algiers square. The reaction of the authorities was, at last, brutally effective. Twenty thousand regular troops besieged the OAS stronghold of Bab el-Oued in Algiers, using aircraft and artillery to eliminate OAS snipers on the rooftops.

After 90 per cent of French people – excluding the *colons*, who were not allowed to vote – had approved the Evian Agreements, the OAS launched a scorched-earth strategy, Operation Apocalypse, setting fire to hospitals and schools as well as the huge BP oil refinery in Oran. Two hundred and thirty Muslims were gunned down in one week, including seven elderly cleaners murdered on their way to work and nine Muslim patients lying in their hospital beds. In a single year the OAS killed 1,400 people, 80 per cent of them Muslims.[45]

The French government had calculated that 100,000 *colons* might leave Algeria in the first year of independence. FLN warnings about suitcases or coffins clarified minds. In June 1962 alone, 350,000 Europeans headed for the docks and airports. By the autumn some 1,380,000

Europeans had left. They were followed by former *harkis* fleeing FLN death-squads, exiled to a land that seethed with indiscriminate resentment against all Arabs. In Algeria French troops watched passively as nationalist guerrillas marched into the major cities. On 4 July the French flag was lowered and replaced by the green and white crescent banner of independent Algeria. Half a million people had died in an eight-year war, the vast majority of them Muslims.

The poisonous end of the French Empire gives the final and absolute lie to the myth of the *mission civilisatrice*, just as the sleazy means employed by de Gaulle's right-hand man Jacques Foccart to maintain France's informal empire in black Africa shame the General's memory. In Algeria Ahmed Ben Bella briefly became the darling of the non-aligned Third World until deposed in 1965 by the deadly Houari Boumédiène, who gave up all pretence at democracy. Enveloped in romantic myth, the dogmatism and violence of these years entered into independent Algeria's DNA. France's Algerian expatriates also bolstered the metropolis's political right in a way that Britain was ultimately spared because of the much smaller numbers of European settlers in its more volatile colonies. Royal Tunbridge Wells never threatened to become Aix, Orange or Toulouse, despite its many retired colonial colonels. That was not true of the dominant Conservative Party, to whose troubles in Africa we should turn.[46]

13. TERROR AND COUNTER-TERROR: KENYA

The Image of Africa

By the late 1940s Kenya had become a favoured location for film-makers requiring Technicolor skies, smiling natives and lions that roared on cue, an exotic backdrop for Hollywood stars with manly chests playing big white hunters. *King Solomon's Mines* brought Stewart Granger and Deborah Kerr, and *The Snows of Kilimanjaro* Gregory Peck and Ava Gardner. But *Mogambo* was the big one. At Christmas in 1952 Nairobi's Government House hosted Clark Gable, Grace Kelly and Gardner. Gardner's husband Frank Sinatra sang 'White Christmas' to a perspiring audience that included the Governor Sir Evelyn Baring and his wife Lady Molly. Kenya also attracted the world's attention that year when Princess Elizabeth, on a tour with Prince Philip, learned at Treetops Safari Lodge that her father George VI had died and that she was queen. It would later win renown from the discovery of the oldest human ancestor by the naturalists and archaeologists Louis and Mary Leakey, and Joy Adamson's story about the orphaned lion cubs she successfully returned to the wild, as told in the book *Born Free*, which so many children won as a school prize.[1] Into this colonial idyll intruded the Mau Mau 'emergency', which confronted two characters so representative of their respective cultures at that time as to merit the term 'paradigmatic'.

'The Great One'

The Barings occupied Government House in Nairobi for seven years, starting in September 1952, though Sir Evelyn's appointment came six months earlier. He had injured his hand and, besides, letters from his predecessor Sir Philip Mitchell were more concerned with the delicacies of how to socially sidestep divorcees than with unrest in the colony. Though aged only sixty-one, the outgoing Governor was an exhausted man who had ceased to travel through his vast domain. His Directorate of Intelligence and Security was similarly confined to Nairobi, which largely explains why warnings about trouble ahead, including detailed reports from Louis Leakey, were ignored.[2]

The youngest son of Lord Cromer, the 'Maker of Modern Egypt', Evelyn Baring had every advantage in life, not the least being the enormous wealth of the banking branch of the family, which he affected to disdain. Educated at Winchester, the traditional factory for senior British civil servants, he achieved a first-class honours degree in history at New College, Oxford, before following in his father's footsteps to pursue a career in the empire. His earlier career was spent in the Indian Civil Service, where work involved widening his competence as a magistrate, and play included sticking wild pigs with a lance and dodging the annual 'fishing fleet' of hopeful girls sent out to look for husbands by ambitious parents. But there was no chance of Baring being hooked, as he explained to his eccentric mother Katie: 'snobbery, that most excellent of failings, protects your son absolutely'.[3]

Connections and nepotism guaranteed steady promotion, but in 1933 an attack of amoebic dysentery, which permanently damaged his liver, forced him to abandon India. He spent six years working for the family bank in London, during which time he married Molly Grey and so joined himself to her extremely distinguished family. When Evelyn was made a peer in 1960 he took the title of Baron Howick in honour of the manor Molly had inherited from her most famous ancestor, the reforming Prime Minister Charles Earl Grey.

By now among the best-connected individuals in Britain, Evelyn joined the Foreign Office in 1938 and in 1942, aged only forty, he was appointed governor of Southern Rhodesia as Sir Evelyn. In its laudatory account of why the youngest ever colonial governor had been appointed, the *Daily Telegraph* commented that Baring was 'a man of the world, a good mixer and has the advantage of a fine physique'. He was indeed strikingly tall and slim, and hence known in Africa as 'the Great One'. Something of the rarefied atmosphere the Barings inhabited is conveyed by the story that, when they boarded a warship bound for Durban, Lady Molly handed the welcoming admiral her handbag, taking him for a porter.

Evelyn would spend the next seventeen years in Africa, first in Southern Rhodesia, then as high commissioner in South Africa, simultaneously governor of the African enclaves of Bechuanaland, Basutoland and Swaziland, and finally as governor of Kenya. Molly ensured that wherever they went the country-house lifestyle of their grand home in Northumberland was replicated. In Rhodesia and Kenya the Barings lived in the high colonial manner in Salisbury and Nairobi, having to endure a suburban villa only in Pretoria. There, unusually in their limited experience of lesser humanity, they could hear their neighbours' gramophone. In general the seigneurial manner worked well with black Africans, less so with the white settlers.

By 1944 Baring had wearied of Southern Rhodesia, where the name of the game was to prevent the local English settlers from emulating their Dutch Afrikaner neighbours by formalizing racial discrimination. Molly's cousin, the Dominion Secretary 'Bobbety' Cranborne (Marquess of Salisbury from 1947), appointed Baring to the high commission in South Africa. There Baring cultivated the friendship of the elderly Prime Minister Field Marshal Jan Smuts, a member of the British cabinet in the two world wars, a big player in the shaping of the post-war world in which both believed the empire could play a key role.

In June 1948 Smuts was ousted by the Afrikaner National Party, which regarded him as a traitor to their race, severing Baring's access to the top level of South African government as it embarked on the creation of apartheid. Baring's lordly manner also became a decided political liability. In 1952 the Conservatives moved him to the lesser post of governor of Kenya.

The Making of Mzee Jomo Kenyatta

The man Governor Baring chose to confront rather than co-opt was born *circa* 1889 as Kamau wa Ngengi in the village of Gatundu, centrally located in what was then known as British East Africa. He was a member of the Kikuyu tribe, who constituted only about 20 per cent of the black African population but who occupied much of the best farmland and were the most advanced in terms of agricultural practice and their willingness to adapt. As he was to all intents and purposes an orphan, his medicine-man grandfather, Kungu wa Magana, became the formative figure in his young life.

At about the age of twelve, his grandfather sent him as a boarder to a Church of Scotland Mission school twelve miles north-west of Nairobi. While there he learned to read and write, was trained as a carpenter and took the name John Peter in Christian baptism, which he changed to Johnstone Kamau. He was also initiated into his tribe through ritual circumcision, rejecting a choice between the two identities and becoming a man of two worlds. Moving to Nairobi, he dressed in raffish Western clothes but affected a colourful beaded belt, called a *kinyata* in Kikuyu, the first step in constructing the identity by which he became famous.[4]

Kamau worked first as a jobbing carpenter, before joining the Nairobi Public Works Department as a peripatetic meter reader, purchasing a motorbike, a bit of land and a shack he called Kinyata Stores. Literate and persuasive in English, he rose quickly in the Kikuyu Central Association (KCA), a political organization formed in 1924 to present the concerns of the Kikuyu to the colonial government. Land was the principal grievance. It was the Kikuyu's misfortune that their lands were those that white settlers most coveted in terms of climate and quality of soil. After the First World War there was an influx of settlers, many of them former military men who knew little about farming and even less about the local culture. They imagined the land was vacant of humanity, not realizing that African pastoralists practised transhumance, moving back and forth over hundreds of miles to find grass and water, and that the Kikuyu shifted their farms to avoid soil depletion.

Additional vexations included whites' lack of respect for ancestral burial grounds, sacred trees and the like. Although the element of semi-legal dispossession was as great an irritant here as elsewhere in the world, it was not a simple morality tale of white villainy as trumpeted in recent works of ahistorical advocacy. On the reserves Kikuyu chiefs and elders disposed of substantial lands, and were just as keen on protecting their property from squatters and their herds from the skeletal beasts of their poorer fellows as any white farmer. Furthermore they had their tribal police, officially recognized by the British authorities, to back them up. Rebellious young males were encouraged to leave, for this was as much an inter-generational conflict within the Kikuyu as it was a rebellion against white rule.[5]

A substantial part of the Kikuyu population became rootless, eking out a living as squatters on white farms. All had to carry a record of their birthplace, fingerprints, employment history and wages in a small tin strung around their necks. Those who became squatters on white-owned property found themselves subjected to forced labour, in particular the important task of excavating terraces to prevent soil erosion. The squatters' small herds were constantly subjected to veterinary procedures designed to stop diseases jumping to prize European livestock. They were tolerated so long as the white settlers did not know how to make the land they occupied profitable, but once they mastered such cash crops as coffee or tea, and developed large beef and dairy herds, it was time for the squatters to go. Since they were unwelcome back on the Kikuyu reservations, which had their own demographic pressures, many younger Kikuyu migrated to the slums of Nairobi, where they became a restive underclass, while those in regular employment were radicalized by trade unions protesting against the dire wages they received.

Young Kamau worked his way up to secretary-general of the KCA, editing its newspaper *Muigwithania* and making an impressive presentation on Kikuyu land problems to the Hilton Young Commission in Nairobi in 1928. The association sent him to London the following year to represent Kikuyu interests directly to the Colonial Office. Apart from a brief return visit in 1930–1 to see his wife Grace Wahu and their young children, Kamau would remain in Britain until 1946, using the name Johnstone Kenyatta and marrying an Englishwoman while his presumably more informal African marriage was still in being. What-ever transformed him into one of the most revered African nationalist leaders largely happened in the dingy London bedsits he inhabited for sixteen years of cold and hardship, alleviated by handouts from his white liberal and Presbyterian friends.

In 1929 he paid a brief visit to Bolshevik Russia, returning there in 1932–3, where as 'James Joken' he attended the Lenin School and the Communist University of the Toilers of the East (thereby following in the steps of Ho Chi Minh), whose offerings included paramilitary train-ing and indoctrination in Marxist-Leninism. Like many another black African he soon discovered that Russian racism was of an even more virulent kind than he had encountered in Britain. As to the supposed indoctrination, when a South African Communist accused him of being 'petty bourgeois', he replied, 'I don't like the petty thing. Why don't you say I'm a big bourgeois?'[6] 'James Joken' left Russia abruptly when Stalin reversed the orthodox Communist line on imperialism to court the Western powers after the advent of Hitler in Germany.[7]

Although Britain's MI5 knew that Communism had little appeal to Kenyatta, the colonial administration in Kenya was to make much of his time in Moscow. In fact it left almost no imprint on him and was merely one of the identities he tried out, encouraged to dabble in Marxism by the clever African Americans and Trinidadians he met in London, and, unlike the majority of Western 'useful fools', permanently put off it by his experience of Stalin's police state.

In fact Kenyatta was very far from being 'progressive'. Although he remained a Christian, he broke with the Church of Scotland for its con-demnation of the Kikuyu practice of female circumcision, which pri-vately he opposed. This was a clever tactical move, in line with the KCA's pose as the defender of ancestral ways against Western interlopers and their agents, the tribal chiefs, whose authority of course rested on tradi-tion. Independent schools, staffed by teachers who refused to observe the Church's line, were created to rival the mission schools.[8]

During his long sojourn in London Kenyatta eked out a modest liv-ing, as a spear-waving African extra in Alexander Korda's 1934 film *Sanders of the River*, while attending classes by the great anthropologist Bronisław Malinowski at the LSE. Under Malinowski's guidance, he produced *Facing Mount Kenya* in 1938, a hymn to the primordial paradise that was East Africa before the disruptive white serpent arrived. Parts of the book are intensely lyrical, as when thunder and lightning are attributed to the creaking joints of Ngai the sky god as he stepped from one mountaintop to another.[9] It was a brilliant work of semi-fiction, with academic trappings.

For the cover the nearly-fifty-year-old author posed wearing a cloak and brandishing a fake spear, with a beard modelled on that of the Emperor Haile Selassie. With the aid of a friend Kenyatta went through the alphabet trying combinations of sounds until they alighted on Jomo as the appropriate name to accompany Kenyatta.[10]

While Kenyatta settled into the role of stage African, affecting a fez and cloak, large garnet rings on his fingers and a silver-topped cane as well as his trademark beaded cummerbund, the fecund Kikuyu were bursting through the demographic limits of their territorial reservations, at the same time as the white settlers were expanding their holdings, a process accelerated by the boom in commodity prices following the outbreak of war in 1939. More demobbed British soldiers flooded into Kenya after 1945 to benefit from a scheme to expand agricultural settlement. By contrast, many of the 75,000 demobilized Kenyan African soldiers who had fought for Britain drifted into heavily segregated Nairobi, by now much more than a dusty or muddy railhead, where some of them joined criminal gangs.[11] Moreover, 100,000 squatters without any firm title were displaced from prime agricultural land to more remote and infertile territory between 1946 and 1952.[12] To bolster their solidarity the squatters took binding oaths, a practice adopted from men radicalized by the slums of Nairobi.

This was all a world apart from the sleepy West Sussex village of Storrington, where Kenyatta spent the Second World War tending tomatoes and lecturing to army educational classes. In 1942, by now divorced, he married the thirty-two-year-old Edna Clarke, whose parents had been killed in a bombing raid. After sixteen years in England, Kenyatta had astute things to say about the inhabitants. 'The English are a wonderful people to live with in England,' he wrote to his daughter Margaret, the child he had had with Grace Wahu.[13]

The 1941 Atlantic Charter seemed to promise much, bringing in its wake much frothy talk on the BBC about the future of European colonies. To the official response that it was a question of fitness for self-governance, Kenyatta and his fellows, like Kwame Nkrumah from the Gold Coast, responded, 'who is to be the judge of our fitness, and by what standards will this verdict be pronounced?' In September 1946 Kenyatta bade farewell to his Edna and their own child and set sail for East Africa. At Mombasa he was reunited with Grace Wahu and their two children, a son aged twenty-five and the eighteen-year-old Margaret. At each stop on the journey to Nairobi women made the Kikuyu trilling sound every time he alighted, which suggests a considerable degree of prior mobilization and organization. Tribal connections ensured that Kenyatta's future was bright when he was made head of an Independent Teachers' College, with a view to training teachers who he hoped would become a future political network. In June 1947 Kenyatta became president of the Kenyan African Union (KAU), which since the banning of KCA in 1940 had become the main vehicle of Kikuyu nationalism. Although he would have preferred to embrace the other major tribes, the Kamba, Luo and Masai, they so feared Kikuyu domination that they preferred to stick with the British. While Kenyatta was undoubtedly the movement's figurehead, within the KAU much more radical figures slipped into leadership positions. Kenyatta himself was under permanent police surveillance and had to be very cautious, but the more obscure actors suffered no such inhibitions. From early 1952 the bodies of police informers began to appear as the KAU radicals cleaned house.

The Setting

The settlers' behaviour as they fanned out in the White Highlands between Nairobi and Lake Victoria could be brutal. One colonial official reported: 'there is no atrocity in the [Belgian] Congo – except mutilation – which cannot be matched in our Protectorate'.[14] Once colonial policing was introduced such behaviour died down, but the settlers learned to institutionalize their power through domination of the all-white Legislative Council introduced in 1920. By the 1930s they numbered around 30,000, and they undoubtedly put their stamp on the country. A gulf of incomprehension divides contemporary Britons from those times. Most whites were wiry, hardworking farmers living in glorified shacks, with enough Swahili to say 'jambo' (hello) or 'kwa heri' (goodbye) to the help. But the richest indulged in every kind of vice, which gave the whole of Kenyan white society an international reputation for tawdry scandal.[15] As Evelyn Waugh noted when he visited in 1930 as a special correspondent for *The Times*, this was like generalizing the antics of a handful of upper-class rakes in Belgravia or Mayfair to the clerks and managers of London.[16]

Although the settlers spoke constantly of the superiority of white civilization, there was not much of it in evidence among them, as visiting intellectuals like Julian Huxley sneered. They were devoted to sports and to heavy drinking in hotels and clubs, with the abrupt sunsets acting like a starting pistol. The places where they gathered were strictly segregated. When a customs officer played tennis with an Anglo-Indian doctor at the Mombasa Sports Club, he was taken aside and told he was an embarrassment to the European community. As a Jew, Alderman Izzie Somen could not join the exclusive Nairobi Club even after he became the mayor of the city.[17] By the mid-1940s the settlers had organized as a proto-party called the Electors' Union, with Michael Blundell as their sophisticated spokesman.

Of the Barings, the American travel writer John Gunther wrote: 'Sir Evelyn is one of the most aristocratic aristocrats I have ever met . . . [He and his wife] were fastidious, generous, with beautiful manners and refinement – healthy people too – but they made Government House in Kenya resemble a stately island lost in time, drowned in forces nobody could comprehend.'[18]

The last point was also true of a British intelligence-gathering operation confined to Nairobi. Among the Kikuyu, oaths had long been used to cement contracts involving land or marriage, with 'unhealthiness' the penalty for infringements. Christianity meant that oaths were sworn with a Bible in one hand. The more radical members of the KAU developed the oathing ceremonies of the displaced squatters into a means of political mobilization. At some point members of protection rackets in the Nairobi slums began to take oaths among themselves and (under duress) from those they preyed on. For that was the literal meaning of the term Mau Mau – 'greedy eaters' being a plausible translation – that came to be applied to the Kikuyu resistance movement against egregious white domination. Their oaths drew on animist practices and glorified gang rituals.

Such rituals appealed to the Mau Mau's core supporters: rural have-nots and urban 'wild boys' impatient with the slow traditional path to becoming a fully fledged man through acquiring a stake in society as it existed. Coerced oath-taking spread through the Kikuyu community, with the object of deterring people from becoming police informers and to create an informer-free space in which to operate their criminal enterprises. Oaths were administered at night, under arches of banana leaves studded with sheep's eyes, and involved animal and human menstrual blood, urine and animal parts. Sometimes participants were obliged to commit bestiality. When naked husbands and wives took the oath, they were bound together by the intestines of goats. Unsurprisingly, Europeans concluded that something darkly demonic or at least essentially pathological was afoot, whereas African loyalists tended to view the Mau Mau as 'lost boys' or reckless delinquents. By 1950–1 the most advanced oaths had become a call to bloody revolution:

If I am sent to bring in the head of my enemy and I fail to do so, may this oath kill me.

If I fail to steal anything I can from a European may this oath kill me.

If I know of an enemy to our organization and I fail to report him to my leader, may this oath kill me.

If I ever receive any money from a European as a bribe for information may this oath kill me.

If I am ever sent by a leader to do something big for the house of Kikuyu, and I refuse, may this oath kill me.

If I refuse to help in driving the Europeans from this country may this oath kill me.

If I worship any leader but Jomo, may this oath kill me.[19]

Acknowledging Kenyatta as a symbolic figurehead was no proof that he either initiated or directed Mau Mau violence. In fact, the head of MI5,

Sir Percy Sillitoe, was categorical that 'Our sources have produced nothing to indicate that Kenyatta, or his associates in the UK, are directly implicated in Mau Mau activities, or that Kenyatta is essential to Mau Mau as a leader, or that he is in a position to direct its activities.' Its leadership was much more decentralized and self-selecting and hence difficult to track than would have been the case had it been the handiwork of one man.[20]

Initially, Mau Mau violence was deployed against those Kikuyu loyalists who refused to take such oaths; many of them were Christians who regarded such rituals as satanic. Following prosecutions of those who administered such oaths, in August 1950 the Mau Mau society was proscribed, without the colonial government having much of an idea of what it was. Attacks on loyalist Kikuyu continued, and there were dozens of cases of arson on remote farms, where the dry grass suddenly blazed up. When the police investigated such incidents, they encountered a wall of silence, with the result being a Collective Punishments Ordinance in April 1951, under which recalcitrant villages could be fined the huge sum of £2,500.

The government also encouraged what wits called 'Her Majesty's Witch Doctors' to administer counter-oaths, based on anthropological 'traditions' invented by Louis Leakey. In return for their fees, these elderly gentlemen used a goat's hoof or sacred stone to induce the oath taker to vomit out the Mau Mau oath, although usually this involved a spit and the words 'I emit it', all helped along with a few prods of the rifle butt by African policemen.[21] In mid-May 1952 the first mutilated corpses appeared, usually of informers, with those who reported finding the bodies also murdered.[22] In a particularly shocking incident, a Kikuyu Christian who refused such an oath was strangled to death. A couple of weeks after his burial, Mau Mau insisted his neighbours exhume the corpse, which they were obliged to hack to pieces, touching decomposing parts to their mouths.

With Baring yet to grace his colony with his presence, the acting Governor Henry Potter yielded to settler pressure for drastic measures to deal with these incidents of murder and arson as well as more general unrest. In September 1952 curfews were introduced, printing presses were controlled and the police were allowed to attest a suspect's confession in court. Judges soon realized that these were being beaten out of people, although none of them allowed this to lead to acquittals.[23] Within a week of Baring's arrival in the colony the paramount chief of the Kiambu district was ambushed and shot dead as his car returned from a session of a Native Tribunal in which he sat as a judge. Baring attended his funeral, catching sight at the graveside of Jomo Kenyatta, who a few weeks before had denounced Mau Mau in front of a crowd of 30,000 people.

The initial British response was to attempt to 'nip the insurgency in the bud' through massive coercion. Unlike in Malaya, the authorities in Kenya did not have the option of deporting their enemy to their country of origin. Sir Percy Sillitoe of MI5 and his top team were brought in to make Special Branch intelligence collection more efficient, but although many of the tactics employed in Malaya were adopted in Kenya they were not part of an overall, integrated plan. For this Baring's arrogance bears the primary responsibility. As the number of killings mounted, he requested authorization from London for a state of emergency. In preparation for Operation Jock Scott, a list of 150 names of people to be arrested was compiled, at the head of which was Jomo Kenyatta.

On 20 October 1952 the 1st Battalion of the Lancashire Fusiliers was flown in from Egypt, to reinforce the eight battalions of King's African Rifles present in the theatre. At midnight the Kenyan police picked up two-thirds of the 150 people on the list. Moderates awaited arrest, while the real radicals like Dedan Kimathi and Stanley Mathenge escaped into the forest. Kenyatta was arrested at his residence in the school compound at Githunguri and flown to Lokitaung, a remote desert station near the Ethiopian border. He had his own small house, alongside another where four guards from a different tribe lived. Meanwhile senior policemen toiled through the ton and a half of papers they had scooped up during his arrest, finding nothing incriminating.[24] In a legalized farce, Kenyatta and five KAU colleagues were relocated to a remote area called Kapenguria, technically as free men, where they were rearrested so that they could be tried in obscurity rather than in Nairobi in whose vicinity their alleged offences had been committed. They were charged with controlling and directing Mau Mau, and became notorious as 'the Kapenguria Six'.

Ransley Thacker, formerly of the Supreme Court of Kenya, was picked to preside over the trial. He requested and received a secret payment of £20,000 to ensure his future safety in Kenya. An impressive defence team included a member of India's upper house and Denis Pritt, a British Marxist MP and Queen's Counsel. Every obstacle was put in the defence team's way, starting with locating them in a town thirty miles from the court, where even getting a meal was complicated by the colour bar against Pritt. The prosecution case was flimsy, reliant on one witness who claimed to have seen Kenyatta administer an oath – on a date before Mau Mau had been legally proscribed. Thacker was biased and vindictive against the defendants and their counsel, frequently repairing to Nairobi for consultations. Six years later it transpired that the prosecution's chief witness had been paid to perjure himself in return for an airfare to England, the fees for a university course, subsistence for his family and a guaranteed job back in Kenya.

After the initial hearings, Thacker went to Nairobi to ponder whether to dismiss or proceed. Whatever doubts he had were dispelled when the Mau Mau slaughtered a young couple called Roger and Esme Ruck on their remote farm. Hitherto, when the Mau Mau had struck at Europeans (and it is worth bearing in mind that the thirty-two Europeans killed in the emergency were fewer than those who died in road accidents) the victims had been elderly loners who were easy prey. Roger and Esme were hacked to death with panga knives on the veranda of their home; their six-year-old son Michael met the same fate in his bed amid his toys. A thousand white settlers descended on Government House in an ugly mood. A middle-aged woman screamed, 'There, there, they've given the house over to the fucking niggers, the bloody bastards!' when the visiting Sultan of Zanzibar was incautious enough to appear on the balcony, while below him enraged settlers pressed against African policemen guarding the Barings, burning them with cigarettes. At a mass meeting in Nakuru bullish settlers demanded that 50,000 Kikuyu be shot to avenge the Rucks.

Thacker returned to Kapenguria in a grim mood. The lead prosecutor spent a fortnight smearing Kenyatta as a Soviet stooge, and trying to fabricate a connection with Mau Mau. The background continued to militate against dispassionate justice. In March 1953 several hundred Mau Mau killed seventy-four men, women and children in the loyalist village of Lari, committing unspeakable atrocities. The following day, relatives of the victims in the Home Guard and Kenya Police Reserve struck back at suspected Mau Mau sympathizers in the area, killing a far greater number. Thirty miles away, another Mau Mau gang attacked a police post in Naivashu, making off with a significant cache of weapons and freeing 170 Mau Mau suspects from an adjacent detention camp.

Thacker found Kenyatta and the others guilty and sentenced them to seven years' hard labour. They were sent back to Lokitaung, which had been converted into a prison, its barbed wire augmented by Kamba guards, who hated the Kikuyu inmates, while the local Turkana tribes-men were told they could hunt down and kill escapees. In Kenyatta's absence the authorities destroyed his college at Githunguri and pulled down his home at Gatundu. Aged sixty, he was spared manual labour and instead functioned as the group cook while tending vegetables. On completion of his sentence in April 1959 he was restricted to a purpose-built colony at Lodwar, where he could move only 800 yards from his dwelling.

Johnnie Shows that Bwana is Boss

Kenyatta's personal fate was separate from that of Mau Mau, although imprisonment accelerated his transformation into nationalist leader in waiting. The partial decapitation of the Mau Mau political leadership was accompanied by collective punishments, mass screening and a spe-cial tax levied on the Kikuyu to subsidize the costs of fighting the Mau Mau. In active Mau Mau hotspots livestock was confiscated, notionally to encourage informants to come forward. In a very tense atmosphere, even innocent events could turn deadly. When a large group of Kikuyu gathered to witness a dumb boy miraculously cured, a much outnum-bered party of African policemen panicked at the sight of so many pan-gas and shot sixteen of them dead. As a result of this incident the police were ordered to use buckshot rather than bullets.[25]

From the end of 1952 Mau Mau raids quickened. On Christmas Eve there were five separate attacks on senior African members of the Church of Scotland, in which the victims were speared or hacked to death. On New Year's Day 1953, two white bachelor farmers were killed when fifteen Mau Mau burst in before the victims could rise from the dinner table to get their guns. For this was a society where it had become advisable to have a loaded revolver near to hand at all times as detailed instructions called 'Your Turn May Come' advised: 'The speed with which you can have a gun in your hand may well mean the difference between life or death.'[26] Robert Broadbent, the MI5 security liaison officer in Nairobi, slept with a revolver under the pillow, blissfully unaware that a Mau Mau arms cache was hidden in his own kitchen.[27] 'Women Put Guns in their Handbags' figured as a headline in Britain's right-wing *Daily Mail*, which along with the left-wing *Daily Mirror* gave regular coverage to events in Kenya.[28]

In line with what the French military were doing in Algeria, the Aberdare Range and Mount Kenya were declared prohibited zones, where anyone was liable to be shot. The definition of a weapon was extended to agricultural tools or a spear that the bearer might have had innocent reasons to possess. On the Kikuyu Reserve those who failed to respond to a challenge could be shot too. During the first three months of 1953 thousands of Kikuyu loyalists were encouraged to join Home Guard militias to defend people and property against Mau Mau attacks. More and more Kikuyu were screened to identify Mau Mau activists and supporters, who were held in an ever larger number of detention camps. The constant harassment served as a recruiting sergeant for the Mau Mau cause – if you were going to be treated as Mau Mau, you might as well join them.[29] So did the policy of expelling squatters from the Rift Valley or from the slums of Nairobi. They were not welcome in the Kikuyu reservations and often joined the Mau Mau bands for want of any alternative.[30]

Britain had signed the Geneva Convention in 1949, though it contrived to avoid ratifying it until 1957 to allow itself as much latitude as possible in dealing with insurgents. Similarly, Britain may have been one of the original signatories to the Council of Europe's Convention for the Protection of Human Rights and Fundamental Freedoms, but it ensured that derogations existed to exempt its colonies from it. However, the development of global mass media meant that the metropolis could no longer turn a blind eye to what happened at the behest of local colonial authorities. In both Algeria and Kenya the traditional collusion failed.[31]

In 1952 the local authorities requested the blueprints for gallows to be built beyond Nairobi.[32] By mid-1953 capital crimes included administering or participating in Mau Mau oaths, membership of Mau Mau gangs, being found in possession of arms, ammunition and explosives or being discovered in the company of such persons. With so many suspects being detained the wheels of justice turned too slowly in the eyes of the settler community and the majority Kikuyu loyalists, which presented the authorities with the challenge of pre-empting vigilante justice. In response the British government gave in to Baring's request for a series of Emergency Assize Courts.[33]

It was not the finest hour for British jurisprudence. The judges, who sat alone in these courts, gave credence to dubious confessions and to the evidence of witnesses who had survived Mau Mau massacres by keeping their heads down. In one notorious case where the accused had the seemingly watertight alibi that he had been in jail during the massacre at Lari, the police were on hand to testify that on the day in question he had escaped for a few lethal hours. The judge sentenced him to death, although the conviction was quashed on appeal.[34] The seventy-one men executed for the Lari massacre were only the first to be hanged in a draconian and largely successful effort to prevent Kenya succumbing to lynch law. In normal times half of the death sentences passed in Kenya were commuted to terms of imprisonment. Of the 1,468 Mau Mau convicted of capital crimes, 1,068 were hanged. By contrast there were 226 hangings in Malaya and only twelve Zionist terrorists executed in Palestine between 1938 and 1947. Although in both cases more British civilians, policemen and soldiers lost their lives than in Kenya, the threat of mass vigilantism was absent.

The Mau Mau murder of the Ruck family intensified white-settler pressure on Baring to involve them more intimately in the anti-Mau Mau campaign. The settlers formed a United Kenya Protection Association, with its own seventy-man 'Commando' or death squad. To counter such pressures, the War Office despatched Major-General Robert 'Looney' Hinde, who in 1944 had been removed from his brigade command in Normandy, as director of operations. Hinde declared that 'we must heed the example of Malaya and ensure that repressive measures do NOT result in an unbridgeable gap of bitterness between us and the Kikuyu'. His stated plan was to prevent the spread of Mau Mau, stop terrorist attacks and 'stamp out Mau Mau and the ideology behind it'. But when the Mau Mau murdered a farmer who had been a wartime soldier and POW, Hinde's sympathies swung towards settlers who wanted to wage a 'gloves off' war in which vengeance would be meted out by their own police force and the Home Guard militias. Once it became apparent that he was prepared to tolerate vigilantism, Hinde was sacked. However, the police continued to kill with impunity, joking that *simama* (halt) meant 'goodbye'.[35]

Hinde was replaced by Lieutenant-General Sir George 'Bobbie' Erskine with the title of commander-in-chief. His early military career had started in Ireland and India. He went on to win the DSO at El Alamein in 1942, although later in Normandy Montgomery lamented his lack of aggression on the battlefield. He made up for it as commander of British forces in Egypt in 1949–52, using considerable force to suppress nationalist guerrillas in the Canal Zone. Erskine had a low estimation of some of his own forces and took a violent dislike to the 'middle class sluts' as he described the white settlers – and he did not just mean the women. He kept a written authorization to declare martial law in his spectacle case, which he opened and snapped shut whenever the settlers tried his patience.

Erskine immediately stopped the practice of keeping scorecards of Mau Mau killed and paying £5 per kill by way of bonus. He dismissed the brigade commander of the King's African Rifles and court-martialled KAR Captain Griffiths for shooting two Kikuyu prisoners. Unable to make the charge of murder stick, Erskine insisted the court try him for torture instead, because he had cut trophy ears from the victims before murdering them. Griffiths spent five years in a British prison, an almost unique case when most British personnel who committed acts of barbarity were never even indicted. Erskine was exceptional too in that he was firmly of the opinion that Mau Mau was not an atavistic cult, which was how Colonial Secretary Lyttelton, Governor Baring and most of the settlers perceived it. Instead he regarded it as the product of maladministration and brutal policing, not to speak of the economic exploitation practised by the settlers.

In late June 1953 Erskine launched Operation Buttercup. This was a large-scale probing mission that took in the villages of the Kikuyu reserve at Fort Hall as well as the adjacent forested areas where the Mau Mau operated. To increase spatial coverage, Erskine agreed that the police needed beefing up, incorporating the white-officered Home Guard, which added another 25,000 men and women to the settlers' own all-white Kenya Police Reserve, which was in turn augmented with imported 'Kenya Cowboys' from the European war's flotsam and jetsam. Stationed in encampments surrounded by barbed wire and watchtowers, the Home Guard performed badly: they tried to buy off the Mau Mau with arms and ammunition, and tended to bolt at the first sign of trouble. They also extorted money and goods from the Kikuyu they were supposed to be protecting. In yet another precursor of events in Afghanistan in the twenty-first century, the pervasive violence served as cover for both sides to settle private scores.

Under close press scrutiny, Erskine made it a priority to seek the moral high ground, in which endeavour he was aided by the barbarity of the Mau Mau. So the conflict was cast as a struggle against savagery rather than against Communism, the usual suspect, to prevent the internationalization of the conflict by meddling Americans or Nehru's India striking poses at the UN.[36] Evidently, the behaviour of some elements of the security forces undermined the claim. To sort out the police, who were the worst offenders, Arthur Young, the London Police Commissioner who had been successful in Malaya, was appointed Kenya's new commissioner of police, arriving in March 1954. One of his first acts was to restore the autonomy of the Criminal Investigation Department to investigate police abuses and atrocities. Young lasted until December. Two innocent Kikuyu farmers were tortured and killed at a loyalist interrogation centre, with the connivance of British officials who falsified evidence and committed perjury. Although a judge unravelled the truth, Baring suppressed the written judgment. Young resigned and returned to London, and was with difficulty persuaded to tone down a resignation letter that blamed Baring for what the police had been doing.[37]

In Kenya white judges and juries more usually found excuses for whatever the police did, assuming that wholesale bureaucratic cover-ups did not prevent such incidents reaching court. Brian Hayward, the nineteen-year-old leader of a screening team sent to Tanganyika in October 1953 to vet 8,000 Kikuyu being repatriated to Kenya, was found to have systematically tortured those he suspected were Mau Mau with the aid of ten African members of his team. One victim was so badly beaten that he begged to be killed. The judge showed much sympathy for the defendants: 'It is easy to work oneself up into a state of pious horror over these offences, but they must be considered against their background. All the accused were engaged in seeking out inhuman monsters and savages of the lowest order.' Hayward was convicted and given a token sentence that he served by working for twelve weeks as a clerk in a hotel. Baring compounded matters by reinstating him as a district officer, although Erskine later managed to have him dismissed.[38]

Meanwhile, in January 1954 the army captured Waruhiu Itote, known as General China because of his wartime service with the KAR in Burma. Disorientated after demobilization, Itote had been oathed in 1950, before becoming an administrator of oaths himself, and an experienced Mau Mau killer. In August 1952 he moved to the forests, from which he launched a series of fearsome raids to massacre government loyalists, their wives and children. Finally his band ran into an army patrol and, after being shot twice and injuring his leg, he surrendered. Surprised to be treated well and offered his life, Itote revealed everything he knew, including the fact that he had commanded 4,000 men, the largest single concentration of Mau Mau. On Prime Minister Churchill's instructions he was prevailed on to relay surrender terms to his comrades in the forests. A KAR unit not informed of this arrangement ambushed a large group of Mau Mau on their way to surrender, driving the rest back into the hills.

In April 1954 Erskine launched Operation Anvil, based on the 1946 Operation Agatha, when the Zionist leadership had been rounded up in Palestine. In the small hours of 24 April some 20,000 British and African troops interdicted all movement in and out of Nairobi. For four weeks the security forces screened the entire male population, paying special attention to the Kikuyu inhabitants of the densely populated sub-districts of Bahati, Pumwani and Kariokor, before turning to the predominantly Asian suburb of Eastlands out near the airport. Basic inspection of an array of documents Kikuyu were required to have about them led to suspects being taken to a transit camp at Langata, one of three camps erected prior to the operation. Notes were made on each individual, which frequently developed into a substantial file. Tribal elders and hooded informers were brought in to identify Mau Mau, a practice that left plenty of room for mere malice.

Alleged Mau Mau were moved to two camps at Mackinnon Road and Manyani where, in line with Allied classification of Nazis in post-war Germany, they were designated 'black', 'grey' and 'white'. Most of the 'blacks' and 'greys' were subject to emergency detention orders under which they could be held without trial for two years. Twenty-four thousand people, roughly half the adult male Kikuyu population of Nairobi, were detained. By the end of 1954 there were 70,000 in captivity. The greatest number formally detained in Malaya had been 1,200, in Palestine 500.[39]

While Anvil certainly dampened down Mau Mau activity in the capital, it was a desperately indiscriminate operation that swept up even brave Christian opponents of the terrorists. Richer Kikuyu often evaded detention by doling out bribes, but others were taken away, leaving Home Guard units free to loot their shops and homes. The Home Guard became a permanent intimidating presence in some of Nairobi's slums, but at least the remaining inhabitants could drink beer and smoke cigarettes, which the Mau Mau had banned on pain of death or mutilation. This was one of the many ways in which the Mau Mau had alienated potential supporters. Another was their campaign to burn down Church schools, which outraged the vast majority who recognized that education was the only way to achieve prosperity.

The Nairobi operation was matched by the creation of protected villages in Central Province, another strategy copied from Malaya, and designed to isolate the Mau Mau from their food and supplies. People who had traditionally lived in scattered settlements were scooped up and their villages burned. They were corralled into tight groups of around 500 people, after first having to build the new round huts themselves, together with excavating the spike-filled moats that surrounded them.[40]

By the end of 1955 there were 804 such villages, containing 1,050,899 people. It is worth noting that, as a proportion of the target population, this eclipsed what the French did in Algeria or the Portuguese in Angola and Mozambique.[41] The wretched inhabitants of these villages were subjected to all manner of chicanery and coercion by the Home Guard protecting them. A further disgusting detail is that since many of the inmates were women, whose husbands were in detention camps, they were frequently raped.[42]

The Mau Mau were forced into harsher environments such as swamps and the deep forests, where their morale and discipline crumbled. Although this terrain was too altitudinous for the sole available helicopter, the RAF was licensed to drop much bigger bombs (weighing 500 or 1,000 pounds) than the twenty-pounders used on areas where the Mau Mau were mixed up with civilians. In September 1954 a Mau Mau leader called Gitonga Kareme surrendered after twenty of his gang had been obliterated by RAF bombing. Between November 1953 and June 1954 the RAF killed or wounded 900 Mau Mau insurgents.[43] British troops also tracked the Mau Mau into the forests. They destroyed a Mau Mau gang lurking in the Dandora Swamp, capturing its leader, Captain Nyagi Nyaga, and although he was extremely co-operative with his CID and Special Branch interrogators, he was sentenced to death and hanged along with sixteen of his comrades. Nyaga was a seasoned fighter, but many of his co-accused were either men whom Mau Mau had sprung from a prison – and had little choice in joining the society – or who claimed they had been kidnapped and press-ganged. That defence did not save them, even when one of the hard-core Mau Mau fighters confirmed it was true.

The last Mau Mau redoubts were in the forest of the Aberdare Range and Mount Kenya, where trees gave way to dense bamboo as one got higher, and the bamboo gave way to hard scrabble and rock. Here Mau Mau bands established well-concealed camps, ringed by sentries and provisioned by volunteers from nearby villages. They learned how to use animal or bird sounds to communicate, and while their British opponents lumbered noisily through the undergrowth laden with heavy gear, the Mau Mau could run for up to seventy miles a day. They made do with berries and plants, and overcame Kikuyu taboos to eat elephant or monkey meat. The ability to extract honey from African beehives was a much prized skill. Gradually they replaced their ragged uniforms with items fashioned from furs and animal hides. But, like the Chinese Communists in Malaya's jungles, they were increasingly prone to paranoia and depression.[44]

Major infantry operations such as Operation Hammer in February 1955 involved a sharply worsening cost-benefit ratio for the attacking force. In Hammer nine battalions killed 161 Mau Mau, which worked out at £10,000 per kill. Out of this impasse emerged the innovation, pioneered by the then Major Frank Kitson, of false-flag operations or 'pseudo gangs', initially involving Kikuyu loyalists from the Kenya Regiment, and then rebels who had been successfully turned to operate against their former Mau Mau comrades. Contrary to myth there was little role for white policemen and settlers 'blacking up' with actors' greasepaint or burned cork for these missions.[45] In October 1956 Ian Henderson, a white Special Branch officer, used Kitson's methods to track down the able if psychopathic Dedan Kimathi, the only major Mau Mau leader still at large. He became the last Mau Mau member to be hanged when he was executed in Nairobi prison on 27 December 1956.[46]

In June 1957, Sir Evelyn passed on to the Colonial Secretary Alan Lennox-Boyd a secret memorandum written by Eric Griffiths-Jones, the Attorney-General of Kenya. The memorandum described the abuse of Mau Mau detainees. Sir Evelyn wrote a covering letter stating that inflicting a 'violent shock' had been the only way of dealing with Mau Mau insurgents.

Though the Mau Mau uprising had been militarily defeated by this date, its aftermath was deeply embarrassing for the British government, which found itself arraigned by both domestic and international opinion. The reasons arose from the so-called rehabilitation process or 'Pipeline' into which Mau Mau suspects were fed and shunted between camps whose regime notionally reflected whether they were categorized as 'grey' or 'black'. The camp gates were emblazoned with such historically unfortunate exhortations as 'Labour and Freedom', as well as 'He Who Helps Himself Will Also Be Helped'. These camps were barbed-wire compounds dominated by watchtowers, with images of the young Queen Elizabeth II juxtaposed to those of Jomo Kenyatta, who within a few years she would be greeting like a long-lost uncle. Loudspeakers boomed out commands and exhortations day and night.

The Kenyan concentration camps bear comparison with the worst, excepting Nazi death camps. They were places where people were dehumanized and randomly brutalized (or just murdered) by men over whom the colony's authorities exercised no control whatsoever. They undermined the British people's belief that their colonial regimes were superior to those of their European competitors, let alone the idea that the British 'don't do that sort of thing'. It in no way diminishes British responsibility that many Kikuyu loyalists enthusiastically supported and participated in the process.[47]

There was both a scandal and a government cover-up. Despite being systematically smeared for their efforts, a few local whistleblowers brought the disgraceful conditions in the Kenyan detention camps to the attention of Labour politicians at Westminster such as Fenner Brockway, Barbara Castle and John Stonehouse. Just when the metropolitan and colonial governments thought they had bluffed their way past a succession of scandals in Kenya, they were hit by the worst of them all. It had a history.

In 1957 senior members of Baring's administration had decided drastically to reduce in number the 30,000 or so detainees who were still classified as 'black'. By overestimating the capacity of Kikuyu land to support released detainees it would be possible to free large numbers of them, provided they could be psychologically broken first. That put the spotlight on the most irremediably 'black', who were thought to exert an untoward influence on the less committed majority. Special measures would have to be employed to break that core group of recalcitrant Mau Mau, who were reclassified more precisely as Ys and Zs or even Z1s and Z2s, the latter being the most stubborn.

To effect this new course, dubbed Operation Progress, Carruthers 'Monkey' Johnston, the Minister for African Affairs in Nairobi, appointed thirty-four-year-old District Officer Terence Gavaghan as head of rehabilitation. Gavaghan's only obvious qualifications were that he was very large and extremely brutal. The Kenyan Attorney-General Eric Griffith-Jones helpfully provided a specious lawyerly distinction between 'compelling' and 'punitive' force, which led to the policy being tacitly approved by both Governor Baring and Colonial Secretary Lennox-Boyd.[48]

In November 1958 the Kenya Commissioner for Prisons imparted the new line to Commandant G. M. Sullivan, newly appointed to Hola detention centre on the Tana River, which housed the worst of the worst detainees. He received support from John Cowan, the Senior Superintendent of Prisons, as he set about breaking those detainees who were still refusing to work. Cowan suggested saturating the place with a riot squad of Africans who would outnumber the detainees by five to one, and Johnston and the Minister for Internal Security and Defence authorized it. In February 1959 massive force was used to induce eighty-five detainees to work after they had sat down on the ground. Eleven of them were beaten to death by guards with pickaxe handles. When news of the atrocity reached Nairobi, Baring and the senior officials involved conspired to pass off the deaths as the result of drinking contaminated water, and quickly shunted the affair over to a supposedly compliant magistrate's inquest. When a doctor and nurse who were present testified that the men had been beaten to death, Baring instituted merely disciplinary, as opposed to criminal, proceedings against Sullivan and his deputy Walter Coutts. He even recommended Cowan for an MBE. The smooth lawyerly scum who legitimized these acts remained entirely unaffected.[49]

News of the latest outrage filtered back to British politicians, partly through the good offices of Kenyatta's lawyer Denis Pritt. Starting with credulous reports in the *East African Standard*, by June 1959 the 'Hola Scandal' had made *Time* magazine in the US. The subject of Hola occupied an all-night debate in the House of Commons on 27–28 July. Hitherto Lennox-Boyd had been able to deflect Labour calls for a public inquiry into conditions in Kenya's camps. When the government sought to defend its clumsy cover-ups with reference to the 'morale' of the colonial civil service, one Labour member countered with the dubious claim that 'we cease to rank as a great power, but moral power we still have'. He also acidly commented that 'of course the colonial civil servants were jolly good chaps, and it was very unfair to attack them, whatever they did. That is what [Dr] Crippen's friends said: they all said that he was an extremely nice chap, but, after all, he had murdered his wife.'

More dangerously for the Colonial Secretary, the Tory MP Enoch Powell – who had resigned from the Treasury eighteen months before – was also incensed.[50] Powell was known to his own leader as the 'Fakir', and Macmillan had even asked for him to be seated further down the Cabinet table to avoid his staring eyes. It has to be said that the detestation was mutual, since Powell thought the Prime Minister was a Whig 'actor-manager' and not a true Tory.[51]

Powell had decided by the early 1950s that the Commonwealth was a sham, and that, without India, which he loved, empire was beyond Britain's means. In the early hours of the morning he rose to speak and in his flat Midlands accent forensically demolished the claim by Lennox-Boyd, Baring and others that one could not use metropolitan methods to counter an African insurgency. Attempts to justify the deaths at Hola by calling the victims 'sub-humans' met his withering scorn: 'I would say that it is a fearful doctrine, which must recoil on the heads of those who pronounce it, to stand in judgement on a fellow human-being and to say, "Because he was such and such, therefore the consequences which would otherwise flow from his death shall not flow."' Acceptance and assignment of responsibility for one's actions were part and parcel of the representative government which Britain sought to introduce to Africa. Finally, Powell attacked the moral relativism of applying different standards to different peoples. 'We must be consistent with ourselves everywhere. All Government, all influence of man on man, rests on opinion. What we can do in Africa, where we still govern, depends on the opinion which is entertained of the way in which this country acts and the way in which Englishmen act. We cannot, we dare not, in Africa of all places, fall below our own highest standards in the acceptance of responsibility.'[52] If anything induced the British to pack up and go, it was the moral disaster that it had inflicted on itself, a disaster British politicians and civil servants systematically covered up until 2012 by destroying or doctoring the written records of the former colony.

The eventual settlement also engraved injustices into independent Kenya. The Swynnerton Plan of late 1953 proposed the creation of a solid class of Kikuyu yeoman farmers, allowed to grow cash crops such as coffee. With so many Mau Mau suspects in detention, it was a simple matter to resurvey land and to reward loyalists with solid title to the vacant holdings of detainees. This meant jobs for the willing boys on a grand scale. Loyalist Kikuyu of humble means were blessed with much official favour in terms of trading licences or loans to purchase something as modest as a bicycle. The administration operated whitelists as well as blacklists for employers, who were encouraged to discriminate on behalf of loyalists. Loyal Kikuyu were recruited into the lower reaches of the administration, whence they rose higher and were favoured when the colonial regime gerrymandered an anti-Mau Mau electorate in the transition to Kenyan independence. The aim was to ensure that, when Mau Mau detainees were released, they would never attain the critical mass needed to dominate the majority, something over-insured by denying them the Certificates of Loyalty without which one could not vote. As a measure to prevent a possible breakdown of law and order it was a great success. However, the structure became the backbone of the authoritarian, bureaucratic and deeply corrupt state that Kenyatta would impose on independent Kenya, which his successors have done little or nothing to reform. Kenya was one of those colonies where the Americans were content to allow the British free rein. The developing Cold War forced them to think about Africa in a more focused way. But in the beginning policy towards this huge continent was almost a blank slate as its affairs did not concern them.

14. THE COLD WAR COMES TO AFRICA

A Blank Slate

In February 1950, US diplomats from across sub-Saharan Africa convened in Lourenço Marques, the capital of Portuguese Mozambique. US Assistant Secretary of State George McGhee chaired the conference. The purpose of the gathering was to fill the void in US policy towards Africa, which had been neglected. Washington had fewer diplomats in the whole of Africa than in West Germany.

The conference participants endured a series of briefings on the problems of each European colony, coloured by their belief that they were riding the wave of the future and could safely scorn the past. 'The East African authorities are still living in the age of Queen Victoria,' said one. Communists were not a significant problem anywhere, though the colonial powers were exaggerating the threat of Communism in Africa to avoid concessions to nationalist movements. Since it did not want to sink the NATO boat by destabilizing Europe's colonies, the US favoured lengthy periods of grace so that, having built the foundations of stability, newly independent states would avoid anarchy, from which only the Soviets might benefit. 'It is necessary to keep in mind that we are not in a position to exercise direct responsibility with respect to Africa,' said McGhee. 'We have no desire to assume the responsibilities borne by other peoples and, indeed, our principles, our commitments, and our lack of experience all militate against our assumption of such obligations.'[1]

While McGhee acknowledged diffuse humanitarian goals, US policy was very much of its time regarding the regressive potential of black Africa: 'the American negro is to Africans in Central Africa as the present day white American is to the common man in the days of Charlemagne'. Thus, he continued, 'without the discipline and control of Western nations, ancient antagonisms would burst their present bounds and numerous races or tribes would attack traditional enemies in primitive savagery. The native people of Africa tend always to mistrust the leadership of their own kind because in themselves they have not yet as a people achieved sufficient evolutionary stature to understand the existence of motivation other than the compulsion of self-interest of a very low order or fear.'[2]

As the 1950s unfolded the growing band of newly sovereign states had minds of their own regarding their strategic destinies. Foster Dulles was intensely suspicious of Third World neutralism and non-alignment, as advertised at the Bandung Conference in April 1955, regarding them as 'a transitional stage to communism', even though 'neutralism' had been the US's default diplomatic stance, barring a brief participation in the First World War, from the Republic's inception until December 1941. After the British Gold Coast became independent Ghana in early 1957, Vice President Nixon took the lead in pushing Washington to rethink its overall policy towards the continent. After touring northern Africa, Nixon lobbied for a separate Bureau of African Affairs at the State Department, for increased economic aid and for progress to be made on domestic civil rights, if only to stymie Soviet propaganda on the issue in Africa. The US administration was too witless to advertise the fact that African students at the Friendship University in Moscow were routinely abused and beaten in the streets by Russian racists.[3] The first policy statement on sub-Saharan Africa was NSC 5719, issued five months after Nixon's visit: 'Premature independence would be as harmful to our interests in Africa as would be a continuation of nineteenth-century colonialism, and we must tailor our policies to the capabilities and needs of each particular area as well as to our overall relations with the metropolitan power concerned.'[4]

The domestic rhetorical pace on Africa was set by the Democrat Senator John F. Kennedy, who was boosting his own standing in foreign policy to counter the expertise of Nixon, his most likely opponent in a run for the presidency. Kennedy became the leading light of the Senate Foreign Relations Sub-committee on African Affairs, and African nationalism was a powerful wind filling his sails. In September 1956 he spoke of:

the Afro-Asian revolution of nationalism, the revolt against colonialism, the determination of people to control their national destinies . . . In my opinion, the tragic failure of both Republican and Democrat administrations since World War II to comprehend the nature of this revolution, and its potentialities for good and evil, has reaped a bitter harvest today – and it is by rights and by necessity a major foreign policy campaign issue that has nothing to do with anti-Communism.

In July 1957 he delivered an outspoken attack on French policy in Algeria. When would the French learn that colonies are 'like fruit that cling to the tree only till they ripen'? When would the Eisenhower administration learn that 'tepid encouragement and moralizations to both sides, cautious neutrality on all the real issues, and a restatement of our obvious dependence on our European friends, and our obvious dedication to the principles of self-determination, and our obvious desire not to become involved' was not a coherent policy?[5] Thereafter, every ambitious African leader beat a path to Kennedy's office to enjoy face time with the charismatic young Senator, among them the Angolan Holden Roberto and the Kenyan labour activist Tom Mboya.

Much of Kennedy's interest in Africa was designed to compensate for his non-interest in domestic desegregation because of the electoral importance of Southern Dixiecrats. But in one respect he did bring new thinking to US relations with Africa. He did not reflexively link the nationalist ferment happening within European colonies with the Cold War threat from the Soviets. After nationalist forces had triumphed, he adopted a much more nuanced approach towards Third World non-alignment. He distinguished between Soviet clientelism and 'true' or 'real' neutralism, in which Third World nations were critical of both superpowers while maintaining order and stability and practising economic diversity and political pluralism at home. The US could accommodate such diversity of outlook; until Khrushchev arrived on the scene, the Soviet Union could not. African states would not need to become military allies or mini-Americas; instead, the US could achieve 'victory through denial' by simply ensuring that they did not become puppets of the Soviet Union. This went together with a belief in the usefulness of strongmen in undeveloped societies unfit for democracy, a stance Kennedy took over from the Eisenhower administration.[6]

Sverdlovsk, Cuba and the Congo

Policy towards Africa was inseparable from a sudden ratcheting up of Cold War tensions. The advent to power of the Castro regime in Cuba in 1959 meant that any Third World radical was liable to be viewed through a similar optic, added to which was the fall-out from the U-2 spy plane incident the following year. In May 1960, a weary Eisenhower prepared for a summit conference in Paris as the prelude to a visit to the Soviet Union later in the year. The previous September Khrushchev had managed to show his more personable side during an historic visit to the US. He came to revel in the technological achievement that on 4 October 1957 had seen Russia put a Sputnik in orbit around the Earth, emitting bleeps for radio hams the world over. Here indeed was proof of the superiority of socialism, he said, even though his fellow countrymen had never seen a banana or an orange, and had to wait decades for a car.[7] Much hinged on Eisenhower making a success of the intervening Paris summit with Khrushchev before his reciprocal trip to Moscow later in the year. The auguries for a nuclear test ban treaty seemed fair, and Ike hoped to revive the Open Skies idea of mutual aerial inspections of rocket-launch sites, not realizing that the Soviets would have to reject it to conceal how small their nuclear arsenal was compared to the Americans'. While candidate Kennedy cynically declared the reverse to be the case and denounced a 'missile gap' he knew did not exist, the reality was that the US had 150 ICBMs and the Soviets a mere four, as confirmed by U-2 spy planes. Although Ike was very aware that these over-flights were illegal and provocative, he rather too casually allowed the CIA one final pre-summit U-2 flight over the Soviet Union, codenamed Operation Grand Slam. The mission was supposed to be completed before 1 May but in fact took place on that all too auspicious date in the Soviet calendar.

Previously U-2 flights had operated from Greenland, darting in and out to photograph the ICBM sites at Plesetsk, about 500 miles north of Moscow. The dense northern network of Soviet anti-aircraft defences made it advisable to vary the route and the latest flight involved taking off from Peshawar in Pakistan, turning north towards Sverdlovsk, then north-west over Plesetsk to land at Bodo in Norway. At 11 a.m. on 1 May villagers in Povarnia near Sverdlovsk heard an explosion and spotted what they thought was a balloon in the sky. It turned out to be a parachute with the U-2 pilot, Gary Powers, attached. The KGB hastened to the scene. The U-2 had been disabled by an S-75 Surface-to-Air missile equipped with a proximity fuse. In Langley the CIA received the ominous signal 'Bill Bailey didn't come home.' The news did not unduly perturb Eisenhower, as the U-2s were fitted with self-destruct devices and the pilot was supposed to remove himself from the equation with a poisoned pin – which Powers thoughtfully stopped his KGB interrogators fiddling with since a single prick was fatal.

Although the U-2 flights were an open secret to all except the American public, Ike persisted in denying their existence. The space agency NASA was prevailed on to issue a statement lamenting the loss of a weather-research plane over Lake Van in Turkey, which did not explain what it was doing near Sverdlovsk. Khrushchev lured Eisenhower into maintaining these fictions, until he revealed that the Soviets had most of the U-2 and that Gary Powers was 'quite alive and kicking'. Eisenhower persisted in his visit to the Paris summit and walked into a Soviet propaganda trap. At the opening meeting he never got the chance to forswear any future U-2 flights, for the Russian leader started shouting. At one point the chairman, de Gaulle, interjected: 'The acoustics in this room are excellent. We can all hear [Mr Khrushchev]. There is no need for him to raise his voice.' When Khrushchev rekindled his choler, shouting 'I have been overflown!', de Gaulle sympathized, saying he had been overflown too, eighteen times, by a Soviet spy satellite. 'As God sees me, my hands are clean,' replied Khrushchev.[8] Both he and the American President had turned bright red in the face under the emotion of it all. 'We couldn't possibly offer our hospitality to someone who had already, so to speak, made a mess at his host's table,' Khrushchev said, and the Soviet delegation walked out. A dejected Ike flew home, the autumnal peace efforts of his presidency a failure.[9]

Tribes and Bribes

It was in this tense atmosphere that events in the Congo suddenly impressed themselves on Washington's attention. The Congo was a huge expanse of savannah and lush jungle straddling the Equator and extending from the West African coast to the interior. It was around a third of the size of the USA and equivalent in area to Western Europe. Since it bordered nine other states, Congo's fate could not be ignored. The Belgian King Léopold (after whom the capital city was named) had ruthlessly exploited the Congo before international outrage resulted in the colony being taken over by the Belgian state in 1908. The Belgians had divided the colony into six vast provinces. It had roads, which have long since disappeared from today's Democratic Republic of the Congo, as well as remarkably good medical services. Missionaries from the Roman Catholic Church dominated education. The Belgian Flamands were much given to drunken expatiation on what they called *la mentalité bantoue*, meaning the Conradian darkness just beneath the surface of even the few native *évolués*, a term we have already encountered in Algeria.[10]

The Congo's thirteen and a half million Africans were divided into 200 tribes, speaking over 400 dialects. Its rich natural resources were unevenly distributed, with diamonds in south-central Kasai Province and copper, cobalt, tantalum and uranium in southerly Katanga neighbouring Rhodesia. Katanga was like a corporate fiefdom divided up among Belgian, British and South African conglomerates.

Throughout this vast sprawling country, unified only by an immense dirty brown river, Europeans monopolized all skilled positions, for only nineteen native Congolese were university graduates.[11] From the late 1940s Congolese who had enjoyed a secondary education formed old boys' associations, which together with socialist and Catholic study groups evolved into political parties. In the beginning these mirrored tensions in metropolitan Belgium between rival supporters of *laïcité* and religious education, but as time went on some forty parties reflected tribal divisions, whatever the outward ideological coloration.[12]

In late January 1960 representatives of the Congolese parties attended a round-table conference in Brussels, the goal of their hosts being to perpetuate Belgian administration and economic control after the Congo became nominally independent by 30 June. In May national elections were held. There were three main political figures: the Bakongo nobleman Joseph Kasavubu, the firebrand all-Congolese nationalist Patrice Lumumba from the Tetela tribe in Orientale Province and, in Katanga Province, the Balunda leader Moshe Tshombe, a Methodist businessman who was the best regarded in Western circles.

Belgium was ceding independence, but calculated that it would continue to rule. Belgians controlled business, the civil service and the officer corps of the army, which was exclusively European above the rank of sergeant. Following the election, Kasavubu became president and Lumumba prime minister. The former dreamed of restoring the ancient Bakongo kingdom, but Lumumba was a pan-African nationalist close to Kwame Nkrumah in Ghana. He had also been in contact with Soviet diplomats in Guinea and in Brussels. At the independence celebrations on 30 June, King Baudouin made an emollient speech, but walked out when Lumumba altered the tone of the occasion with a biting, unscheduled address:

We have known sarcasm and insults, endured blows morning, noon, and night, because we are 'niggers'. Who will forget that a Black was addressed in the familiar *tu*, not as a friend, but because the polite *vous* was reserved for Whites only? We have seen our lands despoiled under the terms of what was supposedly the law of the land but which only recognised the right of the strongest. We have seen that this law was quite different for a White than for a Black: accommodating for the former, cruel and inhuman for the latter.[13]

Retrospective sainthood has invested Lumumba with an aura he did not enjoy in life. Although undoubtedly charismatic, he had spent a year in prison for embezzling at the post office where he worked as a clerk, before becoming sales manager of a brewery. He was a disorganized thinker but a gifted demagogue, which was not a quality prized by Western governments scarred by the memory of Mussolini and Hitler – and he reminded Americans of Fidel Castro.[14]

Immediately after independence Congolese government officials awarded themselves handsome pay rises, enabling former clerks to acquire cars. Two disastrous consequences flowed from this act of self-indulgence: the higher salaries would have to be paid by raising the tax take from Kasai and Katanga, which increased the desire of the local Congolese to keep the money for themselves; and the largesse was not extended to the Armée Nationale Congolese (ANC), where the senior Belgian military commander scrawled 'Before Independence = After Independence' on a blackboard for the benefit of his troops. Drunken and mutinous soldiers roamed the streets of Léopoldville, attacking Europeans, who fled in large numbers across the Congo River to neighbouring Brazzaville in the French Congo. 'We are the masters now' was a common refrain. A Soviet delegation sent to establish diplomatic relations was set upon and managed to get free only by exclaiming 'Khrushchev!' and 'Sputnik!'[15]

Lurid accounts of rape and white flight in European newspapers gave the Belgians a fresh excuse to meddle. They shipped in 1,800 paratroopers, who sought to restore order with their customary lack of finesse, killing twelve Congolese soldiers on disembarking at the port of Matadi. Their presence caused the Congolese to panic. Following independence, mining interests led by the Belgian Union Minière du Haut Katanga encouraged Tshombe to secede. The educated African front men of the new state, complete with its flag of crosslets on a red and green background, regarded their fellow Africans with much the same contempt as did the whites. In fairness to the foreign interests, their primary concern was to cordon off Katanga from the chaos in the rest of Congo, for they always maintained secret contacts with the authorities in Léopoldville behind Tshombe's back.[16] Kasavubu and Lumumba tried to fly in to Elisabethville, the capital of Katanga, but found that European mercenaries had blocked the runways with burning oil drums.

While Kasavubu and Lumumba were away, the ministers they left behind in the capital appealed to the US for 3,500 troops to suppress the military mutiny. They were rebuffed by an administration that thought the UN was better placed for such a role. Kasavubu and Lumumba turned to the UN instead. Within three days the UN Secretary-General Dag Hammarskjöld had secured a resolution ordering Belgium to remove its forces so as to enable the Congolese government to function. The US joined the Soviets in favouring the despatch of a UN peacekeeping operation while the Europeans abstained. The Swedish Hammarskjöld worked the telephones to assemble a force of Ethiopians, Ghanaians, Moroccans and Tunisians for Operation Safari, to be led by General Carl Carlson von Horn, another Swede. Ninety US planes airlifted the bulk of this 12,000-strong force into the simmering former colony. The UN might have seemed neutral to any Westerner, but it was ominous that when they met the new troops Congolese officials inquired, 'L'ONU? C'est quelle tribu?' What tribe is that?[17]

Close acquaintance with Lumumba had not made Washington hearts grow fond. In July 1960 he spent three days in Washington, and against a background of reports of European women being raped in the Congo asked his State Department minders for a woman. What did he have in mind? 'Une blanche blonde,' he replied. After meetings in which Lumumba sat staring at the ceiling and mumbling to himself in between bouts of fervid utterance, senior officials at State formed the not unreasonable view that he was unbalanced. He was also reported to smoke hashish, which in 1960 made him a 'drug addict'. On his final day in Washington, Lumumba thanked the Soviet Tass news agency for Soviet food aid to Congo, which seemed to confirm the official Belgian view, echoed by the US Ambassador to Brussels, that he was a Communist. In reality Lumumba was more like Ghana's Kwame Nkrumah or Guinea's Sékou Touré than Castro, but the CIA's Allen Dulles was convinced that Lumumba would have to go.[18]

Frustrated by the UN's refusal to crush the Katangan secessionists, an enraged Lumumba declared that 'We will take aid from the devil or anyone else as long as they get the Belgian troops out.'[19] The Russians were soon in evidence. The first Ambassador, Mikhail Yakolev, and three KGB officers moved into a rented villa in Léopoldville. From mid-August 1960 Soviet aircraft based in Ghana flew Eastern Bloc technicians and a hundred motor vehicles to the Congo. They also delivered ten Ilyushin transport aircraft to enable Lumumba to move his forces around the vast country.[20] For while the UN had come to restore peace, Lumumba was bent on restoring his grip on the whole country, and the Russians were going to help him.

The modest Soviet presence in turn drew in the CIA. Lawrence Devlin, a former army officer who had joined the CIA in the late 1940s, opened a new station in Léopoldville. On his first night in the capital, drunken Congolese soldiers mistook him for a Flamand and played Russian roulette with a gun to his head. Devlin signalled Bronson Tweedy, head of the Agency's new Africa Division, that 'Congo is experiencing a classic Communist effort to take over the government.' Lumumba had long been in contact with the Soviets, but it was a moot point whether or not he was a Communist. A mercurial radical might have been more accurate, but the effect was the same.[21]

The American response was disproportionate, not helped by the fact that some senior officials believed the Congolese had only recently descended from the trees.[22] At an NSC meeting on 1 August 1960, Eisenhower resolved to stymie Soviet intervention in the Congo. Assuming that they would try to Balkanize the Congo, he determined to consolidate it – but not under Lumumba. On 18 August the NSC reconvened to consider Devlin's alarming report. When Ike made clear his belief that Lumumba was fronting for the Soviets, it had an effect akin to Henry II's supposed exclamation 'Who will rid me of this turbulent priest?' with reference to Archbishop Thomas à Beckett. Whatever Ike's precise phrasing, National Security Assistant Gordon Gray told the CIA that the President had expressed 'extremely strong feelings on the necessity for very straightforward action' against Lumumba.[23] Allen Dulles agreed to proceed 'as vigorously as the situation permits or requires . . . within the bounds of necessity and capacity'. On 26 August he personally signed off on a cable to Devlin, making the 'removal' of Lumumba 'an urgent and prime objective'.[24] Devlin was authorized to spend up to $100,000.

Soon, whenever Lumumba appeared in public rented crowds gathered to shout 'Down with Lumumba!' He was his own worst enemy. He had insisted that the UN force, which was not his to command, be diverted to crush the Katanga secessionists, only to be menaced by a new separatist movement under Albert Kalonji in the central diamond-rich province of Kasai. When UN Secretary-General Hammarskjöld refused to use his forces in this way, Lumumba accused him of being in the pay of Belgian mining interests. Relations between the two men were dreadful. Since the UN was preventing Lumumba's troops from flying into Katanga, Soviet planes flew ANC troops from the Benalulua tribe under the command of the army chief (and Lumumba's uncle) General Victor Lundula into Kasai instead. Lundula's troops failed to recover control of the province, but did massacre about a thousand members of the Baluba tribe. By this time the UN and its allies had explicitly decided to back Kasavubu, although the home governments of the African 80 per cent of UN troops supported the more radical Lumumba.

The Congo had slipped into anarchy. Each day Africans and Europeans seeking rescue mobbed UN posts. The new and highly effective SIS station chief Daphne Park, a dead ringer for Miss Marple even when younger, once had to chase away an intruder in her suburban house by shouting 'I am a witch! And if you don't instantly go away your hands and feet will drop fall off.' This worked. In several provinces communications were impossible. When one official asked for plans of the provincial telephone system, the new chief of communications proudly handed him the telephone directory. When Moroccan UN troops alighted upon a hospital, they found the head male nurse (the new Director) and an 'assistant' poised to perform an appendectomy on a terrified patient who had received no anaesthetic.[25] Although the Moroccan troops were the best of the bunch, some of the senior UN personnel were questionable. The Ghanaian contingent was commanded by a British general. He once blithely described the ANC as 'the nigger in the woodpile' to the distinguished Afro-American diplomat Ralph Bunche.[26]

While Lumumba 'governed' the Congo via a bank of ten telephones in his office, a real foe quietly worked on his downfall. Since there were no weapons (or guards) in the US embassy, Devlin purchased small arms from Congolese soldiers. He recruited a network of agents, and forged contacts with Kasavubu, Foreign Minister Justin Bomboko, Chief of Police Victor Nendaka and Colonel Joseph Mobutu, the young former journalist whom Lumumba had appointed deputy to General Victor

Lundula. Unknown to the hapless Lumumba, Mobutu had been working for Belgian intelligence for at least two years. On 5 September 1960, President Kasavubu announced the dismissal of Lumumba, who retaliated by dismissing Kasabuvu, something he lacked the legal right to do. Lumumba also lacked the armed power to prevail, as most of the troops loyal to him were now in South Kasai, which he hoped would be the springboard for retaking Katanga.[27]

The UN force prevented Lumumba's troops returning to Léopoldville, thereby effectively taking sides in a civil war. A British UN official, Brian Urquhart, supplied Lumumba's troops with enough beer to put them to sleep, while Ethiopian UN soldiers blocked the runway from which they might have taken off in Soviet aircraft. The UN also disabled Radio Congo, from which Lumumba might have rallied supporters in the capital. Although Lumumba managed to persuade both houses of parliament to back him by stationing his goons in the chambers, he had not reckoned on the ambitious Mobutu, who sought out Devlin for a quiet word. 'The President and the Prime Minister have dismissed each other,' he said. 'Political games! This is no way to create a strong, independent, democratic Congo!' Greatly exaggerating the Soviet threat, Mobutu expressed his readiness to mount a coup, which would pave the way for a government of Congolese technocrats. All he required was the assurance of immediate US recognition of the new regime. Devlin was not authorized to license a coup, but he did just that.

The coup against Lumumba duly took place on 14 September 1960, Devlin having prevailed on Mobutu to keep Kasavubu as president to provide a semblance of legitimacy, permitting the US to recognize the regime without more ado. Kasavubu in turn appointed the new team of 'technocrats', of whom only Justin Bomboko had any experience in government. Mobutu spent the night of the coup drinking whisky in UN headquarters, listening to the announcement of his own putsch on the radio.[28] By morning he had Lundula under house arrest and replaced him as chief of staff. At Devlin's insistence Mobutu changed the name he proposed for the new regime from College of Commissars to College of Commissioners. Devlin and the Binza Group (named after the suburb where Kasavubu and Mobutu lived) decided everything of any importance, with any dissent trumped by Mobutu's control of the army. What Devlin never knew was that Mobutu also sought advice from Daphne Park. It was a tense time. On 17 September the Soviet and Czech embassies were closed and the diplomats expelled. Ambassador Yakolev was thrown into an army truck like a sack of potatoes and driven to the airport.[29]

While the US administration seemed to be playing with a straight bat through the UN, darker operations were afoot. Lumumba remained in the Prime Minister's residence, guarded by Ghanaian UN troops under the orders of his friend Kwame Nkrumah. On 19 September Devlin was informed that a colleague known as 'Joe from Paris' would be arriving in Léopoldville later that month. 'Joe from Paris' introduced himself outside a café: he was Sidney Gottlieb, head of the CIA medical division and an authority on lethal toxins. He handed Devlin a package of tubes of toothpaste containing cobra venom, and surgical gloves to handle them. Unimpressed, Devlin put in a request for a rifle with a telescopic sight to be sent by diplomatic bag.

The standoff around Lumumba continued and he even ventured out, protected by his UN bodyguards, into the capital's bars where people vied to touch their saviour. When Devlin suggested that Kasavubu should have Lumumba arrested, they discovered another obstacle in Hammarskjöld's personal representative, the Indian Rajeshwar Dayal, a personal favourite of Prime Minister Nehru. Dayal detested Americans and as a high-caste Brahmin viewed the Congolese as Untouchables. His wife went to Brazzaville in a UN helicopter to do her shopping. He oozed the condescension he had learned from the British. 'Mr Devlin, I so admire America and Americans,' he sneered on one occasion. 'You make the very best air-conditioners, the best refrigerators, so many fine machines. If only you would concentrate on making your machines, and let us ponder for you.' Dayal insisted that the Commissioners lacked the legitimacy to issue arrest warrants, and Hammerskjöld backed him.[30]

Since Devlin had many tasks, the CIA despatched another senior agent, Justin O'Donnell, to resume covert action against Lumumba. Devlin showed O'Donnell the package of toxins stored in his safe, which O'Donnell remarked 'wasn't for somebody to get his polio shot up to date'. Since O'Donnell himself had problems about personally killing Lumumba, the obvious solution was to deliver him into the hands of his local enemies. To that end the CIA set up an observation post outside

Lumumba's residence, and recruited an agent within. A key break-through was the intelligence that Lumumba would forsake his UN guards if he knew he could make it to his power base in Stanleyville, the capital of Orientale Province ruled by his protégé Antoine Gizenga, a move which the UN was refusing to sanction.[31]

When, after prolonged debate, the UN General Assembly finally accredited the Kasavubu regime in the teeth of Soviet opposition, Lumumba knew it was time to flee. Realizing his UN guards would soon be withdrawn, on 27 November 1960 he slipped out of his residence during a thunderstorm and headed for Stanleyville 1,300 miles away. He never made it. Devlin was flying back from briefing his bosses in Rome when he saw the headline 'LUMUMBA CAPTURED' of a fellow pas-senger's newspaper.

Lumumba was flown back to Léopoldville in early December, where he was severely beaten at the airport by ANC troops who were oblivious of the TV cameras recording the incident. Transferred to the sinister ANC base called Camp Hardy at Thysville, at the narrow western end of the Congo, his prospects briefly improved when the garrison came close to mutiny against Mobutu. After that his only hope lay with the fact that John F. Kennedy was to be sworn in as president on 20 January 1961. In case the new President should intervene to prevent it, on 17 January Lumumba and two of his supporters were bundled on a plane to Kasai, which was ruled by one of his most implacable enemies. Learning that UN troops were at the airport, the plane diverted to Elisabethville in Katanga. While in the air Lumumba was so badly beaten that the Belgian radio operator vomited and the terrified Australian flight crew locked themselves in the cockpit. Lumumba was taken to a villa about eight miles outside Elisabethville, where he was foully tortured before being shot by executioners commanded by the Belgian Captain Julien Gat. His corpse was dissolved in acid.[32]

There were tearful demonstrations in Moscow outside the Belgian embassy, while the new Friendship University was renamed Patrice Lumumba University. The adverse reaction to Lumumba's death would help shape future US policy, which was carefully calibrated to woo mod-erate African leaders. In the short term, US policy in the Congo was clarified by Under Secretary of State George Ball, who brought order into the clamour of competing voices of the Africanists, Europeanists and international-organization experts. Although it made economic sense to back the Katanga secession, it would alienate both the African states and the UN. In the worst scenario, it might result in the Balkanization of the whole of sub-Saharan Africa. Moreover it would allow Gizenga to pose as the champion of national unity from his Lumumbist base in Orientale Province, from where he was bombarding Khrushchev with requests for military assistance. On all these grounds Ball decided to back the central Congolese government and the UN peacekeeping effort, even though Washington was intensely suspicious that the UN was pursuing its own foreign policy. The optimum solution was to force Tshombe into negotiations with Kasavubu, who in turn would be encouraged to find a federal solution to Congo's regional and tribal problems. Since the Africans had withdrawn their forces from the UN mission in protest at Lumumba's murder, they were replaced by around 5,000 tough Gurkhas and Sikhs.[33]

The squeaky-voiced Kasavubu was neither dynamic nor charismatic, so the US had to find a more plausible figurehead. They identified Cyrille Adoula, the head of the Congolese labour movement, as the most convincing candidate for prime minister. Together with the UN, US diplomats organized a conference of Congolese parliamentarians at Lovanium University, fifteen miles outside the capital, to legitimize the new regime. Alcohol and women were banished until proceedings concluded. When it became clear that the absent Gizenga might emerge triumphant despite all their best efforts, the CIA was ordered to swing the votes in Adoula's favour. The US outbid Adoula's Soviet-backed rival with bribes including cars as well as cash coupled with threats of a military coup if Gizenga won.[34]

The next task was to reunify the country. While the Belgians secretly supported Tshombe in Katanga, they also urged other Western nations not to recognize his government in order to prevent a dilution of their influence. The main supporters of the breakaway state were highly conservative chiefs such as Tshombe's sinister Interior Minister, Godefroid Munongo, who believed that Lumumba was a modernizing Satan, and the large European community, which in the new dawn of Katanga embraced blacks whom its members despised. Since Tshombe had reason

to mistrust his own forces, he recruited 400 more reliable white mercenaries, notably the French soldier of fortune Robert 'Bob' Denard and
the South African 'Mad Mike' Hoare, to lead them. The spirit of the
Algerian OAS had come to the Congo.[35] There was no love lost between
the mercenaries and the UN. At one diplomatic cocktail party, a Swedish UN colonel felt something pressed into his back. Turning round, he
saw that a French mercenary had jabbed him with part of a human face:
'You are betraying the last bastion of the white man in Central Africa.
You will get a knife in your back one of these days,' he warned the
Swede.[36]

There was general lawlessness in Katanga, where the two top UN
civilian officials were kidnapped and assaulted by Tshombe's drugged
thugs just as they arrived at a dinner to honour US Senator Thomas
Dodd, ironically a figure nicknamed 'the Senator from Katanga' in his
own country. Urquhart, one of these officials, was head-butted, kicked
and then repeatedly hit with rifle butts in the back of a truck. The wife
of the US Consul exclaimed, 'Why, if it isn't that nice Mr Smith!' as her
husband's car passed the truck in which a UN representative of that
name was being beaten up alongside Urquhart. While Smith was freed,
Urquhart was detained until a UN Gurkha colonel threatened to blow
up Tshombe's palace if he was not released. Urquhart had the satisfaction of bleeding all over the seats of the fancy white convertible sent by
Tshombe.[37]

The UN sent Brigadier K. A. S. Raja, commander of the 99th Infantry Brigade, the Indian component of the UN peacekeeping force, and
the Irish envoy Conor Cruise O'Brien to compel both shadowy Belgian
civilian advisers and the mercenaries to leave, and to negotiate an end to
the Katangan secession. 'Who is Conor O'Brien?' Prime Minister Macmillan once asked in rhetorical exasperation at being obliged to contemplate the Congo. His own reply was 'an unimportant, expendable man'.
It was not the least of Macmillan's errors of judgement.

O'Brien was born in 1917 in a Dublin suburb, to a journalist and
teacher with sufficiently independent views in this clerical state to send
him to a non-denominational school. From there he went to Trinity College, Dublin, that residual redoubt of Anglo-Irish Protestantism.[38]
O'Brien grew up knowing that while one uncle had been killed by the

British during the Easter Rising, another had perished in British uniform on the Western Front. His identity became further blurred when in 1939 he married into a liberal Presbyterian family from Belfast, where he was working as a supply teacher. The Irish exemplar was not to prove the key to remoter problems, though many have entertained this delusion since in other times and contexts.[39]

In 1942 O'Brien joined the Irish Department of Finance, transferring after a couple of years to the Department of External Affairs. For an Irishman with an anti-colonial background, the newly founded United Nations beckoned, a forum in which a very small nation could punch above its weight by striking moral poses. By this route O'Brien arrived at the breakaway province of Katanga as Hammarskjöld's delegate in June 1961.

O'Brien met Munongo, who always wore dark glasses, and Tshombe, who had gone into politics as a more lucrative alternative to grocery. Dealing with the latter was as easy as trying to squeeze an eel into a bottle.[40] O'Brien's remit was to remove the European mercenaries as the prelude to a political settlement of the Katanga secession. He confidently announced that Operation Rumpunch, which began in August 1961, had been successful because he had got the Belgian civilian advisers out, but he failed to realize that the expelled mercenaries were simply returning via Rhodesia. He was horrified when Irish UN troops at Jadotville were compelled to surrender by a combined force of Belgian settlers and Katangese gendarmes led by mercenaries and supported by a Fouga Magister jet. O'Brien took it on himself to launch a second operation, codenamed Morthur (the Hindi word for 'smash'), which imposed UN control on many parts of Katanga by dispensing with the concept of minimal force by employing heavy weapons. Morthur could not prevent Tshombe's mercenary-officered gendarmes from burning down many villages loyal to the central government, which in turn triggered a refugee crisis with 75,000 people ending up in UN-administered camps. It also failed to capture Tshombe, who fled to Northern Rhodesia.

Chastened by the Bay of Pigs fiasco in Cuba, on which more later, Kennedy refused to help the UN force with air support, notwithstanding the fact that the US was largely paying for Hammarskjöld's increasingly autonomous Congolese operation. The British were also obstructive, prohibiting weapons flights to cross Uganda. After the French had also refused financial support, Hammarskjöld decided to try to mediate with Tshombe in person. He died when his aircraft crashed en route from Léopoldville to Ndola in Northern Rhodesia, where he hoped to broker a meeting between Tshombe and Adoula. Though some persist in claiming that the Swede was assassinated, in fact the crash was probably due to pilot error during a night flight.

Different elements of the US administration gave Kennedy conflicting advice. Non-interventionists thought the Congo 'has a right to its own War of the Roses', while others wanted the US to contribute military assistance to UN operations, a view forcefully argued by UN Ambassador Adlai Stevenson. While Kennedy vacillated about whether to bolster the UN force with American planes and troops, the new UN Secretary-General – the Burmese U Thant – abandoned his lifelong pacifism and ordered UN forces to suppress army mutineers in Kivu Province after they had abducted and murdered thirteen Italian airmen serving with the UN.

Despite many misgivings, Kennedy decided to put US prestige on the line. Threatening to deploy jets and helicopters, he helped the UN broker a ceasefire, and sent his personal plane to fly Tshombe to Kitona for talks with Adoula. Placed under house arrest by Mobutu, Tshombe promptly agreed to merge his 18,000 troops with those of the central government, and to take his place in parliament in Léopoldville. The secession seemed to be over, but just as Kennedy was congratulating himself on his successful mediation Tshombe was freed and reneged on the agreement, with his southern power base seemingly as secure as ever. The only positive development was that Adoula and Mobutu finally suppressed Gizenga's rebellion in Orientale. Gizenga survived imprisonment for the next two and a half years on the malarial island of Bula Bemba.[41]

Meanwhile the Soviets had returned to the Congo, with a diplomatic mission consisting mainly of KGB officers, which was initially based in Gizenga's Stanleyville. The pro-Western Adoula put obstacles in the way of their accreditation for as long as he could, as did the CIA. Having failed to bug the premises the Soviets would occupy before they arrived, Devlin hired a colourfully attired witch doctor to dance and chant in front of the embassy, cursing anyone who entered, to inhibit the KGB's ability to recruit Congolese agents.[42] According to Second Secretary Yuri Viktorov:

> We immediately faced the problems of food, clothing, and service. Shops were empty; all that we could buy there were American chickens, which seemed to have been frozen during World War II, and sometimes fish. At the local markets, there were lots of tropical fruit at a very low price – bananas, pineapples, papaya, mangoes etc. But there were no fruits to which we were accustomed – apples, pears, plums etc. Only occasionally could we buy meat, and what was especially bad, there was almost no milk or other dairy products.

Consumer durables could only be bought across the river at Brazzaville in French Congo, though even there there was not much to be had to furnish a flat in Moscow, let alone a country dacha, the humdrum goals of all Soviet diplomats and their spouses.[43]

Kennedy threw his weight behind State Department plans for a graduated economic embargo on Katanga's cobalt and copper, while pressuring the big mining interests to pay their corporate taxes directly to the central government rather than to Elisabethville. US transport aircraft flew UN forces and their supplies wherever they needed to go. After Katangan forces had shot down a UN helicopter on Christmas Eve 1962, the UN launched Operation Grand Slam after a delay caused by British reluctance to supply the UN's Indian aircraft with bombs. The Katangan air force was destroyed and ground forces moved quickly enough to prevent Tshombe from realizing his threat to blow up all the mines under his control. Brushing aside Tshombe's attempts to buy himself time through more negotiations, U Thant ordered his troops to press ahead until in late January 1963 Tshombe threw in the towel and fled, ultimately to Franco's Spain.

That May Kennedy received the thirty-two-year-old General Joseph Mobutu in the White House. Outside in the Rose Garden, as they posed for pictures, Kennedy remarked, 'General, if it hadn't been for you, the whole thing would have collapsed and the Communists would have taken over.' Mobutu modestly agreed: 'I do what I am able to do.'[44] Since the UN force was about to depart, Mobutu asked whether the US might provide the arms and technicians needed to help modernize the Congolese army. He inquired whether he and ten fellow officers might receive parachute training at Forts Bragg and Benning. All this could be arranged, said a 'delighted' President.[45] In 1965 Mobuto deposed Kasavubu to rule Zaire, as he renamed the Congo in 1971. He would be warmly regarded by Nixon, Carter – with Zaire receiving half of US aid to sub-Saharan Africa during his presidency – Reagan and George H. W. Bush.

The crisis in the Congo has become a textbook example of the almost intractable problems that statesmen face in real time and within a kind of fog of conflicting forces and inadequate intelligence. While the CIA conspiracy to murder Lumumba has given plenty of reasons for retrospective moral outrage, it is worth considering the imponderables and uncertainties of a foreign policy crisis that combined a local risk of anarchy with the real prospect of Soviet aggrandizement in a strategically crucial area of Central Africa. Belgium, Britain and France all had their separate agendas, as did some of the African participating nations. Nor was US attention constant, as Kennedy had to deal simultaneously with the challenges of the Berlin Wall and the Cuban Missile Crisis. Finally, it was unfortunate that the largest peacekeeping operation in UN history involved a state larger than Western Europe, and that the armed mission exceeded both its capacities and its original mandate. While O'Brien revelled in a world-level role not enjoyed by any Irishman before or since, peacekeeping was probably not best done with fighter-bombers and tanks.[46]

Guinea and Ghana

The Congolese crisis was a violent version of a rapidly developing Cold War in Africa.[47] Elsewhere the contest was less sanguinary, though still conducted in deadly earnest in this vast proxy venue. West Africa was a major theatre. In Soviet eyes, the former French colony of Guinea, about the same size as Great Britain or Oregon but containing half the world's known reserves of bauxite, represented the best 'window into Africa'. Its president, Sékou Touré, was an aristocratic Marxist-Leninist postal workers' union activist. In 1958 Touré's party won a referendum for immediate independence and a rejection of the new French Community, the only Francophone African colony to opt for such a repudiation.

The rest gained their independence two years later, but in Guinea the French were spitefully vindictive. All French administrators and technicians left almost overnight, ripping out telephone cables and even smashing light bulbs. What could not be burned was tipped into the ocean. In addition, there was the more general problem that the colonial powers had never linked infrastructures between adjacent countries. This did not apply just to roads, but even to telecommunications. If you wanted to make a telephone call from the Guinean capital of Conakry to Freetown in Sierra Leone (eighty miles away), the calls had to be routed through either London or Paris.[48]

The Soviet embassy opened in Conakry in April 1959 and military hardware followed, with three light tanks making a big impression at a Soviet-style parade. The East Germans installed an urban public address system, but Africans tired of blaring propaganda. Trade deals also ensued, but an anti-capitalist Soviet economy produced little to trade and Guinea had nothing with which to pay for it. As a Radio Moscow correspondent explained to a US acquaintance: 'We gave them what they wanted, and they didn't know what to do with it.' The Soviets kept altering the terms of barter so that iron ore and bauxite had to be added to consignments of bananas and oranges. This was part cheap buy-in, part an attempt to extend Soviet influence to West Africa.

A hodgepodge of badly made Eastern Bloc equipment and spoiled Chinese rice turned up to rust or rot on Conakry's docks, for despite mass famine at home Mao could export 15,000 tons of rice to Guinea in 1960.[49] Soviet largesse included lavatory bowls for homes with no bathrooms or plumbing (even in the presidential palace, Touré had to go to the ground floor to wash his hands since the water pressure was unable to reach his second-floor offices). Six tons of quill pens were accompanied by enough tinned crabmeat for half a century, although the snowploughs famously left to rust were in fact supposed to be brush cutters. Machines and vehicles lacked French-language maintenance manuals and so ended up rusting in ditches. Bigger capital projects disappointed: a print works operated at below 5 per cent capacity; a radio station was erected over an iron-ore vein, which interfered with its signals; and a tomato cannery was built in an area that had neither water nor tomatoes.[50]

Faced with this reality Touré turned westwards, especially to finance his favourite project, the Koukoure hydroelectric dam needed to power a huge aluminium smelter at Boku. In December 1961 he expelled the Soviet Ambassador Daniel Solod on a trumped-up charge of fomenting a teachers' strike and halved the number of Soviet advisers and technicians in Guinea. The following October he visited Washington, where he was well received. Returning home, Touré denied the Soviets landing and refuelling rights at a runway they had earlier built, and which they needed to circumvent the US naval quarantine around Cuba. Khrushchev responded by cutting all aid to Guinea, remarking that 'the President behaves like a boor; don't give him any assistance'. Soviet–Guinean relations took a further turn for the worse after the KGB tried to abduct and fly out an attractive Russian teacher who had fallen in love with a Haitian diplomat. A sharp Guinean customs officer prevented her removal and the word spread that the Russians had objected to the relationship because the Haitian was black. In the end Touré did not get much more than warm words from the US and eventually turned to the Gulf Arabs for funding.[51]

The Soviets also initially enjoyed good relations with the pan-Africanist Kwame Nkrumah, leader of Ghana, previously the British colony of the Gold Coast, and the first black African nation to achieve independence. The country started independent life from a higher base than Guinea since it had $200 million in the bank and a good civil service. A low-level Soviet delegation attended independence celebrations in Accra in March 1957; the US sent Nixon. Nkrumah wanted to dash for industrialization and modernization, his key project being the River Volta Dam, and to that end tacked back and forth between the US and USSR in opportunistic fashion. A Soviet embassy opened and a trade deal was concluded, involving the Russians taking 20,000–30,000 tons of cocoa beans. Attempts to widen commerce failed since the Soviets were unfamiliar with credit, payment on instalment or the need to display and explain their wares at local trade fairs. As Soviet farm managers could not turn a profit from giant agricultural collectives at home, what hope was there to do the same in Ghana?

The Americans regarded Nkrumah's close relations with the Soviets, central planning and various crackbrained socialist experiments with suspicion. But they nonetheless loaned him $37 million, with a further $97 million for the private consortium that was studying the feasibility of the dam. Like Guinea, Ghana refused the Soviets landing and refuelling rights during the Cuban Missile Crisis. Strategic defeat in the Congo and disappointing results in Guinea and Ghana inclined the Russians to look elsewhere for a foothold in sub-Saharan Africa, in the troubled Portuguese colonies of Angola and Mozambique to which the aged dictator António de Oliveira Salazar clung like grim death.[52]

Weary Men with Glazed Eyes and the White Redoubts

Among those who believed that Salazar was right to hang on were British supporters of white settlers in Rhodesia.[53] The British government was coming to another conclusion. The abrupt end of the French and Belgian empires in Africa put pressure on the British not to be the last to leave the party, especially since by loitering they attracted the focused hostility of Asian and African states at the UN. Did Britain really wish to end up in the same boat as Salazar's Portugal? France's futile war in Algeria was a fate the British government wished to avoid. 'It was idle dreaming to think that Britain, by force, could hold her position,' said Iain Macleod, Colonial Secretary in the crucial period from October 1959 to October 1961. 'If General de Gaulle with a million men couldn't hold Algeria, then we couldn't hold about a third of the continent.'[54]

What Britain did in Africa also affected relations with the US, where Kennedy was a great champion of independence movements – except in his own Latin backyard – and with India because of the many sub-continentals the British Empire had imported to East and Southern Africa. The chaos engulfing the Congo was a terrible warning of what might happen if majority rule were conceded without adequate preparation – but black nationalists also threatened chaos if the white minority clung to power for too long. These were loaded questions for the Conservative Party. While de Gaulle was never sentimental about the *pieds noirs*, British Conservative governments could not ignore their voters' favourable opinion of their 'kith and kin', supported by Conservative newspapers. In the 1950s and 1960s empire was as divisive and poisonous for the Conservatives as Europe would be from the 1980s onwards.

Harold Macmillan took it upon himself to lance the boil. The droopy-eyed Premier with the languid manner and the bons mots was personally innocent of what became outright decadence as symbolized by the 1963 sex scandal known as the Profumo Affair which finished off his administration. After an unhappy boyhood at Eton Macmillan enjoyed two years at Balliol College, Oxford, before the First World War intervened to end the Edwardian 'Indian summer'. His war record was distinguished by many acts of bravery, in the course of which he was wounded three times. Like most of his generation, it was hard to shake loose the feeling that their most talented contemporaries had been immortalized in bronze or stone at the threshold of their potential.[55]

After the war Macmillan entered the family publishing business, where he was a success, and then became a Conservative MP in 1923.[56] Six years later his wife Dorothy embarked on the lengthy affair with the bisexual Bob Boothby and Macmillan had a nervous breakdown. Under the influence of his friend John Maynard Keynes he became an advocate of economic planning, which joined his patrician concern for the disadvanted as a sort of political philosophy, though condescending guilt might better describe it. He had another 'good war' as minister resident at Allied Headquarters in Algiers. He handled the fractious French with aplomb (he spoke the language fluently) and forged enduring friendships with Eisenhower and his US counterpart Robert Murphy. However, during the January 1943 Casablanca conference, Macmillan shared with the future Labour Party intellectual Richard Crossman an hauteur that remained for the rest of his life: 'We, my dear Crossman, are Greeks in this American empire. You will find the Americans much as the Greeks found the Romans – great big vulgar, bustling people, more vigorous than we are and also more idle, with more unspoiled virtues, but also more corrupt. We must run Allied Forces Headquarters as the Greeks ran the operations of the Emperor Claudius.'[57]

On his return to Britain, Macmillan switched parliamentary seats from northern Stockton to suburban southern Bromley. Ideas he had promoted before the war became commonplace, as the Tories endeavoured to shape themselves around the nationalizations and statist planning of the newly elected Labour government.

When the Conservatives returned to office in October 1951, Macmillan became minister of housing. Older than either Eden at the Foreign Office or Butler at the Exchequer, Macmillan thought himself better than either. After Churchill's belated departure, Macmillan became Eden's first foreign secretary. Given Eden's claims to unique expertise, it was not a happy relationship. In December 1955 Eden made Macmillan chancellor of the exchequer. A year later the top job became vacant because of Suez, and in January 1957 Macmillan became prime minister.

At the start of his premiership, Macmillan commissioned several policy studies, including 'a profit and loss account' for each colony. Economic objections to granting independence were discarded. Rather, the colonies were defended on the grounds of moral responsibility, whether to the Asian minorities Britain had transplanted to African settings as a penny capitalist class, or to the white settlers who, with the aid of African labour, had made the colonies what they were. An abrupt abdication of responsibility towards the minorities was regarded as immoral.

There was a further consideration. The pervasive American fear that Communism would flourish in places denied their independence was less evident than British concern that the post-1948 apartheid regime in South Africa might exert a gravitational pull on the white settlers of Kenya, plus North and South Rhodesia, which with Nyasaland had become a Central African Federation in 1953.[58] A parallel defence review, undertaken by Duncan Sandys, recommended reducing expenditure from 10 to 7 per cent of Britain's GNP by 1962. To achieve this, the armed forces were to be slimmed down drastically and made all-volunteer services. A reduction in numbers from 690,000 to 375,000 men by the end of 1962 had obvious bearings on Britain's ability to fight major counter-insurgency wars. A third review concerning how Britain might best match ends and means during the decade ending in 1970 concluded that the Atlantic alliance with the US was the chief means of containing the Soviet threat, with Europe and the Commonwealth in supporting roles.[59]

Another consideration, this time a domestic one, influenced Macmillan as he prepared for a grand tour of Africa in early 1960. His party was divided into three shades of opinion about decolonization: imperial diehards, pragmatists and those who did not think very much about anything.[60] The Suez shambles had alienated many of the brightest young people and Macmillan hoped to recapture their moral imaginations by projecting a 'big picture' for post-imperial Britain. This became an urgent consideration once the horrors of Hola became general knowledge, and a judicial inquiry described Nyasaland (where Dr Hastings Banda and other nationalists had been imprisoned in the course of Operation Sunrise) as 'a police state'.[61]

With his Commons majority increased to over a hundred following the election in October 1959, Macmillan's six-week tour of Africa began in January 1960 in independent Ghana where Nkrumah welcomed the sixty-five-year-old British Prime Minister. The next stop was Nigeria, which was about to become a Dominion and which was scheduled for independence in 1963. There Macmillan casually observed that the Central African Federation was not necessarily permanent. This was news to Sir Roy Welensky, the Federation's Prime Minister.[62] Welensky was a tough operator, the son of a Lithuanian Jew and an Afrikaner mother who nonetheless thought of himself as '100 per cent' British. He had come up the hard way, as a railway union activist who in his youth had also been Rhodesia's heavyweight boxing champion. Macmillan's patrician charm was water off a duck's back when they conferred at Salisbury's Government House. 'The sight of big powers scuttling out of colonial responsibilities makes me sick,' said Welensky.

But this was as nothing to the storm Macmillan ran into on 3 February, when he ventured forth from Bechuanaland – one of the three high-commission enclaves within the Union of South Africa – to address parliament assembled in Cape Town. British commercial, sporting and wartime ties with South Africa were multiple. These bonds were shredded by the ascendancy of Boers with a grudge born out of the suppression of their independent republics at the turn of the century, men who sounded like a Dutch version of German Nazis.[63] Undeterred by the grim faces in his audience, Macmillan said:

the most striking of all the impressions I have formed since I left London a month ago is of the strength of this African national consciousness. In different places it takes different forms, but it is happening everywhere. The wind of change is blowing through this continent, and, whether we like it or not, this growth of national consciousness is a political fact. We must accept it as a fact, and our national policies must take account of it.

This was met with icy silence and restrained applause at the end. Thunderous clapping greeted the South African Premier Hendrik Verwoerd, when he reminded Macmillan that the white man had rights in South Africa too, their presence long predating that of Bantu migrants.

The winds of change became a gale once Iain Macleod became colonial secretary. When Macmillan said, 'Iain, I've got the worst job of all for you,' Macleod knew he was going to the Colonial Office, despite never having visited a British colony, although his youngest brother was a farmer in Kenya. His sibling reported that an African who had fought the Japanese on behalf of the British 'didn't take kindly to removing his hat in his own country in the District Commissioner's Office to ask for a pass to visit a cousin in the next village'.[64]

The son of a medical doctor from the island of Lewis, Macleod grew up in Yorkshire, where his father practised, but he remained a middle-class Scot in a party of upper-class Englishmen. He was a successful professional card player whom the war sobered up, an ideas man who adorned the new Research Department of a party in which the term clever was a veiled insult. He became an extremely effective speaker on health questions, and an advocate of One Nation Toryism, while penning a regular bridge column for the *Sunday Times*.

After coming to Churchill's attention in May 1952, the thirty-eight-year-old bright spark became minister of health in the new Conservative government. Three years later Eden appointed Macleod to his cabinet as minister of labour, which kept him clear of responsibility for the Suez debacle, and suited him to be the new broom Macmillan was looking for to liquidate the empire.

Knowing next to nothing of the colonies enabled Macleod to pursue a few key ideas. He recognized the illogic of Britain granting independence to West African nations while denying it in East Africa because of the white settler minorities. For, regardless of anything decided in

Whitehall, a rapid chain reaction was occurring in Africa. The quality of British colonial administration, which in some parts of Africa was undeniably good, could not be an excuse for denying Africans the right to govern themselves. Macleod rejected the idea that white settlers knew what was best for the African majorities and declared his aim to proceed 'not as fast as the Congo and not as slow as Algeria'.[65]

Macleod lifted the state of emergency in Kenya, which meant the release of the remaining detainees, with the former 'terrorist' Kenyatta becoming an interlocutor. As a lifelong gambler, Macleod was eminently suited to the ensuing conferences in which black and white men sat around a table, arranging the constitutional frameworks for new East African nations. During conference sessions he first let each delegate deliver the setpiece speech he had burning in his pocket, to clear the air for detailed bargaining. He was ruthless in encouraging fissures between moderate whites and the diehards, while of course there were exploitable fissures among the blacks too, for beneath the fancy political party acronyms lured deep anxieties about one tribe dominating others, as well as an all too human desire to get their hands on the levers and rewards of independent statehood.[66] In this cumulatively exhausting manner the tracks were cleared for Tanganyika, Uganda and Kenya to become independent nations.

The fate of the Central African Federation caused the most acrimony. Established in 1953, this was the great black and white hope – so to speak – of British sponsorship of a multiracial polity, distinctive in feel from the grim Calvinist redoubt of Pretoria. Actually, for a black person – referred to as 'It' and debarred from using urban pavements – the tangible differences between Southern Rhodesia and South Africa were marginal.[67]

Opinion in the Conservative Party was as divided about the white settlers as it was united in doubting the ability of the black Africans to govern themselves. Macmillan regarded Kenyan and Rhodesian whites as the deracinated scum of the earth and belittled Welensky's patriotism as the outpourings of 'an emotional Lithuanian Jew'. Macmillan and Macleod were not above misleading Welensky to the effect that Britain would never tolerate black secession from the Central African Federation, not least because the cattle and tobacco farmers of Southern Rhodesia would find themselves in trouble without the copper of Northern Rhodesia (it shared the Copper Belt with Katanga) or Nyasaland's labour pool.

In fact, the Federation was a British delusion of an essentially idealistic kind. Whites were very unevenly distributed across the three constituent territories, which also had five governments if one includes the British. As far as the northern Africans were concerned, the Federation was simply a constitutional confidence trick enabling white domination of Southern Rhodesia. This was why the Monckton Commission into the Federation's future in October 1960 recommended swift moves to majority African rule in Nyasaland and Northern Rhodesia, and parity between whites and blacks in the federal assembly. In so far as it touched on Southern Rhodesia – apart from recommending the relocation of the federal capital – it was to suggest that it should divest itself of racially discriminatory practices that associated it too closely with South Africa.[68]

These manoeuvres appalled 'Bobbety' Salisbury, the Cecil family dynast after whose grandfather the Southern Rhodesian capital was named. Salisbury liked Welensky and white Rhodesians in general, even as he grew to dislike the slippery Macmillan and Macleod, whom he regarded as a Scots cardsharp. After Welensky had supplied Salisbury with confidential correspondence from Macmillan, the Prime Minister put his former colleague under MI5 surveillance. Salisbury himself formed a covert Watching Committee to subject Macmillan to a war of attrition. He also sought to counteract the liberal Conservatism of the Macmillan/Macleod variety by patronizing the ultra-reactionary Monday Club. On 7 March 1961, the aged Salisbury roused the House of Lords from its usual torpor with a vitriolic defence of the white man in Africa. Although the speech was remembered for his 'too clever by half' comment about Macleod, its target was really Macmillan. At times the speech turned truly personal:

> It is not considered immoral, or even bad form, to outwit one's opponents at bridge. On the contrary, the more you outwit them, within the rules of the game, the better player you are. It almost seems to me that the Colonial Secretary, when he abandoned the sphere of bridge for the sphere of politics, brought his bridge technique with him. At any rate, it has become, as your Lordships know, the convinced view

of the white population in Eastern and Central Africa that it has been his object to outwit them, and that he has done so successfully.[69]

There was some truth in this: Macleod's approach to politics was indeed as a game he played to win. While Macmillan and Salisbury eventually restored outward civilities – though it was 'Dear Prime Minister' rather than 'My dear Harold' thereafter in correspondence – Macmillan decided that Macleod was a liability and dumped him. Under his successor, Reggie Maudling, the Federation was dissolved in 1963 and a year later Nyasaland metamorphosed into Malawi and Northern Rhodesia into Zambia, led by Hastings Banda and Kenneth Kaunda respectively. There was general confidence that having these moderate African states in the Commonwealth (and hence truly out of South Africa's dangerous orbit) outweighed anything the aggrieved white Rhodesians could manage. That proved a false calculation with the rise of the Rhodesian Front and its dogged leader, Ian Smith, who in 1965 declared Unilateral Independence to defend a way of life, with its barbecues and swimming pools, more American than British if my memories of the 1960s are at all accurate. While the Americans tended to regard Africa as a British thing, or at least the parts of it we have been considering (other than Algeria), in their own hemisphere their policy had always been to prevent outside interference. Sometimes this involved their own aggressive interventions.

15. BACKYARD BLUES: CUBA

Mare Nostrum

The US has always felt proprietary about Latin America and in particular the Caribbean basin. It proclaimed hemispheric hegemony in the 1823 Monroe Doctrine, seven decades before it had the navy to enforce it. During the US imperialist spasm under Presidents William McKinley and Teddy Roosevelt, Cuba and Puerto Rico were taken from Spain in 1898, and in 1903 Panama was detached from Colombia to ensure US ownership of the planned inter-oceanic canal. The US intervened five times in the isthmus before 1903 and further four times in the next fifteen years. In 1905, after he had placed the Dominican Republic under 'customs receivership' to protect creditors, Teddy Roosevelt declared the US to be 'the policeman' of the Caribbean and sent the Marines into Honduras, the first of five such interventions over the next twenty years.

Successive presidents ordered US military interventions in the 'backyard', although the 'Progressive' Democrat Woodrow Wilson was much the most robust in coercing democracy. US troops were sent into Cuba in 1906–8 and 1912, and they were a more or less permanent feature in Honduras (1905–25), Nicaragua (1912–33), Haiti (1915–34) and the Dominican Republic (1916–24), while the Mexican port of Vera Cruz was shelled and occupied in 1914. The failure of direct interventions to bring about any permanent change in what one under secretary of state called 'rotten little countries' led President Franklin Roosevelt to announce the 'Good Neighbor' policy in 1933, a switch to informal methods of control, with dollars replacing bullets and stability ensured through local strongmen.[1]

There is no question that the cascade of US military interventions sits heavily on the historical record. The fact that they were wrapped in paternalist verbiage (Wilson's 'a world fit for democracy' springs to mind) simply added insult to injury. The maverick Marine Major-General Smedley Butler, one of the most decorated soldiers in US history, had this to say about his own career:

I spent 33 years in active military service and during that period I spent most of my time as a high class thug for Big Business, for Wall Street and the bankers. In short, I was a racketeer, a gangster for capitalism. I helped make Mexico safe for American oil interests. I helped make Haiti and Cuba a decent place for the National City Bank boys to collect revenues. I helped in the raping of half a dozen Central American republics for the benefit of Wall Street. I helped purify Nicaragua for the Banking House of Brown Brothers. I brought light to the Dominican Republic for the American sugar interests. I helped make Honduras right for the American fruit companies. Looking back on it, I might have given Al Capone a few hints. The best he could do was to operate his racket in three districts. I operated on three continents.[2]

By 1960, US direct investment in Latin America totalled over $8 billion, which represented a quarter of all US overseas investment. US capital was preferentially invested in extractive enterprises, although North Americans also had large land-holdings and ranches too. Latin America also accounted for 20 per cent of US foreign trade, and in the case of Cuba the US bought 74 per cent of the island's exports and supplied 65 per cent of its imports.[3] In many parts of Latin America US ambassadors were potentates in the land, often the second most important persons after the presidents. New embassy buildings employed a lot of plate-glass frontage, engraved with the bald eagle, to suggest modernity, transparency and power. But the money actually expended on policy initiatives in Latin America suggested that the Eisenhower administration did not really believe in the Communist threat there. Compelling evidence of Soviet activity in the Western hemisphere in the 1950s was minimal.

Indeed the Russians were barely present, for until 1960 Moscow maintained embassies only in Argentina, Mexico and Uruguay. Trade with the Soviet Union was a very modest 2 per cent of Latin America's annual total, and did not compete with US interests at all, since Americans did not need grain or beef from Argentina or Uruguay.[4]

The Duck Test

At his confirmation hearings, Foster Dulles compared the situation in Latin America in the 1950s with China in the 1930s: it was not going to be 'lost' on his watch.[5] In mid-March 1953 National Security Council document 144/1 outlined US policy towards the region: to ensure continued Latin American support for the US within the UN; to encourage orderly economic and political development; to guarantee the flow of commodities and strategic raw materials; and to combat Communism, both internally and through joint hemispheric defence. The more detailed annexe said that 'overriding security interests' might require unilateral US intervention even though 'this would be a violation of our treaty commitments, would endanger the Organization of American States (OAS) . . . and would probably intensify anti-US attitudes in many Latin American countries'.[6]

In March 1954, Dulles received overwhelming backing at the Tenth Inter-American Conference at Caracas to extend 'the Monroe Doctrine to include the concept of outlawing foreign ideologies in the American Republics'. This was a restatement of the 1904 Roosevelt Corollary to the Monroe Doctrine, under which Teddy Roosevelt had arrogated a right to 'stabilize' regimes in the region by sending in the Marines to pre-empt European interference in their revolutions, civil wars and debt crises. Seventeen governments approved Dulles's proposal; Argentina and Mexico abstained. Guatemala's President Jacobo Árbenz Guzmán was the naysayer.[7]

Although he had not been expressly named, Árbenz was the target of what he called Dulles's 'internationalization of McCarthyism' for in truth he was scarcely a threat to the US. Árbenz was the first leader in Guatemala's 130-year history to benefit from a peaceful and legitimate transfer of power. But his agrarian reforms brought him into conflict with the United Fruit Company, known to local opponents as 'the Octopus'. The tentacles were very long. Ann Whitman, Eisenhower's personal secretary, was married to Ed Whitman, United Fruit's chief Washington lobbyist, while as a corporate lawyer Dulles himself had represented the company on many occasions. Árbenz effectively flunked what in 1950 the US Ambassador in Guatemala City described as the 'duck test': 'Suppose you see a bird walking around in a farmyard. This bird wears no label that says "duck". But he certainly looks like a duck. Also, he goes to the pond and you notice he swims like a duck. Then he opens his beak and quacks like a duck. Well, by this time you have probably reached the conclusion that the bird is a duck, whether he's wearing a label or not.'[8]

Apparently free to topple governments around the world, and emboldened by the overthrow of Iran's Mossadeq, the CIA repeated the trick in Guatemala with Operation PBSUCCESS in June 1954. Like Mossadeq, Árbenz suffered a loss of nerve and failed to rally the popular support that would have called the bluff of the minimal forces deployed against him. A year after the coup, CIA officers were still vainly combing Guatemala's government records for any evidence of Communist infiltration of the overthrown regime; however Árbenz's wife did say that her husband believed 'the triumph of Communism in the world was inevitable and desirable'. What Guatemala got instead was a gang of right-wing thugs – and the US a puppet. 'Tell me what you want me to do and I will do it' were the first words the figurehead of the coup, Colonel Carlos Armas, said to Vice President Nixon when he came to Washington to pay his respects.[9]

The US Information Agency and the Inter-American Organization of Workers were the principal tools for combating 'Communist' subversion. USIA flooded Latin American newspapers and radio stations with comic strips and radio scripts, and the IAOW backed labour leaders of the right cast of mind, but neither was a big budgetary item. Nor, intriguingly, was the military assistance budget: $400 million was appropriated, but very little of it translated into weapons deliveries. The co-ordination of hemispheric defence was viewed as pointless and the State Department was adamant that Latin American nations should be discouraged from wasting money on modern weapons.

Much more crucial were the personal bonds forged between Latin

American military officers and their US counterparts – not least because of the prevalence of military dictatorships in the hemisphere. The ones in the 'backyard' tended to wear comic-opera uniforms and to have their chests emblazoned with self-awarded medals, often just for murdering their own people. The Dominican Republic dictator Rafael Trujillo was known as 'Chapitas' (Bottletops) because of this habit, although he was also referred to as 'the Goat' because of his relentless exercise of a latter-day *droit de seigneur.* Trujillo was a product of the National Guards trained by the Americans to maintain political stability after they withdrew their Marines. He ruled the Dominican Republic from 1930 until his death in 1961 at the hands of assassins given sniper rifles by the CIA. Killing him was primarily a balancing act so that Latin sympathies would not be so outraged when the CIA organized the death of Fidel Castro.[10] Another dictator to emerge from a National Guard was Anastasio Somoza, who ruled Nicaragua with what really involved an iron fist from 1936 until his assassination twenty years later.[11]

In February 1953 Foster Dulles recommended to Eisenhower, 'you have to pat them a little bit and make them think that you are fond of them'.[12] Both Manuel Odría (dictator of Peru) and Marcos Pérez Jiménez (dictator of Venezuela) received the Legion of Merit, the highest award the US confers on foreigners. The fawning conduct of some US ambassadors towards corrupt tyrants was embarrassing. As in the case of Pakistan's Ayub Khan, uniform spoke unto uniform, in this case strongmen like Paraguay's General Alfredo Stroessner.

Despite the absence of a Communist threat, the administration used its second major review of policy towards the region to widen the scope for intervention along the lines of Guatemala. In September 1956, NSC 5613/1 included the ominous warning that, 'if a Latin American state should establish with the Soviet bloc close ties of such a nature as seriously to prejudice our vital interests, the United States would be prepared to diminish governmental economic and financial cooperation with that country and take any other political, economic, or military actions deemed appropriate'. No sooner had the administration adopted this line than its major figures effectively denied the basis for it. In November 1957 Foster Dulles told journalists: 'we see no likelihood at the present time of Communism getting into control of the political institutions of any of the American Republics'. The following year his brother Allen testified to Congress that Communism in Latin America was not 'a situation to be frightened of as an overall problem'.[13]

There was considerable, if episodic, evidence that many people did not love the US. In May 1958, during a state visit to Venezuela, where Pérez Jiménez had recently been overthrown, the limousine carrying Vice President Nixon and his wife Patricia was spat on and attacked by rioters in Caracas. This was a blow to the American belief that they were universally respected, and some 85,000 Washington bureaucrats were given time off to line the streets when Nixon returned, brandishing placards saying 'Don't Let Those Commies Get You Down, Dick'.[14] The experience resulted in a curious bifurcation of US policy, although top policy-makers remained convinced that excitable Latins loved (or at least needed) authoritarian men on horseback.[15]

The term 'Latin America' dates from the French attempt to install an emperor in Mexico during the US civil war, when they dreamed of establishing a Latin empire to counter the 'Anglo-Saxons'. *Plus ça change . . .* European critics are even more prone than the citizens of that part of the continent that has appropriated the word 'America' for itself to facile generalizations about the other nations of the hemisphere. Chile has experienced only three *coups d'état* since 1830, whereas its neighbour Bolivia has had a blur of them. The ethnic mixes are just as varied, ranging from all-African Francophone Haiti, through largely Amerindian Guatemala, Ecuador, Peru, Bolivia and Paraguay, to virtually all-European Argentina and Uruguay, and (pre-Castro) Cuba, where blacks and mulattos were a quarter of the population. Paradoxically, the foundations for the remarkably untroubled modern history of little Costa Rica were laid by José 'Pepe' Figueres, who seized power from a democratically elected president in 1948 and promptly abolished the army, nationalized the banks, and granted women and blacks the vote. Despite being a rancher, he also instituted land reform. What he did not do was indulge in strident anti-*yanqui* rhetoric, for he had studied at MIT and had two successive American wives, with the result that, although balefully regarded by the CIA, he was the poster boy of the State Department, and Costa Rica became an island of peaceful democracy surrounded by variously extreme anti- and pro-US guerrilla movements and dictators. The State Department ensured that Somoza did not kill him.[16]

In August 1958 Eisenhower, despite the indignities endured by his Vice President, welcomed the Ambassador of newly democratic Venezuela with the words: 'authoritarianism and autocracy of whatever form are incompatible with the ideals of our great leaders of the past'. These fine words were not matched with economic assistance, however much they represented a rhetorical departure from traditional US policy – Ike's belief in free trade over taxpayer-funded aid was too strong for that. Latin Americans wanted a regional Marshall Plan, as though over a century of self-government had produced a situation akin to a Europe devastated by war. When Brazilian President Juscelino Kubitschek called for a $40 billion Operation Pan America in 1958, the response was an Inter-American Development Bank, with the US providing 45 per cent of its one-billion-dollar capitalization. It was a relatively small beginning; nonetheless Eisenhower would claim paternity rights over the more ostentatious aid programmes of his successor John Kennedy.[17]

Gangster Island

The duck test was at the heart of the US response to a mounting crisis in Cuba during the last years of the Eisenhower administration. The Platt Amendment to the constitution imposed on Cuba in 1901 had symbolized the island's subordination to the US, curtailing its ability to conduct an independent foreign policy and to contract unsupervised loans. The US also acquired long leases on two naval bases, including Guantanamo Bay. While Franklin Roosevelt rescinded the Platt Amendment in 1934, and Cuba became one of the most prosperous Hispanic American republics, the relationship with the US remained neo-colonial and a burning affront to Cuban nationalists.

Unfortunately, although the island could boast a culturally vibrant and generally free society, Cuban politics were stunningly corrupt and, especially in the autonomous national university, extremely violent. It was ruled dictatorially from 1952 onwards by the mulatto Fulgencio Batista, a former army sergeant who had cunningly taken over a

US-sponsored revolution in 1933 against the dictator Gerardo Machado and acted as kingmaker in the elections that followed. In 1940 he won the presidency for himself in fair elections, with the full backing of Cuba's labour unions and the tiny Communist Party (which he had legalized), and promulgated a constitution inspired by collectivist ideas that was considered the most 'progressive' outside the Soviet Union. There were two Communists in his government, though that did not unduly discommode the Americans. The constitution forbade him to succeed himself and he retired to Florida's Daytona Beach in 1944.[18]

After his return to Cuba, Batista rapidly shed his earlier respect for constitutional proprieties. When it became apparent that he was not going to win the 1952 elections, he and his military supporters seized power. Political parties were suspended and elections deferred. The US government recognized the new regime, which was also welcomed by the US investors who controlled the island's sugar industry and enjoyed a quota arrangement that guaranteed US purchase of 40 per cent of the annual harvest at a generous price. Increased world demand for sugar during the Korean War gave Cuba the second highest per-capita GDP in Latin America, making it an irresistible prize for Batista and the shady cronies he had acquired during his eight-year exile.

Batista had become an intimate of Italian-Americans with such *noms de guerre* as 'Joe Bananas' or 'Fat Joe'. The leaders of US organized crime, Salvatore 'Lucky' Luciano, Meyer Lansky, Albert Anastasia and Santo Trafficante, had agreed to turn Havana into the 'Latin Las Vegas', and a key entrepot for North African heroin destined for the US. The deal was done in 1946, with crooner Frank Sinatra providing the night's entertainment. Batista was brought in on it early, becoming co-owner of Havana's Hotel Nacional with Luciano and Lansky.

By the mid-1950s the island was attracting 300,000 US tourists a year and Batista pledged to provide dollar for dollar matching funds for investors in Cuba's burgeoning hotel and gaming sectors. Anyone investing $1 million in a hotel or $200,000 in a nightclub would automatically receive a gaming licence, without such inconveniences as criminal background checks. As in earlier eras of prosperity, Americans travelled, many of them drawn to the thriving sex trade in a Havana thronged with whores and offering floor shows such as the one featuring

'Superman' and his fourteen-inch penis. They also tried their luck at gaming tables, while overall the mobsters enforced their own brand of justice by breaking the fingers of cardsharps and scam artists.

A quarter of the Batista government's 'dollar for dollar' was paid back to the President personally, and the police required over a million a month in protection money. In return the Mafia investors were exempted from formal taxation for ten years, and were freed from import duties on building materials, equipment and furnishings. Havana was soon lit up with garish casinos and clubs, including an entire wing of the Nacional that Lansky refurbished for high rollers, and where Eartha Kitt entertained the punters on opening night. Thereafter, Mrs Marta Batista's shadowy representative appeared each night with a big bag, one of the means whereby the Batistas amassed a fortune estimated at $300 million, not counting the brother who simultaneously pillaged the nation's parking-meter revenues.

Legitimate business was no more ethical. The telecoms giant AT&T presented Batista with a gold-plated telephone, still displayed in Havana, in return for hiking local call charges. The unrestrained rapacity of US investors, legal or illegal, compounded deep nationalist resentments. The place was ripe for a Latin Nasser; instead it got a Latin Lenin, although it took the US time to decide who it was dealing with. It took the Latin Lenin some time to decide who he was too.[19]

Castro Becomes Fidel

Fidel Castro was the second of five illegitimate children borne by a housemaid to an illiterate Galician immigrant who had built up a 10,000-acre sugarcane estate in eastern Oriente Province, an enterprise which employed 500 workers. Castro was brought up by his maternal grandparents, who lived in a shack, and was later sent to foster parents while he and his younger brother Raúl attended a Jesuit school in Santiago de Cuba. It was not until he was seventeen that his father finally married his mother and formally recognized his children by her. Thus, although he was indeed from a prosperous background – when he arrived at the University of Havana in 1945, it was in his own car – Castro grew up with the resentments of a 'poor white'.

Six foot three and powerfully built, at school Castro excelled at sports, particularly baseball. In 1949 he was offered a contract by the New York Giants. He turned them down.[20] He read voraciously, counting Alexander the Great, Napoleon, the Spanish Fascist José Antonio Primo de Rivera and Lenin among his heroes. It is not difficult to see how his early life also gave him a precocious passion for social justice. Although enrolled to study law at the university, he was clearly destined for politics and spent much of his time exercising his vocal cords. University politics were indistinguishable from gang warfare, and Castro became accustomed to carrying a gun.[21]

Had he been associated with left-wing politics, the CIA might have red-flagged him. But Castro neither waddled nor quacked nor bore any resemblance to the Communist duck. Quite to the contrary, at Havana University his mortal enemy was Rolando Masferrer, who had been a Communist Party enforcer in the Lincoln Battalion of the International Brigades in the Spanish civil war. Elected to the House of Representatives in 1949, under Batista Masferrer was to run Oriente Province as his personal fief, employing a murder squad known as 'the Tigers'.

In 1948 Castro took part in the violent disorders in Bogotá that accompanied the establishment of the Organization of American States. Young nationalists from all over the continent had gathered to protest against what the demagogic Argentine dictator Juan Domingo Perón denounced as a new manifestation of US imperialism; but the assassination of the populist Liberal Party leader Eliécer Gaitán detonated an anarchic civil war in Colombia known simply as *la Violencia*. The experience was defining in a way that whatever books Castro had read were not.

Castro may have struggled through a bit of Marx, but unlike his younger brother Raúl he did not join the Communist Youth Movement. The Communists were far too cautious, waiting for history to take its inevitable course, and Fidel was impatient to become a protagonist. He grew infatuated with the idea of being a revolutionary, of striking martial poses and giving 'the people' an authentic voice – a voice that could ramble on for hours at a stretch, without speaking notes.

Although he had married and started a family with the daughter of one of Batista's political henchmen, the coup of 1952 thwarted Castro's ambition to become a congressman. Still only twenty-seven, he felt a sense of urgency and on 26 July 1953 he and 150 followers launched attacks on the Moncada army barracks in Santiago de Cuba and at Bayamo in his home province. The aim was to seize weapons with which to arm a wider revolt. The attackers were outnumbered and half of them were captured, tortured and murdered. Adverse public reaction to such brutality benefited Castro by the time he surrendered four months later, and instead of being murdered he was tried and sentenced to fifteen years' imprisonment. At his trial he depicted himself as the spirit of historic Cuban liberties denied and pronounced that 'history will absolve me'. Following the rigged November 1954 elections, Castro was among those who gained from a general amnesty of political prisoners.

He, Raúl and the twenty or so members of his 26 July Movement went to Mexico, determined to return and overthrow Batista's government. They set up a guerrilla training camp on a farm about twenty miles outside Mexico City. There a fellow spirit entered Castro's life, the Argentine medical student Ernesto Guevara Lynch, known as 'Che' from a term unique to River Plate Spanish akin to 'pal' in English. Guevara had fled Guatemala at the time of the CIA coup, an experience that left him with a faith in revolution as a biological process, which 'cleanses men, improving them as the experimental farmer corrects the defects of his plant'. He was not especially clean himself, since never washing or changing his clothes was a mark of revolutionary authenticity. Like Raúl Castro, Guevara was better versed in Marxism than Fidel, although neither man could match his charisma.

On 24–25 November 1956, Castro and eighty-two armed adherents set sail for Cuba on the yacht *Granma*, paid for by the President Batista had deposed in 1952. Within a short time of landing they were almost annihilated in their initial contact with Batista's troops. Fifteen survivors escaped to the Sierra Maestra, the mountain range along Cuba's south-east coast in Oriente Province. Although the terrain was unpromising, the area was inhabited by peasant squatters aptly known as *precaristas*, whose hatred of the authorities made them invaluable allies of the small guerrilla band. Much the greater part of the resistance to Batista was carried out in the cities, where a vicious cycle of terrorist attacks and retaliatory police torture and summary executions simultaneously granted Castro's band the time necessary to establish themselves in the mountains while eliminating potential rivals to his leadership.

Castro's apotheosis into Fidel, the romantic, bearded legend in olive combat fatigues, came courtesy of the *New York Times*. A journalist called Herbert Matthews ventured into the Sierra Maestra, where he reported: 'The personality of the man is overpowering. It was easy to see that his men adored him . . . Here was an educated, dedicated fanatic, a man of ideals, of courage and of remarkable qualities of leadership . . . one got a feeling that he is now invincible.' Matthews did not notice that the 'hundreds' of fighters he observed in the guerrilla camp were a far smaller number rotated repeatedly into view by Raúl. Matthews's report caught the imaginations of many Americans and he was only the first of many foreigners, including some usually hard-headed Russians, to succumb to Fidel's magnetic presence.

Even the CIA station in Cuba did not buy Batista's charge that Fidel was a Communist, and he was regarded favourably by the State Department, which badly wanted the gangster regime gone. Adding to his lustre, the Cuban Communist Party supported Batista and disdained Castro's band of 'adventurers'. The Catholic Church gave qualified support to the resistance and even provided the guerrillas with a resident chaplain, while a major Cuban sugar baron donated $50,000. Raúl Castro and Guevara might talk Marxism late into the night, but at this stage the Movement was simply a patriotic front, combining moderate liberals with fervent anti-Communists backed by Trujillo, who hated his fellow dictator and whose agents in February 1957 shot their way into Batista's palace in a failed attempt to kill him. It was also overwhelmingly white and middle class, as Cuba's blacks and mulattos generally supported the mulatto Batista, and the labour unions were a pillar of his regime.

Even when his force was only 150 strong, Fidel acted as if he was ruling his part of Oriente Province, with his own newspaper and radio station. He issued decrees calling for non-payment of taxes to the government, and criminalizing anyone who joined the armed forces after 5 April 1958. But this was after the crucial blow struck by the US government, which on 13 March 1958 placed an arms embargo on Batista, despite the pleading of Ambassador Earl Smith. In a remarkably inept display of opportunism, the British government earned the enmity of the resistance by selling Batista some Sea Fury aircraft, which did nothing to sustain his regime but were to play a key role in defeating the CIA's invasion two years later.

While Batista vainly tried to dislodge Castro from the Sierra Maestra, his opponents daily undermined the regime by attacking bridges, roads and rail links, and with headline-seeking kidnappings and skyjackings. Although captured rebels were usually tortured and shot, Fidel adopted the policy used by Mao in China and ordered that captured government troops should be well treated and released. The rebels also confiscated livestock and distributed them to needy peasants, and provided rudimentary medical services and schools. They also shot the more vexatious landlords' men. The effect of this in combat was readily apparent when column commanders Raúl Castro, Guevara and Camilo Cienfuegos debouched from the Sierra Maestra to wage war along the length of the country.[22]

By early December 1958 the US government was openly pressuring Batista to go, preferably ceding power to a caretaker regime to preserve order. Without even warning his military commanders and mobster cronies, Batista fled at 4 a.m. on New Year's Day, leaving his accomplices to scramble for seats in whatever was able to fly or sail away from the island. He flew first to the Dominican Republic and then to Mexico, being refused asylum in both places. Trujillo clipped him of a few millions on the way through.

A Caribbean Animal Farm

Castro's regime was exceptionally popular, and would remain so for many years. He seemed to be a revolutionary nationalist, a Garibaldi or Nasser, bent on freeing Cuba from colonial shackles, rather than a totalitarian tyrant intent on creating a 'new man' to serve 'the revolution', which he defined in Guevarist terms as a process with no time limit. There was a powerful sense of new beginnings, and it was favourably noted that the new masters of Cuba were personally austere with regard to money, although of course they took their pick from among the large number of young women excited by the hot rush of liberation. The new leaders also looked different from the world's other politicians, their bohemian long hair and beards contrasting markedly with the buttoned-down and overly hygienic Americans and the charisma-light chunky Soviets. Fidel was thirty-six, Raúl thirty-one, Guevara thirty-four, Ramiro Valdés, the Minister of the Interior, was thirty, and Manuel Piñeiro, the first General Directorate of Intelligence chief, a mere twenty-eight.

The first revolutionary government briefly reflected the popular-front approach of the 26 July Movement. Manuel Urrutia, a respected judge who had defied Batista, became president, while a prominent lawyer became prime minister. Respected members of the legal opposition to Batista took several important portfolios, joined by younger figures from the Movement. They agreed to postpone elections for eighteen months and to abolish political parties. Given the viciousness of the Batista regime, a reckoning was inevitable – although it was modest compared with the post-Second World War *épurations* in Europe. By the end of January 1959 some 200 accused torturers and murderers had been executed, seventy shot into a common grave in one night and most without benefit of trial. A few senior *batistianos* were given show trials, the most notorious in a stadium packed with people howling for their blood.

It did not take long for it to become apparent that the law was what Fidel said it was. He was Máximo Líder, his only official post being supreme commander of the armed forces, as befitted a Garibaldian romantic with a wider role as revolutionary inciter-in-chief. He insisted that air force officers who had been acquitted of bombing civilians should be retried and found guilty, while the defence lawyers and supportive witnesses from the first trial were detained and required to recant. Guevara, in charge of the fortress overlooking Havana harbour, was particularly ruthless and arbitrary, and exhibited special animosity against wealthy Cubans. The Villoldo family owned a 30,000-acre farm and several General Motors car dealerships. Guevara sent armed men to storm the home of Gustavo and his wife Margarita, who were dragged away to the fortress. Guevara gave Gustavo the choice of handing his assets to the state or seeing his two sons shot. On 16 February Gustavo Villoldo took a fatal overdose of sleeping pills to avoid this choice. His sons survived and Gustavo Jr would be a member of the CIA squad that directed the operations in Bolivia in 1967 that ended with Guevara shot after capture.[23]

In an early indication that relations with the US would be turbulent, Fidel said that if Washington did not like these trials it could send in the Marines, and then there would be 'two hundred thousand dead gringos'.[24] In a conversation with President Rómulo Betancourt of Venezuela, he volunteered that he was thinking 'of having a game with the gringos'. The Eisenhower administration remained unsure whether Fidel was intent on confrontation or simply raising the stakes towards an eventual settlement, even though from April 1959 onwards the new regime sponsored subversive acts in Panama, the Dominican Republic and Haiti. At a conference of US ambassadors to the Caribbean, those willing to give Castro the benefit of the doubt, including Philip Bonsal, the new man in Havana, outnumbered those favouring a hardline response. The State Department hinted that a major economic assistance programme was possible, but Fidel did not pursue the offer.[25]

Just before his departure on a tour of the US in April 1959, Fidel explained at a reception in the US embassy that elections could not be held before necessary agrarian reforms and general improvements to popular health and education. His unstructured visit to the US distracted from that significant shift in priorities. Predictably he was fêted at various Ivy League universities, where the spoiled offspring of the Western bourgeoisie found much to like in this tropical communitarian, so removed in spirit from the dull puritanism of Moscow or Beijing. Newspaper editors were charmed by Castro's jokes, as were the usual suspects from the American *gauche caviar*. UN delegates were less enchanted when he gave the longest ever speech to the General Assembly.

As far as the US government was concerned, reactions to Fidel were mixed. Following a two-hour meeting the CIA's leading expert on Latin American Communism declared that 'Castro is not only not a Communist, he is a strong anti-Communist fighter.' Vice President Nixon was not so sure: 'I was convinced Castro was either incredibly naive about Communism or under Communist discipline and that we would have to treat him and deal with him accordingly.' Eisenhower repaired to Augusta, Georgia, to play golf and chose not to meet the bearded revolutionary, missing an opportunity to flatter his inordinate vanity by dealing with him as one soldier to another. There was undoubtedly an echo of the attitude dating back to John Quincy Adams, the second US President, who compared Cuba to an apple that, when shaken loose from the Spanish tree, could only 'gravitate' to the US. Otherwise, Fidel ingratiated himself so successfully with credulous Americans that Raúl telephoned to warn him that his own people were saying that the 'Maximum Leader' had fallen into the habitual bad ways of Latin Americans exposed to the perfidious Yankees.[26]

Castro was always keen to stress that the Revolution was olive green, the colour of guerrilla battledress. What made it red instead was that the 26 July Movement was simply too disparate and amorphous to serve as a platform for Fidel's unbounded ambition. Knowing that confrontation with the US was inevitable, Fidel needed the backing of the USSR. In addition, the Cuban Communist Party (Partido Socialista Popular, or PSP) was not only a uniquely well-organized and disciplined body amid the chaos of Cuban politics, it was also ripe for picking after having backed Batista. Fidel could have ordered the prosecution of the leading Communists as collaborators with the hated dictator, but instead chose to co-opt them. Barring a foolish, Soviet-inspired attempt to reassert the 'leading role of the party' in 1968, which ended with Party Secretary Aníbal Escalante and several others sentenced to long periods of imprisonment, the Party became and remained as servile as any in the Soviet Bloc.

Shortly after his return to Havana, Castro presented the cabinet with a draft Agrarian Reform Law, which they were not allowed to discuss. Land over a thousand acres was to be expropriated, in return for interest-yielding government bonds, which in the event were never issued. A National Agrarian Reform Institute (INRA) would run the land as co-operatives or grant sixty-seven-acre plots to individual families. Foreigners could no longer own shares in sugar plantations, and ownership of refining mills was separated from the plantations. Young INRA officials with degrees but no practical experience took over virtually all the livestock farms, fecklessly butchering laying hens and dairy herds, and even a prize pedigree bull worth $20,000. Castro dismissed cabinet members who protested against the folly, and thereafter the cabinet became irrelevant as the real business of government was conducted by decree.[27]

Criticism of the growing influence of Communists was not tolerated. Fidel sacked Pedro Luis Díaz Lanz, the head of the Revolutionary Air Force who had flown in arms and ammunition for the revolutionaries in 1958, and deposed President Urrutia in favour of Osvaldo Dorticós, a wealthy closet Communist. He made himself prime minister by 'popular acclaim', for monster rallies styled as direct democracy had become his preferred means of claiming to express the popular will. By the autumn there were more people in prison than had ever been the case under Batista, and the death penalty, abolished in 1940, was restored for counter-revolutionaries. Brother Raúl, starting with military intelligence or G2, merged the guerrillas with what was left of the army to create the new Revolutionary Armed Forces. One of his first acts was to make a secret request to the Soviets to send a mission of Spanish Communist exiles who had served in the Red Army. Five KGB officers arrived to train a new secret police.[28]

Shortly afterwards, when Díaz Lanz flew an aircraft over Havana dropping anti-Castro leaflets, improperly fused anti-aircraft shells fired by Cuban gunners burst on return to the ground and Fidel accused the US of complicity in 'terror bombing'. The remaining liberals in the government were forced out, and Guevara was appointed director of the National Bank, triggering financial panic and a run on the banks. Investors withdrew over US$50 million in days. In October, Huber Matos, the military commander of Camagüey Province, attempted to resign along with forty of his officers because of Communist infiltration of the army. He was tried for 'betraying the revolution' and sentenced to twenty years in jail. In November the regime suspended habeas corpus indefinitely and the following month all Cubans were encouraged to become informers and to report any overheard criticism of the regime. Eventually this was institutionalized by enrolling 800,000 people in Committees for the Defence of the Revolution.[29]

And on it went, an avalanche of decrees that often contradicted each other, whether by accident or design making the normal conduct of business impossible as managers spent all their time trying to comply. There was also a *Kulturkampf* against black social clubs and Santería religious rituals – which fused folk Catholicism with Yoruba traditions from West Africa – as well as against all private clubs and associations. Santa Claus and Christmas trees were proscribed and rock and roll music banned. The labour unions, cringingly aware that their support for Batista was a sword hanging over their heads, were taken over by the Communists, who promptly requested the abolition of the right to strike. They muffled the freedom of speech that Batista had never dared to suppress by censoring all publications. All radio and TV stations were subsumed into a state corporation. Meanwhile the militarization of Cuban society proceeded apace with the creation of a 100,000-strong militia.[30]

Thorn in the Flesh or Mortal Threat?

It was not US business interests or dispossessed American landowners who decided that Castro had to go, for they lived in hope that they could negotiate compensation for their lost assets; it was an administration worried about US loss of international face and domestic charges of being weak on Communism, aided and abetted by a vociferous exiled Cuban lobby in Miami. Specifically, Eisenhower worried that Castro would inveigle the whole of Latin America into an emerging Third World neutralist camp, to the detriment of global US influence. In February 1959 a secret NSC policy statement stated that 'A defection by any significant number of Latin American countries to the ranks of neutralism . . . would seriously impair the ability of the United States to exercise effective leadership of the Free World, particularly in the UN, and constitute a blow to US prestige.'[31]

As early as mid-March 1959, before Fidel's visit to New York, Eisenhower had approved CIA contingency planning to arm and train Cuban exiles, and to support guerrillas operating on the island. Nixon and the Chief of Naval Operations, Admiral Arleigh Burke, were early anti-Castro hawks. In July, after Esso, Shell and Texaco had refused (for dubious technical reasons) to process Soviet crude oil in their Cuban refineries, Castro expropriated them. Eisenhower stepped up the pressure by cutting the annual US Cuban sugar quota by 700,000 tons, only to see the Soviets and Chinese step in to increase their forward purchases of sugar. In the autumn Castro expropriated all remaining US-owned agricultural, industrial and banking interests. Corporate America had lost $1 billion in investments, but felt it less keenly than the Mob, which had lost $100 million invested in casinos and hotels, as well as the enormously profitable Cuban connection for heroin.[32]

The reds came out from under the bed with Soviet Foreign Minister Anastas Mikoyan's mission to Cuba in February 1960. To compensate for the US cancellation of the sugar quota, Fidel and Mikoyan signed a treaty whereby the Soviets would purchase a million tons of sugar a year for the next four years. The Soviets would also loan Cuba $100 million, and provide oil, steel and fertilizers. It was not enough to compensate for the economic chaos created by the doctrinaire Guevara, who ordered all foreign commercial and industrial enterprises expropriated. Following the mass emigration of managers and technicians, he discovered that not only his team of young industrial engineering graduates but also the Soviets lacked the expertise to run them.

Initially arms were not part of the new treaty, as the Soviets were cautious about the likely US reaction. The Castros bought them from European suppliers instead until on 4 March 1960 a Belgian ship called *La Coubre* loaded with ammunition blew up in Havana harbour, causing widespread devastation. It was on this occasion that the photographer Alberto Díaz Gutiérrez, better known as Alberto Korda, took the iconic picture of Guevara that has adorned countless student walls and gained a new lease of life as a fashion accessory. The explosion was almost certainly the product of negligence, but Fidel clamorously insisted that it was sabotage and demanded Soviet arms to defend the revolution against rising US aggression. Whether they believed it or not, the incident persuaded the Soviets to deepen their commitment. They not only paid for arms shipments from Poland and Czechoslovakia, but also started paying Fidel a personal subsidy in the form of exorbitant fees for the right to reprint his speeches and writings.[33]

Though Khrushchev was keen to maintain peaceful coexistence with the US, there was a countervailing consideration. Competition with Mao's China for leadership of Third World revolutions led Khrushchev to up the ante, lest Cuba follow Albania into the anti-Soviet camp. Speaking to an audience of Moscow teachers on 9 July 1960, Khrushchev said:

> It should be borne in mind that the United States is now not at such an unattainable distance from the Soviet Union as formerly. Figuratively speaking, if need be, Soviet artillerymen can support the Cuban people with their rocket fire should the aggressive forces in the Pentagon dare to start intervention against Cuba. And the Pentagon could be well advised not to forget that, as shown at the latest tests, we have rockets which can land precisely in a preset square 13,000 kilometres away. This, if you want, is a warning to those who would like to solve international problems by force and not by reason.[34]

This was a bluff. Two years earlier, Khrushchev had tried it on with Senator Hubert Humphrey during a rambling eight-hour conversation in the Kremlin. He had gone up to a wall map of the USA, and asked Humphrey where he was born. He then circled Minneapolis with a blue pencil, saying, 'That's so I don't forget to order them to spare the city when the rockets fly.' The reality was that the Soviet planned economy was in semi-permanent crisis, selling gold to purchase imported butter. And worse, when in October 1960 the Soviets tested the new R-16 ICBM, it blew up, killing a hundred technicians and Marshal Mitrofan Nedelin, chief of the new Soviet strategic rocket forces. The R-9 also flopped during flight tests. By this date the US had something of the order of 18,000 nuclear warheads.[35]

In July 1960 Raúl Castro had his first meeting with the Soviet leadership in Moscow. He must have impressed his hosts. The KGB changed the codename for the Castro regime from Youngstye (Youngsters) to Avanpost (Bridgehead) to reflect the fact that the Castros were serious allies. The Castro brothers' main fear was that the US would repeat what it had done in Guatemala, and they had grounds to worry. Within the Republican Party, Nixon's hopes of succeeding Eisenhower were under threat from Senator Barry Goldwater of Arizona, whose main plank was visceral anti-Communism, and the Republicans in turn faced the challenge of the Democrat John F. Kennedy, who made much of the

Iron Curtain having moved within ninety miles of the US mainland. During the 1960 presidential campaign, after Nixon had prevailed on Eisenhower to send a symbolic reinforcement of 1,400 Marines to Guantanamo, Kennedy rightly dismissed the PR exercise as 'too little, too late'.[36] He did not yet know how far planning had advanced into what was to become the most ludicrously sordid episode in US history, a tar-baby he was to embrace with enthusiasm.

Kennedy had the morals of an alley-cat, but Eisenhower was an upright, devout and honourable man. How could he have sanctioned a government conspiracy with mobsters to murder a fellow head of state? The answer lies in the fact that few who had endured the Second World War doubted that it could have been prevented by the timely assassination of Hitler. There was also a precedent for US government involvement with the Mob in the deal made with Luciano, which saw him released from prison in return for Mafia assistance during the invasion of Sicily directed by Ike in 1943.

The Mafia were recruited to kill the Castro brothers and Guevara as a possible alternative to the CIA's planned invasion by a force of exiles, in that the US might intervene directly to 'restore order' after the leaders were dead. Robert Maheu, a former FBI agent, arranged meetings between Colonel Sheffield Edwards (representing the CIA's special plans chief Richard Bissell) and Italian-born Johnny Rosselli, whose real name was Filippo Sacco. As the Mob's man in Los Angeles Rosselli had pressured Hollywood film producer Harry Cohn to cast Frank Sinatra in *From Here to Eternity*, although not by placing the head of a racehorse in his bed as portrayed in Mario Puzo's *The Godfather*. Later he became the Mob's chief representative in Las Vegas. Rosselli linked the CIA with Chicago boss Sam Giancana and Florida boss Santo Trafficante, both of whom nurtured a murderous personal grudge against Castro for the money they had lost in Cuba.

Bissell explicitly informed Allen Dulles that 'contact has been made with the Mafia', including a payment of $200,000 diverted from the budget for the invasion to cover the cost of assassinations, although Giancana declined his fee on grounds of patriotic duty. It would be otiose to list, once again, the many failed attempts to murder Castro. Most of them suffered from the basic sin of over-elaboration, what the Americans call 'trying to be cute', leading Fidel to dub the CIA the 'Central Agency of Yankee Cretins'.[37] A barman was bribed to put a capsule containing botulism bacteria into Castro's milkshake, but stored the capsules in a freezer and could not free them when the time came. Juan Orta, a private secretary in the Prime Minister's office who missed the kickbacks he had once received from the Mob, was also given poison pills by Maheu and Rosselli. As Larry Devlin realized in the Congo, there was no substitute for a proficient sniper.[38]

Of the US and Cuba, Khrushchev once asked 'Why should an elephant be afraid of a mouse?' Kennedy was to ask him the same question with regard to Hungary and Poland, implicitly revealing that he believed the US also controlled a bloc, though he would have denied it. Like Khrushchev, Kennedy was above all concerned that a successful revolution against US authority would have a domino effect – and it did. The Cuban example inspired would-be imitators throughout Latin America, in many cases supported by Cuban agents and arms, and further encouraged by Khrushchev's decision to support national liberation movements throughout the Third World. It was rubber-stamped by the Presidium in August 1961, at the height of the crisis provoked by the Soviet ultimatum demanding the withdrawal of Western armed forces from West Berlin, which ended with the construction of the Berlin Wall, a humiliating admission that the people could be kept in the people's republics only by force.

KGB chief Aleksandr Schelepin drew up a plan to back Latin American revolutionary movements which 'would favour dispersion of attention and forces by the United States and its satellites, and would tie them down during the settlement of a German peace treaty and West Berlin'. The main tools were to be the Cubans and the newly formed Sandinista movement in Nicaragua, which received a modest KGB subvention from the start.[39] With good cause, the US government feared that Cuba had become a Communist spearhead pointed at the totality of US interests in Latin America.[40] Castro confirmed that it was so in the autumn of 1960, when he merged the PSP and the 26 July Movement into a single Cuban Communist Party and pronounced himself a Marxist-Leninist, which was news to brother Raúl and to his Soviet advisers.[41]

All Mouth and No Trousers

Astute though he undoubtedly was, Fidel could not have prayed for a more obliging enemy than the new American President, who remains the benchmark aspired to by all who seek to use style to obscure their lack of substance. John Fitzgerald Kennedy was born outside Boston in 1917 into one of America's richest families, his father Joe having made a fortune in movies, property and stocks and distributing imported spirits. These were real clan Irish, with the father believing that 'family' – in the Mafia sense – trumped all other considerations. In a society still prejudiced against Catholics and the Irish, Joe acquired social respectability sufficient for FDR to appoint him to such posts as chairman of the Securities and Exchange Commission and as one of the most anti-British ambassadors every posted to London. His vicarious political ambitions were initially invested in his namesake elder son, leaving second son John free to pursue a carefree young life.

John or 'Jack' Kennedy had a gilded youth, fitfully laid low by colitis and Addison's disease, which plagued him throughout his life. The family home was a large house at Riverdale in suburban Manhattan. Long summers were spent sailing off Cape Cod, where the family congregated in their own compound at Hyannis Port. There was another place at Palm Springs. The Depression made little impact on the Kennedys; Jack's sole recollection was that his father hired more gardeners.[42] Jack's interests at Harvard were on the social and sporting side, although this period also saw the beginnings of the sex addiction that he indulged for the rest of his life. His combination of money and good looks made him what the British called a 'deb's delight'.

While shadowing his ambassador father to London in the 1930s, Jack was seduced by the lifestyle of the British aristocracy, with whose philistinism he strongly identified. Though he later assumed the airs of a highly cultivated man, and knew how to flatter vain artists and intellectuals, there is scant evidence that he had any serious cultural interests. Camelot, it should be recalled, was just a kitschy musical. Home-movie footage from Hyannis Port shows Kennedy 'goofing off' with a tight

coterie of friends, aggressively playing touch football and above all sailing, which he found relaxing.

His father ensured that much of Jack's medical history was suppressed
when he joined the navy in October 1941. He eventually commanded a
fast Patrol Torpedo boat (PT-109) in the Pacific. After a botched attack
on a Japanese convoy, PT-109 was sliced in half by an enemy destroyer
that was not even aware that the boat was there. Kennedy redressed his
sloppy seamanship by a genuinely heroic effort to rescue his surviving
crew members, which lost nothing in the telling back home.

Aged twenty-eight when the war ended, Kennedy was 'drafted' by his
overbearing father into politics to replace his elder brother, killed piloting a bomber packed with explosives that detonated prematurely.[43] Joe
quite simply bought Jack's election to Congress in November 1946 for
Massachusetts's 11th District, and his money thereafter was the magic
dust that transformed a junior congressman with a very modest track
record into a rising national figure. Jack struck crucial progressive poses,
supporting Third World nationalists and US trade unions, but also pan-
dered to his blue-collar base by adopting a hardline anti-Communist
stance. His younger brother Bobby even worked for the notorious
red-baiter Senator Joseph McCarthy. In 1951 the brothers became more
closely acquainted when they went on a seven-week tour of Israel, Iran,
Pakistan, India, Singapore, French Indochina, Korea and Japan. Jack
returned convinced that the US should align itself with emerging nations,
while helping them combat 'poverty and want' and 'sickness and disease'. Joe's money was again lavishly dispensed to get Jack elected to the
US Senate in 1952, spending $500,000 to secure the support of the *Bos-
ton Post,* which he calculated was worth 40,000 votes.[44]

In September 1953 the youngest Senator acquired another political
asset – his attractive wife Jacqueline Bouvier. The wedding was the society event of the year, though the groom did not suspend his incessant
philandering even on the day itself. Jack was packaged for high office as
no one had ever been packaged before. As a sceptical journalist wrote:
'This man seeks the highest elective office in the world not primarily as
a politician, but as a celebrity. He's the only politician a woman would
read about while sitting under the hair dryer, the subject of more human
interest articles than all his rivals combined.'[45] Since he needed to correct

the impression of being a rich playboy dabbling in politics, it helped when in April 1957 Joe bought a Pulitzer Prize for Jack's ghost-written *Profiles in Courage*, just as he had made London embassy staff available to 'research' Jack's youthful venture into print.

Following his impressive re-election in 1958, which cost Joe a further $1 million, Jack's by now impressive journalistic claque, who never shared with the public their intimate knowledge of his hedonistic life-style, were already speculating where he would put Bobby or his youngest brother Ted after he entered the White House. His nomination as the Democratic candidate and, indeed, his victory in the 1960 presidential election itself, was swung by a back-room deal between Joe and Chicago Mayor Richard J. Daley, who delivered the crucial Illinois vote. The Kennedys dramatized Jack's Catholicism to win ethnic votes. As Harry Truman tartly observed of Joe's influence: 'It's not the Pope I'm afraid of. It's the pop.'[46] There was much portentous talk too during these campaigns of global nuclear annihilation, and of the need for 'new men to cope with new problems and new opportunities' to neutralize those who thought JFK (as he became known) too young for the job, or who, like Eisenhower, thought him a hyper-privileged 'Little Boy Blue'. After defeating the rebarbative, sweaty Dick Nixon by a tiny margin (0.2 per cent) of the popular vote that was delivered by late returns from Illinois, JFK was sworn in as the thirty-fourth President on a chill day in January 1961. His inaugural address is deservedly celebrated for the soaring rhetoric that lit up the occasion.

Playa Girón

When William Crockett was appointed assistant secretary of state for administration he was summoned by Bobby Kennedy, the new Attorney-General. Without looking up, Bobby snapped, 'You work for my brother, the President of the United States, and you do whatever he says. Your job in the State Department is to make sure that all the personnel in the Department understand that they work for the President and that they are loyal to him. So now you know what your job is. Do you know how to do your job? You kick people in the ass so hard that teeth will rattle in all the embassies. That's what you will do. That is how to get your job done!' And the interview was over. Bobby was his elder brother's rat-catching terrier.[47]

Operation Zapata was posited on delusional thinking by Cuban exiles and CIA agents on the island about the degree of local support that an invading force might receive. CIA planning was well under way by early 1960, with exiles training in Guatemala and a powerful fifty-kilowatt medium-wave radio transmitter to broadcast propaganda installed on tiny Swan Island midway between Florida and Cuba. CIA veterans of the successful coup in Guatemala were thick on the ground; indeed the facility of that operation encouraged the new administration to take this further step in Cuba. The tough-talking intellectuals around Kennedy lacked the old soldier's caution instilled in Eisenhower and JFK thought the NSC 'a waste of time'. Having made so much of the Communist menace emanating from Cuba, JFK himself could not afford to be seen as soft seventy days after entering the White House. For as Allen Dulles reminded the new President in briefing sessions, if the invasion was called off the 1,500-strong Cuban exile force assembled in Guatemala would disperse to bruit JFK's weakness across the entire continent. The Republicans would undoubtedly exploit the issue in the elections in 1962.[48]

The CIA bounced the new administration into backing what ceased to involve landing a guerrilla force and became a pathetic replica of a Second World War amphibious invasion, albeit without superior air cover. To the horror of CIA planners in their Quarters Eye barracks near Washington's reflecting pool, Secretary of State Dean Rusk vetoed a landing near the town of Trinidad because of concern with civilian casualties. The alternative chosen was Playa Girón, a beach on the Bay of Pigs (Bahía de Cochinos) on the southern coast of Cuba. This was surrounded by crocodile-infested swamps that spawned clouds of mosquitoes. It was chosen because the swamps would make it difficult to snuff out the beachhead. JFK was also ill served by the Joint Chiefs of Staff, who signed off on a night amphibious landing by a bunch of civilians that, as experienced soldiers, they surely knew had zero chance of success. For reasons of operational secrecy, no attempt was made to co-ordinate the landings with the heavily penetrated resistance inside Cuba. Finally, the keystone assassination of Fidel failed. Shortly before

Zapata was launched Juan Orta lost his nerve and sought asylum in the Mexican embassy. What the CIA did not count on was that JFK would demonstrate a totally unexpected willingness to live with the political fall-out of letting the botched operation fail rather than doubling up on the gamble by committing US armed forces.[49]

Operations began with raids on Cuban airfields by B-26 bombers painted in Cuban air force colours operating from bases in Nicaragua. They were supposed to be flown by Cuban defectors. When one of these planes made an allegedly emergency landing in Miami, an alert journalist paid less attention to the bullet holes in the fuselage than to the plane's aluminium nose, when the noses of all Cuban air force B-26s were of Perspex. He might have noticed that the machine guns were taped up to protect them from Nicaragua's dust. The raids disabled 60 per cent of the small Cuban air force, but the remaining 40 per cent included the British Sea Furies. Brigade 2506 steamed from Nicaragua in the name of Catholic Cuba, with Latin crosses on their badges and bidden Godspeed by Luis Somoza, son and heir of 'our son-of-a-bitch' Anastasio, who requested some hairs from Castro's beard. Cuban intelligence analysts would subsequently declare that between them the men on board the CIA-chartered freighters had owned a million acres of land, 10,000 houses, seventy factories, five mines, two banks and ten sugar mills.

The invasion force received the go signal from CIA officer Howard Hunt, later to figure as the organizer of the Watergate burglary that brought down Nixon in 1974: 'Alert! Alert! Look well at the rainbow. The first will rise very soon. Chico is in the house. Visit him. Place notice in the tree. The tree is green and brown. The letters arrived well. The letters are white. The fish will not take much time to rise. The fish is red.'[50]

The second fateful decision occurred when Rusk telephoned Kennedy, who was at his new Virginian horsey retreat of Glen Ora near Middleburg, on the night of the invasion. Kennedy agreed to rescind his earlier authorization of air strikes by USAF and US Navy pilots to support the invaders. These men died on the beaches as Castro's forces closed in and the Sea Furies blew up the ammunition ship *Rio Escondido*.[51]

Apart from the heroism of the young exiles left stranded by a US administration that had lacked the moral courage to call the whole thing off, there was nothing remotely redemptive about the fate of Assault

Brigade 2506, whose designation honoured an exile who fell during a training accident in Guatemala (2506 had been his membership number). The CIA even managed to contaminate their patriotism by including 194 *batistianos* in their ranks, fourteen of them sufficiently notorious to be put on trial afterwards, with nine shot and the remainder sentenced to long prison terms. Castro subsequently exchanged the survivors for $53 million in food and medicine.[52]

In August 1961, during a meeting of the Organization of American States in Punta del Este, Uruguay, Guevara gave a White House secretary a note for JFK. 'Thanks for Playa Girón,' it said. 'Before the invasion, the revolution was weak. Now it's stronger than ever.' Truer words were never spoken. Castro was justified in proudly proclaiming it 'the first defeat for Yanqui imperialism in Latin America', and it cemented the revolution in the hearts of the great majority of Cubans. For the rest, thousands of suspects were rounded up and hundreds shot, including all the CIA infiltrators and the extraordinarily brave internal resistance members they had made contact with. No wonder the CIA team at Quarters Eye used wastepaper baskets as they threw up.

On 29 December 1962, JFK and Jackie attended a welcoming ceremony for Brigade 2506 survivors at the Orange Bowl stadium in Miami. The President was wise to bring his wife, as she spoke charmingly in Spanish and those present who believed he had betrayed them were constrained to be polite. But the poison contaminated US politics for decades to come, with undying conspiracy theories linking Cuban exiles in the CIA with the assassinations of both JFK and his brother. In fact the Cuban with the most reason to want them dead was Fidel, who became the target of a highly personal vendetta pursued by the Kennedy brothers for making them lose face at the Bay of Pigs. As a result of this, they would pursue Castro with a vengeance, up to and including repeated conspiracies to murder him, and when he and his Soviet patrons went to the brink of war they would match them move for move during the most deadly moment of the entire Cold War.

16. TO THE BRINK:
THE MISSILE CRISIS

A Maze of Options

During the Bay of Pigs fiasco Khrushchev exclaimed, 'Can he [JFK] really be that indecisive?', forgetting his own dithering over Hungary in 1956. It is worth bearing in mind that a broad range of people who knew JFK well, including his father, judged him to be a lightweight. He was in some respects a silver screen on which others projected their yearnings, which helps to explain his lasting status as a liberal icon. Another reason is that he also grew in an office that has diminished many of those who have occupied it. In the minds of those who revere his memory, the violently attenuated promise outweighs the amorality of his private life and of his secret conduct as president.

Although he took public responsibility for the Bay of Pigs, JFK seethed with hostility towards the CIA, sacking Allen Dulles and Richard Bissell shortly afterwards. The Republican John McCone replaced Dulles and the suave Richard Helms, known to his detractors as the 'Eminence Grease', took over from Bissell. But instead of reining in the paramilitary side of the CIA in favour of humdrum intelligence collection and analysis, the gung-ho Kennedys expanded it. They were admirers of Ian Fleming's James Bond books, in which a suave Brit saves the world with fancy gadgets. Whereas Eisenhower had authorized 170 CIA covert operations in eight years of office, the Kennedys licensed 163 in less than three. Top of the list was revenge on Castro, for the Kennedys were unaccustomed to failure.[1]

To ensure that the CIA did the President's bidding, Bobby Kennedy was effectively put in charge of its operational division. Thus was created the paradox of the top law officer in the country directing an organization whose activities were legal only on rare occasions. He brought in Brigadier-General Edward Lansdale, whose legendary status had survived his lacklustre period in Diem's turbulent Saigon. It was naively assumed that as an expert in counter-insurgency he should also be able to mount a grassroots rebellion. Lansdale devised a thirty-two-point plan, adding as an afterthought point 33 – to use chemicals to temporarily incapacitate all Cuban plantation workers during the sugar harvest.[2] Though formally based in the Pentagon, Lansdale took charge of Special Group Augmented, which ran CIA operations in Cuba. CIA analysts were justly sceptical that Lansdale's uprising, codenamed Touchdown Play, could be triggered in a popular police state like Cuba.[3]

Although forbidden by law to operate in the US, the world's largest CIA station, codenamed JMWAVE, mushroomed on the south campus of the University of Miami, with an annual budget of $50 million. This was four times the total the CIA spent on spying in twenty Latin American countries. Disguised as Zenith Technical Enterprises, it housed 300 CIA officers, who recruited thousands of Cuban exiles as agents. The officers all acted as though they were above the law, whether driving around with sub-machine guns and explosives in their cars or being quietly released from jail after being caught driving under the influence. Indiscriminate recruiting saw the ranks swelled by fantasists and psychopaths, and even the sane and sober recruits knew less and less about life in Cuba, creating a shadow country full of repressed people yearning to be free that simply did not exist. Of course, they and the Miami Cubans ignored the really repressed people in the new Cuba, the blacks who had overwhelmingly supported Batista against these middle-class Hispanic revolutionaries.

JMWAVE's major project was dubbed Operation Mongoose. Implementation was assigned to the CIA's Task Force W under a tough ex-FBI man called William Harvey.[4] Bug eyed, purple faced and pear shaped, Harvey went around with a pistol in a holster and another clipped to his belt in the small of his back. He hated Lansdale, whom he contemptuously called 'FM', short for field marshal. He also despised the Kennedys, calling them 'fags' and 'fuckers'.[5] In meetings Harvey liked to annoy Bobby Kennedy by loading and unloading his gun on the table, and on occasion ostentatiously raised a leg to fart. Bobby was present at all Mongoose planning meetings, like one in October 1962 where the minutes read, 'General Lansdale said that another attempt will be made against the major target which has been the object of three unsuccessful missions, and that approximately six new ones are in the planning stage.' Harvey was appalled to find himself named and linked in a memo with the word 'liquidation'.[6]

JMWAVE ran a number of operations against the Castro regime. The CIA soon had command of the third largest navy in the Caribbean. Large CIA mother ships such as the *Rex* and *Leda* towed smaller swift boats within range of Cuba, where they launched black inflatables with teams of saboteurs. Their targets included setting fire to sugarcane plantations and timber yards, and blowing up bridges and rail lines as well as such talismanic sites as the Patrice Lumumba Sulphuric Acid plant. In a raid on 24 August 1962, a thirty-foot boat called the *Juanín* entered the harbour at Miramar, a Havana suburb. On board were six Cuban exile commandos equipped with two .50-calibre machine guns and a 20mm cannon, acquired from a Mafia gun dealer in Miami. For five minutes they poured fire into the illuminated ballroom of the Blanquita Hotel, where Czech and Russian military personnel liked to party on Friday nights. The boat then sped back into the night.[7] Underwater demolition teams were also used to attach limpet mines to ships or to the country's largest floating crane.[8]

All overseas CIA stations were required to establish a Cuban desk, responsible for misinformation and sabotage. Large sums of money were disbursed to European industrialists to damage equipment sent to Cuba, such as lubricants doctored to wear out engines or slightly misshaped ball bearings. A Japanese ship's captain was bribed to collide with a vessel on the River Thames taking Leland buses to Havana. Enormous sums were expended by CIA purchasing agents to deny the Cubans such items as bright stock, a heavy viscous lubricating oil used in engines. As Mongoose seemed not to be delivering the uprising Lansdale had promised,

Helms and Harvey decided to re-explore the Mafia connection they had opened during the Eisenhower administration. They were warned off by FBI Director J. Edgar Hoover, who hated Harvey from his time in the Bureau and was fully cognizant of the CIA's links with the Mafia. Hoover also possessed a political nuclear weapon in the shape of proof that Judith Campbell, one of JFK's favourite sexual partners, had served as his confidential link with Sam Giancana since JFK first became a senator. After Hoover had presented JFK with a top-secret FBI memo on the subject, he ended his affair with Campbell and also the long and close relationship between his family and the Mob.

While the tide of sleaze flowed on in the secret world, in public JFK initiated the economic quarantine of Cuba whose tattered legacy persists to this day. By executive decree in February 1962 he banned most Cuban imports, notably cigars and tobacco products – having first stocked up his personal supply. The US also arm-twisted the OAS to expel Cuba, and fifteen Latin American states broke off diplomatic relations with the Castro regime. That year, 82 per cent of Cuban exports went to Communist countries, which supplied 65 per cent of the island's imports.

Despite all this activity, voters still thought JFK and the Democrats were most weak on the subject of Cuba, leading to enhanced sabre-rattling in the weeks before the mid-term polls in 1962. JFK may have ruled out an unprovoked invasion, but he ordered contingency plans should a viable excuse for a successful invasion arise – which is to say if Mongoose finally produced Lansdale's 'spontaneous' uprising. The plan was for a combined operation known by its February 1962 planning title OPLAN 314-61. On 1 October army and navy commanders were ordered to prepare to execute Operation Ortsac (Castro cunningly spelled backwards), a large-scale amphibious exercise in the Caribbean to begin on 15 October.[9] The KGB knew about this in general terms, and connected it with Castro's public declaration on 1 December that he was a Communist bent on building a Marxist-Leninist society.[10]

The US also resumed atmospheric nuclear tests after Khrushchev had refused site inspections that might have revealed Soviet strategic weaknesses. The GRU (the foreign military intelligence directorate of the Soviet General Staff), usually more dependable than the politicized KGB, falsely reported that only the Soviet test of a fifty-megaton Tsar hydrogen bomb in October 1961 had deterred the US from launching a pre-emptive nuclear strike. Actually, both sides knew that the colossally destructive weapon was unusable. What really worried Khrushchev was that following the installation of highly accurate Minuteman missiles in blast-proof silos in Montana, South Dakota and Wyoming, the US had a nine-to-one superiority in Inter-Continental Ballistic Missiles over the USSR, whose meagre arsenal of SS-7s were relatively inaccurate and required larger warheads. Also, the solid-fuel Minuteman could be launched much more rapidly than liquid-fuelled SS-7s, making them highly vulnerable to a US first strike. The British SIS confirmed much of this detail through GRU Colonel Oleg Penkovsky, who began spying for them in late 1960.[11]

In April 1962 JFK and the visiting Shah of Iran inspected Lantphibex-62, a vast amphibious exercise off Puerto Rico involving 40,000 troops and eighty-four warships. Developments in Cuba itself were also giving Khrushchev concern. Moscow's Cuban Communist friends were losing ground to those like Guevara who were attracted by the vicious élan of Mao's China. To the simple-minded or wilfully ignorant, the Great Leap Forward – a crash collectivization and industrialization programme initiated by Mao in the late 1950s which caused a catastrophic famine – was an example to be followed in the creation of the 'new man'. The Soviet Union seemed part of the problem of imperialism rather than the solution, against which the Chinese appeared to offer the revolutionary solidarity of Third World proletarian nations. The looming split with China might be inevitable, given Mao's determination to be recognized as the Communist world's 'Great Master' in succession to Stalin. But ideological deviation among the satellite countries, among which Khrushchev (but not Castro) counted Cuba, posed a threat to the forward defence of the Soviet heartland.

In fact, to the chagrin of the stolid old men in the Kremlin, their charismatic new Cuban friends effortlessly assumed the role of the revolutionary socialist vanguard supposedly reserved for the Communist Party of the Soviet Union. Romantic style once again trumped ideological substance, and the Russians found themselves under attack from the left, when all their mental processes were geared to dealing with the comparatively arcane deviationism of Yugoslavia's Tito. Castro and Guevara were also reckless, training guerrilla fighters to create trouble even for Latin American countries that had not joined the OAS boycott of Cuba.[12]

All of these factors explain why Khrushchev decided to invest in Cuba more heavily than the arms shipments promised but only partially delivered because of the competing claims of Nasser's Egypt. Stalin had been contemptuous of revolutionaries in the undeveloped world, but his successors were compelled to be more respectful of the revolutionary potentialities unleashed by colonial struggles, and to pay more attention to the educated elites in the civil service or the military in the Third World. Khrushchev decided that the USSR should ride the doctrinally unpredicted wave or else be left behind in what could well be the Marxist-Leninist dream of world revolution. To do so involved co-opting the Cubans, who had won enormous prestige by defeating the Americans, in order to halt their drift towards the perfidious Chinese and to curb the Castro–Guevara combine's pretensions to becoming an autonomous ideological force in their own right.

On 12 April 1962 Khrushchev stopped prevaricating about deliveries of both Surface-to-Air (SAM) missile batteries and the Sopka coastal defence cruise missile system to Cuba, adding ten Ilyushin IL-28 medium bombers that Castro had not requested. Accompanying the weapons were Soviet military technicians to train the Cubans in their use – but also to guard them against misuse. These were purely defensive weapons, fully justified by the ongoing aggression of Operation Mongoose. But, as Mikoyan acknowledged after his first trip to Havana, Castro reminded aged Bolsheviks of when they had been young and daring. It was time for Khrushchev to show daring himself.[13]

Later in April Khrushchev said to his defence chief, Rodion Malinovsky, 'Why not throw a hedgehog at Uncle Sam's pants?' Malinovsky answered that, whereas the Soviets had no SS-7s to spare, they had medium- (MRBM) and intermediate-range missiles in relative abundance. The IRBMs were comparable with the US Army Jupiter missiles that the US had recently installed in Italy and Turkey, and with the US Air Force Thor missiles installed in Britain. The Soviets were not to know that the rival missile systems had already caused a huge bureaucratic row, which had been resolved by the Solomonic decision to phase out Jupiter and Thor in favour of the submarine-based Polaris system. The deployment of Jupiter to Turkey and Italy had been little more than a counter to the view expressed by de Gaulle that the US would never use nuclear weapons to defend Europe, and that the continent should develop its own.

Khrushchev's seemingly casual exchange with Malinovsky marked the beginning of a policy shift from defending Cuba to a projection of Soviet nuclear power into the Western hemisphere. There is little doubt that the Soviets would not have embarked on it were they not convinced that JFK was a weak man who would back down again if challenged robustly. The underhand and mean little pin-pricks of Operation Mongoose also indicated a ruler deficient in moral courage. In geostrategic terms the prize seemed well worth the risk. Putting the M into MAD (Mutual Assured Destruction) by situating a formidable nuclear arsenal ninety miles from the coast of Florida, outflanking the north-facing US early-warning system, would greatly strengthen Khrushchev's hand in negotiations over West Berlin and a whole range of other issues.[14]

Khrushchev's Cuban launch platform would have included forty missiles with one-megaton warheads – R-12 MRBMs and R-14 IRBMs with respective ranges of 1,000 and 2,000 miles – and warheads in the low-kiloton range for eighty cruise missiles with a range of a hundred miles. In addition over 50,000 Soviet technicians and troops would buttress the island's defences, though in the event only 41,000 were sent. A Soviet naval fleet would permanently operate from Cuban waters, including seven submarines carrying R-13 nuclear-tipped ballistic missiles based in the great natural harbour of Cienfuegos.[15] The deployment was in flagrant violation of the formal guarantees Khrushchev had given in April 1961 that the Soviet Union did not have any bases in Cuba and did not intend to establish any. In August 1962, Ambassador Anatoly Dobrynin assured Bobby Kennedy that Khrushchev would not cause trouble during the imminent US mid-term elections, and that he would never arm a third party with the means to wage a nuclear war.

As past masters of *maskirovka* (military camouflage and deception), the Soviets expected to be able to complete the deployment undetected, as they had done with a similar force projection into East Germany in 1959. Operation Anadyr was named after an obscure river on a Siberian peninsula, and KGB-controlled CIA watchers sent back reports of train-loads of fur hats and felt boots apparently heading towards the Arctic. Not even ships' captains were told of their destination until they were at sea, but there was a surprisingly glaring lapse in the order to stop shaving given in June to the troops that were to be embarked. The idea was that they should blend in with their Cuban comrades on arrival. Pallid Slavic skins were also exposed to the sun in the vain hope of acquiring local colour during the long sea voyage; they peeled and glowed red instead.[16]

General Issa Pliyev flew to Havana in July, to prepare the launch sites, although *maskirovka* was to prove inadequate to conceal the equivalent of a major circus in a small town. From mid-July, eighty-five ships were en route to Cuba, some passing by intelligence-gathering nodes such as Gibraltar. While large numbers of troops sweltered below deck, a select few cavorted on deck for the benefit of reconnaissance aircraft. On 30 July, after one spy plane had flown so low that it crashed into the sea, Khrushchev piously asked JFK to suspend reconnaissance flights over Soviet ships in the Caribbean 'for the sake of better relations'. The demands of *maskirovka* aside, the Soviets lacked the necessary shipping to deliver whole systems simultaneously, and missiles and warheads were despatched at considerable intervals, in the event allowing the US some scope to respond short of war.[17]

CIA chief John McCone did not believe it, and after U-2 flights had detected the positioning of top-of-the-range SA-2 SAM batteries on 29 August he sent JFK a memo speculating that they might have been deployed to protect more dangerous systems. However, he did not follow it up and went on a long honeymoon instead. Republican Senator Kenneth Keating was the sole voice warning that the Soviets were up to something destabilizing, but JFK dismissed him as 'a nut'.[18]

US intelligence efforts redoubled as the ships began arriving in Cuba. It was the hurricane season and bad weather hampered aerial reconnaissance, but the fundamental problem was that, from fourteen miles above, U-2 cameras could not conclusively distinguish between a SAM and a ballistic missile under a tarpaulin on a trailer. Yet, as each day passed, the density of SAM coverage made low-level passes over Cuba more perilous, and as the CIA had discovered with the downing of Gary

Powers, even the U-2s were threatened. Photographs taken at a slanting angle by aircraft skirting the island were even less revealing. Agents on the ground, however, reported that some of the trailers were so long that they damaged houses and knocked down telegraph poles when they made sharp turns, firmly indicating that they were carrying something bigger than a SAM.

On 4 September JFK issued a press statement warning the Soviets of the gravest consequences should they be giving Cuba 'significant offensive capability', specifying Soviet bases, Red Army troops and ballistic missiles. This let the Soviets know the US was aware of their game, and that the American public would now know too. The tension ratcheted up. By the end of the month he ordered the Pentagon to plan air strikes to knock out any ballistic missiles that might be identified, and/or to pave the way for an invasion. Later that month a CIA agent reported that the SAMs were being positioned in a trapezoid manner, the known configuration for defending a ballistic missile installation. It was decided to risk a low-level overflight when weather permitted.

On Monday 15 October, JFK received Algeria's Ahmed Ben Bella in the White House. When Ben Bella probed JFK about his intentions towards Cuba, the President said that he would have to invade the island if the Soviets turned it into an offensive base, or if Castro tried to incite revolution in the Western hemisphere. But, JFK added, he might be able to reconcile himself to a 'national Communist' regime akin to those in Poland or Yugoslavia.[19] Hours after Ben Bella had left, analysis of U-2 film taken the day before revealed fixed concrete slabs, and images of R-12 ballistic missiles before their trailers had time to scuttle beneath the palm trees. When JFK was told, he exclaimed, 'He can't do that to me!' When Bobby was shown the briefing boards, he said, 'Oh shit! Shit! Shit! Those sons of bitches Russians.'[20]

Blissfully unaware of this, Ben Bella flew on to Havana, where he was equally warmly welcomed. Algerian war orphans given sanctuary in Cuba cheered him on the airport tarmac. During the visit the Cubans agreed to send a team of doctors to make up the gaps in Algeria's medical services left by the departing French. Everything seemed normal. At the official dinner on 17 October, Ben Bella reported JFK's words to Fidel, and must have been startled by the ostentatious nonchalance with which his friend responded by boasting of his plans to export 'the Revolution' to the whole of Latin America.[21]

Soviet and Cuban intelligence failed to report on how Washington was responding. US options were thrashed out in an Executive Committee of the National Security Council, known as ExComm, though of course all major decisions were JFK's alone. It would take only ninety seconds for his military aides to bring the 'football' containing the nuclear launch codes. ExComm's members included the Defense Secretary Robert McNamara and the Chairman of the Joint Chiefs of Staff General Maxwell Taylor; the CIA's McCone; the National Security Advisor McGeorge 'Mac' Bundy (brother of William Bundy) and Ted Sorenson from the White House; and Dean Rusk, George Ball, Llewellyn Thomas and Charles Bohlen from the State Department. Dean Acheson and Adlai Stevenson, who also attended as elder statesmen, represented the two poles of Democrat foreign policy thinking. Bobby Kennedy was a permanent presence to cover for his brother, who had to maintain his normal schedule in the run-up to the mid-term elections; McGeorge Bundy proved to be ExComm's weathercock, veering from air strikes to blockade and back again, although Acheson was implacably in favour of sending in the bombers. Valued advice came from outside ExComm, when JFK consulted ex-President Eisenhower by telephone. The Vice President was present at many sessions too, but did not say much. When he did it was along the lines of 'All I know is that when I was a boy in Texas, and you were walking along the road when a rattlesnake reared up ready to strike, the only thing to do was to take a stick and chop its head off.' Among the most hawkish, Vice President Johnson would be excluded from an inner ExComm cabal that settled the eventual deal with the Soviets.[22]

All participants were encouraged to maintain their regular public duties, and took effective measures to avoid attracting the attention of journalists. They car-pooled so that there should be no giveaway cavalcade of black automobiles entering the White House and took to using a tunnel from the Treasury building into the White House bomb shelter. Several ExComm members slept in their offices, not just for convenience but to avoid having to lie to their wives. George Ball broke cover by telling his wife to convert their basement into a bomb shelter, with canned food, bottled water and even a Bible for their pious black cook. McGeorge Bundy's wife appears to have been fully aware of what was going on and impressed on him that a violent solution was not necessary. The general climate was caught by Tom Lehrer's song:

> *Oh, we will all fry together when we fry*
> *We'll be French fried potatoes by and by*
> *There will be no more misery*
> *When the world is our rotisserie*
> *Yes, we will all fry together when we fry*

ExComm's undisciplined, unstructured discussions took their toll on all involved. It was not unusual for sessions to go on for thirty hours at a stretch, fuelled by black coffee, sandwiches and cigarettes. Exhaustion manifested itself in short fuses, notably after Adlai Stevenson suggested something that smacked of appeasement. Minds sometimes switched off in the face of a maze of unsatisfactory options. JFK remained serene – according to the official history, relaxing in the evenings by watching films such as *Roman Holiday* with Audrey Hepburn. It is highly improbable that a man who claimed that he got headaches if he went without sex for a day would have sought any other form of relaxation. Possibly his nod to confidentiality was to limit himself to the services of Mary Pinchot Meyer, with whom he may have previously experimented with LSD and who was the ex-wife of Cord Meyer, head of the CIA's International Organizations Division.

There was disagreement about the means, but none about the non-negotiable demand that the ballistic missiles must be removed from Cuba. Bobby Kennedy set the tone by declaring that 'If we go in, we go in hard,' at one point floating the idea of faking an attack on the US base at Guantanamo to give a pretext for invasion, just as Hitler did with Poland in 1939.[23] Taylor was the only serving military officer on ExComm, but throughout the deliberations the other Joint Chiefs of Staff were asked their professional opinions. The easy assumption that civilian doves had to overcome military hawks should be resisted. In fact, there were plenty of civilian hawks, as well as hawkish doves and dovish hawks.[24] Added tension came from the fact that several of the civilians had been subordinates of the Chiefs of Staff during the Second World War, notably McNamara, who had served as a statistician for the strategic bombing offensive conducted by General Curtis LeMay, and had in fact recommended him for the job of air force chief of staff in June 1961.

On one occasion, McNamara was told by General Thomas Power of the Strategic Air Command (SAC) that 'the only way to deal with these barbarians was to blow them all up and I said, "But who's going to win that?" And he said, 'I would be satisfied if there were just two Americans left and one Russian – that would be . . . we would have won." And I said, "Well there'd better be one of them a woman."'[25] The failure of the Joint Chiefs to warn him about the military nonsense of the Bay of Pigs operation had also taught JFK 'to avoid feeling that just because they [generals] were military men their opinions on military matters were worth a damn'.[26]

JFK had an intriguing interaction with LeMay. Every time the two met, JFK 'ended up in a sort of fit'. When Kennedy imagined himself in Khrushchev's shoes, he conjured up a Russian air force general as relentless as LeMay urging the Soviet leader to destroy the US. This helped him appreciate Khrushchev's domestic dilemmas. When Le May exclaimed, 'You're in a pretty bad fix, Mr President,' JFK first asked him to repeat himself and then shot back, 'You're in there with me – personally.'[27] But at the same time JFK appreciated the value of having at his side an air force commander with LeMay's proven ruthlessness should it come to all-out war. There would be no doubt or hesitation there.[28]

ExComm was one of the first high-level policy discussions to be secretly recorded by devices activated by a button under JFK's desk. What began as freewheeling seminar-type discussions, or what Acheson contemptuously called 'a floating crap game', gained greater focus. In perhaps the most remarkable personal transformation, the Kennedys set aside their obsessions with bringing down Castro.

Initially JFK was in favour of taking the missile sites out, and teams were formed to game out the options when discussions deadlocked, with participants required to play devil's advocate against their own preferred strategy, as the NSC under Bobby Cutler had done for Eisenhower. The first discussions rapidly established that there was only one option with regard to such a 'fast track', because air strikes limited to the missile sites would almost certainly escalate to a more general air assault. It was most unlikely that the CIA had been able to identify all the sites; indeed the full effectiveness of *maskirovka* in Cuba was not learned until much later. Post-Second World War analysis of the effects of strategic bombing were not reassuring about the ability of the bombers to win a campaign outright, and once an all-out air assault took place an invasion would follow. Maxwell Taylor's gloomy estimates of the likely loss of US lives in any such endeavour dampened enthusiasm for a pre-emptive strike, as it became clear that a 'graded' military response was a chimera. Conflicting advice from the Joint Chiefs made it very far from their finest hour. Moral qualms did not surface until the high probability of uncontrollable escalation became apparent, with George Ball warning of the negative effects of the US committing its own Pearl Harbor in the Caribbean. Bobby concurred, joking, 'My brother is not going to be the Tojo of the 1960s.'[29]

McNamara reverted to his earlier idea of a blockade, which became known as 'slow track'. Initially he had proposed it as a means of stopping the delivery of further weapons, after air strikes had destroyed those already delivered. After 'fast track' had stalled he revived it as an alternative, tweaked to get around the fact that international law categorized a blockade as an act of war. What if a more limited interdiction, to be called a 'quarantine' to make it more palatable to international opinion, could be devised to interdict the shipment of specific offensive cargoes, reserving a full blockade for a later date if it did not work? Apart from providing a flexibility absent from the 'fast track', the proposed alternative would keep the focus on the Soviets and avoid seeming to make war on Castro's Cuba. It was decided that 'slow track' would be given a week to achieve a result. Meanwhile, at a protracted secret meeting on 22 October, Mikoyan persuaded the Presidium to deny local Soviet commanders the power to launch their weapons independently, and to give the US government an assurance that the weapons would never be put under Cuban control.

On 23 October SAC went to DEFCON 2, the highest state of 'defence condition' alert before war was declared. An eighth of SAC's armada was permanently in the air at any one time and target folders were regularly updated, to increase the nuclear bomb load here or to deliver an airburst there. Twenty-three nuclear-armed B-52s were ostentatiously sent to orbit points within striking distance of the Soviet Union and 145 US-based ICBMs were put on ready alert; no less ostentatiously, the Americans refrained from beginning the highly visible preparations necessary to put liquid-fuelled missiles based overseas on the same level of readiness, so as not to alarm their allies. Meanwhile a huge influx of fighter and fighter-bomber aircraft crammed into airfields in Florida.[30]

'Slow track' was not all that slow, as the quarantine would involve stopping and searching inbound Soviet ships and one of these, the *Aleksandrovsk*, had reached the port of La Isabela in the Dominican Republic a few hours before the quarantine went into effect. This ship was a source of great anxiety to Khrushchev because she was carrying sixty-eight nuclear warheads, twenty-four for the IRBMs and forty-four for the cruise missiles.[31] On the US side, when the quarantine came into force at 10 a.m. on 24 October not much thought had been given to how to respond if the Soviet ships failed to stop, or how to deal with the noisy Foxtrot diesel- and battery-powered submarines that were shadowing them.

That morning an ashen-faced JFK waited to learn whether the Soviets were going to back down. At last intelligence came in that the Soviet ships had halted or were circling. Finally, one after another, the freighters carrying proscribed cargoes turned around, while an oil tanker and an East German cruise ship submitted to inspection and were permitted to proceed. At a Presidium meeting on 25 October Khrushchev tried unconvincingly to present the retreat as a victory. 'Apparently Kennedy slept with a wooden knife,' he announced jovially. Nobody knew what he was talking about, so he explained that 'When a person goes bear hunting for the first time, he brings a wooden knife with him, so that cleaning his [soiled] trousers will be easier'. At this, the tension in the room broke.[32]

A two-day pause brokered at America's behest by UN Secretary-General U Thant may have defused the likelihood of an untoward incident at sea, although by this time McNamara was micromanaging the quarantine. When the Chief of Naval Operations Admiral George Anderson challenged him, McNamara brutally reminded him who was boss, and told him when he swept from the room that he was 'finished'. Anderson was put out to pasture as ambassador to Portugal in 1963.

The problem of the Soviet missiles on Cuba remained, and the possibility of using the Jupiter missiles in Turkey as a bargaining chip, something discussed earlier and discarded, was revived when Kennedy invited eight of the fifteen-strong ExComm group to a private discussion in the Oval Office. Johnson was deliberately excluded. There were two major problems: the missiles had become operational only on 22 October and the Turkish government had told the State Department that they would 'deeply resent' it if they were immediately deactivated; and there was no question of being seen to reward the Soviets for their reckless gamble. The State Department began to manage public opinion as early as 25 October by floating the idea through the influential newspaper columnist Walter Lippmann. On the same day a furious Fidel Castro publicly declared that under no circumstances would he accept US verification of the missiles on the island, which he said were purely defensive.

The outlines of a solution were first mooted at meeting in Washington between Aleksandr Feklisov, a KGB officer, and the ABC journalist John Scali. Feklisov suggested that the Soviets might withdraw their missiles from Cuba in return for a solemn promise that the US would never invade the island. On the same day a signal arrived from Khrushchev that seemed to confirm the informal approach:

Mr. President, we and you ought not now to pull on the ends of the rope in which you have tied the knot of war, because the more the two of us pull, the tighter that knot will be tied. And a moment may come when that knot will be tied so tight that even he who tied it will not have the strength to untie it, and then it will be necessary to cut that knot, and what that would mean is not for me to explain to you, because you yourself understand perfectly of what terrible forces our countries dispose. Consequently, if there is no intention to tighten that knot and thereby to doom the world to the catastrophe of thermonuclear war, then let us not only relax the forces pulling on the ends of the rope, let us take measures to untie that knot. We are ready for this.

This rambling message had been drafted by Khrushchev. A more considered signal linked the missiles in Cuba with the Jupiters in Turkey. Bobby Kennedy came up with the felicitous solution of publicly embracing the first signal, misrepresented as having promised the unconditional withdrawal of the ballistic missiles in Cuba.

On 27 October all such deals seemed to be off when a U-2 was shot down over Cuba and another was chased out of Soviet airspace. McNamara took a Machiavellian approach, seeming to be the strongest advocate of retaliatory air strikes, while letting the rest of the ExComm members know that he had gamed out an air onslaught and follow-up invasion of Cuba, a Soviet counter-attack against Turkey, NATO retaliation in the Black Sea and the likelihood that a nuclear war would follow. The Kennedys and an inner group of six ExComm members then decided to give up the soon-to-be-obsolete missiles in Turkey, although keeping this information from the American public.[33]

Bobby Kennedy worked out the details with Ambassador Anatoly Dobrynin, warning that if the missiles did not leave Cuba 'right away' there might be a 'chain reaction', which chilled the blood of his Soviet interlocutor. Any further Soviet attacks on US planes would meet with instant retaliation that would leave a lot of dead Russians. In his report to Khrushchev, Dobrynin added much entirely false local colour about US generals 'itching for a fight', which Khrushchev dramatized as a potential coup against the President. On 30 October Dobrynin tried to hand Bobby Kennedy a letter from Khrushchev formally acknowledging that the Jupiters would go. Bobby refused to accept it, saying: 'Who knows where and when such letters can surface or be somehow published – not now, but in the future . . . The appearance of such a letter could cause irreparable harm to my political career in the future.' Recalling his father's injunction never to put anything in writing, he also deleted any reference to such a deal from his notes.[34]

For once, Fidel's belligerence worked in favour of the US. The U-2 shoot-down was his doing and at 2 a.m. on Saturday 27 October he drove to the Soviet embassy and raved about Cuban honour and his willingness to die 'with supreme dignity'. He spewed out a torrent of words which Soviet stenographers tried to pare down to a message for Khrushchev. As dawn broke, a text was ready. The key paragraph said: 'If they carry out an attack on Cuba, a barbaric, illegal, and immoral act, then that would be the time to think about liquidating such a danger for ever through a legal right of self-defence. However harsh and terrible such a decision would be, there is no other way out, in my opinion.'[35] The Cuban tail was urging the big red dog to unleash a nuclear war. While this frightening communication wound its way towards the Kremlin, Cuban intelligence radioed its agents in Latin America to prepare to launch a campaign of terrorism and revolution. US embassies and business interests were to be among the targets. Bombs exploded in Venezuela. It is worth noting that Cuban intelligence planned to launch Operation Boomerang, involving the bombing of government buildings, military installations and cinemas in the greater New York area.[36]

Castro's letter had a sobering effect on the Soviets. After waiting a few days, Khrushchev sent a paternal rebuke, reminding Castro that 'above all Cuba would have been the first to burn in the fire of war'. If Castro wanted to commit suicide that was his affair: 'We struggle against imperialism not to die but to make full use of our possibilities, so that in this struggle we win more than we lose and achieve the victory of Communism.' Castro was so annoyed by the Soviet climbdown that he smashed a mirror. Thereafter a contemptuous ditty did the rounds in Havana:

> *Nikita, mariquita,*
> *Lo que se da no se quita!*
> *[Nikita, you pansy,*
> *A gift cannot be taken back!]*[37]

Although the crisis had abated by 29 October 1962, it took months for a settlement to be agreed. On 5 November the *Aleksandrovsk* sailed home with its nuclear warheads, followed by all the MRBM warheads that had already reached Cuba. In late November the Soviets agreed to remove the Ilyushin bombers. Some but not all the tactical nuclear warheads were shipped out on Christmas Day 1962 and the remainder remained strictly under Soviet control until they too were withdrawn. In turn the US ended the naval quarantine. The paramilitary aspects of Operation Mongoose were suspended in early 1963 and the Jupiters in Turkey were dismantled in April. JFK refused to make a formal pledge of non-aggression towards Cuba, reserving the right to take military action should the Castro regime persist in using the island 'as a springboard for subversion'.

Nonetheless that is exactly what Castro did, sponsoring subversion from Guatemala to Chile. With the extravagant JMWAVE station in Miami wound down, a large number of trained, armed and highly motivated exiles were cut loose to raise hell in their own deadly but ineffectual ways. The Kennedys did not give up trying to kill Castro, however, and during a reception on 8 September 1963 at the Brazilian embassy in Havana, Castro gave AP journalist Daniel Harker a three-hour impromptu interview. 'US leaders', he warned, 'should think that if they are aiding terrorist plans to eliminate Cuban leaders, they themselves will not be safe.'[38]

The day before, CIA headquarters had received a report that agent AM/LASH (Roberto Cubela), a medical doctor and revolutionary hero, who in 1956 had gunned down Batista's military intelligence chief outside Havana's Montmartre nightclub, before offering himself to the CIA as an agent, was ready to kill Castro. Cubela felt himself shortchanged in the shareout of power by Fidel. On 29 October he asked the CIA for a high-powered, silenced rifle. At a meeting in Paris on 22 November his case officer gave him a poison pen/syringe instead, at about the time JFK was being assassinated in Dallas. Cubela was arrested in March 1966, but during his trial in Havana all evidence of his dealings with the CIA prior to November 1963 was suppressed at Castro's express command. Sentenced to twenty-five years' imprisonment, he was released after serving only thirteen as the prison's doctor with his own private house. He was often seen outside the prison driving a car. It is very hard to avoid the conclusion that he was a Cuban intelligence plant. Castro himself had a private assassination squad who would kill all those Bolivians involved in the death of Guevara, as well as the exiled dictator Somoza, and make several attempts on the life of Chile's Augusto Pinochet.[39]

There were global ramifications to events in Cuba. Chinese newspapers took the opportunity to laud Castro's heroic resistance in bold type, while comparing Khrushchev to Neville Chamberlain at Munich in 1938. Given that shortly after Munich the Soviets had allied with Hitler, this was very provocative. From grudgingly and belatedly supporting China in its border war with India, the Soviets started selling India MiG-21 jet fighters instead. Relations between the two great Communist powers got steadily worse, while Castro joined China on a global crusade against imperialism. In late 1963 in response to an appeal from Ben Bella a battalion of Cuban troops, together with tanks, artillery and other heavy weapons arrived to support the Algerian regime in a confrontation with Morocco. It was a decisive intervention, and marked the beginning of a long period of semi-independent Cuban involvement in Africa, which tended to lead rather than follow the Soviet line.[40]

Khrushchev's resort to bluff and brinkmanship to force the US into treating the Soviet Union as an equal played a part in his downfall. Ironically, as Mikoyan knew, by the time he was ousted he had achieved something like peaceful coexistence with the Americans. The plot against Khrushchev was triggered not by foreign policy, but by his arbitrary insistence that the length of time Soviet children spend in school should be reduced from eleven to eight years. This reflected a deep peasant anti-intellectualism at a time when the Soviet state needed all the scientists and technocrats it could produce. The initial plotters were President Leonid Brezhnev, Nikolai Podgorny who had joined the Presidium in 1960, the KGB Chairman Vladimir Semichastny and the former KGB chief Aleksandr Schelepin, who was outraged when, during a visit to Egypt, Khrushchev allowed himself to be seated next to the Iraqi Baathist leader Abdel Salam Aref, who had recently exterminated the Iraqi Communist Party. In October 1964 Khrushchev went to his vacation home at Pitsunda on the Black Sea, only to be urgently summoned back to the Presidium where he found Brezhnev sitting in his usual chair. By the time the session concluded, the sixty-nine-year-old Soviet leader found his bodyguards gone and his black Zil limousine replaced by a modest Volga sedan.[41]

While Kennedy's victory in Cuba helped see off his old Soviet opponent, posthumously, he was also responsible for increased US military involvement in South-east Asia, the obsessional commitment which would end in defeat and a bout of as much introversion as a superpower is capable of. Ironically this obsession with stopping the Communists taking over South Vietnam from within and without coincided with mounting evidence that major splits were developing between the USSR and China which might have been exploited a decade before President Nixon made his historic visits to Beijing and Moscow. What was called 'the Bloc' was not as monolithic as it seemed.

17. OVERREACH: VIETNAM

Esau's Birthright: The Sino–Soviet Split

Mao felt that Khrushchev's disparagement of Stalin's reputation merely served the interests of global imperialism. He argued that Stalin's legacy needed cool assessment, so that the 20 or 30 per cent bad could be separated from the 80 or 70 per cent good. 'Stalin is a sword,' he said. 'It can be used to fight imperialism and various other enemies . . . If this sword is put aside completely, if it is damaged, or if it is abandoned, the enemies will use the sword to try to kill us. Consequently, we would be lifting a rock only to drop it on our own feet.' Khrushchev replied that the sword was completely useless and should be abandoned.

Compared with the two-month wait he had endured in 1949, Mao was lavished with attention when he paid his second, and last, visit to Moscow in November 1957 on the fortieth anniversary of the Bolshevik Revolution. He was housed in a palace of Catherine the Great, but slept on the floor rather than in her bed. Hidden microphones picked up Mao's private comments on his hosts, which were withering. Dismissing Khrushchev's belief in peaceful coexistence with the West, Mao said: 'If worse came to worst and half of mankind died, the other half would remain, while imperialism would be razed to the ground and the world would become Socialist.'[1]

Mao's psychopathy surged to a new level when he launched the Great Leap Forward in 1958. Detailed research by Frank Dikötter has established that fifty-five to sixty-five million people perished in this dystopian effort to surpass British industrial output within fifteen years. Even

China's sparrows were not safe from this relentless venture, for they pecked away at grain and had to be kept airborne until they dropped dead by villagers banging pots through the night.[2] Foreign relations were not spared the general hysteria; indeed, they may have been integral to it. This was the year when the Soviets sought to install their communications system for submarines operating in the northern Pacific on Chinese soil, offering the Chinese, who wanted to have their own submarine fleet, what Mao dismissed as a 'military co-operative'. Mao's response to the Soviet Ambassador was so rude that Khrushchev hastened in person to Beijing, where discussions with the Chinese leader went from bad to worse: 'The British, Japanese, and other foreigners who stayed in our country for a long time have already been driven away by us, Comrade Khrushchev. I'll repeat it again. We do not want anyone to use our land to achieve their own purposes any more.' There was rivalry even when the two relaxed. While Khrushchev bobbed nervously in a rubber ring in the shallow end of Mao's pool, the Chinese leader ploughed back and forth like a porpoise, demonstrating his mastery of various strokes, while keeping up a stream of talk translated into Russian by poolside interpreters.

Mao gave his guest no warning that he was about to embark on his own challenge to US Pacific hegemony. He was quite explicit about the 'social imperialist' agenda: 'a tense international situation could mobilize the population, could particularly mobilize the backward people, could mobilize the people in the middle, and could therefore promote the Great Leap Forward in economic construction'. In other words, Mao was going to incite Chinese chauvinism.[3]

On 23 August 1958 the People's Liberation Army rained 30,000 artillery shells in one hour on the Kuomintang-controlled island of Jinmen (Quemoy) off the mainland, killing 600 of Chiang Kai-shek's troops. The US responded, as they were obliged to do under the 1954 defence treaty with Taiwan, with a massive naval build-up in the Taiwan Straits and the deployment of 200 aircraft. With the US threatening war, Soviet Foreign Minister Gromyko rushed to Beijing, where Mao explained that his intention was to lure the Americans into an 'iron noose'. Gromyko was appalled when Mao amplified his strategy. If the Americans were to use nuclear weapons or invade China, the PLA would retreat into the interior, drawing US forces after them. At that point, the Kremlin should 'use all means at its disposal' to destroy them. Gromyko flatly told him that such support would not be forthcoming. His main object of having the Americans and Russians 'dancing and scurrying' about over two miserable little offshore islands achieved, Mao allowed tension to subside.

In view of Mao's cavalier attitude towards nuclear warfare, it was not surprising that the Soviets found excuses not to give Communist China a prototype nuclear bomb and related blueprints as they had agreed to do in October 1957. Further tearing noises were heard, as we have seen, during the Sino–Indian conflict. In September 1958 Khrushchev arrived in Beijing for the tenth anniversary celebrations of the Chinese Revolution, to find no reception party at the airport and no microphone for his carefully prepared arrival speech. At the formal reception, he lectured his hosts on the need for a relaxation of international tensions, and chided them for the recklessness of their recent ventures in the Taiwan Straits and on the Sino-Indian border. The meetings between Chinese and Russians degenerated into insults, so the Russians cut short their scheduled week of talks and left. Shortly afterwards Moscow slashed aid to Beijing, which enabled Mao to blame the Soviet 'revisionists' for the failings of his Great Leap Forward. China increasingly regarded the Soviets as part of the problem rather than the solution, and themselves as the torchbearers of the insurgent Third World.

The CIA's Sino–Soviet Studies Group, set up in 1956, produced a series of 'Esau studies', named after the biblical figure duped out of his birthright by his brother Jacob, which analysed the rift in the making. Agency analysts developed what amounted to heretical views at a time when the prevailing orthodoxy was of a monolithic Communist bloc pursuing common objectives. Those who stressed the role of national differences in Communist parties were accused of having 'nineteenth-century minds', to which they retorted that it was an improvement on having minds locked into the thirteenth century. Bureaucratic caution and suspicions that the split might itself be a 'Commie plot' explain why it took time for these views to feed into policy-making. Among those most sceptical were Eisenhower, Nixon and the CIA's future chief John McCone.

It was not until 1960 that the views of the heretics found their way into the National Intelligence Estimates that the CIA prepared for the NSC, and not until about two years later that State Department officials accepted this new international reality.[4] By early 1962, when 60,000 Muslim Uighars fled Xinjiang for neighbouring Kazakhstan, the Chinese accused Moscow of having suborned them through 'subversive activities'. Moscow replied that since 1960 Chinese troops had flouted the borders, and warned of an 'extremely decisive response'. This was where things were tending. What might have led to a shift in US foreign policy ten years before the Nixon–Kissinger opening to China in 1971–2 was put on hold because the Soviets and Chinese seemed to be co-operating in supporting North Vietnam's war against the South. Despite the fact that Vietnamese national identity had been shaped by a thousand years of implacable resistance to the Chinese, the US saw Hanoi as just a proxy of Beijing, and the Vietnamese civil war as a replay of Korea.[5]

Why Vietnam?

As a senator, John Kennedy had repeatedly advertised his support for South Vietnam. It was, he said, in a flurry of mixed metaphors that we have already quoted, 'the cornerstone of the free world in Southeast Asia, the keystone to the arch, the finger in the dike'.[6] In his inaugural address JFK spoke grandiloquently of Americans as 'watchmen on the walls of freedom'. An activist style swept through Washington, as the 'best and the brightest' moved into their new posts, many of them armchair tacticians and professorial warriors, over-fond of modish social-science modernization theory. For all their conceit about being new brooms, they were mental prisoners of the faith that appeasement had brought about the Second World War, and of the post-war belief in a domino theory that refused to recognize the nationalist fissures in supposedly monolithic international Communism.

A few sceptics reported, from the inside, that much of the administration's relentless activism was pointless. 'We are like the Harlem Globetrotters, passing forward, behind, sidewise, and underneath. But nobody has made a basket yet,' wrote the new National Security Advisor

McGeorge Bundy at the time. Bundy had been brought in from Harvard, where he was a senior academic manager.[7] Although there was an emphasis on youth, a kitchen crowded with young chefs had to accommodate such oldies as Acheson, Averell Harriman and even Douglas MacArthur, for a huge range of advice was solicited, often to no obvious purpose.

Wider events favoured doing *something* about Vietnam. In their pre-inaugural briefing sessions Eisenhower had underscored the importance of Laos, which JFK insisted on pronouncing *Lay-os* to avoid the homonym with *Louse*. He initiated negotiations that included the Pathet Lao over the future of Laos, but until July 1962 Harriman's diplomatic efforts in Geneva proved sterile. In any case the principal conflict was in South Vietnam, where the National Liberation Front (Viet Minh) swelled with southerners returning from training in the North from 10,000 guerrillas in January 1961 to 17,000 by October. It was not essential to make a stand in South Vietnam even if the assumptions about monolithic Communist aggression and falling dominoes were right. The line might as easily have been drawn around SEATO ally Thailand.[8]

As part of his creed of flexible response, JFK preferred to fight the war indirectly. The US Military Assistance and Advisory Group (MAAG) in Saigon received 500 extra personnel, the US having long exceeded the 685 permitted under the 1954 Geneva Accords.[9] Four hundred freshly minted Special Forces operators in their green berets were sent to train the Army of the Republic of Vietnam (ARVN) to conduct hit-and-run raids across the 17th parallel dividing North from South.

The CIA accelerated covert operations in Laos. Using such codenames as Operation Momentum, CIA officers organized and trained 9,000 Hmong tribesmen, whom the Americans ignorantly called Meo, which meant something like 'native' or 'nigger' in Chinese. The aim was to use the fiercely anti-Vietnamese tribesmen to disrupt the Ho Chi Minh Trail, which was becoming the major Viet Minh supply route, snaking along the border inside Laos. Supplies were flown into remote jungle landing strips by such colourful Air America pilots as 'Weird Neil' Houston, while the base chief, Tony Po, lived in a house adorned with strings of ears the Hmong had separated from severed Pathet Lao and Viet Minh heads.[10]

While these limited measures bought time, they did not address how the US might respond if the Diem regime collapsed. Some hawkish members of the administration – such as the Deputy Special Assistant to the President for National Security Affairs Walt Rostow – wanted air and naval operations against North Vietnam, accompanied if necessary by US boots on the ground in the South. An ambitious Polish-Jewish academic from MIT, Rostow had been a target identifier in the Second World War. His enthusiasm for bombing led to his being known as 'Air Marshal Rostow'. A major obstacle to boosting the US presence was President Diem himself, described as 'a weak, third-rate Catholic bigot' by one senior State Department official. While Diem wanted the cornucopia of US aid to continue, he was wily enough to realize that an overt US military presence – involving an autonomous command – would unify his many domestic opponents and give the Communists a powerful propaganda lever against him.

A major difficulty the new administration faced was getting an accurate picture of conditions in Vietnam, on which to build costly nation-building projects – manufactured from turgid sociology and a false analogy with civil engineering. That was why so many high-powered visitors were regularly sent there, for what in reality amounted to guided tours around Potemkin villages. On 5 May 1961 JFK sent Vice President Lyndon Johnson on a tour of Asia, with a key stop in Saigon. As his huge motorcade struggled into the capital Johnson stepped out to dispense pens, lighters and complimentary passes to the US Senate gallery, as he would have in Texas. In public he referred to Diem as 'the Winston Churchill of Asia'. In private conversations, this master of innumerable 'knee to knee' negotiations in the US Senate, where he had been majority leader, found Diem impossible to pin down. 'He was tickled as hell when I promised him forty million dollars and talked about military aid, but he turned deaf and dumb every time I talked about him speeding up and beefing up some health and welfare projects.'

Reporting to JFK on return from his tour, Johnson stressed that the free nations of Asia took a poor view of the search for a Laotian compromise. Diem himself was badly shaken by US willingness to negotiate with the Pathet Lao. Johnson added that support for Diem 'must be made with the knowledge that at some point we may be faced with the further decision of whether we commit major United States forces . . . I recommend we proceed with a clear cut and strong program of action.'[11] Yet Johnson also conjured up the spectre of US troops 'bogged down chasing irregulars and guerrillas over the rice fields and jungles of South-east Asia while our principal enemies China and the Soviet Union stand outside the fray and husband their strength'. This encapsulated the essential problem: JFK could neither withdraw nor escalate.[12]

Subsequent policy discussions were interminable and fractious. Many experts on Europe regarded the entire South-east Asian region as a bad joke, including doves like George Ball and the hawk Dean Acheson. Civilian and military hawks alike saw a massive Soviet and Chinese threat to the whole of South-east Asia, and wanted to deter it through escalating US responses to a series of pre-calibrated trip wires. Rostow recommended ground troops in Laos and air strikes against North Vietnam in retaliation for increased Viet Minh activity. JFK even consulted old MacArthur, who warned that Americans were useless at guerrilla warfare and should avoid it. America's SEATO allies were unenthusiastic about intervention in South-east Asia, and only Thailand would be of much help on the ground. What did Pakistan or the Philippines care about Vietnam?

On 17 October Rostow and General Maxwell Taylor were despatched to Saigon to report, once again, on conditions on the ground and the durability of Diem's regime. Maxwell Taylor spoke French and was known to liberals as the 'good' General, perhaps because he had recently headed the Lincoln Center for the Performing Arts. The two men landed during the worst floods in living memory, with much of the Mekong Delta under water and many of the inhabitants stranded on their roofs. The Viet Cong abducted and murdered a prominent army liaison officer just to remind the arriving American who was really boss.

South Vietnam seemed to Taylor to be undergoing 'a collapse of national morale'. Hidden in a cloud of cigarette smoke, Diem talked at Taylor for over four hours, although Taylor was fortunate here since Diem could often manage ten hours when he got into his stride. He insisted on more US aid while denying his visitors the ability to form their own opinion about what was needed. He also wanted extra US advisers to train a further 100,000 troops. When Taylor met General

Duong Van Minh, who as 'Big Minh' notionally commanded the field army, Minh bitterly criticized Diem for permitting arrangements in which political concerns subverted the army chain of command. Thus Diem loyalist General Nguyen Khanh seemed to have more power than Lieutenant-General Le Van Ty, the Chief of the Joint General Staff, while civilian political bosses gave orders to the troops in their areas. There seemed to be seven intelligence agencies, none of them doing much to defeat the Viet Cong.

In the end, Taylor decided that it was the best of a series of bad options to stick with Diem. Fatefully, he recommended using the floods as an excuse to introduce a small number of US troops, notionally to lend Diem's forces logistical support, but also to lay the foundations for whatever larger US presence might eventually be judged necessary.[13]

Intelligence experts warned that for each added US contribution, the Communists would respond in kind. They were ignored. There was no discussion of the implications of the Sino–Soviet split, nor of how North Vietnamese support for southern revolutionaries related to Moscow and Beijing, nor of international law on countering aggression of the kind that had justified the UN-mandated US intervention in Korea. More-over, although the visiting Americans could not fail to comment on Diem's deficiencies, which State Department officials tirelessly empha-sized, they never addressed one crucial dilemma: if the US took over running the war it would be vilified around the world for neo-colonialism; if it merely continued to advise Diem, there was the dangerous prospect of the tail wagging the dog, or at least a fruitless cycle of mutual decep-tion and manipulation.[14]

While the administration procrastinated about ends, the US 'advi-sory' presence mushroomed. The Saigon CIA station under William Colby from 1959 until 1961 – when he took over the Far Eastern Affairs desk – and his successor John Richardson became a huge operation, with housing, facilities and pay deeply resented by the embassy staff. When Richardson and his wife Ethyl took up residence in a big villa on a leafy street, they found that they could not hire servants. With that attention to local nuance so representative of American officials abroad, they had not appreciated that the house had been used as an interrogation centre by the French army, by their Japanese successors and then by the Viet Minh before the French Sûreté policemen returned. Vietnamese thought the place haunted, and would not enter it until monks were brought in to exorcize the house for a week, while the walls were hung with ghost-unfriendly mirrors.

Although the new wave of CIA officers likewise wished to exorcize the residual spirit of the 'cowboy' Lansdale, the Saigon station took over many of his best operatives, whose names would recur again and again in the history of Vietnam. One of Colby's more lamentable schemes was the Lansdale-esque Project Tiger, involving the air or sea insertion of agents into North Vietnam, of whom the only ones to escape execution were those who had been turned, replicating the success of British counter-intelligence against the Germans in the Second World War.[15]

Nor were the soldiers idle. Under Project Beefup, the number of military advisers rose from 3,205 in December 1961 to 9,000 a year later. MAAG was transformed into a new Military Assistance Command Vietnam (MACV) under General Paul Harkins and its role expanded to piloting aircraft and helicopters on combat missions, with some token South Vietnamese aviator present should anything go wrong or a plane be shot down by the Viet Minh. JFK also authorized the use of defoliants to deny the enemy forest cover, and herbicides to kill off their food crops.

Questioned by the press, JFK denied that the advisers were engaged in combat, even though some were being decorated for valour and others killed in action. He also tried to exercise control over a Saigon press corps that had once largely supported the American engagement but was becoming radically disillusioned by what they heard and saw on the ground. On one occasion JFK personally telephoned the publisher of the *New York Times* to get a foreign correspondent removed.

Illusion and Reality

The Kennedy administration was captive to the doctrine of sub-nuclear 'flexible response'. Counter-insurgency operations were only one item in the tool kit. It also included tactical good deeds of a progressive nature, what nowadays is called 'nation-building'. JFK was sympathetic to hearts-and-minds warfare, involving quarantining the population from the Viet Cong so as 'to put a TV in every thatched hut', while the army pursued and killed the enemy lurking in between. Senior military commanders appreciated that this flexible response might boost their budgets, but were fundamentally wedded to more conventional forms of warfare based on eliminating the enemy with main force, or as they had it: 'Grab 'em by the balls and their hearts and minds will follow.'[16]

As it happened this was the view being pushed in Saigon by Sir Robert Thompson, veteran of the Malayan Emergency, whom Diem had consulted to reduce his dependence on the Americans. Thompson's British Advisory Mission (BRIAM), established in September 1961, proposed a plan to clear the Viet Cong from the Mekong Delta and to secure the population through the creation of 'strategic hamlets'. Thompson's memoirs are filled with lazy patronizing comments about both the Americans and the Vietnamese. The American reputation for efficiency was 'mythical'; 'no American we met had read Mao'. Actually, some of them had, in the original, for Thompson overlooked those thousands of American missionaries whose cosmopolitan children had grown up speaking Mandarin.[17] In his view Vietnam was just Malaya on a bigger scale, for he had no grasp of what made the Viet Cong a very different fighting proposition from the Communists in Malaya. He failed to notice that some of the Americans knew a great deal about what had happened in Malaya, particularly the US foreign service officer Charles Cross and the sinologist Lucian Pye, author of *Guerrilla Communism in Malaya* (1956), which was based on interviews with captured Communists.[18]

There were actually few meaningful lessons to be drawn from Malaya, where the Communist insurgents were ethnic Chinese and the majority population Malay. Furthermore it had taken the British twelve years to get on top of them, in circumstances infinitely more propitious than those prevailing in South Vietnam. One narrow land border between Malaya and Thailand was not comparable with the 800-mile internal frontier of dense jungle, rivers and mountains between Vietnam, Cambodia and Laos. The British had a functioning administration throughout Malaya; in Vietnam a similar set-up had vanished with the French. Vietnam had an abundance of rice, Malaya did not, which enabled the British to use food supplies as a means of population control.

Finally the common threat from Indonesia concentrated both Malay and Chinese minds to accept a federal settlement once the British had promised independence.

Despite these differences, Diem simply rechristened his earlier *agrovilles* 'strategic hamlets' and called for increased aid, which was forthcoming because of the Malayan precedent. By September 1962 some 4,322,034 people (33.4 per cent of the population) were gathered in 2,800 strategic hamlets, corralled within moats and bristling bamboo spikes. The Americans dubbed them 'oil spots', the coalescence of which would exclude the Viet Cong from operating in a given area. While they marvelled at the speed with which all this was done, the Americans were unaware that the official driving the programme so fast, Colonel Pham Ngoc Thao, was a highly placed Viet Minh agent, whose aim was to encourage peasant disaffection. He certainly succeeded.[19]

The problem was that the oil spots were widely dispersed, while the strategic hamlets took little or no notice of how peasants related to ancestral graves or worked their patchwork fields. All intervening areas were declared free-fire zones in which anything that moved could be pulverized with artillery and bombing. While US officials saw the strategic hamlets as an opportunity to introduce modernizing reforms in village life, Diem regarded them primarily as a means of political control. Aid money was now embezzled by an even larger number of corrupt officials, in a country where the pool of educated administrators was modest to begin with. The CIA also spread vast sums of money around, so much that they got the Vietnamese to sign for the few available trolleys the bulky cash was moved on rather than for the cash itself. By contrast, where they were in control, which meant much of the country after dark, the Viet Minh were scrupulously egalitarian, combining this with the systematic assassination of corrupt government officials.[20]

The delusion that these programmes were having an effect confirmed JFK's reluctance to bring the big military club to bear. By the summer of 1962 he was contemplating withdrawing US advisers, starting the following year. One hears echoes of his doubts and dilemmas amid the beating of the war drums around him. For all the specious numerology, he knew that one basic set of figures did not compute. How could he justify sending US combat troops to fight 10,000 miles away, in what seemed a lopsided conflict involving 16,000 guerrillas and an indigenous South Vietnamese army which on paper numbered 200,000? As he astutely remarked: 'The troops will march in; the bands will play; the crowds will cheer. And in four days everyone will have forgotten. Then we will be told we have to send in more troops. It's like taking a drink. The effect wears off, and you have to take another.'[21]

But at the same time JFK's defining fear of seeming soft on Communism prevented him from pushing for a diplomatic resolution of a conflict that was still at the stage of a civil war. He was loath to expand the negotiations over neutralizing Laos into a general settlement in Vietnam, based on de-escalation and mutually agreed partition. Under Secretary of State George Ball, Averell Harriman (newly appointed assistant secretary for Far Eastern affairs) and the US Ambassador to New Delhi John Kenneth Galbraith urged this course on him. Galbraith envisaged using the Indians as a backchannel to Hanoi, and Harriman slipped into a Geneva kitchen to hold clandestine talks with the North Vietnamese Foreign Minister Ung Van Khiem. Khiem, wearing a Soviet suit much too large for him, wasted the opportunity by raging at the seventy-year-old American statesman. Harriman drew himself up to his full height to tower over Khiem, looked the 'insulting little thug' in the eye and told him he 'was in for a long, tough war'.[22]

The Soviets would certainly have come aboard any negotiated settlement. Khrushchev was as exasperated by 'all those silly Laotian names or the individuals to whom these names belonged' as were Americans such as Ball, who described the names as a series of typographical errors. 'Laos, Vietnam, all Southeast Asia,' Khrushchev exclaimed to Harriman. 'You and the Chinese can fight over it. I give up. We give up. We don't want any of it!'[23] The problem was their respective clients, who were not really clients at all. Diem knew he would be an early casualty of any broadening of the Saigon regime to make it more pluralistic, while the North Vietnamese could not be persuaded to pretend that any popular-front arrangement would be anything other than a temporary arrangement prior to their complete takeover of South Vietnam.

Supposedly dependable numbers and not old-fashioned perceptions of linguistic nuances and cultural differences led to insufficient urgency being given to the exploration of these possibilities. Even at this early stage, the US military were quantifying victory in terms of body counts, prisoners taken, numbers of aerial sorties and so on, the only language understood by Defense Secretary McNamara; for this, as David Halberstam argued so persuasively in *The Best and the Brightest*, was above all McNamara's war. He completely eclipsed Secretary of State Dean Rusk, the loyal Presbyterian who saw it as his job to express his own views only in private to the President, and sometimes not even then.

A registered Republican, McNamara was the supreme can-do guy in the Kennedy administration, an academic accountant and statistician turned whizz-kid president of the giant Ford automobile company. Although he looked about as buttoned down as it was possible to be with his slicked-back dark hair and large, black-rimmed glasses, he had read widely and was able to exchange quotations with the academics in the Kennedy entourage. Having made his pile with what were naively thought to be infinitely transferable skills, he was now driven by a desire for power unqualified by any moral considerations. There was something chilling about a man who could spend eight hours watching data slides on Vietnam on a screen, only to call for the projector to be stopped because something on slide 869 did not tally with slide 11. If information did not come to him in the form of numbers or tables, McNamara had difficulty processing it and he was widely regarded as a barely human computer.[24]

The numbers flowing from MACV encouraged optimism, but the soldiers were lying to themselves as much as to Washington. A persistent American complaint was that the Viet Cong would never stand and fight, preferring to hit and run in the way natural to 'raggedy-assed little bastards'. This was to underrate the pressures which the war exerted on Viet Minh commanders; if they failed then their peasant support might leach away. They were also required to undertake self-criticism among their troops, acknowledging and learning from their mistakes. The hierarchical US military insulated senior commanders from the truth and led to the reinforcement of failure, as did the good-old-boy fraternity-ring mafia among senior officers.

In January 1963 intelligence reported three Viet Cong companies grouped around a radio transmitter near the hamlet of Ap Bac, forty miles south-west of Saigon. An entire ARVN division was deployed against them. Instead of fleeing, the Viet Cong dug in and prepared to fight. The attack was a classic pincer operation, landing one force in helicopters despite thick fog, while another closed in with armoured personnel carriers. There was a substantial reserve force, and artillery and air cover. With a ten-to-one ARVN superiority, what could go wrong?

Almost everything, concluded the senior US adviser, Lieutenant-Colonel John Paul Vann, as he circled the battlefield in a spotter plane. After allowing the helicopter pilots to think the landings were unopposed, the Viet Cong unleashed deadly and sustained fire that destroyed five helicopters. The armoured units were slow in going to their relief, and when they did they too were ambushed amid near-total command chaos as Diem's political appointees ignominiously failed their first test of combat. They had also subverted the entire point of the operation by leaving the Viet Cong an escape route, and, to round it off, when another airborne battalion was inserted, it was in the wrong place and a massive friendly-fire episode resulted.

Only because they were such poor shots was the death toll limited to sixty-one ARVN troops dead and a hundred wounded; the Viet Cong had vanished, leaving behind only three dead. They had even taken away their spent cartridge cases for reuse. As MACV proclaimed Ap Bac a major victory because the Viet Cong had conceded the field, a South Vietnamese artillery commander unleashed a pointless barrage on a village he believed deserted but which was actually occupied by ARVN troops. After realizing his mistake he shot the lieutenant acting as a forward observer, which under the circumstances seems to have been justified.[25]

Washing Diem Away

Seldom has an imperial power put its prestige behind a more suicidal group of puppets than the Ngo Dinh clan. Diem's younger brother Nhu and his ghastly wife were bad enough, but it was elder brother Pierre Martin Ngo Dinh Thuc, Archbishop of Hué and the senior Catholic prelate in Vietnam, who did for his family. In May 1963 he prohibited the display of Buddhist banners during the celebrations commemorating the birth of the Gautama, citing a regulation prohibiting the display of non-government flags. Yet a few days earlier Catholics had been encouraged to fly Vatican flags to celebrate Thuc's twenty-fifth anniversary as bishop, to pay for which the mainly Buddhist residents of Hué had been taxed by Ngo Dinh Can, another younger brother, who ran central Vietnam with a private army and his own secret police.[26]

On 8 May 1963 large crowds gathered in Hué to protest against the ban were fired on by Can's thugs, killing nine protesters. Can and Diem blamed the Viet Cong, but in early June a sixty-six-year-old Buddhist bonze called Thich Quang Duc sat down in a lotus position at a Saigon junction and set himself alight with gasoline. What many American observers had regarded as a passive faith, until they saw Quang Duc in flames on the cover of *Life*, quickly became a powerful protest movement.[27]

Six more Buddhist priests immolated themselves with much further publicity, which Madame Nhu crassly described as 'barbecues'. 'Let them burn, and we shall clap our hands,' she said. Although Diem assured the departing US Ambassador Frederick Nolting that he would take no further measures against the Buddhists, in August Nhu's Special Forces (dressed as ARVN infantry) raided pagodas across the land, violently arresting 1,400 monks and sending them to join the already large number of political prisoners. Such operations brought the South Vietnamese army into such public discredit that some of its officers resolved on a coup.

The US government's disaffection with Diem reached breaking point when it learned that Nhu was engaged in secret talks with Hanoi. The North Vietnamese were happy to play along, calculating that once they got the Americans out they could rid themselves of the Ngo Dinhs. This intelligence report on the clandestine meeting arrived in Washington on a Saturday, when the most senior players were away from their desks. Three officials, including Harriman, seized the opportunity to draft instructions to the new US Ambassador, Henry Cabot Lodge, to the effect that if Diem could not rid himself of the Nhus then Diem himself would have to go.

Lodge would play a key role in the coup. He was the incumbent Massachusetts Senator so narrowly defeated by Kennedy in 1952 and was Nixon's running mate in 1960. JFK shrewdly sent him to Saigon as a lightning rod for Republican critics of his policy in South-east Asia. If a man who had twice lost murky elections to JFK was prepared to work for him, then Congressional Republicans should also accept him. Unlike Nolting, the tough patrician Lodge took an instant dislike to Diem. He also mistrusted CIA chief Richardson so much that he used a journalist to blow Richardson's official cover. Lodge's fresh instructions included permission to tell dissident Vietnamese generals that the US would support them 'in any interim period of breakdown of central government mechanisms'. JFK cleared this signal from his Hyannis Port compound, although it is unclear whether he saw the whole cable or only had it read to him over the telephone. When he returned to Washington on Monday he found his cabinet almost at war with itself, as the cats discovered what the mice had done in their absence.

From then on the machinations in Saigon became frankly byzantine. Nhu and Diem had wind of the coup, and the plotters had to proceed with great caution. Lodge's surrogate was Lucien Conein, the CIA's secret liaison with the generals. Conein had been in Indochina for eighteen years, a pulp-fiction spy with a French twist, who crisscrossed Saigon accompanied by a heavy Magnum revolver in case Nhu, who was exhibiting signs of opium-induced paranoia, decided to have him assassinated. Conein met with General Tran Van Don, the notional head of the army, at a dentist's office. The key conspirators included Don's brother-in-law, General Le Van Kim, and General Duong Van Minh, the former corporal known as 'Big Minh'. Like Don, all of them had been shuffled into marginal posts because Diem distrusted their popularity among the troops. Others whose careers would benefit from the removal of Diem and Nhu were recruited, including General Ton That Dinh, commander of Saigon district.

The conspirators had to be careful when meeting their MACV opposite numbers, since they were not apprised of the change in US policy and supported Diem. MACV chief Harkins did not even know that Vietnamese-speaking army signals officers had been brought in from the Philippines to transcribe the take from microphones planted to eavesdrop on the plotters when Conein was not present. Lodge, also, had to be careful because Nhu had comprehensively bugged the US embassy. Preparations for the coup went ahead with apparently routine command changes gradually moving Diem loyalists further from Saigon to prevent them rushing to defend the regime. Astrologers were consulted to divine which date had the most favourable aspects.[28]

There was one hiatus, as a further top-level delegation, led by McNamara and Maxwell Taylor, arrived in late September 1963, with William Colby along for the CIA. The last such visit, by Marine General Victor Krulak and the State Department's Joseph Mendenhall, had prompted JFK's famous quip: 'The two of you did visit the same country, didn't you?'[29] McNamara had been appalled by the idea of removing Diem, not least because MACV's General Harkins was reporting a war almost won. It seemed illogical to change the winning team in such circumstances. Certain aspects of the visit meant that 'the computer' began to be malfunction. While Diem's two-hour opening monologue was nothing unusual – for McNamara had been to Vietnam before – there was the bizarre experience of staying with Lodge, who told him Diem was a lost cause, and then being briefed by Harkins's staff who told him that nothing was wrong. Knowing McNamara's obsession with facts and figures, the military men presented the war in such terms, with Harkins and Taylor beaming at their mastery of flow charts and graphs.

The Potemkin village collapsed when it came to a briefing on a certain province in the Mekong Delta. A young major, answering helpful questions from Maxwell Taylor, affirmed that everything in the Delta was hunkydory. However, McNamara had a copy of a report by a young CIA officer and rural affairs adviser called Rufus Phillips, which had caused serious ructions when it had been discussed by the NSC on 10 September. Phillips sent back a report by a US civilian adviser who bleakly estimated that the Viet Cong were in charge of 80 per cent of villages in the Delta, and affirmed that a US Army adviser had been reporting to his superiors in similar terms, without receiving any response. McNamara asked the young Major if he had read the reports. Yes, he had. Did he agree with them, asked the Defense Secretary. After a pause, for his eyes to flit over Harkins and Taylor, the Major said he did. Why hadn't he reported the same developments? They were 'beyond the parameters set by his superiors'.[30]

As they returned to Washington, McNamara and Taylor drew up their mission report. It included such gems as 'our policy is to seek to bring about the abandonment of Diem's repression because of its effect on the popular will to resist'. Despite concluding that the military programme 'has made great progress and continues to progress', such that a thousand US advisers could be withdrawn by Christmas, the two men agreed that relations with Diem should be 'correct' while a search was made for 'alternative leadership'.[31]

On 1 November the conspirators moved, with Conein bustling about the capital armed with large bags of money. Their task was made easier by Nhu, who out-clevered himself by mounting a phoney coup to draw the real plotters into the open, which meant his own troops were not where they were needed when the real coup took place. Regime loyalists such as the head of Special Forces guarding Diem were arrested and summarily shot. After their pleas to Cabot Lodge were coldly rebuffed, Diem and Nhu managed to flee the palace for the Chinese quarter of Cholon, leaving the conspirators to storm the abandoned building. Trusting in assurances the plotters had given the Americans, Diem and his brother eventually agreed to surrender at St Francis Xavier's Catholic church. When 'Big Minh' sent a select team to pick them up, by gestures he indicated that they must die. Diem and Nhu were bound and loaded into an armoured personnel carrier, and were butchered during the journey into central Saigon. The APC had to be hosed out afterwards.

Diem was briefly replaced by a twelve-man military junta that operated from an HQ near Tan Son Nhut Airport. On 29 January 1964 it was overthrown by a group of younger officers under General Nguyen Khanh, again with American connivance. Khanh was so uncertain about his own future that he took up residence in a villa on the Saigon River, convenient if he had to flee by boat. The CIA reckoned the new regime's longevity in terms of weeks or months.[32]

When he learned that Diem and Nhu had been killed, JFK paled and rushed from the room, suddenly brought face to face with what he and some of the most liberal members of his administration had done. One might legitimately wonder who he and his colleagues thought would replace Diem, for the alternatives were more dismal than him, if they could be identified at all. Three weeks later Kennedy was himself assassinated, so we cannot know whether he would have continued down the blood-smoothed slope or would have found the moral courage to back off. It seems unlikely: he had no reason to believe that South Vietnam was a lost cause, especially with the Ngo Dinhs out of the way, and his fear of being seen as soft on Communism was as strong as ever.[33] Responsibility for Vietnam devolved on a big-hearted but corrupt and cunning man who in domestic policy hoped to begin where FDR rather than JFK had left off. What happened to him deserves the epithet tragic.

18. WATERSHED OF THE AMERICAN CENTURY

The Great Society

News of Kennedy's murder reached Ambassador Lodge in San Francisco as he arrived from Saigon. He continued on to Washington with bad tidings of the progress of the war in Vietnam, a report he delivered on 24 November 1963 to President Johnson. Johnson had been sworn in two days earlier on the aircraft bringing JFK's body back to Washington and he made one thing clear: 'I am not going to lose Vietnam. I am not going to be the President who saw Southeast Asia go the way China went.' This pledge became policy two days later when it was incorporated into National Security Council Action Memorandum (NSCAM) 273.[1]

The hostility felt towards Johnson by the Kennedyites was personal. Bobby, in particular, hated him as the usurper of the deceased legend. The feeling was entirely mutual and Johnson described Bobby as a 'self-righteous little prick', which he undoubtedly was. Acolytes of the dead President could only register a snobbish distaste for his successor's crude vulgarity. The list of offences against good taste was admittedly long, but there is no correlation between good manners and ethical or even decent conduct in office.

Where Johnson grew up in the Texas hill country, everything had to be done by hand since there was no electricity. As a child he had picked cotton and shone shoes himself before discovering a talent for debate. Resembling a bull elephant, he had a far more coherent political vision than his stylish predecessor. He had been a committed New Dealer and as such FDR's favourite son in Texas politics. He never lost that vision, even as he reached pragmatic accommodations with the big oil men and cattle ranchers of his home state. Lying and fighting dirty came as naturally to him as belching and farting in genteel company. In Washington his dominance first of the House of Representatives and then of the Senate was legendary. It was based on physical intimidation and on an encyclopaedic knowledge of the personal foibles of every colleague that rivalled J. Edgar Hoover's. The 'Maharajah of Texas' and his staff occupied twenty rooms in the Capitol after he became Senate majority leader.

He had led a loyal opposition to Eisenhower, supporting his civil rights initiatives and his liberal internationalism, and shaming his fellow Southerners (many of them conservative Dixiecrats already travelling towards the Republican Party, along with much of the South) by accusing them of being obstacles on the South's road to modernization. Even before becoming vice president, he had staffers investigate how many of his predecessors had succeeded to the top job. At Kennedy's inaugural ball, Johnson told the wife of *Time*'s owner: 'Clare [Luce], I looked it up: one out of every four Presidents has died in office. I'm a gamblin' man, darlin', and this is the only chance I get.'[2] The chance came when, in a rented car well behind Kennedy's Dallas motorcade, LBJ was manhandled to the floor by a secret service agent who realized what the three sharp cracks of sound signified.

As president, Johnson undertook a bold reform programme known as the Great Society, including civil rights and better medical care, which was to be achieved through a combination of budget savings, tax cuts and social programmes financed by high private sector growth.[3] Although he was as conventionally anti-Communist as the next American, Johnson's key concern was that the right should not thwart his domestic legislation because of perceived weakness in foreign policy. The last thing he wanted was a major war to drain away the money he wished to use to transform American society. The trick was to avoid another lost China, without getting stuck in a second Korea. In fact, he got Vietnam, with its own draining, gruelling identity. He vividly dramatized his dilemma. The Great Society was the woman he loved, but he was constantly being led astray by 'that bitch of a war on the other side of the world'.[4]

Initially Johnson opted to do 'more of the same and do it more efficiently' in Vietnam, or as he put it, 'by God, I want something for my money [military aid for South Vietnam], I want 'em to get off their butts and get out in those jungles and whip hell out of some Communists. And then I want 'em to leave me alone, because I've got some bigger things to do right here at home.'[5] The policy of 'maximum effect with minimum involvement was set out in NSCAM 288 in March 1964. As a supposedly temporary surge, the number of military advisers was increased from 16,300 to 23,300, with an extra $50 million in economic assistance. Recklessly optimistic General Harkins was the most visible casualty of the new efficiency drive, replaced in June by General William Westmoreland, who was a facts-and-figures man in the mould of McNamara, a corporate man in uniform, and as different from Douglas MacArthur as it was possible to be. An exponent of big-unit warfare, 'Westy' never mastered how to pacify an unconventional enemy with unconventional means in what was not an asymmetric fight. The following month, the Chairman of the Joint Chiefs Maxwell Taylor succeeded Cabot Lodge as ambassador to Saigon after Lodge had decided to return to the US to shore up the shrinking liberal internationalist strain in the Republican Party.

Major decisions to escalate US involvement in Vietnam were a year away, but the rationalization for past and present failures began to shift ominously long before. President de Gaulle's advice in February 1963 to neutralize North and South, which would then block Chinese expansionism, was never seriously considered, and nor was the logic of falling dominoes often disputed. During another visit to South Vietnam in December, McNamara became convinced that the solution was to raise the cost of war to the North. A month later the Joint Chiefs delivered a similar message. The enemy was being allowed to dictate the course of the war, and that enemy was not so much the guerrillas in the South as their leaders in Hanoi. Rostow, now Chairman of the State Department's Policy Planning Council, had been urging the use of graduated bombing to send signals to the North Vietnamese leadership for years.

The concept was powerfully appealing to the air force and navy, for it would enable them to underline their ongoing (budgetary) relevance to a conflict that had hitherto largely been an army affair. After he returned from yet another depressing trip to Saigon in mid-March 1964, McNamara ordered the Joint Chiefs to plan alternative bombing scenarios. The first would be a limited seventy-two-hour blitz in response to major guerrilla provocations. The second version would be a major strategic bombing campaign, designed to smash the North's entire military and industrial infrastructure. This would force Ho Chi Minh to the negotiating table, for otherwise he would see his attempts to build a socialist society in ruins.

The Pentagon conducted two sets of war games in April and September 1964: SIGMA I-64 and SIGMA II-64, with National Security Advisor McGeorge Bundy representing the President. The Red Team (representing Hanoi) included the Far Eastern expert Marshall Green of State and General Earle Wheeler, Taylor's replacement as chairman of the Joint Chiefs. Blue Team had Curtis LeMay, William Bundy and John McNaughton, the academic recently appointed assistant secretary of defense for international security affairs. Honestly conducted, the war games made it apparent that bombing had little or no deterrent effect on Red Team's ability to escalate infiltration of South Vietnam, while every Red Team counter-move exposed new US vulnerabilities. LeMay found it all too much to bear, and in an aside to McGeorge Bundy snarled, 'We should bomb them back to the Stone Age.' 'Maybe they're already there,' replied Bundy.

The games continued with the dice loaded to produce the desired outcome. Even so, the chimera of victory could be achieved only by switching the more able players and raising the levels of what the US was prepared to do, up to and including use of tactical nuclear weapons. 'Mac' Bundy was not impressed, and resolved that if a bombing campaign were unleashed, it would have to be subject to stringent limits.[6]

Getting with the Programme

Planning activity went ahead despite countervailing opinion regarding its assumptions. McNamara believed that the fall of South Vietnam would result in dominoes toppling throughout the rest of South-east Asia, affecting not only Cambodia and Laos, but also Thailand, Malaysia, Indonesia, India and even Australia and New Zealand, not to speak of the Philippines, Korea and Japan. The CIA, which understood what was unique about the Vietnamese Communists, contradicted that view, not least by pointing to the thousand years of antipathy between Vietnamese and Chinese. A report drawn up by the State Department's Policy Planning Council also concluded that bombing the North would have very little impact on its support for the South. Indeed, it might escalate its activities by reconstituting North Vietnamese Army (NVA) forces for deployment in the southern campaign. It would also frustrate, rather than encourage, any will to negotiate in Hanoi. Rostow suppressed the report, on the grounds that State had no business meddling in military affairs. Similar warnings from the Pentagon's internal Defense Intelligence Agency were also ignored.

Unfortunately Secretary of State Rusk did not fight his corner and endorsed McNamara's views, claiming that US credibility in Europe or elsewhere would be undermined if a stand were not taken in Vietnam. That was a lie. Britain and France opposed escalating the war, and de Gaulle was a firm advocate of Vietnam's neutralization. In a growing atmosphere of 'getting with the programme', any dissenting voices found themselves shut out of decisions being taken by fewer and fewer principals. Only George Ball, who had opposed American involvement in Vietnam from the time Kennedy first sent 16,000 'advisers', was left as a licensed devil's advocate, a designation indicating that he was not to be taken too seriously, like Adlai Stevenson over Cuba. Earlier lobbying to oust Diem undermined the authority of State Department dissenters such as Ball.[7]

Johnson was torn between competing pressures, hoping that all the bright, can-do men he had inherited from Kennedy would get him off the hook of his own private agonies. He feared that inaction in Vietnam would result in his political opponents (especially in the Southern states) derailing his ambitious domestic programmes. It would be like Truman and China all over again. 'If I don't go in now and they show later I should have gone, then they'll be all over me in Congress. They won't be talking about my civil rights bill, or education or beautification. No sir, they'll push Vietnam up my ass every time. Vietnam. Vietnam. Vietnam. Right up my ass.'[8] Johnson could not grasp how what he called 'a piss-ant' or 'raggedy-ass little fourth-rate country' could defy the will of a technologically advanced superpower. To negotiate or withdraw would represent a massive loss of face, a concept whose importance to Asians was sneered at by Americans deeply concerned about prestige. In pushing on with the war, Johnson was powerfully supported by America's union bosses, men like AFL-CIO president George Meany who said: 'I would rather fight the Communists in South Vietnam than fight them down here in Chesapeake Bay.'[9]

Contrary to the image of brutality projected on to him by the Kennedyites, Johnson agonized over the human tragedy of war in a way alien to the man he had replaced. Unlike Kennedy he had no schoolboy enthusiasms for special ops or covert warfare. Among the half-million photos of LBJ taken by the White House photographers – he was very vain – there are some with his head slumped down on his desk. In a recorded telephone conversation with McGeorge Bundy in May he said:

I'll tell you . . . I just stayed awake last night thinking about this thing. The more I think of it, I don't know what in the hell it looks to me like we're getting into another Korea. It just worries the hell out of me . . . I don't think it's worth fighting for and I don't think we can get out. And it's just the biggest damn mess that I ever saw . . . I was looking at this sergeant of mine [his valet] this morning. Got six little old kids over there and he's getting out my things and bringing in my night reading . . . and I just thought about ordering his kids in there and what in the hell am I ordering him out there for? What the hell is Vietnam worth to me? What is Laos worth to me? What is it worth to the country?

Bundy replied: 'It is. It's an awful mess.' 'Of course, if you start running from the Communists, they may just chase you right into your own kitchen,' Johnson continued. 'But this is a terrible thing that we're getting ready to do.' 'Yeah, that's the trouble,' Bundy replied, 'and that is what the rest of that half of the world is going to think if this thing comes apart on us . . . That's exactly the dilemma.'[10] Despite all the doubts, Bundy pressed ahead by commissioning target folders, for the magic bullet of bombing had its own momentum. And the 'thing' did indeed come apart.[11]

In Your Guts You Know He's Nuts

Vietnam had a domestic political context, not exhausted by oppositional babyboomer students who by now were listening to 'California Girls', 'I Can't Get No Satisfaction', and 'Stop! In the Name of Love' by respectively the Beach Boys, the Rolling Stones and the Supremes, should one care to remember. In reality, those most disillusioned with the war were the poor whites and poor blacks who had to fight it, not draft-dodging students. Johnson also faced threats from the Republican right and hawkish Democrats. Barry Goldwater, the Republican candidate for the presidential election of 1964, answered the question what he would do in South-east Asia with: 'I'd drop a low-yield atomic bomb on the Chinese supply lines in North Vietnam or maybe shell 'em with the Seventh Fleet.' Democrat strategy was to depict him as a maniac, countering Goldwater's slogan 'In Your Heart You Know He's Right' with 'In Your Guts You Know He's Nuts.'[12] But Johnson also simultaneously feared that the Kennedy clan would use weakness in Vietnam to launch a challenge within the Democrat Party. Against that backdrop came the Tonkin Gulf Incident.

On 2 August 1964, two covert US missions got their wires fatally crossed in the Gulf of Tonkin. The first was a raid by South Vietnamese commandos on islands off the North Vietnamese coast (OPLAN 34A, authorized by McNamara in December 1963). The second was a 'DeSoto' electronic-warfare operation involving the destroyer USS *Maddox*, whose tasks included identifying the positions of North Vietnamese radars as they lit up in response to the South Vietnamese raids. North Vietnamese torpedo boats, chasing the South Vietnamese intruders, naturally assumed that the *Maddox* – lurking ten miles from shore – was part and parcel of the same operation. When they attacked, *Maddox* returned fire, with planes from the aircraft carrier USS *Ticonderoga* joining in to cripple two enemy boats and sink a third. Washington ordered the *Maddox* to resume operations accompanied by the destroyer USS *Turner Joy*.

On 4 August initial reports from the two ships claimed they were under attack from North Vietnamese torpedo boats, having mistaken disturbances on sonar and radar screens on a stormy night for enemy ships. Even as the administration resolved on retaliatory air strikes against the torpedo-boat bases, urgent messages from the *Maddox* spoke of 'freak weather effects' and excitable radar and sonar operators. At the same time McNamara received decrypted North Vietnamese reports of an attack on US ships, but either failed or chose not to note that they referred to the attacks on 2 August rather than two days later.

The President knew instinctively what was going on: 'It reminds me of the movies in Texas. You're sitting next to a pretty girl and you have your hand on her ankle and nothing happens. And you move it up to her knee and nothing happens. You move it up further and you're thinking about moving a bit more and all of a sudden you get slapped. I think we got slapped.'[13] Nonetheless he authorized Operation Pierce Arrow, involving air strikes on the torpedo-boat bases and neighbouring oil-storage facilities at Vinh, which were deemed highly successful.[14]

Johnson seized the opportunity to secure a Congressional resolution authorizing him 'to take all necessary measures to repel any armed attacks against the forces of the United States and to prevent further aggression'. This involved lying about what the *Maddox* was doing, and failing to mention the initial South Vietnamese commando raids to which the North Vietnamese were responding. Since a leak ensured that the press had already reported a second attack, there was no turning back. But that was judged a small price worth paying in what was a successful attempt to neutralize Goldwater, whose robust call to do what the administration was secretly planning to do was unfavourably contrasted with Johnson's apparently moderate and proportionate response to Communist aggression in international waters. After Johnson had won the greatest electoral landslide of modern times, domestic constraints on him were fewer, especially since stopping Communism in South Vietnam was massively popular with the public. Eight months after the incident, Johnson wryly conceded, 'For all I know, our Navy was shooting at whales out there.'

At this point, the Chinese took a much keener interest in Vietnam, beyond the huge quantities of weapons they had supplied to Hanoi in the previous seven years. After the 1954 Geneva Accords they had advised North Vietnam to focus on socialist reconstruction rather than revolution in the South. This agenda changed because Mao saw the utility of miring the US in a conflict in South-east Asia, to distract it from the South China Seas and specifically what Mao was doing at Lop Nor in the Gobi Desert, where his technicians were developing a Chinese atomic bomb. Since Kennedy had vainly consulted Khrushchev about whether they could jointly destroy the site, Mao had good reasons to divert the Americans elsewhere. Vietnam was ideal for this purpose. Ostentatious support for North Vietnam would also promote China's claims to be leading global revolution and draw attention away from the disastrous Great Leap Forward.

In joint meetings held in 1963–4 the Chinese committed themselves to defend North Vietnam in the event of a US invasion. Mao chided his North Vietnamese comrades that they were 'just scratching the surface ... Best turn it into a bigger war.' He reassured them that 'if the United States attacks the North, they will have to remember that the Chinese also have legs, and legs are used for walking'. He did not add that he was quite capable of sending his troops into North Vietnam without Hanoi's permission.[15] The PLA initially moved air and anti-aircraft artillery forces into the vicinity of the border with North Vietnam, and used the British to communicate to Washington the circumstances in which they would certainly be used. At the same time Mao reduced China's own vulnerabilities by relocating arms industries from the coast to the interior, diverting four million people to the endeavour.

Hanoi had no intention of becoming a Chinese puppet and proved adroit at exploiting the deepening animosities between Beijing and Moscow. After the fall of Khrushchev the Soviets delivered $670 million in mainly military aid.[16] Even before the US bombing of the North began, the Soviets supplied SAM-75 missile batteries and 2,500 men to defend Hanoi, while the Chinese sent 100,000 combat engineers to improve and repair roads and railways more rapidly than the US could bomb them. These were followed, from August 1965, by 150,000 Chinese troops to man an enormous number of anti-aircraft artillery batteries. Vast quantities of food and war materials flowed south too, as well as everything from harmonicas to ping-pong balls. The result was a competition to see who could support Hanoi most, with Hai Phong harbourmasters juggling which fraternal nation's ships could dock first. After the Chinese *Red Flag* was shot up by US aeroplanes as a result of being left loitering offshore while priority was given to Soviet ships, Beijing belatedly realized what was going on. By that time the massive reinforcement it had received permitted North Vietnam to launch a major offensive to topple the Saigon regime before the US intervened on the ground.[17]

On 1 November 1964 the Viet Cong struck a US Air Force base at Bien Hoa, where a squadron of old B-57 bombers was parked, destroying six planes and killing five US personnel. Seventy-six more were wounded. Although this incident, two days before the US election, brought no overt response, it did finally tip Ambassador Maxwell Taylor into recommending a major bombing campaign. The idea was to create a greater sense of stability in the South, enabling General Khanh and his colleagues to clean up their act. Although Johnson had declared that he had had enough of 'this coup shit', when Khanh made overtures to the Buddhists to form a broader coalition government he had to go because the Buddhists wanted the Communists included with an eye to a negotiated conclusion to the war, which would end with the US being requested to withdraw its forces. In January 1965 Khanh was forced to resign by Air Vice Marshal Nguyen Cao Ky and General Nguyen Changh Thi, who overthrew the trappings of civilian government. Ky in turn pushed out Thi. 'Mac' Bundy thought them the absolute bottom of the barrel, but they were not. Still to come was General Nguyen Van Thieu, who outmanoeuvred Ky to become the Americans' final man on horseback at the end.

In a last attempt to grasp the situation, on 4 February 1965 'Mac' Bundy paid his first visit to Saigon, though he had been in post for four years. Everything seemed in a state of atrophy and, of course, the Viet Minh kidnapped a senior embassy official to coincide with his arrival. Three days into his visit, the Viet Minh attacked a US helicopter base at Pleiku, killing eight Americans and wounding 126 more. The base hospital resembled a charnel house. The Viet Minh used captured US mortars to destroy ten helicopters on the ground. They must have been sure the US would not respond since Soviet Premier Aleksei Kosygin was in Hanoi at the time. They were wrong.

All the big local players, Taylor, Westmoreland and Deputy Chief of Mission Alexis Johnson, assembled in the MACV command centre to review the attack. Bundy contacted the White House, where Johnson summoned an expanded NSC meeting including the leaders of the House and the Senate. They overwhelmingly approved Bundy's request for retaliatory bombing, and 132 planes were launched from carriers and headed for North Vietnam. After a visit to Pleiku, where he was moved by a very young wounded US soldier, Bundy flew back to Washington drafting a recommendation for a policy of 'sustained reprisal' that had been in the works for months. As he said to a reporter, attacks like Pleiku were 'like street cars' – it was just a matter of which one you chose to board.[18]

Johnson opted for Operation Flaming Dart, which targeted select North Vietnamese regular army barracks. The Viet Minh responded with an attack on a US base at Qui Nhon, killing twenty-three Americans, for which more retaliatory sorties were flown to demolish further barracks. The Soviets were infuriated that the attacks had begun while Kosygin was in Hanoi, and on 10 February Kosygin and the North Vietnamese Prime Minister Pham Van Dong issued a joint communiqué that condemned the attacks and committed the Soviet Union to giving 'all necessary aid and support' to North Vietnam to resist US aggression. This was followed in April 1965 by a further agreement signed in Moscow to provide and maintain what was to become the most comprehensive missile defence in the world.

The reason for the second agreement was that, realizing that Flaming Dart was having no deterrent effect, the Joint Chiefs unfurled Operation Rolling Thunder, a much more sustained campaign involving hitting ninety-four designated targets two days a week over two months. It was a compromise, a calibrated campaign to force the North Vietnamese to negotiate rather than Curtis LeMay's wish for an all-out offensive against the Red River irrigation dykes and other crucial economic targets.

The first planes struck on 2 March, against communications links between Hanoi and southern Vinh, part of a wider effort to destroy transportation choke points and supply dumps. While US planes usually destroyed the targets, the problem was that the enemy soon repaired the damage, or simply found other routes for a logistical effort that relied more on beasts of burden and on human porters. Only thirty-four tons of supplies a day were required for the 6,000 men they were moving south each month. North Vietnamese logistical dispersion meant that an air campaign that was supposed to be under strict civilian control soon involved giving pilots the freedom to bomb targets of opportunity, and the greater use of napalm to inflict horrifying human casualties.

As was already evident from the attacks on Bien Hoa and Pleiku, increasing the number of air bases in Vietnam would require further ground troops to defend them. One general estimated 15,000 more soldiers just to defend a greater-than-mortar-range perimeter around Pleiku. On 8 March Johnson acceded to Westmoreland's request for two battalions of Marines to defend the air base at Da Nang, and they came ashore with howitzers and tanks. Johnson believed he could control future escalation until he found the force levels that broke North Vietnam's will to fight. As he put it, 'I'm going up old Ho Chi Minh's leg an inch at a time.'[19] The seventy-five-year-old Ho, meanwhile, had become a largely symbolic figurehead, living in a simple stilt house in Hanoi, where he did his morning calisthenics and fed carp. While careful to never fall out with the Soviets, Ho spent more time in China, including his birthdays, as, whatever his private distrust of the Chinese, Mao's oft-repeated willingness to unleash a third world war was the ultimate guarantor that Johnson would not invade the North.

The Chinese successfully tested their first nuclear bomb on 16 October 1964. Zhou Enlai urged 3,000 comrades to rejoice in the Great Hall of the People, while Mao penned celebratory verses: 'Atom bomb goes off when it is told / Ah, what boundless joy!'[20] Johnson's military advisers reported that nothing short of a nuclear strike on Lop Nor would be certain to degrade China's atomic capacity in perpetuity.[21] Instead, Johnson pressed on with combating nuclear proliferation in conjunction with the Soviet Union. The price included reassuring regional allies from Australia to India that the US would defend them against a nuclear-armed China. If the US abandoned South Vietnam, it was believed, then either China would become a Pacific hegemon or else nuclear weapons would proliferate among US allies anxious to prevent this outcome. These considerations were a largely unspoken and usually overlooked reason for the decision to pound North Vietnam with conventional ordnance.[22]

Before March 1965 had passed, Westmoreland sought two divisions of infantry to protect Saigon, and the Joint Chiefs said why not send three? On 1 April Johnson approved a further 18,000–20,000 increase in military support personnel, plus two more battalions of Marines and a Marine air squadron. US forces were now to be deployed in offensive counter-insurgency operations for the first time, venturing forth on fruitless patrols that became carelessly routinized until, on the twentieth such patrol, they were ambushed and shot to pieces. On 19–20 April, key US policy-makers convened in Honolulu, where they recommended a 150 per cent increase from 33,500 troops in the country to 82,000. CIA warnings that such an increase would fail to impact significantly on the Viet Minh were ignored. At the same time, Operation Rolling Thunder was extended from eight weeks to six months or a year 'at the present tempo', turning Vietnam into 'a lush tropical bombing range'. In June, Westmoreland requested a further 93,000 troops – bringing his force to 175,000 – for there was still no sign that the Viet Minh were prepared to throw in the towel.[23]

None of this involved a declaration of war, nor had Congress sanctioned anything beyond what had been conceded in the wake of the Tonkin Gulf affair. Mounting opposition to what was afoot by influential columnists spread to a few brave Congressmen. When Senator George McGovern, who had flown thirty-nine bombing missions in the Second World War, tried to remonstrate with him Johnson replied, 'Goddamn it, George, you and [Senator William] Fulbright and all you history teachers. I haven't got time to fuck around with history. I've got boys on the line. I can't be worried about history when there are boys out there who might die before morning.' Not for the last time, personalizing wars in this way as a 'blood sacrifice' by boy soldiers ensured that they continued. Johnson made a few concessions to the idea that bombing was related to negotiations, and Bundy suggested that he announce a South-east Asia Development Corporation designed to pump money into the region and to make South Vietnam as prosperous as South Korea.[24]

But the only money being pumped into Vietnam was the $700 million Johnson requested in May for US military operations. Instead of bolstering South Vietnamese military performance, increased US involvement was matched by a rising frequency of ARVN defeats whenever they encountered Viet Minh forces, now augmented by NVA regulars. Like a primitive man first encountering a screw in a baulk of wood, the US response was to apply more force. The number of fighter-bomber sorties over the North rose from 3,600 to 4,800, while B-52s were used to carpet-bomb enemy-held areas in the South. By the end of 1968, the US had dropped a million tons of bombs on South Vietnam and 643,000 tons on the North. The war had become one of attrition and endurance, though television reported only a sanitized version of helicopters landing and taking off, not the terrifying reality out in the jungles.

Final Straw

Marine Lieutenant-General Charles Cooper's 2002 memoir *Cheers and Tears* contains a unique account of a row between Johnson and the Joint Chiefs after they had requested a private meeting, a rarely exercised right to speak to him directly about their differences of opinion with their titular superior McNamara. Cooper was the junior officer required to hold up the large map brought by Admiral David McDonald. Johnson did not invite the Chiefs to sit while their Chairman General Earle Wheeler spoke for them. Wheeler briefly recommended mining Haiphong harbour, blockading the North Vietnamese coast and unleashing B-52s against Hanoi as an alternative to raising the stakes in the losing land war in the South. McDonald spoke in support of the navy and General John McConnell for the air force. Johnson quietly asked Generals Harold Johnson (army) and Wallace Greene (Marines) if they, whose services had the most to gain or lose, fully supported these ideas. After they had said they did:

Seemingly deep in thought, President Johnson turned his back on them for a minute or so, then suddenly discarding the calm, patient demeanor he had maintained throughout the meeting, whirled to face them and exploded . . . He screamed obscenities, he cursed them personally, he ridiculed them for coming to his office with their 'military advice'. Noting that it was he who was carrying the weight of the free world on his shoulders, he called them filthy names – shitheads, dumb shits, pompous assholes – and used the F-word as an adjective more freely than a Marine in boot camp would use it. He then accused them of trying to pass the buck for World War III to him. It was unnerving, degrading.

Then came the crucial test of moral courage, which even after nearly forty years Cooper did not appreciate that the Joint Chiefs had failed. Johnson asked each in turn what they would do if they were the president of the United States. Each in turn echoed Wheeler's reply to the effect that they could not put themselves in Johnson's shoes and that it was his decision and his alone. 'President Johnson, who was nothing if not a skilled actor, looked sad for a moment, then suddenly erupted again, yelling and cursing . . . He told them he was disgusted with their naive approach, and that he was not going to let some military idiots talk him into World War III [and] ended the conference by shouting "Get the hell out of my office!"' Cooper concluded that 'the Joint Chiefs of Staff had done their duty'. Not so. After a scene like that they should have resigned. By clinging to office they confirmed Johnson's low opinion of them.

The result was that Johnson insisted on being briefed on military operations in real time as well as concerning each US combat death. The phone buzzed throughout the night, reducing the limited rest of a man who worked eighteen hours a day. Locked into what became a personal conflict, the President lost sight of the whys and wherefores of so much effort. Deep depression set in. He hammered the bottle. Any impact that bombing had on North Vietnamese industrial output was neutralized by massive Soviet resupply and the presence of Chinese troops who helped with reconstruction. Including $6 billion in lost planes, every dollar of damage the US caused was costing it $9.60 to inflict.[25]

Nothing the Americans did could stop the Viet Minh from using the 600-mile Ho Chi Minh Trail, on which huge quantities of supplies were moved, loaded on backs both human and animal and on modified bicycles. The war came to be seen in terms of US material versus Vietnamese spirit, a line that proved potent propaganda. But what the Bay of Pigs had done to American prestige in its Latin American backyard, Vietnam did in the wider global neighbourhood. Everything the US did damned it as an imperialist power and, however harsh that verdict may seem, since Vietnam it has stuck, being duly attached even to administrations as leftist (in the American context – centre-rightist in the costive spectrum of British politics) as those of Presidents Jimmy Carter and Barack Obama.

This is not to be wondered at. If this book has achieved no other purpose, I hope it has illuminated the fact that the perceived imperatives of world power shaped the foreign policy of the USA quite as much as they did its European imperialist predecessors. The central contradiction addressed by this book has not been between Americans ideals and practice, but the fact that, unlike the British, French, Dutch, Spanish and Portuguese empires, the USA profited little and lost much from its misconceived adoption of liberal imperialism. For the Europeans it was an alibi adopted to prolong their imperial delusions; the 'best and the brightest' of the American liberal establishment were confident that they could do it better, and in that hubris lay their own and their nation's tragedy. That antipathy to empire was in America's DNA was not the least of history's ironies, a lesson it is relearning even as the writing of this book paralled the withdrawals from contemporary Iraq and Afghanistan, and popular Western domestic disenchantment with improving small wars in what are no longer faraway places, but have become some of the most dynamic economies of the twenty-first-century world.

EPILOGUE: LEGACIES

DEAN ACHESON resumed his career as a Washington lawyer in 1953, while being periodically invited to advise successive US governments, and died of a heart attack at home on his Sandy Spring farm in 1971. He was seventy-eight.

HOUARI BOUMÉDIÉNE deposed Ahmed Ben Bella, President of Algeria, in 1965. Ben Bella lived under strict house arrest until 1980 when he was exiled to Lausanne. After a decade he returned to Algeria. He acted as the chairperson of the African Union's Council of the Wise, before his death on 11 April 2012 aged ninety-three.

RAÙL CASTRO took over the Cuban presidency from the ailing Fidel in 2006, though at the time of writing the latter is still alive too, judging from a private audience in Havana in 2012 with Pope Benedict XVI. An aspirin remains a rare item in Cuba, and mulattos and blacks feel oppressed. Since a BBC journalist wept over the death of Yasser Arafat, one can anticipate the rending of garments and pulling out of hair when Fidel finally shuffles off his mortal coil.

CHIANG KAI-SHEK died in 1975 aged eighty-seven. He and his KMT successors ran Taiwan as a one-party state until the start of the second millennium, although its current multi-party system is being held up as a future paradigm for China's own democratization. Some have wondered – should Chiang's and Mao Zedong's ghosts haunt contemporary

China – which of them would be more approving or disapproving of what they saw.

CHIN PENG, leader of the Malayan Communist Party, at the time of writing still lives in unrepentant exile in southern Thailand. A film about his life, *The Last Communist*, was banned in Malaysia in 2006.

WINSTON CHURCHILL died aged ninety on 24 January 1965 at his home Chartwell in Kent. Following a state funeral in which East End dockside cranes dipped in his honour, he was buried at Bladon, near his birthplace at Blenheim Palace.

ANTHONY EDEN died of liver cancer on 14 January 1977, after retiring with his second wife to Rose Bower at Broad Chalke, Wiltshire. He was seventy-nine.

DWIGHT D. EISENHOWER and MAMIE retired to their farm near Gettysburg. He died of congestive heart failure on 28 March 1969 and is buried near his memorial library in Abilene, Kansas. His reputation as president has markedly improved as time moves on.

KING FARUQ I, weighing 300 pounds and described as 'a stomach with a head', died in exile after choking at Rome's Île de France restaurant on 18 March 1965. He was forty-five. I have met young Egyptians who are nostalgic for his era, a vibrant time in Egypt's cultural life.

GENERAL CHARLES DE GAULLE died of a ruptured blood vessel at home in Colombey-les-Deux-Eglises on 9 November 1970. He had installed an electricity meter and paid for his own stamps and haircuts. He was almost eighty. He has dwarfed all subsequent post-war French leaders.

SAM GIANCANA was shot dead in Oak Park, Illinois, in 1975, while sawn-up pieces of Johnny Rosselli were found floating in a barrel off Florida a year later. Having escaped prosecution one last time in 1986, Santo Trafficante lived modestly in Miami Beach and Tampa, and died peacefully the following year.

PRESIDENT HO CHI MINH died of heart failure aged seventy-nine on 2 September 1969. His body is displayed in a mausoleum on Ba Dinh Square in Hanoi. Saigon was renamed Ho Chi Minh City in his honour. United Vietnam would fight China and invade Pol Pot's Cambodia. The People's Republic of Vietnam is one of the fastest-growing economies in the world, and conducts naval exercises with the US so great are its anxieties about China, which has the autism of all great powers.

LYNDON BAINES JOHNSON died of a heart attack on his ranch on 22 January 1973, aged sixty-four, after a lifetime of physical indulgence. It was the day before a ceasefire was declared in Vietnam.

BOBBY KENNEDY was assassinated by Sirhan Sirhan on 6 June 1968 during his campaign for the Democratic Party nomination. He is buried at Arlington Cemetery near JFK. His murderer remains in prison.

JOMO KENYATTA ruled Kenya until his death from old age on 22 August 1978, when his deputy, Daniel arap Moi, replaced him. Moi ruled, dictatorially and corruptly, until 2002.

NIKITA KHRUSHCHEV lived on a reduced pension of 400 roubles a month in Moscow until his death from a heart attack on 11 September 1971. He was not given a state funeral.

KIM IL SUNG died of a heart attack aged eighty-two on 8 July 1994. Despite many North Koreans being dependent on US food aid to avoid starvation, Kim was embalmed and immortalized in the Kumusan Memorial Palace in Pyongyang. Visitors enter this on travelators. The monument is estimated to have cost anything between $100 million and $900 million. His young grandson Kim Eun rules North Korea.

MAJOR-GENERAL EDWARD LANSDALE died on 22 February 1987 at home in McLean, Virginia, where he lived with Pat Kelly, whom he took up with again after the death of his wife Helen. A memorial Mass was held in a university chapel in Manila.

GENERAL DOUGLAS MACARTHUR died at Walter Reed Army Medical Center on 5 April 1964. He is buried within his own memorial museum in Norfolk, Virginia, where his hundred or more military decorations are displayed.

IAIN MACLEOD died of a heart attack on 20 July 1970, a month after Prime Minister Edward Heath had appointed him chancellor of the exchequer.

HAROLD MACMILLAN, FIRST EARL OF STOCKTON, died aged ninety-two on 29 December 1986 at home at Birch Grove. His last words were 'I think I will go to sleep now.' Some claim greatness because of the housing he built.

MAO ZEDONG ruled China until his death aged eighty-two on 9 September 1976. He was succeeded by the reformer Deng Xiaoping. The ruling Communist Party still venerates Mao's legacy, though not the 100 million deaths he caused, which are said to be the 30 per cent he 'got wrong'.

ROBERT McNAMARA served as president of the World Bank, 1968–81, and died aged ninety-three on 6 July 2009, having very publicly repented of his former ways.

ROLANDO MASFERRER was killed by a car bomb in Miami in 1975.

GENERAL JACQUES MASSU retired from the French army in 1969 and lived at Conflans-sur-Loing until his death on 26 October 2002.

MOHAMMED MOSSADEQ died of cancer on 5 March 1967; Mohammed Reza Pahlavi, Shah of Iran, was deposed in 1979 and, after covert treatment for cancer in the US, died in Cairo in 1980, where he is buried in a mosque next to his brother-in-law King Faruq.

PRESIDENT GAMAL ABDUL NASSER OF EGYPT died suddenly of a heart attack in Cairo on 28 September 1970. A lifelong heavy smoker, he was aged fifty-two. An estimated five million people attended his funeral, including a weeping Yasser Arafat and Muammar Gaddafi of Libya, who fainted twice.

JAWAHARLAL NEHRU died of a ruptured aorta on 27 May 1964, after years of hypertension and chronic overwork. India remains the world's largest democracy. He built it.

KIM 'KERMIT' ROOSEVELT died on 8 June 2000 in a retirement home in Maryland. His memoirs were controversial within the CIA.

MOBUTU SESE SEKO ruled Zaire as a brutal kleptocracy until 1997, when he was driven into exile. He died later that year in Rabat, Morocco, and is buried in a Christian cemetery called Pax. The full name he awarded himself translates as 'The all-powerful warrior who because of his endurance and inflexible will to win goes from conquest to conquest, leaving fire in his wake'. 'Thief' would be shorter.

LUIS TARUC, the Huk leader, was sentenced to twelve years' imprisonment, but was pardoned in 1968 by President Ferdinand Marcos, whom he thereafter supported. He died of a heart attack aged ninety-one in 2005 in Quezon City.

FIELD MARSHAL SIR GERALD TEMPLER died of lung cancer and pneumonia in London on 25 October 1979 after a final pink gin had put him to sleep.

MOSHE TSHOMBE, the Katangan separatist, was exiled to Spain after Congolese independence, while Mobutu's courts tried and sentenced him to death *in absentia*. In June 1967 his plane was hijacked to Algeria, where he was kept under arrest until his death 'from heart failure' in 1969. Who was responsible for the hijacking has never been clarified.

Acknowledgements

Andrew Wylie and Scott Moyers of the Wylie Agency helped shape the initial proposal on which this book hangs like a fat man on a skeleton. I must thank Ron Suskind, whose blending of contemporary history and reportage I enormously admire, for a valuable discussion on how to interweave complex narrative plotlines while he was trying to drive a car in Washington traffic.

I am very grateful to Hugh Bicheno for his expert advice on Cuba and Latin America, and for unravelling the more tortuous paragraphs and sentences with such good grace. Yang Lian explained much about Mao Zedong through the Chairman's poetry, as has my great friend George Walden, who served as a British diplomat in Moscow during the Missile Crisis and in Beijing amid the Cultural Revolution. Professor Frank Dikötter in Hong Kong also recommended some very useful reading on the People's Liberation Army, while Dr John Adamson reminded me of Nehru's world history. Professor Jonathan Haslam set me to rights about Soviet foreign policy through his excellent monograph on that subject. At a very early juncture Professor William Hay made several helpful suggestions about the distinctive traditions within US foreign policy over a much longer period than is directly addressed in this book, notably as refracted through the works of Professor Walter McDougall of Penn State. My wife Linden has constantly reminded me of the needs of the general reader, even if I took a strategic decision to focus on Indian foreign policy in the 1950s and 1960s rather than the last days of the Raj, which her family lived through. Both Wendy Wolf at Viking in New York and Georgina Morley at Macmillan in London have done sterling work on a manuscript whose possibilities they generously and jointly recognized early on. Working with them has been a pleasure, though I let them imagine they terrify me for form's sake. In our sixth collaboration, Peter James has been a sensitive and painstaking editor.

The London Library, the Liddell Hart Military Archive at King's College London and the Imperial War Museum have been hugely helpful with materials, though this is primarily a work of description and interpretation. Finally, I am grateful to the Nonino family for an amazing prize that enabled me to finish the book at my own pace. The book is dedicated to someone I admire, whose company I enjoy and through whose writing I was intrigued by this wider world as a young man – Sir Vidia Naipaul – and to his wife Nadira, who talks so intelligently about Pakistan. They are joined on the dedication page by two other dear friends, Nancy and Andrea, who have shown Lindy and me incredible hospitality in their beautiful home in Venice.

Michael Burleigh
Kennington, London
May 2012

Notes

1: Japan Opens Pandora's Box

1. Peter Thompson, *The Battle for Singapore. The True Story of the Greatest Catastrophe of World War II* (London 2006), p. 39.
2. Margaret Shennan, *Out in the Midday Sun. The British in Malaya 1880–1960* (London 2000), p. 237.
3. Christopher Bayly and Tim Harper, *Forgotten Armies. Britain's Asian Empire and the War with Japan* (London 2004), p. 226.
4. Masanobu Tsuji, *Singapore. The Japanese Version* (London 1962), p. 272.
5. Liddell Hart Archive King's College London (hereafter LHAKCL), Spooner Papers 1/38a, diary entry dated 7 February 1942.
6. Bayly and Harper, *Forgotten Armies*, p. 132.
7. Max Hastings citing M. N. Roy in *All Hell Let Loose. The World at War 1939–1945* (London 2011), p. 417.
8. T. N. Harper, *The End of Empire and the Making of Malaya* (Cambridge 1999), p. 38.
9. David French, *The British Way in Counter-Insurgency 1945–1967* (Oxford 2011), p. 162, and John Dower, *War without Mercy. Race and Power in the Pacific War* (New York 1986).
10. Odd Arne Westad, *Decisive Encounters. The Chinese Civil War 1946–1950* (Stanford, Calif. 2003), p. 71.
11. Chong-sik Lee, *Counterinsurgency in Manchuria. The Japanese Experience 1931–1940*, Rand Corporation Memo RM-5012-ARPA

(1967), pp. 82ff. This is probably one of the most neglected documents in the history of counter-insurgency warfare.

12. Bayly and Harper, *Forgotten Armies*, pp. 113–14.

13. Rana Mitter, *A Bitter Revolution. China's Struggle with the Modern World* (Oxford 2004), p. 178, and pp. 140–1 for the hair and dress points.

14. Jung Chang and Jon Halliday, *Mao. The Unknown Story* (London 2006), pp. 42–5.

15. Ibid., pp. 16–17, is crucial on Mao's worldview.

16. David Apter and Tony Saich, *Revolutionary Discourse in Mao's Republic* (Cambridge, Mass. 1994), p. 259, is based on interviews with Yenan veterans.

17. Jonathan Fenby, *The Penguin History of Modern China. The Fall and Rise of a Great Power 1850–2008* (London 2008), pp. 299ff.

18. Chang and Halliday, *Mao*, p. 250.

19. Ibid., pp. 270–2.

20. Jonathan Fenby, *Generalissimo Chiang Kai-shek and the China He Lost* (London 2005), pp. 440–2.

21. Richard Harris Smith, *OSS. The Secret History of America's First Central Intelligence Agency* (Guilford, Conn. 2005), pp. 241ff, and Maochun Yu, *OSS in China. Prelude to Cold War* (Annapolis, Md 1996).

22. Bruce Cumings, *The Korean War. A History* (New York 2010), pp. 51–7.

23. Charles K. Armstrong, *The North Korean Revolution 1945–1950* (Ithaca, NY 2003), pp. 27–32.

24. Andrew Gordon, *A History of Modern Japan. From Tokugawa Times to the Present* (Oxford 2003), pp. 178ff and 191ff.

25. Hastings, *All Hell Let Loose*, pp. 420–1.

26. Judith Brown, 'India', in Judith Brown and Wm Roger Louis (eds), *The Twentieth Century* (Oxford 1999), vol. 4 of *The Oxford History of the British Empire*, p. 433.

27. Ibid., p. 419.

28. Stanley Wolpert, *Shameful Flight. The Last Years of the British Empire in India* (Oxford 2009), pp. 44–6 and 60–3.

29. Hastings, *All Hell Let Loose*, pp. 422–4.

30. Patrick French, *India. An Intimate Biography of 1.2 Billion People* (London 2011), p. 25, for the holy monkey on the loose in Lucknow.

31. Alan Campbell-Johnson, *Mission with Mountbatten* (London 1985), pp. 200–1.

32. Stanley Karnow, *In our Own Image. America's Empire in the Philippines* (New York 1989).

33. H. W. Brands, *Bound to Empire. The United States and the Philippines* (New York 1992), p. 199.

34. Benedict Kerkvliet, *The Huk Rebellion. A Study of Peasant Revolt in the Philippines* (Berkeley, Calif. 1977, reprinted Lanham, Md 2002), pp. 26ff.

35. Nicholas Tarling, *A Sudden Rampage. The Japanese Occupation of Southeast Asia 1941–1945* (London 2001), pp. 154–9.

36. Mark Atwood Lawrence, *The Vietnam War. A Concise International History* (Oxford 2008), p. 30.

37. Ibid., p. 30.

38. See the excellent essay by Paul Orders, 'Adjusting to a New Period in World History: Franklin Roosevelt and European Colonialism', in David Ryan and Victor Pungong (eds), *The United States and Decolonisation. Power and Freedom* (New York 2000), pp. 63–84.

39. William Duiker, *Ho Chi Minh. A Life* (New York 2000) is the finest life in English.

40. The best account of these years is Sophie Quinn-Judge, *Ho Chi Minh. The Missing Years 1919–1941* (London 2003), pp. 43ff.

41. Stanley Karnow, *Vietnam. A History* (London 1983, revised edn 1994), p. 135.

42. Peter Macdonald, *Giap. The Victor in Vietnam* (London 1993).

43. Duiker, *Ho Chi Minh*, pp. 255–6.

44. Archimedes Patti, *Why Vietnam? Prelude to America's Albatross* (Berkeley, Calif. 1980), pp. 83–8.

45. David G. Marr, *Vietnam 1945. The Quest for Power* (Berkeley, Calif. 1995), p. 289.

46. Ibid.

47. Duiker, *Ho Chi Minh*, p. 323.

48. Jean-Louis Margolin, 'Vietnam and Laos: The Impasse of War Communism', in Stephane Courtois, Nicholas Werth, Jean-Louis

Panne, Andrzej Paczkowski, Karel Bartosek and Jean-Louis Margolin, *The Black Book of Communism* (Cambridge, Mass. 1999), pp. 566–7.

49. Smith, *OSS*, p. 318.

50. Ibid., p. 330.

51. Duiker, *Ho Chi Minh*, p. 361.

52. Martin Thomas, 'French Imperial Reconstruction and the Development of the Indochina War 1950-1954', in Mark Atwood Lawrence and Frederik Logevall (eds), *The First Vietnam War. Colonial Conflict and Cold War Crisis* (Cambridge, Mass. 2008), pp. 131–5.

53. Frank Giles, *The Locust Years. The Story of the French Fourth Republic 1946–1958* (London 1991), p. 58.

54. Macdonald, *Giap*, pp. 78–85.

55. Patti, *Why Vietnam?*, p. 380.

56. Charles Cruickshank, *Special Operations Executive in the Far East* (Oxford 1983), pp. 191ff.

57. Robert McMahon, *Colonialism and Cold War. The United States and the Struggle for Indonesian Independence 1945–49* (Ithaca, NY 1981), p. 35.

58. Ibid., p. 36.

59. See especially John D. Legge, *Sukarno. A Political Biography* (London 1972), pp. 149ff.

60. McMahon, *Colonialism and Cold War*, p. 95.

61. Christopher Bayly and Tim Harper, *Forgotten Wars. The End of Britain's Asian Empire* (London 2007) p. 173.

62. Patrick Heren, 'The Death Knell of the British Empire', *Standpoint* (November 2010), pp. 38–41. The title is misleading since the piece concerns the fate of the Dutch East Indies.

63. Audrey Kahin and George McT. Kahin, *Subversion as Foreign Policy. The Secret Eisenhower and Dulles Debacle in Indonesia* (Seattle 1995), pp. 31–3.

2: Harry Truman's World

1. See Wilson D. Miscamble, 'Roosevelt, Truman and the Development of Postwar Grand Strategy', *Orbis* (2009) 53, pp. 556–8.

2. Joseph G. Goulden, *The Best Years 1945–1950* (New York 1976), pp. 91–2.

3. Robert Dallek, *The American Style of Foreign Policy. Cultural Politics and Foreign Affairs* (New York 1983), p. 172.

4. Alonzo Hamby, 'The Mind and Character of Harry S. Truman', in Michael Lacey (ed.), *The Truman Presidency* (Cambridge 1991), p. 37.

5. David McCullough, *Truman* (New York 1992), pp. 340–2.

6. Robert Dallek, *The Lost Peace. Leadership in a Time of Horror and Hope 1945–1953* (New York 2010), pp. 154–7.

7. Ibid., p. 101.

8. George C. Herring, *From Colony to Superpower. US Foreign Relations since 1776* (Oxford 2008), p. 603, for Truman's words.

9. John Lewis Gaddis, *George F. Kennan. An American Life* (London 2012), p. 268.

10. For an excellent discussion of the evolution of containment, see Henry Kissinger, *Diplomacy* (New York 1994), pp. 447–55.

11. Roy Jenkins, *Churchill* (London, 2001), pp. 810–13.

12. Goulden, *The Best Years*, p. 259.

13. Miscamble, 'Roosevelt, Truman', p. 569.

14. Stephen Ambrose, *Rise to Globalism. American Foreign Policy 1938–1970* (Baltimore 1971), p. 297.

15. Ronald Steel, *Walter Lippmann and the American Century* (Boston 1980), p. 445.

16. McCullough, *Truman*, p. 753.

17. Dallek, *The Lost Peace*, pp. 221–4, is excellent on this shift.

18. See the fascinating history of US embassy architecture by Jane C. Loeffler, *The Architecture of Diplomacy. Building America's Embassies* (New York 1998, revised edn Princeton 2011), pp. 126–31.

19. Robert Beisner, *Dean Acheson. A Life in the Cold War* (Oxford 2006), p. 174.

20. McCullough, *Truman*, pp. 754–5.

21. Andrew Alexander, *America and the Imperialism of Ignorance. US Foreign Policy since 1945* (London 2012), pp. 132–7, has a good discussion of McCarthyism.

22. For an interesting discussion of foreign policy decision-making see Joseph Marion Jones, *The Fifteen Weeks. An Inside Account of the Genesis of the Marshall Plan* (San Diego 1955), pp. 109ff.

23. H. W. Brands, *Inside the Cold War. Loy Henderson and the Rise of the American Empire 1918–1961* (New York 1991), pp. 147–61.

24. Truman Speech to Congress on 12 March 1947 at Yale Law School, Lillian Goldman Law Library, The Avalon Project Documents in International Law and Diplomacy at http://avalon. law.yale. Edu/20th_century/trudoc.asp.

25. Melvyn Leffler, 'The Emergence of an American Grand Strategy 1945–1952', in Melvyn Leffler and Odd Arne Westad (eds), *The Cambridge History of the Cold War*, vol. 1: *Origins* (Cambridge 2010), p. 68.

26. Howard Jones, *'A New Kind of War': America's Global Strategy and the Civil War in Greece* (New York 1989).

27. McCullough, *Truman*, p. 742.

28. Tim Weiner, *Legacy of Ashes. The History of the CIA* (London 2007), pp. 26–7.

29. Saki Dockrill, *Eisenhower's New-Look National Security Policy 1953–61* (London 1996), p. 49.

30. L. Douglas Keeney, *15 Minutes. General Curtis LeMay and the Countdown to Nuclear Annihilation* (New York 2011), pp. 28–37, is excellent on the evolution of SAC.

31. David Holloway, *Stalin and the Bomb. The Soviet Union and Atomic Energy 1939–1956* (New Haven, Conn. 1994), p. 218.

32. McCullough, *Truman*, pp. 747–64.

33. Walter Isaacson and Evan Thomas, *The Wise Men. Six Friends and the World They Made* (New York 1986), pp. 406–8.

34. William I. Hitchcock, 'The Marshall Plan and the Creation of the West', in Leffler and Westad (eds), *Cambridge History of the Cold War*, vol. 1, p. 156.

35. Dallek, *The Lost Peace*, p. 240.

36. Hitchcock, 'The Marshall Plan and the Creation of the West', pp. 160–4.

37. David Ellwood, *Rebuilding Europe. Western Europe, America and Postwar Reconstruction* (London 1992), pp. 89–93.

38. Kissinger, *Diplomacy*, pp. 456–60.

39. Robert McMahon, *Colonialism and Cold War. The United States and the Struggle for Indonesian Independence 1945–49* (Ithaca, NY 1981), p. 244.

40. Ibid., p. 248.

41. Ibid., p. 256.

42. Jung Chang and Jon Halliday, *Mao. The Unknown Story* (London 2006), p. 392.

43. Ross Terrill, *Mao. A Biography* (Stanford, Calif. 1999), p. 217.

44. Odd Arne Westad, *Decisive Encounters. The Chinese Civil War 1946–1950* (Stanford, Calif. 2003), p. 69.

45. Ibid., p. 238.

46. David Halberstam, *The Coldest Winter. America and the Korean War* (London 2008), p. 234.

47. Ibid., pp. 152 and 224.

48. David Galula, *Counterinsurgency Warfare. Theory and Practice* (Westport, Conn. 1964, reprinted 2006), p. 35.

49 Talk with the American correspondent Anna Louise Strong, August 1946, at http://www.marxists.org/reference/archive/mao/selected-works/volume-4/mswv4. 13.htm.

50. Sergei N. Goncharov, John W. Lewis and Xue Litai, *Uncertain Partners. Stalin, Mao, and the Korean War* (Stanford, Calif. 1993), pp. 84ff.

51. Jongsoo Lee, *The Partition of Korea after World War II* (New York 2006), p. 90.

52. Halberstam, *The Coldest Winter*, pp. 73–81, deftly sketches Kim Il Sung's character without the apologetic tendencies evident in some revisionist US writing of a more self-flagellating kind.

53. Max Hastings, *The Korean War* (London 1987), pp. 38 –42.

54. Allan R. Millett, 'The Korean People', in William Stueck (ed.), *The Korean War in World History* (Lexington, Ky 2004), pp. 13–39.

55. Goncharov, Lewis and Litai, *Uncertain Partners*, p. 133.

56. Gye-Dong Kim, 'Who Initiated the Korean War?', in James Cotton and Ian Neary (eds), *The Korean War in History* (Manchester 1989), p. 39.
57. Bruce Cumings, *The Korean War. A History* (New York 2010), pp. 111ff.

3: Arab Nationalism, Jewish Homeland

1. John Darwin, *The Empire Project. The Rise and Fall of the British World System 1830–1970* (Cambridge 2009), pp. 313–19.
2. On the British in Iraq see Kwasi Kwarteng's astute and unsentimental *Ghosts of Empire. Britain's Legacies in the Modern World* (London 2011), especially pp. 51ff. I am grateful to Kwasi Kwarteng for letting me see an early proof of his remarkable book.
3. Gholam Reza Afkhami, *The Life and Times of the Shah* (Berkeley, Calif. 2009), p. 74.
4. Manucher Farmanfarmaian and Roxane Farmanfarmaian, *Blood & Oil. A Prince's Memoir of Iran, from the Shah to the Ayatollah* (New York 2005), pp. 209–12.
5. Christopher de Bellaigue, *Patriot of Persia. Muhammad Mossadegh and a Very British Coup* (London 2012), pp. 83–6.
6. Farmanfarmaian and Farmanfarmaian, *Blood & Oil*, pp.114–22, and Ryszard Kapuściński, *Shah of Shahs* (London 2006), p. 23, for the ban on photographing camels.
7. Amin Saikal, *The Rise and Fall of the Shah. Iran from Autocracy to Religious Rule* (Princeton 1980), pp. 19–25.
8. See Bellaigue, *Patriot of Persia*, for these biographical details.
9. Odd Arne Westad, *The Global Cold War. Third World Interventions and the Making of our Times* (Cambridge 2007), p. 62.
10. Claremont Skrine, *World War in Iran* (London 1962), especially pp. 211ff.
11. Bellaigue, *Patriot of Persia*, pp. 120ff.
12. For Soviet pressure on Turkey see Jamil Hasanli, *Stalin and the Turkish Crisis of the Cold War 1945–1953* (Lanham, Md 2011).

13. H. W. Brands, *Inside the Cold War. Loy Henderson and the Rise of the American Empire 1918–1961* (New York 1991), pp. 141–5.

14. Robert Beisner, *Dean Acheson. A Life in the Cold War* (Oxford 2006), pp. 38–43.

15. Tarek Osman, *Egypt on the Brink. From Nasser to Mubarak* (New Haven, Conn. 2010), p. 37, and Trevor Mostyn, *Europe's Belle Epoque. Cairo and the Age of the Hedonists* (London 1987).

16. For the above see mainly Robert Stephens, *Nasser. A Political Biography* (London 1971), pp. 21–37.

17. Trefor Evans (ed.), *The Killearn Diaries 1934–1946. The Diplomatic and Personal Record of Lord Killearn (Sir Miles Lampson), High Commissioner and Ambassador to Egypt* (London 1972), pp. 206–19, for the relevant diary entries.

18. This was a more pervasive view. See Ronald Hyam, *Britain's Declining Empire. The Road to Decolonisation 1918–1968* (Cambridge 2006), p. 92, on Nigerians for the first time meeting Brits who were less well educated and articulate in English than themselves.

19. Frank Giles, *The Locust Years. The Story of the Fourth French Republic 1946–1958* (London 1991), pp. 129–32; Robert Merle, *Ben Bella* (London 1967), p. 47, talks about the 'coldness and reserve of the Algerians'.

20. Edward Behr, *The Algerian Problem* (London 1961), p. 45, quoting Ferhat Abbas.

21. Martin Evans, *Algeria. France's Undeclared War* (Oxford 2012), pp. 23–4, is good on this background.

22. Maurice Larkin, *France since the Popular Front. Government and People 1936–1996* (Oxford 1997), p. 226.

23. The best account of these rivalries is by Behr, *The Algerian Problem*, pp. 42ff. Behr covered Algeria for several magazines in the 1950s.

24. Martin Evans, 'Patriot Games: Algeria's Football Revolutionaries', *History Today* (2010) 60, pp. 20–5.

25. Alistair Horne, *A Savage War of Peace. Algeria 1954–1962* (London 1977, reprinted New York 2006), pp. 74–9.

26. Evans, *Algeria. France's Undeclared War*, p. 89.

27. Kathryn Hadley, '"A French Policeman Lost his Head": The Origins of the Algerian War of Independence', *History Today*, 22 September 2010, online version with British diplomatic cable electronic annexe.

28. Jean-Louis Planche, *Sétif 1945. Histoire d'un massacre annoncé* (Paris 2006), pp. 136ff; Marcel Reggui, *Les Massacres de Guelma. Algérie, mai 1945. Une enquête inédite sur la furie des milices coloniales* (Paris 2008); and Annie Rey-Goldzeiguer, *Aux origines de la guerre d'Algérie 1940–1945. De Mers-el-Kébir aux massacres du Nord-Constantois* (Paris 2006), pp. 302–3.

29. Giles, *The Locust Years*, p. 135.

30. Clyde Sanger, *Malcolm MacDonald. Bringing an End to Empire* (Liverpool/Montreal 1995), p. 160.

31. Michael Burleigh, *Blood and Rage. A Cultural History of Terrorism* (London 2008), pp. 95–6.

32. Naomi Shepherd, *Ploughing Sand. British Rule in Palestine* (London 1999), pp. 67–9.

33. LHMAKCL Stockwell Papers 6/26, 'Lessons from Palestine', including the paper 'Relations of Military Commanders with the Civilian Population'.

34. Brands, *Inside the Cold War*, p. 181.

35. Bruce Kuniholm, 'US Policy in the Near East: The Triumphs and Tribulations of the Truman Administration', in Michael Lacey (ed.), *The Truman Presidency* (Cambridge 1991), pp. 322–7.

36. A brilliant evocation of upper-class Anglo-Saxon Protestant society is E. Digby Baltzell, *The Protestant Establishment. Aristocracy and Caste in America* (New York 1964).

37. Cited in Wm Roger Louis, *The British Empire in the Middle East 1945–1951. Arab Nationalism, the United States, and Postwar Imperialism* (Oxford 1984), pp. 401–2.

38. Benjamin Grob-Fitzgibbon, *Imperial Endgame. Britain's Dirty Wars and the End of Empire* (London 2011), pp. 46–8.

39. Ibid., pp. 48–52.

40. Christopher Andrew, *The Defence of the Realm. The Authorized History of MI5* (London 2009), pp. 350–64.

41. David Cesarani, *Major Farran's Hat. Murder, Scandal and Britain's War against Jewish Terrorism 1945–1948* (London 2009) faithfully mounts the Zionist case against Farran.

42. Grob-Fitzgibbon, *Imperial Endgame*, pp. 73–4.

43. LHMAKCL Stockwell Papers 6/26, 'Lessons from Palestine', including Lt-Col. J. H. M. Hackett, 'Reports', p. 4.

44. Christopher Sykes, *Crossroads to Israel. Palestine from Balfour to Bevin* (London 1965), p. 397.

45. Keith Jeffrey, *MI6. The History of the Secret Intelligence Service 1909–1949* (London 2010), pp. 689–97.

46. Andrew, *The Defence of the Realm*, p. 359.

47. Sykes, *Crossroads to Israel*, pp. 381–4.

48. Grob-Fitzgibbon, *Imperial Endgame*, pp. 93–100.

49. On this see Wiebke Bachman, *Die UdSSR und der Nahe Osten. Zionismus, ägyptischer Antikolonialismus und sowjetische Aussenpolitik bis 1956* (Munich 2011), pp. 122–32.

50. Benny Morris, *1948. The First Arab–Israeli War* (New Haven, Conn. 2008), pp. 81–2.

4: Some More Victorious than Others

1. Andrew Rotter, 'Chronicle of a War Foretold. The United States and Vietnam 1945–1954', in Mark Atwood Lawrence and Fredrik Logevall (eds), *The First Vietnam War. Colonial Conflict and Cold War Crisis* (Cambridge, Mass. 2008), p. 290.

2. Robert Dallek, *The American Style of Foreign Policy. Cultural Politics and Foreign Affairs* (New York 1983), p. 143.

3. Theodore White and Annalee Jacoby, *Thunder out of China* (New York 1946), p. 129.

4. Jonathan Fenby, *Generalissimo. Chiang Kai-shek and the China He Lost* (London 2005), p. 438.

5. Westad, *Decisive Encounters. The Chinese Civil War 1946–1950* (Stanford, Calif. 2003), pp. 91–4.

6. Richard Harris Smith, *OSS. The Secret History of America's First Central Intelligence Agency* (Guilford, Conn. 2005), pp. 259–60.

7. David Halberstam, *The Coldest Winter. America and the Korean War* (London 2008), p. 230.
8. Smith, *OSS*, pp. 458–9. He lived on as the John Birch Society, founded thirteen years after his death.
9. Ernest May, 'China, 1945–1948: Making Hard Choices', in Ernest R. May and Philip D. Zelikow (eds), *Dealing with Dictators. Dilemmas of US Diplomacy and Intelligence Analysis 1945–1990* (Cambridge, Mass. 2006), pp. 17ff.
10. David McCullough, *Truman* (New York 1992), p. 475.
11. John Robinson Beal, *Marshall in China* (New York 1970), p. 194.
12. Halberstam, *The Coldest Winter*, p. 229.
13. May, 'China, 1945–1948', p. 30.
14. Ibid., pp. 43–7.
15. Robert Service, *Stalin. A Biography* (London 2004), pp. 478–82.
16. Dmitri Volkogonov, *Stalin. Triumph and Tragedy* (London 1991), pp. 498ff.
17. Herbert Feis, *Between War and Peace. The Potsdam Conference* (Princeton 1960), pp. 177–8.
18. Robert Dallek, *The Lost Peace. Leadership in a Time of Horror and Hope 1945–1953* (New York 2010), p. 122.
19. Adam B. Ulam, *Expansion and Coexistence. The History of Soviet Foreign Policy 1917–67* (New York 1968), pp. 270ff.
20. Odd Arne Westad, *The Global Cold War. Third World Interventions and the Making of our Times* (Cambridge 2007), pp. 54–8.
21. For these points see Anne Deighton, 'Britain and the Cold War 1945–1955', in Melvyn Leffler and Odd Arne Westad (eds), *The Cambridge History of the Cold War*, vol. 1: *Origins* (Cambridge 2010), p. 115, and Douglas Waller, *Wild Bill Donovan. The Spymaster Who Created the OSS and Modern American Espionage* (New York 2011), p. 286.
22. Jongsoo Lee, *The Partition of Korea after World War II* (New York 2006), p. 51.
23. David Dilks (ed.), *The Diaries of Sir Alexander Cadogan, OM, 1938–1945* (London 1971), entry dated 25 July 1945, p. 772.

24. William Taubman, *Khrushchev.The Man and his Era* (New York 2003), pp. 211–18, and Simon Sebag Montefiore, *Stalin. The Court of the Red Tsar* (London 2003), pp. 526ff, have a depressing verisimilitude.

25. Robert Conquest, *Stalin. Breaker of Nations* (London 1991), p. 270, for the Pasternak citation.

26. Dallek, *The Lost Peace*, p. 184.

27. Vladimir Pechatnov, 'The Soviet Union and the World 1944–1953', in Leffler and Westad (eds), *The Cambridge History of the Cold War*, vol. 1, pp. 109–10.

28. Robert Beisner, *Dean Acheson. A Life in the Cold War* (Oxford 2006), p. 36.

29. John Lewis Gaddis, 'The Insecurities of Victory: The United States and the Perception of the Soviet Threat after World War II', in Michael Lacey (ed.), *The Truman Presidency* (Cambridge 1991), especially, pp. 268–72.

30. Dallek, *The Lost Peace*, p. 112.

31. Alex Danchev and Daniel Todman (eds), *Field Marshal Lord Alanbrooke. War Diaries 1939–1945* (London 2001), entry dated 23 July 1945, p. 709.

32. Roy Jenkins, *Churchill* (London 2001), pp. 791ff.

33. Kenneth O. Morgan, *Labour in Power 1945–1951* (Oxford 1984), pp. 236–8, for the benign view; Correlli Barnett, *The Lost Victory. British Dreams, British Realities 1945–1950* (London 1995), pp. 40–5 for a cold shower of truth.

34. John Darwin, *The Empire Project. The Rise and Fall of the British World System 1830–1970* (Cambridge 2009), p. 546.

35. Memorandum by Keynes, 'Top Secret', dated 28 September 1944, Treasury 160/1375/F17942/010/5, cited by Wm Roger Louis, 'The Dissolution of the British Empire', in Judith Brown and Wm Roger Louis (eds), *The Twentieth Century* (Oxford 1999), vol. 4 of *The Oxford History of the British Empire*, p. 331.

36. Geoffrey Warner, 'Bevin and British Foreign Policy', in Gordon Craig and Francis Loewenheim (eds), *The Diplomats 1939–1979* (Princeton 1994), p. 105.

37. Barnett, *The Lost Victory*, p. 55.
38. See David Egerton's article 'Declinism' in *London Review of Books*, 7 March 1996 (and Correlli Barnett's replies), for the substance of these paragraphs.
39. Ibid., pp. 190ff.
40. John Darwin, *Britain and Decolonisation. The Retreat from Empire in the Post-War World* (London 1988), p. 76.
41. 'Ice-Floes near Norfolk', *The Times*, 20 February 1947, p. 4.
42. For vivid individual accounts see David Kynaston, *Austerity Britain 1945–51* (London 2007), pp. 185ff.
43. Dominic Sandbrook, *Never Had It So Good. A History of Britain from Suez to the Beatles* (London 2005), p. 45.
44. J. G. Ballard, *Miracles of Life. An Autobiography* (London 2008), p. 124.
45. Alan Bullock, *Ernest Bevin. Foreign Secretary 1945–1951* (Oxford 1985), pp. 97–8.
46. Ibid., p. 90.
47. Morgan, *Labour in Power*, pp. 207–8.
48. Warner, 'Bevin and British Foreign Policy', p. 109.
49. Ronald Hyam, *Britain's Declining Empire. The Road to Decolonisation 1918–1968* (Cambridge 2006), p. 142.
50 Darwin, *The Empire Project*, p. 528: the phrase was Margery Perham's.
51. Hyam, *Britain's Declining Empire*, p. 131.
52. Morgan, *Labour in Power*, p. 252.
53. *The Times*, 6 April 2011.
54. Mark Atwood Lawrence, 'Forging the "Great Combination": Britain and the Indochina Problem 1945–1950', in Lawrence and Logevall (eds), *The First Vietnam War*, p. 108.
55. See Jonathan Fenby, *The General. Charles de Gaulle and the France He Saved* (London 2010).
56. Frank Giles, *The Locust Years. The Story of the Fourth French Republic 1946–1958* (London 1991), p. 74.
57. Ibid., p. 27.
58. Rod Kedward, *La Vie en bleu. France and the French since 1900* (London 2005), p. 381.

59. Maurice Larkin, *France since the Popular Front. Government and People 1936–1996* (Oxford 1997) is exceptionally clear on these developments.
60. Giles, *The Locust Years*, p. 35.
61. Anthony Clayton, *The Wars of French Decolonization* (London 1994), p. 15.
62. Giles, *The Locust Years*, p. 138.
63. Martin Evans and John Phillips, *Algeria. Anger of the Dispossessed* (New Haven, Conn. 2007), pp. 53–5.

5: 'Police Action': Korea

1. Dae-Sook Suh, *Kim Il Sung. The North Korean Leader* (New York 1989), pp. 114–19.
2. Sergei N. Goncharov, John W. Lewis and Xue Litai, *Uncertain Partners. Stalin, Mao, and the Korean War* (Stanford, Calif. 1993), p. 135.
3. Bruce Cumings, *The Korean War. A History* (New York 2010), p. 144.
4. Robert L. Beisner, *Dean Acheson. A Life in the Cold War* (Oxford 2006), pp. 326–31.
5. For a detailed discussion of the genesis of NSC 68 see ibid., pp. 236ff.
6. Melvyn Leffler, 'The Emergence of an American Grand Strategy 1945–1952', in Melvyn Leffler and Odd Arne Westad (eds), *The Cambridge History of the Cold War*, vol. 1: *Origins* (Cambridge 2010), p. 86.
7. James Chace, *Acheson. The Secretary of State Who Created the American World* (New York 1998), pp. 272–9.
8. Walter Isaacson and Evan Thomas, *The Wise Men. Six Friends and the World They Made* (New York 1986), p. 497.
9. Beisner, *Acheson*, pp. 329–30.
10. Robert Dallek, *The Lost Peace. Leadership in a Time of Horror and Hope 1945–1953* (New York 2010), p. 311.
11. Suh, *Kim Il Sung*, p. 121.

12. Chen Jian, *Mao's China and the Cold War* (Chapel Hill, NC 2001), p. 87.

13. Eric F. Goldman, *The Crucial Decade – and After. America 1945–1960* (New York 1960), pp. 146ff.

14. Dallek, *The Lost Peace*, p. 315.

15. Goldman, *The Crucial Decade*, p. 173.

16. David Halberstam, *The Coldest Winter. America and the Korean War* (London 2008), p. 136.

17. William Manchester, *American Caesar. Douglas MacArthur 1880–1964* (New York 1978), pp. 468ff, for vivid characterizations of the General.

18. Goldman, *The Crucial Decade*, p. 177.

19. Halberstam, *The Coldest Winter*, p. 143.

20. Manchester, *American Caesar*, p. 576.

21. Dallek, *The Lost Peace*, pp. 323–4.

22. Goldman, *The Crucial Decade*, p. 178.

23. Cumings, *The Korean War*, pp. 190–9, for details of southern atrocities.

24. Jian, *Mao's China and the Cold War*, p. 88.

25. Yu Bin, 'What China Learned from its "Forgotten War" in Korea', in Mark Ryan, David Finkelstein and Michael McDevitt (eds), *Chinese Warfighting. The PLA Experience since 1949* (Armonk, NY 2003), p. 124. I am grateful to Frank Dikötter for this and other guidance about China.

26. Jung Chang and Jon Halliday, *Mao. The Unknown Story* (London 2006), p. 442.

27. Halberstam, *The Coldest Winter*, p. 402.

28. Ibid., p. 383.

29. Max Hastings, *The Korean War* (London 1987), p. 390.

30. Shu Guang Zhang, 'Command, Control and the PLA's Offensive Campaigns in Korea 1950–1951', in Ryan, Finkelstein and McDevitt (eds), *Chinese Warfighting*, p. 108.

31. For the Chinese army see Russell Spurr, *Enter the Dragon. China at War in Korea* (London 1989).

32. George Mitchell, *Matthew B. Ridgway. Soldier, Statesman, Scholar, Citizen* (Mechanicsburg, Pa 2002), p. 51.

33. Reginald Thompson, *Cry Korea. The Korean War. A Reporter's Notebook* (London 1951, reprinted 2009), p. 309.
34. Hastings, *The Korean War*, p. 266.
35. Ibid., pp. 257–72, gives the clearest account of these changes in policy and the role of the British in shaping them.
36. Mitchell, *Matthew B. Ridgway*, p. 56.
37. Jian, *Mao's China and the Cold War*, pp. 95–6, for this important theme.
38. For these observations see Zhang, 'Command, Control and the PLA's Offensive Campaigns in Korea', pp. 108–14.
39. For detailed descriptions of these battles see Kenneth Hamburger, *Leadership in the Crucible* (College Station, Tex. 2003).
40. Jian, *Mao's China and the Cold War*, pp. 97–9.
41. Kathryn Weathersby, 'Stalin, Mao and the End of the Korean War', in Odd Arne Westad (ed.), *Brothers in Arms. The Rise and Fall of the Sino-Soviet Alliance 1945–1963* (Stanford, Calif. 1998), pp. 105–6.
42. Goldman, *The Crucial Decade*, p. 186.
43. Cumings, *The Korean War*, p. 159.
44. Mark O'Neill, 'Soviet Involvement in the Korean War: A New View from the Soviet-era Archives', *Magazine of History* (2000) 14, pp. 1–10.
45. Jonathan Fenby, *The Penguin History of Modern China. The Fall and Rise of a Great Power 1850–2008* (London 2008), pp. 369–70.
46. Dallek, *The Lost Peace*, p. 335.
47. Stephen E. Ambrose, *Eisenhower*, vol. 2: *The President 1952–1969* (New York/London 1984), pp. 30–5.
48. Dallek, *The Lost Peace*, p. 355.
49. Jian, *Mao's China and the Cold War*, p. 116.
50. Hastings, *The Korean War*, p. 490.
51. Robert McMahon, *The Limits of Empire. The United States and Southeast Asia since World War II* (New York 1999), pp. 44ff.

6: 'Emergency': Malaya

1. A. J. Stockwell, 'The United States and Britain's Decolonization of Malaya 1942–57', in David Ryan and Victor Pungong (eds), *The United States and Decolonization. Power and Freedom* (New York 2000), p. 193.
2. Harry Miller, *Menace in Malaya* (London 1954), p. 41. This account of the early years of the Emergency by a *Straits Times* reporter is exceptionally useful.
3. As plausibly maintained by Anthony Short, *In Pursuit of Mountain Rats. The Communist Insurrection in Malaya* (London 1975, reprinted Singapore 2000), p. 34.
4. Miller, *Menace in Malaya*, p. 60.
5. Margaret Shennan, *Out in the Midday Sun. The British in Malaya 1880–1960* (London 2000) is a fair-minded account of the European contribution to Malaya's development.
6. Ibid., pp. 167–8, for examples, and David Cannadine, *Ornamentalism. How the British Saw their Empire* (London 2002).
7. Benjamin Grob-Fitzgibbon, *Imperial Endgame. Britain's Dirty Wars and the End of Empire* (London 2011), p. 151, for these statistics.
8. A. J. Stockwell, 'Imperialism and Nationalism in South-East Asia', in Judith Brown and Wm Roger Louis (eds), *The Twentieth Century* (Oxford 1999), vol. 4 of *The Oxford History of the British Empire*, p. 470.
9. For this important point see Karl Hack, '"Iron Claws on Malaya": The Historiography of the Malayan Emergency', *Journal of Southeast Asian Studies* (1999) 30, pp. 118–19.
10. T. N. Harper, *The End of Empire and the Making of Malaya* (Cambridge 1999), pp. 94ff.
11. Notably David French, *The British Way in Counter-Insurgency 1945–1967* (Oxford 2011) is exemplary.
12. See the important discussion by Karl Hack, 'The Malayan Emergency as Counter-Insurgency Paradigm', *Journal of Strategic Studies* (2009) 32, pp. 383–414.
13. Christopher Bayly and Tim Harper, *Forgotten Wars. The End of Britain's Asian Empire* (London 2007) p. 173, quoting Howe.

14. Short, *In Pursuit of Mountain Rats*, pp. 80–1.

15. Shennan, *Out in the Midday Sun*, p. 315.

16. Noel Barber, *The War of the Running Dogs. How Malaya Defeated the Communist Guerrillas 1948–1960* (London 1971), pp. 20ff.

17. Piers Brendon, *The Decline and Fall of the British Empire 1781–1997* (London 2007), p. 454, and Bayly and Harper, *Forgotten Wars*, pp. 449–56, for the most detailed and fair-minded account.

18. Miller, *Menace in Malaya*, p. 86.

19. French, *The British Way in Counter-Insurgency*, pp. 75–82, has a good discussion of the legal framework.

20. A. J. Stockwell, 'Sir (Gerard) Edward James Gent', *Oxford Dictionary of National Biography* online edition, pp. 1–3.

21. Meaning nursemaids, house servants, drivers and water carriers in English.

22. Robert Thompson, *Make for the Hills. Memoirs of Far Eastern Wars* (London 1989), p. 88.

23. Joshua Rovner, 'The Heroes of COIN', *Orbis. A Journal of World Affairs* (2012) 56, pp. 215–32, is an important corrective to the inspired-hero view of counter-insurgency warfare.

24. David Cesarani, *Major Farran's Hat. Murder, Scandal and Britain's War against Jewish Terrorism 1945–1948* (London 2009), pp. 28ff.

25. Miller, *Menace in Malaya*, p. 89.

26. French, *The British Way in Counter-Insurgency*, p. 97.

27. Leon Comber, *Malaya's Secret Police 1945–60. The Role of the Special Branch in the Malayan Emergency* (Monash, Australia 2008), p. 84.

28. Han Suyin, *My House Has Two Doors* (London 1982), p. 81.

29. Richard Miers, *Shoot to Kill* (London 1959), pp. 79ff.

30. Ibid., pp. 152–3.

31. Barber, *The War of the Running Dogs*, p. 143.

32. A. F. Derry, *Emergency in Malaya. The Psychological Dimension* (Latimer 1982), p. 6.

33. Miller, *Menace in Malaya*, pp. 181–6.

34. Hack, 'Malayan Emergency', p. 390.

35. John Cloake, *Templer. Tiger of Malaya. The Life of Field Marshal Sir Gerald Templer* (London 1985), p. 201.

36. Ibid., p. 204.
37. Phillip Deery, 'The Terminology of Terrorism: Malaya 1948–52', *Journal of Southeast Asian Studies* (2003) 34, p. 246.
38. Cloake, *Templer*, pp. 226–7.
39. Ibid., p. 262.
40. Jeremy Lewis, *Shades of Greene. One Generation of an English Family* (London 2010), pp. 364–71.
41. Stockwell, 'The US and Britain's Decolonization of Malaya', pp. 198–9.
42. Cloake, *Templer*, p. 223.
43. Shennan, *Out in the Midday Sun*, pp. 329–30.
44. Cloake, *Templer*, p. 263.
45. John Oldfield, *The Green Howards in Malaya (1949–1952). The Story of a Post-war Tour of Duty by a Battalion of the Line* (Aldershot 1953), pp. 50–1.
46. Short, *In Pursuit of Mountain Rats*, pp. 349–50. For a vivid account by an officer in the South Wales Borderers who served in Malaya from 1955 onwards see Miers, *Shoot to Kill*.
47. Grob-Fitzgibbon, *Imperial Endgame*, pp. 198–201.
48. Miller, *Menace in Malaya*, p. 225.
49. For examples see LHMAKCL Stockwell Papers 7/6, leaflet No. 1579 dated 17 February 1953, 'Communist Reward'. Also online examples at National Malaya and Borneo Veterans' Association UK (http// www.nmbva.co.uk/).
50. Barber, *The War of the Running Dogs*, pp. 190ff.
51. Miers, *Shoot to Kill*, pp. 79–90, for the regime in Communist camps.
52. Short, *In Pursuit of Mountain Rats*, pp. 459ff.
53. French, *The British Way in Counter-Insurgency*, pp. 215–18, refutes the idea that the British army had a better learning curve than the Americans. Contemporary American military experts like Thomas Nagl are unduly respectful of British exemplars.
54. These matters are expertly discussed by Karl Hack in Octavian Manea, 'Setting the Record Straight on Malayan Counterinsurgency Strategy: Interview with Karl Hack', *Small Wars Journal*, 11 February 2011.

7: By Huk or by Crook: The Philippines

1. Benedict Kerkvliet, *The Huk Rebellion. A Study of Peasant Revolt in the Philippines* (Berkeley, Calif. 1977, reprinted Lanham, Md 2002), p. 53.
2. Ibid., p. 42.
3. Vina A. Lanzona, *Amazons of the Huk Rebellion. Gender, Sex and Revolution in the Philippines* (Madison, Wis. 2009), p. 7.
4. On the origins of the Huks see Kerkvliet, *The Huk Rebellion*, pp. 26ff.
5. LHMAKCL M/F 515 OSS/State Department Intelligence and Research reports, Part II 'Postwar Japan, Korea and Southeast Asia', for the plight of the Philippines in 1945.
6. Kerkvliet, *The Huk Rebellion*, p. 113.
7. H. W. Brands, *Bound to Empire. The United States and the Philippines* (New York 1992), p. 239.
8. Kerkvliet, *The Huk Rebellion*, p. 147.
9. Douglas Macdonald, *Adventures in Chaos. American Intervention for Reform in the Third World* (Cambridge, Mass. 1992), pp. 142–3.
10. For these details see Cecil B. Currey, *Edward Lansdale. The Unquiet American* (Boston 1988, reprinted Washington, DC 1998), pp. 21–4.
11. Jane C. Loeffler, *The Architecture of Diplomacy. Building America's Embassies* (New York 1998, revised edn Princeton 2011), p. 42, with information from someone familiar with the facts.
12. Ibid., pp. 70–2.
13. Lanzona, *Amazons of the Huk Rebellion*, pp. 144–56.
14. Lawrence Greenberg, *The Hukbalahap Insurrection. A Case Study of a Successful Anti-Insurgency Operation in the Philippines 1946–1955* (Washington, DC 1987), p. 53.
15. Macdonald, *Adventures in Chaos*, p. 152.
16. Currey, *Edward Lansdale*, p. 91.
17. Edward Geary Lansdale, *In the Midst of Wars. An American's Mission to Southeast Asia* (New York 1972, reprinted 1991), pp. 36ff, gives the flavour of their relationship.

18. Jonathan Nashel, *Edward Lansdale's Cold War* (Amherst, Mass. 2005), pp. 27ff, is good on Lansdale's public relations background.
19. Greenberg, *The Hukbalahap Insurrection*, p. 86.
20. Lansdale, *In the Midst of Wars*, p. 75.
21. Currey, *Edward Lansdale*, p. 101.
22. Ibid., pp. 102–3.
23. Ibid., pp. 98–100.
24. Lanzona, *Amazons of the Huk Rebellion*, pp. 138–42.
25. Macdonald, *Adventures in Chaos*, p. 134.
26. Nashel, *Edward Lansdale's Cold War*, p. 34.
27. Macdonald, *Adventures in Chaos*, p. 177.
28. Brands, *Bound to Empire*, pp. 251–2.
29. Lanzona, *Amazons of the Huk Rebellion*, p. 262.
30. Kerkvliet, *The Huk Rebellion*, p. 245.

8: Parachute the Escargot: Indochina

1. Chen Jian, *Mao's China and the Cold War* (Chapel Hill, NC 2001), p. 124.
2. William J. Duiker, *Ho Chi Minh. A Life* (New York 2000), pp. 421–3.
3. Howard R. Simpson, *Tiger in the Barbed Wire. An American in Vietnam 1952–1991* (Washington, DC 1992), pp. 60–1. This memoir by a former US Foreign Service officer is easily the most subtle account of the war in Indochina.
4. See the vivid accounts in Norman Lewis, *A Dragon Apparent. Travels in Cambodia, Laos and Vietnam* (London 1951, new edn 2003), p. 35.
5. Bernard Fall, *Street without Joy. The French Debacle in Indochina* (Harrisburg, Pa 1961, reprinted Mechanicsburg, Pa 2005), pp. 254–5.
6. George C. Herring, *America's Longest War. The United States and Vietnam 1950–1975* (Boston 2002), p. 24.
7. Andrew Rotter, 'Chronicle of a War Foretold: The United States and Vietnam 1945–54', in Mark Atwood Lawrence and Frederik

Logevall (eds), *The First Vietnam War. Colonial Conflict and Cold War Crisis* (Cambridge, Mass. 2008), p. 300.

8. 'The French MacArthur', *Time Magazine*, 24 September 1951.
9. Fall, *Street without Joy*, pp. 39–40.
10. Peter Macdonald, *Giap. The Victor in Vietnam* (London 1993), pp. 100–1.
11. Anthony Clayton, *The Wars of French Decolonization* (London 1994), p. 61.
12. Marilyn B. Young, '"The Same Struggle for Liberty": Korea and Vietnam', in Lawrence and Logevall (eds), *The First Vietnam* War, pp. 207–11.
13. Martin Windrow, *The Last Valley. Dien Bien Phu and the French Defeat in Vietnam* (London 2005), p. 117.
14. Jian, *Mao's China and the Cold War*, pp. 132ff.
15. Lewis, *A Dragon Apparent*, p. 317. Lewis spent some time with an active Viet Minh unit which operated in marshes near Saigon.
16. Simpson, *Tiger in the Barbed Wire*, pp. 25–6.
17. Ibid., pp. 109–10.
18. Ibid., p. 18.
19. Ibid., p. 32.
20. 'We Must Attack', *Time*, 28 September 1953, for a profile of Navarre.
21. Simpson, *Tiger in the Barbed Wire*, p. 83.
22. Ibid., pp. 90–1.
23. Jian, *Mao's China and the Cold War*, p. 134.
24. Fall, *Street without Joy*, pp. 62–3.
25. Jian, *Mao's China and the Cold War*, p. 134.
26. Windrow, *The Last Valley*, p. 429.
27. Peter Grose, *Allen Dulles. Spymaster. The Life and Times of the First Civilian Director of the CIA* (London 2006; first published as *Gentleman Spy. The Life of Allen Dulles*, London 1995), p. 410
28. Andrew Rotter, 'Chronicle of a War Foretold', p. 303.
29. A. J. Langguth, *Our Vietnam. The War 1954–1975* (New York 2000), pp. 77–8.
30. Herring, *America's Longest War*, p. 47.
31. Simpson, *Tiger in the Barbed Wire*, p. 127.

32. Robert McMahon, *The Limits of Empire. The United States and Southeast Asia since World War II* (New York 1999), p. 67.

33. Frances Fitzgerald, *Fire in the Lake. The Vietnamese and the Americans in Vietnam* (New York 1972), pp. 83–4.

34. Kathryn Statler, 'After Geneva: The French Presence in Vietnam, 1954–1963', in Lawrence and Logevall (eds), *The First Vietnam War*, pp. 270–2.

35. McMahon, *The Limits of Empire*, pp. 76–7.

36. Kathryn Statler, 'Building a Colony: South Vietnam and the Eisenhower Administration 1953–61', in Kathryn Statler and Andrew Johns (eds), *The Eisenhower Administration, the Third World, and the Globalization of the Cold War* (Oxford 2006), especially pp. 107–13.

37. Simpson, *Tiger in the Barbed Wire*, p. 79.

38. Ibid., p. 152.

39. Edward Geary Lansdale, *In the Midst of Wars. An American's Mission to Southeast Asia* (New York 1972, reprinted 1991), pp. 232–3.

40. Fitzgerald, *Fire in the Lake*, pp. 97–8.

41. Cecil B. Currey, *Edward Lansdale. The Unquiet American* (Boston 1988, reprinted Washington, DC 1998), p. 182.

42. Langguth, *Our Vietnam*, p. 99.

43. Stanley Karnow, *Vietnam. A History* (London 1983, revised edn 1994), pp. 242–56, is excellent on this phase of the Diem regime.

44. Statler, 'Building a Colony: South Vietnam and the Eisenhower Administration', pp. 103–7.

45. Jonathan Nashel, *Edward Lansdale's Cold War* (Amherst, Mass. 2005), pp. 149ff.

9: Sometimes Special Relationship

1. Carlo D'Este, *Eisenhower. Allied Supreme Commander* (London 2004).

2. Stephen Ambrose, *Eisenhower*, vol. 1: *Soldier, General of the Army, President Elect 1890–1952* (New York/London 1983), p. 430.

3. Ibid., pp. 514–15 and 525.

4. Ibid., p. 529.

5. George W. Ball, *The Past Has Another Pattern. Memoirs* (New York 1982), p. 114. Ball was a Stevenson campaign aide in 1952 and 1956.

6. Ibid., p. 129.

7. J. Ronald Oakley, *God's Country. America in the Fifties* (New York 1990), p. 131.

8. Emmet John Hughes, *The Ordeal of Power. A Political Memoir of the Eisenhower Years* (New York 1963), pp. 74–7.

9. Richard Challener, 'The Moralist as Pragmatist: John Foster Dulles as Cold War Strategist', in Gordon Craig and Francis Loewenheim (eds), *The Diplomats 1939–1979* (Princeton 1994), p. 143.

10. See Peter Grose, *Allen Dulles. Spymaster. The Life and Times of the First Civilian Director of the CIA* (London 2006; first published as *Gentleman Spy. The Life of Allen Dulles*, London 1995), pp. 145–255, for this part of the men's careers.

11. Richard H. Immerman, *John Foster Dulles. Piety, Pragmatism, and Power in US Foreign Policy* (Wilmington, Del. 1999), pp. 31–2.

12. Ibid., p. 32.

13. Ambrose, *Eisenhower*, vol. 2: *The President 1952–1969* (New York/London 1984), p. 21.

14. William Inboden, *Religion and American Foreign Policy 1945–1960. The Soul of Containment* (Cambridge 2008), pp. 238–9.

15. Hughes, *The Ordeal of Power*, pp. 204–9.

16. Aleksandr Fursenko and Timothy Naftali, *Khrushchev's Cold War. The Inside Story of an American Adversary* (New York 2006), pp. 149–52.

17. Peter Hahn, 'The United States and Israel in the Eisenhower Era: The "Special Relationship" Revisited', in Kathryn Statler and Andrew Johns (eds), *The Eisenhower Administration, the Third World, and the Globalization of the Cold War* (Oxford 2006), pp. 225–38.

18. Imboden, *Religion and American Foreign Policy*, pp. 289ff.

19. Colin Dueck, *Hard Line. The Republican Party and US Foreign Policy since World War II* (Princeton 2010), p. 89. Dueck's outstanding book is highly recommended for what follows.

20. George C. Herring, *From Colony to Superpower. US Foreign Relations since 1776* (Oxford 2008), p. 647.

21. L. Douglas Keeney, *15 Minutes. General Curtis LeMay and the Countdown to Nuclear Annihilation* (New York 2011), pp. 89–90.

22. Ibid., pp. 112–13.

23. 'Weather Control as a Cold War Weapon', *Smithsonian Museum Magazine*, 5 December 2011, on blogs.smithsonianmag.com.

24. Robert A. Strong, 'Eisenhower and Arms Control', in Richard Malamson and David Mayers (eds), *Reevaluating Eisenhower. American Foreign Policy in the Fifties* (Urbana, Ill. 1989), p. 243.

25. Dueck, *Hard Line*, p. 97.

26. Saki Dockrill, *Eisenhower's New-Look National Security Policy 1953–61* (London 1996), p. 23, is excellent on the NSC.

27. Dueck, *Hard Line*, pp. 89–90.

28. Cody M. Brown, *The National Security Council. A Legal History of the President's Most Powerful Advisers* (Washington, DC 2008), pp. 17ff.

29. Immerman, *John Foster Dulles. Piety, Pragmatism, and Power*, pp. 59–61.

30. John Lewis Gaddis, *George F. Kennan. An American Life* (London 2012), pp. 485–8.

31. Kenneth Osgood, 'Words and Deeds: Race, Colonialism, and Eisenhower's Propaganda War in the Third World', in Statler and Johns (eds), *The Eisenhower Administration*, pp. 3–16.

32. See the brilliant study by Nicholas Cull, *The Cold War and the United States Information Agency. American Propaganda and Public Diplomacy 1945–1989* (Cambridge 2008), pp. 107–8.

33. See Hugh Wilford, *The Mighty Wurlitzer. How the CIA Played America* (Cambridge, Mass. 2008), pp. 106–8, and David Caute's important *The Dancer Defects. The Struggle for Cultural Supremacy during the Cold War* (Oxford 2003), which corrects Frances Stonor Saunders, *Who Paid the Piper? The CIA and the Cultural Cold War* (London 1999). Interested readers might also consult Peter Coleman's *The Liberal Conspiracy. The Congress for Cultural Freedom and the Struggle for the Mind of Postwar Europe* (New York 1989), which I strongly recommend.

34. Dominic Sandbrook, *Never Had It So Good. A History of Britain from Suez to the Beatles* (London 2005), especially pp. 48–61, is exceptionally astute on these issues.
35. Roy Jenkins, *Churchill* (London 2001), pp. 836–42.
36. Evelyn Shuckburgh, *Descent to Suez. Diaries 1951–56* (London 1986), entry dated 3 December 1953, p. 112 .
37. Jenkins, *Churchill*, p. 868, makes this point.
38. David Carlton, *Anthony Eden. A Biography* (London 1981), pp. 327–8.
39. Peter Hennessy, *Having It So Good. Britain in the Fifties* (London 2006), p. 357. Hennessy is a remarkably well-informed guide to the high politics of this period.
40. Shuckburgh, *Descent to Suez*, entry dated 19 November 1952, p. 54.
41. John Colville, *The Fringes of Power. Downing Street Diaries 1939–1955* (London 2004), entry dated 31 December 1953, p. 616.
42. Ibid., entry dated 7 January 1953, p. 620.
43. Robert H. Ferrell (ed.), *The Eisenhower Diaries* (New York 1981), entry dated 6 January 1953, pp. 222–3.
44. Colville, *The Fringes of Power*, entry dated 4 December 1953, p. 639.
45. Hennessy, *Having It So Good*, pp. 389ff, for a very unboring discussion of British relations with Europe.
46. Carlton, *Anthony Eden*, p. 337.
47. Stephen Ambrose, *Eisenhower*, vol. 2, p. 21.
48. Carlton, *Anthony Eden*, pp. 340–4.
49. Shuckburgh, *Descent to Suez*, entries dated 30 April–2 May 1954, pp. 185–6.
50. Donald Cameron Watt, *Succeeding John Bull. America in Britain's Place 1900–1975* (Cambridge 1984), p. 130.
51. Shuckburgh, *Descent to Suez*, entry dated 4 May 1954, p. 190.
52. Hennessy, *Having It So Good*, pp. 165ff, and David Holloway, *Stalin and the Bomb. The Soviet Union and Atomic Energy 1939–1956* (New Haven, Conn. 1994), pp. 314–17.
53. Hennessy, *Having It So Good*, pp. 341–56.

54. Peter Catterall (ed.), *The Macmillan Diaries. The Cabinet Years 1950–1957* (London 2003), entry dated 14 March 1955, pp. 405–6, for the crucial meeting.

55. D. R. Thorpe, 'Anthony Eden', *Oxford Dictionary of National Biography* online edition, pp. 1–28.

56. Hennessy, *Having It So Good*, especially p. 375.

57. Christopher de Bellaigue, *Patriot of Persia. Muhammad Mossadegh and a Very British Coup* (London 2012), pp. 150–7, charts these events very well.

58. James Bamberg, 'William Milligan Fraser', *Oxford Dictionary of National Biography* online edition.

59. For insights into Mossadeq see Roy Mottahedeh, *The Mantle of the Prophet. Religion and Politics in Iran* (Oxford 2005), pp. 115ff.

60. Manucher Farmanfarmaian and Roxane Farmanfarmaian, *Blood & Oil. A Prince's Memoir of Iran, from the Shah to the Ayatollah* (New York 2005), pp. 228ff.

61. Stephen Kinzer, *All the Shah's Men. An American Coup and the Roots of Middle East Terror* (New York 2008), pp. 96–7.

62. Bellaigue, *Patriot of Persia*, p. 173.

63. Ibid., pp. 178–80.

64. Wm Roger Louis, 'Musaddiq, Oil, and the Dilemmas of British Imperialism', in his *Ends of British Imperialism. The Scramble for Empire, Suez and Decolonization* (London 2006), pp. 758–60, is excellent on these aspects of the crisis.

65. Bellaigue, *Patriot of Persia*, pp. 184–5.

66. Stephen Dorril, *MI6. Inside the Covert World of Her Majesty's Secret Intelligence Service* (New York 2000), pp. 586–8.

67. H. W. Brands, *Inside the Cold War. Loy Henderson and the Rise of the American Empire 1918–1961* (New York 1991), pp. 253ff.

68. C. M. Woodhouse, *Something Ventured. The Autobiography of C. M. Woodhouse* (London 1982), pp. 125–6.

69. Richard Clegg, 'Christopher Montague Woodhouse (Baron Terrington)', *Oxford Dictionary of National Biography* online edition, and Woodhouse's memoir *Something Ventured*.

70. Miles Copeland, *The Game Player. Confessions of the CIA's Original Political Operative* (London 1989), pp. 187–91. When Copeland understates his role in Iran, alarm bells should ring.

71. Donald Wilber (pseudonym?), 'Overthrow of Premier Mossadeq of Iran: November 1952–August 1953', CIA Clandestine Service History, p. 7. The original is dated March 1954. The electronic version available at http://www.nytimes.com/library/world/mideast/041600iran-cia-index.html continues to evolve, with heavily redacted parts gradually revealed. (Hereafter CIA History).

72. Brands, *Inside the Cold War*, pp. 281–3.

73. CIA History, pp. 9–10.

74. Bellaigue, *Patriot of Persia*, pp. 226–30.

75. Grose, *Allen Dulles*, pp. 266–7.

76. CIA History, p. 37.

77. Ibid., pp. 73–4, on the role of radio.

78. Dorril, *MI6*, p. 596.

79. Brands, *Inside the Cold War*, p. 237.

10: Hungary and Suez

1. All these biographical details are from William Taubman's gripping *Khrushchev. The Man and his Era* (New York 2003), pp. 18ff.

2. Jonathan Haslam, *Russia's Cold War. From the October Revolution to the Fall of the Wall* (New Haven, Conn. 2011), p. 148.

3. Aleksandr Fursenko and Timothy Naftali, *Khrushchev's Cold War. The Inside Story of an American Adversary* (New York 2006), pp. 25ff.

4. Vojtech Mastny, 'Soviet Foreign Policy 1953–1962', in Melvyn Leffler and Odd Arne Westad (eds), *The Cambridge History of the Cold War*, vol. 1: *Origins* (Cambridge 2010), p. 315

5. Robert Service, *Comrades. Communism. A World History* (London 2007), p. 313.

6. Taubman, *Khrushchev*, pp. 236ff.

7. Arkady Shevchenko, *Breaking with Moscow* (New York 1985), pp. 78–9. This memoir of a high-ranking defector is excellent on conditions of service for Soviet diplomats.

8. Ibid., p. 82.

9. Fursenko and Naftali, *Khrushchev's Cold War*, p. 58.

10. Service, *Comrades*, p. 319.

11. Ibid., pp. 290–4.

12. Tim Weiner, *Legacy of Ashes. The History of the CIA* (London 2007), p. 129.

13. Haslam, *Russia's Cold War*, p. 171.

14. Fursenko and Naftali, *Khrushchev's Cold War*, pp. 178 –82.

15. Shu Guang Zhang, 'The Sino-Soviet Alliance and the Cold War in Asia 1954–1962', in Leffler and Westad (eds), *Cambridge History of the Cold War*, vol. 1, p. 364.

16. Peter L. Hahn, *The United States, Great Britain, and Egypt 1945–1956. Strategy and Diplomacy in the Early Cold War* (Chapel Hill, NC 1991), p. 213.

17. Eugene Rogan, *The Arabs. A History* (London 2009), pp. 123–32, is excellent on the Urabi revolt.

18. The essential issues are well described by Ronald Hyam, *Britain's Declining Empire. The Road to Decolonisation 1918–1968* (Cambridge 2006), pp. 221ff.

19. Keith Kyle, *Suez. Britain's End of Empire in the Middle East* (London 1991, revised edn 2003), p. 40.

20. Wm Roger Louis, 'Prelude to Suez: Churchill and Egypt', in Wm Roger Louis, *Ends of British Imperialism. The Scramble for Empire, Suez and Decolonization* (London 2006), p. 612.

21. Lord Moran, *Winston Churchill. The Struggle for Survival 1940–1965* (London 1966), entry dated 10 January 1952, p. 362.

22. Louis, *Ends of British Imperialism*, p. 609.

23. Robert Stephens, *Nasser. A Political Biography* (London 1971), pp. 101–8.

24. Miles Copeland, *The Game Player. Confessions of the CIA's Original Political Operative* (London 1989), pp. 142ff.

25. James Jankowski, *A Short History of Egypt* (Oxford 2000), pp. 136 –7.

26. Stephens, *Nasser*, pp. 122–37.

27. Eden memo dated 16 February 1953 in John Kent (ed.), *Egypt and the Defence of the Middle East*, British Documents on the End of Empire Project (London, 1998), part 2, no. 361, pp. 563–4.

28. Evelyn Shuckburgh, *Descent to Suez. Diaries 1951–56* (London 1986), p. 75.

29. Louis, 'Prelude to Suez', pp. 617–21.

30. Peter Hahn, 'The United States and Israel in the Eisenhower Era: The "Special Relationship" Revealed', in Kathryn Statler and Andrew Johns (eds), *The Eisenhower Administration, the Third World, and the Globalization of the Cold War* (Oxford 2006), pp. 230–5.

31. Hyam, *Britain's Declining Empire*, p. 231.

32. Stephens, *Nasser*, p. 142.

33. Humphrey Trevelyan, *The Middle East in Revolution* (London 1970), pp. 86ff.

34. Kyle, *Suez*, pp. 60–1.

35. Tony Walker and Andrew Gowers, *Arafat. The Biography* (London 2003), pp. 12–19.

36. Hahn, *The United States, Great Britain, and Egypt*, p. 159.

37. Miles Copeland, *The Game of Nations. The Amorality of Power Politics* (New York 1969), pp. 157–60.

38. Kyle, *Suez*, pp. 78–80.

39. D. R. Thorpe, *Supermac. The Life of Harold Macmillan* (London 2010), p. 332.

40. Copeland, *The Game Player*, pp. 165–6.

41. Hyam, *Britain's Declining Empire*, p. 232.

42. Jonathan Pearson, *Sir Anthony Eden and the Suez Crisis. Reluctant Gamble* (Basingstoke 2003), pp. 112–15.

43. Ibid., pp. 60ff.

44. David Carlton, *Anthony Eden* (London 1986), p. 412.

45. Thorpe, *Supermac*, pp. 344–7.

46. Pearson, *Sir Anthony Eden and the Suez Crisis*, pp. 140–1.

47. Ann Lane, 'Sir Ivone Kirkpatrick', *Oxford Dictionary of National Biography* online edition, pp. 1–4.

48. Pearson, *Sir Anthony Eden and the Suez Crisis*, pp. 156–7.

49. Kyle, *Suez*, p. 331.
50. Carlton, *Anthony Eden*, pp. 435–41, and Hyam, *Britain's Declining Empire*, pp. 229–30.
51. Peter Grose, *Allen Dulles. Spymaster. The Life and Times of the First Civilian Director of the CIA* (London 2006; first published as *Gentleman Spy. The Life of Allen Dulles*, London 1995), pp. 434–5.
52. Hahn, *The United States, Great Britain, and Egypt*, p. 231.
53. Fursenko and Naftali, *Khrushchev's Cold War*, p. 136.
54. Kyle, *Suez*, p. 467.
55. Thorpe, *Supermac*, p. 364.
56. Piers Brendon, *The Decline and Fall of the British Empire 1781–1997* (London 2007), p. 496.
57. Carlton, *Anthony Eden*, pp. 460–1.
58. Rogan, *The Arabs*, p. 304.

11: With Us or against Us: The Sub-Continent

1 Andreas Hilger, 'The Soviet Union and India: The Years of Late Stalinism', *Parallel History Project on Cooperative Security* (September 2008), pp. 1–5.
2. Robert McMahon, *The Cold War on the Periphery. The United States, India and Pakistan* (New York 1994), p. 46.
3. Kwasi Kwarteng, *Ghosts of Empire. Britain's Legacies in the Modern World* (London 2011), pp. 89ff.
4. H. W. Brands, *Inside the Cold War. Loy Henderson and the Rise of the American Empire 1918–1961* (Oxford 1991), pp. 198–9.
5. Judith Brown, *Nehru. A Political Life* (New Haven, Conn. 2003), p. 236.
6. McMahon, *The Cold War on the Periphery*, pp. 16–17.
7. C. L. Sulzberger, *A Long Row of Candles. Memoirs and Diaries 1934–1954* (Toronto 1969), entry dated 29 April 1950, p. 548.
8. Andrew Rotter, *Comrades at Odds. The United States and India 1947–1964* (Ithaca, NY 2000), p. 19.

9. Dennis Kux, *The United States and Pakistan 1947–2000. Disenchanted Allies* (Washington, DC 2001), pp. 27–31 and 38–42.

10. McMahon, *The Cold War on the Periphery*, p. 56.

11. Brands, *Inside the Cold War*, pp. 211–23.

12. See the brilliant account by the contemporary *Times* journalist Neville Maxwell, *India's China War* (London 1970), pp. 126–7.

13. Kux, *The United States and Pakistan*, p. 18.

14. George McGhee, *Envoy to the Middle World. Adventures in Diplomacy* (New York 1983), p. 97.

15. Sulzberger, *A Long Row of Candles*, entry dated 22 April 1950, p. 541.

16. Rotter, *Comrades at Odds*, pp. 232–3.

17. McMahon, *The Cold War on the Periphery*, pp. 131ff.

18. Ibid., p. 211.

19. Ronald Steel, *Walter Lippmann and the American Century* (Boston 1980), p. 504.

20. Iftikhar Malik, *The History of Pakistan* (Westport, Conn. 2008), pp. 129ff.

21. Maxwell, *India's China War*, pp. 148–9.

22. Brown, *Nehru*, p. 260.

23. K. M. de Silva, *A History of Sri Lanka* (Colombo 2005), pp. 624–5.

24. Maxwell, *India's China War*, pp. 395–9.

25. Brown, *Nehru*, pp. 318ff, is brilliant on this conflict; Peter Worthington, 'War in the Clouds', *The Indian Quarterly*, Vol. 1 (2012), p. 115.

26. Maxwell, *India's China War*, p. 475.

12: Losing by Winning: Algeria

1. Jacques Valette, *La Guerre d'Algérie des Messalistes 1954–1962* (Paris 2001), pp. 23–6.

2. Robert Merle, *Ben Bella* (London 1967), pp. 68–94.

3. Anthony Clayton, *The Wars of French Decolonization* (London 1994), pp. 111–12.

4. Edward Behr, *The Algerian Problem* (London 1961), pp. 189–92.

5. 'Au Peuple Algérien' issued 31 October 1954, in Mohammed Harbi and Gilbert Meynier (eds), *Le FLN. Documents et histoire 1954–1962* (Paris 2004), pp. 36–8.

6. Alistair Horne, *A Savage War of Peace. Algeria 1954–1962* (London 1977, reprinted New York 2006), pp. 105ff.

7. Behr, *The Algerian Problem*, p. 76.

8. Olivier Todd, *Albert Camus. A Life* (New York 1997), p. 331.

9. Frank Giles, *The Locust Years. The Story of the Fourth French Republic 1946–1958* (London 1991), pp. 254ff.

10. Horne, *A Savage War of Peace*, p. 123.

11. Ted Morgan, *My Battle of Algiers. A Memoir* (New York 2005), pp. 107–8.

12. Giles, *The Locust Years*, pp. 267ff, and more generally Martin Thomas, 'Algeria's Violent Struggle for Independence', in Martin Thomas, Bob Moore and L. J. Butler, *Crises of Empire. Decolonisation and Europe's Imperial States 1918–1975* (London 2008), pp. 228ff.

13. John Nagl, *Learning to Eat Soup with a Knife. Counterinsurgency Lessons from Malaya to Vietnam* (Chicago 2005) is an interesting examination of institutional amnesia and the military learning process.

14. David Galula, *Pacification in Algeria 1956–1958* (Santa Monica, Calif. 2006).

15. 'General Marcel Bigeard' obituary *Daily Telegraph* online dated 20 June 2010.

16. Morgan, *My Battle of Algiers*, pp. 111–12.

17. Paul Aussaresses, *The Battle of the Casbah. Terrorism and Counter-Terrorism in Algeria 1955–1957* (New York 2002), pp. 132–41.

18. See George J. Andreopoulos, 'The Age of National Liberation Movements', in Michael Howard, George J. Andreopoulos and Mark R. Shulman (eds), *The Laws of War. Constraints on Warfare in the Western World* (New Haven, Conn. 1994), especially pp. 203–9.

19. Clayton, *The Wars of French Decolonization*, pp. 134–5.

20. Ian Beckett, *Modern Insurgencies and Counter-Insurgencies. Guerrillas and their Opponents since 1750* (London 2001), pp. 159–60.

21. Morgan, *My Battle of Algiers*, pp. 123ff, is especially forthright on this ghastly preening individual.

22. Martin Evans, *Algeria. France's Undeclared War* (Oxford 2012), pp. 194–8, is good on the international context.

23. Horne, *A Savage War of Peace*, pp. 405–6.

24. Irwin Wall, *France, the United States, and the Algerian War* (Berkeley, Calif. 2001), p. 28.

25. Ibid., pp. 162–3. See also Raymond Aron, *The Dawn of Universal History. Selected Essays from a Witness to the Twentieth Century* (New York 2002), especially pp. 423–60.

26. C. L. Sulzberger, *The Test. De Gaulle and Algeria* (London 1962), p. 5.

27. Wall, *France, the United States, and the Algerian War*, p. 158.

28. Benjamin Stora, *Algeria 1830–2000. A Short History* (Ithaca, NY 2001), p. 111.

29. Stanley Hoffmann, 'The Foreign Policy of Charles de Gaulle', in Gordon Craig and Francis Loewenheim (eds), *The Diplomats 1939–1979* (Princeton 1994), pp. 228ff, is a perceptive portrait.

30. Jonathan Fenby, *The General. Charles de Gaulle and the France He Saved* (London 2010), pp. 380ff for general background, and p. 484 for 'not French' quotation, is excellent on de Gaulle's state of mind in this crucial year.

31. Evans, *Algeria. France's Undeclared War*, p. 292.

32. Horne, *A Savage War of Peace*, pp. 284–7.

33. Giles, *The Locust Years*, p. 351.

34. Evans, *Algeria. France's Undeclared War*, p. 253.

35. Sulzberger, *The Test*, p. 108.

36. Ibid., 108–13.

37. Horne, *A Savage War of Peace*, pp. 344–6.

38. Behr, *The Algerian Problem*, pp. 160ff.

39. Fenby, *The General*, p. 465.

40. Horne, *A Savage War of Peace*, p. 456.

41. Pierre Meallier (ed.), *OAS: la guerre d'Algérie vue de Bône à travers les tracts OAS* (Nice 2004), p. 9.

42. Olivier Dard, *Voyage au coeur de l'OAS* (Paris 2005), pp. 94ff.
43. Paul Henissart, *Wolves in the City. The Death of French Algeria* (London 1970) is a fast-paced history of the OAS.
44. Stora, *Algeria 1830–2000*, pp. 82–3.
45. Henissart, *Wolves in the City*, pp. 411–12, for the death toll.
46. Martin Evans and John Phillips, *Algeria. Anger of the Dispossessed* (New Haven, Conn. 2007).

13: Terror and Counter-Terror: Kenya

1. C. S. Nicholls, *Red Strangers. The White Tribe of Kenya* (London 2005), p. 258.
2. Richard Frost, *Enigmatic Proconsul. Sir Philip Mitchell and the Twilight of Empire* (London 1992), pp. 252ff.
3. Charles Douglas-Home, *Evelyn Baring. The Last Proconsul* (London 1978), p. 52. This brilliant satire, for one assumes it is such, deftly draws out Baring's character
4. Jeremy Murray-Brown, *Kenyatta* (London 1972), p. 75. Many of the details of Kenyatta's life recounted here draw on this exemplary biography.
5. As explained by Daniel Branch, *Defeating Mau Mau, Creating Kenya. Counterinsurgency, Civil War, and Decolonization* (Cambridge 2009), pp. 29ff.
6. Christopher Andrew, *The Defence of the Realm. The Authorized History of MI5* (London 2009), pp. 455–6.
7. Murray-Brown, *Kenyatta*, pp. 169–71.
8. David Anderson, *Histories of the Hanged. Britain's Dirty War in Kenya and the End of Empire* (London 2005), pp. 18–21.
9. Jomo Kenyatta, *Facing Mt Kenya. The Tribal Life of the Gikuyu* (New York 1965), pp. 222ff.
10. Murray-Brown, *Kenyatta*, p. 196.
11. Anderson, *Histories of the Hanged*, p. 27.
12. On the squatters see Vincent Harlow and E. M. Chilver (eds), *History of East Africa* (Oxford 1965), vol. 2, pp. 346–8.
13. Guy Arnold, *Kenyatta and the Politics of Kenya* (London 1974), p. 32.

14. Murray-Brown, *Kenyatta*, p. 63.
15. Piers Brendon, *The Decline and Fall of the British Empire 1781–1997* (London 2007) is good on 'white mischief'.
16. Evelyn Waugh, *Remote People* (London 2002), p. 138.
17. Nicholls, *Red Strangers*, p. 245.
18. John Gunther, *Inside Africa* (New York 1955).
19. Benjamin Grob-Fitzgibbon, *Imperial Endgame. Britain's Dirty Wars and the End of Empire* (London 2011), pp. 214–15, for examples of Mau Mau oaths from British army documents.
20. Andrew, *The Defence of the Realm*, p. 454.
21. Branch, *Defeating Mau Mau*, pp. 39–46.
22. Anderson, *Histories of the Hanged*, p. 47.
23. Grob-Fitzgibbon, *Imperial Endgame*, pp. 220–1.
24. Murray-Brown, *Kenyatta*, p. 258.
25. Grob-Fitzgibbon, *Imperial Endgame*, pp. 238–9.
26. 'Your Turn May Come' is reproduced as Appendix 1 in Peter Hewitt, *Kenya Cowboy. A Police Officer's Account of the Mau Mau Emergency* (Johannesburg 2008), pp. 321–5.
27. Andrew, *The Defence of the Realm*, pp. 457–8.
28. Joanna Lewis, '"Daddy Wouldn't Buy Me a Mau Mau": The British Popular Press and the Demoralization of Empire', in E. S. Atieno Odhiambo and John Lonsdale (eds), *Mau Mau and Nationhood* (Athens, Ohio 2003), pp. 227ff. This collection of essays is easily the best single source on Mau Mau.
29. John Lonsdale, 'Mau Maus of the Mind: Making Mau Mau and Remaking Kenya', *Journal of African History* (1990) 31, p. 396.
30. Branch, *Defeating Mau Mau*, pp. 89–90.
31. David French, *The British Way in Counter-Insurgency 1945–1967* (Oxford 2011), pp. 79 and 230 for chapter and verse.
32. Ibid., p. 93.
33. In Ian F. W. Beckett, *Modern Insurgencies and Counter-Insurgencies. Guerrillas and their Opponents since 1750* (London 2001), p. 125.
34. Anderson, *Histories of the Hanged*, pp. 162–3.
35. Grob-Fitzgibbon, *Imperial Endgame*, pp. 254–5.

36. A. S. Cleary, 'The Myth of Mau Mau in its International Context', *African Affairs* (1990) 89, pp. 227–45.

37. Anderson, *Histories of the Hanged*, pp. 300–7.

38. Caroline Elkins, *Britain's Gulag. The Brutal End of Empire in Kenya* (London 2005), p. 83.

39. Beckett, *Modern Insurgencies and Counter-Insurgencies*, p. 125.

40. Branch, *Defeating Mau Mau*, pp. 107–15.

41. French, *The British Way in Counter-Insurgency*, p. 121.

42. Elkins, *Britain's Gulag*, pp. 246ff, for multiple examples.

43. Stephen Chappell, 'Airpower in the Mau Mau Conflict', *Small Wars and Insurgencies* (2011) 22, pp. 495–525.

44. Kennell Jackson, '"Impossible to Ignore their Greatness": Survival Craft in the Mau Mau Forest Movement', in Odhiambo and Lonsdale (eds), *Mau Mau and Nationhood*, pp. 176ff.

45. Frank Kitson, *Gangs and Counter-gangs* (London 1960), pp. 77ff, and Anderson, *Histories of the Hanged*, pp. 285–6.

46. Ian Henderson and Philip Goodhart, *The Hunt for Kimathi* (London 1958) is a tedious *Boy's Own* adventure account of the capture of Kimathi. One of the authors (Goodhart) went on to be a prominent 'wet' Conservative MP, that is opposed to Prime Minister Margaret Thatcher.

47. Elkins, *Britain's Gulag*, especially pp. 152–232, gives exhaustive evidence of brutality in these camps.

48. Ibid., pp. 315ff.

49. Philip Murphy, *Alan Lennox-Boyd. A Biography* (London 1999), pp. 208–14.

50. Elkins mistakenly writes that Powell had left the Tory Party; he had resigned from a junior Treasury post in the Macmillan government in support of the Chancellor of the Exchequer Peter Thorneycroft who went too, but he remained a backbencher.

51. See also Simon Heffer's outstanding *Like the Roman. The Life of Enoch Powell* (London 1998), pp. 252ff.

52. *Parliamentary Debates* (Hansard), Fifth Series, vol. 610, House of Commons Session 1958–9. (London 1959), pp. 232–7 (Enoch Powell) and p. 239 (Leslie Hale) quotations.

14: The Cold War Comes to Africa

1. George McGhee, *Envoy to the Middle World. Adventures in Diplomacy* (New York 1969), p. 128.
2. John Kent, 'The US and the Decolonization of Black Africa, 1945-63', in David Ryan and Victor Pungong (eds), *The United States and Decolonization. Power and Freedom* (London 2000), p. 170.
3. Thomas Noer, 'New Frontiers and Old Priorities in Africa', in Thomas G. Patterson (ed.), *Kennedy's Quest for Victory. American Foreign Policy 1961–1963* (New York 1989), pp. 254–5.
4. James Meriwether, '"A Torrent Overrunning Everything": Africa and the Eisenhower Administration', in Kathryn Statler and Andrew Johns (eds), *The Eisenhower Administration, the Third World, and the Globalization of the Cold War* (Oxford 2006), p. 184.
5. Richard D. Mahoney, *JFK. Ordeal in Africa* (New York 1983), p. 20.
6. Noer, 'New Frontiers and Old Priorities', p. 257.
7. See Francis Spufford's outstanding semi-fictional *Red Plenty: Inside the Fifties' Soviet Dream* (London 2010). This vividly brings to life the clunky technology of the times.
8. William Taubman, *Khrushchev. The Man and his Era* (New York 2003), pp. 461ff.
9. Stephen Ambrose, *Eisenhower*, vol. 2: *The President 1952–1969* (London 1984), pp. 568–80.
10. Michela Wrong, *In the Footsteps of Mr Kurtz. Living on the Brink of Disaster in the Congo* (London 2001) is a vivid account of Congolese history.
11. Madeleine Kalb, *The Congo Cables. The Cold War in Africa – From Eisenhower to Kennedy* (New York 1982), p. 49, is based on a wealth of declassified US documents.
12. Colin Legum, *Congo Disaster* (London 1961), especially pp. 49ff, explains this process most clearly.
13. Ludo De Witte, *The Assassination of Lumumba* (London 2001), p. 2.
14. For the identification of Lumumba with Castro see Charles Cogan and Ernest R. May, 'The Congo, 1960–1963: Weighing Worst

Choices', in Ernest R. May and Philip D. Zelikow (eds), *Dealing with Dictators. Dilemmas of US Diplomacy and Intelligence 1945–1990* (Cambridge, Mass. 2006), p. 57.

15. Sergey Mazov, *A Distant Front in the Cold War. The USSR in West Africa and the Congo 1956–1964* (Washington, DC 2010), p. 88.

16. R. F. Holland, *European Decolonisation 1918–1981* (London 1985), pp. 186 –7, is good on the business community in Congo.

17. Brian Urquhart, *A Life in Peace and War* (London 1987), p. 149.

18. Kalb, *The Congo Cables*, p. 27.

19. Mahoney, *JFK. Ordeal in Africa*, p. 38.

20. Legum, *Congo Disaster*, p. 167.

21. Larry Devlin, *Chief of Station Congo. Fighting the Cold War in a Hot Zone* (New York 2007), p. 77.

22. Meriwether, 'A Torrent Overrunning Everything', p. 185.

23. Mahoney, *JFK. Ordeal in Africa*, p. 41.

24. Peter Grose, *Allen Dulles. Spymaster. The Life and Times of the First Civilian Director of the CIA* (London 1995), pp. 502–3.

25. Urquhart, *A Life in Peace and War*, p. 132.

26. 'Baroness Park of Monmouth', *Daily Telegraph*, 25 March 2010, obituary and private information from one of her service subordinates in the 1970s.

27. Georges Nzongola-Ntalaja, *The Congo from Leopold to Kabila. A People's History* (London 2007), pp. 143–4.

28. Urquhart, *A Life in Peace and War*, p. 169.

29. Mazov, *A Distant Front*, p. 118.

30. Ibid., p. 103.

31. Kalb, *The Congo Cables*, pp. 149ff.

32. Nzongola-Ntalaja, *The Congo from Leopold to Kabila*, pp. 111–12.

33. George W. Ball, *The Past Has Another Pattern. Memoirs* (New York 1982), pp. 232ff.

34. Noer, 'New Frontiers and Old Priorities', pp. 263–4.

35. Conor Cruise O'Brien, *To Katanga and Back. A UN Case History* (London 1962) contains vivid accounts of the main players and of the smell of Katanga at the time.

36. Ibid., pp. 201–2.

37. Kalb, *The Congo Cables*, p. 312.
38. Conor Cruise O'Brien, *Ancestral Voices. Religion and Nationalism in Ireland* (Dublin 1994).
39. 'Conor Cruise O'Brien', *Daily Telegraph*, 19 December 2008, anonymous obituary.
40. O'Brien, *To Katanga and Back*, p. 121.
41. Noer, 'New Frontiers and Old Priorities', p. 266.
42. Devlin, *Chief of Station, Congo*, pp. 194–5. It was actually Daphne Park's idea.
43. Mazov, *A Distant Front*, p. 179.
44. Cogan and May, 'The Congo', p. 86.
45. Kalb, *The Congo Cables*, pp. 371–2, for this exchange.
46. Paul Kennedy, *The Parliament of Man. The United Nations and the Quest for World Government* (London 2007), pp. 83–5.
47. William Attwood, *The Reds and the Blacks. A Personal Adventure* (New York 1967), p. 60, makes this valuable point. Attwood was US ambassador to Guinea in the Kennedy era.
48. Ibid., p. 53.
49. Alaba Ogunsanwo, *China's Policy in Africa 1958–1971* (Cambridge 1974), p. 89.
50. Ibid., pp. 68–9.
51. Mazov, *A Distant Front*, pp. 190–7.
52. Ibid., pp. 197–218.
53. R. F. Holland, *European Decolonisation 1918–1981* (London 1985), p. 294.
54. Robert Shepherd, *Iain Macleod* (London 1994), p. 162.
55. All described at interminable length in Simon Ball's *The Guardsmen. Harold Macmillan, Three Friends, and the World They Made* (London 2004). Of course they were Guards *officers*, and they did not 'make a world' either.
56. H. C. G. Matthew, 'Maurice Harold Macmillan', *Oxford Dictionary of National Biography* online. edition, p. 4. See also Ferdinand Mount, 'Too Obviously Clever', *London Review of Books*, 8 September 2011.
57. D. R. Thorpe, *Supermac. The Life of Harold Macmillan* (London 2010), p. 170.

58. Hyam, *Britain's Declining Empire*, pp. 252–3.
59. L. J. Butler, 'British Decolonisation', in Martin Thomas, Bob Moore and L. J. Butler, *Crises of Empire. Decolonization and Europe's Imperial States 1918–1975* (London 2010), p. 98.
60. Dan Horowitz, 'Attitudes of British Conservatives towards Decolonization in Africa', *African Affairs* (1970) 69, p. 22.
61. Ball, *The Guardsmen*, p. 349.
62. Thorpe, *Supermac*, p. 454.
63. Ronald Hyam and Peter Henshaw, *The Lion and the Springbok. Britain and South Africa since the Boer War* (Cambridge 2003) is easily the best guide to Anglo-Afrikaner relations.
64. Shepherd, *Iain Macleod*, p. 155.
65. Hyam, *Britain's Declining Empire*, p. 261.
66. Shepherd, *Iain Macleod*, p. 177.
67. Piers Brendon, *The Decline and Fall of the British Empire 1781–1997* (London 2007), p. 581.
68. John Darwin, *Britain and Decolonisation. The Retreat from Empire in the Post-War World* (London 1988), p. 273.
69. Shepherd, *Iain Macleod*, pp. 225–7.

15: Backyard Blues: Cuba

1. Lars Schoultz, *Beneath the United States. A History of US Policy toward Latin America* (Cambridge, Mass. 1998), p. 209.
2. Hans Schmidt, *Maverick Marine. General Smedley D. Butler and the Contradictions of American Military History* (Lexington, Ky 1998) p. 291. This essay appeared in the 1935 issue of the socialist magazine *Common Sense*. At the time Butler – nicknamed 'Old Gimlet Eye' – was the most decorated Marine in the Corps history with sixteen medals, including (twice) the Medal of Honor.
3. Thomas G. Paterson, 'Fixation with Cuba: The Bay of Pigs, Missile Crisis, and Covert War against Castro', in Thomas G. Paterson (ed.), *Kennedy's Quest for Victory. American Foreign Policy 1961–1963* (Oxford 1989), p. 127.

4. Stephen Rabe, 'Controlling Revolutions: Latin America, Alliance for Progress, and Cold War Anti-Communism', in Paterson (ed.), *Kennedy's Quest for Victory*, p. 108.

5. Schoultz, *Beneath the United States*, p. 339.

6. FR 1952-1954 4:1-10 and Annex to NSC 144, 6 March 1953.

7. George C. Herring, *From Colony to Superpower. US Foreign Relations since 1776* (Oxford 2008), pp. 369ff, explains this very well.

8. Richard H. Immerman, *John Foster Dulles. Piety, Pragmatism, and Power in US Foreign Policy* (Wilmington, Del. 1999), p. 109.

9. Herring, *From Colony to Superpower*, p. 685.

10. Alexandra von Tunzelmann, *Red Heat. Conspiracy, Murder and the Cold War in the Caribbean* (London 2011), pp. 196–7, is excellent on the Dominican Republic, as well as on Cuba and Haiti

11. Herring, *From Colony to Superpower*, pp. 473–4.

12. Stephen Rabe, 'Dulles, Latin America, and Cold War Anticommunism', in Richard H. Immerman (ed.), *John Foster Dulles and the Diplomacy of the Cold War* (Princeton 1990), p. 163.

13. Ibid., p. 178.

14. Schoultz, *Beneath the United States*, pp. 351–2.

15. Ibid., 328–31.

16. On Figueres see David Atlee Phillips, *The Night Watch. 25 Years inside the CIA* (London 1977), pp. 62–3. In 1955 Phillips spent three days in San José as guest of Pepe and Karen Figueres though they did not learn of his profession until 1977.

17. Thomas Zoumaras, 'Eisenhower's Foreign Economic Policy: The Case of Latin America', in Richard Melanson and David Mayers (eds), *Reevaluating Eisenhower. American Foreign Policy in the Fifties* (Urbana, Ill. 1989), pp. 155ff.

18. Hugh Thomas, *Cuba. A History* (London 1971, revised edn 2001), pp. 446ff.

19. For the sordid details see T. J. English, *Havana Nocturne. How the Mob Owned Cuba . . . and Then Lost It to the Revolution* (New York 2007).

20. Tunzelmann, *Red Heat*, pp. 40–1.

21. Hugo Abedul and R. Gerald Hughes, 'The Comandante and his Labyrinth: Fidel Castro and his Legacy', *Intelligence and National Security* (2011) 26, pp. 533–4, is a detailed demolition of the dictator's biographical mythologies.

22. Volker Skierka, *Fidel Castro. A Biography* (Cambridge 2004), p. 53.

23. Jacqui Goddard, 'Man who killed Che to avenge father's death awarded $2.8bn', *The Times*, 25 August 2011, p. 39.

24. Michael Grow, *US Presidents and Latin American Interventions. Pursuing Regime Change in the Cold War* (Lawrence, Kan. 2008), p. 32.

25. Thomas, *Cuba*, p. 729.

26. Abedul and Hughes, 'The Comandante', pp. 548–9, is good on US attitudes to Cuba.

27. Skierka, *Fidel Castro*, p. 82.

28. Aleksandr Fursenko and Timothy Naftali, *'One Hell of a Gamble'. Khrushchev, Castro, and Kennedy 1958–1964. The Secret History of the Cuban Missile Crisis* (New York 1997), p. 12, and Brian Latell, *Castro's Secrets. The CIA and Cuba's Intelligence Machine* (New York 2012) for the KGB and the Cuban secret service.

29. Tunzelmann, *Red Heat*, p. 179.

30. Skierka, *Fidel Castro*, p. 87.

31. Grow, *US Presidents and Latin American Interventions*, pp. 41–2.

32. Skierka, *Fidel Castro*, p. 95.

33. Fursenko and Naftali, *'One Hell of a Gamble'*, p. 45, report one $8,000 payment for his recent speeches in February 1961. Capable of speaking for four or six hours at a stretch, Castro hoped he might be paid by the word.

34. Ibid., p. 52.

35. Aleksandr Fursenko and Timothy Naftali, *Khrushchev's Cold War. The Inside Story of an American Adversary* (New York 2006), pp. 429–30.

36. Grow, *US Presidents and Latin American Interventions*, p. 49.

37. Skierka, *Fidel Castro*, pp. 103–4.

38. Grow, *US Presidents and Latin American Interventions*, pp. 26 and 91.

39. Fursenko and Naftali, *Khrushchev's Cold War*, pp. 378–9.

40. Paterson, 'Fixation with Cuba', p. 129, citing Walter Lippmann's shrewd remark

41. Grow, *US Presidents and Latin American Interventions*, p. 50.

42. Robert Dallek, *John F. Kennedy. An Unfinished Life 1917–1963* (London 2003), p. 31.

43. Ibid., p. 118.

44. Ibid., pp. 165–8.

45. Ibid., p. 225.

46. Ibid., p. 235.

47. Jane C. Loeffler, *The Architecture of Diplomacy. Building America's Embassies* (New York 1998, revised edn Princeton 2011), pp. 131–2, citing her interview with Crockett

48. Grow, *US Presidents and Latin American Interventions*, pp. 52–4.

49. Paterson, 'Fixation with Cuba', pp. 134–5.

50. The best account of the invasion is by Howard Jones, *The Bay of Pigs* (Oxford 2008).

51. Phillips, *The Night Watch*, pp. 106–8.

52. Jones, *The Bay of Pigs*, p. 107.

16: To the Brink: The Missile Crisis

1. Tim Weiner, *Legacy of Ashes. The History of the CIA* (London 2007), p. 180.

2. Cecil B. Currey, *Edward Lansdale. The Unquiet American* (Boston 1988, reprinted Washington, DC 1998), p. 242.

3. Lawrence Freedman, *Kennedy's Wars. Berlin, Cuba, Laos, and Vietnam* (Oxford 2000), pp. 154–6.

4. Bayard Stockton, *Flawed Patriot. The Rise and Fall of CIA Legend Bill Harvey* (Dulles, Va 2006), pp. 143ff.

5. Evan Thomas, *The Very Best Men. The Daring Early Years of the CIA* (New York 1995, reprinted 2006), pp. 289–90.

6. Gerald Ford Library, Ann Arbor, Mich., 'Minutes of Meeting of the Special Group (Augmented) on Operation MONGOOSE', 4 October 1962. This document was declassified in 1997.

7. Taylor Branch and George Crile, 'The Kennedy Vendetta: Our Secret War on Cuba', *Harpers Magazine* (August 1975), p. 60, is based on interviews with many participants in these ventures.

8. Brian Latell, *Castro's Secrets. The CIA and Cuba's Intelligence Machine* (New York 2012), p. 99.

9. Kai Bird, *The Color of Truth. McGeorge Bundy and William Bundy. Brothers in Arms. A Biography* (New York 1998), p. 244.

10. Aleksandr Fursenko and Timothy Naftali, *'One Hell of a Gamble'. Khrushchev, Castro, and Kennedy 1958–1964. The Secret History of the Cuban Missile Crisis* (New York 1997), pp. 149–51.

11. Jonathan Haslam, *Russia's Cold War. From the October Revolution to the Fall of the Wall* (New Haven, Conn. 2011), pp. 196–9, has much valuable Soviet material.

12. Odd Arne Westad, *The Global Cold War. Third World Interventions and the Making of our Times* (Cambridge 2007), pp. 160–7.

13. William Taubman, *Khrushchev. The Man and his Era* (London 2003), pp. 532–3, is very convincing on Khrushchev and his inner circle during the missile crisis.

14. George C. Herring, *From Colony to Superpower. US Foreign Relations since 1776* (Oxford 2008), p. 707.

15. Fursenko and Naftali, *'One Hell of a Gamble'*, pp. 188–9.

16. Aleksandr Fursenko and Timothy Naftali, *Khrushchev's Cold War. The Inside Story of an American Adversary* (New York 2006), p. 451.

17. Robert Dallek, *John F. Kennedy. An Unfinished Life 1917–1963* (London 2003), p. 537.

18. George W. Ball, *The Past Has Another Pattern. Memoirs* (New York 1982), p. 287.

19. Fursenko and Naftali, *'One Hell of a Gamble'*, pp. 221–2.

20. Haslam, *Russia's Cold War*, p. 206, and Freedman, *Kennedy's Wars*, p. 169.

21. Fursenko and Naftali, *'One Hell of a Gamble'*, pp. 229–30.

22. Robert A. Caro, *The Years of Lyndon Johnson*, vol. 4: *The Passage of Power* (New York 2012), p. 222.

23. Evan Thomas, *Robert Kennedy. His Life* (New York 2000), p. 213.

24. Maxwell D. Taylor, *Swords and Plowshares. A Memoir* (New York 1972), pp. 267–8.
25. Haslam, *Russia's Cold War*, p. 207.
26. Dallek, *John F. Kennedy*, p. 368.
27. Ernest R. May and Philip D. Zelikow (eds), *The Kennedy Tapes. Inside the White House during the Cuban Missile Crisis* (New York 2002), p. 117.
28. Warren Kozak, *Lemay. The Life and Wars of General Curtis LeMay* (Washington, DC 2009), pp. 332–54.
29. Ball, *The Past Has Another Pattern*, p. 291.
30. L. Douglas Keeney, *15 Minutes. General Curtis LeMay and the Countdown to Nuclear Annihilation* (New York 2011), pp. 282–3.
31. Fursenko and Naftali, 'One Hell of a Gamble', p. 247.
32. Fursenko and Naftali, *Khrushchev's Cold War*, p. 483.
33. Bird, *The Color of Truth*, pp. 238–9.
34. Thomas, *Robert Kennedy*, p. 231.
35. Michael Dobbs, *One Minute to Midnight. Kennedy, Khrushchev, and Castro on the Brink of Nuclear War* (London 2008), pp. 204–5.
36. Ibid., pp. 284–5.
37. Volker Skierka, *Fidel Castro. A Biography* (Cambridge 2004), p. 138.
38. Howard Jones, *The Bay of Pigs* (Oxford 2008), p. 164.
39. See former CIA officer Brian Latell, *Castro's Secrets*, which I first read in serialized form in the *Miami Herald*, 1–5 May 2012.
40. Piero Gleijeses, 'Cuba's First Venture in Africa 1961–1965', *Journal of Latin American Studies* (1996) 28, pp. 171–81.
41. Fursenko and Naftali, *Khrushchev's Cold War*, pp. 532–8.

17: Overreach: Vietnam

1. William Taubman, *Khrushchev. The Man and his Era* (London 2003), p. 341.
2. Frank Dikötter, *Mao's Great Famine* (London 2011) is the definitive account of these horrors.

3. Chen Jian, *Mao's China and the Cold War* (Chapel Hill, NC 2001), p. 77.

4. See Harold P. Ford, 'Calling the Sino-Soviet Split', CIA Library, Center for the Study of Intelligence, Studies in Intelligence 1998/99, pp. 57–71 (pdf), accessed at https://www.cia.gov/library/ center-for-the-study-of-intelligence/csi-publications/csi-studies/ studies/winter98_99/art05.html, pp. 1–14.

5. Kay Möller, *Die Aussenpolitik der Volksrepublik China 1949–2004. Eine Einführung* (Wiesbaden 2005), p. 59.

6. George W. Ball, *The Past Has Another Pattern. Memoirs* (New York 1982), p. 364.

7. George C. Herring, *America's Longest War. The United States and Vietnam 1950–1975* (Boston 2002), p. 94.

8. Maxwell D. Taylor, *Swords and Plowshares. A Memoir* (New York 1972), p. 228.

9. Lawrence Freedman, *Kennedy's Wars. Berlin, Cuba, Laos, and Vietnam* (Oxford 2000), p. 311.

10. Evan Thomas, *The Very Best Men. The Daring Early Years of the CIA* (New York 1995, reprinted 2006), pp. 282–3.

11. Randall B. Woods, *LBJ. Architect of American Ambition* (Cambridge, Mass. 2006), p. 389.

12. Stanley Karnow, *Vietnam. A History* (London 1983, revised edn 1994), p. 266, makes this crucial point.

13. Taylor, *Swords and Plowshares*, pp. 238ff.

14. Freedman, *Kennedy's Wars*, p. 326.

15. John Prados, *William Colby and the CIA. The Secret War of a Controversial Spymaster* (Lawrence, Kan. 2009), pp. 74ff.

16. Walter Isaacson and Evan Thomas, *The Wise Men. Six Friends and the World They Made* (New York 1986), p. 637.

17. Like US Foreign Service officer Charles T. Cross, the author of the revealing *Born a Foreigner. A Memoir of the American Presence in Asia* (Lanham, Md 1999), who was far more generous to Thompson than he was towards the Americans. Cross was born in Nationalist China, and then served in Indonesia, Malaya, London, Hong Kong and Vietnam.

18. Robert Thompson, *Make for the Hills. Memories of Far Eastern Wars* (London 1989), pp. 124–8.
19. Karnow, *Vietnam*, p. 274.
20. Herring, *America's Longest War*, pp. 105–6.
21. Robert Dallek, *John F. Kennedy. An Unfinished Life 1917–1963* (London 2003), p. 450.
22. Isaacson and Thomas, *The Wise Men*, p. 636.
23. Freedman, *Kennedy's Wars*, p. 355.
24. David Halberstam, *The Best and the Brightest* (New York 1969), p. 213, for an astute assessment of McNamara.
25. The classic account of Ap Bac is in Neil Sheehan's marvellously intelligent *A Bright Shining Lie. John Paul Vann and America in Vietnam* (New York 1988), pp. 203–5.
26. Robert Shaplen, *The Lost Revolution. Vietnam 1945–65* (London 1966), pp. 191–2.
27. See the valuable passages in Frances Fitzgerald, *Fire in the Lake. The Vietnamese and the Americans in Vietnam* (New York 1972), pp. 130–4.
28. Karnow, *Vietnam*, pp. 317ff, on the key conspirators.
29. Dallek, *John F. Kennedy*, p. 677.
30. Halberstam, *The Best and the Brightest*, pp. 278–84.
31. Ibid., pp. 284–5.
32. Herring, *America's Longest War*, pp. 134–5.
33. Dallek, *John F. Kennedy*, pp. 693–4.

18: Watershed of the American Century

1. David Halberstam, *The Best and the Brightest* (New York 1969), p. 298.
2. Robert A. Caro, *The Years of Lyndon Johnson*, vol. 4: *The Passage of Power* (New York 2012) p. 115.
3. Randall B. Woods, *LBJ. Architect of American Ambition* (Cambridge, Mass. 2006), p. 433.
4. James T. Patterson, *Grand Expectations. The United States 1945–1974* (Oxford 1996), p. 598.

5. Ibid., p. 508.
6. Kai Bird, *The Color of Truth. McGeorge Bundy and William Bundy. Brothers in Arms. A Biography* (New York 1998), pp. 276–7.
7. Halberstam, *The Best and the Brightest*, pp. 370–1.
8. Ibid., p. 530.
9. Patterson, *Grand Expectations*, p. 608.
10. Woods, *LBJ. Architect of American Ambition*, p. 510.
11. Bird, *The Color of Truth*, p. 281.
12. Woods, *LBJ. Architect of American Ambition*, p. 540.
13. Gordon M. Goldstein, *Lessons in Disaster. McGeorge Bundy and the Path to War in Vietnam* (New York 2008), p. 123.
14. Bird, *The Color of Truth*, pp. 286–9.
15. Jung Chang and Jon Halliday, *Mao. The Unknown Story* (London 2006), pp. 586–7.
16. Jonathan Haslam, *Russia's Cold War. From the October Revolution to the Fall of the Wall* (New Haven, Conn. 2011), pp. 222–3.
17. Chen Jian, *Mao's China and the Cold War* (Chapel Hill, NC 2001), pp. 207–29.
18. Halberstam, *The Best and the Brightest*, pp. 532–3.
19. Mark Atwood Lawrence, *The Vietnam War. A Concise International History* (Oxford 2008), p. 91.
20. Chang and Halliday, *Mao*, p. 590.
21. Jim Mann, 'US Considered '64 Bombing to Keep China Nuclear Free', *Los Angeles Times*, 27 September 1998.
22. Francis Gavin and James Steinberg, 'The Unknown Unknowns', *Foreign Policy*, 14 February 2012, pp. 1–3.
23. Goldstein, *Lessons in Disaster*, pp. 176–7.
24. Woods, *LBJ. Architect of American Ambition*, p. 605, for the exchange with McGovern.
25. George C. Herring, *America's Longest War. The United States and Vietnam 1950–1975* (Boston 2002), p. 179, for these statistics.

Select Bibliography

Abedul, Hugo and Hughes, R. Gerald, 'The Comandante and his Labyrinth: Fidel Castro and his Legacy', *Intelligence and National Security* (2011) 26, pp. 531–65

Abella, Alex, *Soldiers of Reason. The Rand Corporation and the Rise of the American Empire* (Orlando, Florida 2007)

Alexander, Andrew, *America and the Imperialism of Ignorance. US Foreign Policy since 1945* (London 2012)

Alexander, Martin and Keiger, J. F. V. (eds), *The Algerian War and the French Army 1954–62. Experiences, Images, Testimonies* (London 2002)

——(eds), *France and the Algerian War 1954–62. Strategy, Operations and Diplomacy* (London 2002)

Ambrose, Stephen, *Eisenhower* (New York/London 1983–4) vols 1–2

Anderson, David, *Histories of the Hanged. Britain's Dirty War in Kenya and the End of Empire* (London 2005)

Andreopoulos, George, 'The Age of National Liberation Movements', in Michael Howard, George Andreopoulos and Mark R. Shulman (eds), *The Laws of War. Constraints on Warfare in the Western World* (New Haven, Conn. 1994), pp. 191–213

Andrew, Christopher, *The Defence of the Realm. The Authorized History of MI5* (London 2009)

Applebaum, Anne, *Iron Curtain. The Crushing of Eastern Europe 1944–56,* (London 2012)

Armstrong, Charles K., *The North Korean Revolution 1945–1950* (Ithaca, NY 2003)

Arnold, Guy, *Kenyatta and the Politics of Kenya* (London 1974)

Aron, Raymond, *The Dawn of Universal History. Selected Essays from a Witness to the Twentieth Century* (New York 2002)

Attwood, William, *The Reds and the Blacks. A Personal Adventure* (New York 1967)

Aussaresses, Paul, *The Battle of the Casbah. Terrorism and Counter-Terrorism in Algeria 1955–1957* (New York 2002)

Bachmann, Wiebke, *Die UdSSR und der Nahe Osten. Zionismus, ägyptischer Antikolonialismus und sowjetische Aussenpolitik bis 1956* (Munich 2011)

Bakevich, Andrew, *American Empire. The Realities and Consequences of US Diplomacy* (Cambridge, Mass. 2002)

Ball, George W., *The Past Has Another Pattern. Memoirs* (New York 1982)

Ball, Simon, *The Guardsmen. Harold Macmillan, Three Friends, and the World They Made* (London 2004)

Baltzell, E. Digby, *The Protestant Establishment. Aristocracy and Caste in America* (New York 1964)

Barber, Noel, *The War of the Running Dogs. How Malaya Defeated the Communist Guerrillas 1948–1960* (London 1971)

Barnett, Correlli, *The Audit of War. The Illusion and Reality of Britain as a Great Nation* (London 1986)

——, *The Lost Victory. British Dreams, British Realities 1945–1950* (London 1995)

——, *The Verdict of Peace. Britain between her Yesterday and the Future* (London 2001)

Bayly, Christopher and Harper, Tim, *Forgotten Armies. Britain's Asian Empire and the War with Japan* (London 2004)

——, *Forgotten Wars. The End of Britain's Asian Empire* (London 2007)

Beckett, Ian F. W., *Modern Insurgencies and Counter-Insurgencies. Guerrillas and their Opponents since 1750* (London 2001)

Beisner, Robert, *Dean Acheson. A Life in the Cold War* (Oxford 2006)

Bellaigue, Christopher de, *Patriot of Persia. Muhammad Mossadegh and a Very British Coup* (London 2012)

Blundell, Michael, *So Rough a Wind* (London 1964)

Bonsal, Philip, *Cuba, Castro, and the United States* (Pittsburgh 1971)

Boot, Max, *The Savage Wars of Peace* (New York 2003)

Bowie, Robert and Richard Immermann, *Waging Peace. How Eisenhower Shaped an Enduring Cold War Strategy* (New York, 2000)

Bradley, Mark, *Vietnam at War* (Oxford 2009)

Branch, Daniel, *Defeating Mau Mau, Creating Kenya. Counterinsurgency, Civil War, and Decolonization* (Cambridge 2009)

——, *Kenya. Between Hope and Despair 1963–2011* (New Haven, Conn. 2011)

Branch, Taylor and Crile, George, 'The Kennedy Vendetta: Our Secret War on Cuba', *Harpers Magazine* (August 1975), pp. 49–63

Brands, H. W., *Inside the Cold War. Loy Henderson and the Rise of the American Empire 1918–1961* (Oxford 1991)

——, *Bound to Empire. The United States and the Philippines* (New York 1992)

Brendon, Piers, *Ike. The Life and Times of Dwight D. Eisenhower* (London 1987)

——, *The Decline and Fall of the British Empire 1781–1997* (London 2007)

Brocheux, Pierre and Hémery, Daniel, *Indochina. An Ambiguous Colonisation 1858–1954* (Berkeley, Calif. 2009)

Brown, Judith, *Nehru. A Political Life* (New Haven, Conn. 2003)

Bullock, Alan, *Ernest Bevin. Foreign Secretary 194–195* (Oxford 1985)

Butler, L. J., *Britain and Empire. Adjusting to a Post-Imperial World* (London 2002)

Campbell, Arthur, *Jungle Green* (London 1953)

Cannadine, David, *Ornamentalism. How the British Saw their Empire* (London 2002)

Caro, Robert A., *The Years of Lyndon Johnson*, vol. 4: *The Passage of Power* (New York 2012)

Catterall, Peter (ed.), *The Macmillan Diaries. The Cabinet Years 1950–1957* (London 2003)

——(ed.), *The Macmillan Diaries. Prime Minister and After 1957–1966* (London 2011)

Cesarani, David, *Major Farran's Hat. Murder, Scandal and Britain's War against Jewish Terrorism 1945–1948* (London 2009)

Chang, Jung and Halliday, Jon, *Mao. The Unknown Story* (London 2006)

Chevenix Trench, Charles, *Men Who Ruled Kenya. The Kenya Administration 1892–1963* (London 1993)

Clarke, Peter, *The Last Thousand Days of the British Empire. The Demise of a Superpower 1944–47* (London 2007)

Clayton, Anthony, *The Wars of French Decolonization* (London 1994)

Cleary, A. S., 'The Myth of Mau Mau in its International Context', *African Affairs* (1990) 89, pp. 227–45

Cloake, John, *Templer. Tiger of Malaya. The Life of Field Marshal Sir Gerald Templer* (London 1985)

Cohen, Michael and Kolinsky, Martin (eds), *Demise of the British Empire in the Middle East. Britain's Responses to Nationalist Movements 1943–55* (London 1998)

Cohen, Warren, *Empire without Tears. America's Foreign Relations 1921–1933* (New York 1965)

Colville, John, *The Fringes of Power. Downing Street Diaries 1939–1955* (London 2004)

Comber, Leon, *Malaya's Secret Police 1945–60. The Role of the Special Branch in the Malayan Emergency* (Monash, Australia 2008)

Copeland, Miles, *The Game of Nations. The Amorality of Power Politics* (New York 1969)

——, *The Game Player. Confessions of the CIA's Original Political Operative* (London 1989)

Cotton, James and Neary, Ian (eds), *The Korean War in History* (Manchester 1989)

Craig, Campbell, *Destroying the Village. Eisenhower and Thermonuclear War* (New York, 1998)

Craig, Campbell and Logevall, Frederik, *America's Cold War. The Politics of Insecurity* (Cambridge, Mass. 2009)

Craig, Gordon and Loewenheim, Francis (eds), *The Diplomats 1939–1979* (Princeton 1994)

Cross, Charles T., *Born a Foreigner. A Memoir of the American Presence in Asia* (Lanham, Md 1999)

Cull, Nicholas, *The Cold War and the United States Information Agency. American Propaganda and Public Diplomacy 1945–1989* (Cambridge 2008)

Cumings, Bruce, *North Korea. Another Country* (New York 2004)

——, *The Korean War. A History* (New York 2010)

Currey, Cecil B., *Edward Lansdale. The Unquiet American* (Boston 1988, reprinted Washington, DC 1998)

Cutler, Robert, *No Time for Rest* (Boston, 1966)

Dalin, David G. and Rothman, John F., *Icon of Evil. Hitler's Mufti and the Rise of Radical Islam* (New York 2008)

Dallek, Robert, *John F. Kennedy. An Unfinished Life 1917–1963* (London 2003)

——, *Lyndon B. Johnson. Portrait of a President* (London 2004)

——, *The Lost Peace. Leadership in a Time of Horror and Hope 1945–1953* (New York 2010)

Dard, Olivier, *Voyage au coeur de l'OAS* (Paris 2005)

Darwin, John, *Britain and Decolonisation. The Retreat from Empire in the Post-War World* (London 1988)

——, *After Tamerlane. The Global History of Empire* (London 2007)

——, *Unfinished Empire. The Global Expansion of Britain* (London 2012)

Deery, Phillip, 'The Terminology of Terrorism: Malaya 1948–52', *Journal of Southeast Asian Studies* (2003) 34, pp. 231–47

De Witte, Ludo, *The Assassination of Lumumba* (London 2001)

Dikötter, Frank, *The Age of Openness. China before Mao* (Hong Kong 2008)

——, *Mao's Great Famine* (London 2011)

Dockrill, Saki, *Eisenhower's New-Look National Security Policy 1953–61* (London 1996)

Douglas-Home, Charles, *Evelyn Baring. The Last Proconsul* (London 1978)

Dueck, Colin, *Reluctant Crusaders. Power, Culture, and Change in American Grand Strategy* (Princeton 2006)

Duiker, William, *Ho Chi Minh. A Life* (New York 2000)

Elkins, Caroline, *Britain's Gulag. The Brutal End of Empire in Kenya* (London 2005)

English, T. J., *Havana Nocturne. How the Mob Owned Cuba . . . and Then Lost It to the Revolution* (New York 2007)

Evans, Martin, *Algeria. France's Undeclared War* (Oxford 2012)

Evans, Martin and Phillips, John, *Algeria. Anger of the Dispossessed* (New Haven, Conn. 2007)

Faligot, Roger and Kauffer, Remi, *The Chinese Secret Service. Kang Sheng and the Shadow Government of Red China* (New York 1987)

Fall, Bernard, *Street without Joy. The French Debacle in Indochina* (Harrisburg, Pa 1961, reprinted Mechanicsburg, Pa 2005)

Farmanfarmaian, Manucher and Farmanfarmaian, Roxane, *Blood & Oil. A Prince's Memoir of Iran, from the Shah to the Ayatollah* (New York 2005)

Fenby, Jonathan, *The General. Charles de Gaulle and the France He Saved* (London 2010)

Feraoun, Mouloud, *Journal 1955–1962. Reflections on the French–Algerian War* (Lincoln, Nebr. 2000)

Ferguson, Niall, *Empire. The Rise and Demise of the British World Order and the Lessons for Global Power* (New York 2003)

——, *Colossus. The Rise and Fall of the American Empire* (London 2004)

Ferrell, Robert H. (ed.), *The Eisenhower Diaries* (New York 1981)

Findlay, Douglas, *White Knees, Brown Knees. The Canal Zone 1951–1954. The Forgotten Years* (Edinburgh 2003)

Fitzgerald, Frances, *Fire in the Lake. The Vietnamese and the Americans in Vietnam* (New York 1972)

Freedman, Lawrence, *Kennedy's Wars. Berlin, Cuba, Laos, and Vietnam* (Oxford 2000)

French, David, *The British Way in Counter-Insurgency 1945–1967* (Oxford 2011)

Frost, Richard, *Enigmatic Proconsul. Sir Philip Mitchell and the Twilight of Empire* (London 1992)

Fursenko, 'One Hell of a Gamble'. Khrushchev, Castro, and Kennedy 1958–1964. The Secret History of the Cuban Missile Crisis (New York 1997)

——, Aleksandr and Naftali, Timothy, Khrushchev's Cold War. The Inside Story of an American Adversary (New York 2006)

Gaddis, John Lewis, The United States and the Origins of the Cold War 1941–1947 (New York 1972)

——, The Cold War. A New History (New York 2005)

——, George F. Kennan. An American Life (London 2012)

Giles, Frank, The Locust Years. The Story of the Fourth French Republic 1946–1958 (London 1991)

Goldman, Eric F., The Crucial Decade – and After. America 1945–1960 (New York 1960)

Goldstein, Gordon M., Lessons in Disaster. McGeorge Bundy and the Path to War in Vietnam (New York 2008)

Gosnell, Jonathan, The Politics of Frenchness in Colonial Algeria 1930–1954 (Rochester, NY 2002)

Goulden, Joseph G., The Best Years 1945–1950 (New York 1976)

Greenstein, Fred, The Hidden Hand Presidency. Eisenhower as Leader (New York, 1982)

Grob-Fitzgibbon, Benjamin, Imperial Endgame. Britain's Dirty Wars and the End of Empire (London 2011)

Grose, Peter, Allen Dulles. Spymaster. The Life and Times of the First Civilian Director of the CIA (London 2006; first published as Gentleman Spy. The Life of Allen Dulles, London 1995)

Grow, Michael, US Presidents and Latin American Interventions. Pursuing Regime Change in the Cold War (Lawrence, Kan. 2008)

Hack, Karl, 'British Intelligence and Counter-Insurgency in the Era of Decolonisation: The Example of Malaya', Intelligence and National Security (1999) 14, pp. 134–45

——, 'Corpses, POWs and Captured Documents: British and Communist Narratives of the Malayan Emergency, and the Dynamics of Intelligence Transformation', Intelligence and National Security (1999) 14, pp. 211–41

——, '"Iron Claws on Malaya": The Historiography of the Malayan Emergency', Journal of Southeast Asian Studies (1999) 30, pp. 99–125

——, 'The Malayan Emergency as Counter-Insurgency Paradigm', *Journal of Strategic Studies* (2009) 32, pp. 383–414

Halberstam, David, *The Fifties* (New York 1993)

——, *The Coldest Winter. America and the Korean War* (London 2008)

Han Suyin, *My House Has Two Doors* (London 1982)

Harlow, Vincent and Chilver, E. M. (eds), *History of East Africa* (Oxford 1965)

Harper, T. N., *The End of Empire and the Making of Malaya* (Cambridge 1999)

Haslam, Jonathan, *Russia's Cold War. From the October Revolution to the Fall of the Wall* (New Haven, Conn. 2011)

Hastings, Max, *The Korean War* (London 1987)

——, *All Hell Let Loose. The World at War 1939–1945* (London 2011)

Heffer, Simon, *Like the Roman. The Life of Enoch Powell* (London 1998)

Henissart, Paul, *Wolves in the City. The Death of French Algeria* (London 1970)

Hennessy, Peter, *Never Again. Britain 1945–51* (London 1992)

——, *Having It So Good. Britain in the Fifties* (London 2006)

Herring, George C., *America's Longest War. The United States and Vietnam 1950–1975* (Boston 2002)

——, *From Colony to Superpower. US Foreign Relations since 1776* (Oxford 2008)

Hewitt, Peter, *Kenya Cowboy. A Police Officer's Account of the Mau Mau Emergency* (Johannesburg 2008)

Hilger, Andreas (ed.), *Die Sowjetunion und die Dritte Welt. UdSSR, Staatssozialismus und Antikolonialismus im Kalten Krieg 1945–1991* (Munich 2009)

Holland, R. J., *European Decolonisation 1918–1981* (London 1985)

Horne, Alistair, *A Savage War of Peace. Algeria 1954–1962* (London 1977, reprinted New York 2006)

Horowitz, David, 'Attitudes of British Conservatives towards Decolonization in Africa', *African Affairs* (1970) 69, pp. 9–26

Hughes, Emmet John, *The Ordeal of Power. A Political Memoir of the Eisenhower Years* (New York 1963)

Hyam, Ronald, *Britain's Imperial Century 1815–1914. A Study of Empire and Expansion* (London 2002)

——, *Britain's Declining Empire. The Road to Decolonisation 1918–1968* (Cambridge 2006)

Immerman, Richard H., (ed.), *John Foster Dulles and the Diplomacy of the Cold War* (Princeton 1990)

——, *John Foster Dulles. Piety, Pragmatism, and Power in US Foreign Policy* (Wilmington, Del. 1999)

Inboden, William, *Religion and American Foreign Policy 1945–1960. The Soul of Containment* (Cambridge 2008)

Isaacson, Walter and Thomas, Evan, *The Wise Men. Six Friends and the World They Made* (New York 1986)

Jackson, Robert, *The Malayan Emergency and Indonesian Confrontation. The Commonwealth's Wars 1948–1966* (Barnsley 1991)

James, Lawrence, *The Rise and Fall of the British Empire* (London 1994)

Jeffrey, Keith, *MI6. The History of the Secret Intelligence Service 1909–1949* (London 2010)

Jenkins, Roy, *Truman* (London 1986)

Jones, Howard, *'A New Kind of War': America's Global Strategy and the Truman Doctrine in Greece* (New York 1989)

——, *The Bay of Pigs* (Oxford 2008)

Jones, Joseph Marion, *The Fifteen Weeks. An Inside Account of the Genesis of the Marshall Plan* (San Diego 1955)

Kalb, Madeleine, *The Congo Cables. The Cold War in Africa – From Eisenhower to Kennedy* (New York 1982)

Karnow, Stanley, *Vietnam. A History* (London 1983, revised edn 1994)

Kedourie, Elie, *The Chatham House Version and Other Middle Eastern Studies* (Hanover, NH 1984)

Kedward, Rod, *La Vie en bleu. France and the French since 1900* (London 2005)

Keeney, L. Douglas, *15 Minutes. General Curtis LeMay and the Countdown to Nuclear Annihilation* (New York 2011)

Kennedy, Paul, *The Rise and Fall of the Great Powers. Economic Change and Military Conflict from 1500 to 2000* (New York 1989)

——, *The Parliament of Man. The United Nations and the Quest for World Government* (London 2007)

Kerkvliet, Benedict J., *The Huk Rebellion. A Study of Peasant Revolt in the Philippines* (Berkeley, Calif. 1977, reprinted Lanham, Md 2002)

Kinzer, Stephen, *All the Shah's Men. An American Coup and the Roots of Middle East Terror* (New York 2008)

Kitson, Frank, *Gangs and Counter-gangs* (London 1960)

Korbonski, Andrzej and Fukuyama, Francis, *The Soviet Union and the Third World. The Last Three Decades* (Ithaca, NY 1987)

Koya, Zakiah, 'Life behind a Barbed Wire Fence', *New Straits Times*, 31 August 1998

Kozak, Warren, *LeMay. The Life and Wars of General Curtis LeMay* (Washington, DC 2009)

Krauze, Enrique, *Redeemers. Ideas and Power in Latin America* (New York 2011)

Kux, Dennis, *The United States and Pakistan 1947–2000. Disenchanted Allies* (Washington, DC 2001)

Kwarteng, Kwasi, *Ghosts of Empire. Britain's Legacies in the Modern World* (London 2011)

Lacey, Michael (ed.), *The Truman Presidency* (Cambridge 1991)

Langguth, A. J., *Our Vietnam. The War 1954–1975* (New York 2000)

Lansdale, Edward Geary, *In the Midst of Wars. An American's Mission to Southeast Asia* (New York 1972, reprinted 1991)

Lanzona, Vina, *Amazons of the Huk Rebellion. Gender, Sex and Revolution in the Philippines* (Madison, Wis. 2009)

Larkin, Maurice, *France since the Popular Front. Government and People 1936–1996* (Oxford 1997)

Latell, Brian, *Castro's Secrets. The CIA and Cuba's Intelligence Machine* (New York 2012)

Lawrence, Mark Atwood, *The Vietnam War. A Concise International History* (Oxford 2008)

Lawrence, Mark Atwood and Logevall, Fredrik (eds), *The First Vietnam War. Colonial Conflict and Cold War Crisis* (Cambridge, Mass. 2008)

Lee, Jongsoo, *The Partition of Korea after World War II* (New York 2006)

Leffler, Melvyn and Westad, Odd Arne (eds), *The Cambridge History of the Cold War* (Cambridge 2010) vols 1–3

Legge, John D., *Sukarno. A Political Biography* (London 1972)

Legum, Colin, *Congo Disaster* (London 1961)

Lewis, Norman, *A Dragon Apparent. Travels in Cambodia, Laos and Vietnam* (London 1951, new edn 2003)

Likimani, Muthoni, *Passbook Number F.47927. Women and Mau Mau in Kenya* (London 1985)

Loeffler, Jane C., *The Architecture of Diplomacy. Building America's Embassies* (New York 1998, revised edn Princeton 2011)

Lonsdale John, 'Mau Maus of the Mind: Making Mau Mau and Remaking Kenya', *Journal of African History* (1990) 31, pp. 393–421

Louis, William Roger, *The British Empire in the Middle East 1945–1951. Arab Nationalism, the United States, and Postwar Imperialism* (Oxford 1984)

——, *Ends of British Imperialism. The Scramble for Empire, Suez and Decolonization* (London 2006)

Lowe, Keith, *Savage Continent. Europe in the Aftermath of World War II* (London 2012)

Lynn, M. (ed.), *The British Empire in the 1950s* (Basingstoke 2006)

Lyttelton, Oliver, Viscount Chandos, *The Memoirs of Viscount Chandos* (London 1962)

McCullough, David, *Truman* (New York 1992)

Macdonald, Douglas J., *Adventures in Chaos. American Intervention for Reform in the Third World* (Cambridge, Mass. 1992)

McMahon, Robert, *Colonialism and Cold War. The United States and the Struggle for Indonesian Independence 1945–49* (Ithaca, NY 1981)

——, *The Cold War on the Periphery. The United States, India and Pakistan* (New York 1994)

——, *The Limits of Empire. The United States and Southeast Asia since World War II* (New York 1999)

——, *The Cold War* (Oxford 2003)

Mahoney, Richard D., *JFK. Ordeal in Africa* (New York 1983)

Majdalany, Fred, *State of Emergency. The Full Story of the Mau Mau* (London 1962)

Manea, Octavian, 'Setting the Record Straight on Malayan Counterinsurgency Strategy: Interview with Karl Hack', *Small Wars Journal*, 11 February 2011, pp. 1–11

Marr, David G., *Vietnam 1945. The Quest for Power* (Berkeley, Calif. 1995)

May, Ernest, *American Imperialism. A Speculative Essay* (Chicago 1991)

May, Ernest R. and Zelikow, Philip D. (eds), *Dealing with Dictators. Dilemmas of US Diplomacy and Intelligence Analysis 1945–1990* (Cambridge, Mass. 2006)

——(eds), *The Kennedy Tapes. Inside the White House during the Cuban Missile Crisis* (New York 2002)

Meallier, Pierre (ed.), *OAS: la guerre d'Algérie vue de Bône à travers les tracts OAS* (Nice 2004)

Melanson, Richard and Mayers, David (eds), *Reevaluating Eisenhower. American Foreign Policy in the Fifties* (Urbana, Ill. 1989)

Merle, Robert, *Ben Bella* (London 1967)

Miers, Richard, *Shoot to Kill* (London 1959)

Miller, Harry, *Menace in Malaya* (London 1954)

Mitchell, George, *Matthew B. Ridgway. Soldier, Statesman, Scholar, Citizen* (Mechanicsburg, Pa 2002)

Mitter, Rana, *A Bitter Revolution. China's Struggle with the Modern World* (Oxford 2004)

Möller, Kay, *Die Aussenpolitik der Volksrepublik China 1949–2004. Eine Einführung* (Wiesbaden 2005)

Montague, Ludwell Lee, *General Walter Bedell Smith as Director of Central Intelligence, October 1950–February 1953* (University Park, Pa 1992)

Morgan, Kenneth O., *Labour in Power 1945–1951* (Oxford 1984)

Morgan, Ted, *My Battle of Algiers. A Memoir* (New York 2005)

Morris, Benny, *1948. The First Arab–Israeli War* (New Haven, Conn. 2008)

Mottahedeh, Roy, *The Mantle of the Prophet. Religion and Politics in Iran* (Oxford 2005)

Murphy, Philip, *Alan Lennox-Boyd. A Biography* (London 1999)

Murray-Brown, Jeremy, *Kenyatta* (London 1972)

Nagl, John, *Learning to Eat Soup with a Knife. Counterinsurgency Lessons from Malaya and Vietnam* (Chicago 2005)

Naipaul, Vidia, *India: A Million Mutinies Now* (London 2010)

——, *The Masque of Africa* (London 2011)

Nashel, Jonathan, *Edward Lansdale's Cold War* (Amherst, Mass. 2005)

Neustadt, Richard and May, Ernest, *Thinking in Time. The Uses of History for Decision Makers* (New York 1986)

Nicholls, C. S., *Red Strangers. The White Tribe of Kenya* (London 2005)

Nzongola-Ntalaja, Georges, *The Congo. From Leopold to Kabila. A People's History* (London 2007)

Oakley, J. Ronald, *God's Country. America in the Fifties* (New York 1990)

O'Brien, Conor Cruise, *To Katanga and Back. A UN Case History* (London 1962)

——, *Ancestral Voices. Religion and Nationalism in Ireland* (Dublin 1994)

Odhiambo, E. S. Atieno and Lonsdale, John (eds), *Mau Mau and Nationhood* (Athens, Ohio 2003)

Ogunsanwo, Alaba, *China's Policy in Africa 1958–1971* (Cambridge 1974)

Oldfield, John, *The Green Howards in Malaya (1949–1952). The Story of a Post-War Tour of Duty by a Battalion of the Line* (Aldershot 1953)

Pakenham, Valerie, *The Noonday Sun. Edwardians in the Tropics* (London 1985)

Paterson, Thomas G. (ed.), *Kennedy's Quest for Victory. American Foreign Policy 1961–1963* (Oxford 1989)

Patterson, James T., *Grand Expectations. The United States 1945–1974* (Oxford 1996)

Patti, Archimedes, *Why Vietnam? Prelude to America's Albatross* (Berkeley, Calif. 1980)

Paxman, Jeremy, *Empire. What Ruling the World Did for the British* (London 2011)

Phillips, David Atlee, *Night Watch. 25 Years inside the CIA* (London 1977)

Porter, Bernard, *The Absent-Minded Imperialists. Empire, Society and Culture in Britain* (Oxford 2004)

Prados, John, *Keepers of the Keys. A History of the National Security Council* (New York, 1991)

Quinn-Judge, Sophie, *Ho Chi Minh. The Missing Years 1919–1941* (London 2003)

Ramsden, John, *An Appetite for Power. A History of the Conservative Party since 1830* (London 1999)

Rees, David (ed.), *The Korean War. History and Tactics* (London 1984)

Rodman, Peter, *More Precious than Peace. The Cold War and the Struggle for the Third World* (New York 1994)

Rogan, Eugene, *The Arabs. A History* (London 2009)

Rothman, Hal, *LBJ's Texas White House* (College Station, Tex. 2001)

Rotter, Andrew, *Comrades at Odds. The United States and India 1947–1964* (Ithaca, NY 2000)

Ryan, David and Pungong, Victor (eds), *The United States and Decolonisation. Power and Freedom* (New York 2000)

Ryan, Mark, Finkelstein, David and McDevitt, Michael (eds), *Chinese Warfighting. The PLA Experience since 1949* (Armonk, NY 2003)

Sandbrook, Dominic, *Never Had It So Good. A History of Britain from Suez to the Beatles* (London 2005)

Sanger, Clyde, *Malcolm MacDonald. Bringing an End to Empire* (Liverpool/Montreal 1995)

Schoultz, Lars, *Beneath the United States. A History of US Policy toward Latin America* (Cambridge, Mass. 1998)

Schwarz, Bill, *Memoirs of Empire*, vol. 1: *The White Man's World* (Oxford 2011)

Service, Robert, *Comrades. Communism. A World History* (London 2007)

Shaplen, Robert, *The Lost Revolution. Vietnam 1945–65* (London 1966)

Shen, Zhihua, Li Danhui, *Learning to One Side. China and its Allies in the Cold War* (Washington D.C. 2011)

Shennan, Margaret, *Out in the Midday Sun. The British in Malaya 1880–1960* (London 2000)

Shepherd, Naomi, *Ploughing Sand. British Rule in Palestine* (London 1999)

Shepherd, Robert, *Iain Macleod* (London 1994)

Shevchenko, Arkady, *Breaking with Moscow* (New York 1985)

Short, Anthony, *In Pursuit of Mountain Rats. The Communist Insurrection in Malaya* (London 1975, reprinted Singapore 2000)

Shuckburgh, Evelyn, *Descent to Suez. Diaries 1951–56* (London 1986)

Simpson, Howard, *Tiger in the Barbed Wire. An American in Vietnam 1952–1991* (Washington, DC 1992)

Skierka, Volker, *Fidel Castro. A Biography* (Cambridge 2004)

Skrine, Claremont, *World War in Iran* (London 1962)

Smith, Jean Edward, *Eisenhower in War and Peace* (New York, 2012)

Smith, Richard Harris, *OSS. The Secret History of America's First Central Intelligence Agency* (Guilford, Conn. 2005)

Spurr, Russell, *Enter the Dragon. China at War in Korea* (London 1989)

Statler, Kathryn and Johns, Andrew (eds), *The Eisenhower Administration, the Third World, and the Globalization of the Cold War* (Oxford 2006)

Steel, Ronald, *Walter Lippmann and the American Century* (Boston 1980)

Stephens, Robert, *Nasser. A Political Biography* (London 1971)

Stockwell, A. J. (ed.), *Malaya. The Communist Insurrection 1948–1953*, vol. 3 of S. R. Ashton (ed.), *British Documents on the End of Empire*, Series B (London 1995)

Stueck, William (ed.), *The Korean War in World History* (Lexington, Ky 2004)

Suh, Dae-Sook, *Kim Il Sung. The North Korean Leader* (New York 1989)

Sulzberger, C. L., *The Test. De Gaulle and Algeria* (London 1962)

——, *A Long Row of Candles. Memoirs and Diaries 1934–1954* (Toronto 1969)

Sykes, Christopher, *Crossroads to Israel. Palestine from Balfour to Bevin* (London 1965)

Tarling, Nicholas, *Britain, Southeast Asia and the Onset of the Cold War 1945–1950* (Cambridge 1998)

——, *A Sudden Rampage. The Japanese Occupation of Southeast Asia 1941–1945* (London 2001)

Taylor, John, *An American Soldier. The Wars of General Maxwell Taylor* (Novato, Calif. 1989)

Thomas, Evan, *Robert Kennedy. His Life* (New York 2000)

——, *The Very Best Men. The Daring Early Years of the CIA* (New York 1995, reprinted 2006)

——, *Ike's Bluff. President Eisenhower's Secret Battle to Save the World* (New York, 2012)

Thomas, Hugh, *Cuba. A History* (London 1971, revised edn 2001)

Thomas, Martin, Moore, Bob and Butler, L. J., *Crises of Empire. Decolonisation and Europe's Imperial States 1918–1975* (London 2010)

Thompson, Reginald, *Cry Korea. The Korean War. A Reporter's Notebook* (London 1951, reprinted 2009)

Thompson, Robert, *Make for the Hills. Memories of Far Eastern Wars* (London 1989)

Todd, Olivier, *Albert Camus. A Life* (New York 1997)

Toye, Richard, *Churchill's Empire. The World that Made Him and the World He Made* (London 2010)

Trevelyan, Humphrey, *The Middle East in Revolution* (London 1970)

Tunzelmann, Alexandra von, *Indian Summer. The Secret History of the End of Empire* (London 2007)

——, *Red Heat. Conspiracy, Murder and the Cold War in the Caribbean* (London 2011)

Vickers, Adrian, *A History of Modern Indonesia* (Cambridge 2005)

Walden, George, *China. A Wolf in the World?* (London 2008)

Waldron, Arthur (ed.), *China in Africa* (Washington, DC 2008)

Wall, Irwin, *France, the United States, and the Algerian War* (Berkeley, Calif. 2001)

Walter, Calder, *Empire of Secrets. British Intelligence, the Cold War and the Twilight of Empire* (London 2013)

Watt, Donald Cameron, *Succeeding John Bull. America in Britain's Place 1900–1975* (Cambridge 1984)

Wenqian, Gao, *Zhou Enlai. The Last Perfect Revolutionary* (New York 2007)

Westad, Odd Arne, *Decisive Encounters. The Chinese Civil War 1946–1950* (Stanford, Calif. 2003)

——, *The Global Cold War. Third World Interventions and the Making of our Times* (Cambridge 2007)

White, Luise, *The Comforts of Home. Prostitution in Colonial Nairobi* (Chicago 1990)

Windrow, Martin, *The Last Valley. Dien Bien Phu and the French Defeat in Vietnam* (London 2005)

Woodhouse, C. M., *Something Ventured. The Autobiography of C. M. Woodhouse* (London 1982)

Woods, Randall B., *LBJ. Architect of American Ambition* (Cambridge, Mass. 2006)

Worthington, Peter, 'War in the Clouds', *The Indian Quarterly*, Vol 1 (2012)

Wrong, Michaela, *In the Footsteps of Mr Kurtz. Living on the Brink of Disaster in the Congo* (London 2001)

Yu, Maochun, *OSS in China. Prelude to Cold War* (Annapolis, Md 1996)

Zhihua, Shen and Danhui Li, *After Leaning to One Side. China and its Allies in the Cold War* (Stanford, Calif. 2011)

Zoumaras, Thomas, 'Eisenhower's Foreign Economic Policy: The Case of Latin America', in Richard Melanson and David Mayers (eds), *Reevaluating Eisenhower. American Foreign Policy in the Fifties* (Urbana, Ill. 1989)

Index